Foundations of
Nursing
Practice

· ·

Foundations of
Nursing
Practice

Edited by

Richard Hogston and Penelope M. Simpson

palgrave

Published by
PALGRAVE
Houndmills, Basingstoke, Hampshire RG21 6XS and
175 Fifth Avenue, New York, N. Y. 10010
Companies and representatives throughout the world

PALGRAVE is the new global academic imprint of
St. Martin's Press LLC Scholarly and Reference Division and
Palgrave Publishers Ltd (formerly Macmillan Press Ltd).

ISBN 0–333–71423–7 paperback

This book is printed on paper suitable for recycling and made from fully managed and sustained forest sources.

A catalogue record for this book is available from the British Library.

10   9   8   7   6   5   4   3
08 07 06 05 04 03 02 01

Editing and origination by
Aardvark Editorial, Mendham, Suffolk

Printed In Malaysia

Contents

Notes on Contributors   *page* vii

Acknowledgements   x

Introduction: What is Nursing?
PENELOPE M. SIMPSON   xi

1 **Managing Nursing Care**
   RICHARD HOGSTON   1

2 **Promoting Health**
   GRAHAM WATKINSON   24

3 **Safety in Practice**
   FRAN BOXALL AND SOMDUTH PARBOTEEAH   48

4 **Eating and Drinking**
   PENELOPE M. SIMPSON   93

5 **Elimination**
   BARBARA MARJORAM   133

6 **Respiration and Circulation**
   RUTH SADIK AND DEBRA ELLIOTT   167

7 **Movement and Mobility**
   MOLLY COURTENAY   216

8 **Wound Management**
   NADIA CHAMBERS   240

9 **Social Behaviour and Professional Interactions**
   PHIL RUSSELL   267

10 **Understanding Ourselves**
   CATHERINE THROWER   294

11 **Reflective Practice**
   IAN DOUGLAS   315

12 **The Politics of Health Care**
SUSAN MOORE   345

13 **Nursing Practice in an Interprofessional Context**
JANET McCRAY   370

14 **Challenges to Professional Practice**
MELANIE JASPER   389

Answers to Test Yourself! Questions and Activities   421
Index   435

Notes on contributors

NADIA CHAMBERS MA, PGDipEd, BSc(Hons), ENB HA, RGN is a Senior Lecturer in Adult Nursing Studies (Developing Professional Practice) and course leader for the BSc(Hons) Nursing at the School of Health and Social Care, University of Portsmouth. Her clinical practice focus is tissue viability, especially in elderly care. Recent research includes an illuminative evaluation of continuing education in the principles of wound care, collaborative action research into nurses' self-efficacy in wound care and a study of work into how, why and when primary health care nurses involve patients in the nursing management of chronic leg ulcers. Nadia is a member of the Tissue Viability Society and has presented work at the Fifth and Sixth International European Wound Management Association Conferences and the First International Conference for Evidence-Based Nursing.

MOLLY COURTENAY PhD, MSc, BSc, CertEd, RGN, RNT has a nursing background in the general medical and intensive care setting. She has worked as a lecturer in several academic institutions and completed a PhD in 1996 in the area of infection control. She works independently as a research and clinical development consultant and freelance writer, and is presently involved in research, examining the use of larva therapy in the management of wounds. Commencing January 1999, she will be running the Nurse Prescribing programme at Reading University and also teaching their Biological Science modules.

IAN DOUGLAS BA(Hons), RNT, RCNT, RGN is a Senior Lecturer in pre- and postregistration and continuing education at the School of Health Studies, University of Portsmouth. Ian's area of speciality is accident and emergency nursing, his main research interests being in the area of childhood accidents. He has held responsibility for the reflective practice programmes at Portsmouth since their inception.

DEBRA ELLIOTT MSc, BSc(Hons), RNT, CertEd(FE), CertHE, RGN is a Ward Manager of the Emergency Medical Unit at Southampton General Hospital. She previously spent 5 years as a Senior Lecturer at the School of Health Studies, University of Portsmouth, seconded by Queen Alexandra's Royal Naval Nursing Service, in which she served for 10 years. Debra has extensive clinical experience gained in the NHS and the Services within intensive care, coronary care and acute and emergency medicine, her main interest being resuscitation, particularly advanced life support.

RICHARD HOGSTON MSc(Nurs), PGDipEd, BA(Hons), RN is Nursing Officer for Education and Training at the NHS Executive. He was formerly Principal Lecturer/Subject Leader for Nursing Studies at the School of Health Studies, University of Portsmouth, where his main teaching and research interests concentrated upon quality and management together with expertise in curriculum development.

MELANIE JASPER MSc, BNurs, BA, RN, RM, RHV, NDNCert, PGCEA is a Principal Lecturer working primarily in the Centre for Health Research in the School of Health and Social Care, University of Portsmouth. She is Course Leader for the MSc in Nursing Studies and focuses her teaching in the area of critical nursing theory and research methodologies. She has particular interest in the development of reflective writing in professional development, and in the use of portfolio construction in lifelong learning.

JANET McCRAY MSc, BSc(Hons), RNT, RN(LD), CertEd is currently a Principal Lecturer in Primary Care and Disabilities in the School of Health and Social Care, University of Portsmouth. When working in practice, Janet had a wide range of experiences supporting people with learning disabilities, largely in community settings. More recently, she has developed educational programmes that enhance interprofessional working, in particular between nurses and social workers. She now works in the field of primary care and disability studies.

BARBARA MARJORAM TD, MA, RN, CertEd is a Teaching Fellow at the School of Nursing and Midwifery, University of Southampton. She combines over a quarter of a century of both clinical and teaching experience. Her previous publications have been on the use of information technology in nursing.

SUSAN MOORE MSc, MBA, PGDipEd, BA(Hons), DipN(Lond), CertGer, RMN, RGN is Ward Manager of an assessment and treatment unit within the Department of Psychiatry of Old Age, Oxord Mental Healthcare NHS Trust. She has been a nurse for 24 years. In that time she has been a manager, teacher and clinician. Her abiding interest is in working with older people with mental health problems, including the sociology and social policy applied to this specialty.

SOMDUTH PARBOTEEAH MSc, SRN, RCNT, RNT, CertEd, DipN(Lond) is Senior Lecturer in Adult Nursing at the School of Health Studies, University of Portsmouth and is involved in teaching life sciences and nursing practice in the field of nurse education. His research interest includes the use of knowledge maps as a heuristic device for integrating theory and practice.

PHIL RUSSELL MSc, MA, BA(Hons), DipNE, RNT, RN is a Senior Lecturer at the School of Health and Social Care, University of Portsmouth. He is a nurse and practising counsellor with a particular interest in bereavement and palliative care. He teaches counselling, health psychology and interpersonal skills to a wide range of health-care professionals.

RUTH SADIK BA(Hons) Health Studies, RNT, RCNT, RSCN, RGN, CertEd(FE) is presently completing an MSc in Child Health at the RCN Institute of Advanced Nursing Education. She has taught applied physiology relating to respiratory disorders in both adults and children. She is a Senior Lecturer in Child Health and Child Branch Co-ordinator at the School of Health Studies, University of Portsmouth, with a particular interest in the nursing of clients with respiratory conditions.

PENELOPE M. SIMPSON MSc, DipEd, CertEd, DN(Lond), RCNT, RN has been nursing for more than 30 years. Nutrition, surgical nursing and health promotion are her main interests, and she believes in leading by example. She is Senior Lecturer in the School of Health Studies, University of Portsmouth, and helps to run a rest home for the elderly. Her published work to date includes the nutritional impact of alcohol on elderly people and surgical nursing.

CATHERINE THROWER MSc, BSc(Hons), DipNE, RNT, RN, RM is a Senior Lecturer in the School of Health Studies, University of Portsmouth. She gained an honours degree in Psychology in 1989 from Portsmouth Polytechnic, and an MSc in Health Psychology in 1996 from City University, London. She has worked in nurse education since 1989, specialising in dementia. Her clinical experience has been predominately in care of the older adult, with a specific role as an Advanced Nurse Practitioner in Dementia Care from 1993 to 1995, and a Lecturer Practitioner in Dementia Care from 1995 to 1997.

GRAHAM WATKINSON MA(Ed), RN, RNT, CertEd gained primary health-care experience as a nuclear submariner in the Royal Navy responsible for health physics, atmosphere and radiation control before training as a nurse. Postregistration courses in coronary care and intensive care nursing were followed by nursing practice as a charge nurse and nurse manager. As well as teaching on a variety of nursing courses, Graham is the Health Promotion Advisor to the University of Portsmouth.

Acknowledgements

Many thanks to Richard Hogston, who started the whole project, to Ann Meardon for tireless typing and endless revisions, to Elizabeth, Gary, Anna and David for technical help, to the many student reviewers of all the chapters, and especially to my husband, David, for his patience throughout.

PENELOPE M. SIMPSON

Introduction:
What is Nursing?

This text is designed to be used as a study guide to support many aspects of your learning throughout the common foundation programme. Each chapter has been written by an enthusiastic subject specialist, and we hope that their passionate interest is infectious. The chapters are not meant to be read in any particular order but to be tackled when they feel relevant to your progress and experience. The interactive style is intended to make you think, with various activities to enliven the text and enable you to apply your knowledge in practice settings. Constant reference is made to complementary texts, current evidence and further reading. Objectives give you an idea of what you can achieve by working through each chapter, and a running glossary within the chapters will enhance your vocabulary and understanding. Cross-referencing within and between chapters increases the coherence of the text. Client case studies draw on all four branches of nursing and feature a range of settings to encourage you to reflect upon your reading and its application to clients. At the end of the chapters, review questions enable you to check your knowledge gain.

Each of the chapters discusses a particular topic. In Chapter 1, the five stages of the problem-solving approach to care known as the nursing process will be used to help you to focus on the example of the client in pain. You will be enabled to map your own concept of health and, through Chapter 2 on health promotion, identify the concept of health gain. Nurses tend to deal with uniquely vulnerable clients, and nursing can carry risks to nurses, so Chapter 3 will identify some of the many safeguards, legal and otherwise, available to protect you and your clients. Eating and drinking, normal enough activities, can pose particular problems for clients so you will be encouraged in Chapter 4 to look at your own knowledge and habits, aiming to help clients to achieve optimum nourishment for their changing needs. Logically, elimination follows and Chapter 5 will help to dispel some taboos and myths, with a healthy emphasis on achieving and attaining relative normality across the life span. Chapter 6, on respiration and circulation, will explore the nurse's role in assessing and implementing the care of clients with difficulties in breathing and maintenance of the circulation. Other body systems, their purpose and functioning, and what can go wrong will be explored in Chapter 7, covering the musculoskeletal system, the skin, lever systems and movement. The role of the nurse and professional responsibilities, including accountability, will be clearly explained in Chapter 8, on wound care. Working in a team is a key part of nursing, and social behaviour and professional interactions will enhance your skill in therapeutic and other communication; this topic is covered in Chapter 9. Knowing yourself better, the subject of Chapter 10, will enable you to give of yourself to clients and colleagues without being diminished. The image of nursing that you started out with is likely to be much changed as you progress, and reflective practice, explained in Chapter 11, will be one tool for this. As nursing takes place in a political arena, nurses should be political, and The Politics of Health Care (Chapter 12) will help you to understand the climate in which current developments were conceived. Interprofessional practice (Chapter 13) will be a clear focus for the future, as will challenges to professional practice (Chapter 14), enabling you to look forward to the next part of your programme. The chapter contents reflect the authors' views and in no way commit the Department of Health.

We hope you enjoy the book, finding it stimulating and thought provoking, and we wish you well in your nursing career.

Chapter

1

Managing Nursing Care

RICHARD HOGSTON

Introduction

The purpose of this chapter is to explore how nurses manage care; it will take you through a five-stage problem-solving approach known as the nursing process. At the end of the chapter you should be able to:

- Define the stages of the nursing process

- Undertake a nursing assessment

- Identify nursing diagnoses from the assessment data

- Devise and implement a plan of care

- Evaluate your actions

- Consider the link between evaluation and quality of care.

Throughout the chapter, a working example using a client who is experiencing pain will be used to demonstrate how each of the stages of the nursing process is applied. The chapter also provides an opportunity for you to undertake some exercises that will assist you with your care-planning skills.

What is the Nursing Process?

nursing process

a five-stage problem-solving framework enabling the nurse to plan individualised care for a client

The nursing process is a problem-solving framework that enables the nurse to plan care for a client on an individual basis. The nursing process is not undertaken once only, because the client's needs frequently change and the nurse must respond appropriately. It is thus a cyclical process consisting of the five stages shown in Figure 1.1. The nursing process originated in the USA and was formally introduced into the UK in 1977 when the then General Nursing Council introduced its revision of the nursing syllabus. It was an attempt to move nursing away from its traditional 'task-orientated' approach to a more scientific and individualised one.

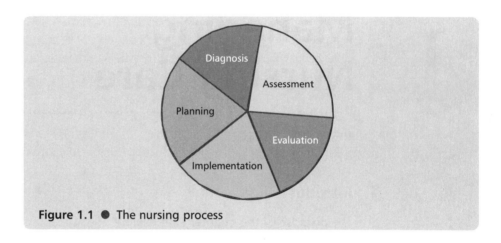

Figure 1.1 ● The nursing process

The nurse is an autonomous practitioner whose responsibilities are now governed by the United Kingdom Central Council for Nursing, Midwifery and Health Visiting (UKCC) *Code of Professional Conduct* (UKCC, 1992). This requires nurses to be accountable for the care that they prescribe and deliver with the nursing process, enabling them to document their actions in a logical and rational manner. Today, one's ability to use the nursing process is governed by the learning outcomes of preregistration courses as outlined by the statutory body, the UKCC, and embedded in parliamentary statute. This states that conditional to registration is the ability to:

> identify the physical, psychological, social and spiritual needs of the patient or client and awareness of the values and concepts of individual care. The ability to devise a plan of care, contribute to its implementation and evaluation, and the demonstration of a problem solving approach to the practice of nursing. (UKCC, 1989)

Failure to keep a record of nursing care or to use the nursing process can lead to a breakdown in the quality of care that is provided. The Clothier Report (HMSO, 1994), which was published following the inquiry into Beverley Allitt (the nurse who was convicted of the murder of children in a hospital in Grantham, Lincolnshire), noted how:

> Despite the availability of a nurse with responsibility for quality management, there were no explicit nursing standards set for ward four. In addition the nursing records were of poor quality and showed little understanding of the nursing process. (Para 5.10.15)

Thus the importance of understanding and using a systematic approach (such as the nursing process) to the provision of nursing care cannot be overestimated.

There has been some debate within the profession over the number of stages in the nursing process, some suggesting four and others five. With a four-stage approach, the nurse does not have time to reflect on the assessment data that have been collected and moves from assessment to planning. The five-stage process enables the nurse to identify the client's nursing diagnosis in order to plan the appropriate care.

The nursing process should not be seen as a linear process. It is a dynamic and ongoing cyclical process (Figure 1.1). For example, assessment is not a 'one-off' activity but a continuous one. Take the example of the individual who is in pain – it is not enough to make a pain assessment that may warrant an intervention; the nurse then needs to make a reassessment having evaluated whether the pain-relieving intervention has been successful.

The nursing process is a problem-solving activity. Problem-solving approaches to decision-making are not unique to nursing. The medical profession uses a specific format based upon an assessment of the body's systems. A number of questions are asked in a systematic manner to enable the doctor to make a diagnosis based upon the information that has been collected. Problem-solving approaches are also taken outside the health-care field. Car mechanics undertake a sequence of activities in order to diagnose what is wrong with your car when you tell them that there is a squeak or a rattle.

Stage One: Assessment

Sources of assessment data

Activity 1

Think about the client and other sources that you may be able to consult to assist you in conducting a comprehensive assessment. Write them down in a list.

Before beginning to consider what sort of information you might need to collect, we need to consider the skills that are necessary to ensure that the data analysed are comprehensive. Assessment is not an easy process; it includes collecting information from a variety of sources. However, the quality of the assessment will depend on one's ability to put together all the sources at one's disposal. Spend a few minutes on Activity 1.

The sources that you have listed in Activity 1 have probably included the following:

- Your client
- Relatives, friends and significant others
- Current and previous nursing records
- The records of other health professionals such as doctors, physiotherapists and so on
- Statements and information from the police, ambulance personnel, witnesses at an accident scene and others.

Your client

The first and most important source for data collection is obviously the individual whom you are assessing. However, it will not always be possible to obtain all the information you require for a number of reasons, so you will also need to consult other people.

Friends, relatives and significant others

If you are assessing a baby, most of the verbal information you require will be obtained from his or her parent(s) or guardian(s). With a child, you will need to qualify some of your information through the same source. In the case of an adult who is unconscious or is having difficulty breathing, you will again need to obtain data from friends, relatives, ambulance personnel, the police and so on. The same applies if the client has difficulty understanding as a result of dementia or severe learning disabilities.

Nursing, medical and other records

It will not always be possible to have immediate access to existing records, especially in an emergency or with a first consultation. However, these sources hold valuable information that you need to analyse. They provide details that may assist and prompt you. If the client has been admitted to a hospital, you may have a letter from the GP, district nurse, health visitor or community psychiatric nurse. Similarly, on discharge from hospital, you will provide discharge information if community-based professionals need to be involved. Telephone calls to these professionals, visits and case conferences may also feature.

Skills

Activity
2

Spend a little while thinking about what sorts of skill you need in order to conduct your assessment. Write them down as a list.

Having considered some of the sources at your disposal, we now need to think about what other factors have a bearing on a successful assessment. Spend a few minutes on Activity 2.

As we are beginning to see, the process of assessment is a complex one. Although we have identified some of the sources of information, the quality of the information that is collected depends upon a number of other factors. In your list from Activity 2, you may have included:

- Listening
- Observing
- The use of verbal and non-verbal communication and open and closed questions
- Physical examination
- Measurements.

You will find a detailed examination of how the nurse can most effectively use some of these skills in Chapter 9, which you may wish to consult before reading on.

Listening

One of the most important features of an assessment interview is the nurse's ability to listen to the client. This means giving the client time to answer your questions. You will appreciate from your own life experience that when you are asked a question, you want time to think and then answer without interruption. Interrupting prematurely may lead to clients withholding information or not feeling that you are really interested in what they have to say. Although it is important for you to focus on the information you require and not digress, the fact that Mrs Jones has been admitted as an emergency and is due to collect her children from school in an hour will be the only thing of interest to her until you are able to contact someone who can collect her children.

Observation

Observation can in itself provide the nurse with a great deal of information. The bluish tinge (cyanosis) seen around the mouths, nailbeds and faces of some breathless patients could be indicative of respiratory distress and will be an indication of how little oxygen is circulating in their blood. A yellowish tinge to the skin (jaundice) may be indicative of biliary disease. Similarly, facial and other body expressions may give you an indication of pain.

Open and closed questioning

closed questions
those designed to elicit a simple 'yes' or 'no' answer

open questions
those in which clients can express their answers in as many words as they choose

Both of these methods of communication need to be used when collecting information. The use of closed questions allows the client who is, for example, breathless, anxious, in pain or depressed to answer with a simple 'yes' or 'no'. Open questions, however, will allow you to provide your clients with a full opportunity to tell you the history of their illness or perhaps their pain.

Physical examination

The physical examination of clients allows you to observe and make a judgement about their symptoms. You will be able to judge the integrity (state) of the skin, which is an important consideration in an immobile client. Physical damage such as wounds can be seen, as can even the small puncture marks left by an intravenous drug abuser. Skin that feels very warm and moist to the touch may be a sign of pyrexia.

Measurements

Measurements come in many forms, for example the taking of a blood pressure, pulse or temperature. Also included here is the use of other assessment tools such as a nutritional analysis, pressure sore risk calculator (for example Norton or Waterlow) or pain chart.

Data collection

Activity 3

Select a friend or relative and ask them if you can spend about 20 minutes undertaking a health assessment. Now take a blank piece of paper and collect the information that you feel is important in making some decisions about your chosen person's health status.

As we have seen, in order for nurses to be able to plan care for their clients, they have to be able to gather information that will enable them to make informed decisions. But what information do nurses need to gather, what questions should they ask and how much do they need to know? The answer is determined on an individual basis, the nurse collecting both subjective and objective information.

Before looking in detail at what information should be collected, undertake Activity 3.

From the activity, in addition to name, age and date of birth, you may have collected some of the following information:

Physical health information
- Current and past health problems
- Nutrition and dietary information
- Patterns of activity and rest
- Stamina
- Physical parameters
- Factors affecting health (cigarettes, alcohol and so on)
- Dental, hearing, vision and so on
- Elimination patterns
- Sexual history.

Psychological information
- How does the client react to stress, challenge and so on?
- What are the person's hopes, expectations, demands and so on?
- Communication
- Values and beliefs.

Social health information
- What is the person's lifestyle?
- Employment/unemployment details
- Family or other responsibilities
- Leisure
- Exercise
- Social environment/networks.

How did you decide what you needed to ask, how did you decide to word the questions, and did you collect everything to enable you to feel that you had conducted a thorough assessment?

Framework for assessment

One way of organising the information that you need to collect is by using a nursing framework. The 'activities of living' framework devised by Roper *et al.* (1986) uses a list of the clients' activities of living (Chart 1.1) as a framework for assessment, the nurse systematically collecting the physical, psychological, sociocultural and economic aspects of those activities.

Breathing, one of the activities of living, will now be used as a framework to demonstrate the type of information that the nurse needs to collect during an assessment. At any given time during the assessment process, it may be necessary to concentrate more on one activity than another.

Breathing

The information that the nurse needs to collect about this and any activity of living depends on the answers to certain trigger questions. For example, you may start off by asking your client if she has any problems with breathing. Even though the answer may be 'no', you would, as a professional, need to investigate further. The client whom you are assessing may not feel that she has a problem with breathing, but consider the following questions:

1. Do you smoke? The answer here may be 'yes', even though the client has said she has no problems with breathing. Indeed, she may still feel that she does not have any problems. However, this is a trigger for further questioning.
2. Do you suffer from any breathlessness? The answer at the outset may again be 'no', but if you ask what about running up the stairs or running for a bus, the client may admit that, yes she does then, but this is because she does not usually do any exercise.
3. Taking this one step further allows the nurse to extract even more information about the status of the client's breathing: Do you cough? The answer may be

Chart 1.1 ● The activities of living

- Maintaining a safe environment
- Breathing
- Eliminating
- Controlling body temperature
- Working and playing
- Sleeping
- Communicating
- Eating and drinking
- Personal cleansing and dressing
- Mobilising
- Expressing sexuality
- Dying

Activity 4

Read the client profiles in Casebox 1.1. Choose one of the profiles and, for any two of the activities of living, write down the information that you would need to collect during a nursing assessment.

'no', but when prompted the client may admit to coughing for a little while in the morning, although this clears rapidly and she thinks nothing of it.

For a normal healthy young adult, the nurse may still perceive at this stage that, although the client is partaking in health-damaging behaviour, she does not actually have a problem with breathing in the short term. In the long term, however, the consequences are obvious. At this stage in the assessment process, it may be sufficient to make a note of the information gathered so far and, when it comes to planning care, the action that will be prescribed will include health education about smoking. This will be expanded in the section on planning and implementation below.

Summary and worked example

This section has introduced you to the nursing process and looked in some detail at assessment. The activities should have enabled you to experience some of the issues that you need to consider when undertaking a nursing assessment. We have examined the skills that the nurse needs to use when assessing clients, and have been introduced to one assessment framework that may assist the nurse during the process. By way of a summary of the information that needs to be gained when undertaking an assessment, the following section takes pain as an example and outlines the questions and methods that can be employed when assessing a client's pain. This will then be revisited as we consider the other four stages of the nursing process later in the chapter. Having read this summary, you may like to return to the client profile that you chose and identify the information you feel would be important for your chosen profile. Alternatively, you might like to take the opportunity to participate in the assessment process during your practice placements in the common foundation programme.

Pain Assessment

The assessment of pain is a complex activity that involves a consideration of physical, psychological and cultural aspects of the individual. Because pain is a subjective experience, the nurse needs to be able to summarise the information gained against some objective criteria. This is essential for diagnosis and for evaluating the effectiveness of interventions. Only the person experiencing the pain knows its nature, intensity, location and what it means to them. One of the most widely used and accepted definitions of pain was put forward by McCaffery (1979), who suggests that pain is 'whatever the experiencing person says it is and exists whenever he says it does'. This is important to remember because a number of research studies have been conducted suggesting that nurses fail to assess pain and pain relief systematically (Seers, 1988) and that they tend to

Casebox 1.1

- Joan Harris is a 69-year-old lady who tripped and fell over a protruding pavement slab this morning while out shopping. She has been admitted to the orthopaedic ward of her local NHS Trust hospital suffering from a fractured neck of femur. Mrs Harris is pale, and is anxious about who will look after her cat while she is in hospital. She is complaining of severe pain in her hip and knee, and has grazes and cuts to her lower leg.

- Andrew Holly is 5 years old and has been admitted to the accident and emergency department of the local NHS Trust hospital. He is complaining of a very sore and painful arm, is very withdrawn and is sobbing. He is accompanied by his mother, his 2-year-old sister and their newborn baby brother.

- Alison Simpson, 21 years old, lives in a hostel for people with mental health problems. She has no close family, having left home at 18. She finds it difficult to develop relationships and is suspicious of people who try to befriend her. Alison is very withdrawn and has attempted to take her own life through unsuccessful overdoses of paracetamol on two occasions. She was found this morning slumped in a corner, covered in blood and complaining of extreme pain in her left hand. On the floor nearby was a razor blade, and on examination she had severe lacerations to her left forearm.

- Amanda Cohen is 29 years old and has profound learning disabilities. She lives in staffed residential accommodation with two other young women. For 2 weeks, Amanda has been showing signs of distress – hitting her face, lifting her jumper and crying. It was thought at first that this might be because of premenstrual tension. At length, someone thought to arrange a dental inspection, under anaesthetic. The dentist found a particularly nasty dental abscess. (Adapted from NHSE, 1993.)

overestimate the pain relief obtained from analgesics and underestimate the patient's pain (Hunt, 1995).

Assessments of the patient's pain experience

To begin with, it is essential to identify the characteristics of the client's pain. This means that the nurse should consider:

- The *type* of pain: Is it crampy, stabbing, sharp? How the client describes the pain may help in the diagnosis of its cause. Myocardial (heart) pain is often described as stabbing, but biliary pain as cramping or aching.
- Its *intensity*: Is it mild, severe or excruciating? Pain assessment scales are helpful here. The nurse can ask the patient to rate the pain on a scale of 0–10, zero being no pain and 10 intolerable pain. With children, a range of pictures showing a child changing from happy to sad can be used. Colour 'mood' charts have also been used with a series of colours from black through grey

to yellow and orange, and are very useful for clients who have difficulty grasping numbers or articulating exactly what their pain is like.

- The *onset*: Was it sudden or gradual? Also find out when it started and in what circumstances. What makes it worse? What makes it better? What was the patient doing immediately before it happened?
- Its *duration*: Is it persistent, constant or intermittent?
- *Changes in the site*: There may be tenderness, swelling, discolouration, firmness or rigidity. With appendicitis, a classic sign is movement of pain from the umbilicus to the right iliac fossa. In a myocardial infarction (heart attack), pain classically radiates down the arm, and with biliary pain it can radiate to the shoulder.
- Its *location*: Ask the patient to be as specific as possible, for example indicating the site by pointing.
- *Any associated symptoms*: Chart 1.2 shows some of the common symptoms of disease that can influence the response to pain.
- *Signs* such as redness, swelling or heat.

Summary

Table 1.1 provides a summary of some of the issues to consider when assessing pain. In essence, this section demonstrates how much detail the nurse needs to collect when making a full assessment of the client's pain. Consider your own experiences of pain, both personally and from clients you have nursed in clinical practice, and reflect on how comprehensive the assessment was.

Stage 2: Nursing Diagnosis

The second stage of the nursing process is making a nursing diagnosis. This enables the nurse to translate the information gained during the assessment and to identify the nursing problems. In order to avoid confusion, it is worth noting that 'diagnosis' is not a concept unique to medicine: car mechanics diagnose mechanical problems, teachers diagnose learning difficulties, and consequently nurses diagnose nursing problems.

The language of nursing diagnosis originated in North America in the 1970s in an effort to move the art, science and theoretical basis of nursing forward, and has recently been described as a strategy for advancing the professional

Chart 1.2 ● Common symptoms of disease that influence the response to pain

● Anorexia	● Malaise and lassitude	● Constipation	● Diarrhoea
● Nausea and vomiting	● Cough	● Dyspnoea	● Inflammation
● Oedema	● Immobility	● Anxiety and fear	● Depression
● Dryness of the mouth			

Table 1.1 ● Assessment of pain

Initial sympathetic responses to pain of low-to-moderate intensity	Parasympathetic responses to intense or chronic pain	Verbal responses	Muscular and postural responses
Increased blood pressure	Decreased blood pressure	Crying	Increased muscle tone
Increased heart rate	Decreased heart rate	Gasping	Immobilisation of the affected area
Increased respiratory rate	Weak pulse	Screaming	
Decreased salivation and gastrointestinal activity	Increased gastrointestinal activity	Silence	Rubbing movements
			Rocking movements
Dilated pupils	Nausea and vomiting		Drawing up of the knees
Increased perspiration	Weakness		Pacing the floor
Pallor	Decreased alertness		Thrashing and restlessness
Cool, clammy skin	Shock		Facial grimaces
Dry lips and mouth			Removal of the offending object

status of nursing as well as a method for defining and organising nursing care (Lutzen and Tishelman, 1996). In 1980, the American Nurses Association (a regulatory body similar to the UKCC), in its standards of practice, defined nursing as:

> The diagnosis and treatment of human response to actual or potential health problems. (Carpenito, 1995)

In North America and elsewhere, nursing diagnosis is now the driving force for nursing (Wake *et al.*, 1993; Fonseca du Cruz *et al.*, 1994; Leih and Salentijn, 1994) and a taxonomy (or list) of recognised nursing diagnoses has been developed by the North American Nursing Diagnosis Association (NANDA). Because of the cultural differences between the USA and the UK and the fact that the structure, process and content of nurse education are fundamentally different, using the diagnostic labels provided by NANDA could cause confusion (Webb, 1992). However, the benefits in clinical settings have been positively described by Mills *et al.* (1997) and Hogston (1997).

nursing diagnosis

the second stage of the nursing process, often described as a 'nursing problem', for which the nurse can independently prescribe care

Nursing diagnosis is a critical step in the nursing process, depends on accurate and comprehensive nursing assessment and forms the basis for nursing care planning. Nursing diagnosis is the end-product of nursing assessment. A clear statement of the patient's problems as ascertained from the nursing assessment is increasingly being referred to as a nursing diagnosis (Roper *et al.*, 1986). For example, Gordon (1987) suggests that a nursing diagnosis 'Describes actual or potential problems that nurses, by virtue of their education and experience, are capable and licensed to treat'. More recently, Weber (1991) stated that a nursing diagnosis is 'A statement that describes the actual or potential health problems of a client based on a complete holistic assessment. The problem/s must be at least partially resolved through nursing interventions.' Furthermore, the International Council of Nurses' (ICN) definition for the purposes of the International Classification for Nursing Practice (ICNP) defines a nursing diagnosis as 'Terms for nursing factors, recorded as diagnoses or problems, indicating a reason for nursing care' (*International Nursing Review*, 1995).

This provides a reasoned argument for defining patients' problems as nursing diagnoses and was the definition adopted by Hogston (1997) in an article published on nursing diagnosis in the UK. In summary, the key components of what constitutes a nursing diagnosis are outlined in Chart 1.3.

Activity 5

Return to the two activities of living that you assessed during Activity 4. Try to identify one actual and one potential nursing diagnosis. Use the guidelines in Chart 1.3 to ensure that your diagnoses meet the criteria.

Making a nursing diagnosis

Nursing diagnoses can be actual or potential. Actual diagnoses are those which are evident from the assessment. An example is pain due to a fractured neck of femur.

On the other hand, potential diagnoses are those which could or will arise as a consequence of the actual diagnoses. For example, an individual who is normally active but is confined to bed is at risk of becoming constipated or developing a pressure sore. In this instance, two potential diagnoses arise:

- Potential risk of constipation as a result of enforced bedrest
- Potential risk of pressure sore development from enforced bedrest.

● Stage 3: Planning Nursing Care

There are two steps to the planning stage:

- Setting goals
- Identifying actions.

Chart 1.3 ● Key components of a nursing diagnosis

A nursing diagnosis:
- is a statement of a client's problem
- refers to a health problem
- is based on objective and subjective assessment data
- is a statement of nursing judgement
- is a short concise statement
- consists of a two-part statement
- is a condition that a nurse can independently prescribe care
- can be validated with the client

Source: Adapted from Shoemaker (1984), Bellack and Edlund (1992) and Iyer *et al.* (1995).

goal

the intended outcome of a nursing intervention, sometimes referred to as an objective

A goal is a statement of what the nurse expects the client to achieve and is sometimes referred to as an objective. In other words, goals are the intended outcomes and can be short term or long term. Goals are client centred and must be realistic, being stated in objective and measurable language. They help the nurse and the client to define how the nursing diagnosis will be addressed. Goals serve as the standard by which the nurse can evaluate the effectiveness of the nursing actions.

When writing goals, they need to conform to the MACROS criteria; they should be:

- **M**easurable and observable so that the outcome can be evaluated
- **A**chievable and time limited
- **C**lient centred
- **R**ealistic
- **O**utcome written
- **S**hort.

Using the example of pain, the short-term goal would be that the client will state that he is comfortable and pain-free within 20 minutes. However, the long-term goal is that the client states that he feels in control of his pain within 12 hours. (It is important to remember, however, to take account of non-verbal clues discussed earlier – is the client really pain-free?) With the move to shorter hospital stays and the emphasis on care in the community, it may not always be necessary to formulate both long- and short-term goals for all problems. However, it is always better to have a number of short-term goals that are reached so that new goals can be set rather than having a long-term goal that takes weeks to achieve. With Mrs Harris (see Casebox 1.1 above), who will have surgery for her hip, this will be a series of goals that progress her towards full mobility following her operation, for example: 'Mrs Harris will walk one way to the toilet unaided by [enter date]. Mrs Harris will be able to climb one set of stairs by [enter date].' This avoids a long-term goal that reads 'Mrs Harris will be fully mobile by [enter date]'.

Action planning

The next stage is to plan the nursing care that will ensure that clients achieve their goals. This is where the nurse prescribes nursing actions that can then be implemented and evaluated. In 'care-planning' language, these are the nursing actions – the prescribed interventions that are put into effect in order to solve the problem and reach the goal. It is against these actions that the nurse may, when evaluating care, have to make some adjustments if the actions have not been effective. In today's NHS, when we are seeing a decreasing number of registered nurses against an increase in those of bank and agency nurses and

Activity 6

For the diagnoses that you identified during Activity 4, try to identify one short-term and one long-term goal for your chosen client. Remember to ensure that they meet the MACROS criteria.

unqualified health care support workers (HCSWs), documenting the prescribed nursing care ensures a degree of continuity. In this way, the care plan can be seen as the diary of the client's nursing care. When planning nursing care, use the REEPIG criteria, which will ensure that your plan of care is:

- **R**ealistic: It is important that the care can be given within the available resources, otherwise it will not be achievable.
- **E**xplicit: Ensure that statements are qualified. If you suggest that a dressing needs changing, state exactly when. This will ensure that there is no room for misinterpretation.
- **E**vidence based: Nursing is a research-based profession. In the planning of nursing care, the research findings that underpin the rationale for care must be considered.
- **P**rioritise: Start with the most pressing diagnosis. Given that time is of the essence, the first priority may be, for example, to plan care for the client's pain.
- **I**nvolvement: The plan of care should involve not only the client, so that he or she is aware of why such care is needed, but also the other members of the health-care team who have a stake in helping the client back to health, for example physiotherapists and dietitians.
- **G**oal centred: Ensure that the care planned meets the set goals.

Returning now to the example of pain, the nurse needs to make decisions about what sorts of intervention will most effectively relieve Mrs Harris's pain. This involves not only decisions about prescribed medications, but also other considerations such as how often the pain assessment tool should be used, and what alternative non-pharmacological methods, such as comfort through pillows, the use of skin traction for the leg and distraction therapy, can be implemented. The nursing care plan for Mrs Harris may therefore detail the following nursing actions:

Activity 7

Return to the client for whom you chose to identify nursing diagnoses and goals. Consider what nursing care you would need to plan in order to achieve those goals.

- Give the prescribed analgesic and monitor its effects. Record them on the pain chart.
- Apply skin traction.
- Nurse on a bed equipped with a pressure reduction mattress.
- Ensure 2-hourly changes of position by attaching a trapeze pole to the bed, and encourage Mrs Harris to change her position regularly.
- Ensure that Mrs Harris has a supply of chosen reading/writing materials and access to the television and radio.

Stage 4: Implementation

Implementation is the 'doing' phase of the nursing process. This is where the nurse puts into action the nursing care that will be delivered and addresses each

Chart 1.4 ● Other members of the health care team

- Physiotherapist
- Community psychiatric nurse (CPN)
- Speech therapist
- Health visitor
- District nurse (DN)
- Podiatrist

- Social worker
- Occupational therapist
- Dietitian
- Key worker
- School nurse
- GP

of the diagnoses and their goals. The nurse will undertake the instructions written in the care plan in order to assist the client in reaching the goal(s). This will involve a process of teaching and helping clients to make decisions about their health. It also involves deciding upon the most appropriate method to provide nursing care and the liaison and involvement of other health professionals. Look at the list of health professionals in Chart 1.4. Do you know what their primary roles and functions are and when you might need to involve them?

Managing Nursing Care in the Clinical Environment

A number of different approaches to the delivery of nursing care are available to nurses. These include task allocation, patient allocation, team nursing, primary nursing, the key worker and caseload management. In addition, under the requirements of *The Patient's Charter* (DoH, 1991), each patient is required to have a 'named nurse' who will be involved in caring for the client while nursing care is required. The benefits or otherwise of each of these methods need to be considered in the light of the skill mix of available staff (that is, the number and grade of qualified and unqualified staff) and what it is the nursing team want to achieve. It is difficult to evaluate what is the right approach without a consideration of the benefits or otherwise of each of these methods.

Task allocation

task allocation

the provision of nursing care that centres around a range of tasks allocated to nurses/support workers

Task allocation (also known as functional nursing) is a highly ritualistic method of organising care that centres on nurses and support workers being assigned tasks. However, it has been reported to be practised in 11 per cent of hospital wards (Audit Commission, 1991). Under this system, a nurse will be assigned to undertake the observations of temperature, pulse, blood pressure and respiration. Another nurse undertakes all the dressings, while another nurse takes care of the drugs and so on. This is a very fragmented method of providing nursing care that will ensure the client receives aspects of care from a multiplicity of nurses and support workers, akin to a production line process. The emphasis on tasks naturally removes the notion of individualised client care and, as such, is incompatible with the nursing process.

Client allocation

client allocation
_____
individualised care provided by a named nurse, often assisted by a support worker

One step removed from task allocation is client allocation, practised in 29 per cent of hospital wards (Audit Commission, 1991). Here, total care for a number of clients is undertaken by one nurse, often assisted by a support worker. Although this system means that there is an emphasis on total client care being delivered by an individual nurse for a designated period of time, continuity of care may become compromised if the same clients are not cared for on a regular basis by the same nurse. It is with this system that attention to detail in the nursing care plan needs extra special care because of the number of nurses who may have contact with a client.

Team nursing

team nursing
_____
care provided by a team of nurses/support workers led by a 'team leader'

Team nursing is where a designated group of clients is cared for by a team of two or more nurses (at least one of whom will be a registered nurse) who accept collective responsibility for the assessment, planning, implementation and evaluation of the clients' care. Forty-five per cent of hospital wards have been reported to be using this system (Audit Commission, 1991). Although each team will be headed by a team leader, each registered nurse is accountable for his or her actions in accordance with the Code of Conduct (UKCC, 1992). This is an important point to remember in an effort to counteract criticism surrounding who is ultimately responsible under a system of collective responsibility.

There is a plethora of literature available on team nursing, although much of it compares team nursing with primary nursing and is now rather dated. The literature suggests that many nurses who have striven towards a system of primary nursing have used team nursing as a 'stepping stone' (Wilson, 1991). The seminal research undertaken by Chavigny and Lewis (1984) set out to compare primary and team methods of care delivery and to estimate the effect on both quality and cost. The research found that team nursing tended to promote more client contact than did primary nursing, that clients' satisfaction was high, but that there were no significant differences in cost or quality. In contrast, the research conducted by Reed (1988) concluded that, compared with team nursing, primary nursing affords an increase in the quality of care and increased job satisfaction for nurses. Walsh and Ford (1989) have described how team nursing and client allocation evolved as the successor to task allocation on the premise that being cared for by a team rather than an array of nurses led to more holistic care. They suggested that team nursing really resembles a small-scale version of task allocation, especially if there is a lack of continuity between shifts when the same team may not be on duty, leading to fragmentation. Consequently, there has to be a commitment against assigning tasks to each team member.

With student nurses, team nursing has received a positive press. Lidbetter's (1990) small-scale study describes how students working in a hospital ward practising team nursing spent more time working alongside a qualified nurse and rated their skill acquisition and evaluation of the effectiveness of client care higher than did those from a ward practising primary nursing. Students were also, as a learning experience, afforded the opportunity to assume the role of team leader under supervision.

Primary nursing

primary nursing

care provided on an individual basis by a named nurse who, in its purest form, holds 24-hour accountability for the package of care

Primary nursing has been described as a professional patient-centred practice (Manley, 1990). In this, the primary nurse accepts full responsibility and accountability for his or her clients for the duration of the clients' stay. In its purest form, the implication is that the primary nurse has 24-hour responsibility 7 days a week (Manthey, 1992). In reality, a team of associate nurses continues to provide nursing care under the direction of the primary nurse and in his or her absence. Again, accountability and autonomy rest with the individual registered nurse under the Code of Conduct (UKCC, 1992). There is a great deal of literature on the efficacy of primary nursing. Some of the debates centre around the difference between primary nursing and the named nurse. For a full and lively debate on the issue, the reader is referred to the chapter on primary nursing in *New Rituals for Old* by Ford and Walsh (1994).

Key worker

A popular technique in the field of learning disabilities and mental health nursing, clients are attached to a named key worker who is responsible for the assessment, planning, implementation and evaluation of care. The key worker will make judgements about when other members of the multidisciplinary health-care team need to be involved and for what purpose. The relationship between client and key worker is normally a long-term one because of the longer-term nature of this type of nursing.

Caseload management

This is the most popular method of organising nursing care in the community setting. It revolves around the designated named nurse with extended qualifications in health visiting/district nursing who acts as the caseload manager. Caseloads are normally organised either geographically or by GP attachment. Each

Activity 8

From your own experiences in clinical practice, what method(s) of care organisation have you experienced? Write down two positive aspects and then consider whether one of the other methods described above would have been suitable and why.

caseload manager leads a team of qualified nurses and health-care support workers. Continuity of care is maintained because the teams are organised to ensure that a member of the team is available every day of the week; as such, it is less affected by the demands of the shift system in hospitals. Each registered nurse is accountable for her own actions (UKCC, 1992), the caseload manager being responsible for ensuring that the skill mix and resources are adequate.

Stage 5: Evaluation

At the beginning of this chapter, it was noted that the stages of the nursing process need to be seen as ongoing rather than as once-only activities. This means that the final stage, evaluation, is in reality the end of the beginning and where the process in essence restarts. One of the key components of quality nursing practice is the nurse's ability to make a clinical judgement based upon a sound knowledge base. Evaluation is about reviewing the effectiveness of the care that has been given, and serves two purposes. First, the nurse is able to ascertain whether the desired outcomes for the client have been achieved. Second, it acts as an opportunity to review the entire process and determine whether the assessment was accurate and complete, the diagnosis correct, the goals realistic and achievable, and the prescribed actions appropriate. The nursing process provides nurses with a tool by which client outcomes are regularly monitored, and can be seen as a vehicle for improving the quality of nursing care and ultimately benefiting the client (Fitzpatrick *et al.*, 1992). Increased costs of health care are requiring managers throughout the professions to reduce costs and seek the most cost-effective options. The population at large is more informed about health-care matters and is arguably a less passive recipient of health care, demanding a detailed and open explanation for their care (Hogston, 1995). It is therefore the responsibility of each nurse to ensure that the prescribed care takes account of these issues. Given that nursing records are legal documents that could be used in a court of law, extreme care and accuracy are essential components of the care plan to which the registered nurse puts her signature.

Methods of evaluating nursing care

Having discussed the importance of evaluation and the place that it has in maintaining quality, it is important to consider some of the methods that nurses can use. First of all, undertake Activity 9.

Your list from Activity 9 may have included some of the following:

- Nursing handover
- Reflection

Activity 9

How do you think that nursing care is evaluated? You may have witnessed some methods in your own clinical placements; write them down as a list. If you have not, try to think generally about how you evaluate any service you have received – buying a meal or an item from a shop, for example.

- Patient satisfaction or complaint
- Reviewing the nursing care plan.

Nursing handover

You may have had experience of a nursing handover, which is where a team of nurses hand over information about the nursing care of clients to another group of nurses, usually at the end of a shift, for example from day care to night care. Using the nursing care plan as the focus, nurses share information about the client and the planned care. This serves as a valuable forum for evaluating care through a discussion of its effectiveness. The variety of experiences and professional expertise that a number of nurses have allows a sharing of that information. Its importance was stated by the Audit Commission (1992) as being critical for maintaining continuity of client care.

Reflection

The role of reflection in quality and evaluation has been discussed in some detail in the literature, and Chapter 11 discusses the concept in more detail. Reflection can, however, be both formal and informal. You probably reflect on your experiences both socially with other friends who are nurses and more formally in lecturer-led tutorials. This leads to an analysis of your actions and some of the ways in which you could have done things differently or which you would want to repeat. The use of critical incident analysis, for example, enables the nurse to evaluate a given situation or event and is a tool that is used by qualified nurses in their personal portfolios, which must be kept in order for the nurses to be eligible for triennial re-registration (see Chapter 11).

Patient satisfaction

The appreciation that is sometimes offered by clients through, for example, a letter is an indicator of how satisfied individuals have been with their nursing care. In contrast, a letter of complaint may lead to an investigation into reasons why a client was not satisfied with the care received. Although letters of complaint appear to be on the increase today, this is probably the result of a culture comprising a more informed public. In many ways, such letters lead to an analysis of what went wrong; this may not necessarily be a result of poor nursing care but of other environmental factors. Hopefully, such publicity allows those who have control over resources to evaluate priorities.

Health-care providers are today required to publish statistics about indicators of quality ranging, for example, from how long clients have to wait in accident and emergency departments to the number of clients who receive a visit from the community nurse within the 2-hour appointment time. In the same vein, letters and cards of satisfaction should also be closely monitored.

Reviewing the nursing care plan

Activity 10

Review the assessment, nursing diagnosis, goal(s), planned care and method of implementation for your chosen client and then write an evaluation statement. Remember to ask the questions outlined in the text.

This is where the nurse evaluates the effectiveness of the care that has been given against the set goals and writes an evaluation statement. When evaluating care, it is useful to ask yourself a series of questions about each of the stages of the nursing process, which will provide you with answers about your plan of care:

- Have the short-term goals been met?
- If the answer is 'yes', has the diagnosis been resolved? If so, it no longer needs to be addressed.
- If the answer is 'no', why have the goals not been met? Did they meet the MACROS criteria?
- Was the planned care realistic? Did it meet the REEPIG criteria?
- Has a new diagnosis arisen or a potential diagnosis become an actual one?
- Was the method of care delivery appropriate?
- Was there effective communication within and between the nursing and multidisciplinary teams?
- How satisfied was the client with the care?

Finally, take a look at the completed care plan for Mrs Harris outlined in Figure 1.3 and compare it with your completed care plan.

Information Technology and Care Planning

The place of information technology in health care is having a significant impact on the NHS as advanced computerised information systems record and evaluate everything from finance to personal records. From your own experiences, you may already have seen laptop/palm-top and office-based computers that can record client details and an analysis of nurses' workload. As the NHS network expands, we can expect to see all health-care workers linked by the turn of the century. For nurses, this will provide rapid access to client data such as previous nursing records. There are also currently a number of care-planning computer packages used by different NHS Trusts; you might indeed have seen one. Computerised care planning offers the nurse a number of advantages. It is quick, because there are a number of templates for common nursing diagnoses. Although these are sometimes criticised for moving towards a more common rather than an individualised approach to nursing care, each of the templates has a menu of options that can be tailored to the individual client. The ability to raise at the push of a button a client's previous records is also advantageous and generally allows a more rapid search than a paper-based system. However,

Nursing diagnosis:	Pain due to fractured neck of femur.
Goal: Short term:	Mrs Harris states that she is comfortable with a pain scale rating below 2 within 15 minutes.
Goal: Long term:	Mrs Harris feels that she is in control of her pain and that it is no longer a major concern for her.
Nursing actions:	Give the prescribed analgesic and monitor its effects.
	Apply skin traction.
	Nurse on a bed equipped with a pressure-relieving mattress.
	Ensure 2-hourly changes of position by attaching a trapeze pole to the bed and encourage Mrs Harris to change her position regularly.
	Ensure that Mrs Harris has a supply of chosen reading/writing materials and access to the television and radio.
Evaluation:	Mrs Harris states that she is comfortable and her pain scale rating remains below 2.

Figure 1.3 ● Worked example of a care plan for Mrs Harris

computerised care planning is only as effective as the person who operates the system and generates the care plan. The skills of assessment, identifying nursing diagnoses and goal-setting, and the required nursing actions, can only be effective if the nurse has a sound knowledge base and uses the skills outlined within this chapter. The profession should, and indeed does, welcome the move to more electronic-based systems, if only because it is fast and usually efficient.

Chapter Summary

This chapter has introduced you to a systematic method for the delivery of nursing care through a framework known as the nursing process. You have been introduced to the five basic stages of assessment, diagnosis, planning, implementation and evaluation. Through the vehicle of structured activities, you have been offered the opportunity to develop a care plan for a chosen client. At this stage, you may feel that the nursing process is a complex activity that demands a great deal of thought and practice. However, your skills and experiences will continue to grow and develop as your professional career continues. Working through a structured chapter such as this is no substitute for practice and experience, but the principles of care planning and the issues you need to consider are offered as the basis of accountable nursing practice. You may have been surprised, for example, at how complex and comprehensive the process of assessment is. The depth of material that you need to collate when undertaking a pain assessment, for example, may have led you to reflect on the importance of probing and accurate questioning. As you progress in your chosen professional career, you will find that your ability to plan care will become greater. The important point to remember is that the whole practice and process of nursing is ever changing. New strategies, treatments and knowledge arrive almost daily. New research informs nursing practice and must be incorporated into one's professional repertoire. The process of nursing, like the process of learning, is an ongoing rather than a once-only activity.

Test Yourself!

1. Name the stages of the nursing process.

2. Give two reasons for using the nursing process.

3. What sort of information needs to be collected during a nursing assessment?

4. How many types of nursing diagnosis are there?

5. What are the two stages of the planning phase?

6. What criteria should goals conform to?

7. How can the nursing care plan be evaluated?

References

Audit Commission (1991) *The Virtue of Patients: Making the Most of Ward Nursing Resources*. HMSO, London.

Audit Commission (1992) *Making Time for Patients: A Handbook for Ward Sisters*. HMSO, London.

Bellack, J.P. and Edlund, B.J. (1992) *Nursing Assessment and Diagnosis,* 2nd edn. Jones & Bartlett, London.

Carpenito, L.J. (1995) *Nursing Diagnosis: Application to Clinical Practice*, 6th edn. J.B. Lippincott, Philadelphia.

Chavigny, K. and Lewis, A. (1984) Team or primary nursing care? *Nursing Outlook* **32**(6): 322–7.

Clothier Report (1994) *The Allitt Inquiry. Independent Inquiry Relating to Deaths and Injuries on the Children's Ward at Grantham and Kesteven Hospital During the Period February–April 1991*. HMSO, London.

DoH (Department of Health) (1991) *The Patient's Charter*. DoH, London.

Fitzpatrick, J.M., While, A.E. and Roberts, J.D. (1992) The role of the nurse in high quality patient care: a review of the literature. *Journal of Advanced Nursing* 17: 1210–19.

Fonseca da Cruz, I.C., Yoshica, M.R., Barbosa, M.A., Narchi, N.Z., Queriroz, A.L., Imanchi, R.M. (1994) Classification for nursing practice in Brazil. *International Nursing Review* **41**(2): 45–6.

Ford, P. and Walsh, M. (1994) *New Rituals for Old: Nursing Through the Looking Glass*. Butterworth Heinemann, Oxford.

Gordon, M. (1987) *Nursing Diagnosis: Process and Application*, 2nd edn. McGraw-Hill, New York.

Hogston, R. (1995) Evaluating quality care through peer review and reflection: the findings of a qualitative study. *International Journal of Nursing Studies* **32**(2): 162–72.

Hogston, R. (1997) Nursing diagnosis: a position paper. *Journal of Advanced Nursing* **26**: 496–500.

Hunt, K. (1995) Perceptions of patients' pain: a study of assessing nurses' attitudes. *Nursing Standard* **10**(4): 32–5.

International Nursing Review (1995) ICNP team drafts new definitions. *International Nursing Review* **42**(5): 134.

Iyer, P.W., Taptich, B.J. and Bernocchi-Losey, D. (1995) *Nursing Process and Nursing Diagnosis,* 2nd edn. W.B. Saunders, Philadelphia.

Leih, P. and Salentijn, C. (1994) Nursing diagnoses: a Dutch perspective. *Journal of Clinical Nursing* **3**(5): 313–20.

Lidbetter, J. (1990) A better way to learn? *Nursing Times* **86**(29): 61–4.

Lutzen, K. and Tishelman, C. (1996). Nursing diagnosis: a critical analysis of underlying assumptions. *International Journal of Nursing Studies* **33**(2): 190–200.

McCaffery, M. (1979) *Nursing Management of the Patient with Pain*. J.B. Lippincott, Philadelphia.

Manley, K. (1990) Intensive care nursing. *Nursing Times* **86**(19): 67–9.

Manthey, M. (1992) *The Practice of Primary Nursing*. King's Fund, London.

Mills, C., Howie, A. and Mone, F. (1997) Nursing diagnosis: use and potential in critical care. *Nursing in Critical Care* **2**(1): 11–16.

NHSE (National Health Service Executive) (1993) *Learning Disabilities*. DoH, London.

Reed, S.E. (1988) A comparison of nurse-related behaviour, philosophy of care and job satisfaction in team and primary nursing. *Journal of Advanced Nursing* **13**: 383–95.

Roper, N., Logan, W. and Tierney, A. (1986) *The Elements of Nursing*, 2nd edn. Churchill Livingstone, London.

Seers, K. (1988) Factors affecting pain assessment. *Professional Nurse* **3**(6): 210–16.

Shoemaker, J. (1984) Essential features of a nursing diagnosis. In Kim, M.J., McFarland, G. and Mclane, A. (eds) *Classification of Nursing Diagnoses*. C.V. Mosby, St Louis.

UKCC (United Kingdom Central Council for Nursing, Midwifery and Health Visiting) (1989) *The Nurses, Midwives and Health Visitors (Registered Fever Nurses) Amendment Rules and Training Amendment Rules Approval Order.* Statutory Instrument No. 1456. HMSO, London.

UKCC (United Kingdom Central Council for Nursing, Midwifery and Health Visiting) (1992) *Code of Professional Conduct for the Nurse, Midwife and Health Visitor,* 3rd edn. UKCC, London.

Wake, M.W., Murphy, M., Affara, F., Lang, N., Clark, J. and Mortensen, R. (1993) Towards an international classification for nursing practice: a literature review and survey. *International Nursing Review* **40**(3): 77–80.

Walsh, M. and Ford, P. (1989) *Nursing Rituals: Research and Rational Actions*. Butterworth Heinemann, Oxford.

Webb, C. (1992) Nursing diagnosis… or two steps back. *Nursing Times* **88**(7): 33–4.

Weber, G.J. (1991) Nursing diagnosis: a comparison of text book approaches. *Nurse Educator* **16**(2): 22–7.

Wilson, J. (1991) Step by painful step. *Nursing Times* **18**(87): 42–4.

Chapter 2

Promoting Health

GRAHAM WATKINSON

Introduction

This chapter will provide the reader with a broad introduction to health and health promotion. It is intended to stimulate thought and challenge areas of life that are often taken for granted, promoting discussion and reflection. At the end of this chapter you should be able to:

- Express what health means to you

- Identify contemporary challenges to health

- Recognise that health promotion is a wide concept that includes health education

- Define the key *Health of the Nation* targets

- Discuss the role of the nurse as a health promoter

- Evaluate health.

Throughout the chapter, exercises are given to provide an opportunity for you to explore the notion of health in a holistic way.

In 1993, the NHS Management Executive set out the nursing, midwifery and health visiting contribution to health and health care. The imperative for nurses, midwives and health visitors to work in partnership with other professionals was stressed. Through collaboration, the overarching outcome of improving the general health and life expectancy of the whole population could, they felt, be achieved.

It would be inappropriate to attempt to condense, and therefore gloss over, material within a chapter that only a whole text on health promotion could cover. Further reading is therefore considered essential to permit the reader to gain a good grasp of the many facets of health promotion. To this end, suggested texts can be found at the conclusion of this chapter.

What is Health?

Before we can examine health promotion, and the integral function that it has within contemporary nursing, we need to define just what health is. Most people know what it is like to experience health on a day-to-day basis. Nevertheless, when you ask someone what it is like to be healthy, or perhaps the less personal question 'What is health?', you inevitably get an answer or definition that seeks to explain what ill-health is. It seems easier to turn the question around by asking what it is like not to be healthy and then to speculate that the reverse is health. Unfortunately, if you do this, you fall into the trap of oversimplification, which this chapter will seek to clarify.

Health is a slippery concept to grasp in comparison with ill-health, which seems so solid and tangible. The following examples have all been drawn from real-life situations. To maintain confidentiality, clients' names have been changed. Try to justify whether these people are healthy.

Example 1

Jill, a student nurse, was on a short placement to a special school for children with health problems. It cared for and educated a whole range of children whose needs were different from those who passed through what can be called the normal state education system. Many children were playing in the school playground when a 6-year-old girl named Samantha caught Jill's attention. Bending down to listen to the child's breathless voice, Jill picked Samantha up and sat her on her knee. She had seen the child playing joyfully a few moments earlier as though she had not a care in the world. After a few minutes of conversation, Samantha stated that she needed a heart transplant. 'There is nothing wrong with my heart', she pointed out. 'The loving part works just fine, it's the pumping part that has a problem.' Clearly, in the medical sense, this child is indeed very sick, yet having watched her at play and talked with her, Jill was taken aback by the composed, almost matter-of-fact way in which the child had come to terms with a life-threatening illness. Indeed, she had a very positive outlook on her potentially negative condition.

Example 2

Annie, who is 42 years old, has been married to Jim for 20 years. Unfortunately, shortly after they were married, Annie had a road traffic accident. This resulted in her being hospitalised and undergoing an exploratory laparotomy for abdominal pain. During the surgery, the surgeon discovered that Annie had an ovarian cancer that had been asymptomatic until the accident. The diseased organ was successfully removed, and there were no other signs of injury. Was Annie

asymptomatic
_____
without symptoms

healthy before her accident? Clearly not, it appears. However, as far as she was concerned, she certainly was.

Example 3

This final example concerns two people and the intimate relationship that they share. Rachel, a 21-year-old married woman, looked forward to the birth of her first child. Her pregnancy had been relatively straightforward as far as she was concerned, with some morning sickness during the first trimester (third) of pregnancy. A routine ultrasound scan had demonstrated that all was progressing well, and there were no specific concerns for mother or child. When Sam was born at full term (40 weeks) weighing over 3.6 kg (8 lb), Rachel went through an unexpectedly difficult labour, the prime reason being that Sam had a larger than normal head. A diagnosis of hydrocephalus was made. This resulted in Sam having many epileptic fits during the first few months of his life. Rachel coped very well with Sam. Unfortunately, during his first Christmas, Sam's fits became more severe, progressing to status epilepticus. The consequence of all this was that Sam sustained some brain damage due to a prolonged period of apnoea. He is now not expected to ever walk or indeed feed himself. Would you consider Rachel to be healthy in her present circumstances, looking forward to perhaps many years caring for her son? What about Sam, and the potential he has for development? How does he fit into your definition of health? Perhaps he doesn't.

Consideration of these three very different examples, involving four individuals, will demonstrate that health takes on many different forms. You may, of course, argue that these examples all involve great deviation from the 'normal', whatever that is. Is someone who has a headache healthy? Is a hangover the residue of having a great time, or is it a transitory unhealthy state?

hydrocephalus

an excess of cerebrospinal fluid inside the skull ('water on the brain')

status epilepticus

an almost continuous succession of epileptic attacks

Activity
1

What does being healthy mean to you (as a daughter/ son, wife/husband, parent, member of a student group or community, and so on)? Write your answer on a separate sheet of paper. You may wish to review/revise this over time. You might like to file this within your portfolio.

● Some Concepts of Health

Enabling people to achieve better health is a fundamental part of good nursing practice, whether in the community or in an acute hospital setting. Whether involved in primary prevention, secondary health care, tertiary rehabilitation or palliative care, a nurse who thinks critically about those he or she seeks to help may be able to promote their health and alleviate their suffering. At a superficial level, this seems obvious, so why is it so difficult to achieve continually in practice with all clients and patients? Perhaps we need to be more critical and define what we mean by health. First of all, consider your own definition of health, as in Activity 1.

Many experts agree that it is difficult to define precisely what health is, although over 50 years ago the World Health Organisation (WHO) put forward a definition that many writers have used as a substructure to build upon:

> A state of complete physical, mental and social well-being and not merely the absence of disease and infirmity. (WHO, 1947)

This definition is very exclusive, in that it excludes so many people from ever achieving or hoping to achieve this elusive state of perfectionism. Is health the same as well-being? Could Sam (see above) aspire to this? Dubos (1979, p. 9) states that:

> Health and disease cannot be defined merely in terms of anatomical, physiological, or mental attributes. The real measure is the ability of the individual to function in a manner acceptable to himself and to the group of which he is part.

Pike and Forster (1995, p. 5) complement Dubos' statement by arguing that it is important to take into account people's own perceptions and views on health and that different people will see and express these in different ways. Furthermore, Seedhouse (1986), in his book of the same title, describes health as the 'foundations for achievement'. The idea that health is a particular, precisely determined, fully informed 'structure' to which each individual can strive is, he argues, absurd. It is as nonsensical as the supposition that there can be a faultless person.

Seedhouse (1997, p. 137) has developed these ideas further into what he calls the foundations theory of health promotion. Fundamental to this theory is the extent to which a person's autonomy reflects his or her health status. Providing that the foundations for health are complete in the context for that individual, he or she may be in a position to attain optimal health. (A simplified version of this theory is included in Figure 2.1. Readers are strongly advised to consult the original text – see Further Reading.)

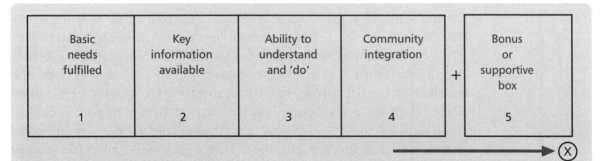

Figure 2.1 ● The foundations theory of health promotion (adapted from Seedhouse, 1997; see text)

According to the foundations theory, providing that a person can stand upon the four central boxes (with support from the fifth when, and as, required), he or she will have a high level of health. Movement towards (X) will require additional provision or maintenance. Consequently, if any of these boxes are damaged or missing, only a lower level of health can be achieved.

Check back to Activity 1 and review your statement about what health means to you. You may wish to revise this.

Challenges to Health

Our health is in a dynamic state of continuity and change. It is constantly being challenged, stressed, abused and even enhanced by our genetic make-up and lifestyle, and by our wider ecological environment. It is truly amazing that, for the majority of people, their health seems to be in a stable state most of the time. As we head into the new millennium, our ideas about health and illness are changing. Conquered infectious diseases of the past are ridiculing modern antibiotic therapy through developed resistance. The media propagate the notion that 'superbugs' with flesh-eating powers lurk within our hospitals each time they are informed of a case of necrotising fasciitis, or when methicillin-resistant *Staphylococcus aureus* (MRSA) closes down yet another hospital ward. According to Emmerson *et al.* (1996), however, there is no evidence of an increase in infection rates from MRSA since 1980.

Other organisms that were routinely killed by simple hygiene methods are now reasserting their influence, perhaps because of our complacency. Yet it only takes a few *Escherichia coli* (*E. coli*) bacteria in the wrong place at the wrong time to cause acute, even life-threatening, illness. During the winter of 1996/97, *E. coli* 0157 food poisoning occurred in North Lanarkshire. This resulted in the deaths of 18 elderly people and close to 400 reported cases of infection. The source of the outbreak was strongly associated with cooked meat products sold by a local butcher. Food hygiene can thus be seen to be an important aspect of caring for sick and vulnerable people.

Health may be affected in a more insidious way as a result of intensive farming methods, perhaps where animals are fed contaminated or the wrong types of food, resulting in, for example, the bovine spongiform encephalitis (BSE) crisis. The word 'crisis' is chosen thoughtfully, as indeed it has been a crisis for the British beef industry, let alone the many thousands of cattle that have been prophylactically destroyed in an attempt to reconcile lost beef markets across Europe and win back consumer confidence. BSE is, at the time of writing, considered by some 'experts' to be transmissible to man, resulting in Creutzfeldt–Jakob disease (CJD). The causative virus in BSE and CJD is a 'slow virus', an agent inducing slow, degenerative encephalopathy (cerebral dysfunctions here characterised by disorientation and excitability of the central nervous system). The Department of Health (DoH) publishes monthly updates on the number of deaths and probable cases of CJD in the UK. New variant CJD (nvCJD), the hitherto unrecognised variant of CJD discovered by the National CJD Surveillance Unit and reported in the *Lancet* on 6 April 1996, has been shown to account for 23 definite and probable cases up to the end of November 1997 (DoH, 1998). Precisely defining the number of cases is difficult because of the complexities of data collection and the different varieties of CJD. Sporadic cases appear to occur spontaneously with no identifiable cause and, according to DoH statistics (1998), account for 85 per cent of all cases. In contrast, iatrogenic infection appears to have occurred accidentally as the result of medical intervention, for example from contaminated neurosurgical instruments, dural grafts and treatment with human growth hormone.

iatrogenic

arising as a result of diagnosis or treatment

Challenges to health may happen in a crude cyclical fashion, whereby diseases pose no real threat until safeguards are removed or 'fail-safe' conditions are disrupted, often through complacency or neglect. This may be true for tuberculosis (TB), which could be said to be revisiting the UK (even though it was never completely eradicated). An opportunistic infection, TB seems to be almost endemic where the most vulnerable are at risk, because of poor or inadequate housing and diet. Those who live as part of society's underclass in a state of relative poverty fall victim to it. This heterogeneous group consists of the disempowered, the frail, the elderly, the single parent with no real chance of escaping welfare under the present system and the long-term unemployed. There seems to be a sense of hopelessness within some communities, which squeezes health and vitality out of the everyday lives of the disenfranchised.

The Goldfish Bowl Society

The goldfish bowl society (Figure 2.2) is an oversimplification that attempts to illustrate how equal access to basic 'essentials' such as nutritious food and warm, dry housing is not available to all. TB kills, albeit slowly. Yet if you have a healthy immune system and are adequately nourished and housed, your body and the environment will rebuff these disease-causing organisms (pathogens).

Promoting Health

Promoting health and preventing ill-health can be seen as a complex business even from the few illustrations given above. The BSE problem involves the interests of commercial organisations and agriculture, also having a political element, with potential global repercussions. The jobs and livelihoods of some farmers and those within the beef industry are at stake. There is, of course, the possibility of widespread trans-species infection. Tuberculosis has its roots in poverty, involving the homeless and the vulnerable. *Escherichia coli* food poisoning, like so

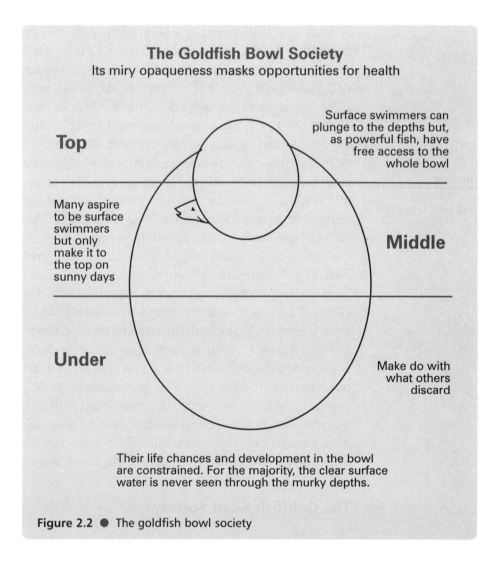

The Goldfish Bowl Society
Its miry opaqueness masks opportunities for health

Top

Surface swimmers can plunge to the depths but, as powerful fish, have free access to the whole bowl

Many aspire to be surface swimmers but only make it to the top on sunny days

Middle

Under

Make do with what others discard

Their life chances and development in the bowl are constrained. For the majority, the clear surface water is never seen through the murky depths.

Figure 2.2 ● The goldfish bowl society

many other bacterial infections, is preventable if scrupulous hygiene standards and thorough food preparation are implemented.

Some key aspects of health promotion are thus beginning to emerge: organisational, social, individual and environmental. Kelly *et al.* (1993) argue very forcibly that health cannot be effectively promoted unless these four aspects are combined in an integrated approach. Their main objection is that many health-promoting activities focus lower than these four levels without the key element of integration.

Two further aspects to health promotion are the political and the spiritual. This is not to say that these aspects have to be overtly integrated to achieve health. Nevertheless, unless they are accounted for in a thoughtful manner, intolerance and non-receptiveness will result at worst in failure and at best partial success. Thus nurses need not only carefully to consider the client's political values and spiritual beliefs, but also be aware of their own. Nurses and others involved in the promotion of health should take a more critical stance. Seedhouse (1997, p. 147) views health promotion as an 'endeavour to help individuals, ...ultimately as a task for governments'. It is they who can ensure that everyone's chances for health are maximised throughout an individual's life span.

The spiritual aspect of health is rarely referred to within general health promotion texts, but within nursing this aspect may be a most important part of the client's health. It especially comes to the fore when an individual crisis occurs, be it acute or chronic, or indeed in the terminal stages of life. A schematic representation of these aspects is shown in Figure 2.3.

According to Petersen and Lupton (1996), everyone is being called upon to play their part in creating a healthier, more ecologically sustainable environment through attention to 'lifestyle' and involvement in various collective and collaborative endeavours. All these concerns, expectations and projects are being articulated through an area of expert knowledge and action that has come to be known as 'the new public health'. This takes as its foci the categories of 'population' and the 'environment', conceived in their widest sense to include the social, environmental, organisational, political, spiritual and individual. Let us attempt to examine each of these six key components. There will, of necessity, be some overlap and integration.

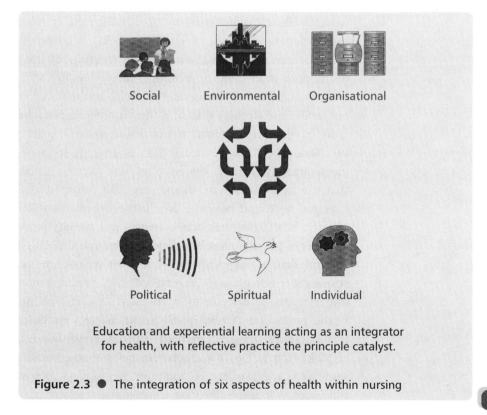

Social   Environmental   Organisational

Political   Spiritual   Individual

Education and experiential learning acting as an integrator for health, with reflective practice the principle catalyst.

Figure 2.3 ● The integration of six aspects of health within nursing

Social health

The social group into which we are born, or subsequently move, may have an influence on our health for better or for worse. It may shape, constrain or indeed enable health to be realised. Factors such as class, gender, ethnicity and age may sway an individual's genetic predisposition. Biology, lifestyle behaviour and the environment all influence health. Much research has focused on the growing links between social class and health inequalities. The Black Report of 1980 (DHSS, 1980) provided a modern benchmark of the relationship between mortality, morbidity and social class. The major findings of the report were that:

1. Throughout the life span, those in the lower social classes had higher death rates than those above them.
2. At birth, children born into a lower social class were of a lower weight, often because of poor maternal diet.
3. The ill-effects of major diseases were more profound in the lower social classes than those at the top of the social scale.

The economy of the 1990s adds a different slant worthy of mention. The middle classes are now feeling the effect of financial stress that may affect their health and well-being. International competition for work results in the 'downsizing' of companies and further casualisation of labour. Middle and senior management are now experiencing what was once within the realm of the working classes: short-term contracts and insecurity. A job for life is becoming a thing of the past, today's emphasis being on flexibility and diversity. Not everyone can cope with managing the enormity of this type of change, often resulting in strains within seemingly secure families.

As Graham (1987) suggests, the social and material circumstances in which people live are strongly linked to their individual behaviour. The continual existence of widespread inequalities in health some 50 years after the foundation of the National Health Service (NHS) is an indication of its inability to tackle inequalities. The NHS is geared to respond to present need, dealing with illness; that is what it is good at. In the very near future, it will have to shift towards expected need and how the present need can promote health by building on effective health maintenance strategies and primary prevention. It is not simply a matter of pouring more and more money into the NHS, thereby perpetuating a growing demand as technology caters for what were once unrealised needs. A strong governmental stand is required now to redirect money from the high-tech, often tertiary, care sector to be invested in long-term health maintenance and health promotion. A sustainable health strategy cannot be realised if medium- and long-term strategies are not resourced. Prevention is better than cure.

Kickbusch (1996) illustrates the point that economic efficiency is not the same as a caring society. For example, key players such as Rupert Murdoch and Bill Gates, who respectively have a vast global telecommunications network and a software empire, are building a global marketplace. But building a caring society is much more than linking health gain with profit margins. Just think about the type of work undertaken by the Missionaries of Charity founded by Mother Teresa of Calcutta.

Activity 2

The local community is often seen as a microcosm of the wider society. How does this constrain or enable the life chances of those in your social surroundings?

Socially determined deprivation damages health. The poor tend to be more socially isolated and lack the social support that tends to achieve health. Social cohesion and the sense of solidarity that this brings are perhaps the most important influences on health status. For example, the two World Wars of the twentieth century caused unprecedented distress and disruption; however, the social solidarity, elimination of unemployment and diminishing differences of living standards rapidly increased life expectancy (Bradshaw, 1994, p. 54). The notions of equal opportunities, social justice and egalitarian principles are required both across and throughout society to enable social health to be fully achieved.

Environmental health

The environment in which we live, work and play has a direct impact upon the state of our health. Peterson and Lupton (1996) state that the shortage of rain, ozone depletion and the greenhouse effect puts public health in a global dimension. International air travel has created what has been termed the 'global village', whereby a traveller can literally have breakfast in one continent, lunch in another and dinner in yet another. If the aircraft's cabin has not been spray-disinfested, so might some insects. Public health experts and environmentalists have turned their attention to 'saving the sick planet'. Within this, the modern city has become the focal point for intervention because of its distortion of true nature. Its spaces and places have become sites for controlling pathology. There has been a rapid increase in the growth of modern mega-cities with high population densities and often inadequate safe water and sanitation. The link between urban conditions and health status has a nineteenth-century ring.

At the Earth Summit in Rio de Janeiro in June 1992, many world leaders signed a global environment and development action plan known as Agenda 21. The aim of this plan was to ensure that development to meet the needs of the present does not compromise the ability of future generations to meet their own needs. The WHO suggested that an ecologically sustainable development should include the prevention and control of environmental health risks while ensuring equitable access to healthy environments. Five key areas of agreement covered a wide range of issues from climate change, biodiversity and sharing resources more equitably, to managing forests, economic growth and overseas aid.

More recently, at the Earth Summit in New York, Irwin (1997) reported that the five main agreements made in Rio de Janeiro had not been fulfilled. The freezing, at the 1990 level, of carbon dioxide emissions, mainly from exhaust fumes and industry, may only be achieved by Britain and Germany by the millennium, whereas most G7 countries will fail to met this objective. In America, emissions have actually increased by 13 per cent since 1995. The protection of endangered species to ensure biodiversity has had some modest success, but this is being undone as deforestation destroys approximately three species every hour. Overseas aid for sustainable development, instead of being increased, has actually decreased. So why is Agenda 21 important and relevant? Over two-thirds of the Agenda 21 plan cannot be delivered without the commitment and co-operation of local government, in which a lead role is played by local authorities. By 1996, each authority had been encouraged to have its own development strategy at the local level that should involve partnerships within the community.

Using food as an example, consider how the production and transportation of what we eat has changed over recent years. Many of our shops and supermarkets are located so far from our homes or workplaces that they require special trips to get there. The use of cars inevitably results in a lack of exercise which contributes, internally, to the deposition of fatty tissue within our arteries, and in the burning of non-renewable fossil fuels which contributes, externally, to air pollution (Lang, 1997, p. 17). This last fact, according to HM Government (1993), has been further compounded by the fact that the distance food is transported has risen by over 50 per cent between 1979 and 1993. The growth in road freight transport conveying the commodities of food, drink and tobacco has increased by more than one-third during this same period (MAFF, 1994).

Organisational health

Most employers stress that their workforce is their greatest asset. Employees spend as much as half their adult lives at work, thus the working environment and the nature of the work clearly have a significant impact on health. In 1997, the Confederation of British Industry conservatively estimated that over 187 million working days lost annually through sickness and absenteeism cost over £12 billion. The benefits of a healthier workforce should be viewed not purely in financial terms but as an integral part of good management. Health promotion at work is an investment in people.

Organisational health is complex and multifaceted. As an example of a large organisation, health in the university will be examined as it is a place where students of nursing study, so it should provide a familiar setting to readers. A health-promoting university is much more than a place where people go to be educated (although this is its main business). It is concerned with introducing a new culture, rather than simply just a few health promotion projects, into our educational settings. Commitment to health promotion as a core value of its mission and the development of its organisation in total is the overall goal. Within this setting, health is viewed as being everyone's business. Why should a university be involved in the health-promoting concept?:

Activity 3

What environmental issues sustain or prevent the achievement of good health in the city or town where you live or study? You may wish to draw up a list of the enabling and ruinous forces that interact on health. How have these environmental issues affected people in your community, those whom you nurse?

- Most universities are large employers; they form a significant part of the local community.
- Both students and staff spend a large percentage of their time within the university environment.
- Young adult students are at university at a time when they are forming attitudes, behaviours and beliefs that may stay with them throughout their adult life.
- Students will themselves play a major part in influencing the health of others, as policy-makers, educators, parents, partners, employers and members of future society.
- There are potentially huge resource savings to be made by becoming more efficient and effective.

In 1995, the University of Portsmouth and local health authority made a joint appointment of a health promotion adviser (HPA) to co-ordinate a university-wide health-promoting initiative. A health needs assessment was performed with both students and staff, which resulted in a report being published and a prioritised 3-year action plan developed. While an assessment identifies problems, only doing something about them makes the exercise succeed. The HPA is made available for students and staff by being situated in the students' advice centre, which is part of the Students' Union. A short summary of the work already completed is set out below:

Access to primary health care – ensuring that all new students register with a GP and dentist; student induction talks supported by displays to increase registration uptake. This information is also available on the World Wide Web under health from the University Home Page (to access this from outside the university via the Internet the address is: http://www.port.ac.uk).

Work with a primary focus on student health
- Peer education project on mental health
- 3-day Mental Health Fair – an annual event before the main examination period
- World Aids Day disco
- Development of sexual health peer education project
- Women's health issues
- Men's health issues
- Drugs panel education
- Meningitis awareness campaigns – especially during the first weeks of each new academic year
- Sensible drinking
- Physical activity
- Non-smoking as the norm in parts of the Students' Union.

Work with a primary focus on staff health

- Lunch-time sessions for stress management
- Stress management workshops for departments
- Team-building within departments
- Development of a working group to implement staff health ideas, working towards the Healthy Workplace Award
- Drugs education and development of a framework for residential staff
- Sexual health
- Smoking cessation
- Increasing physical activity.

The aims of these initiatives are to enable students and staff to fulfil their potential through:

1. Reduced levels of absenteeism
2. Achieving personal organisational goals
3. Improving morale, especially the staff's – while stress is an individual experience, organisational stress affects groups of staff in similar ways
4. Better social relationships throughout the university
5. Increased networking across faculties and departments
6. Reduced utilisation of clinical services (through awareness).

The health-promoting university initiative works very closely with a variety of local and national organisations, creating new networks with key partners including the WHO. There is much more to be done to achieve a healthier potential for everyone who experiences university life, but at least a start has been made, together with the organisational commitment to accomplish this.

Political health

Since the creation of the National Health (illness) Service 50 years ago, which was arguably the greatest politically egalitarian act in recent times, successive governments have sought to make it more effective and efficient. The past two decades have witnessed a drive to make it perform like a business.

The Health of the Nation (DoH, 1992) White Paper set out the government's strategy for improving the health for those in England, laying out a set of priority health targets.

The notion of 'health gain' is expressed pragmatically within the White Paper (DoH, 1992, p. 13). It has two broad aims: first, to reduce premature mortality, thus increasing life expectancy; and second, to add 'life to years', ameliorating morbidity. These ideas originated from the Health for All initiative (WHO, 1985) in which the following six principles were highlighted:

Activity 4

Being a full-time student impinges on family and social life. What organisational support do you get to enable you to achieve your potential as a nurse?

Activity 5

Students' unions are dynamic and lively places, usually exhibiting a diversity of ages, cultures and ethnic groups. What health issues do you think need addressing? What is being done about these issues? How could you become involved?

- Right to health
- Equity
- Empowerment
- Community participation
- Accountability
- Partnerships.

Modern health care is now becoming more focused on a primary care-led NHS. The pattern of health promotion and health education is shifting away from an illness model to one that seeks to underpin health from a much wider perspective. The opportunities to help and advise individuals, families and communities are unparalleled and will undoubtedly become a focus and a challenge well into the new millennium. A brief description of the key areas will be given before illustrating how local health authorities can build on these targets for specific local needs.

The initial key areas

The initial key areas (DoH, 1992) were:

1. Coronary heart disease and stroke
2. Cancers
3. Mental illness
4. HIV/AIDS and sexual health
5. Accidents.

The environment was added as part of this health strategy in 1996. The government's role has been to facilitate action at a high level, providing networks for health across all ministerial departments. The government has tackled legislation, regulation, the allocation of resources and monitoring and assessing changes in health in order to provide, hopefully, reliable information for all those they seek to serve. Key areas with objectives that lead to quantifiable targets were stated along with action to progress these. A brief outline is given below, together with the 1991 mortality figures in brackets from *The Health of the Nation* (DoH, 1992). Figures 2.4 and 2.5 outline the response of one local authority to this strategy.

Coronary heart disease and stroke
Coronary heart disease (CHD) remained the single largest cause of death in England (26 per cent), while strokes accounted for around 12 per cent of deaths.

Major risk factors include cigarette smoking, raised plasma cholesterol level, elevated blood pressure and lack of physical activity. The potential for reducing both morbidity and mortality through modifying these risk factors seems

1. Health improvement targets and monitoring graphs
2. Coronary heart disease
3. Strokes
4. Hypertension
5. Food and health
6. Lung cancer
7. Breast cancer
8. Cervical cancer
9. Skin cancer
10. Family planning
11. Sexually transmitted diseases other than AIDS
12. HIV/AIDS
13. Alcohol misuse
14. Accident prevention
15. Mental health strategy
16. Oral health strategy
17. Continence strategy
18. Prevention of suicide strategy

Figure 2.4 ● An example of local health authority strategies guided by the *Health of the Nation* strategy (Portsmouth and Southeast Hampshire, Department of Public Health, 1995)

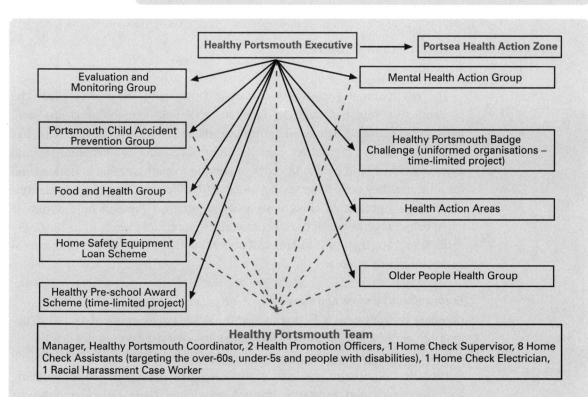

Figure 2.5 ● Healthy Portsmouth Initiative (adapted from Wingham and Nazareth, 1997)

obvious. Targets have been set for both CHD and stroke to reduce the mortality rate by 40 per cent in those under 65 years and by 30 per cent in those between 65 and 74 years of age by the year 2000.

Cancers

Cancers accounted for around 25 per cent of deaths in 1991. While there are many types of cancer all with a different aetiology, the potential to prevent, treat and cure them varies considerably. The targets specifically identify the following cancers:

aetiology

the cause of a condition; also the study of all the factors involved in the development of a disease

- Breast: a reduction in mortality rate of 25 per cent by the year 2000
- Cervical: a mortality reduction of 20 per cent by the year 2000 (baseline 1986)
- Skin: to halt the year-on-year increase by 2005
- Lung: to reduce the mortality rate by 30 per cent in men and 15 per cent in women under 75 years by 2010.

Mental illness

Mental illness is a leading cause of disability and ill-health, resulting in approximately 14 per cent of certified sickness. It is estimated to account for 14 per cent of NHS inpatient costs. Depression and anxiety have a prevalence of between 2 and 7 per cent in the adult population, with a lifetime risk of over 20 per cent. Psychotic illnesses, like affective psychosis and schizophrenia, are less common albeit more severe. The aim is for a significant improvement in the health of those with mental illness, with a reduction of 15 per cent in the overall suicide rate and of 33 per cent for those with severe mental illness.

HIV/AIDS and sexual health

The human immunodeficiency virus (HIV) causes the acquired immune deficiency syndrome (AIDS). This key area deals also with sexually transmitted diseases, encompassing family planning and unplanned pregnancy. The government acknowledges that reliable statistics are very difficult to obtain in this complex area of HIV/AIDS. No-one really knows the size of the problem in England, although, as we learn more about the disease process, the epidemiology is becoming more sophisticated.

The main objectives are: to reduce the incidence of HIV and other sexually transmitted infections; to provide for their effective prevention, diagnosis and treatment; to develop the surveillance and monitoring systems; to provide effective family planning services; and to reduce the number of unplanned pregnancies (a 50 per cent reduction in conception rate of the under-16s by the year 2000).

Safer sexual practices, together with the use of condoms to reduce the infection risk, are stressed. Those who inject drugs and share equipment are noted to be at significant risk of HIV as well as hepatitis B and C. A reduction in this practice by the year 2000 to just 5 per cent of the 1990 level is hoped for.

Accidents

Accidents cause death and have a high incidence of morbidity, especially among people under 30 years of age.

Reductions in the number of deaths for children under 15 years, young adults aged between 15 and 24 years and people aged over 65 have been separately targeted, with reductions of 33 per cent, 25 per cent and 33 per cent respectively by 2005. The government has based its strategy on a better co-ordination of agencies to prevent accidents, for example local authority involvement in planning, building control, highways, housing, social services, education, environmental health and the emergency services. Also involved are the public health promotion of accident prevention to enable people to be better informed, and taking action on specific types of accident and considering vulnerable groups.

Activity
6

Giving power back to clients or patients and working with them to meet their needs must be at the very heart of nursing, suggest Brown and Piper (1997), as they represent the aggrandisement of human care by enabling potential to be fulfilled. In which ways does the political agenda enable or hinder nurses in working in partnership with their clients?

Health promotion receives a relatively small amount from the entirety of the health budget. The prevailing political philosophy towards societal health needs will affect the relationship between national and local government. At her first major speech to the Royal College of Midwives on 15 May 1997, Tessa Jowell, the Minister for Public Health (a new post created by the incoming Labour government), set out to tackle the inequalities that give rise to ill-health alongside the service that provides treatment and care. By tackling the wider influences that detract from health, such as poverty, poor housing, unemployment and polluted environments, government can make an impact on health inequalities.

Smoking has been recognised as the greatest single cause of preventable illness and premature death in the UK, yet the powerful tobacco lobby has managed to convince politicians that banning tobacco advertising is not in their political interest. Many people still smoke, the largest increase in smoking rates being seen in teenagers, especially girls. Smoking during pregnancy has consistently shown a significant statistical relationship between maternal smoking and the risk of sudden infant death syndrome. The planned ban on tobacco advertising and the consequent removal of tobacco sports sponsorship is undoubtedly a courageous political step, one long overdue.

Spiritual health

A person's spiritual dimension enables him or her to move from self-interest to care for another, or allows a greater enjoyment in the fullness of life. While the word 'spirituality' has associations with religious activity, spirituality 'is to be that state in which a person finds his view of life (spiritual life) to be matched by his experience within it' (Langford, 1993, p. 6). The spiritual dimension perhaps acts as a means of integrating the other dimensions of life. It is ulti-

Activity 7

Find out what support is available to help meet the spiritual needs of clients. Make a note of the services and any useful contact addresses. How could you help someone who has a value base different from your own?

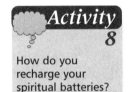

Activity 8

How do you recharge your spiritual batteries?

mately concerned with issues and life principles, and is often seen as a search for meaning. Spirituality, it may be argued, therefore permeates every aspect and moment of living. It involves eating, drinking, working, creating, showing love, sharing laughter and tears, worshipping and dying. Langford (1993) goes on to suggest that all these activities are equally 'spiritual' occasions.

Nursing can be physically and emotionally draining. Dealing with life-and-death situations can be both rewarding and exhausting. Nurses perhaps need four things to assist them in assisting others:

1. A confidant, a friend, preferably someone outside the family, with whom they can share deeply issues concerning work and their emotional reactions. A confidant enables a person to be aware of him- or herself and keep a balance by being alert to possible problems.
2. Peer support offers mutual support and the chance to talk through issues that others can understand because they share the same experience. A student cohort provides a variety of characters, each person then being able to relate to someone who is the right person for them.
3. Doing something completely different – taking time out, developing a hobby or going on holiday – can help to recharge the nurse's spiritual battery.
4. Developing their spiritual base to withstand a multitude of questions, pressures and changes as they progress through their nursing careers.

Individual health

An individual's life chances for health will be dependent on the five other aspects of health (social, environmental, organisational, political and spiritual) and how they interrelate. We have already considered the basic essentials for health maintenance: no wars or civil disturbance, assured personal safety, good housing, safe clean water and sewage disposal, and nutritious uncontaminated food.

Present health status is not fixed but is very much dependent upon what has gone before and, to an extent, what the future holds. Although we cannot predict the future with absolute accuracy, a future without hope would be severely detrimental to health. Conversely, when individuals are given hope for their future, they can overcome enormous threats and challenges to their health. Think back to Annie with the ovarian cancer or to young Samantha waiting for a heart transplant.

Individuals' past health history may show a balance in their personal life. There may be a negative health course, as in the case of Sam. The present health balance depends on the six aspects contributing to well-being and functioning as determined by the individuals and those who share life with them. Future health potential is dependent upon strong integration of these six aspects of health, supporting and enabling a positive self-concept, having developed coping skills as part of the individual's health resource repertoire.

Activity 9

Make a list of the aspects of your own life in which good health could be improved. Be realistic. From this list produce a plan that could be implemented over a 4-week period. Think about how the success of your plan could be evaluated. Implement the plan and, after 4 weeks, evaluate it. Within health promotion, we need short-term gains to encourage and motivate us towards longer-term benefits.

Let us take an everyday example of a life skill and relate this to individual health and the potential for maintaining or improving it. In a study undertaken on behalf of the National Food Alliance by MORI (1993), fewer than half the national sample of children could boil an egg or bake a potato. We are all consumers of food, but individuals are being deskilled or underskilled when it comes to preparing and cooking. Conversely, however, there is an abundance of advice within the media, from television programmes to magazines, on how to cook. Convenience and fast foods have played a part in the deskilling process, but fast food can be nutritious. Fast Food Fit is a campaign developed by Portsmouth City Council to help families on low budgets to cook nutritious food. It has a number of healthy recipes that can be prepared quickly and at a low cost. This scheme is likely to spread to cover university students, many of whom find cooking boring, cannot afford decent wholesome food or prefer a 'liquid diet', with the threats to health that this may bring.

● The Role of the Nurse as a Health Promoter

Investment in the health sector is rapidly becoming an amalgam of public and private partnerships, with some key individuals involved in joint societal efforts. While it is evident that the responsibility for health promotion does not lie with the health sector alone, nurses nevertheless have an unequal contribution to make to alliances created in the pursuit of health. Within the UK, this is especially so as nurses form the largest body of health-care professionals orchestrated by the NHS, with an immeasurable number of client and patient interactions.

The United Kingdom Central Council for Nursing, Midwifery and Health Visiting (UKCC) Code of Conduct (UKCC, 1992) set standards within a professional framework to regulate the conduct of members. Sixteen core statements make up the code, which is founded upon the practitioner being professionally accountable in safeguarding and promoting the interests of individual patients and clients within the context of society. These core values and characteristics of acceptable practice act in a way to safeguard the public. Specifically practitioners must:

Recognise and respect the uniqueness and dignity of each patient and client, and respond to their need for care, irrespective of their ethnic origin, religious beliefs, personal attributes, the nature of their health problems or any other factor. [point 7] ...Having regard to the physical, psychological and social effects on patients and clients, any circumstances in the environment of care which could jeopardise standards of practice. [point 11] ...The notion of partnership and respect between nurse and client are essential ingredients to good practice and especially promoting health.

Health promotion is not simply something that is done to the client or patient, as in changing a dressing or taking a blood pressure, but instead informs and pervades all aspects of nursing care in enhancing health through:

- Needs assessment
- Planning health gain
- Evaluating interventions and strategies for effectiveness and efficiency.

Knowing those whom we seek to support within our professional capacity as nurses will help us to understand their health needs. 'Knowing the client/patient' has become a buzz phrase within contemporary nursing. Understanding the individual's status in terms of health, beliefs, values and attitudes, along with the structural determinants of health and outside influences, will form a starting point for a needs assessment.

Within the acute illness setting, a nurse's professionalism may be the sustaining presence in the facilitation of the patient's own coping abilities. This contrasts with the episodic and often interventionist nature of the medical relationship. In planning health gain, the power that nursing possesses is often very subtle. As Campbell (1993, p. 27) points out, the positive power of nursing:

> is one which knows when to hold and support without possessiveness, and when to motivate and let go, without bullying or rejection.

It is, or should be, the nature of nursing care that empowers the client or patient, and Campbell (1993, p. 27) goes on to suggest that nursing is a form of health promotion. The notion of health gain is at the centre of health promotion as a core value.

Giving power back to clients or patients and working with them to meet their needs, suggest Brown and Piper (1997), must be at the very heart of nursing as it represents the aggrandisement of human care by enabling potential to be fulfilled.

Within nursing practice, an awareness of the nuances of the patient or client is essential, especially if the observant nurse is to pick up on these cues to potentiate health. Because awareness makes demands upon us, usually in the form of some action, but also equally by just providing a listening ear, it costs us in terms of our time. Continually responding to the demands of others requires effort, patience and a degree of self-denial. It can be painful, especially when you are busy and this is the umteenth time that Mrs Moon has had a commode, or, in the community, when you are dressing Miss Patel's leg ulcer, her cat walks across your sterile field. Nurses may lapse into deaf or partially sighted mode as a coping mechanism. It is important that individual nurses are realistic in terms of what they can achieve within their professional role. One way is through the use of praxis (reflective practice and action) to prevent the adoption of second-rate or diminished care by lowering standards through lack of awareness or inaction. Professional dialogue by discussion with qualified staff and your peers may often help to clarify issues before they become problematic.

Under the framework of the English National Board's (ENB) Higher Award (ENB, 1991), 10 key characteristics form the structure for nurses to develop their practice, of which the sixth key characteristic is health promotion (Chart 2.1). While this award is designed for experienced postregistration nurses, it provides a useful structure on which the novice nurse can begin to build his or her practice. Four principles underpin this framework:

- *Reviewing* practice knowledge skills and expertise
- *Identifying* continuing education needs
- *Designing* modular programmes
- *Assessing* continuing education activities.

Reviewing practice is something that all nurses need to do. For students of nursing, it is particularly valuable as it links so closely with the identification of their learning needs. Designing modular programmes does not, at first glance, seem to be in the remit of student nurses. However, within a supervised capacity, students should develop ways and means of involving patients and clients in strategies to make health gains. These strategies may be individualised (designed specifically for the client) and form part of the client's overall care. Planning for health through raising awareness in an enabling way is crucial. There should be no place for 'victim-blaming', in which often rushed and ill-informed judgements are made based on stereotypical and partial information. Health-promotion strategies will need to be assessed for effectiveness and evaluated in terms of how well they meet the client's needs and the normative needs of the health professionals involved. A schematic model of how this could be approached within nursing is outlined in Figure 2.6.

Chart 2.1 ● English National Board key characteristic 6: health promotion

Promote understanding of health promotion, preventative care, health education and healthy living	Understand and apply the principles and practice of health promotion in the work setting and create, maintain and take responsibility for a healthy work environment	Facilitate responsibility and choice among clients for healthy living, and their ability to determine their own lifestyles	Develop and implement strategies for health care based on understanding of the impact of health trends on resources

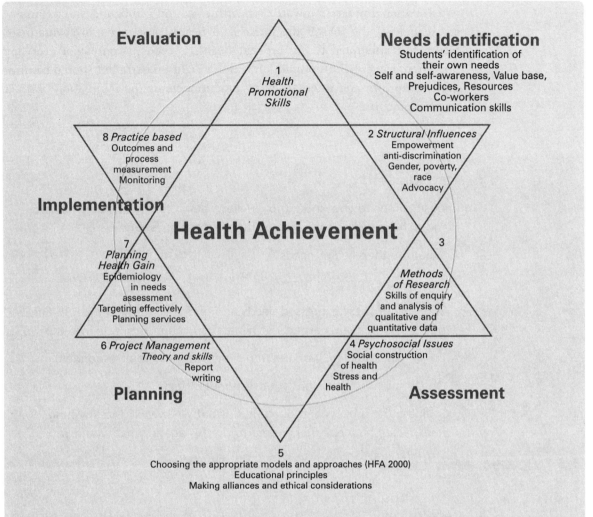

Figure 2.6 ● The role of the nurse promoting health could include the above key areas from planning to evaluation

Chapter Summary

This chapter has explored what health is as a dynamic concept within a flux. It can be a slippery concept to grasp. Contemporary challenges to health have been discussed and some theoretical concepts explained. A model utilising six aspects of health – social, environmental, organisational, political, individual and spiritual – has provided the framework for expanding on these concepts. The activities in these sections will enable readers to relate them to their own setting. In doing so, it is hoped that a greater understanding can be achieved.

Real-life examples have been drawn on to illustrate key points. An overview of the *Health of the Nation* strategy for England has given a baseline against which national progress towards a healthier nation can be measured. Finally, a discourse of the role of the nurse as a health promoter and evaluator of health has attempted to ensure that health is seen in context of everyday nursing practice. Health promotion is not an add-on extra but should be integrated into care and internalised by practitioners as the foundation of good nursing practice.

Test Yourself!

Choose someone you know (not a client but a family member or close friend) who is willing to answer some personal questions.

1. What are their health needs?

2. How do they perceive them?

3. Take one of these expressed needs and plan a strategy to meet it. See how many of the six aspects of health you can incorporate into this.

4. Implement the plan, working in partnership with your respondent.

5. On completion, how does your respondent feel?

6. Evaluate the process and outcomes. What went well? Did anything unexpected happen? If you were to do this again, what would you change?

References

Bradshaw, J. (1994) The conceptualisation and measurement of need. In Popay, J. and Williams, G. (eds) *Researching the People's Health,* p. 54. Routledge, London.

Brown, P.A. and Piper, S.M. (1997) Nursing and the health of the nation: schism or symbiosis? *Journal of Advanced Nursing* **25**: 297–301.

Campbell, A.V. (1993) The ethics of health education. In Wilson-Barnett, J. and Macleod Clark, J. (eds) *Research in Health Promotion and Nursing*, pp. 20–8. Macmillan, Basingstoke.

Department of Public Health (1995) *Health Atlas*. Portsmouth and South East Hampshire Health Authority, Portsmouth.

DHSS (Department of Health and Social Security) (1980) *Inequalities in Health* (Black Report). DHSS, London.

DoH (Department of Health) (1992) *The Health of the Nation – a Strategy for Health in England*. Cmnd 1986. HMSO, London.

DoH (Department of Health) (1993) *A Vision for the Future*. NHS Management Executive, Leeds.

DoH (Department of Health) (1998) Monthly Creutzfeldt–Jakob Figures. Press Release 98/005. 5 January. DoH web site (www.coi.gov.uk/coi/depts/GDH/coi6395d.ok).

Dubos, R. (1979) Mirage of health. In Black, N., Boswell, D., Gray, A., Murphy, S. and Popjay, J. *Health and Disease: A Reader*. Open University Press, Milton Keynes.

Emmerson, A., Enstone, J., Griffin, M., Kelsey, M. and Smyth, E. (1996) The second national prevalence survey of infection in hospitals: overview of the results. *Journal of Hospital Infection* **32**: 175–90.

ENB (English National Board for Nursing Midwifery and Health Visiting) (1991) *Professional Portfolio, Higher Award Learning Outcomes*, Summary Card 2. ENB, London.

Graham, H. (1987) Women's smoking and family health. *Social Science and Medicine* **25**(1): 47–56.

HM Government (1993) *MM20 Overseas Statistics*. December. HMSO, London.

Irwin, A. (1997) The five failures. *Daily Telegraph*, 24 June, p. 13.

Kelly, M., Charlton, B. and Hanlon, P. (1993) The four levels of health promotion: an integrated approach. *Public Health* **107**(5): 320.

Kickbusch, I. (1996) New players for a new era: how up to date is health promotion? *Health Promotion International* **11**(4): editorial.

Lang, T. (1997) *Food policy for the 21st century: can it be both radical and reasonable?* Discussion Paper 4. Thames Valley University, London.

Langford, D. (1993) *Where is God in all this?*, 2nd edn. Countess Mountbatten House, Moorgreen Hospital, Southampton.

MAFF (Ministry of Agriculture, Fisheries and Food) (1994) *Agriculture in the UK 1993*. HMSO, London.

MORI (1993) Poll for Get Cooking Project. National Food Alliance, London.

Peterson, A. and Lupton, D. (1996) *The New Public Health*. Sage, London.

Pike, S. and Forster, D. (eds) (1995) *Health Promotion for All*. Churchill Livingstone, London.

Seedhouse, D. (1986) *Health: The Foundations for Achievement*. John Wiley & Sons, Chichester.

Seedhouse, D. (1997) *Health Promotion Philosophy, Prejudice and Practice*. John Wiley & Sons, Chichester.

UKCC (United Kingdom Central Council for Nursing, Midwifery and Health Visiting) (1992) *Code of Professional Conduct*, 3rd edn. UKCC, London.

WHO (World Health Organisation) (1947) Constitution. WHO, Geneva.

WHO (World Health Organisation) (1985) *Targets for Health for All by the Year 2000*. WHO, Copenhagen.

Wingham, S. and Nazareth, K. (1997) Health Portsmouth Initiative. Unpublished document, Portsmouth City Council.

Further Reading

Ewles, L. and Simnet, I. (1995) *Promoting Health – A Practical Guide to Health Education*, 3rd edn, Scutari Press, London.

Naidoo, J. and Wills, J. (1994) *Health Promotion – Foundations for Practice*. Baillière Tindall, London.

Scriven, A. and Orme, J. (eds) (1996) *Health Promotion: Professional Perspectives*. Macmillan, Basingstoke.

Chapter 3

Safety in Practice

FRAN BOXALL AND SOMDUTH PARBOTEEAH

Introduction

This chapter in divided into four sections: manual handling, control of infection, basic food hygiene and the administration of medications.

The purpose of this chapter is to provide students with the essential knowledge to carry out nursing practice in a manner that will safeguard them and those patients/clients in their care.

By the end of this chapter, you will have an understanding of:

● Safe practice in the delivery of patient care

● The legislation affecting nursing practice

● The administration of medication.

Throughout the chapter, you will be given an opportunity to undertake some exercises that will assist in further developing your competence, knowledge and skills.

Manual Handling

This section describes the role of the nurse in the moving of patients and clients. By the end of this section, the nurse will:

● Have a full understanding of the policies and legislation affecting practice
● Be able to undertake manual handling procedures
● Develop safe manual handling techniques.

In our everyday lives, there will be many times, for example when shopping, doing sport or working, when there is a need to handle equipment or loads, be these objects or people. The majority of individuals undertake such tasks without due consideration of their own or others' safety. In the health-care setting, the need to handle people as well as objects provides an additional risk because people are often unpredictable.

Table 3.1 ● Reporting of manual handling injuries

	1992–93	1993–94
Manual handling injuries	4796	4533
Total injuries	8554	7748
Manual handling injuries related to patient handling	62%	63%

Source: Letter from Dr S.M. Chivers, Director of HSE (1996).

The number of manual handling injuries sustained in the health service sector and reported to the Health and Safety Executive (HSE) under the Reporting of Injuries, Disease and Dangerous Occurrence Regulations (1985) is shown in Table 3.1. Between 1994 and 1997, more than 15 000 manual handling injuries across England were reported to the HSE. The Disabled Living Foundation (1994) has indicated that one in four qualified nurses has taken time off with a back injury sustained at work, this for some meaning the end of their nursing career. Gladman (1993) reported that student nurses are at a high risk of injuries and that the problem may be further compounded by the recent recruitment of older people, who may already suffer from back pain. It is, therefore, imperative to stop manual handling injuries taking their toll on nurses' health.

The estimated annual cost for the NHS of back pain was approximately £480m in 1993 with lost production costs of £3.8bn and benefit payments of £1.4bn (Rosen, 1994).

The law as it relates to manual handling is regulated by statute principally in the form of the Health and Safety at Work Act 1974 and the Manual Handling Operations Regulations 1992, the latter introduced under the provisions of the Health and Safety at Work Act to enable the UK to implement the requirements of European Directives on the manual handling of loads. Manual handling operations have been defined within the HSE Directives (1992) as:

transporting or supporting a load, including lifting, putting down, pushing, pulling, carrying or moving by hand or bodily force. This also includes the intentional dropping or throwing of a load.

Under these regulations the employer has a general duty 'To ensure, so far as is reasonably practicable, the health, safety and welfare at work of all employees' (Health and Safety at Work Act 1974) and must avoid the need for hazardous manual handling operations. Employers' responsibilities are listed in Chart 3.1. Where this is not reasonably practicable, the HSE recommends that employers make a suitable and sufficient assessment and take appropriate steps to reduce the risk of injury to the lowest level reasonably possible.

Chart 3.1 ● Health and Safety Act 1974 – general duties of employers

1. To ensure that employees are not exposed to foreseeable risks of injury
2. To develop a no manual handling policy in practice
3. The provision of information, instruction, training and supervision necessary to ensure health and safety
4. The provision and maintenance of a working environment that is safe and without risks to health and adequate as regards facilities and arrangements for welfare at work

Employees have a duty under the Act to take reasonable care of their own health and safety and that of other people who may be affected by their actions, and it is essential that all health-care workers adhere to these regulations. Failure on the part of any individual to follow these regulations may jeopardise patients' safety, and cause serious injury to themselves, which may result in chronic ill-health.

As a student nurse preparing to take on a professional role and faced with manual handling operations throughout your career, you will need to continue to review any relevant new legislation. All employers are required by law to update their employees annually on the principles and practice of manual handling operations.

As safety of the nurse and patient is paramount, nursing education will include instruction on handling operations and guidance on local practice and the use of handling equipment. Teaching staff have a responsibility to provide the correct information, as indicated by law, and students contracted within a school must, also by law, undergo regular updating. Failure to do so may affect their ability to practise.

Patient or client care involves a multidisciplinary team effort in a variety of settings, so it is important that nurses observe and note the type of patient or client group for whom they are caring.

Activity

1

Identify clients in your practice who need to be moved and the resources available to achieve safe and successful handling.

Risk assessment

Risk assessment is an essential component of nursing practice; four main factors need to be considered:

- The task
- The load
- The work environment
- Individual capability.

The task

The nurse should consider whether the task involves:

- Holding the load at a distance from the trunk, for example moving a patient on a divan bed
- Unsatisfactory bodily movement or posture, as with a patient suffering from a stroke
- Excessive or sudden movement of the load, for example with an unco-operative patient
- Frequent or prolonged physical effort, as when moving a patient to give nursing care
- An insufficient rest or recovery period, for example when too many patients require toileting.

It is important to carry out a thorough assessment of the task in hand. Poor posture during manual handling introduces the additional risk of loss of control of the load and a sudden unpredictable increase in physical stresses.

The load

Is the load:

- Heavy or difficult to grasp, for example an obese patient suffering from a stroke?
- unstable or potentially damaging, for example a confused patient?

Within the health-care setting, the patient is referred to as the 'load'. There-fore, size, weight, shape, fragility, stability, the individual's ability to function both physically and mentally, and any attachments that may hinder movement, such as infusion pumps, should be considered. Human beings can display indi-vidual characteristics that may help or hinder manual handling operations. For example, elderly clients may suffer from arthritis, which may limit movement.

The work environment

Aspects of the work environment to consider are:

- Space constraints preventing good posture, for example working in a bath-room or toilet area
- Uneven, slippery or unstable floors, for example when wet
- Variations in the level of floors or work surfaces, for example a low divan bed
- Poor lighting conditions
- Inadequate or insufficient storage facilities.

A safe working environment may be created if necessary by removing obstacles from the vicinity of the patient and reporting aspects of their work environment that require structural modifications. If the environment is not safe, the patient should be moved to a safer area.

Individual capability

Does the job:

- Require unusual strength or height, for example reaching out to a patient on a fixed height bed?
- Put at risk those who are pregnant or who have a health problem?
- Require special knowledge or training for its safe performance?
- Require protective clothing or personal protective equipment, for example nurses' belts, that can hinder posture or movement.

The Manual Handling Operations Regulations do not contain any weight limits below which manual handling can be considered safe. The Royal College of Nursing (RCN, 1996) recommends that all patient handling should be assessed looking at all risk factors rather than purely weight. The numerical guidelines (Figure 3.1) can be used to determine when an assessment is needed. It is assumed that the load can easily be grasped with both hands and that the procedure is being undertaken in a safe working environment.

Ergonomics

ergonomics

the study of the relationship between the working environment and the people within it

Ergonomics can be defined as the study of the relationship between the working environment and the people within it, and is important in the prevention of injury resulting from manual handling activities, ensuring the optimum 'fit' between the people and the work.

Ergonomic processes include risk assessment and the identification and implementation of measures to reduce risk. Posture, the types of furnishing used, their height, position and manoeuvrability, the tasks undertaken and the environment are all assessed in order to ensure that the job is designed to fit the worker and thus reduce the incidence of manual handling injuries.

Assisting with patient movement

When handling patients, the aim is actively to encourage independent movement, the health-care worker assisting as little as possible. Teaching the principles of normal movement can be undertaken collaboratively between the nurses and the physiotherapist.

Any normal movement that the patient can undertake for herself avoids the need for a full lift, and patient preferences and ways of moving should be taken

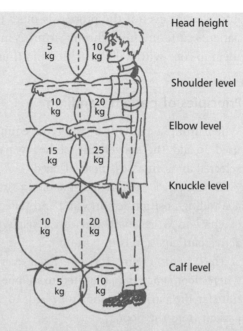

Head height

Shoulder level

Elbow level

Knuckle level

Calf level

Notes:
1. It is important to ensure that the load is grasped with both hands and that the body is in a stable position.
2. If the hands pass through more than one weight zone, the smallest weight figure should be used.
3. The ability to lift or move a load is significantly reduced if it is held at arm's length, or if the hands are raised above the shoulder level.

Figure 3.1 ● Guidelines for lifting and lowering for men

Casebox 3.1

● Mr Jones, a 38-year-old man with learning difficulties has been admitted to your ward with right-sided paralysis and is unable to move his right arm and leg. He is conscious and aware of his admission but is unable to undertake any activities for himself. He weighs 80 kg and has also been suffering from urinary incontinence. He has been placed in the side room that has its own toilet facilities but reduced working space.

Undertake a risk assessment from the above scenario and discuss your findings with your manual handling co-ordinator.

What would you do if the nurse you were working with asked you to lift this patient rather than use the appropriate equipment?

● Assessment should ascertain whether there is likely to be any risk of injury. A more detailed assessment will consider the task involved, the load, the environment and individual capability.

● In this case, you should politely refuse to lift Mr Jones, referring to the *Manual Handling Operations Regulations* (HSE, 1992). An alternative method of moving the patient should be employed.

into account even if the process is more time-consuming. For example, elderly patients suffering from chronic arthritis may have developed strategies that help them to cope with daily activities and thus maintain their independence.

Principles of patient handling

When lifting a patient, a variety of equipment is available which can also be used to aid the movement of heavy patients if required. Hoists should be selected after an assessment of need.

The *Sara 2000* (Figure 3.2) enables a single nurse to raise a patient safely into a standing position for dressing and toileting, allows transfer from bed to chair or chair to wheelchair and can assist with rehabilitation when the patient's active participation is important.

The *Bianca* (Figure 3.3) is a fixed overhead hoist that is particularly useful where floor space is too limited to manoeuvre a mobile hoist. It can be used to transfer the patient to and from bed, to sit the patient up in bed and to lift a patient from the floor.

The *Maximove* (Figure 3.4) is a heavy-duty hoist that can lift up to 188 kg. The tilting spreader bar gives clearance to patients with unsteady head movements and reclines them for secure transfer. The wide lifting range enables the highest treatment beds or even trampolines in the physiotherapy department to be reached.

The *Trixie Lift* (Figure 3.5) is a powered general-purpose hoist for use in nursing homes and domestic situations to lift patients on to most heights of bed and to chairs and toilets, to reposition the patient in bed and for transfer to a car. It can be supplied with advanced electronic weighing scales.

In order to become safe in moving patients either manually or with a hoist a period of instruction followed by direct supervised practice is recommended. Skills laboratories may offer a safe learning environment.

Activity 2

Find out which manual handling equipment is used in your area and which types are most suited for certain tasks. Design a nursing action plan for moving a patient using the four criteria for risk assessment.

Other equipment

There is a vast range of other manual handling equipment, for example patient lifting slings, hand blocks, roller towels and transfer slides, that are being constantly updated and improved by manufacturers. The primary requirement for use is that the equipment is suitable for the user and the task for which it is intended. Equipment must be:

● Compatible with its surroundings
● Compatible with other equipment and mechanical aids
● Designed to avoid or reduce the need for manual handling
● Easy to use, move, adjust and maintain.

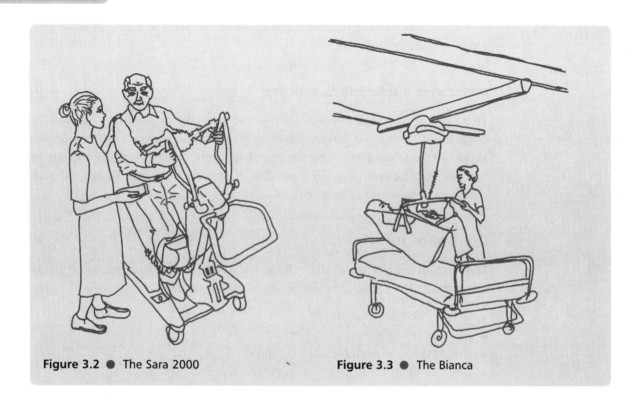

Figure 3.2 ● The Sara 2000

Figure 3.3 ● The Bianca

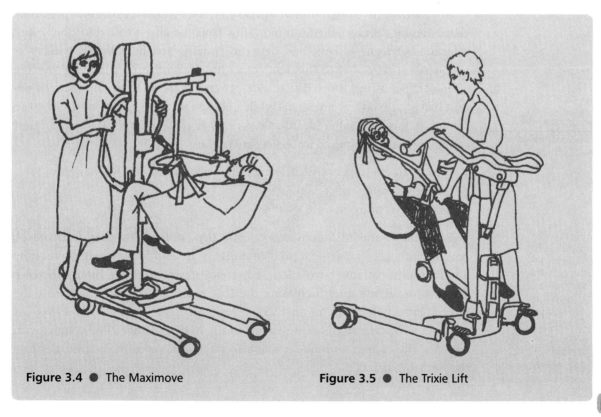

Figure 3.4 ● The Maximove

Figure 3.5 ● The Trixie Lift

The three key words in ensuring the safe use of such handling aids are *suitability*, *availability* and *maintenance*.

Introducing a safer handling policy

The RCN (1996) recommends that health-care workers in the hospital or community should no longer have to lift manually. Specialised equipment should be made available to minimise risk of injury. While hospital Trusts are in the process of developing their policies, health-care workers should take all necessary precautions to ensure their safety.

Control of Infection

This section will describe the role of the nurse in the prevention of cross-infection. By the end of this section the nurse will be able to:

- Define infection control
- Describe hospital-acquired infection
- Understand the need for universal precautions
- Describe the role of the infection control team
- Discuss local infection control policies.

Infection, particularly hospital infection, causes concern because of the associated significant morbidity and mortality. Thus the aim is to reduce the risk of infection between patients, and between patients and health-care workers. A prevalence survey of 18 613 patients in 43 hospitals in the UK in 1980 covering all major specialities showed that 19.1 per cent were infected and that 9.3 per cent had acquired their infections while in hospital (these being known as noso-

nosocomial infections

infections caused as a result of hospitalisation

comial, or hospital-acquired, infections or HAIs) (Meers *et al.*, 1981). The most common hospital-acquired infections are of the:

1. Urinary tract (30 per cent), the majority being in catheterised patients
2. Lower respiratory tract
3. Skin and wounds.

Resistant strains of Staphylococcal infection, difficult to treat and control, have recently become a major problem in HAIs. In addition to greater morbidity and mortality, patients have a longer hospital stay and receive more expensive drugs, thus significantly increasing the cost. During 1987, infections cost the NHS approximately £115m and 95 000 lost bed days (Meers *et al.*, 1981). As nurses are the largest group of workers in the NHS and have close contact with patients, they are in a unique position to integrate preventative strategies into their nursing practice.

The protection of patients

Modern-day care with increased surgical intervention and technological advances on an increasingly elderly population with greater susceptibility to infection heightens the risk of acquiring infection while in hospital. Although some of these nosocomial infections are inevitable, the American Scenic Report (Haley *et al.*, 1985) showed that HAIs can be reduced by as much as 30 per cent.

The most likely means of transmission of infectious organisms from body fluids is by direct contact or the percutaneous inoculation of the infected body fluids. Since it is impossible to identify which patients are infected, the Department of Health (DoH, 1990a) recommends the adoption of 'Universal Precautions' (Chart 3.2) embodying the principles of good practice in the control of bloodborne infections and the spread of infection. In addition, the following basic measures should be taken in order to minimise the risk of patients acquiring infections while in hospitals:

- Employ good hand hygiene.
- Do not touch patients' wounds or dressings unless it is essential; if you have to, always wear gloves.
- Ensure that all equipment for use on patients is sterile or disinfected.
- Ensure general standards of cleanliness.
- Follow specific guidance for patients as required.

Chart 3.2 ● Universal Precautions

1. Skin – Cuts or abrasions of exposed areas should be covered with waterproof dressing, which is also an effective viral and bacterial barrier
2. Gloves – Wear gloves
3. Handwashing – Thorough handwashing in between procedures is necessary
4. Aprons – Wear disposable aprons if there is a possibility of splashing
5. Eyes – Eye protection should be worn if there is a danger of flying contaminated debris
6. Sharps – Extreme care should be taken during the use and disposal of sharps
7. Needlestick injuries – Follow guidelines to avoid injury; in the event of a needlestick injury, follow local policy
8. Conjunctivae/mucous membranes – If splashed, irrigate with copious amounts of water
9. Spillages – Follow local guidelines to deal with spillages. Gloves and aprons should be worn
10. Waste – All contaminated waste should be placed in yellow coloured sacks and disposed of according to local Trust policy

Source: Adapted from DoH, 1990a.

Activity 3

Identify local and national guidelines concerning the control of infection in hospitals and the community.

Activity 4

Identify the different methods of hand decontamination in the different areas of practice such as the hospitals, health centres and patients' homes.

Hand hygiene

Many infections are spread by contact, and the hands are a major vehicle in the transmission of infection (RCN, 1992). Normal skin has a resident population of micro-organisms, and in the delivery of nursing care to patients or clients, other transient organisms are picked up and shed during contact. The aim of handwashing is to remove these transient organisms or to reduce their numbers below the level of an infected dose before they are transmitted to a patient. It is the most important method of preventing spread by contact.

The RCN (1995) recommends thorough handwashing and careful drying on soft, high-quality disposable tissues to remove the majority of resident and transient micro-organisms. All jewellery should be removed before handwashing, and nails should be kept short and clean. Antiseptic detergent solution used in handwashing will help to reduce the number of micro-organisms on the hands. As an alternative, a 70 per cent alcohol rub can be used in between procedures, and staff must follow the recommended guidelines for its use. Hands should be washed following the procedures shown in Chart 3.3.

It is vital, too, that the patient's hands are kept clean. The nurse should, therefore, offer handwashing facilities after the patient has used the toilet, before meals and any other time it is requested.

Laundry

Soiled and contaminated linen can be a source of infection. Linen should be bagged at source when removed from the bed and the hospital's policy for its disposal followed.

Waste disposal

Domestic and clinical waste is likely to contain and support the growth of Gram-negative bacilli; thus all waste should be regarded as heavily contaminated and handled with care. The DHSS gives guidance on the safe disposal of clinical

Chart 3.3 ● Indications for handwashing ....

- Before and after aseptic techniques or invasive procedures
- Before contact with susceptible patients
- After handling body fluids
- After handling contaminated items
- Prior to the administration of drugs
- Before serving meals (see text)
- After removing aprons and gloves
- At the beginning and end of duty
- If in any doubt

waste and on the colour-coding of waste containers, and the NHS has a legal responsibility for the safe disposal of hazardous waste. All waste is classified according to the following categories:

- *Domestic waste*: includes all materials not mentioned below. Domestic waste should be discarded into a black plastic bag that is securely closed.
- *Clinical waste*: includes all materials contaminated with micro-organisms, for example dressings. Clinical waste should be sealed in yellow plastic bags and disposed of by incineration.
- *Sharps*: includes all needles and sharp instruments. Sharps should be discarded into a Sharps box and disposed of by incineration. It may be necessary for a community Trust to organise the safe disposal of waste from the community.
- *Human tissue*: immediately enclose in a yellow bin and transport to the hospital incinerator.

As it is impossible to cover here all the situations that will be encountered, readers are strongly urged to consult their infection control team and check the local policies for guidance.

Activity 5

Identify how the following types of linen are dealt with in your hospital/community: used linen, soiled linen, infected linen, patients' personal clothing and duvets.

Basic Food Hygiene

This section will describe the role of the nurse in food-handling in clinical areas. By the end of this section, you should be able to:

- List the key legislation regarding food safety
- Define food poisoning
- Identify the 10-point code for nurses
- Identify the action to take in the event of food poisoning.

Food safety, food poisoning and consumers' health have recently begun to arouse a great deal of public concern. Since the mid-1960s, the reported number of food poisoning cases in the UK and most other countries of Europe and North America has risen (Sharp, 1992). Whether this increase is real or a result of improved surveillance is unclear, but there has been a significant increase in certain types of food poisoning, such as that by the strain of *Escherichia coli* also known as VTEC (verocytotoxic *E. coli* or *E. coli* 0157), which may lead to kidney failure and death. More resistant types of bacteria such as *Salmonella typhimurium* are also appearing. These multiresistant bacteria cannot be treated by the range of common antibiotics.

Food poisoning outbreaks in hospitals are not uncommon. Between 1978 and 1987, a total of 248 instances of food poisoning were reported in England and Wales, affecting 3000 patients (Joseph and Palmer, 1989). Dryden *et al.* (1994) described a nosocomial outbreak of salmonellosis in two hospitals affecting 22

Activity

6

Have you been ill from eating contaminated food? What symptoms did you have? Undertake a brief survey in your class to find out how many of your colleagues have been affected by food poisoning and what the source of infection was.

food poisoning

an acute illness, normally with a short incubation period, caused by the recent consumption of food contaminated by pathogenic micro-organisms or their toxins

patients and 7 staff in 14 wards, the estimated cost of which was in the region of £33 000.

Food poisoning patterns have also become more complicated. Food poisoning caused by Salmonella and Listeria (Dryden *et al.*, 1994) has decreased in the community, whereas the number of cases of Campylobacter infection has risen, this becoming the most commonly reported type of food poisoning. Such concern about food safety has now culminated in the recognition of the need for stricter controls and new legislation, as shown in Chart 3.4.

Environmental health officers (EHOs) have the power to inspect all premises where food is prepared and consumed, and failure to maintain safe practices may result in prosecution. Accordingly, all food handlers, including nurses, should receive training in food hygiene, the majority of cases of food poisoning being caused by ignorance, bad practice or poor management. The multiplicity of roles for nurses may include food preparation, food handling and assisting clients with their meals, and breaches of hygiene at any time may cause food poisoning.

A variety of diseases can be caused by eating food contaminated with pathogenic micro-organisms or their products, but not all of these diseases can be classified as food poisoning. Food poisoning has been described as an acute illness, normally with a short incubation period, caused by the recent consumption of food contaminated by pathogenic micro-organisms or their toxins. There is disturbance of the gastrointestinal system within a few hours or days of consumption. Although diarrhoea, vomiting and abdominal pain are the most common symptoms of food poisoning, other clinical features such as pyrexia may be present. The clinical features may not all be present at the same time. The cause can be either microbial or non-microbial (Chart 3.5), although bacterial contamination is the most likely.

Chart 3.4 ● UK and EEC food safety legislation

- Food and Drugs Act 1955 (superseded by 1984 Act)
- Food Act 1984
- Food Safety Act 1990
- EC Food Safety Legislation: Directive 89/397/EEC

Chart 3.5 ● Sources of food contamination

- Foreign bodies: for example glass, hair and insects
- Chemicals: for example cleaning products
- Toxins: may be natural, for example red kidney beans
- Micro-organisms   – bacteria, for example Salmonella
  – viruses
  – fungi
  – prions (identified as the agent causing the human form of bovine spongiform encephalitis, BSE)

A review of over 500 outbreaks of salmonellosis in England during the 1970s and 80s (Sharp, 1992) showed the main contributory factors, several of which co-existed, to be:

- Food prepared too far in advance: 42 per cent
- Food stored at room temperature: 30 per cent
- Food cooled too slowly before refrigeration/freezing: 22 per cent
- Reheating food at the wrong temperature: 13 per cent
- Using contaminated food, undercooking poultry/meat: 25 per cent
- Inadequate thawing of frozen food: 11 per cent
- Cross-contamination between cooked and uncooked food: 15 per cent
- Keeping hot food below 63°C
- Food handlers with symptomatic/asymptomatic infections.

Similar factors contribute in other forms of food poisoning, poor temperature regulation compounding all other contributory factors. Micro-organisms require suitable combinations of food, water, time and warmth to multiply (Figure 3.6); given a suitable environment, they can multiply every 20 minutes to levels potentially capable of causing food poisoning.

Our knowledge of the sources of food-poisoning bacteria and of routes of contamination can allow adequate precautions to be taken to prevent illness, especially in the vulnerable group of ill patients in the hospital and the community.

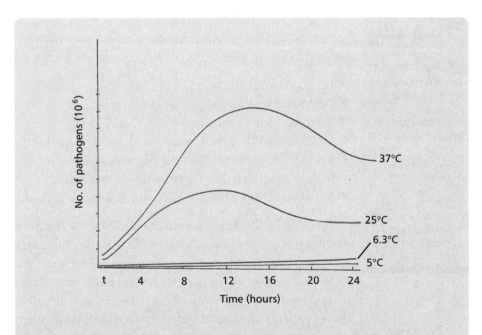

Figure 3.6 ● Diagrammatic representation of a growth curve of a food pathogen. Body and room temperature provide an ideal growth environment

10-Point code for nurses

1. WASH your HANDS
    - before touching food
    - after using the toilet or combing the hair
    - after administering to a patient's needs
    - after handling waste, bed pans or body fluids.
2. TELL your MANAGER immediately if you have any skin, nose, throat or stomach problems.
3. Cover cuts and sores with a brightly coloured waterproof dressing when handling food. (If the plaster is lost in the food, it can easily be identified.)
4. WEAR CLEAN clothing according to hospital policy.
5. NEVER COUGH or SNEEZE over food. Do not pick your nose or touch your lips or mouth when serving food.
6. Keep equipment and utensils CLEAN. (Clean as you go.)
7. KEEP food CLEAN and COVERED.
8. Touch food (both prepared and uncooked) as little as possible.
9. KEEP the lid on all waste sack holders and dustbins.
10. TELL your manager if you cannot follow the rules. Do not break the law.

(Adapted from DoH, 1990b)

Food service on the wards

Activity 7

Describe the food service to patients in isolation and what extra precautions should be taken. Identify whether any of your clients require any special eating or drinking utensils. Explore the range of utensils available for babies, children and those with learning disabilities.

Lukewarm food is potentially dangerous. A moderate temperature allows food-poisoning bacteria to grow rapidly, temperatures between 5°C and 63°C being referred to as the 'danger zone'. While food is being held for service:

- Hot food should be kept hot at above 63°C.
- Cold food should be kept cold at below 5°C.
- Avoid the danger zone between 5°C and 63°C.
- Meals should be served immediately upon arrival on the ward.
- Should there be any delay (if the patient is out of the ward, for example), refer to hospital policy for requesting a fresh meal.
- Microwaves should not be used to reheat or cook food in clinical areas.

The United Kingdom Central Council for Nursing, Midwifery and Health Visiting (UKCC, 1997) has declared that 'Nurses have an implicit responsibility for ensuring that patients are appropriately fed', and, under the UKCC *Code of Professional Conduct* (UKCC, 1992a), nurses also have the responsibility to report to an appropriate person any circumstances in which the safe and appropriate care of patients and clients cannot be provided. While the task of feeding may be delegated to junior members of staff, the overall responsibility remains with the registered nurse.

Ward fridges should be of the larder type, the temperature being checked

Activity 8

Identify the procedure for dealing with patients who develop the signs and symptoms of food poisoning.

daily and recorded on the relevant forms. Ice cream should not be stored in ward refrigerators, and overcrowding should be avoided. Cross-contamination between raw and 'high-risk foods' (for example, trifle) must not be allowed.

Microwave ovens and ice-making machines in clinical areas should be of catering grade, and staff using these should follow the guidelines for their use, cleaning and maintenance. Some microwave ovens produce 'cold spots' in food, so a more even distribution of heat is required, which can be achieved by thorough stirring both during and after cooking. Staff must make every effort to use the hospital catering department for supplying meals for patients.

Failure to follow the guidelines may result in prosecution under the Food Safety Act 1990 and may also be in breach of the UKCC Code of Conduct (1992a).

Administration of Medications

This section will describe the role of the nurse in the practice of drug administration. By the end of this section, the nurse should be able to:

- Understand the legislation and local Trust policies governing the administration of drugs by health-care professionals
- Safely administer drugs to patients by a variety of routes
- Be involved in the storage and preparation of drugs
- Understand how drugs work.

The administration of medicines is considered to be one of the most important responsibilities of the nurse. The nurse is responsible for assessing, planning, implementing and evaluating drug therapies as well as educating patients about their drug regimens. To be effective, the nurse must have an understanding of the fundamental principles of drug action, the purposes of drug use and the nursing actions necessary to bring about beneficial outcomes. The student is advised to consult other textbooks for more comprehensive information on drug actions and pharmacokinetics. Routes such as the intravenous and the epidural using electronic devices, for example pumps, are not described as they require further training at post-registration level.

The UKCC recommends that the administration of medicines should be undertaken 'by a First Level Registered Nurse/Midwife who has demonstrated the knowledge and competencies' (UKCC, 1992a, p. 14) and who can speedily respond to contraindications and side-effects. All practitioners, including student nurses, who are administering drugs must be responsible and accountable for their practice as outlined in the Code of Conduct (UKCC, 1992a).

In the UK, the range of substances intended for medicinal use must conform to standards specified in the *British Pharmacopoeia* or the *British Pharmaceutical Codex* and must satisfy the relevant government legislation listed in Chart 3.6. The implications of these Acts will be discussed below and the reader with a

Chart 3.6 ● Statutes controlling substances intended for medicinal use

- The Misuse of Drugs Act 1971
- The Poisons Act 1972
- The Medicines Act 1968, 1983
- The Prescription by Nurses Act 1992

keen interest for more details is recommend to consult a current copy of the *British National Formulary*. Failure to comply with legal requirements, and any ensuing errors, may result in criminal prosecution.

Before any medication is administered, it is important that the nurse carries out a detailed assessment of the patient, including:

- Medications that the patient is currently taking
- Their frequency and dosage
- Any home remedies being taken
- Other complementary therapies being used
- Allergies to any drugs
- Height, weight, blood pressure, temperature and respiration, as some drug dosages, for example dopamine infusion, are calculated on body mass, and side-effects can affect blood pressure
- General fitness and health, as such information can influence decisions about the routes and methods of drug administration; for example, an emaciated patient may not be able to tolerate deep intramuscular injections
- Diet; for example, if foods such as cheese, yogurt, broad beans, marmite, red wine and beer are administered to a patient who is receiving monoamine oxidase inhibitors (MAOIs), dangerous side-effects may ensue.

Activity 9

Take the medication history of a client you have cared for and discuss any relevant issues with your mentor.

In the UK, certain drugs can be bought over the counter and others must be prescribed by a doctor. In hospitals, medicines should not be administered without a written prescription.

Prescriptions should include information necessary for the safe administration of the drug. The prescription chart should detail:

- The name of the patient
- The date that the prescription was written and the signature of the prescriber
- The medication and dosage
- The route for administering the drug
- The time of administration
- Any specific information, for example that it is to be taken with meals.

Prescriptions are normally written on a standard prescription sheet (usually produced locally and differing between hospitals and in the community). Winslow (1997), in a study of medication prescription orders, found that 78 per cent of signatures were illegible or legible only with effort, thus increasing the risk of medication errors and patient harm. **The nurse should not administer any drug if the prescription is illegible**. It is important that all records of prescribed medicines should be kept together to prevent drug interactions, over-dosage and for monitoring purposes. The following criteria should be adhered to in order to prevent drug errors:

1. The prescription must be **legible**, and the approved or generic name should be used.
2. Details of the client's name and address, the dose required and the frequency and route of administration must be clearly stated. For certain drugs (for example, antibiotics), the proposed duration of therapy should be stated.
3. Controlled drugs, that is, drugs that are subject to the prescription require-ments of the Misuse of the Drug Regulations 1985, should be clearly monitored.
4. A prescription should not be altered once it has been written and should be written out in full again if a change in dose or frequency is indicated.
5. When a prescription is to be cancelled, it should be crossed out and signed and dated by the doctor.
6. In emergencies, telephone orders for the administration of medicines can be accepted by a first-level registered nurse (providing there is local agreement) if the doctor is unable to attend the ward. The prescription must then be written and signed by the nurse, stating that it is a verbal prescription. The doctor's name should be recorded on the prescription sheet and the doctor should sign the prescription as soon as possible. **No telephone orders should be repeated**.

The nurse's first task is to check the prescription for completeness; then he or she can prepare to administer the drug. In preparing medications, it is important to ensure cleanliness of the hands, a clean surface and sterility of all the materials used. All the components must be assembled in a well-lit room and medicines prepared in a safe area away from distraction. A general guide to ensure patients' safety in the administration of medications is to check the 'five rights':

1. The right medication
2. The right amount
3. The right time
4. The right patient
5. The right route.

Right medication

After checking the prescription, the nurse selects the right medication, care-fully checking the labels on the containers. Medications from a container that

controlled drugs

those drugs, such as morphine, subject to the prescription requirements of the Misuse of Drugs Regulations 1985

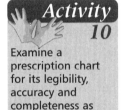

Activity 10

Examine a prescription chart for its legibility, accuracy and completeness as outlined above.

is unlabelled, defaced or illegible must never be used. The nurse should read any instructions pertaining to the medication and check the expiry date. Nurses must never administer a drug prepared by someone else because the nurse administering the drug will still be held accountable for any errors made by others during preparation. Medications must never be decanted from one container. The nurse should be familiar with basic information about the drug including its action, contraindications and side-effects, and current reference books, such as the *British National Formulary*, should be available at all times.

Two nurses, one of whom must be a registered nurse, should be involved in the administration of controlled drugs. The UKCC (1992b) is 'opposed to the involvement of persons who are not registered practitioners in the administration of medicines in acute care settings and with ill or dependent patients, since the requirements of paragraphs 8 and 11 of the document – Standards for the administration of Medicines – cannot be satisfied' (p. 14). All the necessary legal documentation must also be completed immediately after the procedure.

Right amount

To prepare the right amount of medication, the nurse must be familiar with the different measurement systems and common abbreviations used (Chart 3.7).

When preparing liquid medications for oral administration, it is important to shake all suspensions and emulsions to ensure a proper distribution of the drug. A calibrated medicine pot or syringe may be used to draw up the right amount of medication. If the medication is poured from the container, the medicine pot should be placed on a flat surface. To check for accuracy, the pot should be raised to eye level and the measurement read at the lowest point of the meniscus.

Some medications, for example eye drops, are measured with a dropper. The dropper must be held vertically, and the bulb should be slowly squeezed and released until the required dosage is reached.

Chart 3.7 ● Common abbreviations used in prescriptions

p.o.	– by mouth	p.r.n.	– given as necessary	caps	– capsules
s.c.	– subcutaneous	q.d.	– daily	elix.	– elixir
s.l.	– sublingual	q.h.	– every hour	I.U.	– International Units
i.m.	– intramuscular	q.d.s.	– four times a day	kg	– kilogram
i.v.	– intravenous	t.d.s.	– three times a day	g	– gram
e.c.	– enteric coated	b.i.d.	– twice a day	mg	– milligram
s.c.	– sugar coated	a.c.	– before meals	l	– litre
m.r.	– modified release	p.c.	– after meals	ml	– millilitre
stat	– given immediately	tr.	– tincture	guttae	– drops

The administration of injections depends on the drugs prescribed. Some injectables, for example pethidine, are available in liquid form, and the required amount can easily be drawn up. Administering the correct amount also depends on the strength of the drug. For example, heparin is available in 5000, 10 000 or 25 000 units/ml, so the amount injected will vary. Other injectables, such as penicillin, are produced in 'powder form' and require dilution before they can be administered. Where fluid is added, the solution displacement value must be taken into account. This can be found in the literature accompanying the vial and is usually 0.02 ml. If this value is not checked, it can result in erroneous doses being administered. When drugs are supplied at strengths different from the dosages that have been prescribed, the nurse must determine the quantity of drug that is to be administered. Special formulae are available, but it is also essential for the nurse to have a basic knowledge of arithmetic. The student who is experiencing difficulty should consult one of the many drug calculation textbooks now available or seek help from lecturers or mentors.

Right time

In order to achieve maximum therapeutic effectiveness, the doctor will specify the number of times a day the drug is to be given. It is important to adhere to this regimen as closely as possible in order to maintain a relatively constant blood plasma level of the drug (Figure 3.7). Drugs often have to be given with or after meals, and it is important to ensure that the patient understands the reason for this.

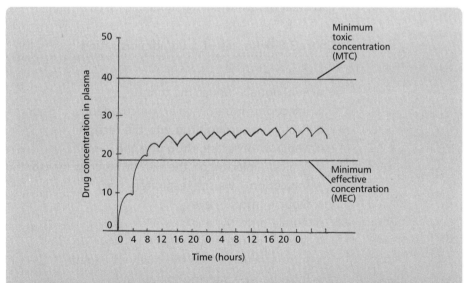

Figure 3.7 ● Plasma level versus time plot of a drug administered at 4-hourly intervals in order to keep the plasma concentration of the drug in an effective but not toxic range

Right patient

It is important to identify the right patient or client, and in a busy hospital or community setting, this is even more important. The following should be employed as a matter of routine regardless of the number of patients involved:

- In acute care settings, check the wrist identity bracelet and the name band on the bed.
- If the patient is not confused, ask him to state his name.
- If the patient questions the dosage, appearance or method of administration, always double-check the prescription and medication.

SPECIFIC POINTS ON CHILDREN'S MEDICATIONS

- If the child is too young, ask the parents to tell you the child's name.

- Children and/or parents have a right to know about the treatments, and they should always be addressed by name.

Right route

The doctor will usually specify the route by which the medication is to be administered, and the nurse administering the drug has the responsibility of ensuring that this is followed. If there are any discrepancies, the doctor should be consulted. If the nurse is concerned about the safety of administering a particular drug, the doctor should be asked to prepare and administer the drug.

Chart 3.8 ● Routes of drug administration

- Oral – given by mouth
- Sublingual – under the tongue
- Injections: intramuscular, subcutaneous, intradermal – into soft tissues
- Rectal – inserting drug into the rectum
- Vaginal – inserting drug into the vagina
- Topical – placing on the skin or mucous membranes
- Inhalation – via the respiratory tract
- Optic – into the eye
- Aural – into the ear
- Nasal – into the nose
- Intra-articular – into the cavity of a joint
- Intrathecal – into the spinal fluid
- Intravenous – into a vein
- Intracardiac – into the heart

Drugs may be administered in a number of ways (Chart 3.8). However, not all drugs may be administered by all the possible routes. When a drug is available in more than one form, the choice of route depends on factors such as the rate of absorption required, the speed of onset, the patient's general condition and any side-effects.

Nurses are not responsible for the administration of drugs by all of these routes but may have to assist doctors, for example with intrathecal administration.

Oral medications

oral route
—————
via the mouth

The oral route is the most frequently used route for drug administration. Oral medications are either in liquid (for example, elixir) or solid (for example, tablet) form. Some tablets (enteric coated) are covered with a substance that does not dissolve until the medication reaches the small intestine. These tablets should never be crushed or chewed because the medication will irritate the gastric mucosa. The administration of oral medication may be carried out by one or two registered nurses, depending on local policy.

Guidelines for oral drug administration

1. Wash your hands.
2. Check the prescription for completeness of date, time, drug to be given, dosage, route, frequency and duration of therapy. Check that the drug has not already been given and is due.
3. The nurse must have a basic understanding of the effects of the drug to be administered.
4. Select and check the required medication for discolouration, precipitation, contamination and expiry date.
5. Prepare the dosage as prescribed. Do not crush enteric-coated, sublingual or sustained-action tablets. Empty the required dose into a medicine pot. To prevent contamination, avoid touching the preparation. If dispensing liquid, the bottle should be held with the label towards the palm of the hand to prevent spillage obscuring the name of the drug.
6. Check the labels on containers again.
7. Take the medication and the prescription chart to the patient. Check the patient's identity (as described earlier) and the drug to be given.
8. Position the patient as upright as possible to aid swallowing, and instruct the patient accordingly. A glass of water or juice (50 ml or more) should be given to facilitate swallowing. The nurse must ensure that the patient has swallowed the medication. Infants and young children should be supported firmly to avoid spilling the medication.

9. Make the patient comfortable and ask her to stay upright for a few minutes.
10. Immediately complete all the necessary records.
11. Clear all the equipment.

Activity 11

Under direct supervision, participate in the administration of oral drugs to clients.

Some patients with a nasogastric tube may have their oral medications administered through it. The principles of managing the nasogastric tube are described in Chapter 4, and the procedure for administering the drug via this route is described in Chart 3.9. Liquid medications will flow easily down the tube; tablets and other solid medications should be avoided if possible but otherwise crushed and combined with a liquid in order not to obstruct the lumen. The medication should not be added to the 'feed'. Instead, the continuous feeding should be interrupted and resumed after administration of the drug. The tube should be flushed with water prior to and after the administration of the drug. Enteric-coated tablets and similar drugs should not be crushed.

SPECIFIC POINTS ON CHILDREN'S MEDICATIONS

● Flush the nasogastric tube with 20 ml water.

Chart 3.9 ● Administering drugs via a nasogastric tube

1. If possible, elevate the patient's head 30–45 degrees to avoid aspiration during and following administration
2. Check the placement of the nasogastric tube by either aspirating a small quantity of gastric contents and testing for acidity or by inserting a small amount of air into the tube while listening with a stethoscope for the entry of air into the stomach
3. Flush the tube with 30 ml of water for adults and 20 ml for children
4. Administer the medication* through a syringe barrel connected to the tubing, as shown in Figure 3.8. Hold the barrel of the syringe about 15 cms (6 inches) higher than the patient's nose and allow the fluid to flow into the stomach by gravity
5. Between medications – flush the tube with 5 ml of water
6. If the patient is on continuous feeding, the feeding is recommenced otherwise the tube is clamped

* Follow guidelines for preparing drugs as outlined above.

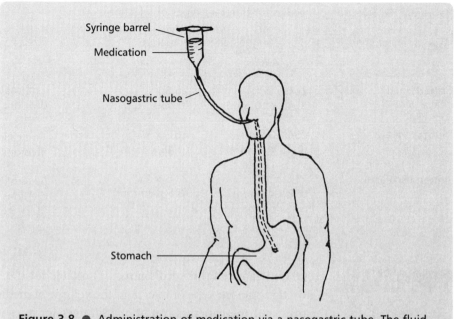

Figure 3.8 ● Administration of medication via a nasogastric tube. The fluid is allowed to flow into the stomach by gravity

Parenteral medications

parenteral route
_____

a route other than via
the alimentary canal

The term 'parenteral' refers to the act of administering drugs by a route other than the alimentary canal. The term is most commonly used to indicate injection routes such as intramuscular, subcutaneous and intravenous. Less common ways by which drugs are administered include intrathecally, intra-articularly, intracardiac and intra-arterially. These more specialised procedures are performed by doctors. Drugs given parenterally have a more rapid effect than those given orally. It is also easy to achieve high plasma levels for effective treatment. Some drugs (for example, insulin) may, if given orally, be destroyed.

When administering drugs by injection, it is important first to select and assemble the correct equipment:

- The patient's prescription
- The medication
- A clean tray
- A sterile syringe and needle
- Alcohol swabs
- **Gloves if necessary.**

There are many different syringes and needles, suiting many different procedures (Table 3.2). It is important to choose carefully according to the procedure;

Table 3.2 ● Selection of needles for different types of injection

Type of injection	Suggested needle gauge		Size of syringe
	Adult	*Child*	
Intradermal	26 G x ⅜" (0.45 x 10 mm)	26 G x ⅜" (0.45 x 10 mm)	1 ml calibrated in 0.1 ml divisions
Subcutaneous	25/26 G x ⅝' (0.45 x 16 mm)	26 G x ⅝" (0.45 x 16 mm)	1 ml calibrated in 0.1 ml divisions
Intramuscular	21 G x 1½" (0.8 x 40 mm)	23 G x 1¼" (0.6 x 30 mm)	5 ml calibrated in 0.2 ml divisions

Activity 12

Identify the different gauge needles that are used for intradermal, subcutaneous, intravenous and intramuscular injections, and for drawing up medications.

intramuscular route

injection into a muscle

Activity 13

Describe the policy for the safe disposal of used needles, syringes, vials and glass ampoules. Describe the actions to be taken in the event of an accidental needle injury.

length and gauge of the needle must be suitable for the injection site, the type of injection site, the type of injection, the volume of medication, the viscosity of the drug and the patient's condition. Syringes for injections range from 0.1 to 5 ml, depending on the volume of drug to be administered.

Gloves should be worn to prevent cross-infection or if the drug is likely to cause skin sensitisation with frequent use. For example, dermatatis can be caused by frequent contact with drugs such as penicillin, streptomycin and chlorpromazine. When cytotoxic drugs are given, vinyl gloves should be worn; goggles and a mask may also be necessary.

Intramuscular injection

The intramuscular route is used to administer medications that are irritating or painful. Skeletal muscles are well perfused with blood and have fewer pain receptors, so pain is minimal, and up to 5 ml of injectate may be given into the large muscles (1–2 ml into the deltoid muscle, for example). To give an intramuscular injection:

1. Collect and check all the equipment to ensure sterility. If the outer packaging is damaged, replace the pack.
2. Wash your hands.
3. Prepare the needle(s) and syringe(s) on a tray. Check for any defects.
4. Check the patient's prescription(s) for completeness.
5. Select the drug and verify it against the prescription.
6. Prepare the drug using gloves if necessary.
7. Administer the intramuscular injection.

Drawing medication from a single-dose ampoule

- Check the ampoule for cracks, cloudiness and precipitation.
- Gently tap the upper area of the ampoule to release any medication trapped at the top of the ampoule.
- Cover the neck of the ampoule or use an 'ampoule breaker' when snapping it open.
- Insert the needle into the ampoule and withdraw the required amount. Avoid contaminating the medication.
- Change the needle and dispose of it as per hospital policy.
- Tap the barrel to dislodge any air bubbles towards the needle and expel the air.

Drawing medication from a multidose vial solution

- Remove the metal cover from the vial and inspect the medication as above.
- Clean the rubber cap with antiseptic solution and let it dry.
- Withdraw the prescribed amount of solution. Two methods can be used to draw the solution:
  - *Method 1*. Insert a 19 G needle into the cap to vent the vial. Insert the assembled needle and syringe, and draw up the required amount.
  - *Method 2*. Assemble the needle and syringe. Fill the syringe with the same volume of air as the medication that will be withdrawn. Insert the needle through the rubber stopper, holding the vial at an oblique angle, and inject the air into the vial. Keep the needle in the solution, invert the vial and allow the medication to enter the syringe. The volume can be adjusted by using the plunger, and the needle is removed when the required amount has been drawn up.
- Change the needle as it may have become blunted/damaged.
- Tap the barrel to dislodge any air bubbles towards the needle and expel the air.

Reconstituting a powdered medication

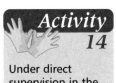

Activity 14

Under direct supervision in the skills laboratory or clinical area, prepare a powdered medication for injection.

- Clean the rubber cap with an antiseptic and allow it to dry.
- Add the required amount of diluent, that is, sterile water, carefully down the wall of the vial, and allow an equal amount of air to escape into the syringe.
- Check for the displacement value of the drug.
- Remove the needle and syringe.
- Shake the vial to dissolve the powder.
- The reconstituted solution can now be withdrawn as described for removing solutions from a multidose vial.

Guidelines for intramuscular injection

1. Identify the patient and explain the procedure. It is important to gain the patient's co-operation.
2. Position the patient for easy access to the injection site, comfort and privacy. Infants and children should be held firmly so that they do not move and thus receive injuries during the procedure.
3. Clean the site with antiseptic.
4. Holding the needle at 90 degrees (Figure 3.9), quickly thrust the needle into the muscle. Leave a third of the needle shaft exposed. If the needle breaks from the hub, it can thus be removed safely.
5. Pull back the plunger. If blood appears, withdraw the needle and repeat the procedure with a sterile needle. Explain to the patient what is happening.
6. If no blood appears, depress the plunger and inject the drug slowly.
7. Quickly withdraw the needle and apply gentle pressure over the puncture site.
8. Position the patient comfortably.
9. Dispose of the needle and syringe as per hospital policy.
10. Complete all the necessary records.

Sites for intramuscular injection

Various sites on the human body may be used for giving an injection. When choosing a site, it is important to identify the anatomical landmarks in order to

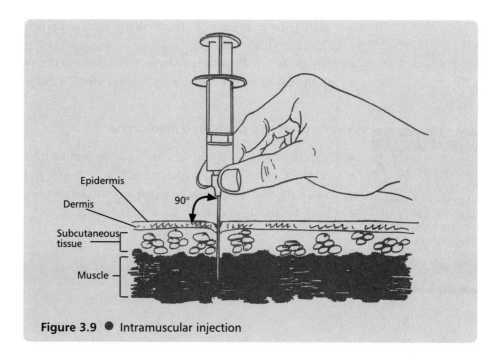

Figure 3.9 ● Intramuscular injection

avoid injuring nerves, striking bones or puncturing blood vessels. The site must also be inspected for its suitability, for example:

- Is there sufficient muscle mass?
- Does the area to be injected have a good blood supply?
- Is there any skin damage?
- Is there evidence of fibrosis or infection?

When patients are receiving frequent intramuscular or subcutaneous injections, for example of insulin, it is important to rotate the injection site to obtain greater drug absorption, decrease tissue fibrosis and cause minimal discomfort to the patient. A rotation chart may be useful in implementing an effective rotation programme.

The most frequently used sites are outlined below.

The deltoid muscle in the upper arm

The deltoid is used for small quantities of injectate, 1 ml or less, of clear non-irritating medication. The muscle is located in the lateral aspect of the upper arm. The injection site (Figure 3.10) is located 4–5 cm below the acromion process and above the deltoid groove in adults, and approximately 2 cm below the acromion process in older children.

The dorsogluteal site in the buttocks

This site (Figure 3.11) is frequently used for injections into the gluteus maximus muscle, this larger muscle mass being the preferred site for larger volumes. The patient should be asked to lie prone with the toes pointing inwards to relax the

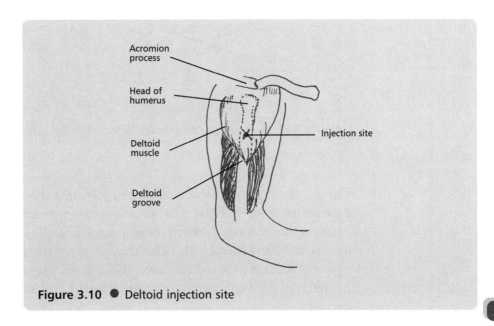

Figure 3.10 ● Deltoid injection site

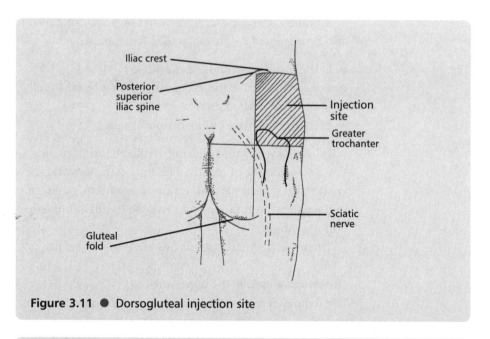

Figure 3.11 ● Dorsogluteal injection site

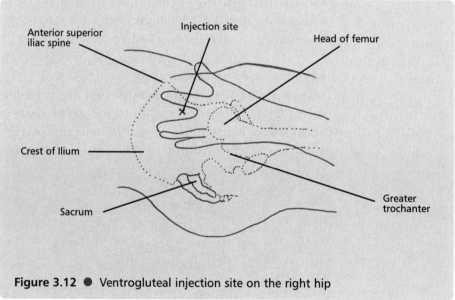

Figure 3.12 ● Ventrogluteal injection site on the right hip

buttocks. The injection site is identified by palpating the anatomical landmarks of the posterior superior iliac spine and the greater trochanter (at the head of the femur). A line is drawn between these two points and a safe injection site is in the area above and lateral to this line. The area below this line should be avoided to prevent damage to the sciatic nerve. This site should not be used in infants or children who have not been walking for at least 1 year since this muscle is not developed.

The ventrogluteal site in the hip area

The injection is given in the gluteus medius and gluteus maximus muscles. The patient is placed on his side or can be allowed to stay in the supine or prone position. To find the injection site on the right hip (the most convenient site for right-handed practitioners), palpate the greater trochanter, the iliac crest and the anterior superior iliac spine. Place the palm of the left hand on the greater trochanter and the left index finger towards the anterior superior iliac spine (Figure 3.12). Move the middle finger away from the index finger to form a V between the fingers. The injection is given into the centre of the V. This is the preferred site for infants and children who have not been walking for a year (Beecroft, 1990; Whalley and Wong, 1995) because the pelvis is concave below the iliac crest and contains a relatively large muscle mass.

The vastus lateralis in the thigh

This muscle is situated in the lateral thigh and can be used for both adults and children. This site (Figure 3.13) is preferable because there are no major blood vessels or nerves in the area. The patient is asked to lie in the supine position with the thigh well exposed, pointing the toe inwards to give a better exposure of the lateral aspects of the thigh. The injection site can be located by dividing the thigh horizontally and vertically into thirds by placing one hand's breadth below the greater trochanter at the top of the thigh and one hand's breadth from the knee. The thigh is then measured vertically, this time by placing one hand's breadth along the middle of the inner side of the thigh and one hand's breadth on the outer side of the thigh, thus creating a rectangle in the middle where it is safe to inject. This strip is between 2 and 4 cm long in children and about 7 cm long in adults. The needle is directed into the tissues at a right angle.

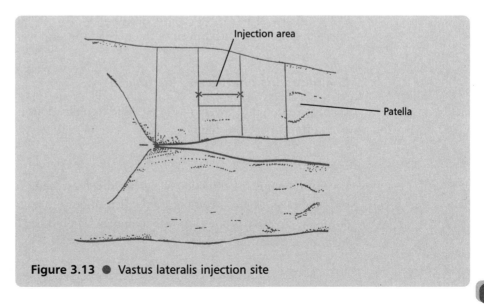

Figure 3.13 ● Vastus lateralis injection site

SPECIFIC POINTS ON CHILDREN'S INJECTIONS

● *Sites for intramuscular injection in infants and children who have not been walking for 1 year*

1. Vastus lateralis in the middle third of femur (Figure 3.13)
2. Ventrogluteal (Figure 3.12)
3. Mid-anterior thigh: injection given in the rectus femoris muscle. This muscle is located on the anterior aspect of the thigh and is quite visible in infants

● *Sites for intramuscular injection in older children who have been walking for more than 1 year*

1. Vastus lateralis (Figure 3.13)
2. Dorsogluteal site in the gluteus medius muscle (Figure 3.11)
3. Deltoid muscle for older children (Figure 3.10)

Z-track intramuscular injection

This technique for intramuscular injection has been primarily reserved for use with medications such as iron preparations that are known to be particularly irritating and can permanently stain the subcutaneous tissue. During this procedure, there is lateral displacement of the cutaneous tissue prior to injection, and the tension is released immediately after injection. When utilising the Z-track technique, the nurse grasps the muscle and pulls it laterally about 2.5 cm until it is taut, holding the tissue in this position. The needle is inserted at a 90 degree angle. After ensuring the position of the needle, the medication is injected. Following withdrawal of the needle, the skin is immediately released.

Complications of intramuscular injections

The nurse should be aware of the possible complications of injections and make every effort to prevent them.

Infection

The introduction of infection via a needle may lead to local (abscesses) or systemic (septicaemia) complications. It is important to maintain strict asepsis during all invasive procedures. All equipment should be sterile, and good handwashing is essential.

Muscle myopathy

Intramuscular injections, by their very nature, cause injury to tissues. Needle myopathy damage can be prevented by good injection technique using the optimum-sized needles. Focal myopathy can be caused by the injectates and by using injectorates of neutral pH.

Wrong route

Injectates may accidentally be given into a vein or an artery, resulting in a rapid physiological response. Depending on the drug used, severe complications and even death may occur. The syringe should be aspirated before the drug is injected. If blood appears in the barrel of the syringe, the needle is withdrawn and an alternative site used. The patient should be informed of the reasons for this. Drugs injected in an artery may cause thrombosis with disruption of the blood supply.

Nerve damage

Nerve damage (to the sciatic nerve) in the dorsogluteal region should be avoided. The nurse should identify the landmarks, as shown in Figure 3.11 and select a safe area for injection. Alternatively, the nurse can select another site such as the vastus lateralis, which carries the least risk.

Subcutaneous injections

subcutaneous route

an injection under the skin

The sites for administering subcutaneous injections include the lateral aspects of the upper arm, the abdomen on either side of the umbilicus, the middle and outer area of the thigh and the back (Figure 3.14). It is important to allow diabetic patients to maintain their own subcutaneous injections while in hospital.

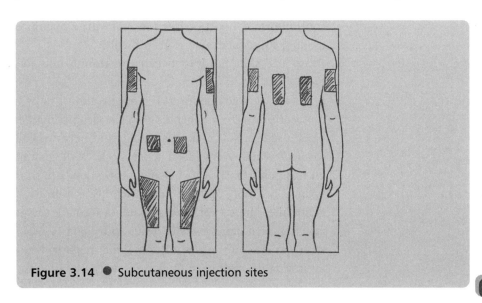

Figure 3.14 ● Subcutaneous injection sites

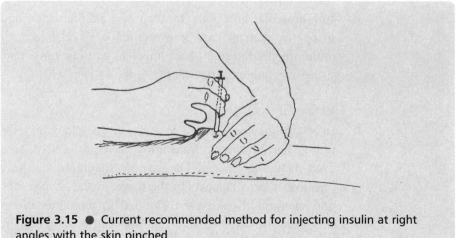

Figure 3.15 ● Current recommended method for injecting insulin at right angles with the skin pinched

Guidelines for administering a subcutaneous injection

1. Explain the procedure to the patient and gain his co-operation.
2. Select the site and assist the patient into position to maintain his comfort and dignity. Expose the injection site; in a viable injection site the nurse should be able to pinch at least 2.5 cm of subcutaneous tissue. Check the rotation chart if one is in use.
3. Wash your hands thoroughly to prevent infection.
4. Prepare medication as outlined in Table 3.2, selecting the correctly sized needle.
5. Clean the injection site with isopropyl alcohol 70 per cent and allow the site to dry. For subcutaneous insulin and heparin injections, alcohol swabs are contraindicated as they interfere with drug action and toughen the skin, making subsequent injections difficult.
6. Grasp the skin firmly between the thumb and forefinger, as shown in Figure 3.15.
7. Maintain the fold and insert the needle almost to its full length at an angle of 45 or 90 degrees depending on the drug being administered, the latter being used for subcutaneous insulin and heparin. Pull back on the plunger to check whether any blood appears (check the manufacturer's instructions on this point first). If no blood appears, slowly push the plunger. When the syringe is empty, quickly and smoothly withdraw the needle and apply gentle pressure to prevent haematoma formation. Studies of subcutaneous injection techniques by McGowan and Wood (1990) showed no difference with respect to bruising outcome when heparin was administered without aspirating the syringe or pressure was used at the site.

8. Safely discard the syringe and needle.
9. Wash your hands.
10. Complete all the relevant records.

Intradermal injections

Intradermal administration is frequently used for diagnostic purposes, the injectate being placed within the layers of the skin just below the epidermis (Figure 3.16). Small amounts of medication, usually not more than 0.5 ml, are administered. The site most often used is the central forearm, but other areas, such as the back and the chest, are acceptable.

Guidelines for giving an intradermal injection

1. Wash your hands. Check the prescription for completeness as described earlier. Prepare the equipment (a 1 ml syringe with a 26 G x 16 mm needle).
2. Explain the procedure to the patient and gain his co-operation.
3. Select the site and assist the patient into position to maintain his comfort and dignity. Select a site with minimal, or preferably no, hair and skin blemishes.
4. Clean the area with antiseptic solution. Avoid using iodine solutions as the residual stain may interfere with interpreting the results of the skin test. If the skin is oily, cleanse the area with acetone to remove any fat deposits. Allow the skin to dry.

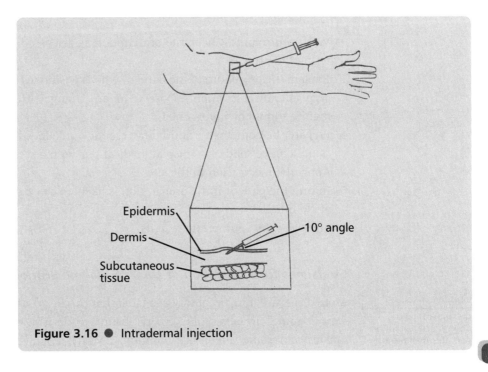

Epidermis
Dermis
Subcutaneous tissue
10° angle

Figure 3.16 ● Intradermal injection

5. Support the patient's arm and stretch the skin taut.
6. Place the bevel of the needle almost flat against the patient's skin and insert the needle with the bevel side up at an angle of 10–15 degrees (Figure 3.16). The needle should be about 3 mm below the skin surface. The medication is slowly injected while watching for a wheal to develop.
7. Once the wheal appears, withdraw the needle.
8. The area should never be massaged as it may interfere with the test results.
9. If the test is carried out to determine sensitivity, follow the text instructions to determine, for example, signs of local reaction.
10. Discard the equipment.
11. Wash your hands.
12. Complete all the relevant records.

Topical medications

topical

applied to the skin or mucous membranes

inunction

rubbing a drug mixed with a fatty base into the skin; also the name given to the mixture

Topical administration refers to the application of medications to the skin or mucous membranes to achieve local or systemic effects. The medication may be incorporated into a base such as an oil, lotion or cream, which is rubbed into the skin (inunction), the area being cleaned with soap and water before application. The inunction can be applied with the fingers and hands, or using cotton wool balls or gauze swabs. If there is a risk of infection or application is to the mucous membranes, gloves should be worn.

Guidelines for the topical administration of drugs

1. Wash your hands. Check the prescription as discussed above before administering the drug.
2. Explain the procedure to the patient, who is positioned to expose the area and carry out any assessments. Observe for any changes. The patient's privacy and dignity should be maintained.
3. Prepare the equipment, and follow aseptic guidelines if there is risk of infection. Remove solid or semisolid medications with a sterile spatula.
4. Apply the medication to the site.
5. Inform the patient if the preparation is likely to cause skin staining or soiling of clothing.
6. Complete the appropriate records.

Guidelines for application of transdermal medications

transdermal route

the application of a drug directly on to the skin, this then being absorbed via the skin

More drugs are now becoming available that can be administered via the transdermal route for example glyceryl trinitrate derivatives (Transderm nitro), opiates and some analgesics (Amitop, EMLA). Following application of the patch, the drug is absorbed through the hair follicles and sweat glands, entering the bloodstream.

Before any patch can be applied, the previous application must be removed from the patient's skin. The prescription is checked to ensure the patient's safety. The new patch is then applied to a clean non-hairy skin surface, the most frequently used sites being the chest wall, the upper arms, the backs of the hands and the ante-cubital fossae, depending on the intended use of the medication. The patches should have labels indicating the date and time of application and the signature of the practitioner.

To prevent inflammation and irritation, the site should be rotated and recorded on a rotation chart. If the patch has been properly applied, the patient is able to shower or bath.

Eye medication

Eye medications are available in two forms: eye ointments and eye drops. The administration of eye drops and eye ointment will initially be the responsibility of the nurse, but he or she may also be involved in instructing the patient as well as other members of the family to administer the medication. It is important that the correct eye is treated. The prescription must be carefully checked and any abbreviations verified. The patient should be informed if her vision is going to be affected after the procedure. Although the eye is not sterile, it is important to use aseptic techniques when performing eye treatment. If infection is present in both eyes, the least affected eye is treated first to prevent cross-contamination. The following general guidelines should be used when administering eye drops and eye ointments.

1. Explain the procedure to the patient, emphasising that her nose may feel as if it is 'running' because the punctum of the eye drains into the nasal space. The patient may also get a taste of the drug at the back of her throat.
2. Ideally, the patient should be lying flat with her head tilted backwards to allow easy access to the eyes. The nurse should stand behind the patient's head as it is easier to administer the drug from that position.
3. Prepare all the necessary equipment. Warm the eye drops and ointments to room temperature.
4. Wash your hands, and put on gloves if necessary.
5. Check the eye and perform eye toilet as necessary.
6. Gently pull down the lower lid to form a pouch, as shown in Figure 3.17. Gently drop the required number of drops into the pouch. Ask the patient to close the eye gently and blink several times. The nurse must wait for 2 minutes before instilling another drug.

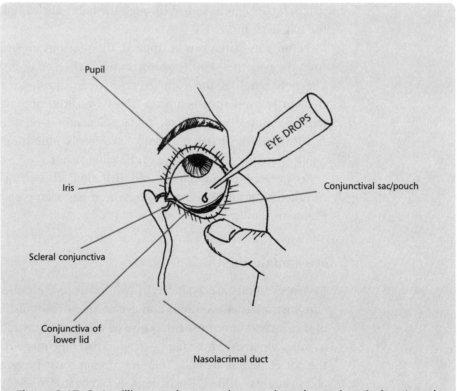

Pupil

EYE DROPS

Iris

Conjunctival sac/pouch

Scleral conjunctiva

Conjunctiva of
lower lid

Nasolacrimal duct

Figure 3.17 ● Instilling eye drops or ointment into the conjunctival sac/pouch

For eye ointment, start from the angle near the nose (the inner canthus) and work towards the ear, gently squeezing the tube along the inner edge of the lower lid. Avoid touching the eye with the sharp nozzle. An eye pad may be applied if requested. Separate tubes/bottles should always be used for the left and right eyes.

7. The patient should be advised not to rub or squeeze the eye. Leave the patient comfortable.

8. Remove any gloves used. Wash your hands.

9. Complete all the necessary documentation.

SPECIFIC POINTS ON CHILDREN'S MEDICATIONS

● The nurse should get extra help so that the head can be held still during eye and ear treatments, to prevent the child rubbing his eyes or ears, and to provide comfort and reassurance.

Ear medications

1. Wash your hands and put on gloves if necessary.
2. Prepare all the necessary equipment and check the prescription for completeness.
3. Warm the medication to room temperature.
4. Clean the outer canal if necessary. Normal saline may be used.
5. Ask the patient to lie on the side with the ear to be treated facing upwards.
6. In adults and children over 3 years old, gently pull the pinna upwards and backwards and instil the prescribed number of drops in the ear canal (Figure 3.18B). In children below 3 years of age, gently pull the pinna downwards and backwards and instil the prescribed number of drops (Figure 3.18A).
7. Advise the patient to remain in that position for 5 minutes.
8. When patient is allowed to sit up, cleanse the external ear of any spillages or leakages, and make the patient comfortable.
9. Remove gloves and wash your hands.
10. Complete all the relevant records.

If both ears are to be treated, wait for 15 minutes between instillations.

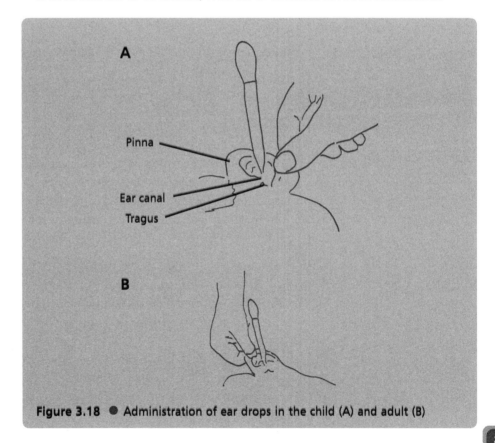

Figure 3.18 ● Administration of ear drops in the child (A) and adult (B)

Nasal medications

A number of drugs, for example nitroglycerine and ephedrine, are available for use as nasal sprays or nasal drops. The nasal drops and sprays should be used appropriately or the drug's effectiveness will be diminished.

Nasal drops may flood the sinuses or dribble down the throat and be ingested. The patient should be advised to expectorate any drug going down the throat rather than swallow it. The timing of these drugs is important, and they should be administered 20 minutes before meals so that the nasal passages will be clear during feeding.

1. Wash your hands and put on gloves if necessary.
2. Prepare all the necessary equipment, and check the prescription for completeness.
3. Get the patient to clear his nasal passages; provide some tissues.
4. For a nasal spray, keep the head and spray container upright. Squeeze the container as instructed and, following each spray, ask the patient to take a deep sniff. Repeat with the other nostril. For nasal drops, it is better if the patient is lying down. Instil the required amount of medication, inserting the dropper approximately 0.5 cm into the nostril. The tip of the dropper should not become contaminated. Young children may be held on the lap with the neck extended.
5. Provide the patient with tissues and make him comfortable.
6. Complete all the relevant documentation.

Rectal medications

rectal route

administration via the rectum

The rectal route is frequently used for the administration of drugs in adults and children. The action of the drug can be local (for example, lubricant suppositories) or systemic (for example, aminophylline). These medications are in the form of a suppository, cream or solution. It is vital that children receiving such medication have been prepared for the procedure, using phrases that the child can understand.

1. Wash your hands.
2. Prepare all the equipment, and check the prescription for completeness.
3. Explain the procedure to the patient and provide privacy.
4. Position the patient on his left side and only expose the buttocks.
5. Put gloves on.
6. The suppository is lubricated with a water-soluble lubricant (KY-Jelly).
7. The buttocks are separated to expose the anus.
8. Ask the patient to take a deep breath and insert the suppository past the anal sphincter. Clean away any excess lubricant.

SPECIFIC POINTS ON CHILDREN'S MEDICATIONS

● When giving a suppository to an infant or toddler, he can lie on his back with his legs flexed. The suppository is inserted using the index finger for children over 3 years. In children of 3 years or less, the little finger may be used.

9. Ask the patient to refrain from pushing the suppository out and make him comfortable. Children and infants may be held or cuddled to distract them. (A commode should be available to avoid any embarrassment.)
10. Dispose of all equipment, and wash your hands.
11. Complete all the relevant records.

Vaginal medications

vaginal route
___

the administration of medication into the vagina

Medications intended for administration via the vaginal route are available in many forms – pessaries, creams and medicated douches – most of which can only be administered using special applicators.

The patient should be encouraged to empty her bladder as she is expected to remain lying down for 20 minutes after insertion of the medication.

1. Wash your hands.
2. Prepare all the equipment, and check the prescription for completeness.
3. Explain the procedure to the patient and provide privacy. Select the appropriate position, either supine with the knees drawn up and legs parted, or left lateral with the knees drawn up.
4. Wash your hands and put on gloves.
5. Lubricate the pessary or applicator.
6. Insert the pessary along the posterior vaginal wall and into the top of the vagina. If using an applicator, insert the barrel of the applicator into the vagina as far as it will go. Squeeze the tube to insert the drug while holding the applicator steady. Withdraw the applicator, and make the patient comfortable.
7. Provide the patient with sanitary towels and advise her to remain in position for 20 minutes.
8. Discard the equipment or clean it for reuse.
9. Remove gloves and wash your hands.
10. Complete all the relevant documentation.

Patient education and compliance in drug administration

Drug therapy can only be effective when the patient co-operates with the drug regimen and correctly takes all the prescribed drugs. In hospitalised patients, drug treatment is closely supervised. In contrast, there is a wealth of evidence indicating that, once discharged from hospital care, many patients fail to continue with their treatment because of:

- Forgetfulness
- A lack of understanding of the illness and/or drugs
- Unclear instructions
- The cost of the medication
- Non-acceptance of the diagnosis
- Inconvenience, such as when at school
- A confusing cocktail of medications
- Side-effects of the drugs, including the fear of addiction.

Failure to complete a course of treatment may result in a poor outcome with a detrimental effect on the patient. The doctor will be concerned at the lack of progress with the drug treatment and may opt to increase the dosage, change to a different drug or question the original diagnosis. The nurse can take positive steps to ensure that the patient co-operates with the drug programme by:

- Effective patient education
- 24-hour containers to ensure that required drugs are taken at the appropriate times
- Starting self-administration while the patient is still in hospital
- A written record of the regimen.

Each patient should be assessed for their willingness to learn about their medications, this information being used by the primary nurse to produce an effective teaching programme ensuring that the patient continues with the treatment following discharge.

General principles when administering medications to children

It is essential to provide safe and effective drug therapy to children. Because of anatomical and physiological differences, the drug's pharmacokinetic properties – absorption, distribution, metabolism and excretion – may be affected. For more details of drug pharmacokinetics in children and infants, the reader is advised to consult textbooks on paediatric pharmacology.

General guidelines for giving medications to children

1. It is important to establish a trusting relationship with the child and to identify any preferences. Always be honest regarding painful injections or distasteful medications. Remain calm.
2. Adequate time should be allowed prior to and after the administration of drugs to comfort the child. It may take longer than expected to explain to the child and to give any instructions that they must follow to enhance the effectiveness of therapy.
3. The nurse should be kind but firm when approaching the child.
4. Organise help to control and support children. Do not interrupt what the child is doing; make medicine-taking a part of it.
5. Identify the child correctly, checking with the parents. If possible, organise drug administration when the parents are present.
6. Explain the procedure to the child and parents. Parents may provide information on how the child likes to take her medication. Offer a choice, for example taking it from the parent or nurse.
7. Avoid mixing medications in milk or essential foods or the child may avoid those foods and develop malnutrition or dehydration.
8. If possible, allow children to participate, for example choosing the juice to be drunk with the medicine.
9. Reward children for taking their medications, but avoid punishing children who are unco-operative.
10. Do not anticipate difficulty: the child quickly picks up your anxiety.
11. Never make a promise you cannot keep.

Specific guidelines when giving injections to children

1. The aseptic and safe-checking procedures should be followed as discussed.
2. Prepare the equipment, and check the prescription for completeness.
3. Explain the procedure to the child in a manner consistent with the child's age and understanding. Audiovisual aids such as booklets or dolls may be used to get the message across. Parents should be informed and involved in supporting the child.
4. Appropriate restraint, for example a blanket, may be required.
5. Select the injection site (see above).
6. The procedure should be undertaken quickly and gently.
7. Support is provided as necessary by the nurse and/or parents.

Giving medications to clients with learning disabilities

Clients with learning disabilities may have varying degrees of mental and physical disabilities, and it may be as difficult for the nurse to explain as for the patient to understand. Following the five 'R's of drug administration (see above) should secure the client's safety. The client may also suffer from physical deformities, which may require adapting methods and in some cases changing the form of the drug and the route of administration. The pharmacist may be able to help with special preparations. Liquid preparations are safer than tablets or capsules. If no alternative forms of medication are available, the tablets should be crushed and mixed with soft foods for easy swallowing. Swallowing may also be stimulated by gentle downward stroking motions over the larynx.

Medication errors

Finally, although medication errors should be avoided at all costs, it is possible that these may occur. Incidents should be immediately reported to the nurse in charge and the doctor. The patient should be monitored for any side-effects and be informed of what has happened. Preventative measures may be taken to control the effects of the drugs. The incident is usually investigated, and if the nurse has been found to be negligent, disciplinary action may be taken by the employing authority and the UKCC. The patient can also take legal action against the nurse or the employer. Thus the advice is to be a safe practitioner.

Chapter Summary

This chapter has revealed some of the key aspects of safe practice in moving patients, preventing cross-infection and food poisoning, and the administration of medicines. Every activity that the nurse undertakes carries considerable risk to the patient as well as to the nurse. By applying the principles described in this chapter, the nurse can ensure that nursing procedures are carried out safely for all.

Test Yourself!

1. Find out the rate of HAI in your hospital.

2. Who are the members of the infection control team?

3. Undertake a survey of hand hygiene in your area of practice.

4. Describe the precautions that nurses should take to reduce the incidence of food poisoning.

5. Describe the signs and symptoms of food poisoning.

6. What precautions should be taken in the event of an outbreak of food poisoning in the wards?

7. Can you describe the responsibilities of the nurse in drug administration?

8. Can you identify at least three injection sites?

9. What special precautions should you take when administering injections to infants and children?

References

Beecroft, P.C. (1990) Intramuscular injection practices of paediatric nurses: site selection. *Nurse Educator* **5**(4): 23–8.

Chivers, S.M. (1996) Letter to *Comfort and Care*. HSE, Bristol.

DoH (Department of Health) (1990a) *Guidance for Clinical Health Workers; Protection against Infection with HIV and Hepatic Viruses*. Recommendations of the expert advisory group on Aids. HMSO, London.

DoH (Department of Health) (1990b) *Food Handler's Guide*. HMSO, London.

Disabled Living Foundation (1994) *Handling People: Equipment, Advice and Information*. Disabled Living Foundation, London.

Dryden, M.S., Keyworth, N., Gabb, R. *et al.* (1994) Asymptomatic foodhandlers as the source of nosocomial salmonellosis. *Journal of Hospital Infection* **28**: 195–208.

Gladman, G. (1993) Back pain in student nurses – the mature factor. *Occupational Health*, February, pp. 47–51.

Haley, R.W., Culver, D.H. and White, J.W. (1985) The American Scenic Report. The efficacy of infection surveillance and control program in preventing nosocomial infection in US hospital. *American Journal of Epidemiology* **121**: 182.

(HSE) Health and Safety Executive (1992) *Manual Handling Operations Regulations – Guidance on Regulations*. HMSO, London.

Joseph, C.A. and Palmer, S.R. (1989) Outbreak of salmonella infection in hospitals in England and Wales 1978–87. *British Medical Journal* **298**: 1161–4.

McGowan, S. and Wood, A. (1990) Administering heparin subcutaneously: an evaluation of techniques used and bruising at the site. *Australian Journal of Advanced Nursing* **7**(2): 31–9.

Meers, P.D., Ayliffe, G.A.J., Emmerson, A.M. *et al.* (1981) Report of the national survey of infection in hospitals in 1980. *Journal of Hospital Infection* **2** (supplement).

Rosen, M. (1994) *Back Pain: Report of a Clinical Standards Advisory Group*. HMSO, London.

RCN (Royal College of Nursing) (1992) *Safety Representatives Conference Committee. Introduction to Methicillin Resistant Staphylococcus Aureus*. RCN, London.

RCN (Royal College of Nursing) (1995) *Guidance on Infection Control in Hospitals*. RCN, London.

RCN (Royal College of Nursing) (1996) *Introducing a Safer Handling Policy*. RCN, London.

Sharp, J.C.M. (1992) Epidemiology. In Eley, A.R. (ed.) *Microbial Food Poisoning*, pp. 125–42. Chapman & Hall, London.

UKCC (United Kingdom Central Council for Nurses, Midwives and Health Visitors) (1992a) *Code of Professional Conduct*. UKCC, London.

UKCC (United Kingdom Central Council for Nurses, Midwives and Health Visitors) (1992b) *Standards for the Administration of Drugs*. UKCC, London.

UKCC (United Kingdom Central Council for Nurses, Midwives and Health Visitors) (1997) *Responsibility for Feeding of Patients*. UKCC, London.

Whalley, L.F. and Wong, D.L. (1995) *Nursing Care of Infants and Children*, 4th edn. Mosby, London.

Winslow, E.H. (1997) Just how illegible are physicians' medical orders? *American Journal of Nursing* **97**(9): 66.

Further Reading

Ayliffe, G.A.J., Collins, B.J. and Taylor, L.J. (eds) (1993) *Hospital Acquired Infections*, 2nd edn, Cambridge University Press, Cambridge.

Burden, M. (1994) A practical guide to insulin injection. *Nursing Standard* **81**(29): 25–9.

Campbell, J. (1995) Injections. *Professional Nurse* **10**(7): 455–8.

Corlett, E.N., Lloyd, P.V., Tarling, C. *et al.* (1997) *The Guide to Handling of Patients*. National Back Pain Association and Royal College of Nursing, London.

Palmer, S.R. and Rowe, B. (1983) Investigation of salmonella in hospitals. *British Medical Journal* **287**: 891–3.

Eating and Drinking

PENELOPE M. SIMPSON

● Introduction

The purpose of this chapter is to encourage you to apply the essentials of nutrition and hydration to your everyday life and that of your clients. At the end of the chapter, you should be able to:

● Describe and explain the principles of a healthy diet and fluid intake

● Enable others to make healthy changes to their food and fluid intake

● Assess the nutritional and hydration status of clients

● Assist clients in achieving optimum nutrition and hydration

● Suggest a range of helpful strategies for use when feeding and hydrating clients

● Extend your range of skills in promoting effective nutrition and hydration

● Promote the dignity of the client needing nutritional support.

There will be reflective activities, activities for you to undertake, reading activities, case histories and review questions to ensure that you interact with the material in a useful and practical way.

Supporting texts you will find particularly helpful are:

Bender, D.A. (1997) *Introduction to Nutrition and Metabolism*, 2nd edn, UCL Press, London, or another introductory nutrition text.

Department of Health (1991) *Dietary Reference Values for Food Energy and Nutrients for the United Kingdom*, Report of the Panel on Dietary Reference Values of the Committee on Medical Aspects of Food Policy. HMSO, London.

Rutishauser, S. (1994) *Physiology and Anatomy*. Churchill Livingstone, Edinburgh, or your own preferred anatomy and physiology text.

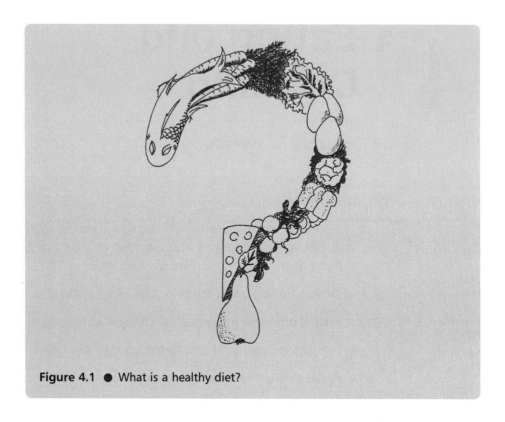

Figure 4.1 ● What is a healthy diet?

What Is a Healthy Diet?

Food is fundamental to physical survival. It is needed for growth, repair and the manufacture of the elements that protect us from disease. Humans will literally eat almost anything to satisfy extreme hunger. Once survival is ensured, other factors, for example age, culture, history, religion, access, taste and preferences, come into play. Most of us believe that we are eating a balanced diet.

At the rock-bottom physiological level, there are certain fundamentals that the body needs in order to function effectively, not just today, but next week and next year, in order to stay healthy into later life. For example, exclusive breast-feeding is recommended for at least the first 4 months of life to enable the best possible start, as it protects against respiratory diseases and gastroenteritis. However, the ability, motivation or knowledge of clients may be impaired, in which case it is the nurse's responsibility to assist, empower and educate. The United Kingdom Central Council for Nursing, Midwifery and Health Visiting (UKCC) reminded us in the 1997 'Feeding of Patients' letter that even if this task is delegated to others, the responsibility remains that of the nurse who is accountable for all aspects of nursing care.

Concepts of a balanced diet have steadily altered across time in response to beliefs and research. At no other time in history have we had access to so much hard evidence of the impact of food on the human body, from starvation to the so-called diseases of affluence, such as obesity. For some considerable time, nutritional advice was aimed solely at preventing deficiency diseases. The wartime diet, for example, kept people remarkably healthy on surprisingly low levels of protein, fat and sugar.

nutrition

the study of the effects of food and drink on the body

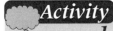

Activity 1

What do you consider to be the main types of food in a normal diet? 'Guestimate' the relative (not actual) amounts, by weight, of food groups that your body needs. For the answer, see Figure 4.3.

Despite considerable 'hype' from those with vested interests and frivolous speculation from irresponsible journalism, there *is* a clear consensus about a balanced diet, which has remained relatively consistent over the past few years. The Committee on Medical Aspects of Food Policy (COMA) published comprehensive recommendations for nutrient consumption in its 1991 report *Dietary Reference Values for Food Energy and Nutrients for the United Kingdom* (DoH, 1991). This replaced the recommended daily allowances (RDA) single figures with ranges for different populations. Later, in July 1992, the government published *The Health of the Nation* (DoH, 1992), a national strategy that set health targets, including ones for eating behaviour, nutritional status and diet-related diseases.

The message is that, whatever you read in the lighter end of the press, experts agree on the information given in the most recent nutrition textbooks. But, unfortunately, consensus does not sell newspapers.

Food substances can be divided into macronutrients, which make up the bulk of our energy and nutrient intake, including carbohydrates, proteins and fats (lipids), and essential micronutrients, which are the vitamins, minerals and trace elements. These will be dealt with in turn below.

Macronutrients

Carbohydrates

carbohydrates

a group of organic (carbon-containing) compounds, comprising starches and sugars, that make up the body's main source of energy

Carbohydrates are needed for fuel and can be divided into two main groups; starches and sugars. Starches are made up of long chains of sugar units: polysaccharides.

The most useful starchy foods include bread, rice, cereals, pasta, potatoes, flour, pizza base, cornflour, crispbread, chapattis, poppadums and porridge. These tend to be filling, which is important for children, rather than fattening; it is what you add to them that makes the difference. Minor sources of starch include cakes, biscuits and pastry. These are more likely to be fattening because they contain high levels of hidden *trans*-fatty acids (see below) as well as sugar. Sugars may be monosaccharides (for example, glucose, fructose and galactose) or disaccharides (sucrose, lactose and maltose) and can be divided into:

- *Intrinsic sugars*, which are contained within plant cell walls
- *Extrinsic sugars*, which are free in solution in the food, as in fruit juice, added sugar and honey in foods and lactose in milk.

Processed foods, chocolates, sweets and snacks are dense sources of sugars. There is evidence that a high sugar intake is a factor in mature-onset diabetes and atherosclerosis, obesity and dental caries (COMA, 1989).

The aim of a healthy diet is to increase the proportion derived from starches to 51 per cent of energy and reduce that from sugars. Infants should gain 40–50 per cent of their total energy from carbohydrates, 40 per cent of this being lactose (milk sugar). Children need about 50–100 g per day of non-milk sugars, one gram of carbohydrate providing 17 kilojoules (kJ), or 3.75 kilocalories (kcal) of energy. The 1991 COMA recommendation was to reduce the level of non-milk sugars, especially sucrose and honey, to 11 per cent of food energy. For the average adult, this is 60 g per day. Identifying how much sugar in its various forms can be found in processed foods can help you to determine your sugar intake.

Activity 2

Look at the food labels in your possession, and list how many different names for sugars you can identify. Were you taking in more sugar than you realised?

Protein

proteins

organic nitrogenous compounds essential as a building material for growth and repair

Proteins are found in meat, fish, eggs, pulses (peas, beans and lentils), nuts, tofu, soya and textured vegetable protein (TVP). It is also found in smaller amounts in bread (11 per cent protein in wholemeal, 9 per cent in white), other cereals and potatoes.

Protein is needed to supply nitrogen for growth (in children), defence and repair, such as wound healing and replacing blood loss. A small amount of protein is continually lost from the body throughout life in hair (adults losing more than 100 hairs a day), shed skin scales (a large proportion of dust), shed gut lining (a major constituent of faeces) and enzymes and other proteins secreted into the gut and incompletely digested. There is also a turnover of body proteins. Tissue proteins are continuously being broken down and replaced. Although there is no change in the total amount of protein in the body, an adult with an inadequate intake of protein will be unable to replace any loss and will thus use up tissue protein. This is broken down into urea and excreted as nitrogenous waste in the urine, faeces and sweat. For healthy adults, an intake of 0.75 g protein per kg bodyweight (0.75 g/kg) in 24 hours is generally considered acceptable, with increased requirements during pregnancy and breastfeeding. Breastfed infants need 8 g per day in total for the first month of life and 2–3 g/kg thereafter.

Activity 3

List the sources of protein in your diet. If you weighed your daily intake, how would it compare with your carbohydrate intake? Check your finding against the 'tilted plate' (Figure 4.3). Do you need to make any adjustments?

amino acids

the building blocks from which proteins are constructed; the end products of protein digestion

Protein is made from 20 different amino acids, which are classified into:

- *Essential*, which cannot be synthesised in the body
- *Semi-essential*, which can be supplied by the metabolism of certain amino acids providing they are consumed in adequate amounts
- *Non-essential*, which can be synthesised from carbon and other precursors in the body.

For further details, consult Bender (1997).

There is some evidence that a diet with a high proportion of protein from animal sources (high biological value/'first-class' protein) is associated with kidney stones (see Chapter 5) and osteoporosis (see Chapter 7). If the protein intake is over twice the reference nutrient intake (sufficient for 97 per cent of population), it has been noted that calcium appears in the urine. Thus if you find that you are eating a lot of animal protein compared with carbohydrate, it is expensive financially, physiologically and ecologically.

It is perfectly possible to get all the protein needed from vegetable sources (low biological value/'second-class' protein), providing that the right amount, combination and range of protein-containing foods are consumed, that is, proteins from different plant sources eaten together. These include:

- Nuts and cereal: a peanut butter sandwich, or muesli with nuts
- Beans and rice: a casserole or salad
- Beans and cereal: for example hummus (chickpea spread) and bread
- Lentils and rice: as in soup.

These are known as complementary combinations. The major principle of a vegetarian diet, therefore, is that pulse dishes must be eaten with bread, rice or other cereal foods.

One gram of protein gives 16 kJ (4 kcal) of energy.

Fat

fats

a group of energy-rich organic substances comprising triglycerides, cholesterol and fatty acids, which are needed for cell structure and function

The major dietary fats are triglycerides, cholesterol and fatty acids. Fat is found in solid fats and liquid oils, in dairy products and as hidden fat in food, for example between muscle fibres in meat, as oils in nuts, cereals, vegetables and fruit (especially avocados), or as fat used in the processing and cooking of foods.

There is a requirement for essential fatty acids, which play an important role in cell structure and function. They cannot be formed in the body so must be gained from the diet. The two main essential fatty acids are linoleic acid (an omega-6 fat; see below) and alpha-linolenic acid (an omega-3 fat; see below).

Vitamins A, D, E and K are fat soluble, found in fatty or oily foods, and will also be discussed below. Their absorption from the gut requires an adequate amount of fat in the diet since they are absorbed dissolved in fats.

For adults and children, it is recommended that no more than 33 per cent of food energy (calories) should come from total fat. This can be subdivided into:

- 10 per cent from saturated fatty acids, for example butter
- 6 per cent (10 per cent maximum) from polyunsaturated fatty acids, for example sunflower oil or sardines
- 12 per cent from mono-unsaturated fatty acids, for example olive oil
- 2 per cent from *trans*-fatty acids, for example biscuits (hydrogenated vegetable oil).

For infants, the figure is 40–50 per cent of the total energy intake.

The fatty acids that make up the fats of our diet can be, in chemical terms, saturated or unsaturated. In saturated fatty acids, there are only single bonds between the carbon atoms that make up the molecule, whereas in unsaturated fatty acids, there may be one (mono-unsaturated) or more (polyunsaturated) double bonds between carbon atoms. In general, fats that contain mainly saturated fatty acids are solid at room temperature, while those which contain mainly unsaturated fatty acids, especially mono-unsaturates, are liquid at room temperature although they solidify when chilled.

Saturated fats are mainly of animal origin and encourage the body to produce more low-density lipoprotein cholesterol (LDL cholesterol; see below), increasing the risk of heart disease. They may also make the blood more prone to clotting. Certain cancers, such as those of the bowel and the breast, have been linked to high intakes of saturated fats (Sanders, 1994).

Polyunsaturated fatty acids bring down the total blood cholesterol level by decreasing both high-density lipoprotein (HDL; see below) and LDL. The two main types are omega-3 and omega-6. Omega-3 fatty acids have either a short or a long chain structure, the latter tending to reduce the inflammatory response, which can help those with rheumatoid arthritis. They also make the blood less likely to clot, thus reducing the risk of a heart attack (Sanders, 1994). Two servings of oily fish or 14 g of walnuts a week are recommended. Omega-6 sources include polyunsaturated margarine and corn, sunflower, rapeseed and soya bean oils.

Polyunsaturated fat must not be increased above 15 per cent of food energy as it is the ratio of saturated to unsaturated fat that is important. The current advice is to replace saturated fats with a mixture of poly- and mono-unsaturates.

inflammatory response

the body's non-specific immune response to injury, characterised by redness, heat, swelling and pain

Chart 4.1 ● Examples of types of fat and their sources

- Saturated: red meat, dairy products, lard, suet, biscuits, palm and coconut oils
- Polyunsaturated:
  - Omega-3: oily fish: mackerel, halibut, pilchards, sardines, herrings, trout, salmon; walnuts
  - Omega-6: polyunsaturated margarine; corn, sunflower and soya bean oils
- Mono-unsaturated: olive oil, rapeseed oil, blended vegetable oil, avocados, nuts
- *Trans*-fatty acids: hard margarine, biscuits, cakes

Activity
4

Look at the food labels on your groceries. How many contain *trans*-fats? Do the food labels identify how much saturated fat is present? Is the fat content of the food more than 33 per cent of the total number of calories? This can help you to identify whether more than 33 per cent of your food energy comes from fat.

Mono-unsaturated fat reduces LDL ('lethal') cholesterol but maintains or slightly increases HDL ('healthy') cholesterol. HDL cholesterol actually removes fats from the walls of arteries and from other body tissues, ferrying it to the liver, where it is broken down into bile. It also protects against oxygen-related tissue damage (oxidation), thought to contribute to heart disease, cancer and rheumatoid arthritis (Sanders, 1994).

Trans-fats are polyunsaturates that have been artificially hardened by adding extra hydrogen. They are thought to be at least as unhealthy as saturated fat and have been linked to an increased risk of heart disease and rheumatoid arthritis. *Trans*-fats increase LDL cholesterol and may reduce levels of HDL cholesterol (Sanders, 1994). Hydrogenated fats/oils can be noted on processed food labels.

Cholesterol is essential for life, being present in the membranes of animal and plant cells, and is important for the formation of oestrogen and other sex hormones. Most cholesterol in the body is manufactured in the liver from saturated fatty acids contained in digested meat and dairy products. Once the fatty acids have been produced, globules of fat cling to proteins in the blood to form lipoproteins. These ferry the cholesterol around the bloodstream. It is only when levels are too high or too low that health is at risk; this is especially so for LDL cholesterol (the 'lethal' variety), which is related to the development of atherosclerosis and ischaemic heart disease.

The main dietary factor that affects the concentration of cholesterol in plasma is the intake of fat. Sources of cholesterol in the diet include eggs, offal and shellfish. The current advice is to take no more than the equivalent of one egg per day. Both the total amount of fat and the relative amounts of saturated and unsaturated fat affect the concentration of cholesterol in LDL cholesterol. High intakes of total fat, especially saturated fat, are associated with undesirably high concentrations of LDL cholesterol. Relatively low intakes of fat, with a high proportion as unsaturated fat, are associated with a desirable lower LDL concen-

Table 4.1 ● Percentages of fats in common sources

	Mono-unsaturated	Polyunsaturated	Saturated
Butter	33	3	64
Hard margarine	49	13	38
Soft margarine	44	23	33
PUFA margarine	17	63	20
Coconut oil	7	2	91
Corn oil	31	52	17
Olive oil	74	11	15
Sunflower oil	34	52	14

Source: Adapted from Bender (1933, p. 21).
PUFA = polyunsaturated fatty acid.

tration. Regular aerobic exercise appears to increase HDL cholesterol levels. The balance in the bloodstream should be, for example, less than 4.0 mmol/l of LDL and greater than 1.0 mmol/l of HDL (Higgins, 1997).

It is difficult to eat enough of a very low fat diet to meet energy requirements, so it is inappropriate for growing children. Infants need to gain 40–50 per cent of their total calories from fat in the first year of life. Most people in the UK usually have too much fat in their diet, averaging 40 per cent of calories, which contributes to obesity and other diseases of affluence. In many foods, the flavour and lubrication of the food comes from the fat component, enhancing the pleasure of eating; the 'mouthfeel' of chocolate is an example.

One gram of fat gives 37 kJ (9 kcal) of energy. It is therefore the most energy-dense form of food.

Energy

Activity 5

Look at two food labels from similar products, perhaps one labelled 'healthy eating', and compare the energy figures.

One calorie is the amount of heat needed to raise the temperature of one gram of water by 1°C. This is not a practical level when studying human nutrition so kilocalories (kcal) are used, each kilocalorie being 1000 calories, the amount needed to raise one kilogram of water by 1°C. For international use, joules are used to measure energy output. These are also very small units so kilojoules (kJ; 1000 joules) and megajoules (MJ; 1 000 000 joules) are used instead.

Conversion: 1 kcal = 4.186 kJ; 1 kJ = 0.239 kcal

The metabolic fuels are fats, carbohydrates, protein and alcohol. For people whose body weight is within the healthy range, energy intake should be enough to maintain a reasonably constant body weight with an adequate amount of exercise. Requirements are also related to age and physical activity levels.

A physically active body with lots of metabolically active muscle needs more than a more sedentary one with a higher percentage of body fat. A baby boy needs 2.89 MJ (960 kcal) per day, a girl of the same age 2.69 MJ (645 kcal). By the time the boy is 11–14 years old, he will need 9.27 MJ (2220 kcal), the girl 7.92 MJ (1845 kcal). The average daily energy requirements of adults aged 19–50 years are 10.60 MJ (2550 kcal) per day for men and 8.10 MJ (1940 kcal) per day for women. Male physiology is metabolically more active as it is geared to laying down muscle. Breastfeeding may increase a woman's energy requirements by as much as 2.40 MJ (570 kcal) per day. As we get older, our metabolism slows down; for example, women need 209 kJ (50 kcal) per day fewer for every 5 years after the age of 27.

If a person does not consume enough energy, tissue breakdown will take place to make up the deficit. If too much energy is consumed, it is stored as glycogen or fat. If you look at how active you were 10 years ago, before the advent of answerphones and remote controls, you probably expended more energy than now, getting up to answer the telephone or change television channels. You may also have used the bus and walked or cycled more than at present.

Although we have a requirement for energy sources in the diet, it does not matter, in theory, how the requirement is met. There is no necessity as such for a dietary source of carbohydrate, for example. The body can make as much as it requires from proteins, albeit expensively. Similarly, there is no need for a dietary source of fat apart from the essential fatty acids. A dietary source of alcohol is non-essential (see below). However, some dietary elements are needed for specific purposes, for example fibre, which used to be called roughage.

non-starch polysaccharides

indigestible substances in plant cells that aid the transit of food through the gastrointestinal tract; also commonly known as fibre or roughage

The terms 'roughage' and 'fibre' should be replaced by 'non-starch polysaccharides' (NSPs). NSPs are a collection of indigestible substances found in plant cells, the main function of which is to aid the passage of food through the bowel and ease elimination. Sources include fruit and vegetables, whole grains, wholemeal bread, cereals, beans and pulses. There is no fibre in animal food sources such as milk, meat, cheese and eggs. The COMA report of 1991 (DoH, 1991) recommended an increase in average consumption from 12 to 18 g per day to reduce constipation, diverticular disease and the risk of colorectal cancer. Men should eat 20 g, women 16; there are no current specific recommendations for children.

There are two sorts of NSP: soluble and insoluble.

- *Soluble NSP* dissolves in the gut and helps to maintain healthy blood glucose levels by a sort of slow-release effect. The richest sources are pulses, oats (for example porridge), barley (for example, pearl barley in soups), rye (for example, bread), beans and lentils, but it is also found in fruits and vegetables. Soluble NSP may help to lower high blood cholesterol levels, probably by combining with bile acids and cholesterol in the intestine and preventing their being absorbed.
- *Insoluble NSP*, as it travels through the digestive system, soaks up moisture, forming bulk that aids the easy passage of waste products. It is found in wheat-based breakfast cereals, bread, rice, maize, pasta, fruits and vegetables. Bran hurries the food through, reducing the absorption of micronutrients (vitamins and minerals), producing a sort of scouring pad effect, and should thus be used with great caution.

Getting enough NSP in the diet means eating a *varied* selection of fruits and vegetables as whole and unpeeled as possible. Take account of current recommendations about pesticide residues on carrot skins, cutting the tops and tails off and peeling them. Five fruits/vegetables a day is best for most people. (Figure 4.2).

The diet should contain plenty of whole grains (rather than completely white, refined versions), wholemeal bread (as brown and granary bread is coloured with caramel or burnt sugar), cereals, rice and pasta. Enough NSP will cause

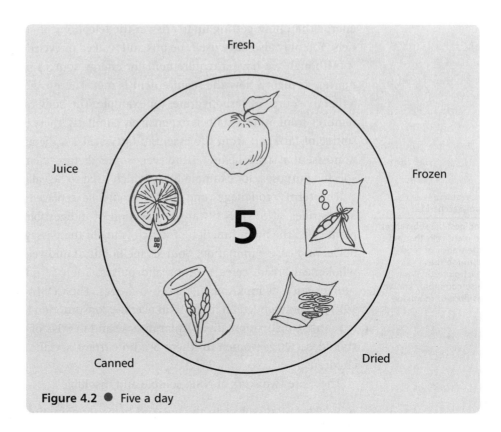

Figure 4.2 ● Five a day

easy bowel actions; too much will lead to diarrhoea and wind. The action of colonic bacteria upon NSP produces methane. Any increase in NSP should be gradual, and the fluid intake may have to be increased.

Fluid

Water is the main constituent of the body, comprising about 60 per cent of adult body weight. The body gains some water from foods, but adults need to drink another 1.5–2.0 litres of fluid daily to replenish water in every cell of the body and ensure efficient functioning at all levels. The healthy adult's fluid requirement can be estimated as 30–35 ml/kg per day. Children (Table 4.2) and people

Activity

6

Look up water and electrolyte balance in your preferred anatomy and physiology text (for example Rutishauser, 1994, pp. 237–52). Why is a detailed knowledge of normal fluid and electrolyte balance necessary for nurses?

Table 4.2 ● Fluid requirements for children

Body weight	Fluid needed
1–10 kg	100 ml/kg
11–20 kg	1000 ml, plus 50 ml/kg over 10 kg
<20 kg	1500 ml
>20 kg	1500 ml, plus 20 ml/kg over 20 kg

Casebox 4.1

Tania is 9 years old and lives with her parents and younger brother in a terraced house with a small garden in a large town. The children are driven to school, to church and to various activities with their friends. They are allowed to take any food or drink from the kitchen whenever they want. Tania's parents are concerned that she is getting very overweight for her height but are frightened of the possibility of anorexia nervosa. Tania's ankle and knee joints are beginning to be painful, and her skin shows stretch marks. Her parents have taken her to see their GP, who has referred them to the practice nurse for some advice.

What would be the main principles of this advice?

- As Tania is still growing, she must not lose weight but slow the rate of gain.

- Activity levels must be considerably increased, building up steadily, over time, to the benefit of the whole family.

- Food freely available to the children will have to be 'healthy', high fibre, low sugar and low fat.

- Tania may be encouraged to drink water, rather than cola, juice or carbonated drinks, when she is thirsty and with meals.

- Energy-dense foods will have to be reserved for treats, and any changes made must not compromise the growth and development needs of Tania's younger brother.

- The practice nurse may be involved in supporting this process.

anorexia nervosa

A psychiatric disorder characterised by intense fear of becoming overweight, even when emaciated

Activity 7

Work out the fluid requirement of one of your clients from the information given above. How do you know that he or she is drinking enough fluid? Remember not to include alcohol in your calculations, as it is dehydrating.

with cardiac or renal problems may need less. Much of this water can be gained from foods with a high water content.

One way to tell whether the fluid intake is correct is that urine is pale and plentiful; dark and scanty urine is a sign of dehydration. The body needs more fluid if it is sweating, as a result of hot conditions or pyrexia, or losing more through diarrhoea and vomiting (see Chapter 5). Nine litres of fluid pass through the average adult gastrointestinal tract daily, 7.7 litres of which is reabsorbed in the small intestine.

Physiologically, the body copes best with plain water, so it should not always have flavourings that are too strong, stimulating, dehydrating or calorific. There are problems of pollution of fluid intake with coffee, tea, cola, sugar and alcohol. Many children never drink plain water, with consequent concerns about dental caries, obesity and the overconsumption of additives.

Body composition alters as it gets older. Elderly people have a higher percentage of body fat to fluid, younger people having more fluid. Therefore, in an older body, there is less fluid to dissolve drugs such as alcohol.

Micronutrients

Leaving the macronutrients, we will now turn our attention to the micronutrients: vitamins and minerals.

Vitamins

vitamins
_____
complex organic compounds vital to metabolic processes

Vitamins are needed in very small amounts. They are relatively complex organic compounds that have essential functions in metabolic processes. Some cannot be synthesised in the body so must be provided by the diet. There is constant turnover of the vitamins; thus they must be replaced. For example, vitamin C is water soluble, needing constant replenishment as there is no storage facility in the body. Water-soluble vitamins are absorbed from the upper intestine. Fat-soluble vitamins are absorbed with fat in food.

For estimated average requirements, see *Dietary Reference Values for Food Energy and Nutrients for the United Kingdom* (DoH, 1991). The supplements that many people take are controlled by food legislation, which is less restrictive than drug legislation. As a result, vitamin labels still refer to a recommended daily allowance single figure, which was replaced in 1991 by the precisely targeted dietary reference values tables (DoH, 1991).

The main vitamins are discussed below.

Vitamin A (retinol, carotene)

Vitamin A (retinol, carotene) is needed for healthy mucous membranes and skin, colour and night vision, and a healthy immune system. In children, it helps to ensure correct bone development and growth. It is one of the antioxidants, which help to protect against bowel cancer and heart disease. It is fat soluble and is found in liver, milk, fortified margarine, butter, eggs, fish liver oils, carrots and leafy green vegetables. It is stored in the liver and released when needed.

Two groups of compounds have vitamin A activity: retinol in animal foods, and carotene from red and yellow fruits and vegetables, especially carrots. Beta-carotene is found in green and orange vegetables. Vegetarians can convert this to vitamin A. Beta-carotene is much less toxic as it is more easily excreted.

Vitamin B group

These are water soluble vitamins.

B1 (thiamin)
Vitamin B1 (thiamin) is needed for the metabolism and release of energy from carbohydrate, fat and alcohol. It is found in brewer's yeast, pork, ham and other meats, fortified breakfast cereals, broccoli, peas, green beans and orange juice.

B2 (riboflavin)

B2 (riboflavin) is necessary for energy metabolism. Sources include liver, milk, fortified cereal products, eggs, plain chocolate, fish and pulses.

B3 (niacin, nicotinic acid, nicotinamide)

Vitamin B3 (niacin, nicotinic acid, nicotinamide) is required for tissue oxidation. It is found in milk, meat products, instant coffee, brewer's yeast, potatoes, bread and fortified breakfast cereal.

B5 (pantothenic acid)

B5 (pantothenic acid) is part of the co-enzyme A molecule. It is needed for energy metabolism. Although it is found in all living matter, good sources include liver, kidney, yeast, egg yolk, peanuts and some vegetables. It is not found in sugar, confectionery, cola, margarine, lard, corn starch or alcoholic spirits.

B6 (pyridoxine)

B6 (pyridoxine) is needed for protein metabolism, the nervous system and the regulation of action of some hormones. It can be found in liver, whole grain cereals, bananas, beans and legumes, nuts and seeds (especially sunflower seeds), chicken, tuna and beef. Small amounts are found in fruits and vegetables. Intestinal flora synthesise large amounts of the vitamin, some of which is available for absorption.

B12 (cyanocobalamin)

Vitamin B12 (cyanocobalamin) is essential for red blood cell production, a healthy nervous system and the synthesis of DNA and RNA (genetic material). Sources include offal, other meat and meat products, fish and eggs, with small amounts in dairy products.

It is absorbed in the distal ileum, deficiency most often being caused by a lack of absorption. Intrinsic factor, produced by the parietal cells of the stomach, is needed for the absorption of vitamin B12. As there are no plant sources, strict vegetarians and vegans may be short of this vitamin without suitable supplementation. Yeast extract may be helpful.

Post-gastrectomy patients will require injections of B12. Tapeworm infestation or bacterial overgrowth may make the vitamin unavailable as they assimilate it for their own use.

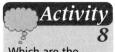

Activity
8

Which are the wholegrain cereals? What loaf is fortified with folic acid? Is yours? Why is this relevant?

Folate/folic acid

Folate/folic acid is necessary for red blood cell production, nervous system functioning and the synthesis of DNA. It can be gained from offal (which cannot be consumed during pregnancy), raw green leafy vegetables and wholegrain cereals.

Lack of folate/folic acid during the first few weeks of pregnancy can lead to neural tube defects, such as spina bifida (failure of the spinal column to close).

Vitamin C (ascorbic acid)

Vitamin C (ascorbic acid) is required for the integrity of the connective tissues, the production of adrenal hormones and wound healing (see Chapter 8). It is antioxidant, water soluble and found in potatoes (especially their skins), fruit juice, citrus and other fruits and green vegetables. It helps to increase iron absorption from vegetable sources. In megadoses of 1 g or more per day, it may reduce the severity and duration of the common cold. Smokers and those taking the contraceptive pill have increased requirements as a result of increased excretion and decreased storage.

Deficiency causes scurvy, resulting in bleeding gums, loosening and loss of the teeth, delayed wound healing (see Chapter 8), lowered resistance to infection and damage to bone and connective tissue. Untreated scurvy is fatal. Sailors used to ransack the colonies looking for fruits high in ascorbic acid, hence the nicknames Pom (short for pomegranate) in Australia and Limey (for limes) in America. Those at risk of deficiency include children from low income and larger families who are unlikely to eat many fruits and vegetables or drink natural fruit juice. Faddy eaters of any age are at risk if they eat few fruits or vegetables.

Over 1000–2000 mg per day can cause diarrhoea and gastric upset. High doses may trigger oxalate kidney stones in those who are susceptible. Suddenly stopping a high intake may cause rebound scurvy because of an enhanced turnover of the vitamin.

Vitamin D (calciferol, ergocalciferol)

Activity 9

Why might a client confined to bed become deficient in Vitamin D? What could be the long-term effects? (See also Chapter 7.)

rickets

undermineralisation of bone, causing abnormalities in the shape and structure of bones owing to a poor absorption of calcium

Vitamin D (calciferol, ergocalciferol) regulates calcium absorption and utilisation for healthy bones and teeth. Fat soluble, it is mostly synthesised from the action of sunlight on skin. Vitamin D food sources include fortified margarine, oily fish, eggs, fortified breakfast cereals, fortified milks and butter.

A prolonged deficiency of vitamin D results in rickets in young children, Asian, Islamic and Afro-Caribbean children being particularly at risk. Asian girls may not expose their bodies to sunlight and, if they are vegetarian, may eat almost no preformed vitamin D. A diet high in phytate (insoluble fibre from plant cell walls) may reduce the absorption of calcium, which may be a factor in rickets. Chronically ill children and elderly, housebound people may also be at risk of deficiency. Women who have had multiple pregnancies may be at risk of osteomalacia, in which their bones become demineralised. Additionally, clinical conditions that impair fat absorption will reduce vitamin D absorption.

Overdose over time can accumulate in the body, causing high blood calcium and symptoms such as headache and appetite loss.

Vitamin E/alpha- and beta-tocopherols

Vitamin E/alpha- and beta-tocopherols are needed for the protection of cell membranes and lipids against oxidative damage and can help to protect against heart attacks. These antioxidants are fat soluble, being found in vegetable and nut oils, wholegrain cereals, eggs and dark green leafy vegetables. The amount needed by the body depends upon the intake of polyunsaturated fatty acids.

Vitamin K/K1/K2

Vitamin K/K1/K2 is essential for blood clotting and energy metabolism. Fat soluble, it is found in vegetables, especially cabbage, sprouts, cauliflower and spinach, margarines and vegetable oils and animal liver.

Lack of vitamin K may cause the blood to take longer to clot. This can be noted in clients who have been on a very low fat diet because of stones in the gall-bladder, giving rise to pain when they eat fatty foods, or those taking warfarin. Small numbers of newborn babies may have low levels of vitamin K and are at risk of haemorrhagic disease of the newborn. To reduce this risk, it is usual to supplement the mother or administer a single oral prophylactic dose of vitamin K to neonates.

prophylactic
preventing infection or disease

Vitamins are more effectively acquired from food than as supplements. If supplements are really necessary, check that the dose is appropriate, make sure that it is taken with food and spread out across the day rather than all at once. Fat-soluble vitamins must be taken with fatty foods for maximum absorption.

Minerals

minerals
naturally occurring, inorganic substances needed in trace amounts in the diet

In addition to metabolic fuels, protein and vitamins, the body has a requirement for a variety of mineral salts (minerals) in very small (trace) amounts. The requirements of a growing child will be greater than those of a healthy adult who simply has to replace body losses from mineral turnover. A sick person or pregnant or lactating mother will have increased requirements of these micronutrients.

Calcium

Calcium (Ca) is needed for the growth and development of bones and teeth, the correct functioning of nerves and muscles, and blood clotting. It is found in milk, cheese, yoghurt, nuts, pulses, green vegetables and canned fish. The body requires adequate levels of vitamin D to absorb and regulate calcium. Absorption may be reduced by excess NSP intake and phytate.

In deficiency states, bone calcium is mobilised to maintain essential functions, leading to rickets and osteoporosis. If a child has a low calcium intake, he

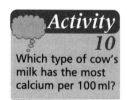

Activity 10

Which type of cow's milk has the most calcium per 100 ml?

hypercalcaemia
————————
excess calcium in the blood

may fail to achieve peak bone mass by 30, which will increase the likelihood of osteoporosis in later life. Those at risk include children who dislike or do not take milk and dairy products, and fail to replace them with a calcium-fortified milk substitute (for example soya). Acute deficiency may cause tetany (muscle spasms) due to loss of neuromuscular regulation.

Overdoses of calcium supplements in people with poor kidney function cause calcium to accumulate and may contribute to kidney stones or the calcification of blood vessels. Overdosage of vitamin D may cause abnormal calcium deposits in soft tissues or hypercalcaemia

Phosphorus

Phosphorus (P) is a component of all cells, necessary for energy storage, membrane function, growth and reproduction. Eighty-five per cent of the body's stores are found in bone. Sources include milk, milk products, bread, cereal products, meat and meat products, peanut butter and almonds.

Sodium

Sodium (Na) is needed for maintenance of constant body water content and plays an important role in the conduction of nervous impulses. It is found in many foods.

Chloride

Chloride (Cl) is required for maintenance of constant body water content. It is found in many foods.

Sodium chloride

The current recommendation for sodium chloride (NaCl, salt) is a maximum of 6 grams of salt per day for an adult (10 g being equivalent to 2 teaspoonfuls of salt). Too much salt is thought to cause hypertension (raised blood pressure) in those susceptible to it. Processed foods and snacks tend to contain high levels of NaCl.

Potassium

Potassium (K) is necessary for the maintenance of constant body water content, for acid–base balance and for nervous conduction. It is found in vegetables, meat, milk, almonds, fruit and fruit juices.

Iodine

Iodine (I) is needed for the functioning of the thyroid gland, which controls the metabolic rate of the body. It is found in seafish and milk, and table salt in the UK is fortified with iodine. Deficiency is possible in those living far from the sea with no access to seafish.

Iron

Iron (Fe) is essential for red blood cell formation, oxygen transport and transfer, enzyme activation and drug metabolism. There are two sorts: organic/haem iron, found in meat, and inorganic/non-haem iron gained from bread, flour and cereal products, potatoes, green leafy vegetables, red wine, dried apricots and chocolate. Balti cooking is a good source because of iron from the cooking pot. Haem iron is more accessible and more easily absorbed than non-haem iron. Vegetarians may, therefore, be at risk of deficiency. Iron is best absorbed with vitamin C, so the 2 mg of iron found in your fortified breakfast cereal is absorbed better with a glass of orange juice than a cup of tea. Keep that for later in the day (see below).

Lack of iron causes iron deficiency anaemia. Those at risk include faddy toddlers on self-restricted diets, especially those drinking large amounts of cow's milk and squash, with little solid food, vegetarians and schoolchildren eating mostly chips, crisps and cola.

Iron supplements can cause gastric irritation, tarry stools and constipation. Overdosage of iron in those genetically susceptible to iron overload can increase the risk of heart disease.

Zinc

Zinc (Zn) is needed for bone metabolism, the activation of enzymes, the release of vitamin A, growth and healing, healthy immune and reproductive systems, taste and insulin release. Sources include shellfish, meat and meat products, milk and milk products, bread and cereal products and peanut butter.

Features of zinc deficiency include anorexia, failure to thrive in infants and children, weight loss, tremor, dermatitis, fine brittle hair, alopecia (hair loss), hypospermia (a reduced sperm count), pica and impaired taste and smell as well as delayed wound healing. At risk of zinc deficiency are faddy toddlers, children on a vegan diet and older children eating predominantly chips, crisps and cola. One solution is to snack on fortified breakfast cereals, cheese and yoghurt, and eat two portions of protein daily (animal or green leafy vegetables and pulses).

Too much zinc can cause gastrointestinal irritation and may disturb the balance of other important minerals, such as iron and copper, in the body.

Selenium

Selenium (Se) is necessary for part of an enzyme involved in the protection of membranes and lipids against oxidative damage. It is one of the antioxidants found in cereals, fish, offal, meat, cheese, eggs and milk. High-protein sources contain the most selenium. The requirement for selenium declines as the amount of vitamin E in the diet increases.

iron deficiency anaemia

a reduced amount of haemoglobin in red blood cells, causing fatigue, glossitis and paraesthesia (sensations of numbness, prickling or tingling)

anorexia

loss of appetite

dermatitis

inflammation of the skin, shown by itching, redness and skin lesions

pica

eating materials unsuitable as food, for example soil

Activity 11

Look up the structure and function of the gastrointestinal tract, particularly digestion and absorption, in your preferred anatomy and physiology text (for example, Rutishauser, 1994, pp. 107–35, 253–74).

Mineral tailpieces

- *Phytates*, found in high levels in unprocessed wheat bran and soya, can lead to the malabsorption of minerals, especially calcium and zinc.
- *Tannins* (polyphenols), found in tea, can reduce mineral availability.
- *Oxalates*, found in high levels in spinach and rhubarb, can reduce mineral availability.

Activity 12

Did you know that there are over 500 different species of fungi and bacteria that live in your gut? They weigh 2 kg in an adult. What are they for? (See, for example, Rutishauser, 1994, pp. 123–4.)

It would be easy to assume that you or your clients are eating a 'balanced' diet, with very little evidence to support this. It is also possible to get confused by technicalities and unnecessary details when looking at nutrition. This chapter is about eating, so will now look at the *foods* that make up a balanced intake. In the first student activity, you were asked to 'guestimate' the relative amounts, by weight, of food groups that your body needs. This can be summarised either by percentages:

- Fruit and vegetables: 33 per cent
- Starchy foods: 33 per cent

Casebox 4.2

Ms Cohen, a retired civil servant of 60, underwent major hip surgery 2 weeks ago. She has little interest in food, and was identified on admission as being underweight and malnourished.

How may this affect her progress after surgery?

What advice would be needed for her convalescence to be an opportunity to improve her nutritional status?

- Malnutrition will delay her recovery and increase the likelihood of complications. It interferes with respiratory function, partly by loss of diaphragm muscle mass and strength, making Ms Cohen more likely to get a chest infection. Cardiac and immune function are depressed, so she would be at high risk of a wound infection or even a heart attack (myocardial infarct). Ms Cohen's grip strength will be diminished, making it harder for her to mobilise on crutches. Her bone density may also be very much diminished. Malnutrition has psychological effects such as apathy, depression and loss of the will to recover (Rollins, 1997), making Ms Cohen less likely to co-operate with her rehabilitation regimen.

- Ms Cohen needs to be fed as a matter of urgency or she is unlikely to get better. Nutritional support may need to be directed along the lines of food as medicine and considerable efforts employed to coax her to eat and drink, little and often, high-calorie and nutrient-dense foodstuffs. Vitamin supplements may be an option. Her belief systems need to be identified: as she is Orthodox Jewish, is kosher food available? An education programme needs to be implemented to gain her interest in 'eating for convalescence'. Any family, friends or neighbours could be encouraged to bring her favourite foods – Jewish chicken soup is said to boost the immune system. Her community nurse may be recruited to monitor her nutritionally.

Activity
13

In which section of
the tilted plate
would you put
eggs? How would
you classify
potatoes?

- Milk and dairy: 14 per cent
- Meat and alternatives: 12 per cent
- Oils, fats, fatty foods, sugars, sugary foods (and alcohol, if taken): 8 per cent

or by a diagram of a 'tilted plate' (Figure 4.3).

Alcohol

This substance has a long history of bad and good press (Simpson, 1992). It is high in calories and carbohydrate, which, when taken in excess, can be a factor in obesity and vitamin deficiency, especially that of vitamin B1. It is dehydrating so is unhelpful in maintaining the body's fluid balance: hangovers are largely the result of dehydration.

A moderate alcohol intake is associated with raised levels of HDL cholesterol, a protective factor against heart disease (see above). The antioxidant components of alcohol are found, for example, in grape skins, so red wine is a good source. Red wine is thought to protect against heart attacks by preventing arteries furring up with deposits of LDL cholesterol. Polyphenols, abundant in red wine, are believed to block the oxidation of LDLs and thus stop them accumulating on arterial walls (Coghlan, 1997). For health, the best pattern is alcohol absorbed slowly with meals, which is one basis of the Mediterranean diet.

Excessive alcohol intake leads to long-term problems affecting every body system, for example brain shrinkage, stroke, liver damage, cancer of the oesoph-

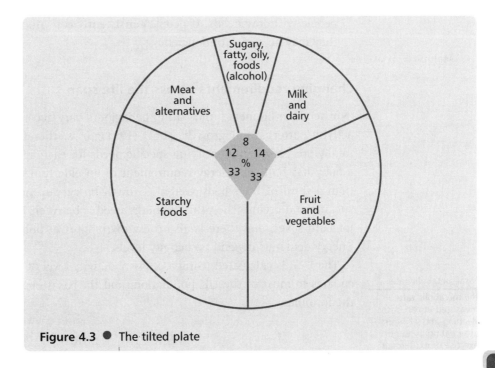

Figure 4.3 ● The tilted plate

agus, heart disease, premature ageing of the skin, loss of secondary sexual characteristics, muscle wasting and bone demineralisation (Bonner and Waterhouse, 1996). Damage is exacerbated by binge drinking.

One unit of alcohol is equal to 8 g of ethanol. For example, 500 ml of 5 per cent alcohol lager will contain 25 ml of pure alcohol, that is, about 3 units. The unit system for healthy intakes needs to be applied with flexibility. Women can take up to 14 units (unless they are pregnant) and men 21 units per week (Marmot, 1995). Two alcohol-free days are encouraged to allow the body to recover. One gram of alcohol gives 29 kJ (7 kcal) of energy.

Getting Enough Nutrients

COMA, in its 1991 report (DoH, 1991), produced ranges for different dietary components, using the following guidelines:

- Dietary reference values (DRVs) is a general term that must be used, as it is a more precisely focused and evidence-based system than recommended daily allowances (RDAs), which produced a single figure for each nutrient, covering every age group.
- Reference nutrient intake (RNI) is the amount of a nutrient that is sufficient for up to 97 per cent of the population.
- Estimated average requirements (EAR) is the estimated average requirement of each nutrient sufficient to meet the needs of half the population.
- Lower reference nutrient intake (LRNI) is the amount of nutrient needed for people with low needs. If people consistently consume less than their LRNI, they may be at risk of deficiency.

Changing requirements across the life span

'Nutrient requirements and eating behaviours vary according to health status, activity patterns and growth' (DoH, 1991); it is, therefore, impossible to be totally precise when identifying specific needs for each age group. For example, a baby has half the energy requirement of an elderly person but is much less than a third of their body weight. Growth has great energy demands, as has sucking and crying. The peak of energy need is between 15 and 18 years of age for both sexes, and there is also the growth spurt at puberty to contend with. Energy demands depend on activity levels.

The EAR is calculated using a physical activity level of 1.4 (Table 4.3), which equates to most of the UK population, and the basal metabolic rate (BMR) in the formula:

$$BMR \times PAL = EAR.$$

basal metabolic rate

the metabolic rate measured at rest, after sleeping and 12 hours after eating, with no exercise or excitement preceding the test

Table 4.3 ● Physical activity level (PAL) for those over 18 years of age

PAL		
1.4		Very little activity at work and in leisure time
1.6	Female	Moderate activity at work/leisure
1.7	Male	Moderate activity at work/leisure
1.8	Female	High levels of activity at work/leisure
1.9	Male	High levels of activity at work/leisure

Assessing nutritional status

Activity 14

Look up metabolism in your preferred anatomy and physiology or nutrition text (for example, Rutishauser, 1994, pp. 266–72). What is the difference between anabolism and catabolism? Why is this relevant to eating and drinking?

anabolism

the building up of body substance; the constructive phase of metabolism

catabolism

the breakdown of body substance; the destructive phase of metabolism

body mass index

a figure derived from a person's height and weight, which indicates whether weight is acceptable

One way of checking whether someone is well nourished is to get him to keep a food diary (see Figure 4.5 below) and then rate it against the 'tilted plate'. One day's intake is not enough information on which to make a judgement, unless it is typical of a very consistent intake. The more information that can be gained, the more accurate the resulting baseline. In order to monitor a client's food and fluid intake, most units have food and fluid charts of varying degrees of formality. The important thing is that they are completed with the best degree of accuracy possible and that the intake is added up and related to the client's needs by someone with the knowledge and interest to ensure that findings are acted upon. There are also local and national nutritional awareness and assessment tools, some research based and validated, many not. Most have a series of questions to be answered, which are scored to identify the client's level of risk of malnutrition. At the very least, every client should, on admission/assessment, be asked the following questions:

1. Have you unintentionally lost weight recently?
2. Have you been eating less than usual?
3. What is your normal weight?
4. How tall are you?

Body Mass Index (BMI)

Questions 3 and 4 above enable the nurse to calculate body mass index (BMI; Chart 4.2), which is a better indicator of health than is weight alone. BMI relates height to weight to indicate healthy ranges of weight.

A BMI below the acceptable range indicates undernutrition (or dehydration), one above the range indicating overweight/obesity (or oedema). This measure is not suitable for infants, children, the pregnant and amputees, and can be difficult in the shrunken older person. If a person has a great deal of muscle he may appear 'obese'.

Chart 4.2 ● BMI

BMI calculation = weight (kg)/height²(m)

Reference ranges for desirable BMI =

    Men: 20.5–25.0, women 19–24

    25–30 overweight

    >30 obese

To determine body fat percentage, multiply the BMI by 1.281 and take 10.13 away from the result for men. For women, multiply the BMI by 1.480 and subtract 7.

Questions 1 and 2 above are essential as unintentional weight loss is significant even if the client has a 'normal' or 'high' BMI. A greater than 10 per cent loss in body weight in less than 3 months signifies that the client is malnourished and should be referred for specialist nutrition advice as there is a risk of increased morbidity and mortality; that is, they are more likely to suffer disease, complications and death.

morbidity

the state of being diseased

Assisting with Nutrition and Hydration

hydration

the state of fluid balance of the body

Activity 15

Most big chemists hold a range of feeding aids and catalogues of equipment. Get hold of some catalogues to see what can be provided for clients. Look at the four 'SEEN' headings (see text) and list as many helpful ideas/equipment as you can in 10 minutes. Identify at least one negative event you have encountered in practice.

The aim of any help is to get optimum food and fluid into clients in a reasonable manner, maintaining their dignity. The only food that is of any use to clients is that which they actually eat and retain, remembering that 'You are what you eat'. Assisting someone with their nutrition and hydration can be placed into four broad areas – social, ergonomic, economic and nutritional (SEEN):

- *Social:* the sociable side of eating.
- *Ergonomic:* the study of work and its environment and conditions to achieve maximum efficiency, as applied to nutrition.
- *Economic/educational:* the best use of time and resources; health promotion/education.
- *Nutrition function:* especially important for the vulnerable client.

Social

Food can and should be an enjoyable break, a pause or punctuation, in the day rather than just fuel. Arrange a change of scene and company if possible by taking clients to a dining room or day room. Get people around tables with upright chairs, away from beds, clatter, telephones, staff and clinical equipment. Identify for each individual the best setting to encourage them to eat, digest and absorb the most nourishment. Watching someone else's food going round like socks in a washing machine may not enhance appetite. A person needing feeding may be best served in privacy to reduce embarrassment and distractions. Involve clients in decisions about their food and drink – its timing, amount and so on (Shepheard, 1998).

Remember that presentation counts. Consider the cleanliness of the surroundings, ensuring that smells are neutral, fresh air is available and the food looks appealing. For blind clients use the 'clockface' to describe what is where on the plate. Braille or large-print menus may also be available.

Sherry as an appetite stimulant can be particularly useful for elderly clients (Simpson, 1992).

Staff might eat their meals with clients to enhance the social function. This can be a useful reminder to those with limited memory who just forget to eat without the external prompt of seeing others doing so.

Ergonomic/physiological

Ergonomics is the study of people, work and its environment, and the conditions to achieve maximum efficiency. It is necessary to know how swallowing works and the physiology of the gastrointestinal tract in order to help the client most effectively in this area.

Gravity feed is the most useful idea on which to base good practice. Sitting the client as upright as possible allows the first third of the oesophagus to work and generate the wave of peristalsis that takes food and fluid (and drugs) into the stomach. If possible, an upright chair drawn up to a table of comfortable height should be used. The client in an armchair may find even an adjustable bed-table too high. In such a case, consider putting a firm pillow under the client to raise her to a more comfortable height. Other strategies include putting the tray on to the edge of the bed if the client can turn to one side in the armchair, sitting the client on the edge of the bed with her feet on the floor if she can support herself, and bringing the bed-table over her knees. Lap-trays with 'beanbag' backs can be used on any height of chair or in bed. For some clients, adjustable chairs should be placed in a more upright position for meals and drinks, and not put back to recline for at least 15 minutes afterwards; this will reduce the chances of reflux.

Clients in bed need to be sitting upright. Pillows should be arranged so that they can lean forward. Clinical equipment might need to be moved out of the way or covered up. Consider the physiological implications of the client being frightened, nauseated or in pain. The effects of stimulation of the gastrointestinal tract by the sympathetic nervous system include a decrease in motility and a drying up of secretions, including a dry mouth, leaving clients unable to utilise what is taken in.

Activity 16

Look up swallowing in your preferred anatomy and physiology text (for example, Rutishauser, 1994, pp. 506–8; see also structure and function of the gastrointestinal tract, especially digestion and absorption, pp. 107–35, 253–74).

---

reflux

a backward flow of food and fluid up the gastrointestinal tract

sympathetic nervous system

part of the autonomic (automatic) nervous system activated in response to fright and other unpleasant stimuli

If clients need help with feeding, sit at the same level so that you can reach comfortably. Try not to rush them or give them too much at any time. A half to a full teaspoonful per mouthful is plenty, and is best placed in the stronger side of the mouth. Ensure that the client can close his lips as the lipseal needs to be maintained to trigger the swallow. Allow two swallows per mouthful to ensure that it is empty. Ask the client to clear his throat to clear the airway; then wait a few seconds before offering the next mouthful. After every few mouthfuls, ask the client to cough, and to do so again at the end of the meal. Listen to his voice, by asking him to say 'Ah ' after every few mouthfuls. A 'wet' or gurgly-sounding voice is an indication to **stop** feeding, as this is a sign of aspiration into the respiratory tract; in such a situation, call for qualified assistance.

When the meal has been completed safely, check the mouth for retained food, which might give trouble later, and remove it with a swab or toothbrush. If the client can cope, a mouthwash will help. After eating or drinking, the client should stay sitting upright for at least half an hour. Blood is diverted to the gut to digest food, so the client may feel chilly after eating. If indigestion is a problem, consider the use of ginger ale (also good for nausea) or peppermint.

Economic/educational

- Know when mealtimes are in order to plan a break in the workload.
- Timing: Try to ensure those needing help with elimination have been encouraged to perform well before mealtimes to reduce unpleasant noises and smells, which act as appetite suppressants.
- If someone needs a commode at a mealtime, wheel them out to a bathroom for privacy.
- Remove bedpans, urinals, commodes and toilet rolls from bedtables and bedsides.
- Handwashing for staff and patients (see Chapter 3) is most important.
- If the family want to visit and help, they could bring in favourite treats if policy allows.
- It might be necessary to discourage other visitors at mealtimes as it distracts the client and diverts the energy needed for eating.
- Is the mouth clean, and are the dentures in place? (If not in use, ensure that dentures are kept in water or they will warp.)
- Do the dentures fit?
- Ensure that pain relief or antiemetic medication is given in time for it to be working well.
- Does the patient need insulin or another medication before meals?
- Employ strategies to reduce breathlessness.
- Time any nausea-inducing therapy to occur after meals.
- Ensure that ventilation is adequate to waft away body smells during meals and the smell of food afterwards.

- Exploit educational opportunities when setting up menu choices.
- Cut up food for those who need it.
- Rearrange the contents of the tray so the client can reach everything. Lift heavy lids and peel off fiddly tops. Are salt and pepper available? Can the client hold the cutlery provided (indeed, is it all there?), or does she need built-up handles or other special cutlery?
- Is fresh water available?
- If a hot drink is delivered too early, put a lid on it and check it again later.
- Supplement the paper napkin with additional protection if needed.
- Would a straw help? This is of no use for stroke patients as their orbicularis oris muscle (the muscle around the mouth) is weak, making their suction power low; straws with valves or a feeder cup may help.
- Does the client need an occasional prompt or gentle reminder, constant attention or feeding?
- Use your awareness of the gastrocolic reflex (putting food in at the top causes the system to shunt into activity) to anticipate needs. Some clients who cannot tell you what they need may go red in the face after tea, coffee or meals, which can mean that they need to defaecate.
- Keeping hot foods hot and cold foods cold enhances their palatability; cold food most improves swallowing.
- If a client has problems with swallowing, has she been referred to a speech and language therapist?
- The easiest consistency to eat is a smooth texture. Soft solids such as ice cream, yoghurt, custard, purée, baked beans (without toast) and mashed potato are acceptable. Normal solids and thickened liquids are more difficult; these include thick milkshakes, yoghurt drinks and thickened soups. Jelly and bananas may help to supplement the fluid intake.
- Food types to be avoided by the client with eating or swallowing difficulties are those which are stringy, crumbly, tough or of mixed texture, or such things as peas, sweetcorn and chips.

Nutrition function

- What are we trying to do for this patient? Are we using nutrition as therapy for:

  – weight gain
  – weight maintenance
  – weight loss
  – wound healing (see Chapter 8)
  – enhancing fibre intake
  – ensuring a balanced intake
  – correcting malnutrition?

- Do we need to keep a food chart so that it can be checked against the 'tilted plate' for:

  - fruits and vegetables: 33 per cent
  - carbohydrate/starchy foods: 33 per cent
  - milk and dairy: 14 per cent
  - protein: 12 per cent
  - fats, fatty foods, sugars, sugary foods and alcohol: 8 per cent?

If there are any doubts about intake, keep a food and fluid intake chart of what has actually been consumed and retained by the patient.

Activity 17

Rate a client's 24-hour food intake against the 'tilted plate' (see Figure 4.3). Are any deficits apparent? What suggestions can you make to remedy these?

- Is the nutrition therapy featured in the care plan? If not, why not?
- Ensure the adequate completion of menu cards, checking for portion size and balance.
- Are we going for the easy option of soup and ice cream? This can be a nutritional disaster if allowed to go on for more than a couple of days, as it is low in nutrients.
- Think about supplements and snacks.
- Avoid tea or coffee just before or with meals as they can fill patients up too much.
- Lots of fluid with food can overfill clients. This can be helpful if one is trying to reduce weight but is unhelpful if trying to enhance the intake of nutrients.
- 1001 ways with mince is very boring, so build in some variety.
- Little and often may help some, so order a sandwich or fruit to be eaten later.
- How flexible are your catering arrangements? Can you get an omelette, sandwich and so on at any time?
- What are the limits? Can a meal be saved and heated in a microwave later on when it suits the patient? (Food hygiene regulations must, of course, be taken into account; see Chapter 3.)
- Use dietitians appropriately. If there is a problem, they can be more helpful than the catering department.
- Does the person need a soft or puréed diet? Keep component foods separate so that an unappetising greyish sludge is avoided.

anosmia

loss of sense of smell

- Those with anosmia and diminished or altered taste sensation (which may be a result of drug therapy) may need to add extra pepper, salt (but not if they have high blood pressure), spices, herbs, vinegar, sauces or garlic. Relatives could provide these, or they could be bought from ward/unit funds.

hemianopia

blindness in half the field of vision of one or both eyes

- Have an awareness of particular client problems. For example, hemianopia after a stroke means that the client ignores one side of the plate, so the plate should be rotated. Paralysis of one side of the face means that food is left in one cheek like a hamster. The client may need help to work the jaw at intervals.

Appetite and Choices

Activity 18

What emotions may be evoked by the smell of frying onions, brewing coffee, or bread baking? What does your favourite person smell of? When you smell this, how do you feel?

The psychology of eating is highly complex, so the reader is advised to consult a psychology text (for example Lyman, 1989) in addition to reading this section. This is also an extremely important area because food and eating are essential aspects of the social and moral aspect of society.

There are four elementary taste sensations, sweet, sour, bitter and salty being all that the tongue can detect. Monosodium glutamate, which enhances flavours, may be added to this list. What adds subtlety to taste is the sense of smell. Taste and smell together equal the flavour system, which can evoke strong emotional responses. The association of odours with emotion is learned.

Flavour includes other characteristics of food, such as temperature and texture. Variety in food seems to stimulate the appetite, and flavour motivates eating by the pleasure derived from its taste, smell and 'mouthfeel'. For this reason, children often come to prefer foods with a high fat content. Social situations and other people also provide cues that stimulate the appetite for certain foods, the presence of other people also generally tending to induce one to eat more. Additionally, changes in a person's nutritional state can affect their motivation to consume certain foods.

Activity 19

What food and drink selections have you made in the past 24 hours? Can you identify some of the factors influencing those selections?

The selection and preparation of food requires a number of psychological processes, including choice, cognition, knowledge and attitudes. Two theories (Lyman, 1989) help to explain how we might select food to produce nutritional balance. One idea postulates an innate recognition of foods containing deficient nutrients, the other that learning occurs to recognise food that makes one feel good and avoid food that makes one feel bad. The other important mechanism in food choice is the tendency to be suspicious of but interested in new foods. We classify food as edible or inedible, having developed attitudes about what makes an object appropriate and desirable as food.

Three factors account for food rejection and acceptance:

1. *Sensory-affective factors*: Like and dislike are based on sensory attributes such as taste, smell and sometimes appearance. Good tastes are accepted; those which are unappealing are rejected as distasteful.
2. *Anticipated consequences*: Acceptance or rejection is based on beliefs about the consequences of ingestion. For example, an elderly person may believe that 'eggs are binding' or that 'bread is fattening'. Rejection of an item because of perceived negative consequences is based on its 'dangerous' nature. Conversely, the acceptance of an item is based on its anticipated beneficial effects.
3. *Ideational factors*: Items are accepted or rejected because of our knowledge of what they are, their origins or their symbolic meanings. Ideational factors are mostly concerned with food rejection. There are two categories of rejected food: inappropriate and disgusting. An example of the latter is many children's attitudes to vegetables.

Casebox 4.3

Miss Quinn, aged 82, has progressive dementia and has lived in a residential care home for 2 years. She wanders restlessly all round the clock and rarely spends more than a few minutes at anything. The staff are concerned that she appears to be losing weight.

What steps could be taken to ensure that this does not become a problem?

- Make every mouthful count, so avoid wasting eating and drinking time on low-calorie fillers.

- Use the fact that she has limited memory to encourage nutritious snacks around the clock instead of expecting her to concentrate for a full meal.

- Instead of a cup of coffee made with water, she could be offered a cup of coffee made entirely with full-cream milk, a little more sugar being added over time.

- Always present a cup of tea with a biscuit, small cake or sandwich.

- Fluid supplements may be prescribed for her and served chilled or heated.

- Has she chocolates, fruit and crisps in her room for constant access?

- Meals can be enriched to enhance the calorie count by adding butter, cream or sugar as appropriate.

Activity 20

Give an example of your own food choices for each category. Try to identify why your choice has developed this way. Then do this activity with a client.

Thus in summary:

- Psychological categories of rejection include distaste, danger, inappropriateness and disgust.
- Psychological categories of acceptance include good taste, its benefits and its appropriateness.
- We consume food because of the perceived benefits or for its own sake, because it tastes good or for comfort.
- We avoid foods because of their dangerous properties, our intolerance or allergy to them or because of dislike or unfamiliarity.

Social factors are important in our acquisition of liking or disliking of foods. For example, parental choice can influence children one way or the other. People develop long-term food preferences that are stable over long periods of time and unaffected by changes in their moods or environment. These can be most resistant to change if a more healthy diet is advised. Some food preferences change from day to day and are more likely to be affected by mood. For example, Lyman (1989) identified that people tended to prefer healthy foods when experiencing positive emotions and junk food when feeling negative. It was also noted that crunchy foods were most likely to be associated with anger, boredom and frustration.

Political, Social and Economic Influences

Many people, for social, economic, geographical and other reasons, are unable to access the basics of a healthy diet without considerable difficulty. Many groups, such as elderly people, the unemployed or those with children, may be living below the poverty line. They may, for example, live on large housing estates, planned without amenities such as shops, clubs, churches or pubs. Shopping for food may involve a bus journey to add to the cost in time and money. Local shops will be more expensive, and have a more limited choice than supermarkets. Low-income families are less likely than higher-income families to eat fresh fruit and vegetables, fish or fresh meat, and more likely to eat fatty foods and starchy 'filler' foods such as white bread, jam, cakes, biscuits and sweets. Vitamin and mineral status is often compromised. Shopping basket surveys have shown that a healthy diet may cost up to 35 per cent more than an unhealthy one. The loss of free school milk and free school meals has not helped those families with children who most need this support to supplement their often meagre diets, and changing benefit patterns do not appear to allow these families to catch up. Thus it seems that the main factors of food deprivation are low income/pension, inadequate benefits, the high cost of appropriate food and its availability. As well as affecting children's growth and development, a poor diet may contribute to dental disease, nutritional anaemia, obesity, low bone mass, coronary heart disease and cerebrovascular disease (stroke).

nutritional anaemia

reduction in the haemoglobin content of red blood cells due to a lack of iron in the diet

---

Casebox 4.4

Raul is 15 years old and has learning disabilities and many physical problems. He is moving to a new care home and the opportunity is being taken to reassess his needs. How may the team assess his nutritional status and identify what assistance Raul requires?

- Measure his height, weight and calculate his BMI.

- Keep a food record over a week to check for likes and dislikes, and overall balance.

- Is Raul getting enough fluid? What are his preferences?

- What capacities has he for chewing and swallowing? Does he need assessing by a speech and language therapist? In what state are his teeth and gums?

- Could the drugs that he is taking (for example, phenytoin) interact with his food?

- How is Raul best positioned for meals, and how much can he do for himself? Does he need a special tilted chair? What about built-up cutlery, moulded to his hand grip? Can occupational therapy help?

Casebox 4.5

Trevor, aged 47, is suffering from depression. He barely has the energy to get himself out of bed in the mornings, is off sick from his work as a storeman and goes to group therapy once a week.

What is likely to be the effect upon his eating pattern and weight?

Trevor will probably suffer from early morning wakening, but his activity levels will be very low. If he eats as much as he used to before he went off sick, and/or eats for comfort, with high levels of refined carbohydrate and fat, Trevor may put on weight. It is also possible that he could lose interest in food, have no appetite and not bother to shop or cook for himself, ending up with weight loss, some of which will be loss of muscle mass from inactivity (see Chapter 7).

Cultural Issues – Ethnic and Religious Practices

Activity 21

Consider why the fish and chip shop is busier on Fridays. Identify the food ideology of a client who comes from a different cultural, ethnic or religious group.

Activity 22

Imagine celebrating a friendly gathering without food or drink. Identify one food that you regard as 'good' and one you regard as 'bad'. Why have these foods come to mean this to you? What is the basis for this belief? Is it rational?

Cultural factors inform food ideology, that is, the collection of customs, attitudes, beliefs and taboos that affect the diet of a particular group. For example, some people may feel that their diet is incomplete without a hot meal at least once a day. For centuries, Roman Catholics consumed no meat on Fridays and Mormons do not consume caffeine or alcohol.

The food ideology of clients is important because it influences their behaviour as well as their motivation to alter their food habits across time. These food habits are acquired as part of primary socialisation in childhood and may be difficult to change, which reinforces the necessity of initially developing good food habits in childhood (Fieldhouse, 1995). Secondary socialisation takes place through the school and workplace, and may contradict food habits learned at home. The attempts by health professionals to change people's eating habits in more healthy directions can be termed 'resocialisation'. This process can be helped or hindered by influences at local, regional and national levels, including such factors as advertising. People may regard foods as 'good' or 'bad', Yin or Yang, 'hot' or 'cold', reward or punishment. The social meanings of food are bound up with notions and traditions of hospitality, expressions of love, friendship, affection and status (Fieldhouse, 1995).

Many world religions, such as Buddhism, Hinduism, Sikhism, Rastafarianism and spiritualism, advocate vegetarianism of varying strictness. Fruitarians eat only fruit, vegans eat no animal products, lactovegetarians eat no eggs, meat, fish or poultry, and lacto-ovovegetarians eat vegetables, pulses, nuts, milk, cheese and eggs.

Chart 4.3 ● Vegetarian tilted plate

....

1 serving of plant oils/margarine/butter

4–5 servings of fruit/vegetables

2–3 servings of pulses/nuts/seeds

3–4 servings of cereals/grains

2 servings of dairy/soya

....

As vegetarianism seems to be on the increase, nurses need to be aware of how a diet can be balanced in the absence of meat, fish, cheese, eggs or dairy products. An alternative 'tilted plate' is outlined in Chart 4.3 and Figure 4.4 for guidance.

Religions and cultures that advocate fasting usually absolve the sick from participating. Yet for many clients, fasting before investigations, surgery or treatment or because of their illness is an unwelcome part of their lives.

● Monitoring Eating and Drinking

Some clients will need close monitoring to ensure that their nutrition and hydration needs are adequately met. Nutritional assessment should be a continuous process, particularly when clients have been identified as being at risk of

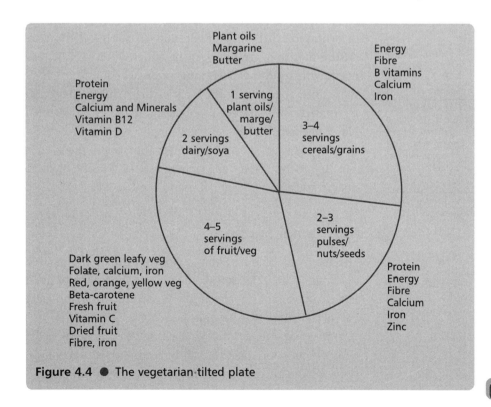

Figure 4.4 ● The vegetarian tilted plate

malnutrition. Simple indicators, such as regular weighing, may be enough if the equipment is available and accurate (Micklewright and Todorovic, 1997). Short-term gains and losses of weight will only reflect body fluid changes. The client's mood may well be affected by nutrition levels. The malnourished patient tends to be apathetic and have poor grip strength and very little motivation to participate in her own care.

Information can also be gained about the client's progress from blood albumin levels. Albumin is synthesised in the liver and transports small molecules including medications, hormones and vitamins. The normal level in adults is 34–50 g/l, and it has a half-life of 20 days. In very ill and malnourished patients, the levels will be below 35 g/l and will decline further if their condition deteriorates. This may mean that their ability to transport drugs around the body could be compromised (McPherson, 1993). Although the albumin level is not a nutritional indicator on its own, it nevertheless gives some idea of the client's condition, and the trend of the readings is significant.

Food charts (Figure 4.5) can be useful provided they are totalled and the findings acted upon. The severely compromised patient may well need referral to a specialist such as a clinical nutrition nurse or dietitian. The key features to check are the calorie and protein intakes. For example, is a male client aged between 19 and 50 achieving 10.60 MJ (2550 kcal) and 55.5 g of protein, and is a female client of this same age eating 8.10 MJ (1940 kcal) and 45 g of protein?

Fluid charts also need to be checked for balance (see Chapter 5). If patients have excessive losses, are being fasted, are vomiting or are being given any form of artificial nutrition or hydration, a careful check is absolutely essential to ensure that they are not over- or underhydrated. (The essentials of caring for a client with an intravenous infusion may be found in Chapter 6.) Some clinicians may pinch the skin on the back of the hand to check skin turgor (for a kinder alternative, see Chapter 5) or monitor the central venous pressure or arterial blood pressure and pulse (see Chapter 6). The presence or absence of oedema may be relevant. 'Low-tech' rehydration techniques, such as rectal infusion or hypodermoclysis (Abdulla and Keast, 1997), are theoretically possible but are not currently in widespread use in the UK.

half-life

the time required by the body to metabolise half of a particular substance

skin turgor

the resistance of the skin to deformation when pinched between the fingers, related mainly to age but also to the level of hydration

hypodermoclysis

the introduction of subcutaneous fluid

Nutritional Support

The mainstay of nutritional support is to use the gastrointestinal tract, if it is working, (enteral feeding) and only use the intravenous (parenteral) route if the gut is unavailable, for example as a result of complete intestinal obstruction. Parenteral support is beyond the scope of this text.

It must be stressed that the best route for feeding is via the mouth, anything else being a poor substitute. Tube feeding has psychological and social implications for the client, and complications may occur. It may be used to provide all the client's requirements or simply be supplemental feeding in those who find it difficult to take in enough orally.

The most straightforward route for gut access is the nasogastric route. A fine-bore polyurethane nasogastric tube (size 10 French gauge [Fr] for an adult,

ONE DAY FOOD RECORD

List below all the food you ate and drank yesterday. For each item check (✓) the appropriate food group. Be sure to total the number of foods eaten for each group.

Self Elderly Person Child Age Pregnant Woman FOODS EATEN	33% Bread & Cereals	33% Fruit & Vegetables	14% Milk & Milk Products	12% Meat & Alternatives	Sugar Alcohol / Fatty Foods 8%
BREAKFAST					
SNACK					
LUNCH					
SNACK					
DINNER					
SNACK					
Total Fluid Volume					
TOTAL NUMBER OF FOODS EATEN FROM EACH GROUP					
Percentage					

Height: Weight: BMI:

Figure 4.5 ● One-day food record

down to size 5 Fr for a very small baby) is inserted for the delivery of liquid feeds. The smallest possible tube is used to reduce the discomfort of leaving it in place and minimise the risk of nasal mucosal ulceration. Contraindications to enteral feeding include clients with:

- Persistent vomiting
- Delayed gastric emptying
- Oesophageal-gastric fistulae
- Oesophageal reflux
- Complex fluid management problems
- Paralytic ileus.

paralytic ileus

paralysis of the intestinal muscle

Activity 23

Look up the pH of gastric juice (see, for example, Rutishauser, 1994, pp.133, 225).

Insertion, by a specially trained nurse or doctor depending on local policy and expertise, is facilitated by the tube's own guidewire. It is essential to check the position of the tip of the tube in the stomach before feeding begins. Once the tube has been inserted, the exit site on the tube is marked to monitor for slippage. Such checking is needed because these tubes can migrate. One way of checking it is in position is to inject air through the tube and listen over the epigastrium with a stethoscope (auscultation). Second, every time the tube is disconnected, the fluid can be aspirated and tested for acidity. This is best achieved after a period of rest from feeding, when the pH of the gastric contents may be approaching normal. If these fail, an X-ray may be needed. Feeding can begin immediately after nasogastric tube insertion.

The main complications of nasogastric tube placement are:

- Malposition at insertion
- Displacement after insertion
- Subsequent occlusion.

Malpositioning of the tube in the trachea or bronchus may cause the accidental intrapulmonary administration of feed, or pulmonary or oesophageal perforation.

Food hygiene is paramount, as these patients are often immunocompromised by their malnutrition (see Chapter 3). Between feeds, the tube must be rinsed through with sterile water (clinical settings) or cooled, boiled water (at home). Fizzy water is sometimes used to dislodge particles and keep the tube clear.

The response to feeds is monitored by:

- Recording the amount given against the client's prescription
- Checking nutritional values gained against the client's requirements
- Noting any side-effects, for example diarrhoea
- Checking the client's weight at agreed intervals.

Complications may include:

- Nasopharyngeal discomfort
- Nasal erosions

- Oesophagitis
- Oesophageal ulceration
- Otitis media (inflammation of the middle ear).

Activity
24
Why is otitis media a complication of nasogastric tube placement? Look at Rutishauser, 1994, pp. 437, 438 and 497 if you do not understand.

Percutaneous endoscopic gastrotomy (PEG)

For clients who need enteral feeding for long periods (more than 4 weeks), a tube is inserted directly into the stomach through the skin. This is performed by specially trained personnel, the client usually receiving local anaesthetic and sedation, in the X-ray department, endoscopy unit or operating theatre. Some tubes may remain in position for as long as 2 years.

Client problems requiring PEG feeding include cerebrovascular accident (CVA; stroke), head injury with brain damage, motorneurone disease, multiple sclerosis and learning disability with multiple physical handicaps. Contraindications for the insertion of PEG include gross ascites, severe obesity, blood clotting abnormalities, oesophageal or gastric varices (varicose veins), gastric ulceration and gastric malignancy.

ascites

excess fluid in the peritoneal cavity

New types of PEG tube become available all the time. Current designs include those with an internal and an external retention disc (Figures 4.6 and 4.7), an internal retaining balloon and an external retention disc or a skin-level button (Figure 4.8). The gastrotomy tube is only removed after 5–6 weeks when a fibrous tract has formed. The skin-level button can then be inserted for long-term feeding.

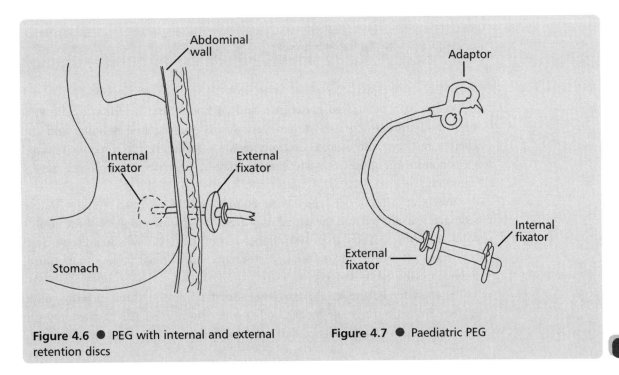

Figure 4.6 ● PEG with internal and external retention discs

Figure 4.7 ● Paediatric PEG

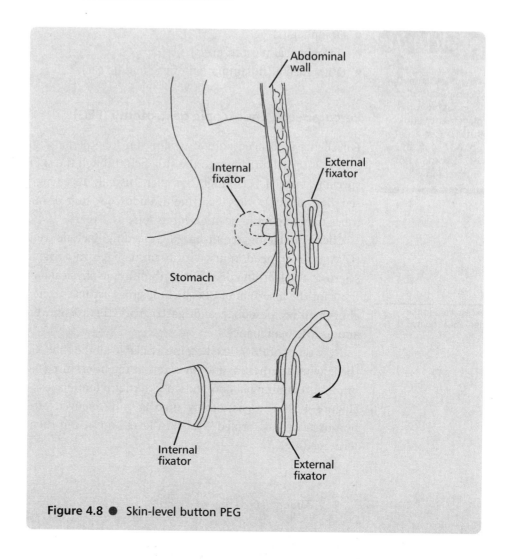

Figure 4.8 ● Skin-level button PEG

Feeding can be started between 6 and 24 hours after insertion of the PEG tube. Full-strength feed is started very slowly for the first 4 hours and the client's response monitored. Continuous slow feeds are recommended to aid gastric absorption, and metoclopramide may be prescribed to enhance gastric emptying.

One hour after a feed has been completed, the residual volume in the stomach is aspirated and measured in order to determine progress. If the adult's residual volume is more than 100 ml, the start of the next feed should be delayed for 1 hour. The residual volume is then rechecked; it must be less than 100 ml before starting the next feed.

Between feeds, the gastrotomy tube must be rinsed through with sterile water (clinical settings) or cooled, boiled water (at home). The gastrostomy site must be observed for gastric acid leak and infection. It is usually aseptically cleaned with normal saline (sodium chloride 0.9 per cent), and a small sterile dressing is applied.

Complications of PEG insertion include:

- Peritonitis (inflammation of the peritoneal cavity)
- The pulmonary aspiration of feed
- Peristomal (around the hole) infection
- Ischaemic pressure necrosis (lack of blood supply as a result of pressure causing tissue death)
- Gastrocolic fistula (an abnormal passage between the stomach and colon)
- Haemorrhage
- A blocked tube.

When the PEG tube is no longer required, endoscopy is needed to remove the internal retaining disc. The balloon is simply deflated.

Clients who are tube-fed miss out on the social and emotional bonds that can be part of eating together with family and friends. It is also important to encourage oral stimulation to maintain chewing and swallowing skills (Townley and Robinson, 1997). This can be fundamentally important in children with disabilities who have never been orally fed. The client must be given the opportunity to see, hear, smell and taste the food before being fed via the tube as the sensory stimulation enables the client's body to prepare for the meal. Oral stimulation is not the same as oral intake, which may be unsafe because of the client's inability to swallow (Townley and Robinson, 1997).

Obesity

For many clients, obesity may be more of a problem than undernutrition. The equation is deceptively simple: the energy expended must be balanced by the energy gained. The body's metabolism slows over time so, as people become less active because of age, illness or labour-saving devices, they need to adjust their intake downwards and try to keep their activity levels up. Nearly half of Britain's population is overweight (a BMI over 25), and one in six is clinically obese (BMI over 30). Obesity reduces a person's life expectancy, the increased weight relating to conditions such as coronary heart disease, diabetes gallstones, hypertension, blood lipid abnormalities, osteoarthritis and respiratory disease, not to mention endometrial and large bowel malignancies.

The obese client may well experience psychological and social problems as well (Thomas, 1998). The role of the nurse is to help them identify the sources and causes of excess calories in their diet (usually fat) and help them make their intake healthier. The distribution of food across the day may affect how many calories are absorbed. Breakfast 'kick-starts' the metabolism; the main meal of the day should be lunch, and the evening meal should be a light one. 'Loading' the calories at the end of the day means that there is little chance to burn them off.

diabetes

the inadequate production or utilisation of insulin, causing a chronic disorder of carbohydrate metabolism

gallstones

concretions forming in the gallbladder or bile duct when the bile contains more cholesterol than can be kept in solution

The changes made should be part of lifestyle modification rather than just 'going on a diet': diets do not work; eating sensibly does. 'Yo-yo' dieting tends to replace fat removed from the hips with fat around the waist, transforming the person from a 'pear' to an 'apple' shape, which increases the risk of coronary heart disease. The best weight loss is a slow one, no more than 1 kg (2.2 lb) per week. If the activity levels are being increased markedly, the weight loss could and should be slower, as muscle is heavier than fat, a pound of muscle being the size of a bar of soap, and a pound of fat, the size of a football. Muscle is more metabolically active tissue and more useful to general health, rendering its owner more resilient. The role of exercise cannot be ignored in terms of the enhancement of mood as well as the burning of more calories (see Chapter 7).

It is possible to slightly restrict the calorie intake of sick clients without detriment to their condition (Sikora and Jensen, 1997).

The role of the nurse is to make sure that any strategies are thought through with the whole team, including a dietitian.

Chapter Summary

This chapter has reviewed the basic essentials of nutrition and hydration, and made suggestions on how to enhance the health-giving benefits of food and fluid, in both the short and the long term. Macronutrients, micronutrients and current recommendations on intake have been described. The assessment of clients' nutritional status is the basis for intervention, and ideas have been offered to assist clients in achieving optimum nutrition and hydration. A range of helpful strategies to use when feeding and hydrating clients, including artificial nutritional support, is outlined to extend your skills in promoting effective nutrition and hydration.

Throughout this process, it must be remembered that securing the well-being and dignity of the client is paramount. Thus education of readers, clients, carers and colleagues in terms of the objectives of care and monitoring the effectiveness of interventions is part of an ongoing process.

Test Yourself!

1. Put the following into a league table according to their energy density in terms of kilojoules (or kilocalories):

   ● alcohol
   ● carbohydrate
   ● fat
   ● protein.

2. List at least two functions of fibre in the diet.

3. Name three sources of fibre in the diet.

4. Work out your fluid volume requirement in 24 hours.

5. What is an antioxidant?

6. Which are the antioxidant vitamins, minerals and trace elements?

7. Calculate your body mass index, and do the same for one of your clients.

References

Abdulla, A. and Keast, J. (1997) Hypodermoclysis as a means of rehydration. *Nursing Times* **93**(29): 54–5.

Bender, D.A. (1993) *Introduction to Nutrition and Metabolism*. UCL Press, London.

Bonner, A. and Waterhouse, J. (eds) (1996) *Addictive Behaviour: Molecules to Mankind*. Macmillan, Basingstoke.

Coghlan, A. (1997) A cheeky little powder and it travels well. *New Scientist* **153**(2070): 4.

COMA (Committee on Medical Aspects of Food Policy) (1989). *Dietary Sugars and Human Disease*. Report on Health and Social Subjects No. 37. HMSO, London.

DoH (Department of Health) (1991) *Dietary Reference Values for Food Energy and Nutrients for the United Kingdom*. Report of the Panel on Dietary Reference Values of the Committee on Medical Aspects of Food Policy. HMSO, London.

DoH (Department of Health) (1992) *The Health of the Nation. A Strategy for Health in England*. HMSO, London.

Fieldhouse, P. (1995) *Food and Nutrition. Customs and Culture*, 2nd edn. Chapman & Hall, London.

Higgins, C. (1997) Measurement of cholesterol and triglyceride. *Nursing Times* **93**(15): 54–5.

Lyman, B. (1989) *A Psychology of Food: More than a Matter of Taste*. Van Nostrand Reinhold, New York.

McPherson, G. (1993) Absorbing effects: drug interactions. *Nursing Times* **91**(23): 30–2.

Marmot, M. (1995) A Not-so-Sensible Drinks Policy. *Lancet* **346**(8992): 1643–4 (letter).

Micklewright, A. and Todorovic, V. (1997) Good old home cooking. *Nursing Times* **93**(49): 58–9.

Rollins, H. (1997) Nutrition and wound healing. *Nursing Standard* **11**(51): 49–52.

Rutishauser, S. (1994) *Physiology and Anatomy*. Churchill Livingstone, Edinburgh.

Sanders, T. (1994) *Dietary Fats: Nutrition Briefing Paper*. Health Education Authority, London.

Shepheard, J. (1998) Learning disability: empowerment. *Nursing Standard* **12**(17): 49–55.

Sikora, S.A. and Jensen, G.L. (1997) Hypoenergetic nutrition support in hospitalized obese patients. *American Journal of Clinical Nutrition* **66**(3): 546–50 (editorial comment).

Simpson, P.M. (1992) Alcohol consumption in the elderly. *Nutrition Research Reviews* **5**: 153–66.

Thomas, D. (1998) Managing obesity: the nutritional aspects. *Nursing Standard* **12**(18): 49–55.

Townley, R. and Robinson, C. (1997) Comfort eating. *Nursing Times* **93**(34): 74.

UKCC (1997) Feeding of Patients (letter). United Kingdom Central Council for Nurses, Midwives and Health Visitors, London.

Further Reading

Ahmad, W.I.U. (ed.) (1993) *Race and Health in Contemporary Britain* (Black Report). Open University Press, Milton Keynes.

Barasi, M.E. (1997) *Human Nutrition: A Health Perspective*. Edward Arnold, London.

Blythman, J. (1996) *The Food We Eat*. Michael Joseph, London.

British Nutrition Foundation (1995) *Vegetarianism: Briefing Paper*. British Nutrition Foundation, London.

Campbell, J. (1993) The mechanics of eating and drinking. *Nursing Times* **89**(21): 32–3.

Carlisle, D. (1997) Formula baby milk: what are the facts? *Nursing Times* **93**(24): 60–2.

Davies, J. and Dickerson, J.W.T. (1991) *Nutrient Content of Food Portions*. Royal Society of Chemistry, London.

Hamilton-Smith, S. (1972) *Nil by Mouth?* RCN, London.

Holmes, S. (1993) Building blocks. *Nursing Times* **89**(21): 28–31.

Jones, D.C. (1975) *Food for Thought*. RCN, London.

King's Fund Report (1992) *A Positive Approach to Nutrition as Treatment*. King's Fund Centre, London.

Orbach, S. (1986) *Fat is a Feminist Issue*. Arrow Books, London.

Paul, A.A. and Southgate, D.A.T. (1991) *McCance and Widdowson's The Composition of Foods*, 5th edn. HMSO, London.

Saunders, T. and Bazalgette, P. (1991) *The Food Revolution*. Transworld Publishers, London.

Thompson, S.B.N. (1993) *Eating Disorders: A Guide for Health Professionals*. Chapman & Hall, London.

Tolonen, M. (1990) *Vitamins and Minerals in Health and Nutrition*. Ellis Horwood, Chichester.

Townsend, P. and Davidson, N. (eds) *Inequalities in Health*. The Black Report. Open Universityn Press, Milton Keynes.

Webb, G.P. and Copeman, J. (1996) *The Nutrition of Older Adults*. Edward Arnold, London.

Whitehead, M. (1992) *Health Divide*. Penguin Social Sciences, Harmondsworth.

Wilson, A.C., Stewart Forsyth, J. Greene, S.A. *et al.* (1998) Relation of infant diet to childhood health: seven year follow up cohort of children in Dundee infant feeding study. *British Medical Journal* **316**(7124): 21–5.

Wolf, N. (1991) *The Beauty Myth*. Vintage, London.

Wykes, R. (1997) The nutritional and nursing benefits of social mealtimes. *Nursing Times* **93**(4): 32–4.

5 Elimination

BARBARA MARJORAM

Introduction

The purpose of this chapter is to explore the urinary and faecal elements of elimination, explaining the normal and abnormal processes and influences on it. At the end of the chapter, you should be able to:

- Explain the development of elimination that an individual experiences throughout the life span

- Identify specimens that may be collected and common abnormalities that may be found

- Understand the causes of constipation and diarrhoea, and the nursing care of clients experiencing these

- Outline the types of urinary and faecal incontinence and the possible treatments and interventions available

- Introduce the different types of stoma and the specific care that clients with them require.

The chapter provides an opportunity for you to undertake activities that will assist you in your understanding of some aspects of client care. It also includes case study scenarios to illustrate points made in the text.

> Elimination of excess water and wastes is a basic need for all forms of life.
> (Lewis and Timby, 1993, p. 173)

Successful elimination in humans depends on the individual having an intact and fully functioning gastrointestinal tract, urinary tract and nervous system.

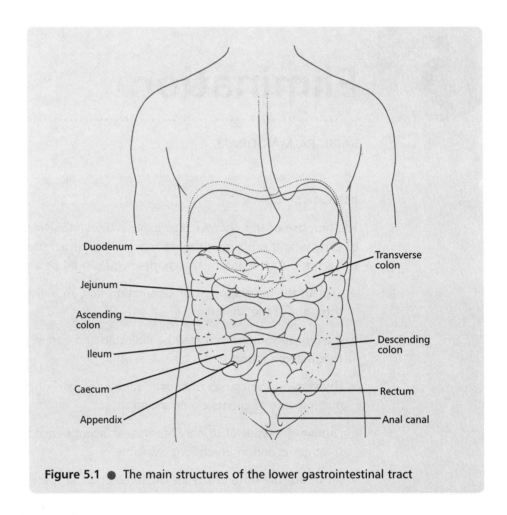

Figure 5.1 ● The main structures of the lower gastrointestinal tract

Labels in figure:
- Duodenum
- Jejunum
- Ascending colon
- Ileum
- Caecum
- Appendix
- Transverse colon
- Descending colon
- Rectum
- Anal canal

Faecal Elimination

The lower gastrointestinal tract (Figure 5.1) includes the small and large intestines. The small intestine (duodenum, jejunum and ileum) is approximately 610 cm (20 ft) long and 2.5 cm (1 in) in diameter in an adult. The partially digested food (chyme) leaving the stomach is moved along the small intestine by peristalsis. The large intestine (caecum, colon, rectum and anus) is approximately 152 cm (5 ft) long and 6 cm (2.5 in) in diameter. The faeces – the waste material of digestion that is passed out of the body via the anus or any other opening (stoma) designed for this purpose following surgery (see below) – in the large intestine are moved along its length in response to food entering the stomach. This gastrocolic reflex, which propels the faeces by mass peristalsis and is associated with eating, usually occurs 3–4 times a day, during or immediately after a meal.

peristalsis

the co-ordinated serial contraction of smooth muscle, propelling food through the digestive tract

gastrocolic reflex

a mass peristaltic movement of the large intestine occurring shortly after food enters the stomach

The defaecation reflex is initiated by the response to faeces entering the rectum. This reflex encourages the internal anal sphincter to relax, and the need to defaecate is conveyed to the brain and interpreted by the individual as an awareness of the need to eliminate faeces.

The 'normal' defaecation pattern varies from one individual to another, some defaecating three times a day, others only once a week.

Development of faecal elimination

Infant

At birth, the muscles of the infant's intestines are poorly developed, and control by the nervous system is immature. The intestines contain some simple digestive enzymes but are unable to break down complex carbohydrates or proteins. The infant can, therefore, only break down simple foods (Cox *et al.*, 1993, p. 266).

meconium
the thick, sticky material that accumulates in the fetus' intestines and forms the newborn's first stools

The infant's first bowel movement usually occurs within the first 24 hours of birth and is meconium, which contains salts, amniotic fluid, mucus, bile and epithelial cells. It is greenish-black to light brown in colour, almost odourless and of a tarry consistency. With the introduction of milk feeding, the characteristics of the infant's faeces change. The infant who is breastfed will have a stool that is bright yellow, soft and semiliquid, whereas the bottle-fed infant's stool will be light yellow to brown in colour and more formed (Cox *et al.*, 1993, p. 266). During the first 4 weeks of life, the infant will have up to 4–8 soft bowel movements per day. This number gradually decreases, and by the fourth week, the number of bowel movements is 2–4 per day. By 4 months of age the infant has gradually developed a predictable pattern of faecal elimination.

Toddler to preschool

The nervous and gastrointestinal systems gradually mature and by the age of 2–3 years are ready to control the faecal elimination function. The infant develops patterns of defaecation, and the parents can, therefore, identify when their child will have success on the potty. Eating stimulates peristaltic activity and defaecation (see above), and this can be used as a sign to take the child to the toilet. As elimination is a natural process, it is important that the child does not feel that it is a dirty or unnatural procedure.

The child, even though toilet trained, can still have 'accidents'. This is often associated when the urge to defaecate is allowed to progress inappropriately. If the child becomes so engrossed in what he is doing, he may ignore the urge to defaecate and become constipated.

Activity 1

For further information, read either Rutishauser 1994, pp. 114–36; Seeley *et al.*, 1995, pp. 808–34; or Marieb, 1995, pp. 813–926.

School-aged child

During the school years, the gastrointestinal system attains adult functional maturity. Individuals with learning disabilities may not reach the indicated maturation milestones because of their disability or lack of perception.

Adolescent

This age is important as developing bowel habits will take them through their adult life. Adolescents often find it difficult to talk about any elimination problem as they develop sexually.

Adult

A healthy adult usually eliminates 100–150 g of faeces per day, 30–50 g consisting of solids and the remaining 70–100 g water. The solids are made up of cellulose, epithelial cells shed from the lining of the gastrointestinal tract, bacteria, some salts and the brown pigment stercobilin. The brown-coloured faeces occur as a result of the breakdown of bile by the intestinal bacteria. If bile is unable to enter the intestines as a result of obstruction of the bile ducts (which transport bile from the gallbladder to the duodenum), the faeces are white.

In adulthood, there may be an increasing incidence of intestinal disorders (colonic and rectal carcinoma, and other gastrointestinal conditions such as irritable bowel syndrome and Crohn's disease). These can be caused by a decrease in the excretion of digestive enzymes (pepsin, ptyalin, gastric acid and pancreatic enzymes). Elimination patterns are affected by changing lifestyle such as, for example, marriage, having children or changes in employment, which may give rise to stress and anxiety.

irritable bowel syndrome

abnormally increased motility of the bowel, often associated with emotional stress

Crohn's disease

a chronic, often patchy, inflammatory bowel disease of unknown origin, usually affecting the ileum

Activity 2

Make a list of all the words you have heard or read that describe bowel habit. You may like to discuss this list with your colleagues. This will help you to understand some of the 'language' your clients may use.

Ageing adult

The decrease in the excretion of digestive enzymes continues. The elimination process may be affected by changing dietary intake caused by a reduced production of saliva, fewer taste buds and the loss of natural teeth, which are replaced by dentures, caps, crowns and bridges.

Specimen collection

Specimens are samples of tissue, body fluids, secretions or excretions (Chart 5.1). Nurses often have responsibility for the collection, labelling and timely, safe transport of samples to the laboratory. The validity of test results, therefore, depends on good practice.

specimens

samples of tissue, body fluids, secretions or excretions

Chart 5.1 ● Why do we collect specimens?

- To identify the nature of any disease or for diagnosis
- To assess the effect of any treatment
- To confirm or eliminate a specific site of the body as a focus of infection or colonisation
- To determine whether a client who has had an infection is still harbouring the pathogen responsible for it. For example, a client who has Salmonella food poisoning may still harbour the bacteria in her stools even though the signs and symptoms have disappeared.

The most common observations the nurse will be required to make of the patient and the specimen are:

- Colour (see above)
- Frequency/time
- Amount
- Consistency
- Odour
- Foreign substances (presence or absence)
- Any pain/discomfort expressed by the client on eliminating.

Activity

3

For further information, read Mallett and Bailey, 1996, pp. 518–19, 525, on specimen collection.

Using these observations, it is important that the nurse makes a clear, accurate and concise report in the client's records.

Faecal specimens

Faeces may be analysed to detect abnormal characteristics or contents, for example blood, parasites, parasite eggs and pathogens.

It is essential that the faecal specimen is not contaminated, so the client is asked to void urine separately into a toilet, bedpan or urinal. Urine can interfere with the examination of the faeces, for example destroying some parasites. The client is then asked to pass the faeces into a bedpan. The nurse transfers approximately 15 g (3 teaspoons) of the faeces into the specimen collection container. Care should be taken not to contaminate the outside of the specimen container with the faeces (the containers usually having a built-in spatula to assist with this).

Altered faecal elimination

Constipation

constipation

the abnormally difficult, infrequent or incomplete passage of hard faeces

Constipation refers to the abnormally difficult or infrequent passage of hard faeces and is caused by a decreased motility of the intestines. Some elderly individuals find it difficult to pass soft, bulky faeces. The longer faeces remain in the intestines, the more water is absorbed from them, which makes them become harder and dryer.

Many individuals wrongly regard themselves as being constipated if they do not defaecate every day. Some individuals who are constipated have episodes of diarrhoea, which can be the result of irritation by the hard faeces of the colon (often termed as constipation with overflow). Therefore, it is essential that a note of the normal bowel habits of clients is included in the admission procedure and recorded.

Causes of constipation

Causes of constipation include the following:

Activity 4

List all the factors that may predispose the individual to constipation.

- *Drugs*: tranquillisers, narcotics, anticholinergics and antacids containing aluminum, these reducing the motility of the intestines.
- *Laxatives*: the abuse of laxatives or frequent enemas. The normal reflexes then diminish, causing the abuser to need more laxative to effect a result and thus become dependent on laxatives.
- *Pregnancy*: limits the space for the faeces to pass through the intestine. Peristalsis slows due to the effect of progesterone causing the excess absorption of water from the faeces.
- *Disease*: obstruction from outside or from within intestine, for example from an abdominal or intestinal tumour, interfering with the passage of faeces. Other causes include irritable bowel syndrome, diverticular disease and neurological deficiencies such as paraplegia and multiple sclerosis.
- *Pain*: for example, from an anal fissure (a longitudinal ulcer in the anal canal) or external haemorrhoids (varicose veins in the anal canal; colloquially known as piles).
- *Psychiatric reasons*: depression, leading to a lack of interest in the surroundings and diet, chronic psychoses and anorexia nervosa, which can cause an imbalance in or an inappropriate dietary intake and therefore low fibre and fluid intake.
- *Diet*: food low in fibre or an inadequate food intake (see Chapter 4).
- *Lack of fluid*: either an insufficient intake of fluid or, rarely, an excessive loss of fluid through vomiting and/or sweating.
- *Immobility*: any disease that predisposes to immobility or any enforced immobility due to bedrest reducing the motility of the gastrointestinal tract.

diverticular disease

a condition in which pouch-like extensions develop through the muscular layer of the colon, affecting the passage of faeces

paraplegia

paralysis or sensory loss of the lower limbs, usually including the bladder and rectum

Casebox 5.1

Mary, aged 32, uses the mental health services for depression and takes her antidepressants as prescribed. She has found it difficult to hold down a job and is at present unemployed, living on benefit payments in her bedsit.

What are the probable impacts of depression upon Mary's elimination status?

Identify the associated symptoms and signs that Mary may experience as a result of her elimination problems?

- A lack of interest in her surroundings and diet, as well as her medication, may cause Mary to be constipated.

- The symptoms and signs that Mary may experience are:
  - Altered bowel habit, of a frequency less than usual
  - Straining on defaecation
  - Abdominal and/or back pain

  - Changing shape of the faeces
  - Hard, formed faeces
  - A palpable abdominal mass
  - Halitosis
  - Headache (because of possible dehydration and the build-up of toxins)
  - Impairment of appetite
  - Increased frequency of micturition (as a result of pressure from the faecal mass).

Casebox 5.2

Zandra, aged 5, was upset by her father's drinking and her parents' subsequent divorce. She has become chronically constipated.

Define constipation.

How would you relieve Zandra's constipation? (See also Chapter 4.)

- Constipation refers to the abnormally difficult or infrequent passage of hard faeces and is caused by the decreased motility of the intestines.

- To relieve Zandra's constipation, first assess her diet and fluid intake, and advise accordingly. Try to assess whether she is depressed because of the divorce, with a view to referring her for counselling if necessary.

- *Ignoring the call to defaecate*: which allows more fluid to be absorbed from the faeces, thus making them harder and more difficult to eliminate.
- *Psychological factors*: unfavourable lavatory conditions, poor hygiene, or having to use commodes and bedpans, which may result in the client delaying the defaecation process.

Care of client with constipation

With the help of the client, a history must be taken of the patient's normal elimination pattern. If a diagnosis of constipation is made, an assessment can be undertaken to aid the planning of the client's care.

It is the nurse's responsibility to promote an understanding of the measures available to overcome constipation. The client needs to be educated about what signs and symptoms are associated with constipation, for example:

- Altered bowel habit, frequency less than usual pattern
- Straining on defaecation
- Abdominal and/or back pain
- Changing shape of the faeces
- Hard, formed faeces
- A palpable abdominal mass
- Halitosis (bad breath)
- Headache (owing to possible dehydration and the build-up of toxins)
- Impaired appetite
- An increased frequency of micturition because of increased pressure on the bladder from an increased mass in the large intestines.

Clients may require advice on:

- Dietary intake: increasing the proportion of fibre (see Chapter 4).
- Fluid intake: increasing fluids and avoiding excess alcohol as this acts as a diuretic. The client should be advised to drink 30–35 ml/kg per day (unless other medical conditions restrict this) (see Chapter 4).

Activity 5

Calculate your fluid intake over 24 hours and compare it with the recommendation of 30–35 ml/kg per day.

micturition

the voiding of urine

Casebox 5.3

Mrs Ghosh is 89 and has been living in a residential care home for 3 years. She used to walk in the garden each day but finds it difficult nowadays, requiring a helping hand for safety.

Mrs Ghosh spends most of her day sitting in either the lounge or her bedroom. Her gums are very sore as her dentures are not fitting properly, so she will only eat 'sloppy' food.

Why does Mrs Ghosh have a potential risk of suffering from constipation (see also Chapters 4 and 7)?

What drugs can treat constipation but when abused cause it?

- There is a risk of constipation because of immobility, ignoring the call to defaecate, possible depression, leading to a lack of interest in her surroundings and diet, a lack of fibre and, because of her immobiliy, drinking only the amount of fluid on offer, which may not be sufficient.

- Laxatives can both treat and predispose to constipation.

Casebox 5.4

Adam, aged 50, has learning disabilities and multiple physical disabilities. He has just moved to a group home in the community. He suffers from chronic constipation as a result of long-term institutional care where he had a poor diet (lacking in fruit and vegetables), restricted access to fluids and little exercise. Previous care to relieve his constipation included enemas and laxatives.

Adam's new GP has advised the discontinuation of the enemas and laxatives as the treatment for his constipation.

What changes to Adam's lifestyle would you consider to improve his elimination problems (see also Chapters 4 and 7)?

- Adam needs to increase his mobility. His diet should be assessed and relevant advice given, emphasising an increase in the amount of fruit and vegetables. Fluid intake should also be assessed. The target is an intake of 30–35 ml/kg per day. Discourage Adam from ignoring the call to defaecate, and gradually reduce his enemas and laxatives.

- Mobility: do more exercise, if other medical conditions allow, to aid in increasing the motility of the gastrointestinal tract.

Although laxatives should be avoided, they may be used only as a short-term measure as prolonged use can lead to dependency, which may result in faecal impaction at a future date.

Other measures to treat constipation include the use of enemas and suppositories. Suppositories are bullet shaped and are designed to melt once they have been inserted into the rectum. Some suppositories soften the faeces and some lubricate the anal canal, whereas others use chemicals to stimulate peristalsis. Other types of suppository that the nurse may use do not promote elimination but are treatments for other conditions, for example infections and pain; these include antibiotic and analgesic preparations. Enemas are solutions that are instilled into the large intestine, the most common being a type of cleansing solution used to empty the lower intestinal tract of faeces.

To insert or introduce a suppository or enema, the client is asked to lie on his left side with the knees bent and drawn up gently towards the abdomen (Figure 5.2). The left side is the preferred side to lie on as the bowel will be angled downwards, which will aid retention of the suppository or enema and help to prevent trauma to the rectum. The suppository or enema is gently introduced into the rectum and the client asked to retain it for approximately 15 minutes to allow the chemicals to stimulate defaecation. Clients often feel that they wish to defaecate as soon as the suppository or enema has been introduced into the rectum because of stimulation from the insertion: the anus and rectum react to

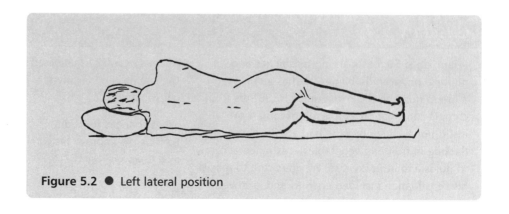

Figure 5.2 ● Left lateral position

the stretching of the muscle by sending the information to the brain that the rectum is full.

For some clients, for example those who are paraplegic/quadriplegic or grossly constipated, the only method of faecal elimination available to them is manual evacuation. The client is required to lie on the left side, and the nurse will remove the impacted faeces by hooking them out of the rectum using a gloved finger or two fingers to break up the faeces. This should only be used in exceptional circumstances and not as a routine alternative to other methods of aiding faecal elimination. **Do not employ the procedure without specific instruction** as there is an associated danger of perforation of the lower gastro-intestinal tract.

Diarrhoea

diarrhoea

the frequent passage of loose, watery stools

Diarrhoea results when movements of the intestine occur too rapidly for water to be absorbed by the intestines. Faeces are therefore produced in large amounts and may range from being 'loose' to being entirely liquid. If the diarrhoea is severe, large amounts of fluid, consisting of ingested fluids and digestive juices together with sodium and potassium, are lost in the faeces; this can rapidly result in dehydration and electrolyte imbalance.

Activity 6

List all the factors that may predispose an individual to diarrhoea.

Causes of diarrhoea

Causes of diarrhoea include:

- *Lack of hygiene*: poor hygiene when preparing food after elimination, causing the contamination of ingested food
- *Laxatives*: laxative abuse
- *Infected food*: *Staphylococcus pyogenes*, Salmonella, *Escherichia coli* (*E. coli*) and Campylobacter

- *Stress*: excitement, stress and anxiety, causing an increased rate of peristalsis so that the faecal material moves faster through the intestines and less water is absorbed
- *Diet*: excessive fibre-rich foods, drinks high in caffeine, which stimulates intestinal motility and allergy to some foodstuffs, causing irritation of the intestine
- *Disease*: diseases such as ulcerative colitis, Crohn's disease, diverticular disease and irritable bowel syndrome can result in swings between diarrhoea and constipation. Malabsorption syndrome can cause fatty diarrhoea (steatorrhoea).

ulcerative colitis

a chronic but inflammatory disease of the large bowel

steatorrhoea

fatty diarrhoea

Care of the patient with diarrhoea

It is essential that fluid balance is maintained as the client can quickly become dehydrated. The nurse must therefore assess the client for signs of dehydration (tachycardia and decreased skin turgor), and the client's input and output of fluid must be accurately recorded. Oral fluid should be high in added potassium and sodium, for example commercially prepared drinks such as Dioralyte or flat cola with a pinch of salt. In severe cases, an intravenous infusion may be required.

A careful and thorough history must be taken from the client to ascertain the possible cause of the diarrhoea. All clients suffering from diarrhoea must be treated as potentially infectious until proved otherwise by laboratory examination of the faeces (see Chapter 3).

Skin care of the perianal region must be maintained as faeces contain digestive enzymes that cause local irritation. Barrier creams may be applied to the area once it has been thoroughly cleaned and dried.

Activity 7

Try the following exercise to assess skin turgor. Pinch the supraclavicular skin (above the collar bone). If a person is dehydrated, the skin fold will remain. In normal hydration, the skin will return to its normal position almost immediately. Older skin reacts more slowly than younger.

Activity 8

Identify the impact of diarrhoea on an individual's lifestyle.

Faecal incontinence

Faecal incontinence is very distressing for the individual as it is difficult to disguise expelled faeces. It is essential that a complete history is taken from the client as it may identify possible causes of the incontinence. These include:

- Disease or injury: permanent or progressive conditions such as spinal cord damage, cerebrovascular accident (stroke) or, multiple sclerosis
- Impacted faeces with overflow (spurious diarrhoea)
- Temporary loss of control caused by diarrhoea
- Laxative abuse
- Pudendal nerve damage after childbirth
- Infection
- Ulcerative colitis or Crohn's disease, which can lead to faecal urge incontinence
- Stress incontinence caused by chronic straining, trauma or a congenital defect, or arising post-partum.

Management of faecal incontinence

The management will depend on the cause but include:

- Administering suppositories or an enema every 2–3 days, if caused by faecal impaction, and then instigating a regimen to prevent recurrence
- Advice on changing the diet to one that is well balanced and high in fibre, with increasing fluid intake (if other medical conditions allow)
- The treatment of diarrhoea
- Controlling and trying to eliminate laxative intake, if the condition has been caused by laxative abuse
- Advising the client to attend to elimination needs after a meal to take advantage of the body's normal gastrocolic reflex
- The use of incontinence aids, such as pads, pants and bed protection
- Pelvic floor exercises (see urinary incontinence, below, for details). For stress incontinence in severe cases, surgery is indicated, for example post-anal repair or after rectoplexy for rectal prolapse.

rectoplexy

the fixation of the rectum by suturing to surrounding tissue

Stoma care

The word 'stoma' is derived from Greek meaning mouth or opening. A stoma is formed following surgical intervention for a disease process, its name being determined upon its site. A stoma, for elimination purposes, is therefore an opening on to the surface of the abdomen through which faecal elimination from either the small or large intestine (or urinary elimination; see the section on urostomy, below) takes place.

The formation of either a temporary or permanent stoma may be the result of elective surgery or an emergency procedure.

Colostomy

colostomy

an opening of the colon on to the abdominal wall

A colostomy is an opening into the colon, which may be temporary or permanent, and is indicated for treatment of the following conditions:

- Malignancy of the colon or rectum
- Diverticular disease
- Inflammatory disease of the intestine (for example Crohn's disease or ulcerative colitis)
- Trauma to the large intestine
- The relief of acute intestinal obstruction or perforation

anastomosis

the joining of two hollow organs

- The protection of a distal anastomosis, the stoma being formed in a position higher in the gastrointestinal tract than the join between the two ends of intestine that remain after a section of bowel has been removed.

A permanent colostomy is required where the distal segment of the large intestine has been removed, for example where the rectum has been excised because of cancer. The stoma is created by bringing the proximal end of the colon out through an opening on to the anterior wall of the abdomen.

A temporary colostomy is usually necessary to divert the flow of faeces away from the distal part of the large intestine. The surgical technique permits the stoma to be closed once the condition requiring the surgery has been resolved.

The faecal material eliminated from a colostomy, especially if it is on the transverse or descending colon, will be semisolid once the initial postoperative period is complete and the client returns to a 'normal' diet.

Ileostomy

ileostomy

an opening of the ileum on to the abdominal wall

An ileostomy is an opening into the ileum and can be indicated for the treatment of the following conditions:

- Inflammatory disease of the intestine (for example, Crohn's disease or ulcerative colitis)
- As a temporary measure to rest the large intestine after major large bowel surgery.

An ileostomy can be a permanent stoma where the colon has been removed (panproctolectomy) or can be temporary to allow the disease process to resolve. If it is a temporary stoma, it can be closed by anastomosis at a later date and the intestine returned to normal functioning.

excoriation

injury to the skin caused by trauma such as scratching, rubbing or chemicals, for example the combination of urine and/or faeces and air

The faecal material eliminated through an ileostomy (Chart 5.2) is liquid in consistency, containing digestive enzymes that can cause excoriation and erosion of the skin if it is not well protected.

Management of a client with a stoma

Preoperative care

The client will require a rigorous preoperative assessment, particularly if presenting with a history of chronic disease, weight loss or anorexia. Such clients may be debilitated, and therefore malnutrition and electrolyte imbalances must be

Chart 5.2 ● Faecal consistency

- Ileostomy: fluid faeces (of a porridge-like consistency), normally 500–800 ml every 24 hours
- Transverse colostomy: unformed faeces, semiliquid
- Descending colostomy: more formed faeces, near to the normal output for that patient

corrected to ensure optimum recovery as a state of catabolism can be detrimental to a client undergoing surgery (Torrance, 1991).

Clients require psychological preparation to prepare them for the change in body image, to reduce anxiety and for reassurance that they can return to their previous place in society.

The stoma nurse should ensure that the client is offered counselling prior to surgery. She, or the consultant if no stoma nurse is available, should mark appropriate sites for the stoma so that the surgery does not interfere with normal activities of living postoperatively (Chart 5.3). The client should be shown and allowed to discuss the appliances available (Figure 5.3).

Chart 5.3 ● Sites to be avoided to facilitate easy management of a stoma

- Old scars
- Bony prominences
- The umbilicus
- The pubic area
- Skin folds
- Where the clothing may interfere, for example around the waistband area

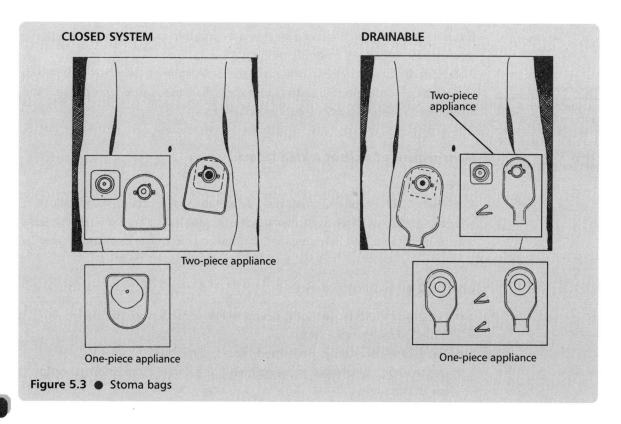

Figure 5.3 ● Stoma bags

Activity 9

For further information, read Mallett and Bailey, 1996, pp. 530–42.

dyspareunia

the occurrence of pain in the labial, vaginal or pelvic region during or after sexual intercourse

haemoserous fluid

serous fluid containing small amounts of blood

flatus

gas in the gastrointestinal tract, which is often expelled through a body orifice, especially the anus

Activity 10

To gain some appreciation of what the stoma client experiences, stick a stoma bag full of slushy Weetabix on to your abdomen and wear it for a few hours, engaging in as many 'normal' activities as possible.

Postoperative care

The client who has a stoma will require a great deal of support, especially in the initial days, weeks and months after its formation. The eliminating process of the body has changed along with body image, and it is therefore essential that 'rehabilitation concerns physical, psychological, social and sexual adjustment' (Salter, 1992). The client, therefore, has to be helped to adapt to the changes.

The patient may initially demonstrate evidence of withdrawal and depression. The process of overcoming this is an important part of nursing care; if the nurses can demonstrate an acceptance of the client, it will give him confidence.

The formation of the stoma concerns not only clients, but also their partners, one reason being that the change in body image may cause psychological difficulties (an inability to accept the change in partner's body image). Clients who have an ileostomy or colostomy may experience sexual dysfunction (impotence in males and dyspareunia in females). Even if they suffer no problems, it may be 2–3 months after the operation before the client is able to return to normal activities, including sexual activity. This may be because of the trauma and oedema at the site of the surgery, or sometimes because of nerve damage.

Care specific to the stoma

Postoperatively, the stoma must be checked regularly to ensure its viability – its colour and size, whether it is retracting or prolapsing (Chart 5.4) and its function. The stoma may initially discharge some haemoserous fluid, and this will be followed, once bowel sounds return, with the passing of some flatus, mucus and fluid. Once a solid food is reintroduced, faecal matter will be discharged from the stoma, often very liquid at first but gradually becoming fluid or semisolid, depending on the stoma site, over the following few days or weeks.

The client will require advice about his diet as some gas-forming foods (for example onions, cabbage, baked beans and spicy food) may lead to excess flatus and pain. The client is, therefore, advised to try out foods gradually in order to identify which cause problems. Clients who have an ileostomy should be advised to increase their fluid intake as their faeces will contain large amounts of water that would previously have been absorbed by the large intestine.

It is important that the client is shown how to care for his own stoma and that he is proficient with its management, for example changing stoma bags, cleaning the stoma and disposing of equipment and soiled stoma bags, prior to discharge.

Chart 5.4 ● Appearance of a normal stoma

- Pinkish red (the colour resembling that of the inside of the mouth)
- Initially postoperatively, it is oedematous

Urinary Elimination

The normal anatomy of the urinary system is shown in Figure 5.4.

Development of urinary elimination

Infant

At birth, both nervous system control and the renal function are immature, causing an inability to concentrate urine and urinary elimination to be involuntary. Urinary output is affected by fluid intake, the amount of activity and the environmental temperature. If the infant is more active or the temperature raised, more fluid will be excreted through the skin and more water vapour via exhaled air.

Toddler to preschool

The bladder increases in size with the growth of the child and is now able to hold more urine. By 2 years of age, the kidneys are maturing and can conserve

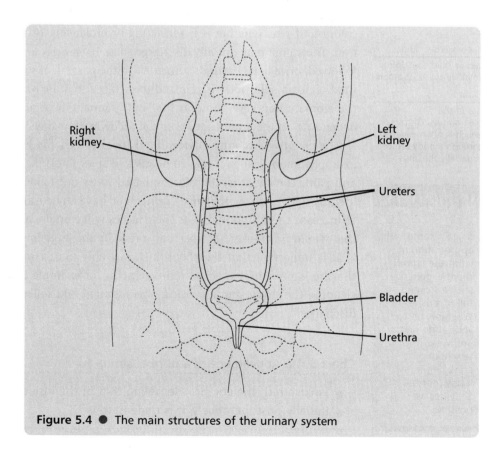

Figure 5.4 ● The main structures of the urinary system

water and concentrate urine almost as well as those of the adult. The nervous system is now matured enough for the toddler to control bladder functioning. Day-time bladder control is attained first, followed by night-time control. Even when toilet training has been achieved, there may be times of regression and 'accidents'.

School-aged child

The urinary system has now reached maturity.

Adolescent and young adult

There are no noticeable changes in urinary elimination during this time.

Adult

There is a decrease in renal function with ageing as the result of a gradual decrease in the number of nephrons. Bladder tone gradually diminishes, and urinary elimination is, therefore, more frequent as the ability to store urine prior to voiding decreases. In a healthy adult the decrease in renal function is so gradual that the effects are minimal until later in the ageing process (Cox *et al.*, 1993, p. 267).

Ageing adult

sclerosis
___
hardening or induration of an organ or tissue

The nephrons continue to decrease in number so renal function gradually lessens. This, combined with vascular sclerosis, decreases the glomerular filtration rate (GFR), thus decreasing the concentrating ability of the kidneys. Waste products are still processed effectively by the kidneys, but the process takes longer (Cox *et al.*, 1993, p. 268).

urethritis
___
inflammation of the urethra

The loss of smooth muscle elasticity affects the bladder and reduces its capacity. Inhibited bladder contraction can result in frequency and a premature urge to urinate. In the older male, the enlargement of the prostate gland can lead to urethritis, especially if there is urinary stasis, which may result in a urinary tract infection (UTI). This leads to dribbling of urine, difficulty in commencing urination, a poor stream, incomplete emptying of the bladder and increased frequency. These changes can cause nocturia (the need to urinate at night) and, therefore, disturbed sleep. The decrease in oestrogen levels in females can predispose to stress incontinence.

Specimen collection

Urine specimens commonly collected are:

- Urine test for *routine screening*, for example on admission or as an outpatient screening procedure.

diurnal
_____
occurring over a
24-hour period

- *Early morning urine* (EMU): because of diurnal variation, the first voided urine of the day is usually the most concentrated and is the preferred specimen when testing for substances present in low concentrations, for example hormones in a pregnancy test.
- *24-hour urine collection*: used to assess the amount of a substance that is lost in the urine. Depending on the substance to be measured, a preservative may be required in the collection bottle, as in the creatinine clearance test (an increased amount of creatinine in the urine being found in the advanced stages of renal disease)
- *Midstream specimen of urine* (MSU): the object of the collection being to obtain a specimen of urine uncontaminated by bacteria that may be present on the following:

Activity
11

List the types of urine specimen you have been asked to collect and why.

  – skin
  – external genital tract
  – perianal region
  – distal third of the urethra.

When a UTI is suspected, macroscopic and microscopic examination of an MSU will identify changes in the urine.

1. *Macroscopic examination*: Although this is by no means diagnostic, the appearance of the urine can provide evidence of infection. Urinary infection, like any other bacterial infection, is associated with an increased number of white cells at the site of the infection and an inflammatory response that results in the production of pus. Pus in the urine (pyuria) renders it cloudy, so the majority of infected urine is cloudy, and some infected urine is foul smelling.

pyuria
_____
pus in the urine

2. *Microscopic examination*: The numbers of white and red cells per mm³ of urine are routinely counted. In good health, urine often contains a small number of these cells along with the occasional epithelial cell shed from the lining of the urinary tract. Fewer than 10 white cells/mm³ is generally considered normal. Counts of between 20 and 50/mm³ are most probably due to infection but are also a feature of renal disease (so further tests may be requested to confirm the diagnosis). Counts of greater than 50/mm³ indicate acute bacterial infection. Infected urine and urinary stasis can lead to crystallisation of the urine, and this and foreign bodies can cause urinary tract stones (Chart 5.5).

Chart 5.5 ● Predisposing factors in urinary stone formation

idiopathic

pathology of unknown
or spontaneous origin

- ● Dehydration
- ● Idiopathic (most common)
- ● Urinary stasis
- ● Chronic urinary infection
- ● Foreign bodies (for example, fragments of catheter tubing)
- ● Disease processes (for example, gout and hyperparathyroidism)
- ● Immobility

Source: Burkitt *et al.* (1990).

Principles of collecting an MSU

Any bacteria present in the urethra are washed away in the first portion of urine voided, which is not collected. Avoidance of other bacterial contamination is achieved by thorough cleansing and a good clean technique (Chart 5.6).

Chart 5.6 ● Collection of an MSU

Protocol for women

meatus

a passage or opening

1. The client should thoroughly wash her hands with soap and water
2. The area around the urinary meatus must be cleaned from front to back with soap and water
3. With one hand, the client should spread her labia, keeping them apart until the specimen is collected
4. The client voids approximately the first 20 ml into the toilet and then passes a portion of the remaining urine into a sterile container. The remaining urine is passed into the toilet
5. The client's fingers should be kept away from the rim and inner surface of the container
6. The specimen is then labelled and, with the investigation request slip, forwarded to the laboratory for testing

Protocol for men

1. The client should thoroughly wash his hands with soap and water
2. The foreskin (if present) is retracted and the urinary meatus cleansed
3. The client voids approximately the first 20 ml into the toilet and then passes a portion of the remaining urine into a sterile container. The remaining urine is passed into the toilet
4. The client's fingers should be kept away from the rim and inner surface of the container
5. The client's foreskin (if present) should be returned to its normal position
6. The specimen is then labelled and, with the investigation request slip, forwarded to the laboratory for testing

Catheter specimen of urine

The catheter specimen of urine (CSU) is taken using an aseptic technique. The catheter bag tubing is clamped (taking care not to damage the tubing) above the specimen portal and left for approximately 1 hour. The specimen portal is cleaned using an injection/alcohol swab and allowed to dry. A sterile needle (21 G x 1½ ") is inserted into the portal, and a specimen of approximately 10–20 ml of urine is withdrawn into the syringe, the needle then being removed and the catheter bag tubing unclamped. The specimen should then be transferred to a sterile container, ensuring that the container is not contaminated. It is important that specimens are taken only from the portal that has been designed for this procedure as any other site may cause the catheter, catheter bag or tube to leak. Urine taken from the catheter bag is too old and possibly too contaminated for an accurate test result.

Urine specimens should, if possible, be taken before antibiotics are commenced as any treatment may affect the result.

Activity 12

List the observations which may be made on a specimen of urine without using a test.

Urine testing for screening

It is important to remember that urine is a body fluid and, therefore, all precautions (as identified in a care setting's control of infection procedure book) must be taken for the nurse's safety.

Clients being admitted to hospital should have a urine test. This is one of the few times that urine is screened, and it can result in the highlighting of any previously undiagnosed medical conditions, for example diabetes mellitus. It will also give a baseline of information about the client and may lead to further investigations.

Activity 13

For exact details on how to test urine for routine screening, read the guidelines that are enclosed with all containers of urine test strips, which will be stocked in your clinical area.

Casebox 5.5

Mrs MacDonnell, aged 72, has visited her GP complaining that her urine has been red.

What urinary test will the GP perform, and what do you expect the result to be?

What foods could Mrs MacDonnell have been eating that would turn her urine red?

- A routine urine test and a midstream specimen of urine (MSU) will be taken. Findings may be positive for haematuria, or negative if the problem is diet related. However, even though Mrs MacDonnell is aged 72, vaginal bleeding

(which could be disease related) should not be ruled out.

- Beetroot or rhubarb could have this effect on her urine.

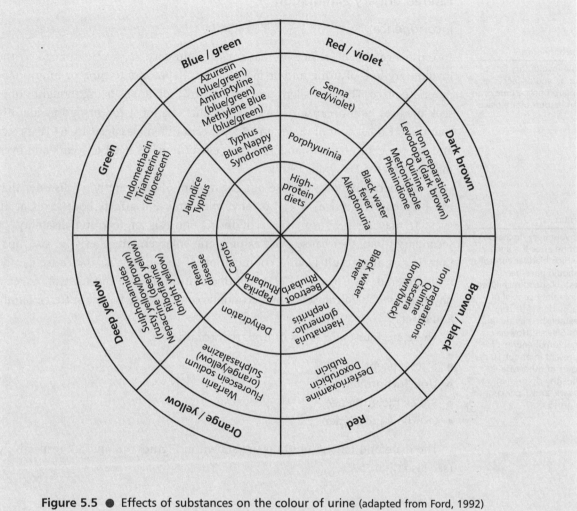

Figure 5.5 ● Effects of substances on the colour of urine (adapted from Ford, 1992)

Activity

14

For further
information, read
Mallett and Bailey,
1996,
pp. 525–6.

The client is asked to void a specimen of urine into a urinal, bedpan, jug or other clean receptacle.

The urine must be observed for colour and odour before being tested with a reagent stick. Normal urine is pale and straw coloured, but the urine may be darker due to loss of extra fluid through perspiration during hot weather or if the client has a limited fluid intake. Normal urine, when fresh, has little smell, but if left it may develop an odour of ammonia. Infected urine may be foul-smelling immediately after voiding and become worse on standing. Urine may change from the normal 'straw' colour because of substances present in it (Figure 5.5).

Altered urinary elimination

Incontinence

incontinence

the involuntary loss of urine and/or faeces at an inappropriate time or in an inappropriate place

Incontinence can be either permanent or temporary. It can be defined as the involuntary loss of urine and/or faeces at an inappropriate time or in an inappropriate place. This is a 'silent problem', many individuals being thought not to seek medical help because of embarrassment. The most recent figures identify that up to 1.6 per cent of males and 8.5 per cent of females aged 15–64 years old, and 6.9 per cent of males and 11.6 per cent of females aged 65 years and over, may be affected (Watson, 1991).

enuresis

involuntary discharge of urine after the age by which bladder control should have been established. In children, voluntary control of urination is usually established by the age of 5 years. However, nocturnal enuresis is present in about 10 per cent of otherwise healthy children at age 5 years, and 1 per cent at age 15

Incontinence is not a disease but a symptom of an underlying disorder that can be mental, physical, social or environmental and affects both sexes at all ages. It may be primary, as in childhood enuresis or learning disability, or secondary to another cause such as prostatic enlargement, obesity or constipation. It can also result from a combination of these, that is, the cause can be multifactorial. As Cheater (1995) identified, 'incontinence can have an adverse physical, psychological, social and economic consequence for the sufferer, family and carers'.

There are four main types of urinary incontinence:

- Stress incontinence
- Urge incontinence
- Reflex incontinence
- Overflow incontinence.

The male and female urethras are shown in Figures 5.6 and 5.7 respectively (see also Chart 5.7).

Chart 5.7 ● The female urethra

- The urethra is embedded in the anterior wall of the vagina
- It runs downwards and forwards behind the symphysis pubis, and opens at the external urethral orifice, which lies just in front of the opening of the vagina
- Its diameter is approximately 0.7 mm
- Its length is approximately 4 cm
- The urethra is 'slit'-shaped rather than cylindrical
- If there is a weakness of the pelvic floor muscles and the urethra becomes more vertical, it is easier for urine to leak out (incontinence)

Source: Haslam (1997)

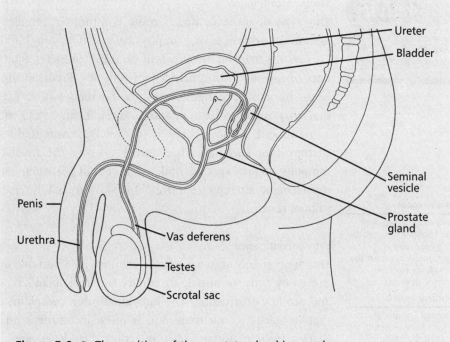

Figure 5.6 ● The position of the prostate gland in a male

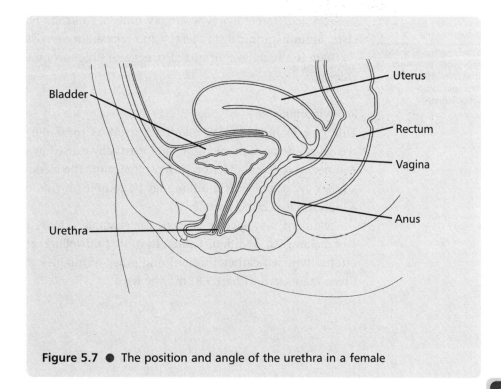

Figure 5.7 ● The position and angle of the urethra in a female

Activity 15

List the causes of stress incontinence.

Stress incontinence

This type of incontinence is more common in females than males. A small amount of urine is leaked on physical exertion, coughing, sneezing or laughing. This results from an incompetent urethral sphincter, which is caused by a weakness of the supporting pelvic floor muscles. Predisposing factors include childbirth, hormonal changes owing to the menopause, vaginal prolapse, obesity, inactivity and constipation, and, in men, it can occur post-prostatectomy.

Treatment includes pelvic floor exercises, weighted vaginal cones, electrical therapy that stimulates the nerves causing the muscles to contract, special tampons, vaginal sponges and, in the case of post-menopausal women, hormone replacement therapy (Pomfret, 1993). Surgical intervention may include a vaginal repair.

vaginal repair

following prolapse of the vagina and uterus, surgical repair is performed to return the structures to their normal position

detrusor muscle

external longitudinal layer of the muscular coat of the bladder

Urge incontinence

This type of incontinence causes the loss of a variable amount of urine and is caused by detrusor muscle instability (unstable bladder), neuropathic conditions and outflow obstruction. The individual often complains of little or no warning that he needs to micturate and is often incontinent on the way to the toilet. Causes include urinary tract infection, bladder stones, an enlarged prostate, urethral stricture, faecal impaction, Alzheimer's disease, cerebrovascular accident, spinal cord lesions and Parkinson's disease. Residual volumes of urine, left in the bladder after micturition, may occur causing urinary stasis and lead to a UTI.

Treatment rarely involves surgery but does include bladder retraining exercises, antimuscarinic drug therapy and relaxation exercises.

There is a high level of mixed stress and urge incontinence, especially in the elderly.

antimuscarinic

opposing the action of muscarine or agents that mimic them, for example atropine and scopolamine

Reflex incontinence

This type of incontinence manifests itself as the failure of the individual to recognise the need to micturate and is usually caused by damage of the peripheral nerves to the bladder or of the spinal cord. The bladder fills and empties on a reflex cycle, and the condition may be combined with incomplete voiding and a high residual urine volume.

Treatment may involve surgery, for example urinary diversion or urostomy (see below). In addition, catheterisation (indwelling urethral, suprapubic or intermittent self-catheterisation) and other techniques, such as the Valsalva or Credé manoeuvre (Chart 5.8) may be used.

Chart 5.8 ● Valsalva and Credé manoeuvres

Valsalva manoeuvre
The client is asked to inhale and then to attempt to forcibly exhale with the glottis (vocal cords), nose and mouth closed. This causes the diaphragm to flatten, thus increasing the intra-abdominal pressure. Unless the urethral sphincter is in complete spasm, the increased pressure forces urine to be voided. It should be noted that any client with cardiac problems should not attempt this procedure

Credé manoeuvre
The client is asked to apply pressure over the symphysis pubis. The pressure may be enough to produce spasm of the bladder or to cause voiding of urine

Overflow incontinence
This type of incontinence is caused by urinary retention with overflow caused by:

● Obstruction from an enlarged prostate, prostatic cancer, urethral stricture or faecal impaction. Treatment includes prostatectomy, urethrotomy and the clearance of faecal impaction.
● Hypotonic bladder (ineffective contraction of the bladder when voiding urine) caused by neuropathy (for example, in diabetes) and anticholinergic medication (for example, imipramine). Treatments include intermittent self-catheterisation, drug therapy (for example, carbachol) to enhance detrusor contractility and a review of drug regimens to ensure that other medication is not the cause of the hypotonia.
● Detrusor–sphincter dysynergia (unco-ordinated muscle activity) caused by neuropathic conditions, for example paraplegia and multiple sclerosis. Treatment includes intermittent self-catheterisation and biofeedback to teach co-ordination.

biofeedback
───────────
a training programme designed to develop one's ability to control the autonomic (involuntary) nervous system

An indwelling catheter should be used only as a last resort for clients with voiding difficulties.

Cystitis

cystitis
───────────
inflammation of the bladder usually occurring secondary to an ascending UTI

Cystitis is the inflammation of the bladder usually occurring secondary to an ascending UTI. It is more common in sexually active females because of the close proximity of the urethra. In the acute stage, clients complain of frequent and painful micturition; in the chronic stage, it is secondary to a lesion with possible pyuria as the only symptom. Antibiotics are used to treat the infection, and the client should be encouraged to drink 2–3 litres of fluid per day (if the medical condition allows) to dilute the urine and decrease the pain on micturition.

If you do not already practise pelvic floor exercises regularly, you should start now by following the instructions in Chart 5.9.

Pelvic floor exercises

Pelvic floor exercises (Chart 5.9) are primarily intended to increase the strength of the levator ani muscles. In women, pelvic floor exercises involve the contraction and relaxation of the muscles that surround the vagina and anus, thus improving their tone. This helps to restore the normal anatomical relationships of the surrounding structures, and urethral sphincter function.

In males, pelvic floor exercises should be taught pre-prostatectomy so that they can help to stop post-micturition dribbling following prostatectomy by improving urethral sphincter function.

Urinary catheterisation

To perceive what clients experience when they are incontinent, wet a pad with water and then wear it next to your skin in the perineal area. Undertake as many everyday activities as possible.

cytotoxic

any substance that is toxic to cells; usually applied to drugs used in the treatment of cancer

A urinary catheter is designed to remove fluid from or instil fluid into the bladder. Urinary catheterisation is a common procedure, 12 per cent of hospital clients (Crow *et al.*, 1996) and 4 per cent of clients in the community (Getliffe, 1990) being catheterised at any one time.

Indications for catheterisation are:

- Pre- and postoperatively to empty the bladder before or after abdominal, rectal or pelvic surgery
- The acute and chronic retention of urine
- To introduce drugs, for example antibiotics and cytotoxic drugs
- To irrigate the bladder in order to remove sediment and/or blood clots

Chart 5.9 ● Pelvic floor exercises

The client needs to sit, stand or lie in a comfortable position and tighten the pelvic floor for approximately 10 seconds. (There should be feeling of tightening the anus but not the buttocks, abdomen or legs.) This should be repeated 10 times. The client needs to imagine that they are stopping a flow of urine. For females learning this exercise, a finger can be inserted into the vagina and 'squeezed'. The client should progress so that, when passing urine, they can stop and start mid-flow; this should be done once per week to check the progress of the exercise regimen. Pelvic floor exercises should be performed at least twice daily

- Trauma, for example any trauma to the pelvis or lower urinary tract (as any oedema resulting from the trauma may cause obstruction) to monitor for blood, and following burns to monitor urinary output
- The accurate measurement of urinary output
- Diagnostic investigations of bladder function
- Incontinence, when all other methods have failed.

Catheters

The nurse should assess the client prior to catheterisation and identify the reason for undertaking the procedure, the length of time the catheter is to remain in situ and the sex of the client. This will help to identify the type of catheter required. The size of catheter will depend upon whether it is clear urine or haematuria to be drained (Chart 5.10). The catheters designed for females are shorter than those designed for males because the adult urethral length in a female is approximately 4 cm and that in a male 20–23 cm.

In the majority of cases, a retaining balloon size of 5 ml volume will be sufficient. The catheter will require 10 ml of sterile water when being inserted as 5 ml will fill the balloon and 5 ml the balloon's inlet tubing. A balloon size of 30 ml volume should be discouraged, its main use being for clients following urological surgery, in particular prostatic surgery.

Common types of catheter
- *Teflon*: The latex is teflon coated to reduce urethral irritation and can be used for clients requiring short- or medium-term, up to 1 month, catheterisation.
- *Silicone*: These catheters are very soft, less irritating and cause less crystal formation than the latex variety. They should be used for clients who require catheterising for more than 2 weeks, the catheters having a life span of approximately 3 months.
- *Hydrogel*: These catheters absorb water to produce a slippery surface and, therefore, decrease friction on the urethra. They are more resistant to encrustation and adherent bacteria. They have a life span of up to 14 weeks.
- *Conformable catheter*: These are designed to conform to the shape of the female urethra (slit shaped) and allow partial filling of the bladder. These catheters are approximately 3 cm longer than the conventional female catheters.

Chart 5.10 ● Catheter size (for an adult)

- Clients with clear urine: 12–16 Fr (Ch)
- Clients with haematuria: 18–22 Fr (Ch)

1 Fr (Ch) is equivalent to 0.3 mm, catheters being measured across the external diameter

Types of catheterisation

There are three types of catheterisation. The most common and probably the best known is the indwelling catheter, the other two being intermittent self-catheterisation and suprapubic catheterisation.

Indwelling catheters

The insertion of a urethral catheter requires an aseptic technique and it is preferable that the client has a shower or bath prior to catheterisation to ensure good hygiene. The balloon size, type of material and size of the catheter used will depend on the reason for catheterisation.

Once the catheter is in situ, meatal and perineal hygiene should be performed. Soap and water is sufficient to clean the meatal and perineal areas, but the nurse or client must ensure that the area is thoroughly dried afterwards (Brown, 1992).

The type of urinary drainage bag will depend upon whether the client is mobile (for example, clients able to continue normal mobility activities or clients in wheelchairs) or has limited mobility (for example, post-surgery or with a medical condition reducing mobility). Clients who are normally mobile may

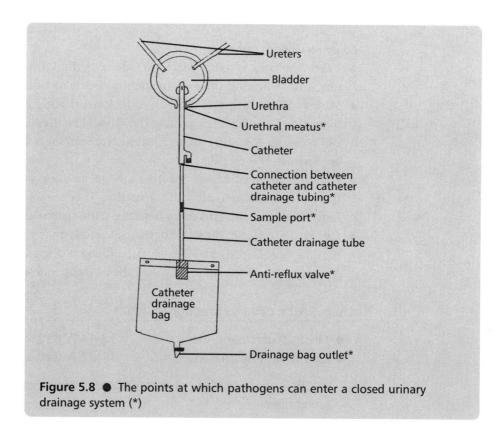

Figure 5.8 ● The points at which pathogens can enter a closed urinary drainage system (*)

benefit from wearing a leg bag during the day, changing to a full-size drainage bag at night. Clients with limited mobility will wear a full-size bag until the catheter is removed or 'normal' mobility is restored.

To empty a urinary drainage bag, the nurse must wash her hands prior to and after carrying out the procedure, as well as wearing gloves during the procedure. The outlet tap of the catheter system should be opened and the urine allowed to drain into a single-use receptacle, the outlet tap being closed after emptying. The urinary drainage bag must hang below the level of the bladder to ensure that urine does not seep back into the bladder, and can be supported by attaching it either to the side of the bed or to a stand specially designed for this purpose. If a leg bag is worn, it must be secured to the client's leg without causing traction to the catheter and, therefore, trauma to the urethra and bladder neck. The tap of the urinary drainage bag must not touch the floor as this will result in contamination and possible UTI (Figure 5.8).

It is important that meatal and perineal hygiene is maintained to reduce the risk of encrustation around the catheter and meatus. The client should, unless medically contraindicated, be encouraged to drink 2–3 litres of fluid every 24 hours in order to reduce the risk of UTI, constipation (as this may cause pressure on the bladder and urethra) and the irritant effect of concentrated urine on the bladder (Getliffe, 1993). Constipation should be avoided as it may contribute towards leakage around the catheter. There is evidence that there is a very high incidence of UTI associated with the use of urinary catheters (Gould, 1994). The principles of care of the patient with a urinary catheter are shown in Chart 5.11.

Chart 5.11 ● Principles of care for the client with a urinary catheter in situ

- Meatal hygiene – to minimise encrustation
- Fluid intake – adequate intake to reduce the risk of concentrated urine irritating the bladder and to reduce the risk of constipation
- Catheter selection – the appropriate size of catheter and balloon, of a material appropriate to the time proposed in situ, a length appropriate to gender, for example, a shorter length for females can prevent accidental trauma from traction
- Catheter drainage bag – position lower than the level of the client's bladder and use effective support
- Catheter drainage bag tubing – ensure that there are no kinks
- Catheter bag drainage outlet – do not allow this to touch the floor as it can cause contamination leading to UTI
- Having a catheter in situ affects body image and sexual activity in the long term. Therefore, psychological support/understanding towards the client and partner is essential

Source: Adapted from Britton and Wright (1990).

Chart 5.12 ● Criteria for clients undertaking intermittent self-catheterisation

Clients should:

- be incontinent of urine (overflow incontinence)
- have good manual dexterity and mobility
- have the mental ability to learn and understand
- show good motivation
- possess an intact urethra
- have a bladder capacity of 100 ml or more

Intermittent self-catheterisation

Intermittent self-catheterisation is the periodic drainage of urine from the bladder. A catheter is inserted into the bladder via the urethra by either the nurse, client or carer, and the bladder is emptied; the catheter is then removed until the next time voiding needs to take place. This method of emptying the bladder is particularly useful for clients who have difficulties in passing urine, for example clients with neurological problems and clients who suffer from urinary incontinence, thus allowing them to gain control of their bladder. Prior to instruction, clients and/or carers should be assessed in terms of whether they are suitable to undertake this procedure (Chart 5.12).

The catheter's length will be determined by the client's gender. For a male, the catheter should be 38 cm long and for a female 20 cm as the female urethra is shorter than the male.

The actual principles and procedure of intermittent self-catheterisation are the same as for the insertion of an indwelling catheter; however, this is a 'clean' procedure rather than an aseptic one. Catheters may be used more than once and may be self-lubricating. Urinary tract infections are lower in incidence than in clients with indwelling catheters.

Suprapubic bladder drainage

A self-retaining catheter is inserted through a suprapubic incision or puncture into the bladder (Figure 5.9). It is a temporary measure to divert the flow of urine from the urethra when the urethral route is impassable or impossible because of, for example:

Activity
18

For further information, refer to Mallett and Bailey, 1996, pp. 590–606.

- Trauma
- Stricture
- Prostatic obstruction
- Pelvic fractures
- Gynaecological operations: vaginal hysterectomy and vaginal repair.

Drainage can be maintained for several months.

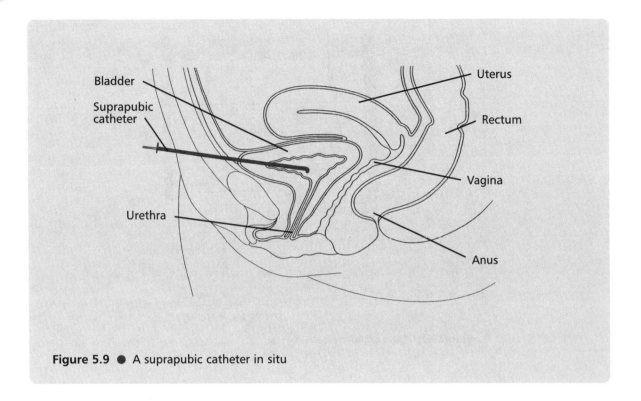

Figure 5.9 ● A suprapubic catheter in situ

Urostomy

urostomy
_____

an opening in the
abdominal wall to allow
the diversion of urine

A urostomy is performed when the bladder is removed or diseased (Chart 5.13). It is an opening from the ureters into a resected section of (usually) ileum, approximately 15 cm in length, which then channels the urine through the stoma that has been formed on the abdominal wall (known as an ileal conduit) and is fashioned into a spout to aid drainage.

Activity *19*

For further information, read Mallett and Bailey, 1996, pp. 530–2, 540–2.

Chart 5.13 ● Indications for urostomy formation

● Malignant disease of the bladder
● Malignant disease of the pelvis
● Trauma
● Neurological damage
● Congenital disorders
● Intractable incontinence

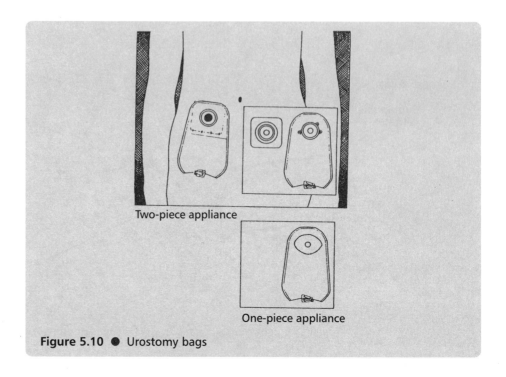

Two-piece appliance

One-piece appliance

Figure 5.10 ● Urostomy bags

Urine that is eliminated through a urostomy can excoriate the surrounding skin if it is not well protected. The urine will constantly 'dribble' from the stoma into a urostomy drainage bag (Figure 5.10). The management of a urostomy is the same as for stoma care.

Chapter Summary

This chapter has explored both the urinary and faecal elements of elimination. It explains the normal anatomy and physiology and then identifies the abnormal processes and influences on elimination. It explores possible treatments, the advice available and nursing care for the conditions identified.

Test Yourself!

1. What information do you need to obtain when making an assessment of your clients' elimination needs?

2. List and explain the factors that may cause a client to become constipated.

3. Identify four types of incontinence.

4. What is the difference between an ileostomy, a colostomy and a urostomy?

5. Identify the psychological factors that affect both urinary and faecal elimination.

6. How much fluid should a healthy individual weighing 65 kg drink in a day?

References

Britton, P.M. and Wright, E.S. (1990) Nursing care of catheterized patients. *Professional Nurse* 5(5): 231–4.

Brown, M. (1992) Urinary catheters: patient management. *Nursing Standard* 6(19): 29–31.

Burkitt, H., Quick, C. and Gatt, D. (1990) *Essential Surgery: Problems, Diagnosis and Management*. Churchill Livingstone, Edinburgh.

Cheater, F. (1995) Promoting urinary continence. *Nursing Standard* 9(39): 33.

Cox, H., Hinz, M., Lubno, M. *et al.* (1993) *Clinical Applications of Nursing Diagnosis: Adult, Child, Mental Health, Gerontic and Home Health Considerations*, 2nd edn. F.A. Davis, Philadelphia.

Crow, R., Chapman, R., Roe, B. and Wilson, J. (1996) *A Study of Patients with an Indwelling Urethral Catheter and Related Nursing Practice*. Nursing Practice Research Unit, University of Surrey, Guildford.

Ford, A. (1992) Feeling off-colour. *Nursing Times*, **88**(5): 64.

Getliffe, K. (1990) Catheter blockage in community patients. *Nursing Standard* 5(9): 33–6.

Getliffe, K. (1993) Care of urinary catheters. *Nursing Standard* 7(44): 31–4.

Gould, D. (1994) A framework for the control of infection. *Nursing Standard* March 30 8(27): 32–4.

Haslam, J. (1997) Floor plan. *Nursing Times* 93(15): 67–70.

Lewis, L.W. and Timby, B.K. (1993) *Fundamental Skills and Concepts in Patient Care*. Chapman & Hall, London.

Mallett, J. and Bailey, C. (1996) *The Royal Marsden NHS Trust Manual of Clinical Nursing Procedures,* 4th edn. Blackwell Scientific, Oxford.

Marieb, E. (1995) *Human Anatomy and Physiology*, 3rd edn. Benjamin/Cummings, Redwood City, CA.

Pomfret, I.J. (1993) Stress incontinence. *Practice Nursing* (15): 25.

Rutishauser, S. (1994) *Physiology and Anatomy: A Basis for Nursing and Health Care*. Churchill Livingstone, Edinburgh.

Salter, M. (1992) Body image and the stoma patient. *Wound Management* 2(2): 8–9.

Seeley, R., Stephens, T. and Tate, P. (1995) *Anatomy and Physiology*, 3rd edn. C.V. Mosby, St Louis.

Torrance, C. (1991) Pre-operative nutrition, fasting and the surgical patient. *Surgical Nurse* **4**(4): 4–8.

Watson, R. (1991) Incontinence in perspective. *Nursing* **4**(39): 7–9.

Further Reading

Alexander, M., Fawcett, J. and Runciman, P. (1994) *Nursing Practice Hospital and Home, the Adult*. Churchill Livingstone, Edinburgh.

Fuller, J. and Schaller-Ayres, J. (1994) *Health Assessment: A Nursing Approach*, 2nd edn. Lippincott, Philidelphia, pp. 185–223.

Getliffe, K. (1995) Care of urinary catheters. *Nursing Standard* **10**(1): 25–9.

Kelly, M. (1994) Mind and body. *Nursing Times* October 19 **50**(42): 48–51.

Chapter 6

Respiration and Circulation

RUTH SADIK AND DEBRA ELLIOTT

Introduction

The purpose of this chapter is to examine factors associated with respiratory and cardiac function. It will explore the nurse's role in relation to assessing and implementing care with clients who experience breathing and circulation maintenance difficulties. At the end of the chapter, you should be able to:

- Monitor and interpret a client's respiratory and cardiac vital signs

- Rationalise common deviations from normal values

- Identify techniques for maintaining cardiorespiratory function

- Assist clients in maintaining effective cardiorespiratory function

- Recognise the signs of cardiorespiratory arrest

- Describe the appropriate response and initial management of a collapsed client.

Respiration

oxygen

a colourless, odourless gas that constitutes one-fifth of atmospheric air

carbon dioxide

the waste product of respiration, which is excreted by the lungs

The purpose of respiration is to ensure that the cells of the body are provided with oxygen and that the waste products of their metabolism, carbon dioxide and water, are excreted. Effective respiration is achieved through the exchange of these two gases within the lungs, which in turn depends on the related structures of respiration being competent. However, the regulation of respiration is controlled by the brain in response to both neural and chemical factors.

While brief overviews will be provided within this chapter, in order to fully understand the anatomical and physiological principles of respiration, including the organs of respiration, pulmonary ventilation, lung volumes and capacities, gaseous exchange, the transport of gases and the control of respiration, you should consult specialist texts on the subject. While your lecturers may recommend alternative texts, Rutishauser's *Physiology and Anatomy: A Basis for Nursing and Health Care* (1994) has a valuable chapter entitled 'Respiration' (pp. 137–56), which will give you the background to the structures in question and their function in facilitating effective respiration. Whichever text you choose, it should be available for reference while working through this chapter.

Respiratory assessment

In order to make a comprehensive assessment, one first needs to understand the way in which air is taken into and expelled from the lungs, carried around the body and utilised by the cells.

Spontaneous respiration depends on regular neural impulses from groups of neurones in the medulla oblongata and pons. The medulla contains two areas of specialised nerves which are known as the inspiratory and expiratory centres, while the pons contain nuclei referred to as the pneumotaxic and apneustic centres which influence and modify the medullary neurones. These areas are required to work together to bring about effective respiration, both voluntary (under our conscious control) and involuntary (unconsciously). Within the

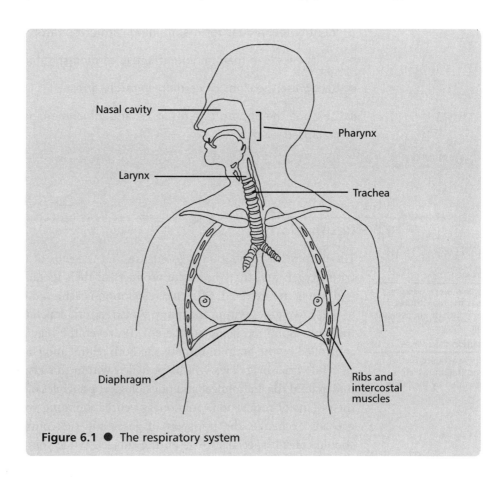

Figure 6.1 ● The respiratory system

voluntary mechanisms are included actions which are non-gaseous in nature such as coughing, swallowing, vomiting and speech.

Involuntary or subconscious respiration, which is needed to sustain life, consists of inspiration, expiration and fine tuning of the system relating to increased need such as when exercising, and decreased need during sleep.

During inspiration, nerve impulses pass from the medulla to the diaphragm and intercostal muscles (Figure 6.1), causing them to contract and enlarge the thoracic cage size, thus lowering the intrapleural pressure. As the outside air pressure is greater than the air pressure inside the lungs, air flows into the alveoli until the intrapleural pressure is equal to atmospheric pressure.

As the lungs expand, stretch receptors within the lung tissue convey nerve impulses to the pneumotaxic centre, which inhibits further inspiration. When muscle contraction ceases and relaxation commences, the stretched muscles recoil to their original length. The thoracic cage and lungs return to their normal sizes, and intrapleural air pressure exceeds atmospheric pressure, forcing air out of the airways into the atmosphere. Expiration is a passive process, dependent only on the inhibition of inspiration.

chemoreceptors

nerve endings or groups of cells that are stimulated by chemicals

partial pressure

the pressure of a gas in a mixture of gases, related to its concentration

The chemical control of respiration is attained by groups of specialised cells in the walls of the aorta and carotid arteries known as chemoreceptors. Their function is to monitor and respond to changes in the partial pressure (denoted by the letter P, see below) of either carbon dioxide (CO_2) or oxygen (O_2) in the blood. Any increase in PCO_2 is transmitted to the respiratory centre, where inspiration is initiated. A small drop in PO_2 acts as a similar trigger, although a substantial decrease can have the effect of depressing respiration. The body can normally maintain the balance between blood PCO_2 and PO_2 through quiet respiration.

The notion of partial pressure is explained by the fact that all gases in a mixture exert their own pressure as if the other gases did not exist. If we take air as an example, this is a mixture, primarily of oxygen (two molecules of oxygen), carbon dioxide (one molecule of carbon and two oxygen), nitrogen (two molecules of nitrogen) and water vapour (two molecules of hydrogen and one of oxygen). The pressure that these gases exert allows them to move across membranes from an area of high concentration to one that has a lower concentration.

Increases in respiratory rate occur in relation to body tissues' demands for oxygen. Factors that increase the demand for oxygen in healthy individuals are exercise, increased body temperature and emotional responses such as laughing or crying. Ineffective breathing patterns occur when the individual 'experiences actual or potential loss of ventilation' (Carpenito, 1990, p. 610).

The health worker's role as part of the multidisciplinary team approach is in the accurate assessment and diagnosis of factors affecting clients' breathing, planning and carrying out effective interventions and evaluating the degree of success.

Physical assessment

Nursing assessment can be made by collecting data from:

- The client, significant others and previous notes
- Observation of the client
- Physical examination
- Laboratory investigations.

accessory muscles of respiration

muscle groups in the neck, back and abdomen that aid respiration by moving the rib cage

The following paragraphs in this section will cover assessment in terms of the quality, rate, pattern and depth of breathing, the colour of the mucous membranes and skin, the presence of cough, the shape of the chest, the equality of movement on both sides of the chest and the use of any accessory muscles of respiration.

Respiratory rate

This is the number of inspirations and expirations recorded in 1 minute without the client's knowledge, while he is at rest (Chart 6.1). Normal respiratory rates for adults and children are shown in Table 6.1, and the effects of exercise on respiration are described in Chart 6.2.

In certain conditions, abnormalities of rate may occur:

bradypnoea

slow but regular breathing as a result of depression of the respiratory centre

- *Bradypnoea:* slow but regular breathing as a result of depression of the respiratory centre. It is a normal phenomenon during sleep but in ill-health may indicate oversedation, opiate poisoning or the presence of a cerebral lesion.

Chart 6.1 ● Hints for assessing the respiration rate

Sitting at the client's right side, reach across and take the pulse in his left wrist while laying his hand on his upper abdominal area. When you have completed this observation, keep hold of the wrist as if you were still counting the pulse. You can then feel the chest or abdomen moving against your hand; count the frequency of movement for 1 minute and then make the other necessary observations

Chart 6.2 ● Effects of exercise on respiration

During exercise, the muscles of the body utilise oxygen and provide carbon dioxide in higher concentrations than when resting. This reduction in PO_2 is identified by the aortic and carotid bodies, and stimulates the respiratory centre to increase the rate of inspiration. This consequently increases oxygen intake and carbon dioxide output

Table 6.1 ● Resting respiratory rates by age

Age	Rate (breaths/minute)	Age	Rate (breaths/minute)
Newborn	50	4 years	23
3 months	40	6 years	21
6 months	35	8 years	20
1 year	30	10–12 years	18
2 years	25	13–adult	12–16

Source: Ramsey (1989) with permission.

tachypnoea

an increased respiratory rate caused by a lack of oxygen or a need for extra oxygen

anaemia

a deficiency of red cells in the blood

shock

inadequate blood flow to the tissues

cardiac failure

occurs when the heart muscle is unable to pump blood effectively around the body

alkalosis

an increase in the amount of alkali in the blood

apnoea

cessation of breathing

● *Tachypnoea:* an increased respiratory rate caused by the body's demands for extra oxygen or by a decreased amount of oxygen being available when the circulation is diminished or respiration impeded. Tachypnoea may be present in anaemia, shock, cardiac failure or alkalosis. It may also indicate infections such as meningitis or pneumonia.
● *Apnoea:* cessation of breathing, although short periods of apnoea may be normal in neonates.

Respiratory rhythm

Normal breathing is effortless, regular and quiet. Each breath takes approximately as long as five heart beats, so for an adult with a pulse rate of 80 beats per minute, one would anticipate their respiratory rate to be 16 per minute.

As the regulatory centres in the brain are immature, the respiratory pattern of newborn babies is more erratic, with periods of bradypnoea and tachypnoea interspersed with periods of apnoea of up to 10 seconds in duration. A typical pattern is represented in Figure 6.2.

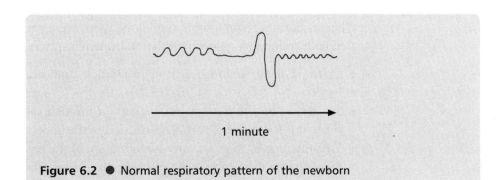

1 minute

Figure 6.2 ● Normal respiratory pattern of the newborn

Changes from the normal pattern of respiration are known as:

- *Dyspnoea*: difficult, laboured breathing, present when the airways are obstructed, as in chronic obstructive airways disease or pulmonary oedema.
- *Orthopnoea*: the ability to breathe without difficulty only when sitting upright. It may be a result of heart failure with pulmonary oedema, or occur in an infant or small child when abdominal pressure is exerted on the diaphragm.
- *Cheyne–Stokes respiration*: breathing cycles of gradually decreasing rate and depth, followed by cycles of increasing rate and depth. This alternating pattern is repeated every 45 seconds to 3 minutes, and there may be periods of apnoea during the cycles. Cheyne–Stokes respiration frequently indicates impending death.
- *Biot's respiration*: periods of rapid, deep breathing interspersed with periods of apnoea, which may indicate fear or metabolic acidosis
- *Kussmaul's respiration*: increased rate and depth of breathing associated with metabolic acidosis.
- *Asthmatic breathing*: prolonged expiration (greater than 2 seconds) accompanied by a wheeze.

Respiratory depth

Respiratory depth is assessed by observing the degree of movement in the abdominal wall in children under the age of 7 years of age, and in the chest wall in older children and adults. The total amount of air inspired and expired in one normal breath is known as the tidal volume, and it can be assessed using a spirometer. Its value differs depending on the gender, age, height and weight of the client; however an approximate figure of 6–7 cm^3/kg can be used.

Hyperpnoea is shallow, rapid breathing usually in an attempt to avoid pain of either a thoracic or abdominal nature.

Respiratory sounds

Whereas normal respiration is soundless, there are a variety of sounds associated with respiratory assessment that indicate respiratory disease:

- *Stridor*: a harsh sound heard on inspiration, indicating obstruction of the larynx.
- *Snoring*: a noise that occurs on inspiration through the nose, usually during sleep. It is indicative of partial obstruction of the upper airway. Causes include inflammation of the nasal mucosa, deviation of the nasal septum, the tongue relaxing into the airway or enlarged tonsils or adenoids. In severe cases, short stoppages in respiration, known as sleep apnoea, may occur.

---

dyspnoea
difficult, laboured breathing

pulmonary oedema
fluid in the alveoli and lung tissue

orthopnoea
the ability to breathe without difficulty only when sitting upright

Cheyne–Stokes respiration
breathing cycles of gradually decreasing rate and depth, followed by cycles of increasing rate and depth

acidosis
a loss of alkali or an increase in acid level in the blood

tidal volume
the total amount of air inspired and expired in one normal breath

hyperpnoea
shallow, rapid breathing

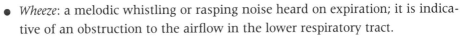

Activity 1

Observe a colleague laughing, excited or upset and assess their respiratory rate, depth and rhythm without their knowledge. Describe the event and behaviour; for example, was the laugh a giggle or a 'belly' laugh? Did you notice that there were changes to all three aspects of the respiratory pattern? In what ways were the rate, depth and rhythm affected?

Activity 2

To help you to identify some respiratory sounds, use a stethoscope to listen to the chest of a colleague or client, preferably one with a smoker's cough or respiratory infection. Is there any difficulty differentiating between the noises made on inspiration and those on expiration. Can you hear the heart beat as well?

- *Wheeze*: a melodic whistling or rasping noise heard on expiration; it is indicative of an obstruction to the airflow in the lower respiratory tract.
- *Grunting*: heard on expiration in infants with severe respiratory difficulty; it is a compensatory mechanism to keep the alveoli from collapsing.
- *Rattle*: audible to the ear on inspiration or expiration and associated with excessive mucus secretion or retention. On forced expiration, if a hand is placed on the mid-sternum, rattles can be felt as a 'fluttering'.
- *Râles and crepitations*: audible with a stethoscope, these are associated with excess fluid in the lungs.

Colour

In health, the skin is warm and well perfused, with pink mucous membranes and nail beds. However, if tissue oxygenation is low or unusually high, there may be noticeable changes in the client's colour. The palms of the hands and feet, the nail beds and the mucous membranes of the mouth and eyes are good places to look in clients of all nationalities for possible changes:

- *Cyanosis*: Blue tinging of the skin with or without involvement of the mucous membranes indicates that there is an abnormally high level of carbon dioxide in the blood. This may be observed in overdoses of drugs that depress the respiratory centre, for example opiates, or in cases where there is a mixing of oxygenated and deoxygenated blood, as in right-to-left intracardiac shunts.
  - peripheral cyanosis: a blue tinge to the hands and feet
  - central cyanosis: blueness of the mucous membranes of the mouth, lips and conjunctivae
- *Cyanosis with dyspnoea*: Laboured breathing and blue extremities may be indicative of damage to the chest wall or lung tissue.

Cough

This is part of a response group that defends the bronchi, trachea and lungs against irritation from a foreign body or excessive secretions. A cough is a sudden, violent expulsion of air from the lungs, which may contain a mix of mucus, cell debris, pus and micro-organisms.

There are numerous types of sputum, indicative of differing disease processes:

- *Mucoid*: has the appearance of raw egg white and occurs in chronic bronchitis
- *Tenacious mucoid*: as above, but it is sticky and difficult to expel; this occurs in asthma
- *Mucopurulent*: thick, sticky and green or yellow in colour, which indicates the presence of infection within the lungs

- *Purulent*: slimy and green or yellow in colour, produced during bronchopneumonial infection
- *Frothy*: a bubbly, white secretion that may appear pink if tinged with blood, which is produced when the client has pulmonary oedema
- *Haemoptysis*: indicates that the client is bleeding into the lungs. The expectorate, that is, the secretions coughed up from the lungs, is bright red and frothy. Haemoptysis may mean that the client is suffering from tuberculosis, carcinoma of the lung or pulmonary embolism.

To enable an accurate diagnosis to be made, the nurse may be asked to collect a sputum specimen to be sent to the laboratory. It may be easier to collect the specimen in the morning when the client awakens, and prior to breakfast. This is because, while the client is recumbent overnight and respirations are shallow, a high volume of secretions may have accumulated, which will be expectorated as the respiratory depth increases. If the client has eaten, food particles may be present in the specimen, making analysis difficult. The principles are outlined below:

- Explain to the client, using methods appropriate to her understanding, that the substance you want to collect is mucus from the lungs and not saliva from the mouth.
- If the client is able to comply with self-collection, give her a covered wide-necked sterile collecting pot to expectorate into the next time she coughs.
- Explain to the client that accidental contamination of the inside of the container by her fingers should be avoided as the laboratory staff need to be certain that any organisms found in the specimen are from the client's lungs.
- If coughing is difficult or the client is exhausted, there are a variety of techniques that the nurse can utilise to ease expectoration. Offering warm drinks or a eucalyptus inhalation may be beneficial.

Once the client has provided a specimen, and you are happy that it is sputum, the pot should be labelled with the client's name, the ward and the date and time of collection, and be dispatched to the laboratory within the hour with the doctor's request form.

The client needs the opportunity to clean her teeth or rinse her mouth after providing the sputum specimen.

Chest shape

In infancy, the thoracic cage is circular, while in the older child and adult, the chest becomes wider from side to side than it is from front to back. Deviations from these shapes are indicative of chronic disease processes. The classical 'barrel' chest that occurs in asthma or chronic bronchitis is probably the most common abnormality.

---

haemoptysis

coughing up blood from the respiratory tract

pulmonary embolism

blockage of the pulmonary artery or one of its branches by foreign matter, usually a thrombus originating somewhere in the venous system

Activity
3

Ask a physiotherapist to show you how he or she intervenes with clients who experience difficulty expectorating. Interventions may include postural drainage, percussion and vibration.

postural drainage

positioning the patient in a way that allows gravity to move fluid from one part of the body to another

percussion

tapping with the fingers on parts of the body

Chart 6.3 ● Causes of airway obstruction

- Anaphylaxis
- Foreign body
- Coma
- Trauma
- Chemical irritants
- Infection
- Near-drowning
- Neurogenic or cardiac causes of pulmonary oedema

anaphylaxis

a potentially fatal reaction occurring when a second exposure to a foreign protein occurs. It consists of breathing difficulty, rapid pulse, sweating and collapse

Nursing interventions

Airway maintenance

hypoxia

lack of oxygen to the cells

Activity 4

Find a client or colleague with a known respiratory infection or cough. Ask them to describe the type of cough and sputum produced. What could be the cause of the cough? Did you review the text to help you determine a cause? Did you perform a respiratory assessment to provide more clues?

'Airway' is the generic term for those parts of the respiratory system through which atmospheric air containing oxygen is inspired and expired to reach the lungs. Where loss of patency occurs in any part of the airway, the flow to the lungs of air containing oxygen is impeded, and a state of hypoxia results. Blockages to airflow may result from the disease process or from mechanical reasons – either a foreign body being inhaled or the tongue relaxing into the airway during periods of unconsciousness. The causes of airway obstruction are listed in Chart 6.3.

In either event, it is essential that the student is able to assist the client in maintaining an effective airway and thus sustaining oxygen delivery to the tissues. Airway maintenance can be achieved by the following methods.

Head tilt/chin lift

This is performed when the client experiences a loss of consciousness; it forces the tongue forward into the mouth and away from the airway. The head tilt in adults, children and infants can be accomplished by placing one hand on the client's forehead and applying a firm backward pressure. The fingers of the other hand are placed underneath the chin to support and lift the chin forward. The preferred degree of tilt is (a) neutral in infants, (b) sniffing in the child, and (c) hyperextension in the adult (British Medical Journal, 1993) as shown in Figure 6.3.

Insertion of a Guedel's (oropharyngeal) airway

An artificial airway is used when the client is unconscious, or the airway is occluded and she is unable to support respiration unaided (Figure 6.4).

The Guedel's airway extends from the teeth to the oropharynx, keeping the tongue in its normal anatomical position. The airway is a concave structure that fits over the tongue. However, the insertion technique differs depending on the age of the client. If the gag reflex is present, an oropharyngeal airway is not used as it may cause vomiting, choking or laryngospasm.

oropharynx

the area behind the mouth from the soft palate to the hyoid bone

laryngospasm

the prolonged contraction of the muscles controlling the vocal cords, which results in the airway being blocked off

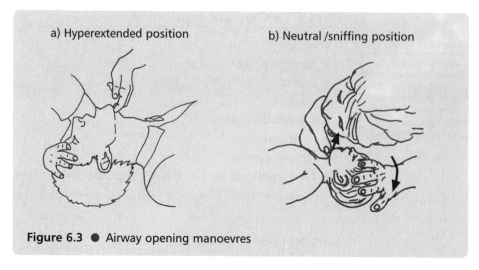

a) Hyperextended position

b) Neutral /sniffing position

Figure 6.3 ● Airway opening manoevres

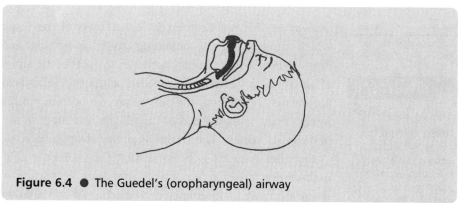

Figure 6.4 ● The Guedel's (oropharyngeal) airway

While you need to be aware of the technique, you will be unlikely to participate in this procedure during your common foundation experience.

Heimlich manoeuvre (Figure 6.5)

This may be applied if a foreign body has been aspirated into the airway and is obstructing the flow of air entry to the lungs. It is an alternating series of mouth-to-mouth ventilations, abdominal or chest thrusts and interscapular back blows. The full manoeuvre is only performed on clients who have stopped breathing as it can prove hazardous for young children and pregnant women if executed while they are still breathing. In infants and children under school age, the rib cage does not protect the liver or spleen, which may be vulnerable to trauma; thus back blows should be the alternative technique of choice for this age group. If used, back blows should be administered with the child lying prone across your thigh, his head hanging over your knee in a head-down position. Using the flat of your hand, administer five sharp slaps between the shoulder

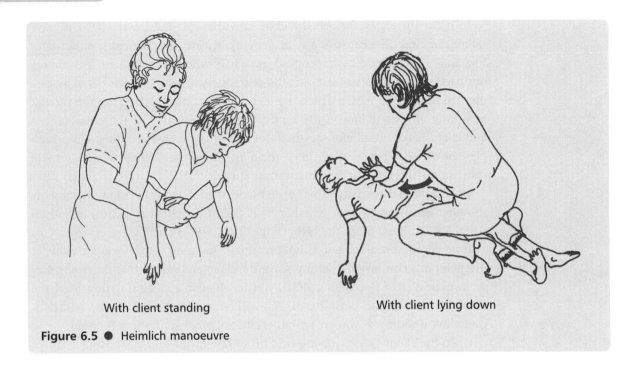

With client standing   With client lying down

Figure 6.5 ● Heimlich manoeuvre

blades. If this fails to dislodge the foreign body, turn the child over and compress his chest five times.

Abdominal thrusts can be achieved by standing behind the client with your hands around his waist. With one fist under the xiphoid process, clench the other fist and pull your arms sharply upwards. This action increases the intra-thoracic pressure, forcing the foreign body out of the airway.

Activity
5

Find out the policy in your clinical area for clients who suddenly collapse or are expected to die. Does your policy include boundaries related to age or mental or physical competence? If there is no policy, do all staff share a common understanding of what to do in such an event?

Cardiac/respiratory arrest

Clinical death is characterised by respiratory and cardiac arrest. In some cases, this is reversible by the prompt application of resuscitative measures, the aim of resuscitation being to 'prevent or reverse premature death in patients with severely compromised or arrested respiration and circulation' (Baskett and Chamberlain, 1997, p. 97). However, there are also times when the order to resuscitate is withheld. This is frequently applied on moral grounds, where resuscitation may deny the client the right to a dignified death, and each case is considered individually. In most instances, the client who is not for resuscitation is known to be going to die or might potentially die from their injuries or disease, and as there can be no generic rules applied to the 'Do not resuscitate' (DNR) or 'Not for resuscitation' (NFR) order, each establishment should have published guidelines relating to this policy. In all cases where a DNR or NFR order is not in place, full resuscitation measures should be employed.

In many instances, the arrest will be unwitnessed, and the rescuer will have no idea of either the cause or any underlying disease. Assessment should therefore follow a methodical process to establish whether the client has airway obstruction, respiratory arrest or cardiopulmonary arrest. This process of assessment is known as 'ABC', which denotes the sequence of checking the airway, breathing and circulation. Only a preliminary assessment of the environment and client is required before resuscitator action is commenced. First aid principles should be followed at all times, including the principle that the rescuer will come to no harm by undertaking resuscitation.

Once an initial assessment has been made, stimulate the client by shaking his shoulder gently and asking whether he is OK. If the client responds, leave him where he is, place him in the recovery position, and get help if necessary.

If he does not respond and is not breathing, summon help. If you are alone at this point in a non-hospital setting, leave the client and ensure that the emergency services are alerted by phoning 999. If you are alone in a medical setting, leave the client and call for the 'crash' team. You will be taught the specific procedure for your clinical setting. If you are within earshot of other staff, shout for help.

Open the client's airway using chin lift or jaw thrust and look, listen and feel for signs of breathing. In the event that opening the client's airway fails to restore ventilation, he requires someone to do it for him. In an emergency situation, this is achieved artificially through mouth-to-mouth resuscitation, or in the infant, mouth-to-nose resuscitation and mouth insufflation:

- With the client lying supine (on his back), open the airway using the chin lift, or the jaw thrust shown in Figure 6.6.
- If using the mouth-to-mouth technique, close off the client's nostrils with one hand while supporting the chin with the other (Figure 6.7). In the infant, this is not required.

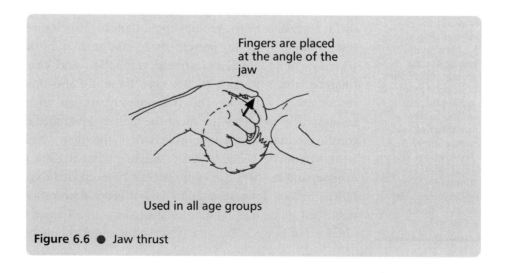

Fingers are placed at the angle of the jaw

Used in all age groups

Figure 6.6 ● Jaw thrust

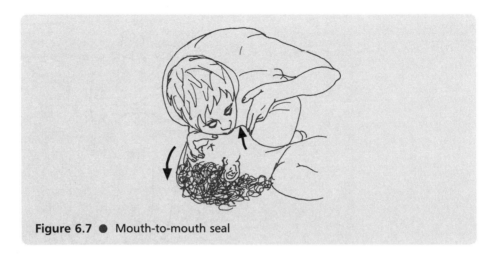

Figure 6.7 ● Mouth-to-mouth seal

- The rescuer takes a normal breath, seals his lips over the client's mouth, or in the case of an infant the nose and mouth, and exhales over the next 1.5–2.0 seconds until the chest rises as with a normal breath.
- Once the client's chest has risen, the rescuer removes his own mouth, and observes exhalation over the next 2 seconds. This should be repeated until two effective rescue breaths have been achieved. Over 1 minute, the rate should equate to normal values of the appropriately aged client. This means 10–12 breaths for the adult, 20 for the infant aged 6 months to 2 years of age and 30 for the younger infant.
- The client should then be assessed for signs of circulation. In the infant, this is achieved by feeling the brachial pulse, and in all other age groups by palpating the carotid pulse for 10 seconds. If you are confident that you have identified signs of circulation, including an appropriate pulse rate, place the client in a recovery position (Figure 6.8). If signs of adequate circulation appear to be absent, commence chest compressions.

If the client has a pulse but is not breathing, continue to ventilate until help arrives.

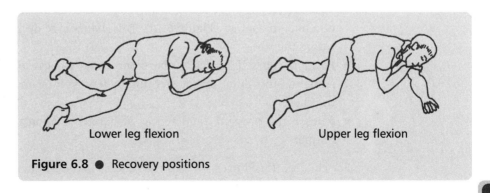

Lower leg flexion   Upper leg flexion

Figure 6.8 ● Recovery positions

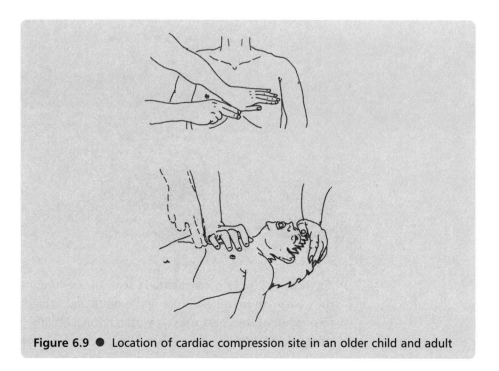

Figure 6.9 ● Location of cardiac compression site in an older child and adult

Compression of the heart is needed when the client's heart abruptly stops circulating blood, and therefore oxygen, around the body. To reinstate cardiac output, the rescuer must perform these compressions at the same rate per minute as the client's normal pulse rate. To perform this on an older child and adult:

- Ensure that the client's chest is resting on a firm surface.
- Kneel at the side of the client and locate the site for compression by placing two fingers on the xiphoid process with the heel of the other hand immediately above them on the sternum (Figure 6.9).
- Remove your fingers from the xiphisternum and place this hand over the other, either grasping the wrist with the thumb or intertwining the fingers. Your fingers are then raised away from the chest wall, leaving just the heels of hands in contact (Figure 6.10). This manoeuvre decreases the risk of fracturing the ribs.
- Position yourself vertically above the client's chest and, with your elbows straight, press down on the sternum to depress it by one-third of the depth of the chest.
- Release the pressure, and repeat at a rate of approximately 60 beats per minute.

For children (aged over 1 year), the process is the same but the rescuer should use only one hand to compress the chest.

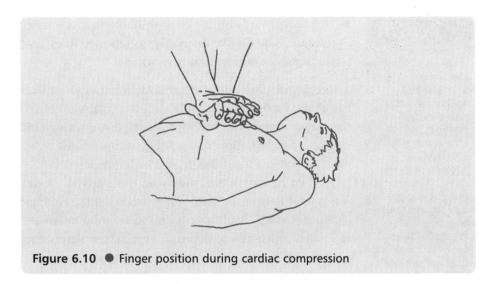

Figure 6.10 ● Finger position during cardiac compression

In infants, if the heart has stopped or is beating at 60 beats per minute or less, cardiac compression should be commenced. As the heart of an infant lies more centrally in the thorax than at any other age, the compression position differs:

- Ensure that the infant's chest is resting on a firm surface.
- Locate the correct site for compression by imagining a line joining the infant's nipples. As can be seen in Figure 6.11, the tips of two fingers are placed on the sternum, one finger's breadth below the intermammilary line. Cardiac compressions are then administered.

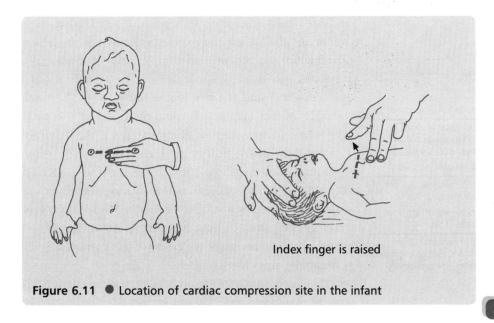

Index finger is raised

Figure 6.11 ● Location of cardiac compression site in the infant

Activity 6

Identify the resuscitation equipment within your clinical area. Who has the responsibility for bringing the equipment to the client? Who checks that the equipment is functional, and how frequently is this done? Does this practice reflect Trust policies and guidelines? List the standard equipment for resuscitation in your area and ensure that you know how it works and connects.

- Press downwards on the chest until the thorax has been compressed by one-third of its depth five times. This is repeated in cycles of five, at a rate of 100 per minute, until medical help arrives.

The above procedures of artificial respiration and cardiac compression are frequently carried out in combination to maintain effective oxygen delivery to the major organs. The ratio for a one-person resuscitation with an infant is 1 respiratory insufflation to 5 cardiac compressions, whereas with an adult or older child it is 2 insufflations to 15 compressions.

Now do Activity 6 and then read on. Did you ascertain that acute hospital wards tend to have a 'crash' trolley where all the equipment and drugs are kept together? On less acute wards and in community areas, minimal resuscitation equipment, such as a back board, oxygen, ventilatory equipment and suction, is available. If the ward has its own trolley, a nurse will usually be first on the scene to fetch the trolley. However, if a group of wards or areas share equipment, a porter may be delegated. Equipment and drugs should be checked, and replaced if necessary, immediately following use. If emergencies occur regularly, a first-level nurse usually checks the 'crash' trolley every day, while in less acute settings, this may be done once a week or even monthly.

Have you asked your assessor or a senior colleague to show you how the equipment works and connects?

Volume measurements

The common units for recording lung function measurements are divided into volumes and capacities, one capacity comprising two or more volumes (Figure 6.12). In healthy individuals, these values are reliant upon age, height, gender and nationality (Kendrick and Smith, 1992). During one normal respiration, the amount of air inhaled and exhaled is known as the tidal volume. The amount of air remaining in the lung on completion of normal expiration is the functional residual capacity (FRC), which is in turn made up of the expiratory reserve volume (ERV) and the residual volume (RV). The total amount of air in the lungs following maximal inspiration is called the total lung capacity (TLC), while the maximal amount of air inspired is the inspiratory capacity (IC).

As airflow obstruction is the main symptom of respiratory disease, the two most important measurements are the TLC and the RV. The peak expiratory flow rate (PEFR) is the maximum flow during forced expiration from TLC and is usually measured by a Wright's meter or Mini-Wright's meter (Figure 6.13). This latter device comes in both low and standard versions. The former is used for clients with severe dyspnoea, elderly clients and young children, while the latter is for adults and older children.

When recording a PEFR, any drugs that the client is taking should be known. Ensure that the pointer or marker on the flow meter is set at zero. When all

total lung capacity

the total amount of air in the lungs following maximal inspiration

inspiratory capacity

the maximal amount of air inspired

peak expiratory flow rate

the maximum flow during forced expiration from full capacity

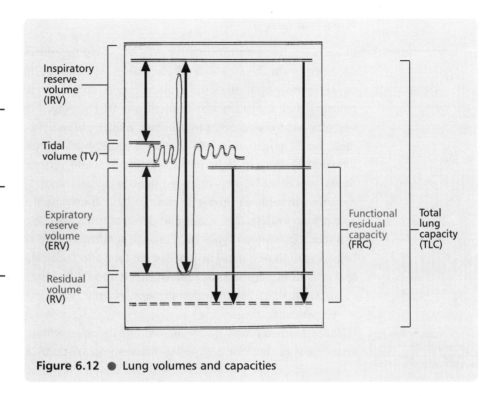

expiratory reserve
volume
___

the maximum volume
of air that can be
expired from the
resting level

residual volume
___

the amount of air
remaining in the lungs
after a maximum
expiration

functional residual
capacity
___

the amount of air
remaining in the lung
on completion of
normal expiration

Figure 6.12 ● Lung volumes and capacities

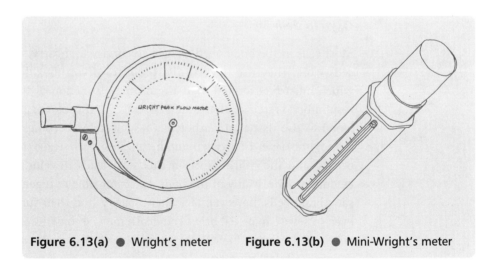

Figure 6.13(a) ● Wright's meter   **Figure 6.13(b)** ● Mini-Wright's meter

restrictive clothing has been loosened, the client is asked to stand or sit upright
and take a deep breath in. With her lips sealed tightly around the outside of the
mouthpiece, she should then be asked to breathe out as hard and for as long as
she can. Three sequential readings should be made, allowing the client to rest
for at least 30 seconds between attempts. The highest reading is then recorded.

Pulse oximetry

Pulse oximetry is a non-invasive way of providing constant information about the client's cardiovascular and respiratory systems by measuring the level of oxygen saturation in peripheral blood. It combines a light-emitting diode (sensor) that transmits red and infra-red light waves through the peripheral vascular bed to be received by a light-sensitive photodiode (detector). The equipment works on the principle that as arterial blood is red, it filters out infra-red light but allows red light to pass through, while venous blood is blue, which filters out red and allows infra-red light to pass through. The photodiode records the intensity of both infra-red and red light transmitted through haemoglobin. To work accurately, the sensor and detector must oppose one another. The pulse oximeter has various types of sensor depending on the site of use, this usually being the digit of a hand or foot, an ear lobe and the bridge of the nose. When a sensor is in place, the skin underneath it should be checked regularly for signs of abrasion or circulatory impairment. Normal values for pulse oximetry are 97–99 per cent.

Pulse oximetry may prove inaccurate in cases where the client has severe anaemia, is in shock or is experiencing vasoconstriction. Cautious use should also be made of oximetry where the client smokes heavily or is suffering from carbon monoxide poisoning, as these factors can compromise the accuracy of the reading.

vasoconstriction

contraction of the blood vessel wall, causing the lumen to narrow

Oxygen delivery

Most cells in the body need oxygen to survive and carry out their functions. As cells work, they use oxygen and produce carbon dioxide as a waste product, which must be excreted. It is the ultimate function of the cardiovascular and respiratory systems, alongside red cells in the blood, to deliver oxygenated blood to the tissues. If either of these systems becomes diseased or compromised, the level of oxygen to the tissues falls. Hypoxia (low oxygen level) occurs, and the continuance of this state leads to cellular death as oxygen is essential to life. Many of the body's cells are able to regenerate and/or compensate; brain cells, however, lack this capacity, and their function may be lost for ever. In severe hypoxia, brain cell death may be so widespread as to bring about death of the individual. Extra (supplemental) oxygen can be administered to support cellular function.

Atmospheric air, containing 21 per cent oxygen, is breathed in through the nose or mouth. This figure can also be expressed as a partial pressure of the constituent gases (see above). The oxygen exerts 21 per cent of the total atmospheric pressure, so the part of the pressure due to oxygen can also be stated as 21 kPa. However, some of the oxygen is lost during the journey to the alveolar air sacs, which at this point contain just 13.2 per cent or kPa of oxygen. While the blood in capillaries surrounding the air sacs already contains some oxygen

(5.3 kPa), it is less than that in the alveolus (13.2 kPa). Gases diffuse from an area of high concentration to one of low, so oxygen moves from the alveoli into the blood until an equilibrium is reached. Carbon dioxide leaves the blood in the same way, diffusing from a high concentration in the blood (6 kPa) to a lower concentration in the alveoli (5.3 kPa). Once in the blood, a small amount of the oxygen dissolves directly, but the majority combines with haemoglobin in the red cells to become oxyhaemoglobin to be conveyed around the body to the cells. Carbon dioxide is more complex and is carried in several forms, carbonic acid, hydrogen carbonate ion and bound to some protein elements where it becomes known as a carbamino compound.

Tissues differ in their requirements for oxygen; there are three main areas that account for 60 per cent of oxygen consumption:

- The brain
- The liver
- Skeletal muscle.

Once in the tissues, oxygen is used to produce adenosine triphosphate (ATP), the fuel for cell maintenance and survival.

Hypoxia can arise when the control mechanisms that ensure adequate oxygen delivery to the cells fail. This may be due to:

1. Deficient oxygenation of the blood through being in a low-oxygen environment, for example during strangulation, suffocation, drowning, inadequate ventilation of the lungs following major abdominal surgery, chest injury, prematurity or paralysis of the respiratory muscles, shunts between the right and left heart (as in infant ventricular septal defect and persistent patent ductus arteriosus) and inflammatory lung disease such as asthma and bronchitis.

2. Inadequate transport of oxygen by haemoglobin as a result of anaemia, a sudden loss of blood or carbon monoxide poisoning.

3. Circulatory inadequacy due to low blood pressure or heart failure.

4. Inability of the cells to use oxygen, which is usually an indication of cyanide poisoning.

ventricular septal defect

an abnormal opening in the septum between the right and left ventricles of the heart

persistent patent ductus arteriosus

a developmental defect leading to an abnormal connection between the pulmonary artery and the aorta

The consequences to the client may be that the cells' ability to produce ATP is lost and so, depending on which tissues are affected, the signs and symptoms the nurse may observe will vary:

- Disorientation and drowsiness if the brain is affected
- Decreased urine output if there is kidney damage
- Muscle weakness
- The skin may appear blue (peripheral cyanosis) or, in central cyanosis, the whites of the eyes, lips, tongue and nails take on a blue tinge
- Tachycardia (rapid pulse rate)
- Changes in respiration rate and depth

- Infant's skin becoming grey and mottled
- The hands and feet becoming cool or cold.

This list is not comprehensive and you may like to add any other observations you make.

Oxygen therapy is, according to Allan (1989), the provision of an atmosphere of increased oxygenation with or without the use of specialised equipment. It is used when the adult's blood oxygen saturation is less than 80 per cent and the infant or young child's is 94 per cent or less (Hazinski, 1995). The factors accounting for this difference are related to the young child's larger consumption of oxygen for cellular growth and function.

As a result of potential dangers, oxygen is treated in the same way as drugs (see Chapter 3) and should as such be prescribed by a doctor. The prescription should include:

- The percentage of oxygen to be administered
- The flow rate in litres per minute
- Whether it is to be continuous or intermittent, or to be given immediately.

As oxygen may need to be administered in an emergency without a doctor present, the ward, hospital or unit should have an agreed written policy to cover this eventuality.

Each oxygen delivery system comprises five basic components:

Activity 7

When on your clinical placement, find out whether there is a policy governing the use of oxygen, and if so, what it recommends. What type of oxygen delivery system is available in your clinical area?

1. An *oxygen supply*: which may be piped to the ward, or come from a portable cylinder that is universally coloured black with a white top marked 'oxygen'. These come in a variety of sizes and are often confused with cylinders containing medical air; a careful check thus needs to be made for accuracy. A portable cylinder for home use holds 300 litres, while cylinders for use with adults in an acute setting hold 3400 litres.
2. A *flow meter*: a device that measures the flow of oxygen in litres per minute.
3. *Tubing*: usually green in colour, although being found in different lengths and diameters, which connects the source to the patient or client.
4. A *delivery mechanism*: mask, cannula, hood, incubator and mechanical ventilator.
5. A *humidifier*: which may be used to warm and moisten the oxygen during delivery.

The choice of method of administration depends upon:

- The concentration of oxygen required
- The client's compliance.

For infants, oxygen is provided via a head hood or box that can provide up to 100 per cent oxygen. The flow rate is set at 7 l/min to prevent carbon dioxide accumulation inside the hood. The hood or box allows both good visibility of the patient's face and access to the infant or child's body without disrupting the flow of oxygen. However, if humidification is used, visibility may be decreased and the child may become cold and wet, which can in turn lead to cold stress and skin irritation. There should be no impedance to the outflow of carbon dioxide, and an oxygen analyser must be used.

Oxygen delivery to newborn babies may be carried out inside an incubator. This allows for the control of environmental temperature and high visibility. The disadvantages are that oxygen concentration is poorly controlled and that, in the humid environment, micro-organisms such as Pseudomonas may grow. Oxygen flow should normally be between 4 and 5 l/min; up to 40 per cent concentrations can be consistently delivered if a head box is used.

A Derbyshire chair can be used optimally for infants and young children, as the oxygen can be consistently administered while the child is sitting in an upright position, allowing for downward displacement of the diaphragm.

Several kinds of disposable face mask, similar to that illustrated in Figure 6.14, are available for both adults and children, these being capable of delivering concentrations of oxygen ranging from 24 per cent to 60 per cent. The nurse should ensure that the nose and mouth are just covered. Masks provide a rapid and accurate delivery to the client, with high visibility. The client may also move around within the confines of the length of oxygen tubing. Disadvantages are that clients cannot eat or speak with the mask on, and if they vomit, it may not be easily noticed.

For clients requiring oxygen administration via a face mask, the nurse should ensure that it fits snugly around the client's nose, otherwise oxygen may blow into the eyes, causing discomfort and possible damage. As oxygen can cause mucous membranes to become dry, leading to inflammation and trauma, both

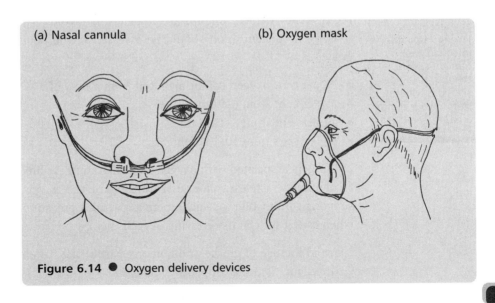

(a) Nasal cannula   (b) Oxygen mask

Figure 6.14 ● Oxygen delivery devices

eye and mouth care are required for clients wearing oxygen masks. When used for infants and children, it might help to position the mask upside down, if the oxygen flow causes problems with their eyes.

Nasal cannulae are reserved for flows of less than 1 l/min or where an infant or child requires less than 24 per cent oxygen. Nasal prongs are usually more comfortable for children and infants, who can eat and vocalise while they are in situ. They are not advocated if the client is mouth breathing.

Nasal catheters are not usually used for infants, who rely predominantly on nose breathing, because irritation to the airways on insertion and removal may cause further respiratory distress. They are advocated for adults and are positioned at the level of the uvula.

Thus, adults can be given nasal cannulae, catheters or face masks. The advantages and disadvantages are the same in adults and children for all three types of system, although an oxygen flow of more than 1 l/min is administered to adults, up to a maximum of 3 l/min. Fluid intake should also be closely monitored to ensure adequate hydration.

Oxygen may need to be humidified because:

- Oxygen from piped or cylinder sources is dry.
- Dry gases lead to drying out of the mucous membrane lining the respiratory system.
- Dry mucus membranes may become inflamed, causing excessive mucous production.

Activity 8

Find out whether it is policy routinely to humidify oxygen. If so, how long should a client be prescribed oxygen before it is humidified? Is there any recent research linking respiratory infection and humidification? If there is, have you shared it with the staff in your clinical area?

As a result, clients needing continuous oxygen therapy may be prescribed humidification. In this, oxygen is bubbled through sterile water at room temperature, picking up moisture and thus increasing its humidity. However, the humidification of oxygen has recently been linked to waterborne infections of the respiratory tract, so it appears to be losing favour as a routine procedure.

Oxygen concentration should be assessed at the point of delivery, but as a guide:

- 28 per cent oxygen can be achieved from a flow of 5–6 l/min
- 35 per cent from 6–9 l/min
- 40 per cent from 8–12 l/min
- 60 per cent from 10–14 l/min.

Dangers associated with oxygen administration are linked to the fact that it is a colourless, tasteless, odourless, transparent gas that is heavier than air and supports combustion. As such, there are various precautions that must be taken when caring for clients receiving oxygen therapy:

1. Avoid the use of grease or oil on any part of the system delivering oxygen to the client, as it may support combustion.
2. No electrical devices should be operated when the client is receiving oxygen.

This includes battery-operated shaving equipment and battery-operated toys for children.

3. Volatile solutions should be used cautiously. Petroleum-based products, which may be inflammable, should not be used to moisten patients' lips.

4. Explain that the client or visitors should not smoke near oxygen supplies.

5. Make sure that you know where the fire extinguishers are positioned or accessed.

Complications of oxygen therapy arise because the prolonged breathing of high levels of inspired oxygen can cause changes in the brain and lung tissue, resulting in fibrosis and decreased efficiency of the relevant organ. In infants, it can also cause a type of blindness known as retrolental fibroplasia.

Clients of all ages with certain types of chronic respiratory disorder require relatively low oxygen levels to maintain breathing. This is known as the 'hypoxic drive'. If oxygen is delivered without due consideration to their underlying disease, it can lead to the cessation of respiration.

Some clients may complain of pain behind their breastbone, which is thought to be related to tracheitis (inflammation of the trachea), and may be an indication for humidification. Humidification during oxygen therapy has itself been linked to an increased risk of chest infection.

When caring for a client receiving oxygen therapy, the nurse should make regular checks (the patient care plan detailing the exact frequency and the observations to be made) on:

- Vital signs, such as respiratory rate, pulse rate, temperature and blood pressure
- The colour of the client's skin and mucous membranes
- The oxygen saturation level, if a pulse oximeter is in use.

Activity
9

You are informed by A&E that a client (of the age group appropriate for your area) with severe dyspnoea is to be admitted to your ward within the hour. The client has bilateral chest movement, an obvious use of accessory muscles and oxygen saturation values of 87 per cent. You are asked by a staff nurse to prepare a bed space for the new arrival. What do you need to do?

Now do Activity 9. Did you remember to prepare an upright position for the client, with a backrest and four pillows for an adult, and a chair for an infant? The client should be easily observable from the nurses' station. You also need the appropriately sized oxygen equipment with humidity, suction and pulse oximetry. As the client is probably mouth breathing, equipment for oral hygiene, a drink and, in the event of the client having a productive cough, a sputum pot and tissues will be needed. In some cases where breathlessness is severe, the older client may appreciate being close to a window or fan to give the impression of an airy environment.

Airway suctioning

While it is unlikely that you will be asked to undertake this procedure, it is performed frequently on medical and surgical wards, and clients with severe physical disabilities often require airway clearance. As such, it is necessary to have some background knowledge about the rationale for airway suctioning.

Suctioning is an essential skill of the nurse caring for the patient who has respiratory compromise. It is used to help maintain a patent airway in cases where the patient is unable to do this herself.

Ineffective airway clearance is the state in which the client experiences a real or potential threat to respiratory status related to an inability to cough effectively. Clients at risk of accumulating secretions in the airway may be diagnosed as demonstrating:

- An ineffective cough reflex
- The inability to remove secretions
- Abnormal breath sounds
- An abnormal respiratory rate, depth or rhythm
- An increased pulse rate
- Pallor or cyanosis of the skin.

This may be as a result of:

chronic obstructive
airways disease

a condition with a
progressive loss of
inspiratory and
expiratory capacity of
the lungs

- An acute or chronic inflammatory response, such as pneumonia or chronic obstructive airways disease
- Burns or trauma to the face, chest or abdomen
- Having an endotracheal or tracheostomy tube in place, which may cause narrowing of the airway or increase the amount of secretions present
- Paralysis of the muscles of respiration through medication or disease.

In times of unconsciousness or paralysis involving the muscles of respiration and the stomach, the patient may be at risk of vomiting and subsequently inhaling vomitus into the respiratory system. This is most acutely possible during, or immediately following, the reversal of anaesthetic agents within the operating department. Impaired levels of consciousness through the ingestion of noxious substances, for example alcohol, or through head injury are causes likely to be seen in the accident and emergency department.

While the art of airway suctioning may appear somewhat barbaric and distressing because of the visual, auditory and aesthetic images it conveys, it is the most effective way of maintaining a clear airway and sustaining life. The nurse is placed in a position of observing a patient who is ineffectively ventilating, and showing all the signs of respiratory distress, yet knowing that the procedure she is about to perform could potentially either save the patient's life or cause untold damage. Both prior to and following the procedure, a reassessment of the patient's respiratory rate, rhythm, depth, effort and sounds should be made.

Activity
10

To acquaint yourself with the principles of airway suctioning, read Lewis and Timby, 1993, pp. 225–9 and Hazinski, 1996, pp. 262–3, making notes in your own words.

Inhaled drug delivery methods

As discussed in Chapter 3, drugs administered directly into the lungs are rapidly absorbed through the alveolar–capillary network into the bloodstream and avoid many of the side-effects associated with the oral forms of the drug. This method is known as 'inhalation' therapy and consists of drugs in either powder or liquid form being breathed into the lungs, thus penetrating the cells directly.

Metered-dose inhalers (MDIs), which deliver a high dosage of drug locally to the lung tissues, rely on pressurised air passing over powder to force the drug deep into the lungs. It is the method frequently used to administer bronchodilators or steroids to clients with asthma or chronic obstructive airways disease. However, the effectiveness of this method is determined by the client's ability to combine activation of the inhaler with inhalation of the drug. Elderly clients, the very young and clients with learning disabilities may be unable to achieve this degree of co-ordination.

The nebulisation of drugs involves compressed gas (either oxygen or air), passing through a quantity of liquid drug within a nebuliser attached to a face mask; this then forms an aerosol spray and is inhaled into the lungs. Little co-ordination is needed so there is a greater compliance of clients who may experience difficulty with MDIs. There are a number of machines available that deliver nebulised drugs to the lungs through a process known as intermittent positive-pressure ventilation. The nurse should familiarise herself with the equipment in order to understand the nature of therapy being given.

Teaching a client to use an MDI

While there are a variety of devices on the market, the principles of action remain the same:

1. Remove the cover of the inhaler.
2. Load the inhaler as instructed by the manufacturer.
3. Ask the client to breathe out gently but not fully.
4. With the client's head tilted backwards slightly, place the mouthpiece between his lips and ask him to breathe in as deeply as possible.
5. Remove the inhaler from between the lips.
6. Tell the client to hold his breath for 10 seconds and then breathe out slowly.
7. Repeat the procedure if necessary.

Circulation

myocardium

the muscular layer of the heart

The purpose of circulation is the provision of an adequate blood flow to vital organs such as the brain and the myocardium. An adequate circulation ensures the delivery of oxygen and nutrients to the body tissues, the removal of carbon dioxide and waste products, and the dissipation of heat from active organs to ensure temperature regulation by redistribution around the body. Effective circulation is achieved via two separate circuits, the systemic and pulmonary circulations, both of which originate and terminate within the heart.

In order to understand the physiological and anatomical principles of circulation, including the cardiovascular system and its components, coronary and peripheral blood flow, the cardiac conduction system and the cardiac cycle, your lecturers may recommend specialist texts on the subject. For example Rutishauser (1994, pp. 77–107) and Hinchliffe and Montague (1995, Section 4) may be useful.

Circulatory assessment

Inadequate circulation results in the ineffective delivery of oxygen to the tissues. The assessment of cardiovascular function includes a physical examination of the patient and assessment of his heart rate, blood pressure, peripheral perfusion and fluid balance. A pain assessment should also be performed.

Physical examination

As discussed in Chapter 1, a physical examination will frequently commence with an initial rapid observation of the client. Consider the client in Casebox 6.1 and determine what general information could be obtained with a rapid initial assessment prior to a detailed cardiovascular assessment.

Heart rate

pulse
_____

the regular expansion and contraction of an artery caused by pressure waves as the heart contracts

The heart rate is most commonly assessed by calculating the pulse rate. The pulse arises from the rhythmical wave of distension in an artery caused by contraction of the left ventricle of the heart, which results in a pressure change within the aorta that can be felt along the arterial wall; this latter is known as the pulse (Chart 6.4).

Casebox 6.1

Davol Singh is a 62-year-old gentleman who has presented to the nurse at his general practice complaining of worsening shortness of breath over the past week. He is accompanied by his wife, who is extremely anxious and worried about his deterioration. Mr Singh is known to be a heavy smoker (35 a day) and suffers from chronic obstructive airways disease.

- Prior to undertaking a full cardiovascular assessment, the nurse could observe the texture, temperature and colour of Mr Singh's skin, which may reveal signs of sweating (cardiac strain), infection or cyanosis (circulatory shutdown).

- A simple question such as 'how are you feeling?' will also help establish mental alertness and degree of respiratory difficulty. (Can the client complete sentences or only gasp individual words?)

Chart 6.4 Hints for pulse measurement

The pulse is detected by placing two fingers over an artery close to a bony or firm surface. The most common site used for pulse rate detection in adults and children over the age of 2 is the radial pulse because it is one of most easily detected and accessible sites. This is felt on the anterior aspect of the wrist (Figure 6.15). The arm should be supported and relaxed, and the palm rotated uppermost. The pulse should be felt with the index and middle fingers over the groove along the thumb side of the inner wrist. Toddlers may need distracting to ensure accurate counting of the pulse. Further sites available for pulse rate palpation are shown in Figure 6.16. In infants, the most common method used for calculating heart rate is by taking the apical rate (see below). When assessing a person's pulse, three factors should be observed: its rate, its strength and its rhythm

tachycardia

an abnormally fast heart rate

Activity 11

Count your resting pulse and respiratory rate. Run up a flight of about 10 stairs five times. Recount your pulse and respiratory rate now, and again after 2 minutes. Chart these readings and note the correlation between the respiratory and pulse rates. Consider what physiological changes have occurred. There is usually a 1:4 or 1:5 differential between the respiratory and pulse rate.

The pulse rate is the number of beats in a 60-second period. Pulse rates are calculated most accurately by counting the beats felt within a period of 60 seconds or, at a minimum, over a 30-second period and doubling the number. Accuracy is particularly important and is most difficult in patients who have a fast or irregular heart rate. Normal heart rates for children and adults are shown in Table 6.2. These rates may vary as a result of age, exercise, posture, temperature, emotions or changes in health status (Marieb, 1992).

An abnormally fast heart rate is known as a tachycardia. In adults, this is considered to occur at over 100 beats per minute, and in children at 20 per cent

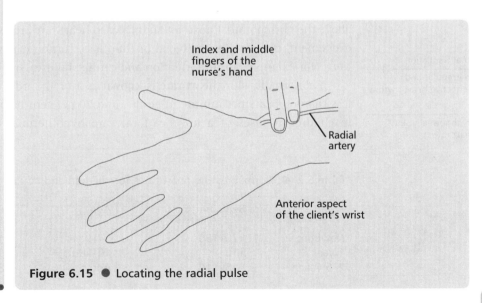

Index and middle fingers of the nurse's hand

Radial artery

Anterior aspect of the client's wrist

Figure 6.15 ● Locating the radial pulse

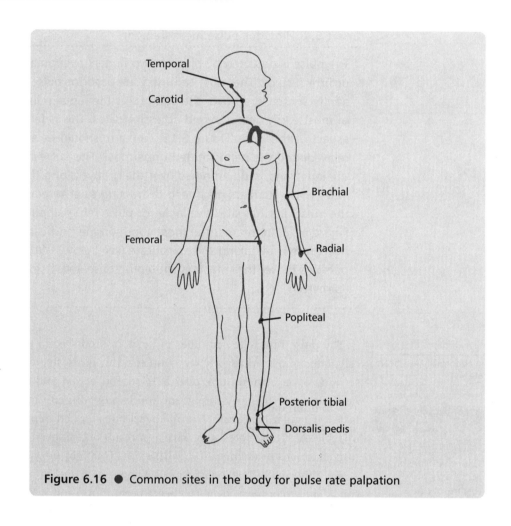

Figure 6.16 ● Common sites in the body for pulse rate palpation

above the normal rate. Causes of an increased heart rate are exercise, stress, fear, excitement, pyrexia (fever), blood or fluid loss, certain drugs and heart conditions (for example, atrial fibrillation and cardiac failure).

An abnormally slow heart rate is known as a bradycardia and is regarded as less than 60 beats per minute in adults, and 20 per cent below the normal rate in children. Causes of a low heart rate are hypothermia, certain drugs (for

atrial fibrillation

an irregular and ineffective heart rhythm

bradycardia

an abnormally slow heart rate

Table 6.2 ● Normal resting heart rates for children and adults

Age	Beats per minute	Age	Beats per minute
Newborn	120–130	5–10 years	110–90
1 year	110	10–adult	90–60
2–5 years	115–110	Adult	80–50

Source: Adapted from Whaley and Wong (1995).

digoxin

a drug that slows and strengthens the heart beat, used for cardiac irregularities

beta-blockers

drugs that slow the heart rate and reduce the blood pressure

Activity 12

By asking a clinical colleague, find out three drugs that can alter the heart rate. Look these up in a pharmacology reference book to see why.

infarction

the death of tissues (necrosis) due to lack of an oxygenated blood supply

example, digoxin and beta-blockers), activation of the parasympathetic nervous system (for example, during sleep or resting), certain heart conditions (for example, heart block, which result from a disorder of the conduction system) and cerebral oedema (excess fluid) following head trauma. A low heart rate may also result from athletic and endurance training.

Now carry out Activity 12. Did you consider:

- Atropine: increases heart rate by acting on the sino-atrial node, sometimes given during bradycardia and cardiac arrest
- Thyroxine: replacement therapy for clients with an underactive thyroid gland, which, if taken in excess, will increase metabolic rate and heart rate
- Adrenaline: resembles the actions of the sympathetic nervous system and thus increases heart rate and output; given during cardiac arrest and anaphylaxis.

The accurate recording and reporting of an abnormally fast or slow heart rate is essential. It will often indicate a sudden change in a person's condition that needs to be assessed and possibly treated. Furthermore, extreme bradycardia and tachycardia result in inadequate filling of the coronary arteries, which can lead to myocardial starvation and infarction. Also, a lack of oxygenated blood to the brain (hypoxia) initially leads to confusion and disorientation, and can give rise to brain damage.

The strength or volume of the pulse is important because it can give an indication of the person's heart function, cardiac output and probable blood pressure. Table 6.3 outlines the relationship between palpable pulse sites and systolic blood pressure. A pulse that is weak and difficult to feel is often described as a 'thready' pulse. A thready pulse will usually be rapid and may be obliterated by pressure on the artery, suggesting that the patient is dehydrated, bleeding or exhausted. In such cases, it may be necessary to feel the carotid or femoral pulse. Cardiac arrest should not be diagnosed when a radial pulse cannot be felt. A very strong and bounding pulse may be a result of infection, stress, anaemia or exercise. An inconsistent pulse pressure within each beat may indicate a Corrigan's or waterhammer pulse, found in children with aortic valve incompetence. The first half of the pulse is normal or full but, after reaching its peak, the wave suddenly recedes under the finger.

Table 6.3 ● Correlation between palpable pulse and systolic blood pressure

Palpable pulse site	Systolic blood pressure
Radial	>80 mmHg
Femoral	>70 mmHg
Carotid	>60 mmHg

The rhythm of the pulse is the pattern in which the beats occur. In a healthy person, the pattern or rhythm is regular because the chambers of the heart are contracting in a co-ordinated manner, producing a regular pulse beat. In children, the pulse is regular, but there is a slight acceleration during inspiration and a slight deceleration during expiration, known as sinus arrhythmia. This may also be present in young, fit adults and is not considered an important deviation. If the pulse rhythm is irregular, it can be of three types: occasional irregularity, regular irregularity or irregular irregularity. An occasional irregularity may be perceived as a missed pulse or 'dropped beat'. This is often the result of an occasional ventricular ectopic (an extra beat, followed by a compensatory pause). This should be reported but might not be treated. A regularly occurring irregularity may be detected as a cyclical event and could be the result of a heart block. Again, these should be reported as they may well reduce the circulation, sometimes with catastrophic effects. An irregularly irregular rhythm is often a result of atrial fibrillation, which is one of the most common irregular cardiac rhythms, occurring in 2–4 per cent of the adult population over the age of 60 years.

Apical pulse rate measurements (heard through a stethoscope placed over the apex of the patient's heart; Figure 6.17) are advocated in children from birth to 24 months of age because, during this period, the pulse rate is quite labile and can be considerably influenced by crying, activity and feeding; apical measurements allow one to obtain more accurate measurements (Whaley and Wong, 1995) and should be counted for one minute. The apical pulse rate is also incorporated into the assessment of adults who have an irregular heart rate and/or

sinus arrhythmia

an irregular heart rhythm following the pattern of respiration

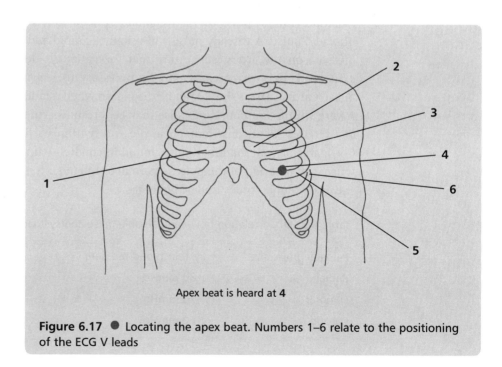

Apex beat is heard at **4**

Figure 6.17 ● Locating the apex beat. Numbers 1–6 relate to the positioning of the ECG V leads

pulse deficit

the difference between apical heart rate and peripheral pulse rate, indicative of a lack of peripheral perfusion

when a measurement of pulse deficit is required. The pulse deficit is the difference between the apical and peripheral pulse rates. The procedure for obtaining these measurements is explained in Mallett and Balley (1996).

Blood pressure

Blood pressure is the pressure exerted by the blood on the blood vessel walls. Each blood vessel has its own pressure, and the pressure in the vessels falls continuously from the aorta to the end of systemic circulation. There needs to be this pressure gradient or fall for blood to flow. During contraction of the ventricles of the heart, blood is ejected into the systemic and pulmonary circulations, which causes distension of the arteries and a rise in arterial pressure. When contraction ends, the arterial walls recoil passively and blood is driven further through the arterial circulation. Arterial pressure therefore rises and falls during the contraction and relaxation of the heart. The maximum pressure is known as

systolic pressure

the blood pressure recorded during contraction of the heart

the systolic pressure, whereas the minimum pressure that occurs during relaxation of the heart is known as diastolic pressure. For a more detailed explanation of the physiology of blood pressure, see Hinchliffe and Montague (1995) or Mallett and Balley (1996).

diastolic pressure

the pressure occurring during relaxation of the heart

Factors determining blood pressure are peripheral resistance, blood volume and cardiac function. Peripheral resistance is the opposition to blood flow and is determined by:

peripheral resistance

the opposition to blood flow

- Blood viscosity ('stickiness'): the greater the viscosity, the greater the resistance
- Blood vessel length: the longer the vessel, the greater the resistance
- Blood vessel diameter: the smaller the tube, the greater the resistance.

Reductions in blood volume can directly affect blood pressure by reducing it dramatically, especially if blood loss (such as haemorrhage) or fluid loss (as in burns or dehydration) is rapid. In these circumstances, the body attempts to rectify the problem with neural controls to supply blood to the vital organs such as the brain, heart and the kidneys by reducing peripheral circulation and directing blood to the major arteries; that is, peripheral resistance is altered to affect blood pressure. Treatment for blood volume loss will be replacement of blood, plasma or fluid at a rate determined to be appropriate to the patient's condition.

stroke volume

the amount of blood ejected from the ventricle during contraction

Cardiac function will determine cardiac output (ml/min), which is equal to the stroke volume (ml per beat) multiplied by the heart rate (beats/min), normal cardiac output being about 5.5 l/min. Change in stroke volume is expressed by the Frank–Starling Law. This law decrees that the critical factor determining stroke volume is the degree of stretch of the cardiac muscle cells just before they contract. The most important factor determining that degree of stretch is the amount of blood returning to the heart (the venous return). Hence we can see that peripheral resistance, cardiac function and blood volume are all interlinked in determining the blood pressure. For further details see Marieb (1992, Unit 4) or Hinchliffe and Montague (1995, Section 4).

The measurement and recording of blood pressure is routinely undertaken in adults and advocated in children aged 8 and over as part of a cardiovascular assessment. The most frequent, non-invasive method of measuring arterial blood pressure is that of using a sphygmomanometer. The frequency of recording will depend on the patient's condition, the reason for admission and the result of the reading. It is therefore essential that the technique is performed accurately, on the same arm each time, and that the patient is prepared prior to the procedure (Figure 6.18, Chart 6.5). Ideally, the patient will not have exerted herself or smoked in the preceding 30 minutes, as these activities can increase the reading. Anxiety also has this effect, and for the patient having a routine blood pressure recording as part of her admission assessment, it is ideal to allow her to settle in her new environment for at least half an hour prior to the procedure. An inspection of patients' charts will frequently show the initial blood pressure to be higher if anxiety has not been allowed for. In an emergency admission, this will be inappropriate, and the blood pressure result will frequently be required as soon as possible, perhaps dictating the patient's treatment (Chart 6.5).

Chart 6.5 ● Hints for taking blood pressure

When undertaking the procedure, the patient should be comfortably seated, or lying if unable to sit, with his arm supported on a pillow at the level of the heart. An appropriately sized cuff (the bladder should encircle the arm) should be used, and tight clothing should be removed. The rubber, inflatable cuff is then applied to the upper arm just above the elbow (over the brachial artery), and the cuff is inflated. Inflating the cuff compresses the brachial artery, and this is continued until no radial pulse can be felt (at this point the artery is collapsed and no blood flows through it distally). The observer should be at eye level with the mercury manometer and the stethoscope placed over the brachial artery (just below the cuff). The cuff is slowly released while listening for audible sounds that indicate flow of blood through the artery and the systolic and diastolic pressures. The Russian surgeon Korotkoff classified these audible sounds into five phases that are now known as Korotkoff sounds (Table 6.4). Controversy exists over whether phase 4 or phase 5 is the best measure of diastolic pressure. What is probably more important is that agreement exists within units and that either method is used consistently when recording blood pressure in the client population. It may also may be useful to note, in the client's records, the phase used

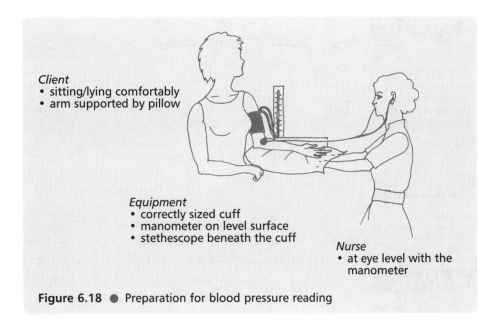

Client
• sitting/lying comfortably
• arm supported by pillow

Equipment
• correctly sized cuff
• manometer on level surface
• stethoscope beneath the cuff

Nurse
• at eye level with the manometer

Figure 6.18 ● Preparation for blood pressure reading

Normal blood pressure values are difficult to define, varying between individuals and in the same person in differing circumstances. Age, sex and race also affect blood pressure values, with blood pressure increasing with age in Western society and being slightly higher in men and in individuals of Afro-Caribbean descent. The factors listed above that affect pulse rate can also alter blood pressure values within individuals. Average blood pressure values are shown in Table 6.5, below.

A persistently high blood pressure reading is known as hypertension. Disagreement exists as to whether this condition should be diagnosed from blood pressure readings or from an epidemiological viewpoint. However most authorities agree that a persistent resting diastolic pressure of over 90–95 mmHg indicates hypertension (Hinchliffe and Montague, 1995). Clinicians are concerned over blood pressure readings because a significantly increased mortality exists for individuals who are hypertensive. The risk increases rapidly with increasing pressure and an individual is most at risk from a cerebral vascular accident or myocardial infarction.

hypertension

persistently high blood pressure

Table 6.4 ● Korotkoff sounds

Phase	Sound	mmHg	Pressure
1	Tapping that is sharp and clear	120	Systolic
2	Blowing or swishing	110	
3	Sharp but softer than phase 1	100	
4	Muffled and fading	90	Diastolic
5	No sound	80	

Activity 13

Find out which Korotkoff sounds are used in your clinical area to determine systolic and diastolic readings. Have you consulted Table 6.4?

Table 6.5 ● Average blood pressure values

Age in years	Systolic pressure (mmHg)	Diastolic pressure (mmHg)
Newborn	80	46
10	103	70
20	120	80
40	126	84
60	135	89

Source: Adapted from Whaley and Wong (1995).

hypotension

persistently low blood pressure

Activity 14

Measure a colleague's resting blood pressure. Using guided imagery, conduct them on a fearful experience and remeasure the blood pressure. Note the differences and consider the physiological changes that have occurred. Try asking your colleague to have a warm bath, and then measure the blood pressure again.

A persistently low blood pressure reading, known as hypotension, is rare. Hypotension is usually transient and is the result of haemorrhage, shock or dehydration. If a patient has a low blood pressure, you may be asked to perform postural blood pressure recordings, the blood pressure being performed in the same arm first with the patient lying and then standing. If a difference exists between the systolic pressures, the patient is said to have a postural fall in blood pressure (postural hypotension); it is particularly significant if the difference is 20 mmHg or more and can indicate a large-volume fluid loss. Always be careful when undertaking this procedure as the patient may faint if the blood pressure is particularly low. Never undertake a standing blood pressure without advice from a trained nurse if the patient is particularly shocked. The alternative option for blood pressure recordings is to undertake a blood pressure on both the left and right arms to compare the difference.

Peripheral perfusion

Peripheral perfusion is assessed by considering the colour, texture and temperature of the skin, the presence of peripheral pulses or oedema and the capillary refill time.

When assessing the colour of the skin, any pallor and/or cyanosis should be noted. Pallor may indicate shock, haemorrhage or poor perfusion and is obviously easier to detect in Caucasian skin. In darker skin, the skin colour may be grey or ashen if severe haemorrhage has occurred. The internal surface of the eyelids can also be inspected, and if these are not their usual reddish colour, this indicates anaemia. Cyanosis, a bluish tinge to the skin or mucous membranes, can be central or peripheral. Central cyanosis is an indicator of poor gaseous exchange and is assessed in the mucous membranes of the mouth. Peripheral cyanosis is an indicator of poor blood flow and becomes apparent when the arterial oxygen saturation is less than 75 per cent (the normal being 96–100 per cent). It is assessed in the extremities and the nail beds (see above for further information).

The texture and temperature of the skin will reveal any localised or generalised warmth or coolness and any signs of sweating. A localised heat reaction may occur following a bite or sting, whereas a generalised heat may be present with an underlying pyrexia or sepsis. Patients who are sweating may also be pyrexial or may have severe pain or blood loss.

Palpation of the peripheral pulses will indicate the presence of arterial blood flow to the extremities (see Figure 6.16 above). If an area of tissue is not adequately perfused, it becomes ischaemic, the metabolic function of the tissue deteriorates, and the damage eventually becomes irreversible (necrosis). During the process of increasing arterial insufficiency, the following signs may be observed: ulceration of skin, thickening of the nails and slow growth of the nails, skin also becoming shiny, scaly and hairless. Oedema and pain in the limb may also be present. Characteristically, the patient will awake in pain at night and hang the limb over the edge of the bed to increase blood supply, thus alleviating the pain. Doppler testing is a non-invasive continuous-wave ultrasonic investigation that can be used to determine blood flow if the pulses are undetectable (an inability to detect this does not necessarily indicate a lack of blood flow). Both limbs should always be checked for pulses or blood flow as this may vary considerably.

Capillary refill time can be assessed using the capillary refill test. The assessor presses her thumb on to an area of the client's skin, which causes it to blanch (go pale owing to blood being squeezed out of the capillaries). The length of time taken for the skin to turn pink again indicates the speed of capillary refill. Longer than 3 seconds usually indicates poor tissue perfusion.

Peripheral oedema usually occurs with congestive cardiac failure and indicates that the heart is unable to function effectively with its workload. Oedema is usually gravitational and may be observed in the feet or legs, or even in the genital area or sacral region if it is excessive. If patients present with these problems, it is essential to elevate their lower limbs to waist level to encourage reduction of the oedema. They may be on diuretic therapy, so fluid balance or daily weights should be ascertained accurately to determine fluid loss. Pulmonary oedema is characterised by acute breathlessness, often with frothy sputum, and is caused by acute left ventricular failure. These patients are often seriously ill and are frequently unable to talk, feeling as though they are 'drowning'. Urgent medical assistance is necessary, and the patients will usually be prescribed oxygen and diuretics.

Fluid balance

A fluid balance record may be requested on clients who have circulatory compromise. Accuracy is essential as it will compare input and output and show whether these are optimal. Ideally, input and output should be the same. If a

---

ischaemia

lack of blood supply to the tissues, usually resulting in acute pain and dysfunction

Activity 15

Try performing a capillary refill test on yourself and then on a colleague. Read the text to ascertain the normal values.

oedema

an effusion of fluid into the tissues

Casebox 6.2

Frances Riteur is an 80-year-old lady with known congestive cardiac failure. Her diuretic therapy has been altered, and the practice nurse is monitoring the effects of her new treatment.

What will the nurse be monitoring?

- Frances will probably be weighed weekly. A maximum weight loss to reduce fluid retention should be no more than 1 kg per day, representing 1 litre of fluid loss per day.

- Any reduction in peripheral oedema will be noted.

- Any reduction in breathlessness will be noted.

- Any improvement in exercise tolerance, appetite and bowel function will also be noted as it may indicate a lessening of cardiac failure.

client has an acute circulatory complication, her cardiovascular output may be ineffective and an adequate urine output will not be produced. Similarly, she may be started on medication to improve the urine output (diuretics), and a fluid chart will reveal the effect. You may also see clients who are weighed daily or twice weekly (instead of having fluid chart monitoring) as a method of assessing the weight/fluid balance.

Pain

The ability to assess and effectively manage a patient's pain is an essential nursing skill. Pain was discussed in Chapter 1, and this section will refer specifically to the assessment, recording and monitoring of pain arising from circulatory problems. As part of the pain assessment, the nurse should identify the location, severity and description of a patient's pain, consider whether there are any precipitating factors or alleviating factors and ascertain the resultant effects on the patient's pain.

An individual may be able to state the location of his pain (for example, central chest pain) or point to it; however, this may be difficult to establish in individuals who do not use English as their main language or who have learning disabilities. Anatomical diagrams and multilanguage tools may be helpful with such patients. Some departments use graphical tools to chart a patient's pain; these can be referred to again in subsequent reviews and evaluations.

The severity of pain is important to establish, various scales existing to assist with this process. The first main tool to assess pain severity is the verbal

Chart 6.6 ● Verbal descriptor pain scale

- None
- Slight
- Moderate
- Severe
- Agony

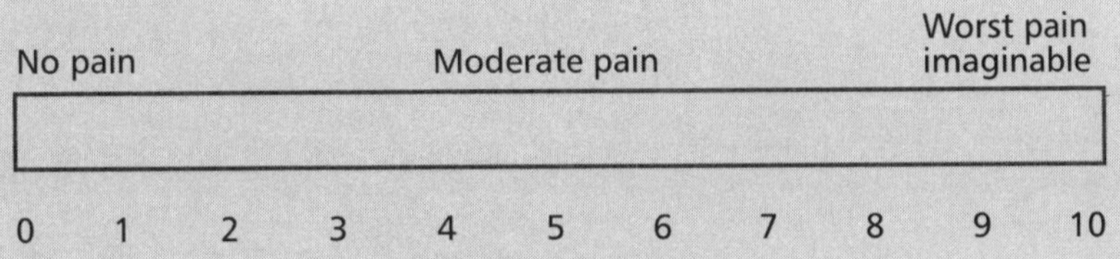

| | No pain | | Moderate pain | | Worst pain imaginable |
| 0 | 1 | 2 | 3 | 4 | 5 | 6 | 7 | 8 | 9 | 10 |

Figure 6.19 ● Visual analogue pain scale

descriptor scale, in which an individual is asked to select a word that describes his pain (Chart 6.6). These scales are quick and easy to use but require an understanding of English or translation to other languages.

Visual analogue scales are usually straight lines with either numbers or describers along them (Figure 6.19). Again, these are quick to use, but they require abstract conceptualising by the patient, which may be difficult if learning disabilities exist.

Last, pain behaviour tools rely on the principle that patients who are in pain exhibit certain types of behaviour (Chart 6.7). These tools require observation of the patient for at least 10–15 minutes and are a subjective assessment of the patient, not including his own perception of his pain.

Ideally, a pain assessment tool allows for a quick but comprehensive pain assessment and provides for the individual interpretation of pain with an assess-

Chart 6.7 ● Pain behaviour scale

- Verbal response
- Body language
- Facial expression
- Behavioural change
- Conscious level
- Physiological changes

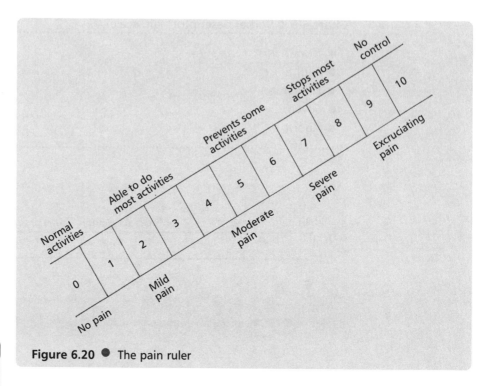

Figure 6.20 ● The pain ruler

claudication

pain in the limbs due to lack of blood supply, which causes limping

ment by the nurse to consider any change in a patient's function. The tool needs to facilitate the ongoing assessment and evaluation of pain and pain control; Figure 6.20 shows a pain ruler that meets these criteria. The Manchester Triage Group have also designed a pain ruler aimed at accident and emergency departments but with obvious uses outside these environments (Mackway-Jones, 1997). The Manchester tool combines the verbal descriptor, visual analogue and pain behaviour tools, which provides for both individual and practitioner assessment.

It is important to remember that patients frequently understate the amount of pain that they are in. This may be seen in the elderly client group who may have become used to chronic pain and have, therefore, adapted to and are able to cope with pain. Children are also a client group who may understate pain, possibly because of fear of the consequences, for example an injection.

The description of pain is necessary to clarify and confirm the location and severity. It may also indicate the probable cause. For example, a client who describes leg pain that is cramping and excruciating, being worse on walking, may have intermittent claudication. Investigations obviously need to be performed to confirm initial suspicions, but it helps the practitioner to prioritise the management of these patients.

Precipitating factors such as exercise, stress, movement, respiration, position, time and duration are helpful in determining the probable cause and possible effects of the pain. For example, chest pain on respiration, particularly inspira-

pericardium

the covering of the heart, comprising two layers – an outer fibrous and an inner serous

tion, may arise from the pleura or pericardium

Alleviating factors such as heat, cold, rest, analgesics, position and distraction may again indicate the cause of pain but may also help with pain management strategies. For example, a patient with angina who complains of chest pain when walking in the cold can be advised to alter her walking habits or to try prophylactic vasodilators such as glyceryl trinitrate (GTN) prior to exercise.

The effects of pain may be minimal or may cause profound physiological changes, for example extreme tachycardia or hyper/hypotension. They may also curtail a patient's activities or lifestyle, so health education advice may be appropriate.

Nursing interventions

Cardiac monitoring

A cardiac monitor displays a graphical representation of the electrical activity occurring in the cardiac muscle fibres. It is a useful tool to assess a client's heart rhythm and also provides information about her condition and progress. Whereas cardiac monitors were once the domain of specialist units, they are now increasingly used in a variety of clinical settings. Chart 6.8 outlines hints on using cardiac monitors.

When a patient is monitored, it is important to remember that the electrocardiograph (ECG) tracing is a tool to assist with the management of a patient and not the reason for managing a patient. It is essential always to consider the patient's condition and the effect of any cardiac rhythm on a patient's well-being. It is also important to note that, during some cardiac arrests, patients can

Chart 6.8 ● Hints on using cardiac monitors

- Ensure that the cardiac monitor is situated in a safe and observable position
- Switch it on at the wall and on the monitor (if appropriate)
- Set the monitor on lead 2 unless told otherwise
- Attach the electrodes on the client's skin surface as shown in Figure 6.21
- The electrodes need to be firmly attached to the patient's skin. This may be difficult if the patient is shocked and sweating. If the leads do not adhere, the following may be useful: abrade the skin lightly (most electrodes have a rough edge to achieve this), dry the skin (iodine solutions are useful, providing no allergy is known) and shave the chest (where the electrodes need placing)
- Ensure that the rhythm tracing is visible and observe it regularly

Casebox 6.3

Joan Hammett is a 52-year-old lady who is recovering from minor surgery carried out 2 days ago. She suddenly complains of central chest pain, which is making her feel dizzy and nauseated. She is known to suffer from ischaemic heart disease but says that this is not the pain she normally suffers.

What could you ask her about the description of pain to help you in your management?

- The site of the pain and any radiation, for example to the neck, arms or back.

- The intensity of the pain and whether anything relieves it.

- The onset and duration of the pain, for example sudden or gradual.

- The consequences of the pain. For example, when she says that she feels dizzy and nauseated, can she concentrate or has this pain taken control of her thoughts?

- Anyone presenting with chest pain potentially has a serious condition such as a myocardial infarction and you should always seek help. The questions above will help the assessor to determine whether the pain is likely to be cardiac in origin.

---

electromechanical dissociation

normal electrical activity of the heart accompanied by a lack of mechanical activity

hypovolaemia

an abnormally low circulating blood volume

polarisation

the resting state of a plasma membrane in which the inside of the cell is negative relative to the outside

depolarisation

loss of the polarised state of a membrane, involving a loss or reduction of the negative membrane potential

have a normal ECG rhythm. This is known as electromechanical dissociation and occurs when electrical activity is normal (hence the normal ECG rhythm) but there is no mechanical activity (and hence no cardiac output), leading to an inability of the heart to propel blood around the body. There are various causes, for example hypovolaemia and pulmonary embolism, but the guiding principle is as follows: look at the patient first and the monitor second.

The normal cardiac rhythm or sinus rhythm has characteristic waveforms (Figure 6.22), and an understanding of these, in addition to the physiology of normal cardiac conduction, will enable you to identify any deviations from the normal ECG. What follows is a basic introduction to ECG interpretation. For a more detailed approach, see Schamroth (1990).

The isoelectric line, or baseline, is seen as a straight line and signifies polarisation of the myocardium. The first wave of the ECG is the P wave, representing depolarisation of the atrial myocardium. Following atrial depolarisation, atrial systole should occur during which blood is expelled from the atria into the ventricles. The P wave is followed by the QRS complex, which represents the depolarisation of ventricular muscle. The Q wave is the first downward (or negative) deflection after the P wave and may not be present with normal conduction. The R wave is the first upward (or positive) deflection after the P wave, and the S wave is the downward deflection that follows an R wave. Following ventricular depolarisation, ventricular systole should occur, resulting in blood being expelled into the systemic and pulmonary circulations. The next deflection

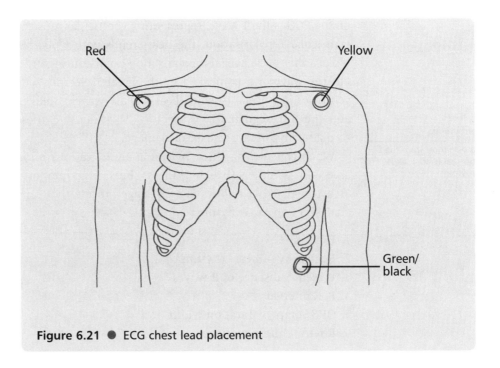

Figure 6.21 ● ECG chest lead placement

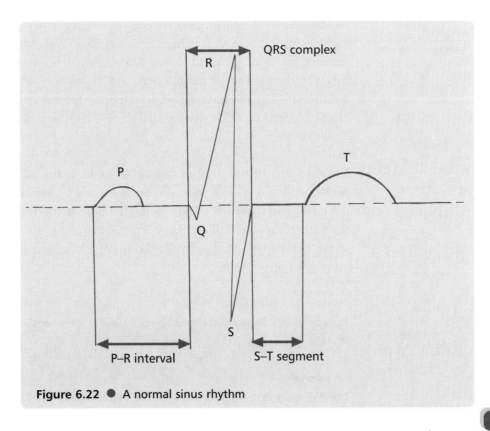

Figure 6.22 ● A normal sinus rhythm

on the ECG is the T wave, representing ventricular muscle repolarisation. During ventricular repolarisation, the heart refills with blood ready to commence the next cardiac cycle. Atrial repolarisation occurs during ventricular depolarisation, but the waveform is masked by the greater electrical activity occurring in the ventricles. A normal or sinus beat has a P wave, a QRS complex and a T wave, and the S–T segment is isoelectric. Alterations to these waveforms indicate cardiac arrhythmias, disease or damage.

When considering ECG rhythm analysis, various information is required to ascertain whether the rhythm is sinus in origin or whether there is an arrhythmia. What follows is a six-stage process that can be used for the basic analysis of an ECG rhythm:

1. Heart rate
2. Regularity of heart rhythm
3. Presence/absence of P waves
4. P–R interval
5. QRS complex duration/width
6. Rhythm interpretation.

arrhythmia

a deviation from the normal (sinus) heart rhythm

Heart rate

The heart rate can be obtained in several ways. If the rhythm is regular, count the number of large squares between two consecutive R waves and divide the number into 300 to determine the heart rate. For example, 5 large squares between two R waves divided into 300 is a heart rate of 60. If the heart rate is irregular, the number of large squares on a 6-second strip can be counted and multiplied by 10. Several types of ECG mark 6-second strips, or 30 large squares can be counted on ECG paper, which represents 6 seconds.

Regularity

The regularity of the rhythm should be noted. If this is not obvious, it can be performed using a ruler or ECG rule, or merely by marking a piece of paper at the top of two complexes and moving it along the rhythm strip to see whether the other complexes fall regularly. Irregular rhythms are unlikely to be sinus in origin except for sinus arrhythmia, in which acceleration and deceleration occur with respiration.

P waves

The presence of a P wave should be noted; it is an essential component of a sinus rhythm.

P–R interval

The P–R interval is measured from the beginning of the P wave to the beginning of the QRS complex. It can be measured in time (0.12–0.20 seconds) or squares

(3–5 small squares on the ECG paper). For a rhythm to be a sinus rhythm, the P–R interval must fall within this duration. If the P–R interval is greater, it may indicate first-degree heart block.

QRS complex

The QRS duration is measured from the beginning to the end of the QRS complex. Again, it can be measured in time (0.08–0.12 seconds) or squares (2–3 small squares on the ECG paper). Beats that are sinus in origin and are conducted normally through the conduction system will be within these parameters.

Rhythm interpretation

Having established all the above you should be able to decide whether or not the rhythm is sinus in origin. Further skills are necessary to determine which other rhythm it could be, but this is beyond the scope of this section.

Anti-embolic precautionary measures

thrombosis

an abnormal condition in which blood clots (thrombi) develop in blood vessels

Patients who are immobile or who have reduced mobility are at risk of venous thrombosis. Venous thrombi are most common in the deep veins of the calf (95 per cent) and result from coagulation in the pocket-like valves of the deep veins owing to venous stasis. Stasis occurs as a result of lying supine (possibly during prolonged surgery or following a major illness), which increases pressure in the leg veins, promoting the stasis or stagnation of the blood. The clinical signs of thrombosis include pain in the calf, especially on dorsiflexion of the foot (Homans' sign), inflammation and localised flushing of the affected limb with associated warmth and swelling. The more serious risk from a venous thrombosis is pulmonary embolism, which results from the dislodging of a clot in the lower limbs. This produces acute dyspnoea and haemoptysis, and can in some instances result in sudden death.

Virchow proposed that three factors, now known as Virchow's triad, were related to the development of venous thrombosis, these being blood flow changes, vessel wall damage and alterations in blood viscosity. Although it is recognised that all three are important, it is now believed that blood flow changes are the dominant component.

Although young, fit, mobile individuals can develop deep vein thromboses (DVTs), the most common cause is a precipitating illness, injury or operation. The greatest risk factors associated with venous thrombosis are a previous history of a DVT, abnormal leg veins, possibly taking oestrogens, heavy smoking, paralysis, congestive cardiac failure, malignancy, pregnancy and hypercoagulability. Precautionary measures can be taken to minimise risk.

hypercoagulability

a tendency towards excessive clotting of the blood

Anti-embolic stockings

Anti-embolic stockings, or graduated compression stockings as they are also known, are a non-invasive, inexpensive, easy-to-use prophylactic method of reducing stasis in the legs. *Bandolier*, the Anglia and Oxford Regional Health Authority magazine that seeks the results of research to provide evidence-based health care, conducted the following meta-analysis. They searched 122 articles, of which 12 were randomised trials with comparable methodology; these revealed that the risk of a DVT was reduced by 68 per cent when using compression stockings. They concluded that, in moderate-risk patients, stockings were a highly effective method of prevention, whereas in high-risk patients, alternative or adjuvant treatment, for example heparin, might be required.

Activity
17

Consider clients of any age who are immobile and at risk of venous thrombosis. What precautionary measures can be adopted to prevent this? Have you considered accompanying a physiotherapist or nurse specialist for the day?

Exercises

Passive/active exercises are an important measure to promote venous return and decrease venous stasis in order to prevent a DVT. Preoperative or bed-bound patients can be taught and encouraged to combine deep breathing techniques and active leg exercises to achieve this. In patients who are unconscious or immobile, exercises can be performed passively for the individual. Further measures to encourage blood flow are regular changes of position, the use of bed cradles to relieve pressure on the limbs and ensuring that top sheets are not tightly tucked in. In some units, intermittent pneumatic compression devices are applied to the calves to assist venous return.

Blood transfusion

A blood transfusion, the administration of either whole blood or one of its components, is a transfer of living tissue from one person to another, and it must, therefore, be remembered that problems can arise. The types of blood/blood product commonly used are whole blood, concentrated (packed) red cells, washed red cells, platelets, plasma and plasma substitutes.

Safety precautions prior to transfusion are as follows. Blood should be stored in a specific fridge (not a domestic fridge) where the temperature is constantly maintained between 2°C and 6°C to prevent bacterial contamination and removed from the fridge no longer than 15 minutes prior to its use. Each hospital will have a local procedure for checking blood that usually involves two nurses, one of whom is a trained nurse, and includes checking the patient's name, date of birth and hospital number, the expiry date of the blood, the blood groups of the donor and recipient, and the serial number of the unit of blood. Once checked, this is recorded either in the patient's notes or on a prescription sheet or checklist. The unit should also be checked for signs of deterioration or damage. If there is any doubt, the blood should not be given but returned to the laboratory and advice requested. The transfusion should be prepared aseptically and the blood administered via a giving set with an in-line filter. Some units use additional filters, and local policies must be checked. Glucose solutions should not be given immediately prior to or following blood administration as they cause the formation of aggregates. You may therefore be asked to 'prime' the giving set with a saline solution prior to commencement of blood.

Observations during transfusion are an integral and essential part of the client's care and should commence with a set of baseline observations prior to commencement of the transfusion. Local policies will vary; however, the patient should be constantly observed and regularly monitored for any signs of transfusion reaction. Reactions can occur very rapidly and are most likely to occur during the initial administration of each unit. Most hospital policies include 15-minute observations during the first hour, followed by either half-hourly or hourly observations of pulse, temperature, blood pressure and respiration during the remainder of the unit. This pattern is repeated for all new units of blood.

Transfusion complications

Circulatory overload occurs from an excess intravascular volume that usually results in pulmonary oedema. This is most likely to occur in chronically anaemic patients who require the additional oxygen-carrying capacity of red blood cells but not the volume. The problem is prevented by using packed cells and giving diuretics. If circulatory overload occurs, the patient should be seated upright and reassured, the transfusion should be discontinued immediately, and medical advice should be sought.

Haemolytic mismatch is one of the most serious complications of a blood transfusion, and clinical problems can arise rapidly following as little as a 10–15 ml infusion of incompatible blood. Problems are due to antigen–antibody reactions, causing acute intravascular agglutination and haemolysis. Early symptoms include fever, shivering, tachycardia, wheeze, rash and hypotension. Further complications are chest tightness, loin pain and oppressive head fullness, which result from agglutination within the capillary beds. The severity of the reaction ranges from mild to severe, with shock and death in some instances. The transfusion should be stopped immediately and any remaining blood sent for analysis. Treatment is symptomatic and is aimed at maintaining a reasonable blood pressure and renal perfusion.

Allergic reactions are fairly common, ranging from mild irritation to anaphylactic shock. Symptoms include flushing, urticarial hives, wheezing, chest tightness, laryngeal oedema and peri-orbital oedema. Anaphylaxis is potentially fatal and requires urgent treatment. This may include intravenous adrenaline to maintain cardiac output, the antihistamine chlorpheniramine (Piriton) given intravenously, intravenous hydrocortisone acting as an anti-inflammatory agent, and salbutamol via a nebuliser as a bronchodilator.

agglutination
the clumping of foreign cells due to the antigen–antibody reaction

haemolysis
the disintegration of red blood cells, causing severe anaemia and possibly jaundice

urticarial hives
a skin condition that manifests as red weals causing intense irritation; it is usually a result of hypersensitivity

Disease transmission is theoretically possible following transfusion and has occurred in the past. Today, all blood in the UK is routinely screened for HIV and hepatitis. It is also extremely rare for blood to be contaminated with micro-organisms, although Gram-negative bacteria can reproduce at 4°C. Reactions include pyrexia, rigor, chest and abdominal pain and the development of septicaemic shock.

Pyrogenic reactions occur from agglutination following mismatch. They are much rarer because of advances in screening techniques, but when they do occur, result in pyrexia and urticaria.

Cold blood can cause ventricular fibrillation when given in large quantities. It is therefore advisable to use a blood-warming device to bring the blood to 37°C if large quantities are required in an emergency.

septicaemic shock

a type of shock usually caused by bacterial endotoxins in the blood

pyrogenic reaction

a reaction that results in pyrexia (a raised temperature of between 37.5°C and 38.5°C), caused by chemicals secreted from white blood cells and injured tissues

Intravenous fluid therapy

A client may receive intravenous fluid therapy when she is unable to maintain fluid balance by oral means. Causes include dehydration due to lack of oral intake, severe vomiting or dehydration, excess urine output or perspiration, severe burns, surgical procedures and unconsciousness. Intravenous fluid therapy is common in acute hospital settings, but it must be remembered that it is an invasive procedure with many potential complications. These include:

- Infection
- Inflammation
- Thrombophlebitis
- Extravasation (infiltration of fluid into the surrounding tissue)
- Septicaemia
- Air or particle embolism
- Circulatory overload
- Anaphylactic reaction.

thrombophlebitis

inflammation of the lining of the veins

The nurse's role is described in Chart 6.9.

Chapter Summary

This chapter examined the key factors related to a client's respiratory and cardiac function. You have learnt how to monitor and interpret respiratory and cardiac vital signs, and how to differentiate deviations from what is normal. You have considered how to assist and maintain respiratory function with supplemental oxygenation, physiotherapy and drugs delivered via inhaler devices. You have also examined techniques to optimise cardiac function, for example pain assessment, cardiac monitoring, anti-embolic therapy, blood transfusion and intravenous therapy. Finally, you have learnt how to recognise and initially manage a cardiorespiratory arrest.

Activity 18

Observe the delivery of intravenous fluids in your clinical area. What precautionary measures are used to ensure that the correct fluid is given to the right patient at the right rate at the right time? Are any electronic devices used for accurate delivery? Is there a policy on which fluids need to be delivered via an electronic device? Do nurses count the drips if no electronic devices are available?

Chart 6.9 ● Hints for intravenous therapy

- Ensure that whoever sites the cannula selects an appropriate site and uses an aseptic procedure
- When sited, the cannula should be firmly secured
- The cannula should be regularly inspected (at least twice a day) for signs of infection and inflammation
- If fluids are being delivered via the cannula, it is essential to ensure that the right fluid is given to the right patient via the right route at the right time at the correct rate
- Most hospitals operate a policy whereby intravenous fluids need to be checked prior to delivery by two nurses, one of whom is a qualified nurse. To ensure that fluids are delivered at the correct rate, electronic pump devices are frequently used in many clinical settings. If these are not available, a formula for calculating the number of drips per minute is required. One such formula is described in Figure 6.23
- The system that is used for delivering the fluids must be inspected for damage and sterility
- It is essential to ensure that the system is free of air bubbles when primed with fluids and during the process of fluid delivery
- All contact with the intravenous system should be aseptic to reduce the risk of infection
- You may also see drugs added to the fluid system. The additives may be prepacked or require adding. In most hospitals, this is a procedure for a trained nurse.

$$\frac{(\text{Number of ml} \times \text{drops/ml})}{(\text{Number of hours} \times 60)} = \text{drops/minute}$$

The following example represents a client who is prescribed 1000 ml (1 litre) of fluid over 4 hours. The giving set in use delivers 10 drops per ml. *Note*: the figure 60 is a given constant representing 60 minutes in 1 hour.

Therefore:

$$\frac{(1000 \times 10)}{(4 \times 60)} = 41.7 \text{ or } 42 \text{ drops/minute}$$

Note: the giving set package must be carefully inspected for the drops/ml as they vary

Figure 6.23 ● Formula for drip rate calculation

Test Yourself!

1. What is the normal respiratory rate for the 2 year-old child?

2. What are Cheyne–Stokes respirations?

3. Describe four types of sputum and their causes.

4. Describe the jaw thrust manoeuvre and when it would be used.

5. List six effects of hypoxia.

6. Where do you assess signs of circulation in the infant and adult?

7. What are the five Korotkoff sounds?

8. How do you assess capillary refill time?

9. Describe the types of pain assessment tool available.

10. Describe five complications of a blood transfusion.

References

Allan, D. (1989) Making sense of oxygen delivery. *Nursing Times* **85**(18): 40–2.

Baskett, P.J.F. and Chamberlain, D. (eds) (1997) The ILCOR Advisory Statement. *Resuscitation* **34**: 97–8.

British Medical Journal (1993) *Advanced Paediatric Life Support: The Practical Support*. BMJ Publishing, London.

Carpenito, L.J. (1990) *Nursing Diagnosis: Application to Practice*. J.B. Lippincott, Philadelphia.

Hazinski, M.F. (1995) *Manual of Nursing Care of the Critically Ill Child*. C.V. Mosby, St Louis.

Hinchliff, S. and Montague, S.M. (1995) *Physiology for Nursing Practice*. Baillière Tindall, London.

Kendrick, A.H. and Smith, E.C. (1992) Simple measurements of lung function. *Professional Nurse* **7**(6): 395–402.

Lewis, L.W. and Timby, B.K. (1993) *Fundamental Skills and Concepts in Patient Care*. Chapman & Hall, London.

Mackway-Jones, K. (ed.) (1997) *Emergency Triage*. BMJ Publishing, London.

Mallett, J. and Balley, C. (eds) (1996) *Royal Marsden NHS Trust Manual of Clinical Nursing Procedures*. Blackwell Scientific, Oxford.

Marieb, E. (1992) *Human Anatomy and Physiology*, 2nd edn. Benjamin/Cummings Publishing, California.

Ramsey, J. (1989) *Nursing the Child with Respiratory Problems*. Chapman & Hall, London.

Rutishauser, S. (1994) *Physiology and Anatomy: A Basis for Nursing and Health Care*. Churchill Livingstone, London.

Schramroth, L. (1990) *An Introduction to Electrocardiography*, 7th edn. Blackwell Scientific, London.

Whaley, L.F. and Wong, D.L. (1995) *Nursing Care of Infants and Children*. C.V. Mosby, St Louis.

Movement and Mobility

MOLLY COURTENAY

Introduction

Movement is vital in many activities, for example in seeking food and avoiding danger. As disease or ageing impairs mobility, the nurse has an important role in promoting the remaining mobility and independence, and enhancing the client's well-being.

On completion of this chapter, you will be able to:

- Describe the musculoskeletal system, skin, lever systems and movement

- Appreciate the importance of physical activity and movement throughout the life span, as well as the importance of exercise on health and physical fitness

- Understand some of the diseases and conditions affecting the musculoskeletal system and mobility

- Appreciate the impact of impaired mobility on social, psychological and physical health

- Understand pressure sore development and the nursing care involved in its prevention

- Appreciate the role of the nurse when caring for the client with impaired mobility.

There are also a number of activities throughout the chapter to enhance learning.

Throughout this chapter you will need access to the following texts:

Brooker, C. (1993) Muscle tissue. In *Human Structure and Function,* pp. 425–38. C.V. Mosby, London.

Hinchcliff, S. and Montague, S. (1996) Skeletal muscles. In *Physiology for Nursing Practice,* 2nd edn, pp. 261–76. Baillière Tindall, London.

Further or alternative texts will also provide the necessary information.

Mobility is generally defined as the ability to move about freely (Ismeurt *et al.*, 1991). For a person to stay fit and healthy, and homeostasis to be maintained, movement is vital. For example, we need to be able to move to seek out, prepare and eat food. We move hurriedly to escape from danger, and twist and turn when sitting or standing just to make ourselves comfortable. There are, however, some people, who, through age, disease or injury, lose their ability to move freely, becoming, to some degree, dependent upon others. A particularly important aspect of the nurse's role when caring for such clients is to promote independence and provide a feeling of well-being.

The Musculoskeletal System

Muscles

Activity
1

Open and clench your fingers as often as you can. How many times can you do this without becoming tired? These muscles are normally used only for gripping things and do not have much stamina. Thus they will tire quite quickly.

The human body is composed of a number of moving parts, perfectly designed for each of the movements that our bodies carry out each day, for example eating, speaking, walking and running. The muscles of the body adjust them- selves and become finely tuned to these regular movements and actions. For example, if certain muscles are used more frequently, and for longer, they increase in size and become stronger. They can also work for long periods of time without tiring; that is, their stamina increases. In contrast, muscles that are used infrequently become weaker and reduced in size.

There are three types of muscle, each of which has a different function and is made up of a different kind of tissue:

- Smooth muscle (non-striated involuntary muscle)
- Cardiac muscle
- Skeletal muscle (striated voluntary muscle).

Smooth muscle

The muscle layers of the body's internal organs, such as the stomach and intestines, are made up of smooth muscle. These smooth muscles, although a lot slower to act than skeletal muscles, expend a lot less energy when contracting. Smooth muscles are responsible for automatic (autonomic) actions such as peristalsis. It is not possible to control the actions of these muscles voluntarily so they are also known as involuntary muscles.

Cardiac muscle

The walls of the heart are composed of cardiac muscle. This is also involuntary.

Activity 2

In the back of each hand, the tendons that run from the forearm muscles to the middle and ring fingers are connected. Place your hand palm down on a table, curl up your middle finger but stretch out the others. Your ring finger is completely immovable.

Activity 3

When our hands are inactive, tension from the muscles and tendons adopting their natural resting positions causes the fingers to be slightly bent. Clasp your hands, interlocking the fingers while keeping the forefingers straight and parallel. Now let your muscles relax. What happens to your forefingers?

cartilage

a non-vascular supporting connective tissue found in the joints, thorax, larynx, trachea, ear and nose

Activity 4

Read and make notes from Hinchcliff and Montague, pp. 261–76, or Brooker, 1993, pp. 425–38.

Skeletal muscle

The body contains approximately 640 skeletal muscles, most of which are attached to the bones of the skeleton by tendons.

Skeletal muscles are arranged in the body in parallel bundles, the cells forming a striped pattern; thus these are known as striped or striated muscles. Skeletal muscles are voluntary muscles as we are able to control their action. They move a part of the body by contracting and pulling on the bone to which they are attached. In order for the body to push, pull and make all its other movements, skeletal muscles are usually arranged in pairs, one on each side of a bone, enabling a bone to be pulled in either direction. Skeletal muscles also tend to work in groups, adjusting and shifting for each of the movements that the body makes. For example, as you move or bend your leg, the muscles in your calf, thigh and buttocks adjust to deal with the leg's new position. This involves some muscles contracting as they take up the strain, and other muscles relaxing as the strain is moved away.

Bones and joints

The framework of the body, or its 'inner scaffolding', consists of bones and joints. These are extremely flexible, adapting to the many demands placed upon them throughout life. For example, exercise helps to make the bones stronger and more resilient, and encourages the joints to stay supple and healthy.

Bones

Bone is a complex organ and is continuously remodelled throughout life. As we pass from childhood into adulthood, the composition of bones changes. A baby's skeleton has more than 300 bones, but many are formed from softer, flexible cartilage. During childhood, this cartilage becomes replaced by true bone. By the time adults have reached their mid-twenties, the skeleton has a final number of 206 fully matured, hardened bones.

There are two types of bone in the adult skeleton:

- Compact bone: This bone makes up 80 per cent of the skeleton and is found in the shaft of long bones, such as the femur.
- Trabecular bone: This makes up the remaining 20 per cent of the skeleton and is found in the vertebrae, the pelvis and the ends of the long bones.

Bones have a number of functions including:

- Supporting body tissue and providing the skeletal framework
- Protecting the organs of the body
- Enabling the body to move
- Acting as a store for mineral salts.

Activity 5

To appreciate the strength of Haversian systems, gather about 60 straws, a lump of plasticine and a book. Cut two rounds out of the plasticine about 3 in in diameter. Using one of these rounds make a tower with the straws, putting the straws in all directions. Make a second tower, but place the straws upright around the edge of the plasticine in a ring. Now press the book on each. You should find that the ring arrangement is much stronger.

Activity 6

Read and make notes from Hinchliff and Montague, 1996, pp. 284–94, or Brooker, 1993, pp. 411–23

synovial fluid

a viscous fluid that acts as a lubricant for joints and tendons

Approximately one-third of each of the body's bones is made up of water, making them not hard and rigid but slightly soft and flexible. Bones have their own blood and nerve supply; they require nutrients and also detect sensation. In other words, bones are alive. When food is scarce, essential minerals are transported from the bones to places where they are needed more urgently.

A typical bone consists of a hard, dense, outer shell called compact bone. This is composed of hundreds of tiny cylindrical units known as Haversian systems, which provide much of the strength of bone. The tube-shaped Haversian units lie in the direction of the greatest stresses on the bone. For example, in the femur they lie lengthways in the bone shaft, so the bone resists buckling.

Weight for weight, bone is stronger than wood, concrete or steel. If the human skeleton were made of steel, and the steel were to equal the strength of bone, it would weigh five times as much.

Osteoblast cells found within the Haversian systems produce a substance called bone matrix. This consists of a mixture of microscopic crystals containing minerals, which make the bone tissue in the walls of these tubes hard, and bundles of fibres made from collagen, which give this tissue some elasticity and resilience. As a result, bones, being slightly flexible, tend to bend rather than snap under a small amount of stress. Within the compact bone is a spongy substance known as spongy, trabecular, or cancellous bone, and in the centre of the bone is a soft jelly-like substance called bone marrow. In children, red marrow occurs in all the bones of the skeleton and makes nearly all the body's new blood cells. From about 5 years of age, red marrow in the limb bones is replaced by yellow marrow. This consists mainly of fibrous connective tissue and fat, and produces far fewer blood cells than does red marrow. At around 25 years old, the production of blood cells takes place in only a few bones, mainly the spine, sternum, collar bones, hip bones and skull.

Joints

Bones are linked together by movable joints, without which it would be impossible to move. We could not nod or shake our heads, run or reach out and grasp things. Human joints are not dissimilar to mechanical joints. For a mechanical joint to function effectively, there needs to be special smooth, hard-wearing substances where the two parts come into contact. In the body, this substance is cartilage. Synovial fluid, found within human joints (Figure 7.1), acts as an oil, lubricating the surfaces of this cartilage and allowing movement to occur smoothly. The body's joints work as a unit, constantly maintaining and occasionally repairing themselves to give the body a lifetime of service.

There are a number of different types of synovial joints including:

- Ball and socket joints, found in the hips and shoulders
- Hinge joints, found in the elbows, knees, toes, fingers and ankles

- Pivot joints, found in the elbows and vertebral column
- Gliding joints, found in the shoulder girdle, hands, feet and vertebral column
- Saddle joints, found in the hands at the base of the thumbs
- Ellipsoid joints found in the wrist, hands and feet.

Synovial joints permit a number of ranges and types of movement:

- *Flexion*: This movement causes the angle between the bones to decrease, for example as the palm of the hand is moved towards the shoulder.
- *Extension*: This causes the angle between bones to increase, for example when the palm of the hand is moved away from the shoulder.
- *Abduction*: This type of movement moves the bone away from the midline of the body, for example when moving the arm out to the side
- *Adduction*: This moves the bone towards the body's midline, for example moving the arm back to the side of the body.
- *Rotation*: This is the movement of a bone around its own axis; for example the radius is caused to rotate when the palm of the hand is turned up and down.

Activity 7

Joints each have a certain position in which the bones fit most securely. Stand upright in a comfortable position: the knee joints are locked, and the muscles do not have to expend energy to sustain this. Now stand with your knees bent: more effort is required.

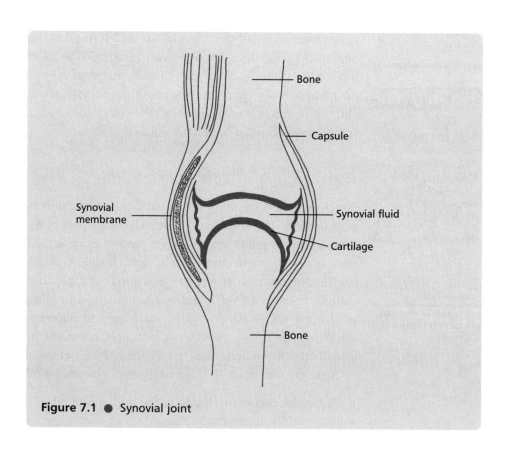

Figure 7.1 ● Synovial joint

Lever systems and movement

fulcrum

the pivot point of the
system

Activity
8

Read and make
notes from
Hinchliff and
Montague, 1996,
pp. 302–14, or
Brooker, 1993,
pp. 465–74.

Movement in humans beings occurs as a result of lever systems. A lever can be visualised as a rigid bar that rotates around a pivot or fulcrum. Basically, a lever moves a load using effort. There are three main types of lever system (Figures 7.2a, b and c), and the body has examples of each, the bone acting as the lever, the muscle supplying the effort, and the body parts, supported by the bone, comprising the load. An example of a first-order lever is the neck joint; in this type of lever, the fulcrum is positioned between the load and the effort. A second-order lever is one in which the load is placed between the fulcrum and the effort, for example when standing on tiptoe. In third-order levers, the effort is in the middle between the fulcrum and the load. This can be seen at the elbow joint.

Exercise and Well-being

Physical activity and movement are basic human needs, important throughout the whole of the life span. As babies and toddlers, we move our limbs around, crawl, walk, jump and run. Between the ages of 2 and 5 children develop many

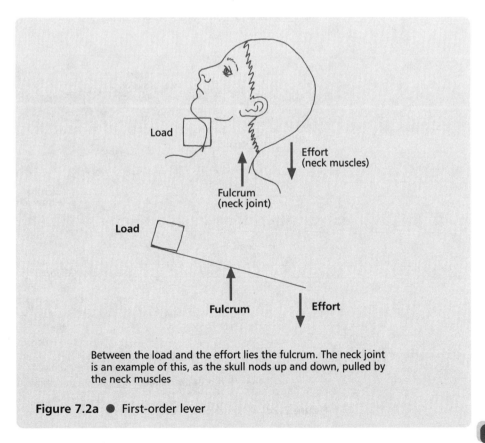

Between the load and the effort lies the fulcrum. The neck joint is an example of this, as the skull nods up and down, pulled by the neck muscles

Figure 7.2a ● First-order lever

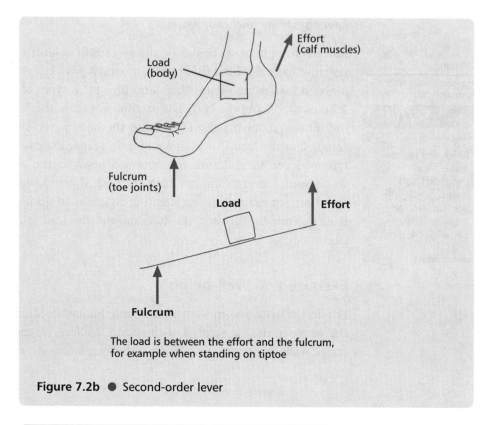

The load is between the effort and the fulcrum,
for example when standing on tiptoe

Figure 7.2b ● Second-order lever

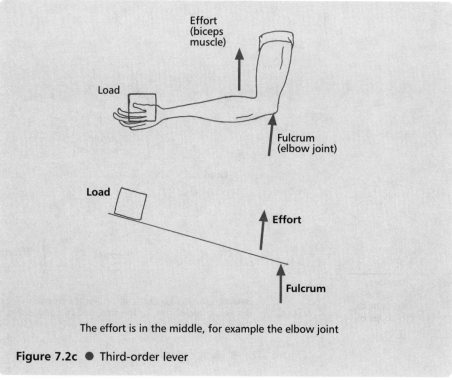

The effort is in the middle, for example the elbow joint

Figure 7.2c ● Third-order lever

skills, for example, those necessary to wash, dress and eat. These not only require mobility, but also dexterity. Most adolescents have boundless energy and are constantly on the move, frequently involved in a number of physically demanding leisure activities such as football and swimming. As individuals pass through adolescence, work, hobbies and pastimes engage them in movement.

The increasing number of elderly people need to be able to move if they are to maintain their independence. If this group exercises regularly, osteoporosis (see below), a problem of increasing magnitude in the elderly, can be prevented or slowed down. Exercise interrupts bone loss and even encourages new bone mass. Furthermore, if the bones are strengthened, they are less likely to fracture. Evidence suggests that a lack of exercise and physical activity can lead to a decrease in fitness and an increase in dependency. Findings from a recent report suggest that individuals over 55 years of age, who failed to carry out tasks of daily living were unable to do so as a result of inadequate strength (Allied Dunbar National Fitness Survey, 1992). A study involving manual workers found that only 4 per cent of those aged between 55 and 60 years old were able comfortably to sustain a walking jog (Bethell, 1992). Although reduced fitness may not result in significant debilitation in this age group, such a reduction in fitness in older age groups may lead to a lack of independence.

There are a number of factors that may prevent people exercising, including a lack of time, a lack of interest or self-discipline, or a lack of understanding of the benefits of exercise. Individuals may also be unaware of how to gain access to suitable exercise programmes. Furthermore, older people may underestimate their physical capabilities, seeing exercise as an activity for the young. However, the development of an appropriate activity programme can mean the difference between dependence and independence, isolation and integration (Dinan, 1994).

Impaired Mobility

During a life span, there are a number of diseases and conditions that can affect the musculoskeletal system and therefore mobility. Some of these disorders are briefly described below.

Muscular dystrophy

muscular dystrophy

a group of diseases characterised by the progressive atrophy of symmetrical groups of muscles

Muscular dystrophy is a condition affecting the skeletal muscles; it is an umbrella name for a group of neuromuscular conditions. Symptoms may vary and can appear at birth or later on in life, but they always involve a progressive wasting and weakening of the muscles. Despite continuing research, the cause of this breakdown and death of muscle fibre is unknown. The damaged fibres attempt to regenerate but fail, and slowly, over several years, the muscle tissue is destroyed, to be replaced by fibrous tissue and fat. The result is a gradually increasing weakness and loss of muscle bulk that causes difficulty in walking and in the use of the arms, and which, over a period of many years, may be increasingly disabling.

Osteoporosis

osteoporosis

a condition in which there is thinning of compact bone by resorption, enlargement of the Haversian systems and a loss of trabeculae from cancellous bone. Bones become fragile and porous, and may fracture spontaneously

Osteoporosis can develop over many years, usually becoming apparent in the over-60 age group. It is particularly prevalent in postmenopausal women although it can occur in childhood or young adults. It affects 1 in 3 women and 1 in 12 men.

Osteoporosis involves thinning of cortical bone by resorption, enlargement of the Haversian systems and a loss of trabeculae from cancellous bone. Bones are fragile and porous, and may fracture spontaneously. Problems encountered include deformity and disability, causing pain, debility and in some cases death. It may also occur as a result of deficient oestrogen secretions during the menopause, or because of the predominance of bone resorption over secretion during old age.

bone resorption

the digestion of bone tissue by osteoclasts, a type of macrophage found in bone

Osteoarthritis

osteoarthritis

a condition in which the joints undergo degenerative changes

Osteoarthritis is a degenerative joint disease. Although this condition is common in the 50–70-year-old group, it can occur in individuals as young as 20. Osteoarthritis occurs in both male and females, and although the cause of this disease is unknown, it is thought that heredity, trauma, congenital factors and pre-existing diseases play a part.

When a joint is affected by osteoarthritis, the normally smooth cartilage becomes rough and cracked, eventually being destroyed. This is thought to occur as a result of digestion of the cartilage by enzymes. During this process, spurs of new bone can be seen at the joint margins. These may then break off and appear in the joint cavity. Osteoarthritis can cause tremendous pain in the movable joints, particularly the large weightbearing joints such as the hips, and joints in the hand. The joint may also become enlarged and, following periods of rest, stiff.

Activity
9

Read and make notes from Hinchcliff and Montague, 1996, pp. 314–19, 278–83 and 294–301.

Rheumatoid arthritis

rheumatoid arthritis

a chronic inflammatory disease affecting the connective tissue

Rheumatoid arthritis is a chronic inflammatory disease affecting the connective tissue. It is three times more common in women than men, normally occurring at the age when careers and family responsibilities are greatest (between 40 and 50 years). The cause of rheumatoid arthritis is not known, but it may be related to an immune mechanism, involve metabolic factors or result from a virus.

Similar to osteoarthritis, rheumatoid arthritis affects the joints. The synovial membrane and joint capsule become inflamed and swollen, which results in the formation of granulation tissue. This leads to fibrous scar tissue, adhesions and possibly calcification. Symptoms commonly include pain, stiffness, fatigue and systematic manifestations such as anaemia. The ability to remain active is compromised.

calcification

the deposition of mineral salts in a tissue

Falls

The changes occurring in joints and muscles as people grow older include:

- A decrease in lean muscle mass
- An increase in body fat
- A decrease in muscle strength
- Demineralisation of the bones.

demineralisation

the loss of calcium and phosphorous from bone

Casebox 7.1

Jane Foster is 65 years old. As a result of an old fracture to her femur, she has a slight deformity of her leg, which interferes with walking. She also has poor vision. Jane is a private person and has no living relatives. The only social contact she has is occasional with a neighbour. Jane is a regular smoker and also likes to drink. Jane's mother suffered from osteoporosis, and Jane is concerned that she may develop this disease.

Describe the clinical development of osteoporosis and identify three factors that can lead to its development. What advice would you give Jane in order to prevent osteoporosis?

- Osteoporosis is initially a silent disease. It can develop over many years and normally becomes apparent in the over-60 age group, being particularly common in postmenopausal women. Bones may fracture spontaneously, leading to deformity and disability.

- Age, the menopause, heredity, diabetes mellitus, hyperthyroidism, Cushing's syndrome (from the oversecretion of glucocorticoids) and acromegaly (from excess growth hormone) are all contributory factors.

- Lifestyle characteristics known to lessen bone loss and fracture risk include: the maintenance of fitness (everyday activities such as dressing, washing and eating help); regular exercise such as running, jogging, swimming and walking to stimulate bone strength; the prevention of falls (reduced environmental hazards, for example loose carpets, wires, footstools, bath hazards, poor lighting and slippery floors); taking care while wearing bifocal spectacles when walking down stairs.

- Jane should eat a nutritionally sound diet (calcium and vitamin D are essential). As people with a high alcohol intake have an increased risk of osteoporosis, Jane should be advised to cut down.

- Smoking, too, is to be avoided as it doubles the risk of osteoporosis, also causing early menopause and reducing bodyweight, which lowers bone density.

Casebox 7.2

David Jones is 72 years old and has a moderate-to-severe learning disability. He cannot speak and his behaviour has been described as autistic. He is also partially sighted. After many years in hospital, he now lives in a small residential home. David has recently developed 'obsessional and ritualistic' behaviour and is continually moving around the room touching, picking up, and moving objects.

What factors may lead to David having a fall? How might the risk of a fall be prevented?

- David's partial vision and continual movement may contribute to a fall.

- The risk of falling can be reduced by tackling environmental hazards, for example not moving the furniture, and by ensuring that David is wearing his glasses.

Osteoarthritis, rheumatoid arthritis and osteoporosis are therefore conditions quite prevalent in the elderly. As a result of these diseases, joints may stiffen and muscle tone may decrease. The individual often develops an awkward gait, and mobility becomes impaired. For example, rising from a sitting position or getting in and out of a car becomes increasingly difficult. Impaired gait and loss of mobility, combined with other physical changes that occur in the elderly, including impaired vision, a confused mental state and a decreased ability to maintain equilibrium, predispose the individual to falling. Contextual factors such as poor lighting, an unfamiliar environment, loose slippers, cluttered equipment and furniture also increase this risk.

People who suffer from impaired mobility will have an associated loss of independence affecting their social, physical and psychological health, with implications for nursing practice. We will now explore this in more detail.

Physical Health

The client with impaired mobility may suffer from a number of problems affecting several of the body's systems; these are outlined below.

Circulatory system

When a person moves, for example during walking, the muscles contract and press upon the veins, causing them to empty. This maintains venous circulation and prevents venous stasis. However, if an individual is immobile, the legs fail to assume or maintain vasoconstriction, resulting in pooling of the venous blood.

stasis
_____
halting of the normal
flow of a fluid

In this situation, a deep vein thrombosis can form in the leg veins. The danger is that this clot, or a portion of it, may become detached and be swept into the pulmonary circulation, causing a pulmonary embolism (see Chapter 6).

Nurse's role

It is essential that the nurse observes for the signs and symptoms of a deep vein thrombosis or a pulmonary embolism. In the case of a deep vein thrombosis, signs include a painful, swollen calf. In the case of a pulmonary embolism, the signs include chest pain and a cough. The nurse's role also involves assisting the client with active and passive exercises and isometric exercises of the extremities.

passive exercises

exercises in which the patient's limb is put through a range of movement by another individual

isometric

muscle contraction with minimal muscle shortening so that there is no movement

Respiratory system

The effect of impaired mobility on the respiratory system is reduced ventilation of the lungs. This decreased ventilation, combined with decreased movement, leads to a decreased stimulation of coughing. Consequently, secretions build up in the bronchi and bronchioles, leading to chest infections.

Nurse's role

It is essential that the nurse observes the client for an inability to cough and raise secretions. It is also important to carry out auscultation of the chest for signs of moisture, and that the patient is frequently repositioned. In order to prevent pneumonia, deep breathing exercises need to be undertaken at regular intervals (at least every two hours), and the client must be encouraged to cough (see Chapter 6).

auscultation

examination by listening to sounds in the body

Gastrointestinal system

Altered diet and fluid intake, combined with a lack of activity, can result in constipation in those clients with impaired mobility (see Chapter 5).

Nurse's role

It is important that the nurse obtains a clear picture from the client of his usual bowel habits, and whether or not he takes anything regularly for constipation. The nurse also needs to observe the client's food and fluid intake. A fluid intake of 2–3 litres a day should also be encouraged, along with a diet high in fibre. The client also needs to be encouraged to be as active as possible. Stool softening agents and suppositories may sometimes be needed (see Chapter 5).

Urinary system

Urinary stasis can be caused by impaired mobility, resulting in the development of a urinary infection or urinary calculi (stones). These occur when crystalline substances such as uric acid, calcium phosphate and oxalate, which are normally excreted in the urine, crystallise out of solution.

Nurse's role

It is important that any history of urinary problems is identified. In male patients, this may involve hesitancy and frequency because of an enlarged prostate gland. It is essential that the nurse records fluid intake and output, and that drinking is encouraged. The signs and symptoms of bladder infection and renal stones must be sought (see Chapter 5).

Musculoskeletal system

Clients with reduced mobility suffer from muscle weakness and atrophy. Bone growth and bone destruction are also affected, leading to osteoporosis.

The role of the nurse in mobilising joints

An essential role of the nurse is to help prevent problems of the musculoskeletal system. Passive exercises of the affected limbs should be carried out regularly, along with active and isometric exercises of the unaffected limbs.

The joints of the body each have their own specific range of movement, usually maintained by the numerous activities that we undertake during our daily lives. These movements stretch the muscles, ligaments and tendons that surround and support each joint, so clients with impaired mobility may experience a loss of function of their joints, resulting in shortening of the muscles, ligaments and tendons. When this occurs, contractures can quickly develop, which can then give rise to further problems. For example, if a foot is allowed to contract in a position of foot drop, the foot will probably not be able to support the foot and leg, and walking will be virtually impossible. A vital role of the nurse when dealing with a client with impaired mobility is to ensure that joints are kept as mobile as possible. In order to do this, each joint must be put through a range of passive and/or active movements. This needs to be undertaken several times a day to prevent stiffness and contractures.

The joints that require exercising include the shoulders, elbows, wrists, neck, fingers, hips, knees, ankles and toes. Exercises not only help to keep the joints mobile, but also promote venous return and lymphatic flow, and prevent excess demineralisation of the bone. If the client is able to move, she can put her limbs

contractures

permanent shortening of muscles and other tissues as a result of disuse, injury or disease

In front of a long mirror, observe the full range of movement for each of your joints

through each of the movements herself. Each of the body's joints have a normal range of movement:

- *Neck*: The neck flexes towards the client's chest and extends out towards the shoulders. Rotation of the neck also occurs from side to side.
- *Shoulders*: The shoulder joints are able to rotate. They also flex forward and extend backwards. Abduction of these joints occurs when the shoulders move away from the body. They adduct when the shoulders move towards the body.
- *Elbows*: The joints in each of the elbows allow the lower arm to flex towards the upper arm and also to extend away from the upper arm.
- *Hips*: The body's hips rotate in a circular motion. They are also able to flex towards the body, and extend and hyperextend away from the body. Adduction occurs when the leg moves towards the body, and abduction when the leg moves way from the body.
- *Knees*: Both knee joints are able to flex and extend.

Find out whether your practice setting has access to physiotherapy services. If possible, arrange to spend some time with the physiotherapist, observing how clients with impaired mobility are treated.

When the nurse carries out passive exercises for the client, it is important that the client does not experience any discomfort. Both the limbs and the joints involved must be supported during the exercises. If the client has a weakness or paralysis of one side of the body, it is important that she is taught how to exercise the affected side herself.

Another way in which the nurse can promote activity is to encourage the client to become involved in her own care, for example, moving independently in bed or a chair, sitting up to wash and eat, and brushing her own teeth; this will increase strength and endurance.

The Pressure Issue

A particularly important area of care in the client with impaired mobility is that of pressure areas.

pressure sores

tissue destruction as a result of tissue overlying a bony prominence being subjected to prolonged pressure from an external object

Pressure sores, also referred to as decubitus ulcers (ulcers developed through lying down) or bed sores (see Chapter 8), can be defined as:

skin ulcerations that occur because of unrelieved pressure in combination with the effects of other variables. (Collier, 1997)

Pressure sores are costly in terms of both an extended stay in hospital and extra medication. The direct cost to the NHS for pressure sores is thought to be as much as £300m, with litigation adding to this figure (DoH, 1993). However, this figure does not take into account the increased suffering incurred by the client. In most cases, pressure sores are avoidable, so the incidence of pressure sores can be seen as an indicator of the quality of health care. It is, therefore, extremely important that everything is done to prevent their development.

In order to understand pressure sores, it is necessary to have an understanding of the anatomy and physiology of the skin (see Chapter 8). To reinforce this information, the structure of the skin is summarised below. Pressure sore development is then examined, along with the associated risk factors.

Skin

The skin (Figure 7.3) is the body's heaviest organ, that of an average adult weighing about 4–7 kg – approximately one-twelfth of the body's total weight. Skin has a large surface area, which spans approximately 2 m². As well as its role as a sensory organ, it has a number of physiological functions including the control of body temperature, the excretion of water and salt, the manufacture of vitamin D, the screening of harmful ultraviolet rays from the sun and protection of the inner organs.

The skin is composed of two layers of tissue:

1. The outer *epidermis*
2. The inner *dermis*.

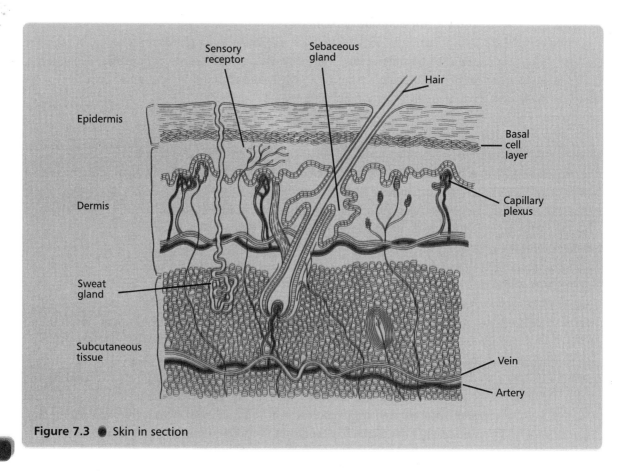

Figure 7.3 ● Skin in section

Epidermis

The skin is continually subjected to mechanical injury. The cells of the basal cell layer within the epidermis are continuously renewed, and it is from these cells that the rest of the epidermis is formed. In one minute 30000–40000 skin cells fall from the body. Each year, up to 4 kg of skin wears away and flakes off our body's surface. Gradually, over a period of about 2 weeks, cells are pushed towards the surface of the skin from the basal layer, during which time their structure and activity change. While still in the basal layer, they begin forming a protein called keratin, this formation of proteins being continued as they move towards the surface. Eventually, as the cells reach the stratum corneum (the outer layer of the epidermis), they are like flattened bags of protein, and the intracellular organelles have disappeared.

The stratum corneum is the major barrier to the loss of water from the body. It has two actions, which restrain the movement of water and limit the loss of water from the skin's surface. First, the matrix in which the cells of the stratum corneum are embedded is rich in lipid. This substance is almost impenetrable to water, which makes it extremely difficult for water molecules to move out of the epidermal cell. Second, protein inside the epidermal cells attracts and holds on to water molecules. As a consequence of these actions, the surface of the skin is normally dry, with very little water lost.

Dermis

The dermis comprises a network of two types of protein: collagen and elastin. The elastin gives the skin its flexibility, and the collagen fibres provide strength. Collagen plays a key role in the formation and healing of pressure sores. It is fundamental in the protection of the body's microcirculation, helping to protect interstitial fluid from pressure. The dermis is also composed of a network of blood vessels, and a number of other structures. These include sweat glands, which are found all over the skin and secrete a dilute salt solution on to the skin's surface; sebaceous glands, found everywhere in the body except non-hairy areas, which secrete sebum containing a mixture of lipids; sensory receptors; and defence cells.

interstitial fluid
the portion of extracellular fluid that fills the spaces between the cells of tissue

There are variations in skin in relation to age, environment and ethnic origin. For example, patches of skin that receive greater wear and tear respond by becoming thicker and tougher, as seen on the soles of feet of someone who habitually walks barefoot. The skin also varies between different parts of the body. For example, non-hairy (glabrous) skin, as on the palms of the hands and the soles of the feet, has an extremely thick epidermis and numerous sensory receptors. Skin with hair follicles (hairy skin), for example on the scalp, has a thin epidermis and many sebaceous glands.

The development of pressure sores and methods of prevention

Pressure sores usually develop as a result of external pressure causing occlusion of the blood vessels and endothelial damage of the arterioles and the microcirculation.

Certain bones, for example the shoulders, elbows, hips, sacrum and heels, lie close to the skin at pressure points. When a person lies or sits, the skin becomes compressed between the bone and the surface of the bed or chair and is stretched. This external pressure is transmitted from the surface of the skin to the bones underneath, compressing the tissue in between. The pressure increases 3–5 times as it travels through the skin, as illustrated by McClemont's cone of pressure (Figure 7.4) (McClemont, 1984). For example, at a bony prominence such as the sacral bone, pressure rises from 50 mmHg to 200 mmHg. This affects the blood supply to the area, and if occlusion of the blood vessels is maintained, anoxia and a build-up of potentially harmful waste ensue. If the pressure is suddenly released, this will result in an increase in blood flow, reaching levels much greater than usual. The resultant red flush is known as reactive hyperaemia. This flush lasts for approximately one-half to three-quarters of the occlusion time. If the vessels of the skin are left intact, there will be no permanent damage. However, if they are damaged, tissue changes will occur, cell membranes rupture and toxic intracellular materials be released. The risk of pressure sore development is greater if the pressure is prolonged.

Pressure sores are caused by unrelieved pressure in combination with other factors, including impaired mobility, poor nutritional status, diabetes, incontinence, reduced fluid intake and oedema. The age of a person is also important as skin changes with age, contributing to the likelihood of skin breakdown. There is a decrease in vascularity and elasticity, and the skin becomes drier. The subcutaneous fat layer of the skin thins, and there is also a reduction in the number of temperature and touch receptors. Therefore, as a person grows older, the skin becomes more easily damaged and takes longer to heal.

During the nursing assessment of a client with a pressure sore, each of the above factors must be taken into consideration. Furthermore, a full description of the altered skin is essential. A standard classification system should be used to describe the sore, and the identification of the stage of sore development helps to determine the most effective intervention. A photograph of the sore, with an indication of its size, is extremely valuable. Such a photograph not only identifies the extent of the problem, but can also be used to evaluate the treatment regimen.

A particularly important feature of treatment is that a consistent approach should be adopted by all those health-care professionals involved in the client's care. Initial care interventions involve identification of those clients at risk of pressure sore development, and pressure sore prevention. Once a pressure sore has began to develop, the interventions will be in accordance with its stage of

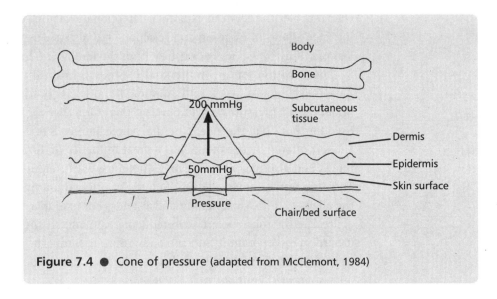

Figure 7.4 ● Cone of pressure (adapted from McClemont, 1984)

development. However, this care will centre upon relieving pressure. Basic nursing interventions involve position change or the relief of pressure, and the use of an appropriate mattress when the patient is in bed. Such mattresses include circulating air mattresses, water beds and egg-crate mattresses. If the client is seated or in a wheelchair, special cushions need to be used. Those clients who spend long periods of time in wheelchairs need to be encouraged and taught to change position regularly by pushing up on the arms of their chairs to relieve pressure. Isometric flexion exercises of the buttocks can be encouraged to increase circulation and relieve pressure.

Other important areas of care include the involvement of the client in a range of motion exercises, ambulation and skin care. It is often extremely helpful if the client's family can be involved in the treatment plan and be given information about pressure sores. It is also important that the client receives adequate nutrition so that healing is promoted. If albumin is being lost from the sore, a diet high in protein is essential. A bladder and bowel programme is also necessary for incontinent patients. (For further information on wound care, see Chapter 8.)

Activity
12

Find out whether your unit uses a pressure sore risk calculator. Obtain a copy and try to identify the original source, for example Norton.

Psychosocial Health and the Implications for Nursing Practice

A client's attitude, acceptance and motivation greatly influence how he copes with his disability. He should be allowed to make decisions involving care at his own pace and be allowed to work within his own limitations. It is vital that the client with impaired mobility receives information and support from the nurse. In this way, clients can begin to regain control over their lives and implement coping strategies. The development of a trusting relationship between the nurse and the client enables the client to explore his emotional reactions to the illness. This may include feelings of isolation and rejection, and also a sense of loss, for example a loss of self-esteem, a loss of status within the family or a loss of independence.

The duration of an individual's illness, intermittent hospitalisations, increased financial strain and emotional and social burdens all put the family under terrific pressure. It is important, therefore, that the client is not viewed in isolation but that the needs of the whole family are considered because the support offered by the family has a great influence on how a person responds to illness and also has a bearing on compliance with treatment and rehabilitation. Thus the nurse should identify failures of understanding of the illness in both the client and his close family and friends. For example, if the family does not appreciate the role of exercise in reducing pain and stiffness, the client may find it hard to incorporate it into the daily routine. Similarly, if a spouse has a poor perception of the disability and pain, she may not acknowledge problems and offer support (Symmons et al., 1996).

When dealing with clients with impaired mobility, the nurse needs to help them to appreciate that their roles may have changed. In situations where clients are unable to return to work, the despondency that this may cause will have repercussions for the family. Loss of a job may cause boredom and a lack of self-esteem (LeGallez, 1993). The nurse needs to encourage and support clients in this situation. This may include referral to the disability employment officer for advice on retraining, or active involvement in a support group. The patient will also require information on benefit entitlement, which can be obtained from the Department of Health and Social Services.

It is clear that the nurse has a number of responsibilities when providing care for the client with impaired mobility. These include:

- Providing the opportunity for both the client and family to articulate their feelings and emotions about the disorder; care provision can then be based on a joint appreciation of the condition
- Providing information on the condition for all family members and the client, the aim being a shared understanding and awareness of the symptoms and the goals of treatment
- Referral to outside help, for example social workers
- Joint goal-setting and sharing of responsibility, thus enabling the client to recognise and accept the help and emotional reassurance provided by the family, while also helping family members to respect the individual.

Disability and Adaptation

An individual's social roles provide a link between that person and society: social roles are determined by society and occupied by individuals. If these roles are disrupted, for example during the working years, or the transitional adolescent years, the effects can be extremely disturbing. The manner in which an individual acts within society has much symbolic value. For example, dressing ourselves has connotations of autonomy, adulthood and independence, but even this simple act may prove impossible for someone with impaired mobility. Thus the social and psychological effects of impaired mobility can be devastating.

The causes of impaired mobility vary greatly and may alter throughout the course of an illness. However, immobility, whatever the cause, can pose a threat to an individual's normal pattern of interdependence with others, which may be particularly traumatic for children and adolescents striving to become independent. In these instances, even mild alterations to relationships can be extremely traumatic. There may be a feeling of being a burden on others, and this might be felt so strongly that help will not be sought when it is needed. Alternatively, individuals may not go out with friends because they think they are an encumbrance. Clients may also worry about the effects their condition may have on their schooling and future job prospects. For example, how will they fare in the job market? Will employers be biased against them? Will they be limited in their choice of career?

The emphasis by today's society on physical achievement and appearance may have disastrous effects on individuals who suffer impaired mobility. For example, in juvenile chronic arthritis, girls who have mildly effused knees may be grossly embarrassed and feel unable to wear short dresses. Teenagers with mobility problems may have only a slight limp but may feel too embarrassed to go out with their friends. Individuals confined to wheelchairs will be unable to participate fully in the usual physical adolescent activities, and a lack of suitable transport may exacerbate this problem.

Thus, people who experience an alteration in mobility often lack confidence in their abilities. This can result in withdrawal from social activities and a feeling of physical and emotional isolation. Individuals may develop an extremely negative self-image as a result of changes brought about by the disease itself, the visibility of the treatment regimen, and also their perceptions of how they are viewed by others. If depression, non-compliance and withdrawal from social situations are to be understood, it is essential that these issues are recognised.

The growing number of elderly disabled living alone increases the risk of social isolation, which, along with loneliness, can lead to a deterioration in both physical and mental health. Research has identified that when the elderly are living alone, they are more likely to suffer from dietary insufficiencies (Walker and Beauchene, 1991). They also suffer losses in relation to their independence, social network and financial status (Folden, 1990). Low self-esteem may develop as a result of feeling unable to support others. Loneliness in the elderly can ultimately result in depression with a risk of self-neglect or suicide (Palinska et al., 1990).

Stereotyping is an important issue confronting the disabled. This literally means that disabled people may be expected to behave in certain ways, for example to be the passive recipients of care. When they comply with this, their behaviour reinforces people's attitudes that they are inferior and incapable of making their own decisions. However, if they do not conform to this role, they are viewed in a negative fashion (French, 1994). It is important that a positive attitude is developed towards disabled people and that the nurse fully understands the meaning of disability.

Aids to normal living when mobility is compromised

Equipment can help to minimise the disabling effects of impaired mobility and also make caring for a disabled person easier. A range of equipment is available for the disabled (Maczka, 1990), including:

- Beds and accessories, for example mattresses, coverings to protect the bed, alarms for clients suffering enuresis, and self-lifting aids
- Chairs, for example ones that adjust and are mobile, high seats, sandbags, footstools and cushions
- Reading and writing aids, for example tape recorders and radios, page turners, and aids for clients with hearing difficulties
- Eating and drinking aids, for example adapted cutlery and plates, drinking aids, non-slip materials and bibs (see Chapter 4)
- Hoists and lifting equipment, for example electric hoists, lifts and stair climbers, and hoists to gain access to cars (see Chapter 3)
- Walking aids, for example frames, crutches and walking sticks
- Household equipment, for example kitchen utensils, cooking appliances and equipment for washing and cleaning
- Clothing, for example special clothes adapted for wheelchair users, hosiery and extra waterproof clothing
- Made-to-measure footwear.

Local hospitals, residential homes and day centres may hold some of the above equipment, so it is possible to try equipment out. If equipment is unavailable, many firms will arrange for their demonstration in a client's home. Disabled Living Centres are also available for individuals to find information about apparatus. Although items are not on sale in these centres, advice on the sources of supply and cost can be obtained.

The Department of Social Security provides several benefits for the disabled person. However, the disabled frequently fail to claim benefits that they are owed. Contributory factors may include a lack of information and knowledge, or the inability to fill in an application form. Consequently, several thousands of pounds of these benefits remain unclaimed each year (Maczka, 1990).

Casebox 7.3

Susan Burton was diagnosed as having juvenile chronic arthritis 10 years ago at the age of 4. During her childhood, she experienced very few problems and participated in most physical and social activities. Recently, however, Susan has become withdrawn. She no longer enjoys swimming or other sports, and she very rarely goes out with her friends.

What factors may have contributed to Susan's behaviour?

What can be done to help her?

- Altered body image, for example as a result of swollen joints, and impaired gait may have contributed to Susan's behaviour.

- Provide support, and encourage Susan to explore her emotions. Involve her family and close friends in discussions. Also encourage Susan to go out with her friends and resume her social and physical activities.

Benefits currently available for the disabled include:

- Attendance Allowance
- Family Credit
- Housing Benefit
- Income Support
- Industrial Injuries and Diseases Disablement Benefit
- Invalid Care Allowance
- Invalidity Benefit
- Mobility Allowance
- Severe Disablement Allowance
- Disability Working Allowance.

Information on each of the above benefits can be obtained from the Department of Social Security.

Chapter Summary

This chapter begins by examining those structures involved in movement and mobility: the musculoskeletal system, skin and lever systems. Physical activity and movement throughout the life span, as well as the effects of exercise on health and physical fitness, are also explored. This is followed by a brief description of the diseases and conditions that affect mobility, and the impact of impared mobility on social, physical and psychological health. Finally, the role of the nurse when caring for these clients is discussed.

Test Yourself!

1. Label Figure 7.5 of a long bone.

2. What are the three major components of bone?

3. Where is compact bone found?

4. What are the functional units of these bones?

5. What are the functions of skeletal muscle?

6. What is muscle tone?

7. When the muscles are at rest, what percentage of the cardiac output do they utilise?

8. What are the functions of joints?

9. Where would you find a third-order lever system in the body?

10. Where would you find a gliding joint?

11. What is the range of movement of a ball and socket joint?

12. How does exercise affect health and physical fitness?

13. What are the effects of immobility on each of the body's systems?

14. What is a pressure sore, and what is the nursing care involved in pressure sore prevention?

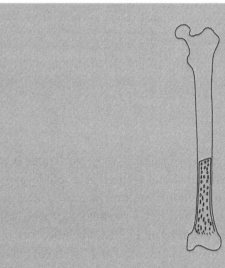

Figure 7.5 ● Long bone to label

References

Allied Dunbar National Fitness Survey (1992) *A Report on Activity Patterns and Fitness Levels*. Belmont Press, Northampton.

Bethell, H.J. (1992) In praise of exercise. *Care of the Elderly* **4**(3): 150.

Brooker, C. (1993) Muscle tissue. In *Human Structure and Function*, pp. 425–38. C.V. Mosby, London.

Collier, M. (1997) Pressure area care: knowledge for practice. *Nursing Times* **93** (Supplement): 1.

Dinan, S. (1994) Fighting fit and over 50. *Practice Nurse* **9**: 441–9.

DoH (Department of Health) (1993) *Pressure Sores: A Key Quality Indicator*. HMSO, London.

Folden, S.L. (1990) On the inside looking out. *Journal of Gerentological Nursing* **16**(1): 9–15.

French, S. (1994) The disabled role. In French, S. (ed.) *On Equal Terms: Working with Disabled People*. Butterworth-Heinemann, Oxford.

Hinchcliff, S. and Montague, S. (1996) Skeletal muscles. In *Physiology for Nursing Practice*, 2nd edn, pp. 261–76. Baillière Tindall, London.

Ismeurt, R.L., Arnold, E.N. and Carson, V.P. (eds) (1991) *Concepts Fundamental to Nursing*. Springhouse, Pennsylvania.

LeGallez, P. (1993) Rheumatoid arthritis: effects on the family. *Nursing Standard* **7**(39): 30–4.

McClemont, E. (1984) Pressure sores. *Nursing* **2**(21) (supplement).

Maczka, K. (1990) *Assessing Physically Disabled People at Home*. Chapman & Hall, London.

Palinska, L.A. (1990) The biocultural context of social networks and depression among the elderly. *Social Science Medicine* **30**(4): 441–7.

Symmons, D., Jones, M., Osborn, J., Sills, J., Southwood, T.R. and Woo, P. (1996) Paediatric rheumatology in the UK: data from the British Paediatric Rheumatology group register. *British Journal of Rheumatology* **23**(11): 1975–80.

Walker, D. and Beauchene, R.E. (1991) The relationship of loneliness, social isolation, and physical health to dietary inadequacies of independently living elderly. *Journal of the American Dietetics Association* **3**: 300–4.

Wound Management

NADIA CHAMBERS

Introduction

The purpose of this chapter is to explore the nursing management of wounds. After working through the chapter, you should be able to:

- Identify and discuss some of the issues surrounding accountability and wound management

- Define the term 'wound' and discuss wound classification

- Describe the use of risk assessment tools in your current area of work

- Describe the recognised stages of the healing process, linking this to the structure and function of healthy skin

- Describe the factors affecting wound healing

- Describe and explain each element of the optimum environment for wound healing

- Describe how each stage of the nursing process may facilitate the nursing management of wounds.

The chapter contains a number of activities that will help to deepen your understanding of this complex topic. Some of these activities require you to access and read the additional texts listed below (or substitute another recommended anatomy and physiology text if necessary).

Additional texts:

Bale, S. and Jones, V. (1997) *Wound Care Nursing: A Patient Centred Approach*. Baillière Tindall, London.

Clancy, J. and McVicar, A. (1995) *Physiology and Anatomy: A Homeostatic Approach*. Edward Arnold, London.

Thibodeau, G.A. (1992) *Structure and Function of the Body*, 9th edn. Mosby Yearbook, St Louis.

A Professional Perspective

tissue viability
_____

the sustained health,
growth and repair of
body tissues

Visit the European
Pressure Ulcer
Advisory Panel
(EPUAP) website on
the Internet (http:
//www.leahcim.
demon.co.uk.epuap)
with a view to
reviewing the
contents and
identifying any
additional relevant
websites.
Download any
potentially useful
information.

The maintenance of tissue viability and the management of wounds is an area of practice that falls clearly within the domain of the professionally qualified nurse. It is an activity that is considered important in terms of both patient comfort and care, and the financial strain placed upon service providers (Cullum and Dealey, 1996).

It has been suggested that the key elements in establishing sound practice include the provision of evidence-based education and the development of good communication networks (Allison, 1995; Edwards, 1995). You may have noticed some of the many journal articles concerned with tissue viability and wound management. You may also be familiar with multidisciplinary associations such as the Wound Care Society, the Tissue Viability Society, the European Wound Management Association and the European Tissue Repair Society. It soon becomes apparent that tissue viability and wound management is a high-profile area of nursing activity. Many NHS Trusts employ clinical nurse specialists for tissue viability, with the distinct remit for managing and co-ordinating care, teaching and research in wound management.

However, it is important to remember that this area of nursing practice is one that most, if not all, practitioners will encounter, both pre- and postregistration.

Accountability in Wound Management

Inherent in the concept of professionalism is the notion of service, and with this the 'duty of care' that is entered into during practice, and for which the professional practitioner is held accountable (UKCC, 1989; Carpenter, 1993). Whenever a professional nurse assesses, plans, implements or evaluates a care intervention, a duty of care arises. The nurse can be held to account for the knowledge base upon which such an intervention is founded and must be able to demonstrate practice within the limits of such knowledge (UKCC, 1994).

The duty of care defines the minimum standard of practice that a patient can expect. In professional nursing practice, this is informed by the *Code of Professional Conduct for Nurses, Midwives and Health Visitors* (UKCC, 1992) as well as national standards such as *The Patient's Charter* (DoH, 1991), professional guidelines (Nelson, 1997) and local policies, guidelines, protocols and procedures. If the duty of care is breached, it is possible that a case of negligence may be brought against either the service provider (organisation) or the individual practitioner accountable for the nursing care involved.

Accountability and responsibility often become confused. Indeed, they are similar concepts. However, a distinction can be made: in order to be held accountable for something, you must have authority over it. This means that you must be in the position to make a decision about a particular course of action. If you are not in such a position, it is your responsibility to say so.

Activity 2

You are in your second clinical placement and it is a particularly busy shift. A health care support worker has reported to the staff nurse that Mr Lyons has a superficial break in the skin over his sacrum. The staff nurse is in the middle of setting up a blood transfusion for another patient and asks you to see Mr Lyons and 'put a dressing on his sacrum'. She assures you that you can do this 'because you are in training'.

Looking at the accountability frameworks, what can you be held accountable for in this scenario and why? What do you think is your prime responsibility?

You may find it useful to discuss this with your colleagues and tutors.

superficial break

where the continuity of the uppermost layer of the epidermis is interrupted

wound

any break in the integrity of the skin and underlying tissues

Chart 8.1 ● Frameworks for accountability

● Legal – common, civil, commercial and criminal law
● Managerial – operational policies and procedures
● Organisational – care delivery systems, contracts
● Professional – codes of conduct, professional lead bodies' mandates, guidelines, recommendations
● Governmental – national standards, citizens' rights
● Moral – personal beliefs and value systems

Source: Adapted from Marks-Maran (1993).

A number of 'accountability relationships' exist within which professional practitioners are required to discharge their duty of care to the client. These are summarised in Chart 8.1. There are times when these different relationships can conflict with one another, for example when moral imperatives conflict with managerial imperatives.

● What is a Wound?

Having identified tissue viability and wound management as a regular nursing activity, and highlighted the importance of accountability in wound management, the next step is to examine what is meant by the term 'wound' and identify the different types that may be encountered.

Any kind of breach in the integrity of the skin or underlying tissues is commonly described as a wound. Wounds can also be classified according to how they were caused, how deep they are, whether they are 'open' or 'closed' or the method by which they are expected to heal. Examples of how these classifications can be interlinked are illustrated in Table 8.1.

● Assessing the Risk

The likelihood of certain wounds developing as a result of pathological processes can be assessed. Such wounds are commonly associated with either:

● Intrinsic (internal) factors such as vascular disease or diabetes, or
● Extrinsic (external) factors such as pressure damage or infection

or a mixture of both.

They can be assessed by examining the risk factors commonly associated with the type of wound.

Table 8.1 ● Examples of wound classification

Description of wound	Cause	Expected mode of healing	Open or closed
Surgical excision	Removal of skin and underlying tissues during surgery	Secondary intention (see Modes of healing later in this chapter)	Open
Surgical incision	Precise cut made during surgery using either a scalpel blade or diathermy	Primary intention (see Modes of healing later in this chapter)	Closed
Burn	Thermal, electrical or chemical	Secondary intention	Open
Laceration ('cut')	Trauma	Primary/secondary intention	Either
Abrasion ('graze')	Trauma	Secondary intention	Open
Puncture ('stab wound')	Trauma	Secondary intention	Open
Venous ulcer	Pathology (intrinsic), for example chronic venous insufficiency	Secondary intention	Open
Arterial ulcer	Pathology (intrinsic), for example atherosclerosis	Secondary intention	Open
Diabetic ulcer	Pathology (intrinsic), for example diabetes	Secondary intention	Open
Pressure (decubitus) ulcer	Pathology (extrinsic), for example pressure, shear or friction	Secondary intention	Open
Fungating	Pathology (intrinsic), for example carcinoma	Neither	Open

diathermy

the application of high-frequency electric currents via a fine, hand-held rod, producing intense, localised heat that may be used to divide tissue and/or seal (cauterise) blood vessels

atherosclerosis

the thickening and calcification of the arteries and narrowing of their lumens that occurs as a result of the deposition of fatty substances (plaques) along the arterial walls

Activity 3

Find out which risk assessment tools are in use where you work. Ask your clinical assessor/supervisor the following: How are the risk assessment tools used? How often is each assessment carried out? Who carries it out? How are the results documented/acted upon? How is the client involved in this?

Assessment may be carried out in a variety of ways, using the nursing process. A number of risk assessment tools have been developed to assist nurses and other health-care professionals in exercising judgement regarding care planning and resource allocation. These include:

● Pressure sore risk assessment tools, for example those of Waterlow (1988) and Norton *et al.* (1975)
● Diabetic foot ulcer risk assessment tool (Plummer and Albert, 1995)
● Nutrition risk assessment tools (see Chapter 4)
● Manual handling risk assessment tools (see Chapter 3).

Healthy Skin and the Healing Process

The ability to support the maintenance of tissue viability and manage wounds effectively is underpinned by a sound understanding of the structure and function of normal, healthy skin as well as a working knowledge of the normal healing process.

Healthy skin

Activity 4

To help you explore the anatomy and physiology of healthy skin refer to your recommended texts (for example Thibodeau, 1992, pp. 63–78 or Clancy and McVicar, 1995, pp. 505–23). Find out the names and characteristics of each of the two layers of the skin.

The skin (Figure 8.1) is the largest and one of the most important organs in the body, forming the primary organ of the integumentary system, which comprises the:

- Skin
- Hair
- Nails
- Sweat glands
- Sebaceous glands
- Sensory nerve receptors.

Activity 5

The skin plays a key role in the homeostatic management of the internal environment. Compile a list of the functions of the skin. Discuss the relationships between skin structure and function, sun damage and the ageing process.

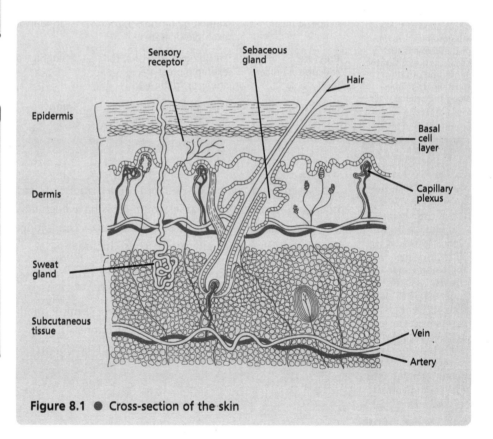

Figure 8.1 ● Cross-section of the skin

The healing process

Normal wound healing is often characterised as a complex, but well-integrated, multiphase process. The phases of this process are usually described separately to facilitate understanding, but it is important to remember that there may be evidence of the different phases of healing within the same wound and that each phase overlaps with the next, often running concurrently. The healing process can be reversed or become static in certain circumstances.

The phases of wound healing

Four main phases have been identified.

Haemostasis

Haemostasis involves wound contraction, which decreases the surface area of the wound, thus reducing bleeding and exposure to contaminants. This process is part of the physiological response to blood extravasation. Released platelets activate the kinin system and release platelet-derived growth factor (PDGF), which stimulates tissue regeneration. Chemical mediators (histamine, adenosine triphosphate and serotonin) attract leukocytes to the injured area by a process called chemotaxis. Healing then progresses.

Inflammatory phase

This phase occurs over 4–5 days and is initiated by the release of prostaglandins, which cause vasodilatation. An inflammatory fluid (infiltrate) containing mast cells, polymorphonuclear leukocytes and lymphocytes (Van Der Kerkhof *et al.*, 1994), then bathes the injured area.

The primary functions of this phase are:

- To cleanse the area of debris: Monocytes enter the area and transform into activated macrophages. These cells clear the debris through phagocytosis.
- To combat potential infective organisms: Neutrophils are activated in the inflammatory response and clear the site of contaminating organisms. This process is augmented by the phagocytic action of the macrophages.
- To initiate angiogenesis (the generation of new blood vessels) and collagen synthesis: Macrophages stimulate the production of angiogenic growth factors such as interleukin. This process, augmented by the activity of mast cells, initiates endothelial division and angiogenesis as well as the regrowth of sympathetic nerve fibres. Fibroblasts migrate to the wound site, initiating the early stages of the next phase.

Proliferative phase

This phase of the wound healing process occurs over a variable time span and

---

extravasation

the leakage of fluid from a blood vessel

kinins

polypeptides present in the blood following tissue injury

chemotaxis

move towards or away from a chemical stimulus

prostaglandins

hormone-like substances that affect vasomotor and smooth muscle tone, capillary permeability, platelet aggregation, endocrine and exocrine functions and the nervous system

angiogenesis

the production/growth of new blood vessels

collagen synthesis

the production of supportive, protein-based, fibrous connective tissue

granulation tissue

red, moist, fragile connective tissue that is characteristic of the proliferative phase of the healing process

is characterised by the formation of granulation tissue. The fibroblasts produce a framework of collagen fibres that support and sustain the products of angiogenesis. The framework is anchored by fibronectin and bathed in proteoglycans. The successful progress of this phase is dependent upon the oxygen and nutrient supply.

Fibroblast activity is sensitive to oxygen supply, which in turn depends upon the vascularity of the wound and surrounding tissues. The growth of capillary buds from undamaged microvessels, forming a network of loops within the wound, is crucial to the level of oxygen supply available during the proliferative phase.

Protein provides the source of the 20 amino acids present in the body (see Chapter 4). These amino acids are described as the building blocks of organic tissue and as such are essential for collagen synthesis, angiogenesis and cell reconstruction (Wells, 1994). If the blood protein levels (measured by serum albumin) are low, wound healing will be impaired.

Essential fatty acids, provided by dietary fat intake, play an important role in cell structure and function. Dietary fat intake is also the largest source of energy, required for wound healing, as well as providing a source of fat-soluble vitamins.

Carbohydrate, in the form of glucose, is the primary energy substrate required for cellular metabolism. If glucose from carbohydrate is unavailable, amino acids will be oxidised to meet the energy requirements of the wound healing process, thus depleting the amino acids available for reconstruction and tissue repair.

hydroxylation

the formation/addition of a hydroxyl (OH) group

Vitamin C is involved in the metabolism of many amino acids and is required for the formation of cross-linking collagen fibres, facilitating the hydroxylation of proline and lysine to hydroxyproline and hydroxylysine – essential components of collagen (Lewis and Harding, 1993). Iron (as well as providing the primary component of haemoglobin, which facilitates the transport of oxygen in the bloodstream) is a co-factor in this process. Vitamin C also enhances wound healing by scavenging potentially harmful free radicals from the surfaces of cells. It has been suggested that the antioxidant vitamin E interacts in this process (Davis et al., 1991).

free radicals

unstable, highly reactive compounds containing an unpaired electron or proton

The B vitamins are involved in enzymatic activity (as co-factors) and are also active in collagen cross-linkage, as is vitamin A, which also acts upon cell surface glycoproteins, effecting epithelial cell proliferation and migration. Zinc is another co-factor in the enzymatic activity associated with collagen and protein synthesis and cell growth. The enzyme lysyl oxidase, instrumental in scar formation, contains copper, a trace element. Many enzymes not only contain, but also rely on, manganese as a co-factor in collagen synthesis, and calcium is a mediator for the enzymes involved in the remodelling of collagen (collagenases).

Two other major processes occur concurrently within the proliferative phase of wound healing – epithelialisation and contraction. The granulation tissue filling the wound bed is gradually resurfaced by epithelial cells, which migrate in from the wound margins or may regenerate as 'islands' on the wound surface. As epithelial cells regenerate and migrate over the wound surface, their eventual contact with one another inhibits further migration, and the epithelialisation process is complete. The process of contraction, initiated in the inflammatory phase, is largely controlled by the activity of myofibroblasts. These specialised fibroblasts contain actin and myosin fibrils (the essential contractile components of muscle tissue), and their activity reduces the surface area of the wound.

Granulation, contraction and epithelialisation mark the completion of the proliferative phase.

Maturation phase

This final phase in the wound healing process is concerned with the remodelling and strengthening of the collagen fibres within the wound. The collagen produced during earlier stages is relatively soft, type III collagen, which has been afforded structural strength through cross-linking of the fibres. During maturation, this is replaced with stronger type I collagen, which is organised into bundles lying at right angles to the wound margins. This ongoing process, facilitated by the activity of fibroblasts and characterised by a gradual reduction in vascularity of the wound site, shrinkage and paling of the scar tissue, can continue over a number of years.

Modes of healing

It is common to refer to the healing process as occurring by one of two modes: primary intention or secondary intention.

Healing by primary intention

healing by primary intention

healing occurring in wounds where the skin edges can be apposed so that there is no scar or granulation tissue

Healing by primary intention refers to wounds where there has been no tissue loss and the skin edges can be brought together, ensuring an absence of dead space in the wound. The four phases of wound healing occur, but there is little granulation tissue produced and minimal wound contraction, epithelial cells migrating along the suture line. Remodelling of the collagen fibres in scar tissue takes place, as previously described, taking 6 months to a year to regain 70–90 per cent of the tensile strength of normal tissue.

Healing by secondary intention

healing by secondary intention

healing in which the edges of the wound are separated, requiring granulation tissue to fill the gap

Healing by secondary intention refers to wounds where there has been tissue loss and the skin edges remain apart. Again, the wound will progress through all four phases of healing, but it will be necessary for the wound bed to fill with granulation tissue, to become resurfaced with epithelium and to contract before and during scar formation.

Reference is sometimes made to an additional mode of healing – healing by

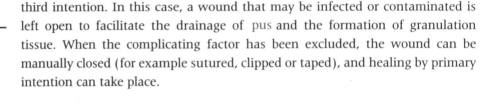

pus
_____
characteristic fluid
composed of exudate,
dead tissue debris,
macrophages and
bacteria

third intention. In this case, a wound that may be infected or contaminated is left open to facilitate the drainage of pus and the formation of granulation tissue. When the complicating factor has been excluded, the wound can be manually closed (for example sutured, clipped or taped), and healing by primary intention can take place.

Activity 6

Consider Figure 8.2. Try to explain how each factor affects wound healing and note how they are interrelated. Now read Chapters 4 and 5 of Bale and Jones, 1997. Try to identify how the factors affecting wound healing are reflected in the nursing care of infants, children and adolescents, and how this may differ from the nursing care of the adult.

Factors affecting wound healing

Wounds do not occur in isolation, and care must be taken to complete a holistic assessment. Initial and subsequent assessments should aim to identify any existing or potential problems that will adversely affect wound healing. The numerous factors to be considered during assessment are illustrated in Figure 8.2.

By reviewing each element in Figure 8.2 and discussing these, where possible, with patients and/or their carers, the nurse will be able to develop an effective care strategy for wound management.

Complications

There are occasions when the wound healing process is interrupted and healing does not progress as anticipated. Commonly observed complications in the wound healing process include the following.

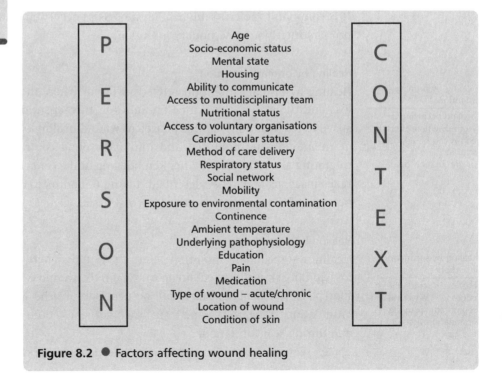

Figure 8.2 ● Factors affecting wound healing

Infection

Normal bacterial colonisation of a wound will not affect the healing process. However, overwhelming numbers, resulting in a clinical infection, interfere with the healing process by 'locking' the wound into a persistent inflammatory phase. This is characterised by localised heat, pain, cellulitis and an increase in exudate (often purulent in nature).

Dehiscence

dehiscence

the separation of a surgical incision or wound

'Dehiscence' is the term used to refer to the 'splitting' open of a closed surgical wound. If the collagen fibres laid down are not strong enough to withstand the internal and external tensions applied to the wound, the newly formed layers of the wound will separate. Dehiscence of a wound is often associated with infection and/or the presence of a haematoma.

Haematoma

haematoma

a collection of blood trapped within the skin or an organ

Haematoma is the name given to a localised 'pocket' of blood and plasma, which can become a breeding ground for bacteria.

Haemorrhage

Primary haemorrhage (severe blood loss during surgery) and intermediary haemorrhage (severe blood loss immediately following surgery) can affect wound strength by interfering with the function of fibroblasts. Secondary haemorrhage (blood loss up to 10 days postoperatively) commonly results in haematoma formation and subsequent infection.

Abnormal healing

hypertrophic scarring

scarring caused by excessive formation of new tissue

keloid scarring

the overgrowth of collagenous scar tissue infiltrating the surrounding skin

Abnormal healing is characterised by abnormalities in scar tissue formation and includes:

- *Hypertrophic scarring*, common in young patients. A large amount of scar tissue is laid down along the incision line, resulting in a raised, fibrous wound site.
- *Keloid scarring*: This is more common in patients with heavily pigmented skin. Again, large amounts of scar tissue is laid down, but in this case the scar tissue infiltrates the skin surrounding the wound site, resulting in large, bulbous growths over and around the wound site.
- *Contractures*: Hypercontraction of the wound during the maturation phase can result in excessive shortening of associated muscle tissue, which, combined with the presence of fibrous scar tissue, inhibits muscular extension.
- *Malignant disease*: Because of the intense cellular activity within a wound, there is the potential for chronic wounds to undergo malignant change. Failure to heal, over an extended period of time, could be associated with such a process.

Activity
7

Can you think of certain measures that could be taken to prevent any of the complications of healing? Discuss your ideas with your colleagues.

The Optimum Environment for Healing

It can be seen, from the preceding sections, that the healing process is not only complex, but also vulnerable to interference from internal and external factors. Our natural instinct, when dealing with vulnerability, is to protect. The efforts that have been made to protect wounds and promote healing have been recorded throughout history (Bale and Jones, 1997, pp. 50–3).

One glance through a hospital formulary, a look around a modern treatment room or indeed an inspection of the contents of a district nurse's car boot will give an indication of the numerous products currently available to facilitate wound management. Such an array can create a certain amount of confusion when deciding which product will be best suited to which wound. In order to avoid this situation, it is worth remembering that although the characteristics of an 'ideal dressing' have been described (Morgan, 1994), few, if any, of the dressings available can conform to every criterion. The choice of dressing material used is only *one element* in creating the optimum environment for wound healing. The other factors affecting wound healing must be taken into account as well.

Thus the optimum environment at the wound/dressing interface would be:

- *Moist*: research conducted over 30 years ago indicated that re-epithelialisation was enhanced when a moist environment was maintained, both within the wound bed and at the wound/dressing interface. This means that the body must be well hydrated and should not have suffered an extensive loss of skin.
- *Protected from bacterial contamination*: the wound requires a physical barrier, and thought must be given to potential sources of infection.
- *Protected from particulate or toxic contamination*: Again, a physical barrier is required, and the environment must be assessed for potential risks.
- *Thermally insulated*: The wound healing process is affected by any variation in the temperature of the wound bed (Morgan, 1994). Not only should any dressing used maintain a stable temperature, but practices such as frequent, unnecessary exposure of the wound, the use of unwarmed cleansing solutions and changes in the ambient environmental temperature must also be assessed.
- *Free from excess exudate*: Although a moist environment is considered to be conducive to wound healing, excess wound exudate (containing micro-organisms and wound debris) will interfere with the healing process, causing wound bed oedema. It will also leak on to the surrounding skin, resulting in the maceration of healthy tissue, as well as providing a potential entry portal for infective organisms.
- *Well perfused*: Gaseous exchange takes place at the wound/dressing interface. A good blood supply will ensure that the oxygen demands of the wound are

wound exudate

a translucent, yellow-tinged fluid, rich in proteins and antibodies, which is produced during the inflammatory phase of the healing process

Activity

8

Find a copy of Morgan (1994) or your pharmacy department's formulary of wound management products. Notice that the dressings listed are divided into groups, for example hydrocolloids. Identify the particular characteristics for as many groups as you can and compare them with the elements described in the text. See if you can identify an example (by trade name) for each group.

met, as well as transporting nutrients to, and removing waste products from, the wound site.

- *Protected from mechanical damage*: Neophyte epithelial cells are extremely delicate and can be easily removed during dressing changes (especially if the dressing material adheres to the wound surface or the surface is rubbed during wound cleansing). Experiments have shown that these cells can also be damaged by the use of certain wound cleansing solutions such as hypochlorite (Leaper, 1996). Thus the environment must be assessed for potential hazards that could cause further trauma.

- *Undisturbed*: Frequent dressing changes, however 'wound environmentally friendly' the dressing is, will interfere with the healing process.

As well as promoting the optimum environment for wound healing, the 'ideal dressing' should be cost-effective, performing in such a way as to maximise the achievement of treatment objectives, and be readily available in both hospital and community settings.

Care Planning in Wound Management

As you will have discovered from working through Chapter 1, one of the most effective methods available for designing a programme of care interventions is the nursing process. The five stages of the nursing process will form the framework for a systematic and holistic review of nursing care, based around a problem-solving approach. One of the benefits of undertaking a systematic approach such as this is that you will be able to demonstrate clearly through documentation not only the decision-making processes involved in designing care interventions, but also – and most importantly – the effectiveness of those interventions.

A good way of exploring care planning in detail is to use a client profile. The profile described in Casebox 8.1 will form the basis for a detailed analysis of care planning in wound management.

Assessment and nursing diagnosis

Morison (1991) suggests that a holistic assessment should form the foundation of any wound management programme. This is an essential nursing activity, and the role of the nurse is to collate and manage the information gathered during assessment in order to generate nursing diagnoses and inform subsequent decision-making. You will recall that the skills required to gather information (see Chapter 1) include:

- Listening
- Observing

Casebox 8.1

Mrs Rosen is a 74-year-old widow and a bilateral amputee with a past medical history of severe arterial disease and non-insulin dependent diabetes mellitus. She lives in a residential home and maintains regular contact with her two children and their families. Mrs Rosen is able to get around independently, using her wheelchair. She is a sociable, chatty lady who enjoys the company of others. Mrs Rosen normally smokes 40–60 cigarettes a day.

She has been admitted to hospital for management of the pressure ulcers that have developed over her ischial tuberosities. On admission to hospital, she appears relaxed and eager to find out about her new surroundings. She is wearing a urine drainage bag on her leg, and this is attached to a urinary catheter. As the ambulance crew transfer Mrs Rosen into bed, she winces several times but quickly regains her composure. There is a damp patch where she has been sitting on the ambulance trolley.

Mrs Rosen sets about organising her belongings; she has a large assortment of sweets, biscuits and fizzy drinks as well as her toiletries, cigarettes and lighter. She moves around the bed with ease, reaching over to pull the locker and table nearer. Having made herself comfortable, she calls the nurse over, apparently eager to do anything she can to assist in the admission process.

---

ischial tuberosities

the bony protuberances present on the ischium (the curved bone which forms the base of each half of the pelvis), commonly known as 'the sitting bones'

Activity 9

Using the information presented in Casebox 8.1, write an assessment of Mrs Rosen and identify any actual or potential problems using the assessment framework in the text.

- Using verbal and non-verbal communication
- Questioning
- Physical examination
- Measurement.

In order to design a comprehensive wound management programme for Mrs Rosen, it will be necessary to review each of the following assessment criteria, identifying any actual or potential problems and stating the related nursing diagnoses. The wound management assessment criteria (adapted from Hallett, 1995) are:

- General physical condition
- Mental state
- Mobility
- Nutritional status
- Continence
- Concurrent disease
- Cardiovascular status
- Pain
- Skin
- Risk assessment.

You will probably have identified the problems described below.

General physical condition

Although Mrs Rosen has a degree of disability associated with bilateral amputation of her legs, she demonstrates a high level of independence. She does not appear to have any difficulty breathing, either at rest or on exertion. She does not appear to show any signs of malaise. There is insufficient information, *at this stage*, to identify problems.

Mental function

Mrs Rosen is alert and appears orientated. She appears to be keen to participate and initiates conversation with the nursing staff. She is aware of her immediate needs and takes steps to meet them independently. No actual or potential problem has been identified.

Mobility

Mrs Rosen's mobility is limited. She is confined to a wheelchair when out of bed but can move herself around the bed using her upper body. She cannot transfer from one surface to another independently.

Actual problems
- Mrs Rosen will be subject to unrelieved pressure while sitting in her wheelchair.
- Mrs Rosen will be subject to additional pressure while in bed.
- Mrs Rosen is unable to transfer independently.

Potential problems
- Mrs Rosen could experience fatigue because of the effort she puts into moving around the bed, and this may lead to unrelieved pressure while in bed.
- Mrs Rosen may lose her balance while moving around in bed, and this may result in injury.
- Mrs Rosen may have a reduced ability to manoeuvre her wheelchair because of unfamiliar surroundings.
- There is a risk of injury (to either Mrs Rosen or the staff) while facilitating movement/manual handling.

Nutritional status

Mrs Rosen is a non-insulin dependent diabetic who appears to have a very sweet tooth! The presence of wounds means that she requires additional protein and vitamins in her diet to effect wound healing.

Actual problems
- Mrs Rosen has an undesirable sugar intake.
- Mrs Rosen has enhanced protein, vitamin and mineral requirements.

Potential problems
- Mrs Rosen may develop poor diabetic control.
- Mrs Rosen may display delayed wound healing.

Continence

Mrs Rosen appears to suffer from urinary incontinence, indicated by the presence of an indwelling urinary catheter. However, it would also appear that the catheter is leaking.

Actual problems
- Mrs Rosen has urinary incontinence, managed by the use of an indwelling urinary catheter.
- The catheter seems to be leaking.
- Mrs Rosen is unable to get to the toilet independently.

Potential problems
- Mrs Rosen is at risk of developing a urinary tract infection.
- There may be trauma associated with the presence of a catheter.
- Mrs Rosen may suffer skin excoriation from leakage of urine.
- Mrs Rosen's wound may be contaminated by leaking urine.
- Mrs Rosen may suffer from constipation as a result of immobility.
- Mrs Rosen may experience faecal incontinence due to immobility, which will result in wound contamination and psychological distress.

Concurrent disease

Mrs Rosen suffers from non-insulin dependent diabetes mellitus. No actual problems have been identified.

Potential problems
- Mrs Rosen may develop poor control of her diabetes because of her dietary sugar intake.
- Impaired wound healing is associated with diabetes.

Cardiovascular status

Mrs Rosen has severe arterial disease, which has led to the amputation of both her legs. She is also a heavy smoker, with no apparent intention of giving up. This will further compromise her cardiovascular system.

Actual problems

- Arterial disease means impaired blood flow to wound sites and impaired healing. Mrs Rosen is a smoker. Smoking exacerbates the effects of cardio-vascular disease as well as being a causative factor for it. It is also a health and safety hazard while Mrs Rosen is in hospital.

Potential problems

- Mrs Rosen may suffer withdrawal symptoms if she reduces or eliminates her nicotine intake.
- Further deterioration of her cardiovascular system will lead to multisystem failure.

Pain

Although Mrs Rosen has not verbally complained of any pain, her facial expression during manual handling indicated that she may have experienced pain.

Actual problems

- Mrs Rosen is not voicing her experience of pain.
- Pain will cause a stress reaction that will interfere with the healing process.

Potential problems

- Mrs Rosen, although she appears cheerful and talkative, may be frightened.
- Mrs Rosen may be reluctant to cause a fuss.
- It may be difficult to assess the level and nature of Mrs Rosen's pain and the effectiveness of any interventions.
- Increasing pain may further limit Mrs Rosen's mobility.

Skin

Mrs Rosen has pressure sores over her ischial tuberosities. It is unclear how many wounds are present or what their status is. There is insufficient information to describe any problems at this stage.

Risk assessment

Mrs Rosen has been admitted with pressure injuries and is therefore at risk of developing additional injuries. However, there is insufficient information to complete a full risk assessment at this stage.

Activity 10

Imagine that you are Mrs Rosen's named nurse and are conducting her initial assessment as part of the admission process. Think carefully about how you can augment the information already gathered from the patient profile. Review your assessment and identify any additional information required, specifying how you would obtain this.

cyanosis

the blue tinge that appears in the skin and/or mucous membranes when the blood oxygen supply is diminished

You may be surprised at how much information can be gathered from the careful reading of a client profile. However, certain areas require clarification so that problem identification can be refined and accurate nursing diagnoses made. You will now need to use the other skills of enquiry, taking into account the factors affecting wound healing described in Figure 8.2, to enhance the data you have already gathered.

Now tackle Activity 10. Your answer may include the following:

General physical condition
You will want to know more about Mrs Rosen's respiratory status. Does she have a cough or wheeze? Are there any signs of cyanosis? Has Mrs Rosen recently suffered from any chest infections? Does she have a history of respiratory disease? What is her general state of well-being?

You will need to use the skills of observation, questioning, listening and physical examination. Your sources of information are likely to be Mrs Rosen's:

- Verbal responses
- Non-verbal responses
- Vital signs, measurements of blood pressure, respiratory rate and depth, pulse rate and rhythm and body temperature.

You may also gather additional information from her:

- Previous medical and nursing notes
- Relatives and carers.

Mental function
Although Mrs Rosen appears to be adjusting well to the situation, you will need to *observe* and *listen* carefully to detect any signs of distress or disorientation. Be aware of the reactions of visitors: are they at all concerned about Mrs Rosen's behaviour?

Mobility
It is necessary to assess the extent of Mrs Rosen's mobility and identify what types of aid to mobility/manual handling may be required. A thorough assessment of mobility can only be effected by direct observation of Mrs Rosen over a period of time (minimum 24 hours) and will need to be repeated regularly. This will also involve questioning.

Your sources of information will include:

- Mrs Rosen
- Members of the nursing and multidisciplinary team
- Staff at the residential care home
- Mrs Rosen's district nurse.

Continence

You will need to establish why a urinary catheter is in situ and how long Mrs Rosen has had a catheter. You will also need to establish whether the catheter is leaking and try to ascertain the cause. Additionally, it will be necessary to find out whether there is infection present and whether the catheter is causing Mrs Rosen discomfort. In order to promote continence and prevent constipation, you will need to establish Mrs Rosen's normal bowel habit. This assessment, like the others, will be ongoing and will rely on your skills of observation, questioning, listening, measuring and recording.

Your main source of information here is Mrs Rosen's:

- Verbal responses
- Physical signs and symptoms: cloudy and/or offensive urine, which on urinalysis may show proteinuria or haematuria; pain, discomfort or retention of urine (see Chapter 5).

Additional information can be gained by liaising with the staff at the residential care home, thus building up a complete picture of Mrs Rosen in her normal environment.

Nutritional status

It will be useful to establish how much sugary food Mrs Rosen consumes and how often. Try to find out how much she understands about diet and diabetes. You could ask Mrs Rosen if she can remember what she has eaten over the past 24 hours and what her favourite foods are. You will also need to establish whether Mrs Rosen is underweight, overweight or obese. It is also vital to know whether there is a degree of protein energy malnutrition; this can be established by investigating serum albumin levels (see Chapter 4). You will use the skills of questioning, listening, observation, measuring and recording.

Sources of information will include:

- Mrs Rosen
- Her family
- Carers in the community
- The results of medical investigations such as blood tests.

Concurrent disease

In order to enhance your information relating to Mrs Rosen's diabetes, it will be necessary to establish a pattern of blood glucose levels over a period of time, starting with a baseline level on admission. You will also need to know whether Mrs Rosen is excreting glucose in her urine. It is important to establish whether she is taking any medication to control the diabetes and whether this has been taken regularly, as prescribed.

Cardiovascular status

The extent of any arterial disease present and Mrs Rosen's understanding of her condition and prognosis should be clarified. You will need to establish the possibility of negotiating a reduction in the number of cigarettes she smokes. Is she willing to give them up for a trial period? How does she feel about this? Your ability to question, listen and observe will be vital in gaining accurate information from:

- Mrs Rosen
- Medical colleagues
- Medical notes
- Carers in the community.

Pain

You will need to establish whether Mrs Rosen is experiencing pain and, if so, its nature, intensity, location, duration and precipitating factors (for example, movement or wound dressing changes). You will need to ascertain her feelings about pain control and prevention (see Chapter 1).

Skin

Assess the quality of the skin in terms of hydration, thickness, elasticity and integrity. Establish exactly how and where the integrity of the skin has been breached, assessing each wound individually and recording:

- *Wound site*: anatomical location
- *Wound dimensions*: diameter or length/width and depth
- *Pressure sore grading*: a numerical value given to pressure sores relating to their severity (Reid, 1994)
- *Wound bed status*: the percentage of wound bed occupied by necrotic tissue (eschar), slough, granulation tissue and epithelial tissue. You may also aim to establish which stage of wound healing is apparent (although this is not always possible)
- *Exudate*: Are levels high, medium or low? Are they increasing or decreasing? Is the exudate purulent or bloodstained?
- *Infection*: Are there any signs or symptoms to indicate wound infection?
- Surrounding skin: Is it intact? Well perfused? Macerated? Inflamed? Eczematous?
- Expected *mode of healing*.

necrotic

dead, devitalised

eschar

dead tissue, characterised by its dry, crusty, black appearance, which adheres to the wound bed

slough

shed dead tissue resulting from injury or inflammation

maceration

the softening and detexturising of tissues due to prolonged exposure to moistness

Risk assessment

Use a risk assessment tool to provide a framework for professional judgement in assessing the level of risk of pressure injury to Mrs Rosen. The initial risk assessment must be completed as soon as possible after admission so that preventative

Activity 11

Try to locate the quality standard(s) for the prevention and management of pressure injury in your workplace. How many of these assessment criteria are reflected within them? Discuss your findings with your colleagues.

measures can be taken. Some areas have particular quality standards relating to the prevention and management of pressure injury, and these will often specify the timeframe within which risk assessment should take place.

Assessment in wound management can be summarised thus:

- Assessment is an ongoing process.
- The nursing diagnosis is arrived at via an assessment.
- The role of the nurse is to gather sufficient information to facilitate the identification of actual and potential problems, to formulate a nursing diagnosis and to provide the knowledge base for planning care interventions.
- The client is recognised as the primary source of information and is involved in information-sharing.
- Secondary sources of information include relatives, carers, friends, other members of the multidisciplinary team, documentation and electronically stored data.
- The primary aim is to assess the client and his environment (local and general) in terms of conduciveness to wound healing.
- The secondary aim is to establish and record wound status, including any factors that may complicate or impair the healing process.
- A risk assessment should form part of the process.

Planning nursing care in wound management

Activity 12

Review your assessment and nursing diagnoses for Mrs Rosen. Select one of the actual problems identified and discuss how care may be planned by explaining how each nursing intervention will affect wound healing, and identifying which other members of the multidisciplinary team may be involved.

Having made a thorough assessment using the previously described criteria and developing a series of nursing diagnoses for Mrs Rosen, you will now be ready to enter the planning stage of the nursing process.

The two stages of planning have been described in Chapter 1, and within the field of wound management, it is important to ensure that, wherever possible, you involve the client in:

- Identifying the broad aim(s) of nursing care in the wound management plan
- Setting specific objectives
- Devising the appropriate intervention
- Identifying other members of the multidisciplinary team who can provide input for care planning.

You will now be starting to understand the complexity of nursing care in wound management. The interventions that relate directly to the wound itself form only one part of a range of activities that are vital to support wound management. However, it is useful to describe and analyse a specific plan of nursing care for the direct management of one of Mrs Rosen's pressure injuries.

Chart 8.2 describes her wound status on admission to hospital. It is now possible to design a nursing care plan for management of this wound, based

Chart 8.2 ● Wound status

Wound 1

- Cavity wound, located over left ischial tuberosity
- Diameter 6 cm, depth 6 cm
- Pressure sore grading of 4.0 (Reid and Morison, 1994; UK consensus of pressure sore severity) – full thickness skin loss with extensive destruction and tissue necrosis, extending to underlying bone, tendon or joint capsule
- Wound bed composed of 70 per cent slough, 30 per cent eschar
- Moderate exudate level
- No signs of clinical infection
- Surrounding skin excoriated and poorly perfused
- Expected mode of healing – secondary intention

upon the assessment of information, and informed by a sound knowledge base in the principles of wound management. Following the previously outlined stages, the care plan will develop as follows.

Identifying the broad aim will be done in conjunction with Mrs Rosen, asking her what she hopes will be the outcome of her period in hospital and carefully establishing how realistic these hopes may be. It will also be necessary to find out the extent to which Mrs Rosen is willing to participate in her care and how keen or reluctant she may be to contribute to certain interventions. In this case, the broad aim may be identified as:

> To create a local environment that will be conducive to and promote wound healing. The expected outcome is that the necrotic tissue will be removed and the formation of granulation tissue will commence.

Specific objectives to be set should be negotiated with Mrs Rosen. They will include:

- Relieving pressure on the wound site
- Cleaning the wound, to encourage the autolysis of necrotic tissue and its removal from the wound bed
- Controlling exudate, to avoid leakage
- Keeping dressing changes to a minimum, changing the dressings only when strike-through or soiling occurs
- Protecting the surrounding skin to prevent further breakdown.

Next, *appropriate interventions* should be devised. Having already established that each objective is a statement of intention, or 'what we want to do', the next

autolysis

the natural breakdown of dead, or foreign, organic material

step involves designing nursing interventions, or 'how we are going to do it'. This can be done by reviewing each objective and:

- Describing the action to be taken
- Identifying the personnel who will be involved
- Identifying the equipment/resources that may be required.

Here is an example:

- Relieving pressure on the wound site (specific objective or 'what we want to do')
- Nursing intervention ('how we are going to do it')
  Action to be taken:
  Install a pressure reduction airwave mattress and wheelchair cushion
  Encourage Mrs Rosen to move from side to side while in bed
  Mrs Rosen to agree to participate and use the prescribed equipment
  Personnel involved:
  Named nurse
  Mrs Rosen
  Equipment officer
  Physiotherapist
  Equipment/resources required:
  Airwave mattress and cushion
  Trapeze pole.

Activity 13

Work through this activity with the support of your clinical assessor/supervisor. Select any one of Mrs Rosen's other specific objectives and, following the framework illustrated in the example in the text, design a nursing intervention to enable you to meet that objective.

Implementing care

The implementation stage of any wound management plan is critical in that:

- You put your planned care into effect
- You delegate elements of planned care appropriately
- You actively involve the client and other members of the multidisciplinary team
- You record which elements of the care plan have been carried out, when and by whom
- You begin to evaluate *as you implement care*, noting the length of time taken to complete an intervention, the ease with which it was undertaken, the degree to which the client was able (or willing) to participate, any associated teaching, helping or educational activities and any changes that occurred while you were implementing care.

If we examine the implementation of one specific objective in Mrs Rosen's care plan – cleansing the wound and controlling exudate – we can take a step-by-step approach to analysing how this intervention may be implemented:

1. On admission, the dressing in place is found to be unsuitable, that is, it does not conform to any of the criteria for an ideal dressing. It is now necessary to *implement* the planned nursing intervention.

2. The nurse selects the appropriate dressing, documenting the selection and giving a rationale, for example:

   Hydrogel selected to instil into wound bed to rehydrate the wound and promote the removal of necrotic tissue by autolysis.

   Adhesive foam dressing selected to cover hydrogel in the wound bed and absorb excess exudate.

3. The use of the dressing is explained to Mrs Rosen, who has an opportunity to examine the dressing and ask any questions.

4. Mrs Rosen is prepared and made ready for the dressing to be applied. She is encouraged to participate in this in anticipation of future dressing changes. She is also encouraged to make any comments throughout the dressing change (for example, to describe any pain or discomfort, and to suggest ways in which she may assist).

5. The nurse prepares for the dressing change following the aseptic technique (Chart 8.3).

6. The nurse decides that the wound needs to be cleansed to remove any loose debris and particulate matter in the wound bed. An appropriate cleanser is selected and used to irrigate the wound bed (Pudner, 1997).

7. The dressing is applied according to the manufacturer's instructions.

8. The area is cleared. Mrs Rosen is made comfortable and given an opportunity to comment or ask any questions.

9. The episode is documented as soon as possible.

Evaluation of care in wound management

You have already discovered that evaluation is concerned with the effectiveness of nursing interventions. At this stage, it is necessary to pose the series of questions described in Chapter 1.

By focusing and reflecting upon what is happening, both during and after the implementation of a nursing intervention, and then recording your findings, the nursing documentation not only serves as a record of events, but also becomes a dynamic, working tool. The description of interactions between client and nurse will provide additional information. This may lead to:

- Further assessment
- Revisions to planned care.

The key to success in making a care plan a 'working' document is your ability to evaluate the effectiveness of the nursing interventions you have designed. In the management of wounds you will need to:

Activity 14

With your clinical assessor/supervisor, and following the local guidelines for aseptic technique, select a hydrogel and a polyurethane foam dressing from the treatment room of your clinical area. Using the principles outlined in Chart 8.3, prepare everything you would need to implement the wound dressing element of Mrs Rosen's care plan.

Activity
15

Consider the wound dressing element of Mrs Rosen's wound management plan. List any possible information you might acquire from Mrs Rosen and your observations. Describe how you might revise the care plan as a result of your findings. Discuss this with your clinical assessor/supervisor.

Activity
16

Undertake an Internet search using the search field 'wound management'. Make a note of: the search engine used (how efficient was it?) and the search field (how productive was it?). Did you need to widen/reduce it? Post your findings on the student notice board and invite comments.

Chart 8.3 ● The principles of aseptic technique

Aseptic technique is a method of carrying out procedures in an environment that is rendered as free from micro-organisms and contaminants as possible. Bree-Williams and Waterman (1996) suggest that this may be achieved by:

- Effective hand decontamination – cleansing (using soap and water, followed by thorough drying) and disinfecting (using a chemical disinfectant or antiseptic solution, followed by drying)
- Creating a sterile field – using a sterilised surface
- The exclusive use of sterilised equipment
- Ensuring that the outer wrappings of sterilised equipment do not come into contact with either the sterile contents or the sterile field
- Using a 'no-touch' (forceps) or sterile-gloved handling technique
- Being aware of sources of contamination (used dressings, bodily contact – especially clothes, skin and hair – contact with non-sterile surfaces, contact with body fluids and aerosol contamination)
- Avoiding the introduction of contaminants into the sterile field
- The safe disposal of contaminants, away from the sterile field
- Achieving competency in aseptic technique, in accordance with evidence-based policy guidelines

- Review the factors affecting wound healing and evaluate the prescribed nursing interventions.
- Review the wound status and evaluate the prescribed nursing interventions.

● Chapter Summary

The effective nursing management of wounds is a complex area of activity involving integrated and systematic assessment, the identification of problems, the generation of nursing diagnoses, and the planning, implementation and evaluation of nursing interventions. This chapter has given you an overview of elements that underpin the principles of the nursing management of wounds, highlighting the importance of ongoing, evidence-based education to inform decision-making in practice, the value of reflection as a way of evaluating your experiences, the varied nature and assortment of tools, frameworks and guidelines available to assist in making a professional judgement and the central role of the nurse in managing care.

Test Yourself!

1. What are the different accountability relationships within which professional practitioners are required to discharge their duty of care to the client?

2. What do you understand by the term 'wound'?

3. How may wounds be classified?

4. What different types of risk assessment may be undertaken?

5. The skin is the primary organ of the integumentary system, what are its components?

6. What are the four main phases of wound healing?

7. The factors affecting wound healing have been described in terms of the *person* and the *context* in which they exist. How many of these factors can you describe?

8. What are the elements required to provide the optimum environment for wound healing?

9. What are the assessment criteria for wound management?

10. What is the purpose of a nursing care plan in wound management?

11. What do you understand by the term 'aseptic technique'?

12. What do you need to consider when you are evaluating nursing care in wound management?

Addresses of Professional Associations

The Tissue Viability Society
c/o Wessex Rehabilitation Association
Odstock Hospital
Salisbury, Wilts SP2 8BJ
Tel: (01722) 336262 ext. 2392

The Wound Care Society
PO Box 263
Northampton NN3 4UJ
Tel: (01604) 784696

The European Wound Management Association
PO Box 864
London SE1 8TT
Tel: 0171-872 3496
e-mail: ewma@kcl.ac.uk

European Tissue Repair Society
Wound Healing Institute
Department of Dermatology
Churchill Hospital
Old Road
Headington
Oxford OX3 7LJ
Tel: (01865) 228264

References

Allison, J. (1995) The effect of continuing education on practical wound management. *Journal of Wound Care* **4**(1): 29–31.

Bale, S. and Jones, V. (1997) *Wound Care Nursing: A Patient Centred Approach*. Baillière Tindall, London.

Bree-Williams, F.J. and Waterman, H. (1996) An examination of nurses' practice when performing aseptic technique for wound dressings. *Journal of Advanced Nursing* **23**: 48–54.

Carpenter, D. (1993) Key working and primary nursing: accountability and professional practice. In Giddey, M. and Wright, H. (eds) *Mental Health Nursing. From First Principles to Professional Practice*, pp. 353–63. Chapman & Hall, London.

Clancy, J. and McVicar, A. (1995) *Physiology and Anatomy: a Homeostatic Approach*. Edward Arnold, London.

Cullum, N. and Dealey, C. (1996) Presentation given to the all party group on skin at the House of Commons. *Journal of Tissue Viability* **6**(1): 20–3.

Davis, M.B., Austin, J. and Partridge, D.A. (1991) *Vitamin C. Its Chemistry and Biochemistry*. Royal Society of Chemists, Cambridge.

DoH (Department of Health) (1991) *The Patient's Charter*. HMSO, London.

Edwards, M. (1995) Healing Practices. *Nursing Times* **91**(11): 62–4.

Hallett, A. (1995) *Guidelines for Practice: Prevention and Management of Pressure Sores*. Portsmouth Health Care NHS Trust, Portsmouth.

Leaper, D. (1996) Antiseptics in wound healing. *Nursing Times* **92**(39): 63–8.

Lewis, B.K. and Harding, K.G. (1993) Nutritional intake and wound healing in elderly people. *Journal of Wound Care* **2**(4): 227–9.

Marks-Maran, D. (1993) Accountability. In Tschudin, V. (ed.) *Ethics, Nurses and Patients*, pp. 121–34. Scutari Press, London.

Morgan, D.A. (1994) *The Formulary of Wound Management Products*. Euromed Communications, Haslemere.

Morison, M. (1991) *A Colour Guide to the Nursing Management of Wounds*. Wolfe Publishing, London.

Nelson, E.A. (1977) Consensus statements. *Journal of Woundcare* **6**(3): 107.

Norton, D., McLaren, R. and Exton-Smith, A.N. (1975) *An Investigation of Geriatric Nursing Problems in Hospital*. Churchill Livingstone, Edinburgh.

Plummer, E.S. and Albert, S.G. (1995) Footcare assessment in patients with diabetes: a screening algorithm for patient education and referral. *Diabetes Educator* **21**(1): 47–51

Pudner, R. (1997) Wound cleansing. *Journal of Community Nursing* **11**(7): 30–6.

Read, J. and Morison, M.A. (1994) Towards a consensus: classification of pressure sores. *Journal of Woundcare* **13**(3): 157–60.

Reid, J. (1994) Towards a consensus: classification of pressure sores. *Journal of Wound Care* **3**(3): 157–60.

Thibodeau, G.A. (1992) *Structure and Function of the Body*, 9th edn. Mosby Yearbook, St Louis.

UKCC (United Kingdom Central Council for Nursing, Midwifery and Health Visiting) (1989) *Exercising Accountability*. UKCC, London.

UKCC (United Kingdom Central Council for Nursing, Midwifery and Health Visiting) (1992) *Code of Professional Conduct*. UKCC, London.

UKCC (United Kingdom Central Council for Nursing, Midwifery and Health Visiting) (1994) *The Future of Professional Practice – The Council's Standards for Education and Practice Following Registration*. UKCC, London.

Van Der Kerkhof, P.C.M., Van Bergen, B. and Spruijt, K. (1994) Age related changes in wound healing. *Clinical and Experimental Dermatology* **19**: 369–74.

Waterlow, J. (1988) Calculating the risk. *Nursing Times* **38**(9): 58–60.

Wells, L. (1994) At the front-line of care. *Professional Nurse* **9**(8): 525–30.

Social Behaviour and Professional Interactions

PHIL RUSSELL

Introduction

This chapter is divided into three sections and is concerned with one-to-one and group interactions. At the end of this chapter, you should be able to:

- Describe the core qualities of therapeutic communication

- Identify six therapeutic interventions and suggest ways in which these might be implemented in your practice

- Describe the difference between primary and secondary groups

- Describe the interdependence of team, task and individual needs

- Discuss the importance of assertiveness to nursing practice

- Describe the process for refusing requests and handling criticism

- Reflect on further areas of study to enhance your own therapeutic communication skills.

The first section of this chapter examines therapeutic communication or the therapeutic use of self. The chapter will start by exploring the meaning of these terms before moving on to ask what sorts of quality are required to enhance communication beyond just conveying information. The last part of this section will examine in more detail some of the tools available to start the process of developing good therapeutic skills that can be used with patients, families and colleagues.

Nurses seldom work in isolation but are more usually part of a team. Groups tend to have their own dynamics, and an understanding of how groups function can help in developing happier and more efficient teamwork. Nurses may work with a variety of diverse groups, for example support groups for patients, therapy groups, commonly found in mental health settings, or families, which form a special kind of group. This section will examine some of the issues important to group dynamics. What constitutes a group? What sort of group are you likely to encounter? What is the role of nurses as group members? What makes effective teams and good leaders?

The third section of this chapter will examine a more specific aspect of inter-action, building on some of the issues raised in the first section. Nurses are at the forefront of care and have an important role in liaising with an extremely wide range of people. In doing so, they sometimes have to deal with difficult situations. This section will examine how, through developing assertiveness, nurses can develop greater self-confidence and work more effectively towards positive working relationships and patient outcomes.

therapeutic

aiding the well-being of an individual

Throughout this chapter, the term 'nurse' will be used for the person who is the provider of the therapeutic communication. The nurse may be from any branch – mental health, learning difficulties or adult nursing. The terms 'client' and 'patient' are often used interchangeably, some branches using the term 'client' more freely than others. To avoid any confusion, the recipient of the ther-apeutic exchange will be referred to as the client.

Finally, this chapter is not intended to be a training manual or a comprehen-sive guide to social interactions. Instead, it offers some signposts on which to base further study, investigation and development.

Therapeutic Communication

therapeutic communication

purposeful communication aimed at enhancing the well-being of an individual

The term 'therapeutic communication' has been chosen in favour of 'interper-sonal skills' or 'counselling'. We all use interpersonal skills all the time whenever we are relating to another person. Sometimes this is constructive, sometimes destructive. To be therapeutic, however, is to aid the well-being of an individual; thus therapeutic communication has the intention of assisting or helping others.

There is evidence to suggest that the communication exchange between nurses and clients, including relatives, is not always as good as it might be (Ley, 1988; Brereton, 1995). There may be many diverse and complex reasons for this. Perhaps the fact that we are all communicating all the time results in a feeling that we do not need to learn how to do something we have been doing all our lives; it seems to be common sense. Perhaps nurses have become complacent about communication. Furthermore, there is a tendency for some nurses to see themselves as people of action rather than words. Many nurses are not comfort-able unless they are 'doing'; this is influenced by the ethos of today's clinical environment and pressures of work. Hewison (1995) found support for the fact that many nurse–client interactions continue to be task orientated, routinised and often superficial.

Nevertheless, nurses do express a desire to communicate well with clients; Buckroyd (1987) found that paediatric nurses wanted to be able to help children in distress but often felt ill equipped to deal with these emotional and difficult interactions. Skilled therapeutic interventions, as Nichols (1989) points out, can minimise the psychological morbidity associated with ill-health, and nurses are ideally placed to provide this kind of care to clients. Therapeutic communication is an essential and central aspect of nursing whichever branch nurses specialise in, and it should not be seen as just the domain of those in mental health settings. Is, then, therapeutic communication the same thing as counselling?

It is difficult to avoid the term 'counselling' when discussing therapeutic communication, but the term 'counselling' has unfortunately become something of a misused term. Indeed, the Oxford dictionary defines counselling as 'to advise, to give advice to people professionally on social problems'. We will look more closely at the notion of advice-giving later in the chapter, but some people, such as financial counsellors or legal counsellors, do just that: they give advice. Other counsellors would never give advice. Some people call themselves counsellors following very brief training, while others undertake years of preparation. According to the British Association for Counselling (BAC):

> The overall aim of counselling is to provide an opportunity for the client to work towards living in a more resourceful way... Counselling may be concerned with developmental issues, addressing and resolving specific problems, making decisions, coping with crisis, developing personal insights and knowledge, working through feelings of inner conflict or improving relationships with others. The counsellor's role is to facilitate the client's work in ways which respect the client's values, personal resources and capacity for self determination. (British Association for Counselling, 1996, para 3.1)

There are, within this statement, some important elements that have significant implications for nursing practice. Nurses will, therefore, be aiming to apply these elements in the care of their clients, regardless of their chosen branch. It might appear from this that nurses are thus engaged in counselling. However, the BAC also states that 'Only when both the user and the recipient agree to enter into a counselling relationship does it become "counselling" rather than the use of "counselling skills"' (British Association for Counselling, 1996, para 3.2). As Burnard (1995a) cautions, counselling and the use of counselling skills are not the same thing. Although they may share many common features, they are different and require a different sort of relationship. Most nurses are engaged in the use of counselling skills rather than counselling, and to avoid confusion, the term 'therapeutic communication' will be used. It is important to stress, however, that although nurses may not by definition be counselling, the outcomes they achieve may be the same, and the value of their contribution should certainly not be underestimated.

This next section will focus primarily on the core qualities that underpin therapeutic communication and some of the skills that can assist in the process and practice of therapeutic communication.

Activity
1

Identify, from the BAC quote, the elements that you feel are important to your chosen branch of nursing. Think of how you might apply these to three or four clients you have had contact with.

Core Qualities

Three particular qualities have been identified as playing an important part in any therapeutic alliance:

1. Empathic understanding
2. Genuineness or congruence
3. Unconditional acceptance.

congruence

a matching between inner feelings and outer behaviour

The requirement for these qualities was first identified in the context of counselling by Carl Rogers, the father of person-centred therapy. Rogers identified these three qualities as being necessary and sufficient to enable constructive personality change (Rogers, 1957). In other words, no other forms of therapeutic intervention are needed. This approach has had a considerable influence on nursing because of the control it gives back to clients, empowering them to make their own decisions and enabling psychological growth. However, nurses are rarely in a position to use these interventions exclusively; to do so risks ignoring many other helpful strategies (Burnard, 1995b). Nevertheless, the three core qualities are considered to be important components in the therapeutic relationship and lay the foundation on which other skills and strategies can be built. They are thus worthy of further explanation.

Empathic understanding

empathic understanding

a capacity to sense accurately the feelings and personal meanings of another person

Empathic understanding is essentially to have a sensitivity for *what* another person is feeling, but not for *how* he or she is feeling. You can never feel exactly the same as other people; their construction of the world will always differ from yours in some way. However, you can be sensitive to what they are feeling and convey this to them in a way that helps them to feel that someone has a valid insight into their world: they feel understood. Rogers (1980) describes empathy as 'a way of being with another person, entering into their world, communicating their sensings'. Nevertheless, it remains a difficult concept to understand and to practise as it is more than just a communication process.

Egan (1994) defines two types of empathy: 'primary empathy' and 'advanced empathy'. The former is a much more straightforward process, although not necessarily simple. It involves listening carefully to what the client is saying and responding in a way that indicates an understanding of what they are saying from their perspective. The latter is a deeper kind of empathy more akin to reading between the lines, picking up not only what the client says, but also what lies behind what is said. As Rogers (1980) suggests, it is 'sensing meanings of which the client is scarcely aware'. It might usefully be compared with being a musician. Some musicians can read the score and play the notes in the correct sequence, but the highly skilled musician sees behind and beyond the notes,

Activity 2

Think of someone you know well. In your mind try to become that person. As that person, write a character sketch of yourself. In other words, try to see yourself through someone else's eyes.

genuineness
_____
the ability to show oneself without putting on a façade

Activity 3

Draw a life line similar to the one in Figure 9.1 and identify the positive and negative influences in your life. Think about how these events have helped to mould and create you, and how they might influence your relationship with your clients.

unconditional acceptance
_____
an attitude that values the worth of another person

understanding the full expression of the music as intended by the composer. Developing these sensitivities appears to come more easily to some than others, but empathic understanding can be enriched with careful reflection on how you respond to clients. What is not required is some sort of phoney understanding. It is important to be genuine with clients.

Genuineness

Genuineness is about being open and honest and is sometimes referred to as congruence or authenticity. This is not to suggest that carers are being dishonest, but it is possible to be deceived about your feelings towards others. The professional mask often worn by nurses can distort the way of being with a client. Genuineness is less to do with telling untruths and more to do with having an openness, an attitude that conveys congruence between what you are thinking and feeling, and what you are saying. It is not hiding behind a uniform or professional role. The very process of professionalisation can result in the taking on of a role that hides the self. Unfortunately, a lack of genuineness can often shine through to clients like a bright light, causing them to withdraw into themselves. Egan (1994) offers some guidance on developing an attitude of genuineness:

- Not overemphasising the helping role, thus avoiding being patronising and condescending
- Being spontaneous: This is not the same as overtly expressing all your present feelings but it does mean not being afraid to express them where appropriate
- Not being defensive: As a nurse, you will not always find you are able to help, but getting to know your own strengths and weaknesses will enable you to be less defensive
- Being open: Where appropriate, do not be afraid to use your own life experience (see Nelson-Jones, 1988, for guidance on appropriate self-disclosure).

Much of being genuine is about having a better understanding of ourselves.

Activity 3 and Figure 9.1 will give you some insight into your own experiences. For example, if you have experienced a loss, this might help you to understand a client better, but it might also make you less tolerant of an angry client who reminds you of your own undealt-with anger.

Unconditional acceptance

Unconditional acceptance or unconditional positive regard is a frequently misunderstood quality. It can appear as though you must like everyone, regardless of what they have or have not done or who they are. Indeed, if you accept

POSITIVE

Started school (5)   Sister born (6)   Happy holiday (11)   Passed A level (16)

- -

Mum in hospital (7)   Had big argument with Dad (12)   Grandparent died (17)

NEGATIVE

Figure 9.1 ● Example of a life line (with age in brackets)

Activity

4

Make a list of clients who might be very difficult to accept because their value system, beliefs or behaviours are very different from your own, for example a drug addict. Think of a client or someone you know whom you do not really like. Write down five positive qualities about that person. Discuss with a colleague how you might better manage working with a client you do not like or whose values and behaviour are opposite to your own.

the statements above about genuineness, then to pretend that you like everyone would mean that you are not being genuine. Unconditional acceptance is about accepting clients as fellow humans entitled to care and respect; this is not the same as liking them as you do your friends, or accepting their behaviour and value systems, which may be at odds with your own. As Mearns (1994) comments, 'Don't confuse unconditional positive regard with liking.' You may not like certain individuals, or their behaviour, but it is not for you to judge them, especially from your position as a carer. Developing the skill of acceptance depends very much on your ability to accept yourself. Fromm (1975) notes that to love others, we must first love ourselves.

None of the above qualities is easy to develop or to execute, although some nurses will find this easier than others. What is of concern is the way in which these qualities are often assumed to exist in an individual just because they have read about them, as if they develop through some osmotic process. They are qualities that take time to develop and must be practised. In reality, they are never fully available to us, so we can only aspire to them. One way to start the process of developing these qualities is to begin reflecting on your interactions with clients and colleagues.

Therapeutic Skills

Heron (1990) has devised a simple but comprehensive model for therapeutic communication referred to as six-category intervention analysis. Within the six primary categories are a wide range of more specific interventions. While the six categories are considered to be exhaustive, the interventions are not and have the capacity for great flexibility. Heron (1990) emphasises that the categories are not a model of counselling but instead a set of analytical and behavioural tools. Many of the interventions are not uniquely identified by Heron, but he provides an effective framework in which all six interventions can be used in one-to-one

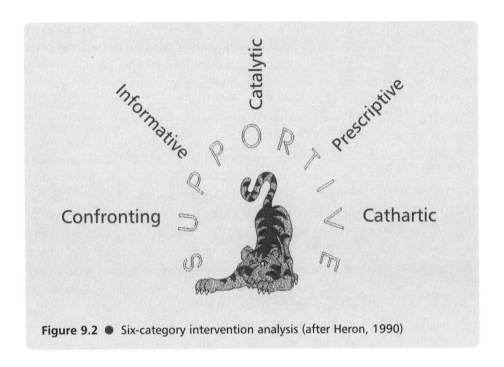

Figure 9.2 ● Six-category intervention analysis (after Heron, 1990)

interactions, including those related to giving information and advice. Figure 9.2 illustrates the six categories.

The first three categories – confronting, informative and prescriptive – are authoritative in that the nurse is taking greater responsibility for guiding the client's responses. The facilitative interventions are catalytic, cathartic and supportive. With facilitative interventions, the authority remains primarily with the client.

No single intervention is more important than another, and none of the interventions seeks to control or take autonomy away from the client. The emphasis is on developing an enabling relationship in which clients can explore their own worlds and make appropriate decisions for themselves.

Catalytic category

catalytic interventions

a set of basic interventions that assist the client with self-discovery and learning

Although there is no hierarchy to the six categories, the catalytic category will be outlined first because it probably contains the most frequently used interventions. Heron describes catalytic interventions in terms of learning and problem-solving. Catalytic interventions enable clients to explore their thoughts and feelings, thus gaining insight and enabling them to be in a better position to make decisions about their future. The skill lies in effective listening and responding in ways that help clients to move on, but at their own pace and with their own agenda. This category requires the nurse to identify which intervention from the toolkit is most appropriate in assisting the client in this explo-ration. The following interventions will be outlined here: listening; simple and selective reflection; paraphrasing; open and closed questions; logical and empathic building; and checking for understanding.

Listening

Before you can listen to others, it is important to give the individual full and free attention. This can be difficult if there is much going on in the immediate envi-ronment and your mind is focused on other issues. Stevens (1971) suggests we have three zones of awareness; a *fantasy zone*, an *inside zone* and an *outside zone*. When your awareness is on fantasy, you are conscious of your thoughts and images; for example, you may be trying to interpret what the person has just said or thinking about your own past or future agendas. When your awareness is inside, you are aware of your own inner sensation. For example, as you sit reading this book, you may be aware of your eyes straining to read the words on the page. With your awareness outside, you are focused on external events, what is going on outside you, such as listening to a client with your attention fully focused on them. If you can learn to distinguish between these zones of aware-ness, it is possible to use them much more effectively, thus keeping your focus out and with the client, fleetingly changing the focus to fantasy to check out your own thoughts and occasionally being aware of your own internal sensations.

One way in which you can demonstrate your attention and interest in clients is by giving them quality time. Even if this is only a couple of minutes, that time can be devoted to the client as quality time rather than being a rushed and haphazard event distracted by your surroundings and what is going on in your head. This, of course, takes practice, but giving quality time to others is one of the most important skills you can offer to clients. In addition, your body language should also convey a message that you are listening with interest to the client. Maintaining good eye contact, a relaxed open posture with a friendly and interested facial expression invites the client to talk to you. The occasional appropriate nod of the head indicates that you are listening and interested. Once you are giving the client your full attention, it is necessary to demonstrate that you are trying to understand their world from their frame of reference. In other words, you are being empathic and not imposing your world, values, beliefs or judgements on the client. Some of the more common interventions you can use to facilitate this process are described below.

Simple and selective reflection

Simple reflection, sometimes known as echoing, is helpful when the client appears stuck. It involves repeating the last word or few words back to the client with the same intensity of expression used by the client. For example, the client may end the sentence saying, *'and I feel very unhappy'*; you respond, *'You feel very unhappy'*, and the client is encouraged to continue the story, *'Yes, ever since...'*. The difficulty in using this intervention is in deciding when it is appropriate and beneficial, as inappropriate use will simply annoy the client.

Selective reflection is similar, involving listening carefully for issues that seem to stand out as being significant and then feeding them back to the client without changing the content: *'You commented a moment ago about how angry you were with your mother'*. This gives the client the opportunity to continue to develop this theme. Care must be taken not to direct the client down avenues of your choosing rather than of the client's choosing. It is easy to think that you know what the client's problem is; in reality, you will often be misguided in your assumption. In both simple and selective reflection, you should be listening for the emotionally charged words the client uses.

Paraphrasing

Paraphrasing is one way of conveying to clients that you have listened to them and have tried to grasp an understanding of what they are saying to you. When paraphrasing, you rephrase what the client has said in your own words. An example of this type of intervention might be:

Client: I'm very worried about my daughter. This problem has been going on for so long, I wonder if she will ever be the same again.

Nurse: It seems like there is no end to your daughter's problem and you're worried she will never be the little girl you used to know.

Open and closed questions

dichotomous

divided into two separate groups

These dichotomous interventions are relatively simple but take practice to master. Open questions invite an open answer, whereas a closed question invites a closed answer. For example, 'Do you have pain?' as an example of a closed question invites a yes or no response, whereas 'how are you feeling?' invites a response much more of the client's choosing. Although it is rather simplistic, as a guide, the 'who' 'what' 'where' 'when' and 'how' questions tend to elicit a more open response. The important word here is 'invites'. A closed question might receive an open response and an open question a closed response. They are better seen as being on a continuum of being more or less open; the more open they are, the greater the opportunity for client self-direction. Closed questions are more frequently asked by the compulsive helper who tends to try to maintain control of the interaction. However, closed questions can be useful in eliciting specific information such as a name or telephone number. 'Why' questions should be used cautiously as they may alienate clients by forcing them to introspect inappropriately. After all, very often if they knew 'why', they would not need help.

Logical and empathic building

Logical building helps to develop a scaffolding for the client by bringing together salient points from the dialogue. Clients are often confused and appear rambling as they try to express their feelings; the nurse can assist by periodically marshalling the various points into some coherent order. For example, you might say, 'It seems as if these are your main concerns, Mr Jones. You are worried about how you will cope if you return to work and who will take care of the children.'

Empathic building is rather like reading between the lines. As you carefully listen to what the client is saying, you are attempting to understand the feeling behind the words. It is important to use other cues such as tone of voice, eye contact and facial expression to help you to understand what the client might be experiencing. Your empathic understanding is then relayed to the client in the form of a statement: 'It sounds as if you are really hurting about...' or 'You are really frightened because...'.

Checking for understanding

It is very important to check periodically that you are, as fully as possible, understanding what the client is saying. This is especially important if you feel that you are becoming confused or if the client is giving contradictory messages. Clarification of the situation can prevent much misunderstanding and helps you to stay within the client's frame of reference.

Cathartic category

As a baby and during infancy, the tendency is to give vent to emotions spontaneously, be they of joy, grief, anger or fear. As you grow older, the responses become modified through modelling, learning or choice, as you decide the best way to master life. You learn perhaps that it is wrong to cry, bad to express anger, that to be fearful might show weakness, or even that it is *not OK* to have fun and enjoy yourself. This may make it difficult to express yourself, particularly at times of crisis. The difficulty with helping others with their emotions is that you may not yet have come to understand your own repressed emotional world. It is one thing to intellectualise and say to the client that it is OK to cry, but if you are sitting there feeling uncomfortable with your own emotions, this may well be conveyed to the client. It is also unhelpful to coerce someone into expressing emotions, such as insisting on a bereaved person crying. Given time, space and permission, clients can choose when and how they want to express their emotions. Working with emotions can be difficult and often requires specific training. However, becoming more responsive to people's emotional needs does not require in-depth training. What it does require is for you to become sensitive to your emotions and to those of your clients. The angry client may awaken memories of an angry parent in your life, or a dying client may provoke memories of an earlier loss. What makes you laugh, cry or get angry? Do you close down your emotions because it is easier that way and you stand less chance of getting hurt? The best way to help clients with their emotions is to be accepting of them and give them permission: permission to be angry parents when they find that their new baby has learning difficulties, permission to fear when they find out they have multiple sclerosis or cancer, permission to cry when in a group therapy session old hurts are uncovered, permission to feel relief when someone they love dies, which releases the loved one from their suffering and themselves from the burden of caring.

Touching, eye contact, listening, being with someone and giving permission are all ways of using cathartic interventions. However, it is also important to be conscious of the cultural perspective. Touch may not in some cultures be acceptable, and eye contact may offend. Do not be afraid to check these things out. Does your eye contact cause the client to withdraw or become more responsive? Ask whether the client would like you to hold their hand.

cathartic interventions

cathartic interventions that seek to enable clients to let go of painful emotions including anger, fear, love and grief, thus releasing tension that has built up within them

Confronting category

confronting interventions

confronting interventions that directly challenge and heighten the client's awareness of restrictive attitudes, beliefs or behaviours of which he or she may be unaware

Confronting interventions are about informing clients of what they are unaware. Because of the nature of confronting, the intervention may be received by clients with some degree of shock as they come face to face with issues that they were either unaware of or not acknowledging. For the nurse, the process of confrontation can also be uncomfortable. The nurse is to some extent making an informed judgement that the client would benefit from the confrontation, but the nurse's fear that he or she may be wrong or may manage the confrontation poorly can lead to anxiety about how to deliver this information. Furthermore, the nurse may become aware of feelings related to previous confrontations in his or her own life. These anxieties can lead the nurse to avoid the issue and 'beat around the bush' or alternatively take a very direct and heavy-handed approach. A more appropriate approach is to take control of these inner feelings and get the confrontation right, in order to convey the confrontation clearly and supportively.

What sorts of issue might be seen as confrontations? There are many potential examples, such as breaking bad news or raising awareness of attitudes and behaviours. The examples below give some indication of how confrontations can be used.

- In a group session, John appears to avoid talking about his feelings:
  'You have explained what you were thinking John, but what is it you are feeling?'

- Mr Patel does not appear to be taking responsibility for looking after his recently fashioned colostomy:

  'I notice you are always asking Nurse Radley to change your colostomy bag.'
- Fasia is a young woman with Down syndrome who is preparing for her first job:

  'Fasia, are you aware that whenever someone speaks to you, you look away?'

  (The nurse demonstrates what Fasia may be unaware of.)
- You notice that the parents of 3-month-old Stephanie, admitted with a chest infection, are irregular visitors:

  'It seems you are unable to visit Stephanie very often.'

Breaking bad news is a further example of a confronting intervention. Maguire and Faulkner (1993) make the point that you cannot soften the impact of bad news as it remains bad news however it is broken. You can, however, break the news in a way that is supportive and gives the client a chance to absorb what is happening. There is insufficient space here to discuss the problems of breaking bad news in detail, but the following (Buckman, 1993) are useful guidelines:

- Prepare the client for the news, offering them privacy and ensuring that they are sitting down.
- Inform them that you have bad news, and then give them the facts in a simple, informative and unambiguous manner.
- Allow them time to take in the news, giving them the choice of being alone or having someone remain with them.
- Finally, be supportive throughout the interaction and offer follow-up help.

Informative category

Why do you need to give information? Clients clearly require information so that they can understand their illness or health problem. Without information, clients are left groundless and are not in a position to make reasoned decisions about their care. It is important that information is given to help clients to understand and maintain control, rather than this just being a duty of the health-care professional. It appears that most people want information about their illness, even if it is bad news (Ley, 1988). It also appears that clients are reluctant to seek out information in health-care settings, often being afraid of wasting the nurses' time, being unsure of whom or what to ask, or sometimes not being sure whether they *can* ask for information. It, therefore, falls to the health-care professional to ensure that quality information is delivered appropriately and in the client's best interest.

Prescriptive and informative interventions are often seen as the easiest to master. Most people feel that they are capable of providing information. It is

informative interventions

interventions that seek to impart new knowledge, information and meaning that is relevant to the client's needs

perhaps this confidence that results in a poor delivery of information. Although clients want and need information, it must be delivered at the right level in the right quantities and at the right time. Too many clients fail to understand the information given to them or forget what they have been told, especially if it is bad news (Ley, 1988). You can perhaps remember occasions when a lecture has been overloaded with information or delivered at a depth or in a manner that leaves you confused. The good lecture provides the right information at the right depth and at the right time in the course, perhaps leaving you to find something out for yourself. This last aspect is often important in mental health nursing, where you may wish to encourage clients to find out some information for themselves and take responsibility for doing so.

Prescriptive category

prescriptive
interventions
_____

prescriptive
interventions that seek
to suggest, advise or
propose ideas to the
client

Prescriptive interventions, such as suggesting a course of action the client might take, attempt to redirect the client's behaviour. A pitfall of this intervention is of its being too prescriptive, thus removing control from the client. What health-care professionals believe is in the clients' best interests is not always how clients themselves see the situation. Nevertheless, the nurse is in possession of much knowledge and may feel that a certain action will be best for the client. The nurse may, therefore, suggest, recommend or propose some action to the client, leaving the situation open for its acceptance or rejection. On other occasions, the nurse may be even more consultative, suggesting a number of options to clients and discussing these in a way that gives them maximum control and choice. On still other occasions, the nurse may be very directive, for example when stopping a diabetic client accidentally overdosing with an insulin injection.

Supportive category

supportive interventions
_____

an attitude of mind that
unconditionally affirms
the worth and value of
the client

Supportive interventions underpin the use of all other interventions. Whatever intervention is being used, it should be used in such a way that supports the individual and not in any way that is destructive. Heron identifies three ways of using interventions. First is a valid way that is appropriate to the needs of the client. In other words, it is the correct intervention delivered in the right way at the right time and in the correct manner. The second intervention style is degenerative, in which, despite the intention, it is used poorly because of a lack of skill, experience, self-awareness or a combination of all three. Finally comes a perverted intervention in which the intervention is used in a deliberately perverse way, to the detriment of the client.

Although the supportive category underpins all other categories, it is also a category in its own right. Such interventions involve the affirmation of others, being with them and demonstrating in a genuine way a care and concern for them. It may involve appropriate touch or appropriate self-disclosure. You demonstrate support for your clients when you willingly do things for them, when you greet them welcomingly and celebrate their achievements, however small they may appear to be. This should be conveyed in an unpatronising way, and you must resist becoming overly nurturing, which may deny clients their independence. The three core conditions identified above are central to the supportive category.

The above interventions provide a useful framework on which therapeutic communication can be developed. What has been presented here is an outline on which you can build. Each of the interventions can be developed and extended, requiring practitioners to research their use and practise their application if they are to be successfully employed.

Working Together – People in Groups

As social animals, people tend to live in groups or be members of a group. There are a whole variety of different groups to which you might belong. For example, you will probably belong to a family, have a group of friends, perhaps belong to a club and be a member of an organisation such as the RCN. You will belong to a large group called 'nurses', you may be a committee member, you will belong to a work group in your clinical area, and, as a student, you belong to a particular intake. Other groups you may come across might be study groups, rehabilitation groups and therapy groups. Nursing involves working as a team with other nurses and working with other professionals as part of a multidisciplinary team. The more effective the teamwork, the better the client care and the better your satisfaction with your work role.

Belonging to a group has many benefits, such as a feeling of belonging, having a shared identity and the benefits of the support you receive from the group. There is a degree of security from belonging to a group in which attitudes and values are similar and in which learning can take place. However, there is also some cost to belonging to a group. You are expected to conform, and you may feel that you are surrendering some of your own personal identity.

The study of groups has interested psychologists and sociologists for a long time and has generated considerable research. This section will confine itself to some of the core issues of groups as a platform for further study.

What is a group?

Most people have a common concept of what a group is, and few of the examples above will have caused difficulty for readers in identifying them as groups. It should also be evident that groups are very diverse and can vary considerably

in their size and function, some being more formal than others. Because of this, definitions are not always helpful, and it is more productive to focus on some of the central characteristics of groups than on definitions. A principal feature of a group is that individuals believe themselves to be members of the group, there being some degree of interdependence and interaction.

Groups can be divided into primary groups and secondary groups. Secondary groups are usually considered to be larger, and members have less direct contact. The hospital in which you work is a larger group, and you may never have contact with many of its members. Nursing as a profession is a large secondary group, as is a political party.

Primary groups tend to be closer and more intimate, all members having face-to-face contact. Such groups might be family groups, friendship groups or small work groups. If you belong to a group, you probably have some expectations of that group, for example the way in which members are likely to behave, some of the attitudes you might expect them to hold, and perhaps a code of conduct, be it explicit or implied. Nurses will be expected to have an attitude of caring and of working in a manner that is in the best interests of the client. These expectations are known as norms and are attained through observation, experience and learning. Although there is invariably a degree of flexibility, it is also an expectation that all members of the group will more or less conform to these norms. Without some conformity, it would be very difficult to operate in a social world. We would be left with a sense of 'anomie', a bewilderment with no frame of reference. Imagine what would happen if, each time you came to work, your group of nursing colleagues behaved radically differently, one day caring, the next not, sometimes wearing a uniform and sometimes casual clothes.

The group you work with in your clinical area is a formal primary group, and this group will have established a set of informal norms and expectations about the group's behaviour. The degree to which members of the group uphold the norms is an indication of the cohesiveness of the group. Other, more formal, norms may be imposed from the hierarchy, and these would also be expected to be adhered to. Needless to say, these two sets of norms may on occasions clash, causing some discontent.

Activity 7

Make a list of the norms for your clinical area. A simple example may be whether or not you wear a uniform. What might the consequences be if the group ignored these norms?

Leadership of groups

Various research studies have identified different styles of leadership and their effectiveness (Lewin *et al.*, 1939; Sayles, 1966; Fielder, 1971). The styles reflect the divide between being autocratic, when one person makes the decisions; democratic, when a consensus of opinion is sought; person centred, in which the leader places greatest emphasis on people; and task centred, in which the emphasis is placed on completing the task. These dimensions are probably best viewed as a continuum rather than as definitive styles of leadership. Good

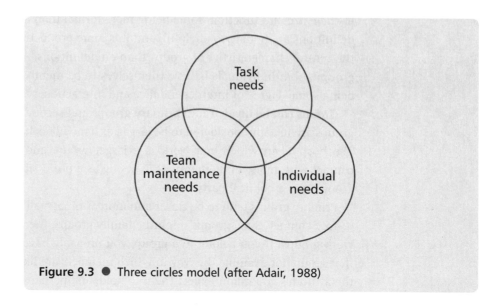

Figure 9.3 ● Three circles model (after Adair, 1988)

leaders, although they may have a predominant style, will adjust their leadership according to the situation (Bass, 1990). For example, it is often important to be autocratic in a cardiac arrest situation, everyone needing to know exactly who is in charge and what needs to be done. On other occasions, such as when deciding on a new policy, a more democratic, person-centred style may be more productive, allowing for open discussion and the sharing of ideas.

Leaders may be emergent, elected or appointed. Emergent leaders are common in crisis situations or when no leader has previously been identified; elected leaders are common in political situations or in committees. In the case of a clinical area, there is usually an appointed leader, someone given the position because of their skills and qualifications. Although you may currently be a student, you will in due course become a staff nurse and will be expected to have some responsibility as an appointed leader.

In maintaining good teamwork, Adair (1988) identifies three broad areas of need to be considered by the leader. These are the 'team' the 'task' and the 'individual', each being equally important and being interrelated, as shown in Figure 9.3.

Maintaining the team

A team is made up of individuals and, as such, takes on its own personality, distinct from that of the individual members. One of the responsibilities of the leader is to form a cohesive group that will together go forward to meet the agreed objective without diminishing the individuality of its members. One of the difficulties often expressed by new staff nurses is how to effect an appropriate distance from the group, one that is neither overfamiliar nor too distant. Adair (1988) suggests that distance should be emphasised if the nurse were known to the staff before adopting the new position, if the nurse feels that staff are becoming overfamiliar and taking advantage of the situation, or when the leader is responsible for implementing unpopular decisions. Distance should be minimised when trying to establish and build trust or where all members are roughly equal in knowledge and experience. The assertiveness skills referred to in the next section of this chapter should help in this respect.

Teams do take time to establish, and Tuckman (1965) suggests that, as groups develop, they pass through a series of stages. Being aware of these stages can help in understanding the progress of a group, and you may be able to identify some of these stages in relation to your group of students and how they have developed since commencing training. The four stages are shown in Figure 9.4.

This process is most clearly seen in the smaller groups that come together to achieve a given purpose, the groups and subgroups formed during nurse training being good examples of these. However, many other groups, such as the group you work with in the clinical area, go through similar stages, and this is often cyclical in nature as the environment and personalities change.

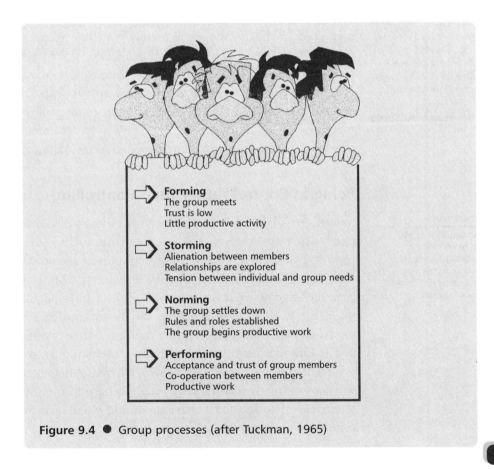

Figure 9.4 ● Group processes (after Tuckman, 1965)

Maintaining the task

The task is the objective to be achieved by the group. Such objectives may be very varied, from the day-to-day care of individuals to establishing new protocols for working practices. The success of such endeavours may depend heavily on the team working together and will require clearly defined objectives. Imagine working with a team and trying to achieve some very ill-defined goal. This will be not only inefficient, but also very frustrating for the team members. When all the team members understand what is required of them and what their role is in achieving the aim, morale and enthusiasm for the task will remain high.

Maintaining the individual

All groups consist of individuals and as such have individual needs and individual skills. The leader must be careful not to undermine these needs but to encompass them. In this way, individuals can be valued and their skills used to maximum effect within the group. Meeting members' needs may be as simple as ensuring regular meal breaks or valuing them as individuals, providing security, trust and a sense of autonomy. Of course, leaders do not always select their own team members, and some members will need more support than others. Harkins (1987) has identified a phenomenon called social loafing in which some members of the group may do as little work as they can get away with. It is a bit like the one member in a tug-of-war team appearing to pull but in fact not exerting any effort at all. The task then becomes all the harder for the other members. By identifying each person's role, encouraging and monitoring progress, and encouraging group support, social loafing can be minimised.

 ## Being in Control rather than Controlling

Assertiveness is sometimes confused with being aggressive, arrogant and getting one's own way. However, it is not about controlling others but about being in control of yourself. It is about respecting yourself and others, recognising that you have rights, including the right to be listened to, while remembering that others have the same rights. It is about good, positive and equitable communication and negotiation so that both people in the interaction feel respected. It is working towards a win–win situation rather than a win–lose or a lose–lose scenario. Some people find that being assertive comes quite naturally to them, others feel less confident and sometimes intimidated, whereas others become aggressive.

There are many reasons why people behave in the way they do, and this is often related to learned behaviour during childhood. Some of the messages commonly conveyed by parents, teachers and the media are shown in Chart 9.1.

---

protocols

regulations or patterns of working

Activity 8

Think of a particular task you might want to achieve as a team, such as implementing a new ward procedure. Using Figure 9.3, blank out the Task area of the three circles. How will this influence achieving your objective? Now blank out the Team area. How will this influence reaching your goal? Finally, blank out the Individual area of the three circles and carry out the same exercise.

---

assertiveness

a positive way of behaving in relationships that is based on honesty, openness and respect for all parties

Chart 9.1 ● Behaviour messages

- Be strong
- Be successful at any cost
- Don't let people walk over you
- Don't be weak
- Stand up for yourself
- Be in control

- Be gentle
- Be kind
- Don't argue
- It is wrong to be angry
- It is selfish to think of yourself

Those in the first column have traditionally been the messages conveyed to boys, and those in the second column the messages to girls. Men traditionally strive to win and see compromise or giving in as weakness and failure. Women have tended to acquiesce, afraid to speak out, especially on their own behalf. The young are often told not to answer back, to have respect for authority. While this may be valid, what they are not told is how to be heard while still being respectful to others, whoever the others may be. Of course, the messages in either of the columns may apply to either sex, and not all women become passive or all men aggressive.

transactional analysis

is a theory of personality and an approach to communication that promotes personal growth and change

The 'I'm OK, you're OK quadrangle', taken from transactional analysis and shown in Figure 9.5, gives us a picture of the different ways in which people might have learned to respond as a result of childhood experiences. In quadrant 1, the aggressive person does not really care about the rights or feelings of the other person: the 'I'm alright Jack' syndrome. In quadrant 2, the person puts himself down; he may be fearful of hurting or offending others and tends to believe that others are better, echoing the 'children should be seen and not heard' approach. This person may be liked but not respected, or may be seen as weak and used by others. In the third quadrant, the person is deceitful. He may

1. AGGRESSIVE I'm OK but you are not OK	2. SUBMISSIVE/PASSIVE I'm not OK but you are OK
3. MANIPULATIVE I'm OK and I'll let you think you're OK but really I don't believe you are	4. ASSERTIVE I'm OK and you're OK

Figure 9.5 ● The 'I'm OK, you're OK' quadrangle

Activity 9

Try to identify situations in which you find it easy to be assertive and ones where you find it difficult. Ask yourself what it is about these situations that makes it easier or more difficult.

be very complimentary to others or be full of excuses and apologies; before you know where you are, you are doing something for him you did not really want to do. You suddenly feel cheated and not quite sure how you got into that situation. The assertive person, shown in quadrant 4, cares both about himself and about others. He speaks clearly about his wants and needs in an unambiguous way but also listens to the needs and wants of others. Although some people's behaviour very obviously matches one of these quadrants, it is more common to take something from each of the four quadrants. It is more usual for us to be able to be assertive in some situations and not others. Some people are assertive at home or with their friends and relations but not assertive at work. Others may be assertive at work but struggle to be assertive in their private lives.

Why assertiveness?

Although assertiveness is important for any group, nurses have been identified as a group that finds being assertive difficult (McCarten and Hargie, 1990). This might be attributed to being a profession whose principal purpose is to care for others. Furthermore, nursing has historically had a tradition of duty and subservience. Becoming more assertive is important for two main reasons. The first is for mental health reasons. Non-assertive behaviour can lead to being pushed aside and not listened to, or to being labelled aggressive. Indeed, these have been some of the common stereotypical portrayals of nurses: the submissive, dutiful carer or the dominant, matronly figure. Both these approaches can lead to increased stress and loss of confidence for the nurse, whereas being assertive affords respect from others and an increase in self-confidence. Second, it is important for the sake of those for whom the nurse is caring and for colleagues and staff working alongside the nurse. Being assertive enables the nurse to be in a position to advocate for the client, be this in relation to a client's direct care or indirectly by challenging working practices. Staff working relationships can be one of the greatest stresses for health-care workers, but by caring for one another, by being open and respectful, working relationships will be enhanced. Hargie *et al.* (1994, p. 273) identify seven functions of assertiveness that will help individuals to:

- Ensure that their personal rights are not violated
- Withstand unreasonable requests from others
- Make reasonable requests of others
- Deal effectively with unreasonable refusals from others
- Change the behaviour of others towards them
- Avoid unnecessary aggressive conflicts
- Confidently, and openly, communicate their position on any issue.

Enhancing your assertiveness skills

There are five central principles to being assertive:

1. Listen carefully to what the other person has to say. This immediately shows some respect for the other person's opinion and feelings. Furthermore, you have the information you need rather than defensively jumping to conclusions.
2. Say what you think and feel. Your feelings and thoughts are as important and relevant as anyone else's. You have the right to be heard.
3. If appropriate, say what you want to happen. Without this, the other person is left guessing what you want. It is important here to be specific.
4. Be persistent. Do not be side-tracked or wrong-footed but stay with the issue in hand, repeating it if necessary until the issue is satisfactorily addressed.
5. Be prepared to compromise. This must be done from a position of choice to bring about a satisfactory conclusion for all involved and not because of coercion or 'just for a quiet life'.

Non-verbal communication

non-verbal communication

communicating without the use of spoken language, for example gestures, body posture and facial expression

In addition to these central aspects, it is important to project yourself in a positive manner using your body language and non-verbal communication. It is no good saying the right things if your body language does not complement what you are saying. Birdwhistell (1970) estimates that up to 70 per cent of social interactions are conveyed via a non-verbal channel; therefore, if your non-verbal communication conveys aggression or passivity, that is what the receiver will be aware of no matter what you are saying. Positive communication requires positive non-verbal communication. It is, of course, important to take into account cultural differences in body language, in which eye contact, proximity and touch may be very different. In principle, eye contact should be direct and appropriate rather than aggressively staring or passively avoiding of eye contact. Good eye contact demonstrates that you are interested in the other person and have nothing to hide. An individual's personal space is also important. We usually stand closest to those with whom we are most intimate and furthest away during normal social encounters (Hall, 1966). Standing inappropriately close can be threatening, whereas standing too far off can be interpreted as withdrawing. Your posture should be upright and open, with an absence of any gestures that could be interpreted as being aggressive, such as finger-pointing, folded arms or the hands on the hips. The tone of voice should be firm but relaxed and gentle. A good understanding of non-verbal communication can enhance interactions, and it is worthwhile taking the time to consider how you use non-verbal communication and to observe how others use it.

Assertiveness techniques

Two aspects of assertiveness will be outlined here – responding to criticism and turning down a request or demand – both of which can be potentially difficult to manage. They also contain many of the central elements of assertion, in particular listening and responding, and three useful techniques: 'the broken record', 'fielding the response' and 'fogging' (see below).

Saying no

Saying no can be particularly difficult for some people. It often raises old anxieties, reminders of when people have said no to us, particularly as children. There is often an underlying fear of hurting or offending others. Furthermore, if you say no, they may not like you, and the feeling of rejection can be painful and frightening. However, to simply agree to a request when you do not want to can mean being taken for granted and used by others. It can also mean not respecting the other person's ability to accept the refusal. Remember that you have the right to say no without feeling guilty. It is the request rather than the person that is being turned down. Nevertheless, some people do seem to have difficulty in understanding that no means no. It is, unfortunately, sometimes necessary to be persistent and explicit in saying no.

Before saying no, take time to consider the request. For example, you may say, 'Can I come back to you in five minutes?' or 'Can I consult my diary before I give you an answer?' If you really do want to say no, say it clearly and unambiguously. You do not have to give a reason, but if it helps then do so, providing that it does not undermine your decision. Remember that it is your choice whether to say yes or no. It is the act of choosing that is so important; you do not then feel you have been railroaded into a decision or have backed down when you really wanted to say no. However, once you have made your decision, then is the time to stick to it. Two techniques can help in sticking to the point.

Broken record

This really is just repeating what you have already said. For example, your manager asks you to do an extra shift, but you have made prior arrangements. After careful consideration, you say 'No, I can't do that shift; I have already made other arrangements.' However, your manager persists. You can respond by saying, 'As I said, I have made other arrangements and I am not able to do that shift.' Remember that this is conveyed not in an aggressive manner, but in a firm and respectful one. In some cases, it may be necessary to repeat yourself several times to reinforce the message, and you should try to use some of the same words each time so that you do not become diverted.

Activity 10

If you find it difficult to use your voice assertively, choose a range of scenarios and try verbalising your response to yourself until you get a feel for the right manner and tone of voice. If possible, stand up and speak into a tape recorder.

Fielding the response

In some ways, this is similar to the above but involves a summarising technique as well as sticking to and repeating your statement. This summarising can be very important because it conveys to the other person that you have heard them and that you understand their point of view. In the following example, you acknowledge the difficulty of the other person and indicate that you would be willing to help if you could, but you also make it clear that you have needs of your own and that these, too, should be respected:

'No I can't work that shift. I realise that you are short of nurses for this shift and if I could help I would, but as I have said, I have made other arrangements.'

Managing criticism

Managing criticism is included because nurses, along with many other professionals, receive criticism as part of their everyday lives. Criticism can be positive if handled well but can be a source of hurt and anger if not constructively imparted. Given constructively, criticism can help you to reflect on your practice and, if appropriate, to modify and enhance that practice.

There are basically three possible responses to criticism. First, criticism may be *invalid*, in which case you can reject it. Second, it can be *valid*, in which case you can accept it. Third, it can be *partly valid*, in which case you can accept the valid aspects and reject the invalid ones (Bond, 1986). However, before any judgement can be made, you must listen to the criticism. Do not reject it immediately and, if necessary, ask for time to think about what you have been told.

Some examples may help to illustrate the three responses.

- VALID
  Staff nurse to student: 'Nurse Kahn, you have forgotten to attend to Mrs Walmsley's dressing.'
  Student: 'Yes I have, I'm sorry. I will go and do it as soon as I have finished this.'
- PARTIALLY VALID
  Staff nurse to student: 'Nurse Reid, you're always late for these meetings.'
  Student: 'I am late for this meeting and I apologise, but in fact I have been here on time for all the other meetings.'
- INVALID
  Staff nurse to student: 'You don't attend any of the ward rounds.'
  Student: 'I do; in fact I have been on every ward round that has taken place when I have been on duty.'

Fogging

A useful technique to use in situations where you feel you are being attacked is that of fogging. Fogging tends to slow the other person down and gives you time to formulate a response. There is often an expectation on the part of the person attacking you that you will immediately disagree. However, if you agree in part with what they are saying, it tends to draw them from their critical parental stance to a more adult stance. An example may help to illustrate this. After being in the difficult situation of breaking bad news to a client, the charge nurse sees the client crying and appears to blame you: *'What have you said to Ms Bland. You have obviously upset her.'* You might respond by saying, *'Yes, she is very upset; I have just explained to her ...'*. Here, you are not agreeing that it is your fault, but you do agree that she is upset. The scene is then set for more constructive dialogue to take place between the charge nurse and yourself.

Conclusion

The very notion of assertiveness can alienate some people. This may be because of their misunderstanding of assertiveness, or because of their observations of people who claim to have been on assertiveness courses. It is, in essence, just good, caring communication. It is communication that respects one's autonomy and the autonomy of others. The techniques of being assertive are relatively straightforward; changing your behaviour may be less easy. What assertiveness training rarely does is address the archaic reasons for why you as an individual communicate the way you do. This is not to say that you cannot improve your communication skills through being assertive, but this needs to be done alongside your own self-awareness. However, it may take time and practice to adjust the way in which you present yourself. Taking small steps in situations you can cope with will be more rewarding than trying to change overnight. Use your reflective practice to examine your own behaviour, and consider situations in which you were assertive and in which you wish you had been more assertive.

Chapter Summary

In the author's recent experience, a client who was about to die, commented that the nurse caring for him seemed to have chosen the wrong profession. It was not her knowledge or technical skills that concerned him but the poor way in which she communicated with him and the other clients around him. Fortunately, there are many examples of good communication to counter this rather sad tale. Clients need more than scientific intervention as part of their care. During your nurse education, you will learn many facts and gain expertise that will undoubtedly be of benefit to the clients in your care. Whatever your chosen branch, your skills must include an expertise in open and caring communication with clients, families and colleagues. Without this, you will be failing in your duty of care. It is possible to enhance your communication style and develop good therapeutic communication skills supported by research-based theory. This chapter has only provided a glimpse into the world of social and professional interactions but provides a basis for further study, reflection and practice.

Test Yourself!

1. Name the three core qualities that are necessary for personal growth and change.

2. Name the six categories of Heron's six-category intervention analysis and give examples of how these may be used in your area of practice.

3. Give five interventions that could be used in the catalytic category.

4. List seven members of the multidisciplinary team in your area of practice.

5. Describe what is meant by a 'primary group' and a 'secondary group'. Give two examples of each.

6. Describe the elements of the three circles model.

7. What are the four stages that Tuckman suggests groups move through as they establish themselves?

8. There are four ways to respond in an interaction, one of which is by being manipulative. What are the other three?

9. What are the five principal stages of being assertive?

10. Criticisms may be 'valid' 'invalid' or 'partially valid'. What are the recommended methods of responding to these types of criticism?

11. How are you going to develop the themes described in this chapter?

References

Adair, J. (1988) *Effective Leadership*. Pan Books, London.
Bass, B.M. (1990) *Handbook of Leadership: Theory, Research and Managerial Applications*, 3rd edn. Collier-Macmillan, London.

Birdwhistell, R.L. (1970) *Kinesics and Context.* University of Pennsylvania Press, Philadelphia.

Bond, M. (1986) *Stress and Self-awareness: A Guide for Nurses.* Heinemann Nursing, London.

Brereton, M.L. (1995) Communication in nursing: the theory–practice relationship. *Journal of Advanced Nursing* **21**: 314–24.

British Association for Counselling (1996) *Code of Ethics and Practice for Counsellors.* BAC, Rugby.

Buckman, R. (1993) *How to Break Bad News.* Papermac, London.

Buckroyd, J. (1987) The nurse as counsellor. *Nursing Times* **83**: 42–4.

Burnard, P. (1995a) Counselling or being a counsellor? *Professional Nurse* **10**(2): 261–2.

Burnard, P. (1995b) Implications of client-centred counselling for nursing practice. *Nursing Times* **91**(26): 35–7.

Egan, G. (1994) *The Skilled Helper*, 5th edn. Brooks-Cole, California.

Fielder, F.E. (1971) Validation and extension of the contingency model of leadership effectiveness: a review of empirical findings. *Psychological Bulletin* **76**: 128–48.

Fromm, E. (1957) *The Art of Loving.* Unwin, London.

Hall, E.T. (1966) *The Silent Language.* Doubleday, New York.

Hargie, O., Saunders, C. and Dickson, D. (1994) *Social Skills in Interpersonal Communication,* 3rd edn. Routledge, London.

Harkins, S. (1987) Social loafing and social facilitation. *Journal of Experimental Social Psychology* **23**: 1–18.

Heron, J. (1990) *Helping the Client: A Creative Practical Guide.* Sage, London.

Hewison, A. (1995) Nurses' power in interaction with patients. *Journal of Advanced Nursing* **21**: 75–82.

Leavitt, H.J. (1951) Some effects of certain communication patterns on group performance. *Journal of Abnormal and Social Psychology* **46**: 38–50.

Lewin, K., Lippitt, R. and White, R. (1939) Patterns of aggressive behaviour in experimentally created 'social climates'. *Journal of Social Psychology* **10**: 271–99.

Ley, P. (1988) *Communicating with Patients.* Croom Helm, London.

McCartan, P.J. and Hargie, O.D.W. (1990) Assessing assertive behaviour in student nurses: a comparison of assertion measures. *Journal of Advanced Nursing* **15**: 1370–76.

Maguire, P. and Faulkner, A. (1993) Communicating with cancer patients: 1. Handling bad news and difficult questions. In Dickenson D. and Johnson M. (eds) *Death, Dying and Bereavement.* Sage, London.

McLeod-Clark, J. (1985) The development of research in interpersonal skills in nursing. In Kagan, C. (ed.) *Interpersonal Skills in Nursing: Research and Applications.* Croom Helm, London.

Mearns, D. (1994) *Developing Person-Centred Counselling.* Sage, London.

Nelson-Jones, R. (1988) *Practical Counselling and Helping Skills.* Cassell Educational, London.

Nichols, K.A. (1989) Institutional versus client-centred care in general hospitals. In Broome, K.A. (ed.) *Health Psychology: Processes and Applications.* Chapman & Hall, London, pp. 103–14.

Rogers, C.R. (1957) The necessary and sufficient conditions of therapeutic personality change. *Journal of Consulting Psychology* **21**(2): 95–103.

Rogers, C.R. (1980) *A Way of Being*. Houghton Mifflin, New York.

Sayles, S.M. (1966) Supervisory style and productivity: review and theory. *Personnel Psychology* **19**(3): 275–86.

Stevens, J.O. (1971) *Awareness: Exploring, Experimenting, Experiencing.* Real People Press, Moab, Utah.

Tuckman, B.W. (1965) Development sequence in small groups. *Psychological Bulletin* **63**(6): 384–99.

● Further Reading

The following books will help to develop the themes referred to in this chapter.

The core conditions

Mearns, D. and Thorne, B. (1988) *Person-Centred Counselling in Action*. Sage, London.

Rogers, C.R. (1980) *A Way of Being*. Houghton Mifflin, New York.

Therapeutic interventions

Burnard, P. (1985) *Learning Human Skills: A Guide for Nurses*. Heinemann Nursing, London.

Culley, S. (1991) *Integrative Counselling Skills*. Sage, London.

Heron, J. (1990) *Helping the Client: A Creative Practical Guide*. Sage, London.

Egan, G. (1994) *The Skilled Helper*, 5th edn, Brooks-Cole, California.

Groups

Adair, J. (1988) *Effective Leadership*. Pan Books, London.

Niven, N. and Robinson, J. (1994) *The Psychology of Nursing Care*. Macmillan, Basingstoke.

Assertiveness

Bond, M. (1986) *Stress and Self-awareness: A Guide for Nurses*. Heinemann Nursing, London.

Other useful texts

Buckman, R. (1993) *How to Break Bad News*. Papermac, London.

Hargie, O., Saunders, C. and Dickson, D. (1994) *Social Skills in Interpersonal Communication*, 3rd edn. Routledge, London.

Nelson-Jones, R. (1988) *Practical Counselling and Helping Skills*. Cassell Educational, London.

Niven, N. (1989) *Health Psychology: An Introduction for Nurses and Other Health Care Professionals*. Churchill Livingstone, Edinburgh.

10 Understanding Ourselves

CATHERINE THROWER

Introduction

The main aim of this chapter is for the reader to appreciate the importance of understanding the self for those working within the health-care profession.

The chapter covers:

- The self-concept
  - The development of self-concept
  - Models of self
  - Self-awareness

- Stress
  - Models of stress
  - Modifiers of stress

- Attitudes
  - Attitude formation
  - Relevance of attitudes for health-care practice.

'Understanding ourselves' may seem a self-evident concept; after all, who should know better about what goes on in our heads than ourselves? How often do we think that others do not understand? Why else would we need to put our point of view in to the public arena but to enable others to understand our perspective? The self is a private world that may in everyday life need little exploration. There are circumstances in which an exploration of understanding the self may seem like luxury, if not indulgence. Do the homeless, the hungry or those in war-torn areas of the globe need to understand their motivation for behaviour? A model proposed by Abraham Maslow places these questions in context.

Maslow's hierarchy of needs (Figure 10.1) is a framework that orders the needs of life. It predicts that there is an order in which needs have to be satisfied to enable individuals to reach their full potential. The lower levels identify the requirement to satisfy physical needs such as hunger and warmth, with a progression through needs such as love and esteem to aesthetics and the final

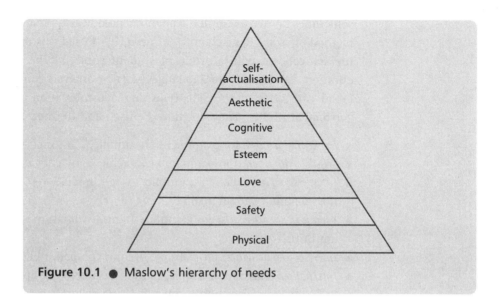

Figure 10.1 ● Maslow's hierarchy of needs

need of self-actualisation (Maslow, 1968). Maslow's theory of growth and development will be further discussed later in this chapter.

As nurses, there is a need to maximise our potential as carers not only to understand what it is to be a professional carer, but also to understand our own motivation for wishing to care and to be able to disentangle our own thoughts and emotions from those of the people we look after. The nature of caring dictates that the people with whom we are in the most intimate contact are the most vulnerable. If we make assumptions about behaviour based on our own past experience and feelings, we may be doing our patients a grave disservice. For example, when a nurse is faced with the death of a patient and grieving relatives, is her distress a sharing of those people's distress and loss, or is it more to do with unresolved issues of grief or mortality in her own life? Thus an understanding of our own thoughts, feelings and behaviour is essential to give the best possible care and to reach one's maximum potential as an excellent carer.

Activity

1

Before reading on, try this brief exercise. Write down 20 answers to the following question: 'Who am I?'

 ## Self-concept

self-concept

the knowledge that a person has about himself

Self-concept is the knowledge that a person has about himself. It is information chiefly acquired by interactions with others (Baron and Byrne, 1997). It is a schema, an organised set of beliefs and feelings that are self-referent. The self-concept influences how we process information about the external social world and its relations to 'me'. The schema holds information about motives, emotions, self-evaluations, abilities and so on (Baron and Byrne, 1997), and we access this self-schema every time we use self-referent information.

Research into the self-concept frequently uses the 'Who am I?' approach, sometimes known as Gordon's phenomenological approach (Gordon, 1968), as a method of study. Rentsch and Heffner (1994) used this methodology to explore the self-concept with a group of student subjects. The researchers asked the question, 'Who am I?' of 230 subjects. Their analysis confirmed Gordon's eight broad categories of the self, reflecting a combination of social identity and personal attributes. These include (Rentsch and Heffner, 1994):

- *Existential aspects*: for example, I am unique, I am special, I am attractive
- *Self-determination*: for example, I can achieve my educational goals
- *Interpersonal attributes*: for example, myself in relation to others, I am a student nurse, I am a daughter/son
- *Ascribed characteristics*: for example, I am a woman/man, I am 19 years old, I am British
- *Interests and activities*: for example, I enjoy football, I like dogs
- *Internalised beliefs*: for example, I am a socialist, I am opposed to fox-hunting
- *Self-awareness*: for example, my beliefs are well integrated, I am a good person
- *Social differentiation*: for example, I am poor, wealthy, I am gay.

However, the self-concept is more than the sum of the answers to 'Who am I?' The schema for self contains information about our past experiences; it contains memories and expectations of the future. Baron and Byrne (1997) maintain that the self is a sum of everything a person knows and what he imagines he can be.

However, to conceptualise this schema as a fixed structure is misleading as there is change over time: the self-concept alters with life events and new learning. It may be that it is vulnerable to change in a short period of time; for example, if a person loses her job, the self-concept will undergo a redefinition from being a person who is employed to one who is unemployed. Of course, the opposite can occur when a person gains employment, passes a driving test or achieves a goal. The concept of self, therefore, is not a rigid percept but is fluid and vulnerable to change.

It is important to understand the effects of change and why this change to the self-image occurs; failure to do so may lead to psychological discomfort as the person resists the redefinition of or addition to self-knowledge. Change can be threatening, particularly if it is enforced rather than chosen.

Development of Self-concept

The sense of self develops as a function of growing older. The child learns about the environment and his relationship to people and objects within that environment by being in the world. The child learns that he is a separate entity within the world rather than symbiotic with the caregiver and the external world. The child learns that objects exist independently of her; that is, the child comes to understand that when she cannot see a toy, it still remains in the world rather than no longer existing. Similarly, the child learns that she exists independently of her environment and that she can act and have an effect on the world, particularly on other people. As a result of interactions with caregivers, friends, teachers and so on, children learn about an 'I' separate from other people and objects (Mischel, 1986). Consequently, the child establishes a self-schema. In early infancy, this is knowledge about the self existing as an independent entity; as the child matures, the schema enlarges. During middle childhood, there is a shift in the self-descriptors from concrete, physical descriptions to social comparisons and psychological descriptors (Brooks-Gun and Paikoff, 1992). Montemeyer and Eisen (1977) asked a group of young people aged from 10 to 18 years to answer the question 'Who am I?' They found that there was an increase in the use of self, ideology and belief references with age and a decrease in physical categories as descriptors.

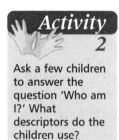

Activity 2

Ask a few children to answer the question 'Who am I?' What descriptors do the children use?

Erikson's Theory of Personality Development

One theoretical framework that places the establishment of the self-schema within a developmental context is Erikson's eight-stage psychosocial theory of development (Erikson, 1959). Each stage has a task of transition or crisis, the resolution of each crisis influencing the subsequent stages. The task is to resolve the conflict between two opposing choices and to balance in favour of a positive or negative outcome. A positive resolution will result in the acquiring of an adaptive strength that will sustain the individual's progress through the next stage of the life span development. Each life crisis gives the individual more knowledge about the world and his relationship to it.

- *Stage 1 – Trust versus mistrust*
  Trust is about learning what to expect from the world. This is not just that the world is a safe place with consistency and nurturing, but also that dangerous people can be trusted to be dangerous (Erikson, 1959). Irregularity and inconsistency will, however, lead to mistrust, and the child experiences anxiety and insecurity.
  Adaptive strength: Hope.

- *Stage 2 – Autonomy versus shame and doubt*
  This is a stage of gaining mastery over the world and, particularly for the young child, over the body. If the child is encouraged to explore her body, there will be a growth of self-confidence, enabling exploration of the physical and social worlds. If constantly criticised, the child will feel ashamed and come to doubt herself.
  Adaptive strength: Will.

297

- *Stage 3 – Initiative versus guilt*
  The child will begin to ask questions to further her knowledge and skills, realising that she has some influence over her environment and the people in it. The child may become successful at manipulating her surroundings, but if reaching out to the world is met with disapproval and reproof, the child will feel inept, resulting in an emerging sense of guilt.
  Adaptive strength: Purpose.

- *Stage 4 – Industry versus inferiority*
  The child is learning about accomplishment and task completion. A sense of industry will feed a sense of an achievement, whereas failure to complete or accomplish will result in a sense of inferiority, which may be lifelong.
  Adaptive strength: Competence.

- *Stage 5 – Identity versus role confusion*
  This was viewed by Erikson as crucial stage of development. Identity is a structure within an organised set of values and beliefs about oneself. These may be expressed in a variety of ways such as occupation, politics, religion and relationships. Erikson maintains that an integrated identity cannot occur before adolescence because of immature cognitive, physical and social development, but failure to integrate during this stage will result in role confusion.
  Adaptive strength: Fidelity.

- *Stage 6 – Intimacy versus isolation*
  This stage presents the young adult with the task of forming intimate relationships with others. It encompasses a sense of connectedness, a fusion of identity with someone else's safe in the belief that you will retain your sense of self intact. The opposing resolution is isolation, a feeling that occurs when a person is threatened by the behaviour of others.
  Adaptive strength: Love.

- *Stage 7 – Generativity versus self-absorption*
  The positive aspect of this task is generativity: an interest in the next generation. The primary interest is in nurturing offspring but, for those without offspring, energies may be directed into creative and altruistic concerns. The opposite of this outwardly directed interest is self-absorption, an indulging of the self as though it were a child, one's one and only child.
  Adaptive strength: Care.

- *Stage 8 – Integrity versus despair*
  This is the final life task in which the individual is faced with integrating the life cycle, an acceptance of one's life as being one's own responsibility.
  Adaptive strength: Wisdom.

Erikson's theory outlines a framework of growth and development that is inevitable and irresistible. Erikson (1959) hypothesised a ground plan for growth, each stage having its time of ascendancy until all aspects of personality are fully developed to form an integrated personality.

---

identity

a structure within an organised set of values and beliefs about oneself

generativity

an interest in the next generation

Resolution in a negative direction means that individuals become restricted in their development and fail to benefit from the adaptive strength associated with each life task. Working with the vulnerable, nurses need to have insight into the self; there is a need to have some understanding of how life tasks have been resolved. Nurses need to access their own thoughts, feelings and motivation for behaviour to be able to have an awareness of how they may respond to the thoughts, feelings and behaviour of others. There is acknowledgement within the field of health care that we need to demonstrate positive regard; nurses aim to promote a sense of value in their patients, but to be successful, we need to have an understanding of the self in terms of our own values, attitudes, thoughts and feelings. We need to be comfortable with ourselves before we can understand others.

Self-awareness

Activity 3

What does it mean to be self-aware?

Reflect on this question and jot down your thoughts.

self-awareness

the condition of being able to analyse motives for behaviour

Rawlinson (1990) defines self-awareness as:

> bringing into consciousness [those] various aspects of our understanding of ourselves.

The 'various aspects' refer to the components of self. Rawlinson differentiates self-awareness from self-consciousness, which, rather than being a constructive appreciation of the self, is a concern for others' perception of our own self.

Self-awareness is a condition of being able to analyse motives for behaviour. Most of the time we act and interact giving scant attention to why, the focus being the consequences or achievement of our goals. Self-awareness is the antithesis of self-consciousness, the latter being a concern with others' opinions and the former a concern with the motives and effectiveness of one's behaviour.

A model of self that illustrates the importance of self-awareness in the growth and development of a confident, effective person is the Johari window (Luft and Ingham, 1955). This model is depicted as a window with four panes, each representing a facet of the self (Figure 10.2).

Public	Blind
Hidden	Unconscious

Figure 10.2 ● The Johari window – four facets of the self

The Johari window is useful in understanding the nature of self-awareness. The aim is to enlarge the public self. The more comfortable we are with what others know about us the easier it is to understand pain at times of change for ourselves and for others. But this is just one model of self; others offer different frameworks in which to strive for self-knowledge.

The public self

This part of self is that information which we know about ourselves and are happy for others to know. This may include name, occupation and marital status. It may also include age (although some people prefer to keep their age a secret), background and personal details. If, for example, I meet anyone from Norfolk, I am, as a person who lived there for many years and has happy memories from that time, immediately prepared, indeed keen, to share my experiences of living there with that person. This is a way of interacting with others that allows me a sharing of common experiences and knowledge with someone I may not know but with whom I share a part of my self-concept, that is, someone who knows and likes Norfolk. This then is public knowledge; it is not a secret as I am prepared to share this knowledge with anyone. These exchanges are not only interactions that we are prepared to be known by, but are also a means of validating beliefs and opinions and affirming the status of 'person'.

The blind self

This is knowledge known to others but not known to the self. This is an area of knowledge that can be threatening. What is it that others are not telling us? It could be that someone's dress is tucked in the back of her knickers or that his fly is undone. More often, it is the psychological, behavioural or social equivalent. The 'other' is able to form a totally different perspective on our behaviour, habits and mannerism of which we are totally unaware. Do you know what you look like from the back view? Do you know what your walk looks like? Others may find our presence pleasing, but, conversely, they may find it unpleasant. The more information that we are given about the blind self, the greater the degree of self-awareness that is allowed to develop. If I am given information about my behaviour of which I have previously been unaware, I have the choice to change or to continue with the knowledge of the effect that this behaviour may have on other people.

Giving an example of knowledge in the blind self is not easy as I do not know what others know about me to which I am not privy. However, when I was sister in a day hospital, I was asked by a member of staff if I would be willing to allow a health-care support worker to be flexible with her time as she had family problems. As part of my self-image was kind and caring, I had no hesitation in agreeing, provided that the day hospital was safe for patients and the care was delivered as it should be. I was curious to know why this woman had not asked me herself. The reply from the staff nurse to this query was that I was unapproachable. This came as new knowledge to me and challenged my existing self-concept as a kind, caring and considerate manager. I could have responded in two ways. First, I could have been defensive. When the self-concept is threatened or challenged, there is a shift to mobilise defence strategies to protect the *status quo*. Hostility is one means of defence: I could have become angry, projecting my feelings of threat on to the other person. A second response is to accept that this was how I appeared to this member of staff and the person on whose behalf she was speaking. These responses will be discussed below.

Defensive response

defence mechanism

a protective strategy employed when the self is under threat

A defence mechanism is a protective strategy employed when the self is under threat. When information is threatening, the self rallies a defence mechanism to maintain an equilibrium. The psychodynamic view proposes that the human organism is unable to tolerate anxiety, and we deal with this state by developing defence strategies that protect against this painful state. Defence mechanisms arise from the unconscious as a way of distorting reality in order to exclude feelings of anxiety from consciousness (Pervin, 1984). Being given information about yourself that is unacceptable will produce a state of anxiety. One way of dealing with this is projection. Projection occurs when internal, unacceptable feelings are projected externally; thus feelings of internal hostility are projected outwards, leading to the perception of the other person as hostile. In the example above, I held the view that I was an approachable manager; this view was under threat. A hostile response would have shifted this internal hostility from the self externally to the staff nurse, invalidating her opinion.

Acceptance

An alternative approach would be to acknowledge the state of anxiety produced by this incongruous information, choosing to alter the image of self conveyed to the world. By accepting the 'other's' perspective, not necessarily as truth but as being a valid opinion, there is a growth in self-awareness. So in my example, I could not accept the truth of being unapproachable, but I did accept that this was how I was perceived by others.

The hidden self

This is the part of the self that is hidden from public gaze. This corner of the window hides that of which we are ashamed, frightened and embarrassed; here lie unacceptable thoughts and feelings. Disclosure of information from this area is threatening and can elicit great anxiety. As an example of the hidden self, we can draw on the literature on carers. Caring for a dependent relative can be a pleasure and enjoyable; it can bring meaning to life and a new perspective to a relationship. However, it is not unusual for carers to feel hostile and angry towards their charge. Admitting that we have these thoughts is a frightening exercise. The dependent person cannot help being ill or disabled; the crying, sleepless baby is vulnerable and helpless. Disclosing feelings of bitterness, resentment, anger and hostility may bring criticism and hostility on the carers themselves, the logic being that, 'If I admit that I feel like hitting X, I will be reviled and ostracised.' The reality may be that, by disclosing these fears, the person will find warmth, understanding and support. Revealing secrets may bring a realisation that others feel like you do and behave like you do, and that behaviour, thoughts and feelings that leave you feeling guilty and ashamed are common to others in similar situations. It is no accident that self-help groups are a popular means of offering support for people caring for dependent relatives. Affiliation with other people in a position similar to our own is an effective way of easing anxiety and lessening a sense of isolation. These groups provide a forum for people to disclose unacceptable thoughts and feelings, facilitating a growth in understanding of the self as carer. There are times when this hidden part of the self needs help to facilitate disclosure, but by accepting this part of the self-concept, it helps the individual to feel more comfortable with the self and as such enables a growth in self-understanding.

The unconscious

This is an interesting but enigmatic area of the self. This is knowledge not known to the self or others, and the question 'Does it exist?' has to be asked. The psychodynamic theory of personality maintains that the unconscious drives behaviour and can be revealed by free association and within dreams. However the antithesis of this is, of course, the behavioural perspective. If it cannot be observed, it cannot be studied, but behaviour can be observed and can, therefore, be attributed to the consequences of action. This is not necessarily to deny the unconscious but to deny the validity of being able to attribute the unconscious as a cause of behaviour. Wittgenstein maintained that when an individual looks inside himself, he finds a beetle in a box, a beetle that only the individual can see and touch (Humphrey, 1984). We all have a beetle, but I do not know what your beetle is like and you have no access to mine. Therefore, what can I say about how your beetle influences your behaviour? If so little of this section of the window is available to the world, the unconscious is a territory to be explored only by the intrepid and with experienced, expert guidance (Humphrey, 1984).

Maslow's Hierarchy of Needs

Maslow's hierarchy is usually depicted as a pyramid with basic needs, such as safety and hunger, forming the base and self-actualisation forming the pinnacle (see Figure 10.1 above). A more appropriate view may to see this structure as a more fluid model. Maslow viewed basic needs as drives that, when they were met, enabled a move to a higher level of need. Not everyone chooses to move beyond a particular level of need; it may be that the rigidity of Maslow's framework provides a safe boundary for the self-concept, but choosing to move to a greater fulfilment of need is to expand self-knowledge, broaden experience and move towards a greater understanding of the courage and anxieties of others.

Rogers' Model of Self

Rogers' model of self consists of all knowledge that we have about the self, all the constituents of 'I' or 'me' (Atkinson *et al.*, 1993). The three dominant features of this model are the real self, the ideal self and the self-esteem. Rogers maintained that we tend to interpret events in the world in relation to the self. We all have a percept of how we are in the world, an image of the self and its relationship to others, objects and events. This image is modelled on the ideal self, the goal for which we strive, the perfect, the self without flaw. The difference between the image we have of the self and the ideal self is the measure of self-esteem, the worth that we attribute to the self. This self-image and level of self-esteem is not necessarily a true reflection of the real self. It is possible for people who outwardly appear successful and competent to have a low self-esteem and to define their self-concept as inadequate. This may be because people set themselves goals that are too high or unachievable, a consequence of which may be, for some, the need for therapy to assist with the attainment of psychological well-being (Atkinson *et al.*, 1993).

Activity
4

What causes you stress? Draw two columns, heading one 'Positive' and the other 'Negative'. List your answers according to whether you find the stressor motivating or threatening.

Self and Sources of Stress

However, when the self-concept is threatened, the resulting discomfort is a manifestation of stress, and the relationship between stress and the self-concept needs to be explored in order to achieve a better understanding of the self.

Selye (1980) maintains that stress suffers from being too well known and too little understood. Nursing is a pressurised occupation. The nurse is put under pressures of time and limited resources, facing daily the pressures of others' pain, discomfort and distress with little time to acknowledge the effect that this may be having on emotions and the self-concept. Certainly, self-esteem has been implicated as a factor influencing our perception of stress. Stress occurs when the demands of the situation exceed the personal resources of an individual, and while a degree of stress is thought to be useful in motivating us to action, there needs to be an awareness of how to maintain a balance between what is motivating (the degree of arousal necessary for successful task performance) and arousal that exceeds an optimum level for effective performance. The experience of the latter is stress, being unpleasant and anxiety-provoking.

Models of Stress

Stimulus-based model

A simple model of stress is the stimulus-based model, which characterises the environment as providing a stressor and the person as experiencing stress or strain. However, while this may offer a description, it does not elucidate the process by which people find themselves under pressure.

Response-based model

The response model offers a more detailed approach. The environment is the source of the stressor or stimulus, and the person's stress is the response. Selye conceptualised this as a non-specific response to excessive demands on individual coping resources. Selye believed that the response did not depend on the nature of the stressor and that the response was a protective mechanism (Cox, 1978). There are three identifiable stages to the response syndrome that form the general adaptation syndrome (GAS).

Alarm reaction

This stage is related to high levels of physical arousal, which causes the release of adrenaline. It is during this initial stage that the organism's susceptibility to the specific stressor increases, and if the severity of the response is great enough, death may ensue. However, with less severe stressors but prolonged exposure, the pituitary/adrenocorticotrophic hormones are released, and the resistance stage of the GAS is initiated.

Resistance stage

During this stage, physical arousal remains high. Adaption occurs as the parasympathetic nervous system attempts to counteract the effects of the sympathetic nervous system. The organism is, therefore, able to resist the debilitating effects of the stressor, but the threshold for eliciting the stress response has been lowered for further encounters with this specific threat or other non-specific stressors.

Exhaustion

If continued exposure occurs, the final stage of the GAS is entered, that of exhaustion. The hormonal reserves are depleted, fatigue results and the felt experience of this stage is frequently that of depression.

Interactional model

This approach to stress incorporates the stress response model with the demand placed on the individual and the subjective perception of that demand. There is an acknowledgement that the consequences of coping strategies will influence the perception of felt stress and that this provides feedback for future action when faced with a similar threat. Cox and Mackay (1978) proposed the man–environment transaction model, which they describe as eclectic, drawing on stimulus and response models. However, it explicitly identifies that a stress system is an individual perceptual phenomenon (Cox, 1978).

The man–environment model has five identifiable stages:

1. Actual capability and demand
2. Perceived capability and demand
3. Psychophysiological changes
4. Consequences of coping responses
5. Feedback.

The feedback component is a particularly important feature of this model as it is the feedback the individual receives from the environment that determines the degree of felt stress and the perceived effectiveness of coping strategies.

Information-processing model

This approach emphasises the importance of cognitive and attentional factors. The individual selectively attends to stimuli and will interpret information as stressful or otherwise by comparing it with past experience (Figure 10.3).

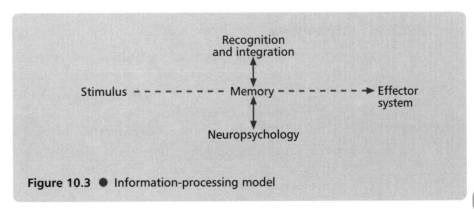

Figure 10.3 ● Information-processing model

Therefore, memory and decision-making play a role in the processing of stimuli, and cognitive appraisal will elicit emotions, such as anxiety, anger, fear and sadness, previously associated with similar situations. This model proposes that stressors and stress responses can only be so if the individual's perception of the situation is that a threat exists. This is in line with the premise that what one individual perceives as a threat, another may view as a challenge. Why is it that one individual will succumb to the debilitating effects of stress, manifest in illnesses such as ulcer, coronary artery disease and depression, while another person in the same circumstances thrives on the motivation of the environment. Kobasa (1979) identifies challenge as a characteristic of the hardy personality, an individual whose susceptibility to illness is less than that of others who may perceive life events as stressful and have less than effective coping strategies.

Factors Affecting Stress

What acts as a source of stress will vary from one individual to another, but there are some events and encounters that have a shared effect; it is the interpretation as either a threat or challenge that differs. The stressful life events model is one model delineating events as sources of stress (Holmes and Rahe, 1967). The Holmes and Rahe social readjustment rating scale was the outcome of research that asked people to rate the degree to which they found life events stressful. The resultant list covers a whole range of general life experiences such as the death of a spouse, marriage, childbirth, moving house, Christmas and going on holiday. However, is the experience of a desirable event the same as that of one with negative consequences or connotations? Is the stress of preparing for Christmas a similar experience to that of losing a job? While there may be emotional strain associated with positive events, there is an expectation of reward that gives a different perspective from events that may have negative connotations.

Why is it that people vary in their response to events and encounters? There are several possible factors that influence this appraisal.

Personality

It seems that some people are predisposed to experience life events as stressful (Watson and Clarke, 1984); some people have a predisposition to negative affectivity, expressing distress and discomfort across a variety of situations rather than responding to specific situations.

The corollary of this is the person who is predisposed to interpret demanding events as challenging and is able to cope effectively. Kobasa (1979) described this personality type as a hardy personality. The hardy personality has three constructs:

- *Challenge*: a willingness to accept change and to face novel situations as opportunities for growth and development
- *Commitment*: the tendency to involve oneself in whatever situations or events one encounters
- *Control*: the belief that one has influence over life events and the assumption of personal responsibility for those events.

Hardy individuals are mentally and physically healthier than others. They seem to appraise events more favourably than other individuals and have more effective coping strategies than non-hardy personality types.

Other personality factors that are related to the way in which people perceive and cope with stress are those of type A (or coronary-prone) and type B personalities. The type A personality was first described by Rosenman and Jenkins in 1975. During a study of the relationship between cholesterol and heart disease among a group of men, one of the subjects' wives suggested that the the real problem was stress. Rosenman and Jenkins undertook a further study of men with heart disease and a group of healthy individuals to identify whether there was a relationship between stress and related personality factors. The comparison showed differences in both behavioural and emotional style. The people with heart disease were more likely to demonstrate type A behaviour, characterised by an orientation to competitiveness, time urgency, anger and hostility.

- *Competitiveness*: Type A people are driven to compete with others and the self. Type A individuals tend to be critical of the self and strive towards their goals without a sense of pride or accomplishment.
- *Time urgency*: Type A individuals are in a constant race with the clock. They tend to be impatient to plan appointments too tightly and to do more than one thing at a time.
- *Anger/hostility*: The type A person is easily aroused to anger and hostility, and this may be expressed in an overt way.

The difference between type A and type B people is the way in which each responds to stressors. The type A person reacts more quickly and with greater strength to stress, interpreting any stressor as a threat to personal control. This pattern of behaviour also seems to predispose such individuals to seek out demanding situations, consequently generating a great deal of stress for themselves. The type B pattern of behaviour is less competitive and driven, and is defined by the comparision made with type A pattern of behaviour rather than by distinctive charactersitics associated with type B.

social support

the perceived comfort derived from a social network that includes significant others, family, friends, community organisations and professional practitioners

Social support

Social support is the perceived comfort derived from a social network that includes significant others, family, friends, community organisations and professional practitioners. There are four broad types of social support:

1. *Emotional*: This is an expression of empathy, caring and concern toward a person. It provides a sense of belonging and being loved at times of stress.
2. *Esteem*: This support is expressed through positive regard. Esteem support enables the development of a sense of worth and competence.
3. *Tangible/instrumental*: This is support that comes from practical help. It may manifest itself in any way from the loan of money to someone doing the shopping or housework, or helping with personal care. This is the support given by someone when individuals are unable to perform a task or activity themselves.
4. *Informational*: This support is derived from advice, direction, suggestion and feedback. This support is manifest as information that allows an individual to make an informed appraisal or decision.

Social support reduces the stress that people experience. Stress has been demonstrated to have detrimental effects on health, and social support has been shown to be protective against these adverse effects. How does social support protect against ill-health? Two theories have been proposed:

- The *buffering hypothesis* proposes that a good supportive network has a protective effect at times of high stress (Cohen and Hoberman, 1983).
- The *direct effect hypothesis* maintains that social support is beneficial regardless of the amount of stress experienced, influencing the appraisal of events as stressful or challenging (Cobb, 1976).

Emotion

Negative events have a greater potential to be interpreted as stressful than positive events, and our emotions will influence the appraisal of a situation. Common emotions associated with stress are fear and anger, whereas a similar event associated with a pleasant emotion may not be interpreted as stressful. For example, if while travelling we are aroused to anger by delays, our interpretation may be that the journey is stressful; however, if the delay in the journey is perceived as an opportunity for time out from a busy schedule, the journey may be described as pleasant.

Recognising stress in ourselves, being able to identify the feelings that indicate stress, is important as the effect that this has on our behaviour within the clinical area will affect the patients for whom we are caring. Similarly, we need to have an understanding of what our patients may be experiencing, not so that we are in position to say, 'Yes, I know how you're feeling and this is how I deal with it' or to be able to evaluate someone else's experience, but so that we, as nurses, can empathise with our patients and provide the support that may be necessary to reduce the adverse effects of that person's experience.

We need to have some understanding of how stress can affect behaviour in order to understand the behaviour of our patients. This may help to enable us to anticipate times when stress may be heightened and when it may be at a minimum. An understanding of how people may appraise a situation as stressful needs to be part of the nurse's repertoire of skills in order to provide care most effectively. Being there for people when the need for support is at its most pressing is one of the most valuable skills of caring. The practice of nursing requires a prioritising when delivering care and being able to anticipate possible stress for patients when making these judgements.

So, making judgements about patients' affect, behaviour and cognition requires skill in empathy and analysis. An understanding of the self is essential to begin the process of analysis. We need to understand our thoughts and feelings to tease out the rationale for the actions and reactions of self and others. We also need to have an understanding of attitudes in order to be able to suspend our subjective evaluations and account for the evaluative judgements of others.

Attitudes

attitude

the sum of one's beliefs and opinions

As we grow from infancy to adulthood, we are influenced by a variety of different pressures from parents, family, friends, school and the media. These pressures form the basis of our attitudes, beliefs and opinions. Attitudes reflect our values, the worth we attribute to events, people and objects. Sharing values is a way of building relationships; we seem to have a natural rapport with those who share our perspective. The way we dress, the music we like, the political beliefs we hold, all contribute to the development of friendships. However, when we nurse, we cannot be that selective. Indeed, in the health-care context, all human life is here. Nurses are charged with being genuine, being warm and demonstrating unconditional positive regard. These are Roger's core conditions necessary to effect change within a therapeutic relationship (Rogers, 1959). How easy is it for these conditions to pertain? There are times when, as nurses, we are required to suspend judgement in order to give our undivided attention. In some cases, this is not difficult. However, in others, our attitudes, beliefs and opinions may block the ability to enter the 'other's' world perspective and give care at an optimum level. Making the effort to know someone's background may make the difference between treating someone as an object in receipt of a service and a person who requires nursing care.

Parkinson's disease

a slowly progressive neurological disorder with resting tremor, muscle rigidity and weakness, shuffling gait and a mask-like appearance

As an illustration of this point, let us consider the experience of a student nurse who was asked to care for a man with Parkinson's disease. The patient had a reputation among the nurses as being difficult. The student said she did not like him, because 'You can't like everyone can you?' This statement requires challenging and analysis in the context of nursing care. When we acknowledge likes and dislikes, we are expressing an attitude. On what are these judgements based? Sometimes they are based on only limited information: our interactions with the patients and possibly the comments of our colleagues. Knowledge can be inaccurate and incomplete, and, as nurses, we need to be prepared to alter our opinions, to allow our knowledge of our patients to be fluid and flexible. How is this achieved? By being non-judgemental. A person-centred approach to care, an approach that starts with the patient before any judgements or decisions, is more likely to facilitate a rapport that will contribute to reducing the impact of the stress of being a patient.

The gentleman with Parkinson's disease had been admitted for a review of his condition. He was slow when mobile and dependent when in bed. He had the typical mask-like expression seen in patients with Parkinson's disease and demonstrated the on/off syndrome when walking. He was perceived by the nurses as demanding because, when he asked for assistance, he was time-consuming and appeared ungrateful for the help. The nurses found him difficult to please, and he always insisted on having things done strictly his way. The student nurse interpreted his behaviour as difficult and hostile, and the consequence was that she judged him as an unpleasant man. Now, this may be an accurate judgement, but an alternative explanation may be that here was a man angry and frustrated at his loss of independence. He was pedantic about his needs; he wanted his way because he was no longer able to perform, without help from another person, activities that most of us take for granted. This patient's expectation was that others would substitute what he would like to do for himself. This nurse needed to develop her skill of empathy to see the world from his perspective. Nurses need to listen to the patient's story (most people have a story if we can make the right connection) and see beyond the label of difficult-to-understand. As nurses, if we label patients as we do our friends and acquaintances, we fail to acknowledge the meaning of our profession, the meaning of care.

Part of this process is to understand attitudes, how they are formed and how they can be changed. Attitudes influence behaviour, and as such we need to have insight into the effect of our own attitudes on our nursing practice. We also need to consider the attitudes of our patients and how these may be influencing their compliance to treatment and their thoughts and feelings about being in a vulnerable, dependent position.

There are three components of an attitude:

1. *Affective*: This consists of the feelings held towards an object or event and is to some degree either positive or negative. This is the component that represents our likes and dislikes.
2. *Behavioural*: This is the observable translation of an attitude. If feelings are positive, we develop an approach tendency or behaviour that increases contact with the object or causes us to engage with that situation. If our feelings are negative, we tend to develop avoidance tendencies or behaviours that distance us from the object or event.

3. *Cognitive*: This is the rationale part of the attitude and defines the object or situation to which the attitude is directed. This encompasses people and groups, and consists of knowledge about the object or situation even though this knowledge may be incomplete.

This three-component model of attitudes is useful in trying to make sense of our experience, but it is based on the the assumption that all three components are consistent. For example, if we hold positive beliefs about an object or event, this should elicit positive feelings and an approach tendency. Is this always the case? Try Activity 5.

Your opinion about smoking may be influenced by whether your parents smoked, whether your friends, the people with whom you wish to affiliate, smoke and whether you smoke. Perhaps you think that smoking in moderation is OK and that people who do not smoke are prudish and boring. You may, however, believe that smoking is a health hazard not just for those who smoke, but also for those of us who have to inhale the smoke from others' cigarettes, making smokers selfish and antisocial if not dangerous. It may be that you hold strong beliefs about smoking because of your experience of its effect on someone you know, or you may have beliefs about smoking but not in such a way that you object to others smoking in your presence.

An alternative model is the expectancy value model. This proposes that we hold attitudes according to what we expect of an object or event and the degree to which this event or object will contribute to our goals and values.

Attitudes are formed by both direct and indirect methods. Direct experiences tend to produce more accurate knowledge on which to form judgements, but indirect methods also have a great influence. These include vicarious experience as well as what others, for example parents, peer group, schools and the media, say and do.

Changing attitudes can be a difficult task but does have real relevance for nurses as it is the attitudes that people have towards health behaviours that influence risky health behaviours and whether people are likely to modify behaviour that will lessen their susceptibility to ill-health. The relationship between the patient and the nurse can be an important factor in changing a person's attitudes. Some of the factors that contribute to attitude change include:

● Trust
● Like and dislike
● Credibility
● Perceived attractiveness
● Individual beliefs
● Self-esteem.

In other words, the relationship between the nurse and patient is important in influencing patients' attitudes. This highlights the importance of the nurse developing interpersonal skills and understanding how to establish and build a rapport.

What happens when our behaviour is inconsistent with our beliefs? When we behave in a way that is contrary to our beliefs, we are left with a feeling of psychological discomfort described as cognitive dissonance. This discomfort may arise, for example, when a person who smokes firmly holds the belief that it is harmful to the self and others, or one who drives a car on a regular basis believes that this is major form of pollution and therefore harmful to self and others. Any behaviour that counteracts our beliefs can lead to a feeling of discomfort, which we try to reduce. Individuals, on the whole, strive for cognitive consistency. As nurses, an understanding of self and motives for behaviour can lead to an attitude change and a greater degree of objectivity when making assessments of patients in our care.

A further issue that needs to be addressed in a discussion of attitudes is that of prejudice. Prejudice arises from a faulty generalisation directed towards a specific person or group of people because they are members of a particular group. A prejudice ignores qualities or characteristics that would negate our opinion, and whereas prejudice is generally thought of as being negative, we may equally ignore negative qualities as well as positive (Oliver and Hyde, 1993). If, as nurses, we believe that people who are short-tempered and particular in the way in which their needs are met are difficult patients, we will adopt a prejudicial approach to people who fit these criteria. The cognitive component of prejudice is more commonly known as a stereotype. One definition of a stereotype is that it is a type of shorthand, a way of understanding without having to go to first principles each time we wish to communicate or understand an event or situation. The knowledge that we hold about the world is organised into schemata, clumps of knowledge that include stereotypes, but by using this shorthand in our professional life, we exclude a great deal of knowledge and information about people that will enrich our understanding and enhance our nursing care.

The student nurse (above) who said she did not like the gentleman with Parkinson's disease had adopted an attitude about this patient based on her belief about how patients should behave and possibly about the nature of Parkinson's disease. However, it suggests that her knowledge about the condition was incomplete, as well as that her attitude towards the patient's behaviour was limited and prejudicial. Knowledge should be acquired as this student progresses through her training. Will an increase in knowledge widen her understanding? The expectation is that it will, and will in turn influence her attitude to patients with Parkinson's disease who remain expressionless, unable to give the usual feedback that helps us to understand our impact on the other person.

Will this increase in knowledge also help to develop the individual's understanding of her action and reaction to patients who may be having difficulty

stereotype

a form of cultural shorthand; shared knowledge or information about an object or event

coming to terms with a redefining of self from independent to dependent? This requires an analysis not just of knowledge in terms of generalising neutral facts to the subjective human experience, but also of the nurse's own thoughts, feeling and behaviours.

Chapter Summary

This chapter attempts to explain why it is important for nurses to have an understanding of the self. It covers issues of the self-concept and its development, self-awareness, stress, attitudes and prejudice.

Nurses need to have an understanding of the self to enable a greater understanding of the people for whom they care. A knowledge of the self will promote empathy by a growth in self-awareness and an insight into the factors that may threaten the self-concept such as stress and prejudice. By understanding our own motivations for behaviour, our own responses to stress, the origins of attitudes and prejudices we will better understand those of the people for whom we care.

Test Yourself!

1. Define the self-concept.

2. What is the difference between being self-aware and self-conscious?

3. Can you define stress?

4. List the factors that may modify the impact of stress.

5. What are attitudes?

6. Why is it important for nurses to have an understanding of attitude change?

7. What are some of the factors in the nurse–patient relationship that contribute to attitude change?

References

Atkinson, R., Atkinson, R., Smith E. and Bem, D. (1993) *Introduction to Psychology*, 11th edn. Harcourt Brace Jovanovich, Fort Worth.

Baron, R. and Byrne, D. (1997) *Social Psychology*, 8th edn. Allyn & Bacon, Boston.

Brooks-Gun, J. and Paikoff, R.L. (1992) Changes in self feelings during the transition towards adolescence. In McGurk, H. (ed.) *Childhood Social Development, Contemporary Perspectives*, pp. 63–90. LEA, London.

Cobb, S. (1976) Social support as a moderator of life stress. *Psychosomatic Medicine* **38**: 300–14.

Cohen, S. and Hoberman, H.M. (1983) Positive life events and social supports as buffers of life change stress. *Journal of Applied Social Psychology* **13**: 99–125.

Cox, T. (ed.) (1978) *Stress.* Macmillan, London.

Cox, T. and McKay, C. (1978) Stress at work. In Cox, T. (ed.) *Stress*, pp. 147–73. Macmillan, London.

Erikson, E. (1959) *Identity and The Life Cycle*. International University Press, London.

Gordon, C. (1968) Self concept: configurations of content. In Gordon, C. and Gergen, K.J. (eds) *The Self in Social Interaction*, Vol. I: *Classic Contemporary Perspectives*. John Wiley & Sons, New York.

Holmes, T. and Rahe, R. (1967) The Social Readjustment Rating Scale. *Journal of Psychosomatic Research* **11**: 213–18.

Humphrey, N. (1984) *Consciousness Regained: Chapters in the Development of Mind.* Oxford University Press, Oxford.

Kobasa, S. (1979) Stressful life events, personality and health. An inquiry into hardiness. *Journal of Personality and Social Psychology* **37**: 1–11.

Luft, J. and Ingham, H. (1955) *The Johari Window: A Graphic Model for Interpersonal Relationships*. National Press, New York.

Maslow, A. (1968) *Toward a Psychology of Being.* Van Nostrand Rheinhold, New York.

Mischel, W. (1986) *Introduction to Personality,* 4th edn. Holt, Rinehart & Winston, Fort Worth.

Montemeyer, R. and Eisen, M. (1977) The development of self conception from childhood to adolescence. *Development Psychology* **13**(4): 314–19.

Pervin, L. (1984) *Personality: Theory and Research,* 4th edn. John Wiley & Sons, London.

Oliver, M.B. and Hyde, J.S. (1993) Gender differences in sexuality: a meta analysis. *Psychological Bulletin* **114**: 29–51.

Rawlinson, J. (1990) Self awareness: conceptual influences, contribution to nursing, and approaches to attainment. *Nurse Education Today* **10**: 111–17.

Rentsch, J.R. and Heffner, T.S. (1994) Assessing self concept: analysis of Gordon's coding scheme using 'Who am I?" responses. *Journal of Social Behaviour and Personality* **9**(1): 283–300.

Rogers, C. (1959) A theory of therapy, personality and interpersonal relationships as developed in the client centred framework. In Koch, S. (ed.) *Psychology: A Study of Science,* Vol 3: *Formulations of the Person and the Social Context*, pp. 184–256. McGraw-Hill, New York.

Rosenman, R.H. and Jenkins, C.D. (1975) Coronary heart disease in the western collaborative group study. *Journal of the American Medical Association* **128**: 307–11.

Selye, H. (1980) The stress concept today. In Kutash, I.L, Schlesinger, L.B. *et al.* (eds) *Handbook on Stress and Anxiety*, pp. 127–43. Josey-Bass, San Fransisco.

Watson, D. and Clark, L.A. (1984) Negative affectivity: the disposition to experience aversive emotional states. *Psychological Bulletin* **96**: 465–90.

Reflective Practice

IAN DOUGLAS

Introduction

This chapter seeks to enable you to gain familiarity with the key features of reflective practice. Specifically, you should become aware that reflective practice is not an isolated phenomenon, but a process designed to assist us to learn from what we do, gaining knowledge and experience not from conventional sources, such as textbooks, journals and study days, but from the richest source of learning – practice itself.

At the end of the chapter you should be able to:

- Identify sources and types of knowledge, and their potential shortcomings in the nurse education setting

- Contrast the media image of nurses against the reality

- Define reflective practice and its contribution to nursing practice

- Identify and utilise reflection-*in*- and *on*-action

- Contrast ritualistic and reflective practice

- Formulate and use critical incident analysis as a means of reflection

- Identify the place that experience plays in developing knowledge

- Discuss how reflection can influence learning in the practice setting.

Each theme within the chapter offers reflective activities to enhance the learning experience, some offering suggested responses for the activities. These are far from exhaustive, so record your own answers in a notebook in order to enhance your own reflective skills.

Reflection – Seeing Ourselves as Others See Us?

Students entering nursing today will naturally encounter many new, seemingly alien, concepts and experiences. They will frequently have entered with a ready-prepared mind-set of what will confront them and the role they will be expected to play.

Many people in our society, and indeed those starting nursing, harbour stereotyped images of what nursing involves and what nurses do. One has to become ill or actually nurse to see nursing truly at first hand. However, the majority of people do not nurse or become ill. Thus most remain in ignorance of the true nature and realities of nursing. A distorted, idealised image of nursing and nurses, possibly perpetuated by the media, frequently remains unchallenged.

Few conversations with actual or potential clients will proceed very far without evidence of the stereotypical nurse image emerging, perhaps through traditionalist associations with activities such as temperature-taking, fevered brow-mopping, back-rubbing and, sadly within our seemingly elimination-fixated culture, even dealing with the ubiquitous bedpans and enemas. Perhaps those indefinable epithets of kindness, dedication, vocation, caring or even angelic will be applied. Thankfully, all are far from reality and are frequently outdated with the emergence of today's research- and evidence-guided practitioner.

Students come from this lay-conceptual environment and can harbour similar anticipatory images of their perceived role, possibly originating years before. None of us will have escaped childhood without at least one encounter with a small girl proudly sporting her first 'Little Nurse' costume, complete with gaudily coloured stethoscope, thermometer and fob-watch. Nursing recruitment campaigns, even in recent years, have perilously focused on such questionable imagery.

On entry into nursing, conflict and dissonance can often result when the reality fails to meet the expectation. Once in the clinical setting, students strive to make sense of the maze of alien activities, roles and terminology encountered. They frequently attempt to gain a grasp of it all by striving to fit it to the public image. As a result, practice can become hesitant, rigid and unimaginative. Unthinking task orientation is frequently the most secure course, as this often best fits the image they believe to be accurate.

Such a haven offers security not only to students. Even for veteran practitioners, Street (1991) observes, survival involves many nurses, midwives and health visitors switching to autopilot, mechanistically attempting to meet demands. Perhaps reluctantly, thoughtful, imaginative and individualised care is not valued as time-economical but more as diverting the practitioner from 'getting the work done'.

Melia (1987), citing Menzies (1960), explains that resorting to routine or ritual is the most common way of coping with stretched resources. Dividing patient care into an array of disjointed, routine tasks is a means of protecting the nurse from the pressures of work. Naturally, the holistic needs of clients are not

Activity

1

Reflect on your experiences of the stereotypical images of nurses and their work. How are we seen by the media, in films and so on? Consider your personal impressions before entering nursing of what you would encounter and what the work would involve. Think about the advice and comments of parents, friends and so on when you announced your decision to enter nursing. Jot your thoughts down, and, in retrospect, consider how accurate they actually were and whether they truly prepared you for the reality of nursing.

met, but the carer achieves solace by striving to maintain expert performance, unfortunately, however, only of routines and tasks.

At first glance, this may appear to paint a rather bleak picture of nursing, but it is not meant to. Numerous exciting initiatives have addressed many of these traditional problems. Not least of these are the establishment of patient allocation and primary nursing approaches to care. Such initiatives are laudable, and students operating within such progressive environments are fortunate.

However, few students will be so lucky as to work within such enlightened practice settings in *every* clinical placement. It is during the times when we are less fortunate that the above propositions will, unfortunately, be all too familiar. For those occasions, reflection can offer a lifeline towards achieving more meaningful practice and learning, even when compelled to work within a task-orientated care environment.

Reflection – Thoughtful Practice

When considering mechanistic approaches to care, most thinking students will immediately realise the flaws. By only addressing the immediate tasks, as such systems do, the work may seem to get done and the routine tasks completed. However, by failing to consider care thoughtfully and critically, individualised needs are not met. It is so much easier to standardise the care given. Everyone receives the same, irrespective of need. The resulting care demands little thought, which might interfere with the primary purpose of finishing the work on time.

However, does detached, unthinking care really save steps, energy and resources? Enlightened practitioners would immediately be dubious of any form of battery-nursing. Routine-driven, standardised care can superficially appear to get the work done faster but ignores one essential fact: it frequently results in dogged repetition of *unnecessary* procedures.

Everyone may not *need* 4-hourly clinical observations, daily fluid balance monitoring, hourly neurological observations, preoperative shaving or daily bed baths. Moreover, the time spent in giving unnecessary care could be better utilised in undertaking *quality* interventions with those who really need them, resulting in more effective, lasting outcomes.

Put another way, the time saved in *not* bed-bathing the whole of bay 6 before coffee-break could be utilised in, for example, giving dietary advice to elderly, postoperative patients. *We* may understand how vital dietary protein is in assisting the healing process, but does the client? It takes time to educate or re-educate such clients, like most people socialised over years into fixed dietary patterns. Yet, for their fullest and quickest recovery, additional and possibly expensive dietary changes or supplements will be needed, and the client needs to fully understand this.

Information-giving or re-education requires time, skill and patience on the part of knowledgeable carers. If lifestyle changes are to be achieved successfully, the new information needs to be carefully packaged and sold. However, it is the courageous nurse, let alone student, who has the audacity to sit down and actually talk to the client when *real* work is going on around them. Despite high ideals, such as supernumerary status for students, many will still be pressurised by their peers into conformity with outdated work schedules.

Quality interactions such as patient education are time-consuming and intellectually demanding, seditious concepts to those who recognise only physical labour as having any real, intrinsic value. Should we then be surprised by the increasing number of media scandals that illuminate the plight of malnourished, dehydrated or otherwise neglected clients? Management responses to such crises frequently involve expensive, futile reactions, perhaps changes in catering arrangements, dietetic consultations, even another Charter or mission statement. In reality, all that is probably necessary is the fostering of a climate that cultivates the provision of 'thoughtful, quality nursing'.

This *thoughtful* element, the desire and opportunity to provide and modify care to the individual rather than the task, are the embryonic roots for reflective practice. When being thoughtful, even critical, we start to consider not just *what* it is we are doing but *how* it is being done, why it is being done this way rather than another, or even whether it needs doing at all. Just because it was done yesterday, is it still needed or justifiable today? Has the client's condition changed or improved, altering his needs? Has new evidence emerged that now challenges a care activity or procedure? Through a thoughtful, questioning process, the minute aspects of care are repeatedly reanalysed to confirm their continuing validity. Without such a reflective approach, task-orientated practice would dominate. Jarvis (1992) cautions that all care activities constantly run the risk of degenerating into habitualised, presumptive and ritualised actions. Superficial, mechanical approaches should have no place in an activity as sensitive as nursing, dependent as it is on the quality of its interpersonal interactions. People are unique and respond best when treated as individuals in a unique and humanistic manner.

Even though many nursing actions may be performed repeatedly, they must nonetheless always be individually planned and monitored. Change in a client's condition, either deterioration or improvement, can be subtle and easily missed when masked by rigid adherence to an unthinking ritual.

Danger exists when people start to be just viewed as cases, virtually becoming dehumanised by their carers. When this happens, clients and patients run the risk of being seen merely as the passive recipients of care, and the danger is increased of care moving from the carefully planned to the taken-for-granted.

Palmer *et al.* (1994) suggest that reflective practice has emerged as a means of overcoming the potential alienation of nurses from their clients brought about

Activity 2

Think about the last week you spent in practice. Critically assess the care you were involved in. Make a list of the care interactions in which you were involved that required little or no thought. From this list, try to identify those which could be seen as 'ritualistic'. Consider now those occasions when time allowed you to sit and talk to your client, perhaps giving advice or reassurance, or just explaining their care in your own way.

Activity 3

Now challenge the two approaches in Activity 2. Which gave you most satisfaction? Which afforded the most learning? Which was directly most beneficial to your client? Pause and reflect on your conclusions.

by today's 'high-speed' care. Although they justifiably caution that reflection should not be perceived as a universal panacea for all the ills of nursing, it does offer practitioners a means by which to interrogate their care, thus avoiding the pitfall of Jarvis's presumptive and ritualised practice. For the student, reflection offers the tools for meaningful learning within the practice setting.

The concept of reflection as a means of enhancing practice is nothing new, perhaps first being considered as early as the 1930s by Dewey (1933). Many others since have contributed to its understanding, among them Habermas (1977), Van Manen (1977), Mezirow (1981), Schön (1983), Kolb (1984) and Boud *et al.* (1985).

Perhaps anticipating the notorious nursing impasse in relating theory to practice, Dewey postulated that, in order for theory to be linked to practice, the process of utilising experience by reflection should be adopted. Dewey contrasted *routine* and *reflective* human action. Routine actions he saw as being driven by impulse, tradition and authority. Here, we risk drawing parallels with the disciplined origins of nursing, for example within the religious orders and the military. More recently, this might be applied to the traditionalist, media images of rigid nursing hierarchies. Visions of tyrannical, matronly figures and demure, obedient student nurses quickly emerge. In these 'routinised' actions, everyday practice is taken for granted. The outcomes can be safely presumed, providing that the routines have been followed. *Process* is subordinated to *product*, the end justifying the means.

Conversely, Dewey (1933) defines reflective action as:

> active, persistent and careful consideration of any belief or supposed knowledge, in the light of the grounds that support it, and the further consequences to which it leads.

Essentially, it demands an open mind, responsibility and the commitment to consider all possibilities and implications, not only to achieve an objective, but also to seek learning from the experience, thus enhancing future practice.

The Reflective Process for Lifelong Learning

Reflection is...

> [the] process of internally examining and exploring an issue of concern, triggered by an experience, which creates and clarifies meaning in terms of self, and which results in a changed conceptual perspective. (Boyd and Fales, 1983)

a process of reviewing an experience of practice in order to better describe, analyse and evaluate, and so inform learning about practice. (Boud *et al.,* 1985)

When the term 'reflection' is used, it can often evoke almost spiritual connotations. In practice, however, reflection should be seen as a learning tool and not merely a random, passive process. It very much has an active element rather than being simply a process of quiet contemplation. It can be learned and taught, and, within reason, controlled and guided. In practice, it should be regarded as a *conscious* process, not essentially happening automatically but rather with a definite purpose in response to an experience.

In nursing, reflection seeks to identify the true value and meaning of our actions in order to quantify, augment, enhance or discard them, and to enable us to replicate them appropriately to their best effect in future interactions. Each situation reflected on must be treated as a unique event if the maximum learning is to be gained.

Nurses constantly meet unique and challenging situations yet frequently fail to acknowledge them as learning opportunities essential to professional growth. Given the pace of today's practice, it becomes all too easy to lapse into presumptive or habitualised care.

Although illnesses and the care we give may appear largely repetitive to us, they are for the client new and unique experiences. Unlike nurses, clients are not exposed to them on a daily basis. When we lapse from viewing the experience from the client's perspective, we cease to function empathically and thus stop interrogating what we do. Pain, anxiety, fear, and ignorance become just detached descriptors for problems in the care plan rather than being the very real human experiences they are. If this happens, we are just a short step from becoming presumptive in our anticipation of the outcomes of our care.

Berger and Luckman (1967) caution that, left unchecked, all human action is subject to habitualisation. They see human actions hierarchically thus:

1. *Creative/experimental actions*: new experiences that are being worked out in practice
2. *Repetitive acts*: acts that are thoughtfully repeated during the normal process of living
3. *Presumptive acts*: actors presuming upon the situation and its outcomes and acting almost unthinkingly
4. *Ritualism*: where participants mindlessly go through the motions
5. *Alienation*: where the need for the action has become lost through mindless repetition, becoming self-destructive.

(after Jarvis, 1992)

In habitual or ritualised care, there is frequently an expectation that the client will conform to a prescribed outcome, and it is not uncommon for clients to be penalised when they fail to do so.

In her seminal work, Stockwell (1984) gave insight into this sinister side of caring and to what it can lead. She gives disturbing examples of the rewards and deterrents that carers will use to impose clients' conformity to the care regimen. Individual needs are subtly suppressed in deference to the need for compliance and order.

Yet, in reality, when the views of the client are not fully explored, an essential component in realistic, effective care-planning is missed. The resulting conformity is achieved by a *power-coercive* imperative rather than the much more desirable *normative-re-educative* approach. This is only a short step from anticipating or presuming outcomes, carers possibly going to extraordinary lengths to ensure compliance. At its simplest, a presumptive interchange might be:

> Mr Brown, you can't possibly still be in pain, you only had your pain killers an hour ago. Mr Wilson and Mr Adams had exactly the same operation and analgesia as you, and they're not in pain.

In this case, the strong signal being given to Mr Brown is to *conform!* Such a scenario may seem far fetched; nonetheless, it will be familiar to many. We all know what we should do, but when we work in an ethos that forces us to ration our resources, coercion to comply can seem justifiable as the most time-economical means of providing care. Conversely, when we nurse reflectively, we maintain responsiveness to the *actual* rather than the *presumed* needs of the client.

No-one is suggesting that we try to reflect on each and every situation or event we encounter. Reflection is a demanding and often disturbing activity, and we would soon burn out. A simple commitment to develop the skills is enough. If we are clear on the advantages that reflection can bring to our practice, there will follow a readiness to develop our reflective skills.

Over time and with practice, the reflective process becomes easier and the skills essential to its use integrated into what we do. However, we need to be clear on the potential benefits. Reflection on our care opens the mind, ensuring flexibility and creativity, rather than merely making our interventions fit predetermined expectations and assumptions.

Although reflection can frequently be spontaneous, structured development of the skills is much more desirable. Atkins and Murphy (1994) offer the reflective framework shown in Chart 11.1. A closer exploration of the stages of this process will help to illustrate the nature and potential of reflection.

Chart 11.1 ● Atkins and Murphy's (1994) reflective framework

- Be aware of uncomfortable feelings or thoughts
- Describe the situation, including thoughts and feelings
- Analyse the feelings and knowledge relevant to the situation
- Evaluate the relevance of the knowledge
- Identify any new learning that has occurred
- Put it into action in a new situation

Be aware of uncomfortable feelings or thoughts

It is all too easy to coast along in our practice, frequently oblivious to the need for minor adjustments or changes. Left unchecked, presumptive and anticipatory action can follow. Conversely, when in tune with our actions, we will often detect shifts from that which is confidently and competently known into areas that are new, untested or uncertain.

Such deviation may generate feelings of insecurity, our actions no longer being guided by what is implicitly known through teaching or experience. Outcomes may seem risky, uncontrollable and unpredictable, and a sense of uncertainty results. Boyd and Fales (1983) speak of this as being 'a sense of inner discomfort', while Schön (1983) calls it 'the experience of surprise'. It is these sensations which best trigger reflection, as it is on such occasions that the potential for learning from a situation is at its highest. The experience need not be unpleasant or merely apply to negative experiences. Heightened awareness can equally be triggered by a positive or fulfilling event, such as being praised or thanked for our care.

The secret of meaningful reflection is to recognise this sense of awareness as a learning opportunity, holding great potential for professional growth. Whether good or bad experiences, for the practitioner, and certainly for the student determined to develop reflective skills, such events should not be allowed to pass unexplored.

There is a great temptation, especially for students, to assume that most events met in practice are common and encountered again and again as we progress through our placements. In reality, every care situation is a one-off, or has unique aspects to its construction. If the maximum learning is not gained from every situation immediately, an invaluable opportunity for improving knowledge, professional growth and insight is lost, possibly never to be repeated. The next time a similar opportunity presents may be far off in the future, perhaps when qualified – and then demanding immediate, *accountable* action. Sadly, responses then may be delayed or inadequate because the opportunity had not been taken to learn from it when it was first encountered.

Care interactions, successful or otherwise, cannot be taken for granted. We only grow professionally by considering *why* events went well or badly, and not by simply accepting their outcome as being inevitable. To do this, we must be in tune with our feelings and recognise the occasions when we experience doubt or uncertainty as powerful triggers for learning through reflection and not, as frequently happens, as occasions when we must dig our heels in and hope to bluff it out.

The reflective and professional practitioner is one who welcomes every opportunity to test, analyse and interrogate practice in the pursuit of excellence, currency and validation, or better still, to have their practice appraised and challenged by peers, even if they are junior. This holds the truest potential for professional growth.

Describe the situation

If the maximum learning is to be gained from an event, it is essential that every single aspect of it must be examined. It is not enough just to gain a superficial overview. All of its characteristics, even the most sensitive and disturbing, need to be explored.

In nursing, where all of the extremes of life and the human condition are encountered, this can frequently be a painful process. In illustrating the student's difficulties in reflecting critically, Palmer *et al.* (1994) speak of the plethora of emotions to which practice exposes us: despair, fear, suffering, disgust, distress and even ecstatic relief. Each should be analysed if the maximum potential for growth and learning is to be achieved. Williams (1996) suggests that such growth might emerge as problems discovered, solutions proposed or attitudes, assumptions and prejudices challenged.

Analyse the feelings and knowledge relevant to the situation

Critical interrogation of a practice situation will require meaning to be drawn from a variety of domains if reflection is to be maximised. Such knowledge may already be possessed, or, alternatively, this may prompt its being sought. For a student, reflecting on a challenging care interaction, it may mean reading up on the salient features or seeking advice from a senior colleague, mentor or tutor. This facilitates the opportunity for shared exploration, the airing of anxieties and the testing of perceptions.

This process of analysing an experience is central to the quality and accuracy of reflection. Through it, attitudes, even prejudices, which might otherwise obstruct the process of healthy and impartial reflection can be confronted and overcome. It is this interrogation of our feelings that determines how we should respond to events, how we can learn from them and what personal changes will result, be they perceptual or behavioural. Boud *et al.* (1985) suggest that this self-interrogation process has four distinct features:

1. *Association*: ideas and feelings arising from the experience being reflected on being tested against perceptions from previous events, experience or attitudes
2. *Integration*: savouring the information and knowledge and identifying links between different parts
3. *Validation*: checking to ensure that impressions emerging from the reflective experience are legitimate
4. *Appropriation*: once the validity of the new knowledge or perception has been verified, assimilating the knowledge or belief into one's own value system.

Evaluate the relevance of the knowledge

After analysis, a clearer understanding of the key features of the event or phenomenon should emerge. As stated earlier, this may involve a change in perception or behaviour in anticipation of our future management of a similar situation. Equally though, the outcome might corroborate a previously held view. Thus the reflective process tests a belief or personal *given*, validating its authenticity.

In a practising profession such as nursing, testing the currency of belief is healthy. It forces the questioning of one's professional values, a process of critical analysis. This is a central feature of all adult learning. We learn best when we are made to rationalise rather than dogmatically accept some long unchallenged concept, even if it is awarded validity by its having achieved the lofty status of a competence. Palmer *et al.* (1994) see such challenging as the emergence of humanistic ideology in clinical practice, rightly confronting other traditional outcomes of learning. It acknowledges the primacy of the *process* rather than the *product* of learning.

The achievement of learning from a reflective episode is, however, not the end of the process. The learning experience is not complete until its relevance is weighed against its implications for our practice. When we reflect and learn from a new event, we store that learning in our professional armoury for use in a future setting. It may never occur, but the mere process of reflective learning will have brought about a dynamic reappraisal of our beliefs – the essence of professionalism.

Identify any new learning

Even when learning has been achieved, the process continues. It is possible that the reflective event has only partially equipped us for practice. The process of learning is not static but must be continually refined and polished. This may demand further action on the part of the reflective practitioner, for example evaluation by a trusted mentor, further reading or plans to undertake an appro-

Activity
4

The reflective
framework (see
Chart 11.1) passed
through six stages.
Choose a significant
learning event from
your own recent
practice and try to
relate it to the
framework, if
possible identifying
each of the stages.

priate continuing education programme or study day. All of these and more may
be necessary in maximising and consolidating the learning.

Put it into action

Like it or not, the process explored here has in reality illustrated a reflective
journey stimulated by real practice experiences. Like any journey, however,
either it can be used to achieve a greater understanding of the scenery passed
through or, conversely, the richness of its staging points can be allowed to erode.
The journey's end is very much the learning we have achieved, but this becomes
redundant if we do not act upon it and allow it influence our future practice.
One journey will never be enough if we are to become seasoned reflective trav-
ellers. It does, however, get easier. Like all travel, every time we wander a route,
the more familiar and less threatening the terrain becomes.

Reflection – Taking Control

By now, you should be starting to see the potential advantages that reflection
brings not only to your practice, but also, more importantly, to your perceptions
of learning. Several authors have stressed the importance of reflection as a
learning tool (Dewing, 1990; Jarvis, 1992; Coutts-Jarman, 1993). Today's
students, through their supernumerary status, enjoy a particular opportunity to
develop in this way. Driscoll (1994) points out that it is, in contrast, a sad reality
that traditionally trained nurses were not routinely encouraged to question their
practice.

Reflection offers a means to add structure to our questioning, a commodity to
be much prized in the culture of nursing (Powell, 1992). However, perhaps
bound by traditional, authoritative perceptions of low status, student nurses still
frequently enter training programmes unaware that they can now enjoy such
freedom in modifying the ways in which they learn.

During their education programme, junior nurses frequently spend much of
their time seeking 'rule book' solutions. This, the technical-rational imperative,
presupposes that there is always a prescriptive answer to everything. For many
years, nurses bound themselves to the notorious Procedure Book, which went
far in perpetuating this restrictive, unthinking approach to professional practice. Similar current issues will be familiar to nurses today. Running parallel
with moves to reduce junior doctors' hours, nurses are once again looking for
rules to guide what they can do. If we are not careful, new, expanded roles may
once again restrict the activities of professional practice to carefully compart-
mentalised skills.

Few could argue with the necessity for policing and auditing one's practice
against defined protocols and standards, but practitioners would be advised to

break away from self-imposed boundaries. In reality, these can generally only control the macro elements of nursing. No protocol can ever be devised that guides our practice in the micro interactions of expert, professional nursing. Schön's (1987) much-quoted 'swampy lowlands' of professional practice are where nursing's most intricate and complex decisions must be made. Often messy and confusing, they frequently defy resolution by formal protocols or traditional types of knowledge.

The UKCC's *Scope of Professional Practice* went some way towards offering guidance for professional decision-making without the need for too many defined rules (UKCC, 1992). It is with each individual practitioner that the potential for professional artistry and growth truly lies.

In the course of our work, we are frequently confronted by problems for which no solutions exist in the literature or through formal guidelines. On these occasions, we are expected to 'think on our feet'. All practitioners will readily agree that nursing practice frequently takes place without the benefit of true evidence. However, this need not hold any anxieties. Providing we critically appraise what we do through reflection, even when in the 'swampy lowlands', we are likely to remain safe.

Benner (1984) alludes to the intuitive characteristic of nursing as being the benchmark of *expert* practice. Nurses accrue clinical knowledge over the course of their careers yet lose track of the exact circumstances in which that knowledge was gained. Benner further refers to the frustration that many expert nurses frequently feel when trying to pass on this expertise to their students. So much of it has been obtained from the myriad of sources to which individual practitioners have been exposed over their careers that it is impossible to isolate the exact circumstances in which the knowledge was obtained. Polanyi (1967) refers to this as 'tacit knowing'.

Mentors naturally try to guide students using sound, theoretically correct sources, but are frequently left frustrated. The exact mechanisms of their expertise have been complex and unique to each individual. Everyone learns differently, assimilating and distilling the experience of their practice in their own way. That process cannot be replicated on demand as its structures, and the conclusions drawn from them, may have been 'lost in the mists of time'. Sadly, the frustration all too frequently results in an authoritarian dismissal such as 'Because it is', 'That's the way we do it around here' or 'Sister prefers it this way', all familiar to most students. Both parties are left frustrated, and potentially rich learning opportunities are left incomplete. Mentors feel they have failed students in not being able to deliver a more professionally robust response, and students feel injured because they have been 'fobbed off' with something dangerously close to an authoritarian demand for unquestioning compliance.

So then, if students are to avoid confrontations and frustration in attempting to gain the maximum information to facilitate their learning, how can progress

Activity 5

Think back on your last week in practice and identify a simple procedure in which you were involved that demanded little thought. Remember that this care may not have appeared 'routine' to the client. Identify the domain of care involved in completion of the activity. Was it:
● Physical or mechanical (psychomotor) – performing a procedure
● Psychological – knowledge, understanding
● Social – implications for family, significant others, work, home
● Emotional or spiritual – fear, anxiety, relief.

Activity 6

Refer back to Activity 5 and reflect on the implications for the client, identifying what additional care might be given related to the remaining domains. Finally, consider how you might next approach a similar care activity, meeting all of the care domains.

be made? It is here that reflection truly comes into its own. Learning nursing can be achieved providing we realise that it not the *quantity* of nursing knowledge that is at issue, but the *quality*; not the *breadth,* but the *depth*. Distillation of this is within the grasp of every student.

Few could argue that, when learning something new, it is best to learn every aspect of it in order to gain the most complete interpretation. Yet how many of us truly do so? The impetus is quite often merely to gain a cursory familiarity and to hope that the rest will somehow fall into place or take care of itself. For example, when we buy a new television set, video or hi-fi, how many of us can truthfully say that we read the instruction manual from cover to cover before attaching the plug? Few of us have the time or the inclination to be so thorough.

Learning nursing can be similar for many students. There appears to be so much to learn that it frequently seems sufficient merely to gain a working knowledge in order to 'survive' in the clinical setting without drawing attention to our 'newness'.

Most nurses can cite an example from their training of when the television analogy applied. Perhaps many will remember the early days of a first clinical placement, having been exposed to the vagaries of the sphygmomanometer and blood pressure taking. What agonies such a simple procedure produced! For most, all that seemed to matter was that they appeared proficient, yet a simple clinical measurement took on the intensity of brain surgery.

However, even when the technique was apparently eventually mastered, how many could honestly have accurately recited fully the implications of peripheral resistance or cardiac output to the reading, let alone have listed the psychological, non-verbal cues to watch out for during the procedure? These might have drawn attention to the patient's acute anxiety at the possibility of suffering hypertension, the implications of this for their lifestyle, and their need for reassurance.

Naturally, to be perceived as acting expertly, one would hope to be able to link all aspects of practice: the pathophysiological, the psychosocial and the nursing characteristics. Yet sadly, many will merely be satisfied to obtain the reading accurately and to continue to replicate it *ad infinitum*. Thus much of the richness of a potential learning experience in seemingly simple practice activities can remain underdeveloped.

Now do Activity 5. Remember that all care, regardless of the domain it takes place within, has implications for the other domains if it is to be achieved to its maximum potential and, of greater importance to the student, if the maximum learning is to be achieved. When you have completed Activity 5, read Activity 6.

Activity 5 required you to think of the widest implications of your care. This is where the maximum learning from even the simple nursing events lies. Your mentor or supervisor may find time to give you the basics of the care to be carried out, the quantity of learning, but you control its breadth – the quality.

It is this extending of each learning event where reflection most offers the opportunity for expanding knowledge and professional growth. Jarvis (1992) suggests that reflection should cause practitioners to 'problematise' their practice, thus constantly extending the knowledge, skills and attitudes demanded by the event.

Types of Reflection

When incorporating reflective processes into our learning and practice, it is prudent once again to stress that reflection is an active rather than a merely passive or random process. As Jarvis (1992) cautions, reflective practice is not simply *thoughtful* practice. Furthermore, reflection is not a unidimensional event but manifests itself in many different forms.

The much popularised work of Schön (1983, 1987) acknowledges the reality that much in professional practice fails to conform to the positivist, technical-rationalism of traditional, professional education. As Palmer *et al.* (1994) interpret, that approach is best suited to problem-solving in the set-piece, contrived world of the laboratory rather than the complex, urgent and often surprising arena of professional nursing practice.

As we discussed earlier, much of our practice is implicit and, although familiar, is often impossible to describe in words. Even more frustrating to the positivist, much of what we do is so complex that it defies rigid control. To attempt to do so would eradicate the responsiveness of the interaction and, with it, much of its richness. Yet much of the effectiveness of our care goes unheralded *because* it is so complex and geared to the uniqueness of the moment. As such, it is difficult to replicate our actions when a similar situation occurs in a future interaction, and once again the risk of resorting to unthinking ritualisation is encountered.

Reflective practice is seen by many as a means of encapsulating the 'essence of practice'. Linked to what we do, Schön postulates that reflection should be operationalised at two points, during and after an intervention – his much-cited reflection-*in*-, and reflection-*on*-action (Schön, 1983).

Reflection-in-action

Reflection-in-action is the process whereby the nurse identifies learning in a new situation as it is encountered and thinks about it while still acting. This is the *active reflection,* which Darbyshire (1993) describes as 'thinking on your feet' or 'keeping your wits about you' rather than working on autopilot. It not only involves thinking about one's practices as they are actualised, but also demands a quantity of preparatory thinking – Van Manen's *anticipatory reflection* (Van Manen, 1977). This relates to the manner in which the care situation is approached, making a tacit comparison with previous experience to ensure that we are not already equipped in some way to deal with what is being met.

It is during the reflection-in-action phase that Atkins and Murphy (1994) see practitioners appraising their range of skills and experiences, and, if appropriate, adapting or modifying them to meet the new situation. As practitioners move towards expert practitioner status, by the accumulation of experience, it is this examination of our practice that Cervero (1988) sees as the true artistry of nursing, described by Powell (1989) as *flexible experimentation* in problem-solving.

Reflection-on-action

Naturally, it is not enough to content oneself with being in tune with one's actions simply as they unfold. There is perhaps too much of a tendency to look back on our actions in a matter-of-fact manner, especially when they have been successful. Obviously, for one to sense that an event has gone well, this infers that similar situations have occasionally gone badly.

It could be argued that, when a nursing action has gone especially well, this is not the time for smug satisfaction, but instead creates more of an imperative to extract exactly *what* features caused it to be so successful. If one can distil the quintessential features that led it to succeed – one's approach, mood, know-ledge-base, experience and so on – something very meaningful has been gained, which can be taken forward into the next similar care intervention. In every sense, it is this which will again truly constitute professional growth.

Greenwood (1993) describes reflection-on-action as a *cognitive post mortem*. Outcomes are reviewed in order to explore the approaches that the practitioner brought to the interaction, their degree of success, and thus concrete evidence for adjustment, augmentation or even rejection. As Atkins and Murphy (1994) put it:

> reflection on action is a very necessary retrospective analysis and interpreta-tion of practice in order to uncover the knowledge used and the accompa-nying feelings within a particular situation.

One should especially note the importance of feelings in this process, considering them as a stimulus or catalyst for further, deeper reflection: Boyd and Fale's (1983) sense of inner discomfort and Schön's (1987) experience of surprise.

● Critical Incident Analysis

The value of reflective practice, and the positive influence it can have on learning, is hopefully becoming clearer. One technique that formally requires you to focus your attention on a practice event for reflective purposes is critical

Activity
7

During your next clinical practice, identify an occasion when you have to force yourself to reflect while carrying out a nursing activity. As it proceeds, consider how it is going and how it relates to your knowledge and beliefs. Afterwards, ask yourself: How did it go? How did I get there? Could I have done it differently? What other knowledge would have been helpful?

incident analysis. You may not have come across this process before, but it is rapidly growing as a reflective learning tool, not just in nursing but in all fields of professional practice.

Crouch (1991) sees the critical incident as 'an observation or activity which was sufficiently complete in itself so as to permit inferences and predictions to be drawn from it'. If maximum learning is to be gained, however, and/or a nursing activity validated, the activity must be subjected to further, formal analysis.

Quite often when significant events occur in our practice, be they positive or negative, the maximum learning is denied because of their complexity. All of the salient features blend into one, and we are simply left with the outcome and any residual feelings about it. Critical incident analysis dissects the event into a 'snapshot in time'. It allows exploration of just one aspect of the event, preferably the moment that determined its outcome and prompted our conclusions on it. The simplest daily nursing activities can be subjected to this process, and, as Crouch (1991) suggests, the effects of care on our clients can be seen or interactions between us and our colleagues illuminated.

Parker *et al*. (1995) acknowledge the importance of meaningful reflection to the critical incident analysis. They advise using the process to focus on the experience (a parallel with Schön's reflection-on-action) and to identify one's feelings about it. The salient features should be documented, extrapolating which domains of learning were influenced or involved during the incident. Were they affective (emotions, values and attitudes), cognitive (knowledge, facts and givens) or psychomotor (practical skills)? Through such analysis, the abstract concepts involved in complex nursing interventions can be broken down into meaningful factors for utilisation in future practice.

Examples of critical incidents and their analysis might help here.

Incident One

The incident took place in a psychiatric assessment unit in the small hours of a night duty and involved Deborah, a second-year mental health branch student. Her description of the incident is given in Casebox 11.1.

Analysis

The analysis is given in Deborah's own words.

My feelings
'On reflection, I realised I was completely out of my depth and had lost control of the situation. It further occurred to me that I had put myself at considerable risk and had possibly irretrievably alienated myself from John. This was *my* environment, not John's. How could I have been so arrogant as to believe that

Casebox 11.1

John had been admitted during the previous day. He was a 50-year-old, homeless man with a psychiatric history and had suffered facial injuries following an assault while on the streets. I had had the opportunity to talk to John before the unit was settled for the night, and he had presented as a confused, lonely man, but was reasonably calm and lucid.

At about 1 am, I got up from the nursing station in response to a noise in the unit and saw John smoking in a part of the ward designated as a no-smoking area. I approached him and advised him that he shouldn't be smoking there, and asked him to put the cigarette out and return to bed. This he did without complaint.

About 2 hours later, I again became aware of move-ment in the same part of the ward and went to investigate. I found John once again smoking in the no-smoking area. Perhaps confident with my previous handling of the situation, I again, this time more forcefully, asked him to put the cigarette out and return to bed. It was then that I realised John was crying and starting to become more agitated. Not really knowing what to do next, I attempted to take the cigarette from him, at which point John physically pushed me away and became abusive. I was confused and frightened, realising I was in an isolated part of the unit and perhaps about to be physically assaulted.

John became progressively more abusive and agitated, but thankfully a trained member of staff came to investigate the disturbance and calmly managed to coax John to a ward annexe, where he calmed down, and eventually returned to bed.

John, possibly feeling abandoned by society, should passively conform to its values and rules.

'I had allowed myself to let my perceptions of status alone control the situation, foolishly feeling I had the right to impose authority over him. I had been blinkered by my determination to stick to the rules. Most of all, I felt guilty that I had not shown the caring or empathy that might have helped John and prevented the situation from escalating.'

The official view

'Although my trained colleagues applauded my alertness and readiness to respond to the situation, I was advised of the dangers of isolating myself with a disturbed patient without first seeking trained support.'

What have I learned?

'After discussion with my mentor, I felt clearer about the incident. I gained invaluable insight into ways of dealing with disturbed psychiatric patients, particularly with regard to communication. I have sought more information from my tutor about management of aggression, and have learned how impor-tant factors such as proximity, posture, eye contact, touch and voice tone are to interactions. Most of all, I've learned that it's all right to make mistakes. That, as a student, I learn from getting it wrong occasionally, providing I look back on the events objectively and carefully.'

Incident Two

This incident involved Alan, a child branch student on his first placement, an acute paediatric ward, and is described in Casebox 11.2.

Analysis

Alan's analysis is given below.

My feelings

'I'd always considered myself to be quite open minded, without too many obvious prejudices. In this case, though, I'd allowed myself to be judgemental before all the facts were known. This had alienated me from Timmy and made his mother feel I was accusing her. Reflecting afterwards, there were so many clues I'd allowed myself to miss. There was obviously genuine love between them. Timmy showed no signs of hesitation or concern with his mother. Despite obvious hardships, the children were clean, happy and well cared for.

'All right, there was some suspicion on admission, but nowhere near concrete enough for me to act in the way I did. Despite the pressures at home, the other children and so on, Tina still found some way be with Timmy while he was in hospital. Hardly the action of an uncaring mother.

'After Timmy was discharged, I talked it over with my assessor. She started off telling me how well I'd been doing, and even cited a couple of examples when I'd correctly used my initiative. She reassured me that, in circumstances like Timmy's, there is naturally an element of concern. But it is not for us, the staff, to pass judgement. On the contrary, to alienate ourselves from the parents can be the worst thing if any further suspicious actions are to be observed. She was very understanding, and reassured me that judgement gets better with experience. Considering I'd made such a fool of myself, her patient explanation and confirmation of my satisfactory progress helped to restore my confidence.'

What have I learned?

'From the incident, I've learned to think thoroughly before forming any opinion, even when there are apparent grounds for it. My assessor was right. If Timmy had been abused, what good would I have been to him by making it so obvious that I was suspicious of his mother. Even if she had been, it's a time for help and support, not recrimination. I've resolved to learn more about non-accidental injury, and my tutor has arranged for me to spend a couple of days with the child protection team during my community placement. Most of all, it's made me

Casebox 11.2

I had been on the ward for about 4 weeks. I'd had to think very hard about coming into nursing, but the time on the ward had convinced me I'd made the right decision. Furthermore, I'd found nursing children especially rewarding.

By the end of the first month, I'd found my feet and was beginning to feel more confident in my practice. Taking more responsibility, voicing my opinions, suggesting changes in care regimes, that sort of thing. Acorn ward is brilliant, and the staff really encourage you. The work is not too taxing, and the children, in general, are not too ill, so not having been really stretched, I began to think I'd seen it all. Then Timmy came in.

Timmy was a loveable 3-year-old. He'd come up from A&E after suffering a pulled shoulder and was naturally very distressed. However, he soon quietened down when he was prescribed analgesia. The problem was, as I began to deduce, that the staff were a bit concerned about the circumstances of his injury. Something about the A&E staff not being happy with the mother's explanation. This was the first time I'd heard the term, 'non-accidental injury'.

Nothing was obvious. He seemed clean, well-dressed and cared for. However, though never previously admitted, Timmy had been seen in the A&E department on two or three other occasions, and this had set the 'alarm bells' ringing.

My problem came when I met Timmy's mother, Tina. Although she seemed perfectly normal, if concerned for Timmy, I found myself unable to interact with her as comfortably as I do normally with the other parents. Try as I might, I could hardly even make eye contact with her, and even found I was almost spying on the woman. You know, watching her when she was with Timmy, yet pretending to be doing something else. I feel sure she must have noticed, as it must have been obvious I was uneasy when she was about.

It all came to a head when I was helping Timmy with his supper. She volunteered to do it, but I made some excuse that it was better that I did it or something. She suddenly blew up, exclaiming, 'For God's sake, I'm not going to kill him!' She got very upset and accused me of treating her like a criminal. The awful thing is, I suspect I probably had been.

I was too embarrassed to go near her again, and naturally my confidence took a nose dive. Whenever Timmy needed care, I found some excuse to be doing something else.

The upshot was that the paediatricians and, I think, the social workers eventually decided that there was nothing suspicious about Timmy's injury. He has four other brothers and sisters, and they were all playing together when the injury happened. His mum, Tina, is a lone parent, and can't be watching them all the time. The A&E staff were probably just being cautious.

It's amazing how rational you can be when the facts are known, but having alienated myself from the mother and having made her feel like a child abuser, I felt pretty wretched. It took all of my courage to go to work the next day, and it made me start to doubt my ability to continue with the course.

grow up and refrain from being too blinkered and idealistic. Accidents, even in the best family circumstances, will always happen. Tina was under great pressure, but despite all the hardships, she was doing her best for her children.

Activity 8

During your next clinical practice, identify an event that went either very well or very badly, or which simply epitomises the norm for that setting. Subject it to critical incident analysis, perhaps using the following headings: context, key players, objective description of the events, why the incident is critical, your concerns and feelings, what was most demanding and most satisfying about the incident, and how it might influence your future practice.

Activity 9

From Activity 8, try to highlight: the reflective learning experience; the pre-existing skills you employed in the situation; any skills you acquired to meet the situation; and what new skills or knowledge you will need in order to meet a similar incident in the future.

'I have learned much from this incident, but most of all I learned something about myself. I feel I will be a better nurse because of it, and, through my assessor's example, ultimately a better staff nurse.'

Deborah and Alan both correctly identify the learning that took place. However, it could have been so different had they merely been content to walk away after the incident, lick their wounds and try to put it behind them. As it was, they utilised critical incident analysis to explore their respective experiences, painful as they were at first, seeking guidance in the process to test their understanding.

The result was that they learned and grew from them and will be far better equipped to deal with similar situations in the future. Note especially the way in which the incident prompted them to seek further sources of formal learning. In essence, the analysis has directed their learning while allowing them to retain control, one of the most significant features of the technique. This is so much more constructive than merely feeling bad or being admonished for getting it wrong. Equally, they alone owned their feelings, and the learning that resulted from reflecting on these was unique to them both and thus all the richer.

Increasingly, nurses are being asked formally to explore reflective aspects of their practice. Initiatives such as Post-registration Education and Practice (PREPP) require this to be done formally through instruments such as the professional portfolio. The nurse should try to perfect these explorations through techniques like critical incident analysis, but equally the technique should be used during clinical placements in order to extract the maximum learning from them.

● Learning from Experience

For the student entering nursing, learning can quite often be seen as a rigid process, out of the control of the recipient. However, increasingly in recent years the value of the students' own experiences and their own interpretations have been correctly seen as of great worth in the process of gaining knowledge.

Burnard (1987) proposed that the potential for knowledge lies in three complementary domains. *Propositional knowledge* is that which is associated with more traditional sources, such as formal lectures, textbooks and so on. *Practice knowledge* is that achieved through a 'hands-on', skills-acquisition mode. However, of equal and possibly greater value is *experiential knowledge,* gained through a direct, personal encounter with a subject, person or event. In the past, much emphasis was placed on the former two sources of knowledge in the preparation of nurses.

As Warner Weil and McGill (1989) state, recognition of the value of the student's experiential or experience-based learning had not been fully recognised until fairly recently. Burnard (1987) defines experiential knowledge, although personal and subjective, as 'a process in which a particular experience is, on reflection, translated into concepts which in turn become guidelines for future experiences'. It always begins with the experience itself, which is then subjected to reflection, analysis and evaluation.

For Parker *et al.* (1995), experience is attending to and organising information in order to make sense of a real world event. Experiential learning can be viewed as synonymous with meaningful discovery through personal involvement in a human experience.

The phenomenon of experiential learning was considered by Kolb (1984), who saw it as offering a model of learning and adaptation. It is consistent with the structure of human cognition and stages of human development and growth, perhaps again paralleling theories of adult learning. Kolb conceives that experiential learning passes through a four-stage cycle:

1. An experience
2. Observation and reflection
3. The formulation of abstract concepts and generalisations out of that reflection
4. Testing the implications of concepts learned on new situations.

Jarvis and Gibson (1985) suggest that the experience can occur within the cognitive, affective or psychomotor dimension. Although it might be facilitated by a teacher or supervisors, it might equally be an everyday event or a spontaneous or vicarious learning opportunity. It is essential that, when such methods are used, the pace must be set by the learner. It is their experience and their learning.

Jarvis and Gibson further caution that if experiential learning is stimulated externally, by a teacher or mentor, the following ground rules must apply:

- The learner must be allowed to think things through for herself and at her own pace.
- She must be allowed to ask sufficient questions to stimulate the process of reflection.
- It is not essential for a conclusion to be reached – it is the process that matters.
- Do not expect student and mentor to reach essentially the same conclusions – whose learning is it anyway?

Let us attempt to gain a greater understanding of Kolb's experiential learning cycle by applying it to a clinical scenario. Attempt to answer the questions posed in the activities below when the text suggests, placing yourself in the part of the subject. Possible responses are given at the end of the scenario.

The cast

- *Student nurse*: Bridget, mother of two, very enthusiastic but a bit apprehensive. First week, first placement.
- *Supervisor*: Debbie, E grade staff nurse. Very experienced.
- *Link tutor*: Peter. Reasonably 'visible' in the clinical area.
- *Patient*: John, 18 years old, stable high cervical neck fracture following a motorcycle accident.

The setting

An acute trauma ward, a six-bedded bay close to the nurses' station, with five elderly male patients, chronically ill and restricted to their beds, and John. Debbie and Bridget were giving care to John, who was completely immobilised in rather threatening cervical traction following a spinal injury, a condition with which Bridget was unfamiliar. There were cords, pulleys and weights, and John was being nursed on a very complex-looking turning bed. Bridget was acutely aware of the potential dangers involved in mishandling this intricate array of equipment. The ever-present risk of dislocation resulting in death or permanent para-lysis or disability was all too apparent.

On initial interview, Bridget revealed her sense of insecurity to Debbie. She told her that she felt threatened by the clients with their unfamiliar diagnoses and the strange terminology employed by the staff, and felt overawed at their familiarity and confidence in administering care. Now carry out Activity 10.

Activity 10

In order to allay Bridget's fears, what might Debbie do or tell her that might make her more confident in dealing with this threatening and alien scenario?

Bridget supported Debbie and was by now feeling free to question all aspects of the care being given. By the end of the shift, having frequently returned to John to give additional support, she was beginning to feel more confident in her abilities. She allowed him to talk at length about his perceptions of his care, his fears and his hopes for a successful recovery. She in turn questioned him and colleagues about different aspects of the care being provided.

The following day Peter, the link tutor, visited the ward. He welcomed Bridget and asked how she was getting on. He asked if there was anything he could offer that might assist her in gaining understanding and confidence in her role during the clinical placement. Refer now to Activity 11.

Activity 11

Such an offer of help frequently occurs. It is done with a purpose that is sadly often missed or misconstrued. What might Bridget and Peter identify as opportunities to assist in this process, with particular regard to her care of John?

By the end of the third day, Bridget was giving John's care with minimal supervision. She informed Debbie that the cord on his traction was too long (the weights being in danger of trailing on the floor). Debbie shortened the cords, explaining the need for non-slip knots, and showed Bridget how to tie them.

Bridget was concerned that John was somewhat isolated and perhaps lonely. In the next bay, there were two other patients of John's age. She suggested to Debbie that perhaps John could be moved there, and this was done.

Bridget recorded this in her reflective diary and the following day discussed it

Activity 12

What additional things might Bridget do to improve the accuracy of her perceptions of this care scenario?

Activity 13

With regard to her proposal to move John, how might she rationalise it?

with Peter. Peter congratulated her on her forethought, and for reflective purposes asked her to analyse the factors that prompted her proposal to move John.

By the end of the week, Bridget was much more confident and was being allowed to play a greater part in her contribution to care. She even proposed a similar movement of patients according to age and condition, and her rationale for the changes was enthusiastically endorsed by her mentor. Now do Activities 12 and 13.

Suggested responses to Activity 10

Debbie should:

- Advise Bridget of the need to be able to talk to John about his condition and perceptions of his care
- Encourage Bridget to be honest about her limitations to her client and, more importantly, to herself
- Carefully consider all aspects of John's care and the equipment involved, and provide Bridget with an opportunity to familiarise herself with the concepts involved
- Encourage Bridget to voice her anxieties, hopes and fears honestly
- Reassure her that reticence and anxiety are normal and indeed healthy
- Suggest that her maturity will convey credibility and empathy to a younger patient
- Explore the elements of Bridget's past experience that might be brought to bear on her care of John
- Advise her that she will be on hand to offer support and advice, and confirm her readiness to do so
- Emphasise the need to discuss and reflect with other students on their care
- Allow Bridget to support Debbie in care provision, gently allowing Bridget to gain familiarity and confidence, while continuously testing for depth of understanding, in essence, providing a role model.

Suggested responses to Activity 11

Peter, with Bridget, should:

- Go through and check Bridget's understanding of the aims and objectives set for the placement
- Identify any immediate anxieties and set additional short-term goals to overcome them
- Relate relevant care to theory already covered in the course
- Check Bridget's understanding of the pathophysiological aspects of John's condition, perhaps through ward tutorials and using the ward and school library

- Guide Bridget through John's case and nursing notes, with a particular emphasis on care plans
- Talk to Debbie to gauge Bridget's progress and ensure that she has realistic expectations for her placement
- Reassure Debbie on his availability to visit the ward to assist and support throughout the placement, and give her licence to ask for this freely as required
- If he has access to any formal sessions on spinal handling, invite Bridget to attend them.

Suggested responses to Activity 12

Bridget could:

- Consult the case notes and care plans to see how care is recorded
- Under supervision, enter her care in the care plans
- Use ward and library reading resources to determine the optimum care for this type of patient
- Discuss her care with John and his relatives
- Discuss and compare her care and understanding of it with other students on the ward
- Take up Debbie's and Peter's offers and consult them whenever clarification is required
- Maintain up-to-date entries of her care experiences in her reflective diary and check its accuracy with either Peter, Debbie or her group tutor.

Suggested responses to Activity 13

Bridget can support her proposal thus:

- John's anxiety will attenuate his sense of isolation
- If the position John is being nursed in restricts his ability to communicate, this too will add to his anxiety
- John has little in common with his fellow patients, who may be too ill to communicate
- The staff cannot be with John all the time
- Younger, perhaps fitter patients may help to keep John occupied and allay his sense of isolation
- Such patients may help to alert staff to any needs John may have, or give support and encouragement.

Look more closely at this scenario, and you will see that it is possible to relate Bridget's experience to Kolb's experiential learning cycle, thus:

The experience
Bridget meets a patient with a spinal injury for the first time and is tasked with contributing to his care.

Observation and reflection
Bridget related to Peter that as John was substantially younger than herself, she had felt an ability to project empathy and understanding not dissimilar from that she experienced with her children, who were of similar age, and that this eased the ability to communicate. In effect, Bridget was correctly utilising her extensive life experience and maturity to gain insight into John's anxieties, perhaps in a way that a more senior, yet younger, colleague might not be able to do.

Formulation of abstract concepts and generalisations out of the reflection
Although perhaps not entirely acceptable to the purist, such a strategy enabled conceptualisation regarding the patient's anxiety state and stimulated theory development on how she might help him. The following day, John looked visibly more relaxed, and with the noisy, expectant approval and encouragement of his peers, was becoming quite cheeky. John's improved mood acted as a reinforcement for Bridget's interventions.

Testing the implications of concepts learned by applying them to new situations
Later that shift, Bridget conferred with Debbie and was, as a result, allowed to make two other moves around the ward, matching patients by age, condition and mobility state.

Experience is a much-cited commodity in professional practice but remains a notoriously difficult factor to quantify. By using the experience of everyday practice events, combined with the principles of formal reflection, students can develop their knowledge in what is, after all, the richest domain of learning, nursing practice itself.

Reflection in the Practice Setting

As was stated earlier, the student entering practice can frequently be overawed by the alien nature of every new environment to which their programme dispatches them. We try to assimilate the skills necessary to demonstrate affiliation with our colleagues so that we will not stand out. Often there is over-eagerness to achieve merely the basic skills and thus acquire just sufficient knowledge necessary for immediate survival. Superficially, this may be acceptable, but the rich seam of knowledge that lies on the periphery of all nursing practice is lost or fails to be acknowledged. Reflecting on our practice experiences from day one of each placement can help to broaden our learning and help us to start taking charge of our development needs from the outset.

The richness of the practice setting can be enhanced in so many ways if the minute features of personal experiences are explored more thoroughly. In an excellent personal account of the positive influence that reflective practice can bring, Palmer *et al.* (1994) cite reflection being used in helping the practitioner to ensure that behaviour remains congruent with professional values and attitudes. Reflection is thus a means of self-monitoring performance against one's aspirations for best practice.

For the student, this could mean ensuring that the maximum potential learning is extracted from every experience, right from the start of training. Equally, it should be tempered by what we already know and bring into nursing. Reflection will facilitate this, as shown in the following scenario, taken a few years ago, from a student in the learning disabilities branch.

Casebox 11.3

Prior to starting the course, Emma had no previous experience of working with people with learning disabilities. Although lacking first-hand insight, she had experience of other voluntary and caring work, and she knew that this was a field in which she could function well. After the introductory block, Emma's set were scheduled to work one shift a week in their practice area. Emma was placed in Grove Villa, a nearby facility for children with severe physical and learning disabilities.

Arriving on the unit at lunch-time on the first day, it was immediately apparent that staffing was a problem, and there was an air of intense activity about the place. Although supernumerary, Emma felt that she should show willingness and help where possible. The Villa was quite old and was imminently due to move to a more modern facility. For now, however, the accommodation consisted of a lounge–diner, a small ward kitchen for making drinks, an L-shaped dormitory and a small bathroom with two baths, six cubicle toilets and six hand-basins. Although the Villa was light and cheerful, ventilation was a little poor, and the building was showing its age.

On arrival, Emma felt acutely aware of her lack of experience and was actually starting to feel a bit nauseated. Lunch had just finished and the lingering smell of food combined with the rather unpleasant odour coming from the lavatories, which were quite close to the door, was unpleasant. Having finished their lunch, the children were being taken to the bathroom area to be washed and use the toilet. The senior member of staff was dispensing medication from the drug trolley.

Everyone was very welcoming when she introduced herself, and, taking her cue from this, Emma asked what she could do. The charge nurse asked whether she would help to wash some of the children, take them to the toilet and, if necessary, help to change their clothes. When she asked whom she should start with, she was assigned to Mark. Mark was aged 7, wheelchair bound and with physical and learning disabilities. She approached him, introduced herself and was greeted with a beaming smile, which she found tremendously reassuring.

After an embarrassing few seconds while she worked out the intricacies of the wheelchair, Emma took Mark through to the bathroom area. Other staff were there with about six other children. The smell in the toilet area was overpowering, and Emma felt quite sick, but she was reassured by one of the staff that she would get used to it. It was a rather tight fit in the bathroom, so a member of staff suggested that Emma should 'do' Mark at his bedside. Feeling a bit clumsy at first, as Mark had been incontinent, Emma finally coped satisfactorily with this, her first exposure to practice.

Activity 14

Imagine you are Emma. How do you think she felt? What preparation should she have received prior to arrival? How could the ward staff have contributed to such preparation?

Activity 15

What potential learning resulted from this brief experience? What pre-existing skills were utilised in the situation? What new skills and knowledge are needed to maximise the learning?

With perhaps a few variations, this scenario will be far from unfamiliar for many students entering clinical practice for the first time, regardless of their chosen branch. The experiences of the first day, or even the first week, often all merge into one, and, if pressed, individual interactions and events are difficult to recall. The overall impressions, such as whether it went satisfactorily or disastrously, will be retained, but minute features, each a potentially rich source of learning, are usually lost in our quest for acceptance by our colleagues.

Students will quickly learn that anxieties and apprehension are not confined to their first placement. Such feelings are very necessary and, although less acute, usually stay with us regardless of how often we change our place of employment. However, those all-important first few hours are vital in easing our passage into becoming a useful member of the occupational group we seek to join. Reflection, both in and on action, can help in this process.

Using these strategies, look back on the scenario just portrayed and reflect on the questions posed in Activities 14 and 15, checking your answers against the text below.

Suggested responses to Activities 14 and 15

- *How do you think she felt?*
  Fearful, anxious, self-conscious, superfluous, a 'spare part', a spare 'pair of hands', threatened, out of her depth, uncertain, unsupported.
- *What preparation should she have received prior to arrival?*
  Orientation with the client group, familiarisation visit to the Villa, insight into ward 'routines'.
- *How could the ward staff have contributed to such preparation?*
  Production of an orientation pack, assignment of a mentor whom Emma could shadow for the first few days, teaching resources, formal introduction to staff and clients, assurance that she was supernumerary and had time to find her feet.
- *What potential learning resulted from this brief experience?*
  THE SPECIFIC LEARNING
  Successfully washing and drying a 7-year-old with physical and learning disabilities.
  THE PERIPHERAL LEARNING
  The location of the Villa
  The mealtime environment and 'routines'
  The responsiveness of her colleagues
  Mark's responsiveness to her
  The time of the medication round
  The operation of the wheelchair
  The location of Mark's bed.

● *What pre-existing skills were utilised in the situation?*
How to find things in a strange environment
How to wash and dress dependent people.
● *What new skills and knowledge are needed to maximise the learning?*
Theoretical input on dignity and privacy
Methods for maximising client independence
Theoretical input on skin care, cross-infection and so on
Incontinence needs and aids.

Although the outcomes of Emma's care of Mark would seem at first glance to be simplistic, it must be remembered that it is usually the simple things that cause the most anxiety when one is new, and act as obstacles to learning.

This was just one snapshot during one shift, perhaps only 15–20 minutes in time, yet following reflection, Emma's real learning achievements, which might otherwise have gone unheralded, can clearly be seen. No matter how small or seemingly insignificant the event, a potential for learning and professional growth will exist. However, real effort is needed, at least at first, to ensure that the breadth and depth of our development and learning are fully accredited. The development of effective, reflective powers will greatly ease this process.

Chapter Summary

Reflective practice is, for many, still a rather nebulous concept with properties that are seen as abstract and vague. Yet it can perhaps be seen that the basic principles of reflection are quite simple, even though their mastery will take a lot longer. However, the time taken in achieving this will be worthwhile.

It is hoped that, through this chapter, students will now be able to define the true structures of the process and will start to develop the mechanisms by which they can implement it into their own personal practice. They are skills worth developing as they really can hold the promise of seeing what we do with greater clarity.

For the student, such development offers a special imperative in that it holds the key to taking charge of our own development and, more especially, our learning. Nurse education programmes, even the most empathic and revolutionary, can only go part way towards equipping us with the skills and insight necessary to becoming an effective practitioner.

The best nursing practice is invisible and anticipatory, buried in the depths of the meaningful, interpersonal relationships we develop with our patients, clients and co-workers. Through reflection in and on our actions, processes such as the analysis of critical incidents, the true worth of experiential learning and the rest, best practice can be unearthed and used to refine our further development, not just during the period of training but throughout our careers.

References

Atkins, S. and Murphy, K. (1994) Reflective practice. *Nursing Standard* **8**(39): 49–56.

Benner, P. (1984) *From Novice to Expert – Excellence and Power in Clinical Nurse Practice*. Addison Wesley, Menlo Park, CA.

Berger, P. and Luckman, T. (1967) The social construction of reality. In Jarvis, P. (1992) Reflective practice in nursing. *Nurse Education Today* **12**: 174–81.

Boud, D., Keogh, R. and Walker, D. (eds) (1985) Reflection: turning experience into learning. In Burnard, P. (1991) Improving through reflection. *Journal of District Nursing* May: 10–12.

Boyd, E. and Fales, A. (1983) Reflective learning – key to learning from experience. In Powell, J. (1989) The reflective practitioner in nursing. *Journal of Advanced Nursing* **14**: 824–32.

Burnard, P. (1987) Towards an epistemological basis for experiential learning in nursing education. *Journal of Advanced Nursing* **12**: 189–93.

Cervero, R. (1988) Effective continuing education for professionals. In Jarvis, P. (1992) Reflective practice in nursing. *Nurse Education Today* **12**: 174–81.

Coutts-Jarman, J. (1993) Using reflection and experience in nurse education. *British Journal of Nursing* **2**(1): 77–80.

Crouch, S. (1991) Critical incident analysis. *Nursing* **4**(37): 30–1.

Darbyshire, P. (1993) In the hall of mirrors. *Nursing Times* **89**(49): 26–30.

Dewey, D. (1933) *How we Think*. DC Heath, Boston, MA.

Dewing, J. (1990) Reflective practice. *Senior Nurse* **10**(10): 26–8.

Driscoll, J. (1994) Reflective practice in practise. *Senior Nurse* **13**(7): 47–50.

Greenwood, J. (1993) Some considerations concerning practice and feedback in nursing education. *Journal of Advanced Nursing* **18**: 1999–2002.

Habermas, J. (1977) Knowledge and human interests. In Atkins, S. and Murphy, K. (1994) Reflective practice. *Nursing Standard* **8**(39): 49–56.

Jarvis, P. (1992) Reflective practice in nursing. *Nurse Education Today* **12**: 174–81.

Jarvis, P. and Gibson, S. (1985) *The Teacher Practitioner in Nursing, Midwifery and Health Visting*. Croom Helm, Beckenham.

Kolb, D. (1984) *Experiential Learning*. Prentice-Hall, Englewood Cliffs NJ.

Melia, K. (1987) *Learning and Working – The Occupational Socialisation of Nurses*. Tavistock, London.

Menzies, I. (1960) A case study in the function of social systems as a defence against anxiety. In Melia, K. (1987) *Learning and Working – The Occupational Socialisation of Nurses*. Tavistock, London, p. 36.

Mezirow, J. (1981) A critical theory of adult learning and education. In Jarvis, P. (1992) Reflective practice in nursing. *Nurse Education Today* **12**: 174–81.

Palmer, A., Burns, S. and Bulman, C. (1994) *Reflective Practice in Nursing*. Blackwell, London.

Parker, D., Webb, J. and D'Souza, B. (1995) The value of critical incident analysis as an educational tool and its relationship to experiential learning. *Nurse Education Today* **15**: 111–16.

Polanyi, M. (1967) The tacit dimension. In Schön, D. (1983) *The Reflective Practitioner*, p. 4. Avebury, New York.

Powell, J. (1989) The reflective practitioner in nursing. *Journal of Advanced Nursing* **14**: 824–32.

Powell, J. (1992) Reflection and the evaluation of experience: prerequisites for therapeutic practice. In Driscoll, J. (1994) Reflective practice in practise. *Senior Nurse* **13**(7): 47–50.

Schön, D. (1983) *The Reflective Practitioner*. Temple Smith, London.

Schön, D. (1987) *Educating the Reflective Practitioner*. Jossey Bass, London.

Stockwell, F. (1984) *The Unpopular Patient*. Croom Helm, Beckenham.

Street, A. (1991) From image to action – reflection in nursing practice. In Palmer, A., Burns, S. and Bulman, C. (1994) *Reflective Practice in Nursing*. Blackwell, London.

UKCC (United Kingdom Central Council for Nursing, Midwifery and Health Visiting) (1992) *Scope of Professional Practice*. UKCC.

Van Manen, M. (1977) Linking ways of knowing with ways of being practical. In Atkins, S. and Murphy, K. (1994) Reflective practice. *Nursing Standard* **8**(39): 49–56.

Weil, S. Warner and McGill, I. (eds) (1989) Making sense of experiential learning: diversity in theory and practice. In Parker, D., Webb, J. and D'Souza, B. (1995) The value of critical incident analysis as an educational tool and its relationship to experiential learning. *Nurse Education Today* **15**: 111–16.

Williams, M. (1996) Reflection, thinking and learning. *British Journal of Theatre Nursing* **6**(5): 26–9.

The Politics of Health Care

SUSAN MOORE

Introduction

This chapter explores the wider context of health care. It looks at how health care policy is made. The first section describes the British political system and the parts of the process that contribute to the formation of health policy. The second section examines some past and present health policies that affect nursing and midwifery practice today. First, the whole structure of the National Health Service is described from its beginnings in 1948 to the 1990 reforms and the introduction of the concept of the internal market, and then to the 1997 changes. Next, we turn to a description of the legal structures that govern the professions of nursing, midwifery and health visiting. Finally, specific branches of practice are discussed in relation to the legislation that provides a framework for practice. After completion of this chapter, the student will be able to:

- Outline the key political institutions involved in the development of social policy

- Justify the need for nurses to have a knowledge of social policy

- Outline the historical development of the British National Health Service

- Describe the key features of policy relating to midwifery, children's nursing and mental health practice

- Discuss the development of the statutory regulation of nursing, midwifery and health visiting.

The Political Process

Why study politics?

This is surely a legitimate question to pose. Why do nurses need to know about political institutions and how social policy is devised, enacted and implemented?

How will this affect the way in which a nurse delivers effective care to a client? What will it matter to a client who is in severe pain or hallucinating, how politically astute the nurse is who offers him help? The immediate answer is that, at this stage in an illness, a client will not be interested in any other skills that a nurse has but those which help to ease the pain or distract him from the hallucinations. Later on, however, a significant proportion of acute illnesses become chronic conditions that affect significant areas of the person's life. It is possible in this situation, where service users and nurses alike are motivated by a need, to influence and improve the service. They are facilitated in doing this if they understand the social and political systems that created it.

It may be argued then that several justifications can be put forward for nurses understanding the process of policy formation in health care. First of all, the nurse is a citizen. It may be argued all citizens should have an understanding of the systems and processes by which decisions are made that affect their lives. Second, the nurse who begins her career at 18 years old may work within the health-care system for upwards of 30 years. In that time, she will have the potential to effect care for a significant number of people. Nurses will be more effective if they understand the history, development, values and beliefs of the health-care delivery system and its institutions within which they operate. Third, in the role of advocate for clients or client groups, it may be helpful to assist them to understand the system and why care is delivered in the way it is. In addition, as care is increasingly delivered outside the hospital setting and in the community, care packages have to be put together with contributions from a range of agencies such as social services, housing and education. Nurses who aim to deliver effective care to clients need to have an understanding of those agencies and the legal frameworks within which they operate. Finally, having gained an understanding of the system, the nurse may seek, either individually or as part of a pressure group, to change or improve health-care policies. For example, the Royal Colleges of Nursing and Midwives and the Community Psychiatric Nurses Association are organisations that seek to influence health policy on behalf of their members.

health policy

the principles that govern public actions to deliver health services

Political values and beliefs

It is important, when considering health policy, to have an understanding of the values and beliefs that shape it. Ranade (1994) argues that the philosophy that provided an impetus for the 1948 National Health Service (NHS) was rooted in the principles of socialism. Before 1948, people were aware of the significant inequalities in health care. Beveridge, the author of the report that provided the blueprint for the NHS, was also concerned with the economic benefits that would result for society if health were improved. These values of shared social responsibility for welfare provision and extensive state economic

socialism

a political doctrine that seeks to organise society on the basis of fairness and equity

intervention continued to dominate the 1950s and 60s. They were based upon the optimistic view that resources invested in health and welfare supported economic growth by improving the quality of the workforce and contributing to full employment.

In the 1970s, academic writing challenged the view that public welfare services were an equalising force in society. It was suggested by the Black Report (DHSS, 1980) that despite 30 years of a welfare state, there were still significant inequalities in health. The medical dominance of health care was also challenged (Illich, 1976, McKeown, 1976). It was argued that medicine was focused too much on science and the promotion of the profession, and not enough on meeting clients' needs.

The values and beliefs that underpinned the policies of the Conservative administrations from 1979 have been summarised by the term the 'New Right'. At that time, the welfare state seemed to be failing, and a 'crisis of welfare' was described in which the growth in the population of older people would coincide with the reduction in the population of wage earners, combined with slow economic growth. This would result in economic disaster. The New Right solution to this problem was to reduce the level of state intervention in the economy. It was argued that market forces were distorted by too much economic planning and regulation. Furthermore, citizens had to fund welfare from taxation, and this resulted in a tax burden that stunted free enterprise. Last, economic decline resulted from having a large public sector that did not contribute to wealth creation.

The New Right also believed that professionals tended to promote their own interests above those of the service, which resulted in inefficiency. In addition, they felt that because welfare was provided by state monopolies, the service was inefficient and wasteful, which would not be tolerated in organisations that were motivated by competition. It was argued from a moral stance that citizens were being coerced in two ways by the welfare state: first, by having to pay more tax because the service was wasteful; and second because, as a prospective consumer, the citizen was offered no choice.

There are significant differences between the 'socialist' and the 'New Right' philosophies. They were the driving force behind the social policy of the time. When policies are described later in the chapter, it will be evident how the dominant political philosophy of the time shaped the form and style of the resultant policy.

How are political decisions made?

It is important to be aware that social policies start with governments. They are the expression of that government's values and beliefs. In order for the nurse to understand, analyse and criticise social policies, he or she must first have some

---

welfare state

a collective term to describe all the government provision, for example education, health or social security, that offers aid to those who need it

Activity

1

Compare the arguments put forward by the 'Old Left' and the 'New Right' for welfare provision. Decide which you think is the most convincing and say why. For a wider discussion of these issues, read Ranade, 1994, pp. 8–23.

understanding of the political system that produces them and the process of government that enacts them.

British central government

In Britain, there is a system of democratic representative government whereby approximately 650 representatives are elected every 5 years by a 'first past the post' or simple majority voting system.

After a general election, the monarch formally requests the leader of the majority party to form a government. The majority party leader then becomes the prime minister. In forming a government, there are over 100 positions to be filled, which will be taken by members of the winning party. The most important positions are those of members of the Cabinet, the executive body of government, which is made up of between 15 and 25 members. These are mainly ministers who lead government departments, but in addition there may be members without departmental responsibilities who have political or co-ordinating roles, for example the deputy prime minister.

The Cabinet is a key body in the decision-making process. Any new policy proposal or change to legislation is discussed, argued through and negotiated within the Cabinet forum. When such proposals need detailed work, it sets up Cabinet committees to complete this. These then refer work back to the Cabinet for a final decision.

Government ministers

A government minister has the role and responsibility of leading a government department, such as the Treasury or the Department of Health. A department consists of a large staff of permanent civil servants who administer it and put policy into effect. Ministers accept responsibility for work carried out in their name and are accountable to parliament.

A government minister can find himself in some considerable conflict as he has to contribute to both developing and co-ordinating central policy and strategy for the government. At the same time, he has a partisan commitment to his department to advance and protect its interests.

There are four main parts to the role of a government minister. First, he puts forward legislation. Second, he has to attend to a high workload of departmental administration, perhaps the development of policy that does not require legislation. Third, the minister has to respond to questions put to him in the House of Commons. These might be probing questions put to him by opposition members of parliament (MPs), designed to embarrass or challenge the government. Equally, they may be questions asked by a member of his own party that are designed to offer him the opportunity to announce new policy or report

the Cabinet

the executive decision-making body of government, made up of Ministers of State, led by the Prime Minister

government minister

the person with responsibility for running a government department

the Treasury

the government department that has the responsibility of receiving the government's financial income, distributing it to other departments and setting the annual budget. The chancellor of the exchequer is its chief minister

favourable statistics. The final aspect of his role is public relations. This will involve a programme of formal visits, speeches and meetings aimed to publicise the work of the department.

The House of Commons

In the UK, the seat of government is the Houses of Parliament. It is situated in Westminster in London and comprises two chambers.

The House of Commons is the chamber within which government policy is presented, debated, negotiated and finally voted upon by MPs. Policy starts as an Act of Parliament. Proposals for change are set out in the form of a 'Bill', which requires skilled presentation and wording. This is done by civil servants, who are permanent government employees. They are engaged in a wide variety of administrative roles within each of the government departments.

Bills have to pass through four stages in both the House of Commons and the House of Lords. Stage one is the 'first reading', which is when the Bill is formally presented to the House. The 'second reading' is when the main principles of the Bill are debated by all parties within the House. The third stage, called the 'committee stage', involves examination of the Bill in detail by a small standing committee. This is the stage during which changes or amendments can be made to the Bill. The final stage is known as the 'third reading' or 'report stage': the revised Bill, having been examined by the committee, is referred back to the House, where it can be amended yet again.

Bill

a draft of proposed legislation. It is work in progress until it becomes an Act of Parliament

The House of Lords

This is the second chamber of government. It is made up of non-elected representatives, senior judges, bishops and peers of the realm, who may be hereditary or life peers. The purpose of the House is to offer a second opinion on Bills that appear before it. It works as a check and a balance to the House of Commons.

Bills go through the same four stages in the House of Lords. This second house can recommend amendments to Bills, but the House of Commons does not have to accept them. The final stage for a Bill to become an 'Act of Parliament' is for it to receive royal assent from the monarch.

The work performed by the ministry

The secretary of state or minister is the statutory head of the department. He or she has a number of junior ministers, themselves elected MPs, who support the secretary in his function. The junior ministers are appointed by the prime minister. They are supported in the administration of the work of the department by a staff of civil servants. It is important to note the differences between these two groups. The ministers may be at the department for a relatively short period of time, during which they may well wish to make their mark and achieve significant policy change. Civil servants, however, are likely to work in one department for the whole of their career. They tend, therefore, to see policy change in the longer term. This can cause some difficulties and disharmony in the promotion of policy change. The most significant civil service role in this context is that of the permanent secretary, the most senior civil servant within a department. This person is in daily contact with the minister and is the minister's source of communication and information about the department.

The Department of Health

The administration of the Department of Health (DoH) is divided into two functions: strategic vision and policy implementation. Strategic vision and direction for the Health Service is devised by the NHS Policy Board. The policy is then operationalised by the NHS Management Executive (NHSME).

The Policy Board is made up of ministers, NHSE chairpersons, the permanent secretary, the chief executive, the chief medical officer and chief nursing officer, a leading clinician from the NHS and people from major industries. The brief for the Policy Board, which is chaired by the secretary of state, is to devise new policies and to evaluate those which have been put into practice.

The role of the NHSME is to carry out tasks that are allocated by the secretary of state and to implement government policy. It has shorter-term objectives for the current financial year but also longer-term objectives, for example those set out in *The Health of the Nation* document (DoH, 1992), that it may be working to achieve over perhaps a 5-year period. Other functions of the NHSME are to promote effective management throughout the NHS and to monitor the performance of health authorities.

Financing policy

An important part of any policy is how it will be funded. Where does the money come from? How is it distributed?, and How much money? are important questions to ask. The NHS provides a good example of how a budget is agreed and subsequently distributed. Money to finance the NHS is derived from three sources: central government tax revenues, national insurance contributions and charges to service users. The largest proportion (81 per cent) is derived from national taxation, national insurance representing 16 per cent and the remaining 3 per cent charges to service users. The allocation of funding for public services is regulated by the Treasury. This is dictated by the economic policy of the current government who, for either economic or social reasons, may decide to restrict or develop spending on public services.

The DoH negotiates with the public services division of the Treasury, submitting revised annual plans for spending to the Treasury. The result of the joint work of these two government departments is to produce the Public Expenditure Survey Committee Report. This is subsequently presented to the Treasury ministers and is studied in the light of the current economic climate and the government's overall strategy. Allocation of funding between various departments is decided finally at Cabinet level, the eventual decisions being set out in the White Paper on Public Expenditure. The end result is that parliament votes the money for the year ahead, for all public expenditure including the NHS.

The DoH then allocates money to the health authorities. Budgets are calculated based upon the size of their resident populations. District health authorities in turn allocate funding to the Trusts, GPs and other providers according to their assessment of and plan for local health needs.

How is policy effected?

The previous sections have described how policy is made at governmental level and the political institutions that support that process. It is equally important to understand how that policy is effected at the level of the workforce. Hill (1993) suggests that policy-making and policy implementation are not two discrete operations but that the two merge. The implementation process influences policy design from an early stage and continues throughout it.

Policy implementation involves several sets of relationships. Initially, there is the relationship between central government agencies, in the case of health policy, for example, the DoH, and local agencies such as health authorities or NHS Trusts. Relationships for policy implementation become more complex when the effective realisation of the legislation involves the collaboration and co-operation of several organisations, each with its own discrete culture and operating system. An example of this may be found in the *Building Bridges* policy for mental health interagency working (DoH, 1995). These guidelines urge a range of agencies such as health, social services, housing, education, the probation service and the police to work together to produce packages of care for people with a severe mental illness.

Policy implementation will also be influenced by the values and beliefs of the practitioners who put the policy into effect. Because there is such a distance between the central controlling agency and the individual who is delivering the service, there can be much room for discretion in how he acts. This can result in a considerable distance between the original principles and objectives of the policy and the actuality of the implementation.

Another important feature that influences policy implementation is finance. For change to take place, extra resources are sometimes required to make that

Activity
2
Are you a politically aware citizen? Which constituency do you live in? What is the name of its MP? Which political party does he or she represent? Does your MP hold a government office? Where and when does he or she hold constituency 'clinics' to obtain feedback and meet constituency residents?
For further reading, see Hanson and Walles, 1990.

change effective, perhaps to provide new environments or to train staff for new roles. In the past few years, for example, several changes have been made to mental health social policy: the introduction of the care programme approach, the supervision register and supervised discharge. All of these changes have had to be introduced by NHS Trusts without additional funding. The adoption of these policies has consequently been quite variable, and change has taken a long time to be effective.

The implementation of policy is a complex, interactive process that shapes the nature of service delivery and also provides the feedback that ultimately results in policy change.

This section has examined the institutions of government and the process by which they develop, enact and implement policy.

● Social Policy and Nursing Practice

In this second section, some of the most important social policy that affects the delivery of health care will be set out. This will look at how the NHS came into being and how it subsequently developed to its present-day form, paying particular attention to the advent of general management and the concept of the internal market. There is then a description of the legislation that governs the professions of nursing, midwifery and health visiting. This will be followed by a survey of policy specific to particular areas of practice such as midwifery, mental health, and children's services.

The beginnings of a National Health Service

The NHS came into existence on 5 July 1948. This universal health system, which was to be free at the point of delivery, had been proposed and outlined in the Beveridge Report (Ministry of Health, 1942). During the Second World War, (1939–45), the government set up an Emergency Medical Service as part of its wartime measures. This required the minister of health to be responsible for the treatment of casualties. Both the voluntary and local authority hospitals that were in existence at that time consequently came under the direction of central government.

As part of this central control, it also took over the financing of the service, which up until that time had been paid for from clients' contributions, local authority rates and the funds of the voluntary hospitals. Very quickly, services such as blood transfusion were organised on a national scale in order to meet the needs of the national emergency. Ernest Brown, the then Minister of Health, announced in 1941 that the government had commissioned an inquiry into the state of the hospitals. This report showed that there were significant inequalities in hospital provision across the country.

In 1942, the Beveridge Report (Ministry of Health, 1942) recommended a universal and comprehensive system of health care that would improve the general health of the nation. It also recommended the adoption of a contributory social security system that would improve on the existing system by protecting citizens against sickness, unemployment and old age.

In 1943, the wartime coalition government announced that it accepted the proposals made by Beveridge and planned to implement them after the war. In March 1946, when the war was over and a new Labour government had been elected, the National Health Service Bill 1946 was published. It set out plans to nationalise all hospitals under appointed Regional Hospital Boards, who in turn were to delegate their authority to Hospital Management Committees. Teaching hospitals (that is, centres that had medical schools) were to be administered separately by Boards of Governors.

The NHS that came into being in 1948 was the product of the bargaining and negotiation that had gone on in the intervening years between interested factions, for example the local authorities, the doctors and the politicians. It represented the product of the art of the possible rather than what in hindsight might be seen to have been the most desirable.

The structure of the NHS was designed in three parts (Figure 12.1). The family practitioner service comprised GPs, dentists, opticians and pharmacists. These were managed by Executive Councils. The second part was the local authority-run services such as environmental health, district nursing, health visiting, child health and ambulances. This part was administered by the medical officer of health and funded partly by central government and partly by local goverment. The third part was the hospitals. The hospitals were divided

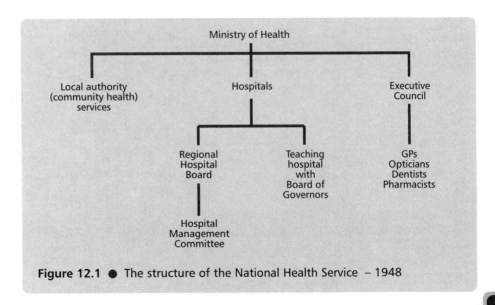

Figure 12.1 ● The structure of the National Health Service – 1948

into two categories. The majority of hospitals came under Regional Hospital Boards. Those designated as teaching hospitals were regulated by separate Boards of Govenors, which related directly to the minister of health.

This tripartite structure, which was set up at the beginning of the NHS, has left its legacy for subsequent generations. Certainly, this structure remained in place until the early 1970s. England was divided into 13 regions, 14 by 1959, and Wales became a region in its own right. The main function of the regional boards was to plan, provide and supervise services.

Reorganisation in 1974

By the early 1970s, it was recognised that the tripartite structure had led to problems of fragmentation. A huge reorganisation was planned of both the health service and local government (Figure 12.2). The legislation created another layer of management in the form of the area health authority. These took responsibility for general policy and the monitoring of services. The whole reorganisation was designed to bring together all health services under the direction of the area health authorities. It also created Joint Consultative Committees, which were to be the bridge between the health service and local authority social services. It created Community Health Councils at district level, whose purpose was to represent the interests of the consumer.

It was not long after its implementation that the 1974 reorganisation came under strong criticism. The focus of this was the delay in decision-making caused

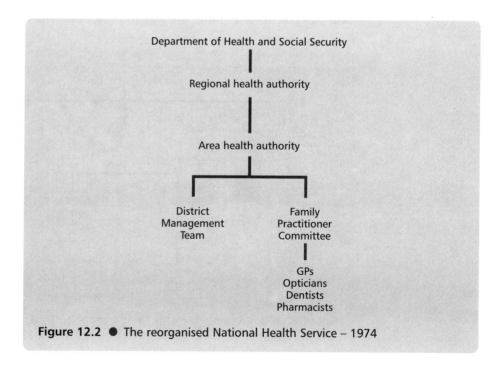

Figure 12.2 ● The reorganised National Health Service – 1974

by the three layers of authority. The 1979 Royal Commission on the National Health Service suggested the removal of one tier of authority. In 1982, the short-lived area health authorities were replaced by district health authorities.

General management

A major piece of health policy occurred in the early 1980s, which changed the way in which the NHS was managed. In 1983, the secretary of state for social services appointed a small team, led by Roy Griffiths, the deputy chairman and managing director of a prominent supermarket chain, to inquire into and give advice upon the effective use of management, manpower and resources within the NHS.

Until the 1980s, the management system employed in the NHS could be described as 'collegial'; that is, each of the various professionals of the service had its own hierarchy of managers. Decisions about how the whole of a service was to be managed were achieved by consensus.

The Griffiths Report (DHSS, 1983) made several significant proposals. First, it proposed changes to the organisation at departmental level. It recommended the creation of a Health Services Supervisory Board, the aim of which was to hold responsibility for the strategic direction of the NHS. There would then be another board responsible to this that would be composed of all professions, which would direct the implementation of the NHS strategy. This would be called the NHS Management Board.

Second, it proposed the role of 'general manager' to be created at all levels of the organisation. The role of the general manager, who might be recruited from any professional background, was to carry overall management responsibility for achieving outcomes. It was expected that decisions would be taken at unit level rather than being passed up a hierarchy.

Third, a process of review that evaluated performance was to be introduced, the aim of which was to reduce costs without impairing the quality of service delivery.

Fourth, clinical doctors were to become more involved in management at a local level. This was to be achieved by the allocation of workload-related budgets to consultants.

Finally, the report asked that more attention be paid to the opinion of the user when developing services.

These main tenets of the Griffiths Report were accepted by the government and put into action by the secretary of state in June 1984. General managers were to be appointed by the end of 1985 at regional, district and unit levels. The posts were to be open to NHS managers of all disciplines, to doctors and to people outside the service. Initially, more than 60 per cent of the posts went to former NHS administrators and treasurers, that is, the same people but with a changed role. Many of the doctors who were appointed were clinicians who had

Activity 3

In your current area of practice, ask local staff to help you draw a diagram outlining the structure of general managers between you and the Chief Executive. List their roles, their responsibilities, the budgets they control and their professional backgrounds.

part-time roles as managers, although some appointments were from outside the service.

This policy resulted in a significant cultural change for the NHS termed 'new managerialism'. This change was in the way in which decisions were made, in the consciousness of budgets and costs, and in the diminished professional autonomy of nurses and doctors. This new business-like approach was fully implemented by the end of the 1980s and created the conditions for the introduction of the NHS reforms of the early 1990s.

Reforming the NHS in the 1990s

The management changes within the NHS did produce significant turbulence for managerial staff and some for clients and practitioners, but this was as nothing compared with the changes wrought by the radical reforms of the NHS and Community Care Act 1990 that were proposed at the end of the 1980s and put into practice in the 1990s.

In 1988, the then Prime Minister, Margaret Thatcher, announced that there was to be a ministerial review of the NHS. This was prompted by sustained and outspoken pressure from the media and opposition concerning the chronic underfunding of the service. One of the tasks of the review was to look at alternative ways of funding the NHS. They were, however, very quickly eliminated as it was discovered that, despite its drawbacks, the British system of funding the NHS out of general taxation was the most effective. The view was taken that, with this system, the Treasury was in a stategic position to police annual increases in NHS revenues.

The review published proposals for reform in the White Paper *Working for Patients* (DoH, 1989). The central idea of the health reforms was that of an 'internal market'. The aim of this system of organisation was to put hospitals and other provider units under competitive pressure to improve the quality and efficiency of the service. The way in which this was achieved was by splitting the functions of funding and the provision of services. Those responsible for funding were to be termed the 'purchasers', and those delivering services the 'providers'. Negotiation between the two was to be formalised in the form of 'contracts'.

There are currently three types of purchaser of secondary care and community health services in the internal market – health authorities, GP fundholders and private clients – the two new institutions created by the reforms being fundholding GPs and NHS Trusts. These were new ideas. The NHS and Community Care Act 1990 set out these new roles, which have been extensively implemented since 1991.

health authority

an appointed body with the responsibility of identifying the health-care needs of a specific population (about 500 000) and commissioning or purchasing that care which is defined in contracts

GP fundholders

What makes a fundholding practice distinctive is that it controls its own budget. In this way, it both provides a primary care service to its clients and can also purchase a limited range of health care for them. It can purchase care from any provider rather than only those within a shared district. Fundholders are distinguished from non-fundholding practices by the fact that their secondary care is purchased on their behalf by the health authority.

There are limits to the extent of purchasing that a GP fundholder can undertake. The budget is limited to standard and inexpensive treatments. GPs are restricted to choosing only from a list of permissible purchases, and there is a fixed financial ceiling for each client. Once treatment requires more than this, the commitment refers back to the health authority. Since 1991, the list of permissible purchases has been extended.

Fundholder status can be granted by the health authority to a practice that has a client list of 5000. A budget is then handed down from the health authority. GP fundholders have three main expenditures: hospital and other secondary services, practice staff and drugs. They are allowed to change the allocation of funds to these three areas of expenditure. For example, money saved from obtaining a cost-effective service from a hospital might be spent on purchasing more staff or improving the decor and equipment in the surgery. They are also allowed to keep any savings they make and carry them over into the next financial year.

A difficulty with this system is that it creates unequal access to health care and treatment. Patients who are registered with a fundholding GP are often able to obtain service more quickly as the GP can purchase it for them. It is also not always the case that patients have a choice between fundholding and non-fundholding GP practices in their locality.

NHS Trusts

NHS Trust

a separate NHS body directly answerable to the secretary of state, which has the responsibilty to provide a health-care service

These are the other major providing body within the NHS. To become a Trust, a hospital or community unit had to demonstrate financial viability. Once Trust status was granted, the organisation left the control of the health authority and became directly responsible to the secretary of state for health. They remain in the public sector as public corporations.

The move to NHS Trusts was undertaken in a series of 'waves' from 1991. Like the GPs, Trust status confers some significant freedoms upon an organisation. A Trust is allowed (within government-set boundaries) to set its own pay levels, to determine the skill mix within the staff group that it employs, to exercise more autonomy in the management of its assets and to return savings and 'profits' back into service improvements.

Contracting

What holds the purchasing and providing functions together is contracting. Health authorities and GP fundholders are both skilled in identifying the health care that they wish to purchase and its standard, kind and content. It is the contract that makes detailed specifications about what is required of the health-care provider.

There are three types of contract. First are 'block contracts', in which access to a specified range of services is purchased in advance of service delivery. Under this arrangement, purchasers do not request, for example, 100 operations but instead the opportunity for any client who requires that treatment within a fixed time period. The second type are 'cost and volume' contracts, whereby a specific set of charges are drawn up for given treatments. Under this arrangement, purchasers might specify, for example, 100 operations at £1000 each. The third type is 'cost-per-case' contracts, whereby a set of charges is drawn up for each individual case.

Continuing development of the NHS

In 1997, the government put forward proposals (DoH, 1997) to continue to reform the organisation of the NHS. The principle of the change is to avoid radical upheavals, the aim being to maintain what was effective from the 1990 reforms and to reorganise what was less than effective. Health authorities will still exist with influence over the assessment of health needs of local populations. The health authority will also be responsible for drawing up a strategy, called a 'health improvement programme', to meet these needs.

The most significant change is to primary care. A new system of 'primary care groups' will be developed. These will consist of representatives of all GP practices in the locality and will also include representation from community nursing and social services. The function of the primary care group will be to contribute to the formation of the health improvement programme, to commission or purchase health services for their population from the relevant NHS Trusts and to monitor their performance.

The aim of the primary care groups is to retain the positive aspects of GP fundholding, which were that the GPs knew the individual health needs of their local population. It is anticipated that this system will eliminate the inequalities of access to health care as health care will be purchased on behalf of the whole locality. The contracts or service agreements will cover longer periods of time than the initial 1-year contracts in order, to enable the development of longer-term strategies.

The NHS has been subject to significant change since its beginnings in 1948. Despite all its tribulations in its first 50 years, it is still warmly regarded by the British public. Nurses, too, enjoy a positive public image.

Activity 4

To identify structures in your locality. Find out who the members of the executive of your local NHS Trust are; with whom they have contracts; and what the annual income of the NHS Trust is. A good source of information is the annual report available from the Trust's headquarters; copies may be available in clinical departments. For further reading, see Holliday, 1995; Allsop, 1995 and Gough *et al.*, 1994.

Regulating the profession

The profession of nursing itself is also subject to social policy and legislation. After a protracted campaign at the beginning of the twentieth century, nurses eventually persuaded the government to create a professional register. This was finally achieved in 1919, when the Nurses Registration Act was passed, creating registers for different parts of the profession. The aim of the register was to protect the public as people would only be admitted to it who had been trained as nurses. Equally, those nurses who did not uphold the required standard of professional conduct would be removed from the register and would not be able to practise as registered practitioners.

The Act also created the General Nursing Council (GNC), a governing body for the profession. It was the role of the GNC to set the standards of education necessary to prepare nurses, examine nurses and maintain the register. Council members were appointed by the minister of health. A similar council was created for midwives.

This system remained in place for 60 years. In 1979, the systems for the regulation of the profession were reorganised by the Nurses, Midwives and Health Visitors Act, creating a new body, the United Kingdom Central Council for Nursing, Midwifery and Health Visiting (UKCC). This brought together all the separate organisations and councils of all the four kingdoms under one administration. Thus all the parts of the profession – nursing, midwifery and health visiting – were regulated by the same body. The principal functions of the UKCC were to establish and improve standards of training and professional conduct.

Nurse education was to be regulated by National Boards for each of the four kingdoms. The function of the Boards was to regulate the quality of the content of nursing education. The Boards received proposals for courses in the form of curriculum documents. They also employed education officers who negotiated with schools of nursing about the quality of the proposals and ensured that they met the Board's regulations. The courses were then approved by the Board for a set period of time, usually 5 years. Schools of Nursing then ran these courses for both pre- and postregistration students, with intermittent supervisory contact from the education officers.

Under the 1979 Act, a proportion of the members of the National Boards were elected by their peers. For example, the English National Board had 45 members, of whom 30 were elected, the remaining 15 being appointed by the secretary of state. Each board would then elect members from its number to sit on the UKCC.

In 1989, this system became subject to review. After only a short time in operation, it was felt that the system of statutory bodies was cumbersome and overly bureaucratic. In 1992, the Nurses, Midwives and Health Visitors Act once again reorganised the statutory bodies, the UKCC becoming the elected body. It is now elected every 4 years. There are designated places for the categories of nurse, midwife and health visitor, and for each of the four kingdoms. Every nurse, midwife and health visitor whose name is held on the register is entitled to vote and indeed to stand for election. In addition, the 1992 Act reduced the size of the National Boards. The membership of the Boards is appointed by the secretary of state, the chairpersons of the Boards also being government appointments. The chair or president of the UKCC is, in contrast, elected from within its membership.

Project 2000

Since its creation, the UKCC has made fundamental changes to the way in which nurses are educated. In 1986, it published a report (*Project 2000: A New Preparation for Practice*, UKCC 1986) that laid out a set of proposals for the reform of preregistration nurse education. The UKCC was aware that health needs and methods of health-care delivery were rapidly changing. The objective of the proposed change was to create a type of nursing practitioner who had been educated to meet these challenges.

The Project 2000 nurse was to be able to practise in both institutional and non-institutional settings. It was seen that a significant proportion of the knowledge needed by practitioners was shared across the range of registers. It was proposed, therefore, to have a 'common foundation' for the first 18 months of the course. In this, the students from all branches of adult, mental health, children's and learning disabilities nursing would all learn together. In the second half of the course, students were to learn in their own branches.

Since Florence Nightingale had set up training for nurses in the nineteenth century, they had been employed on an apprenticeship system. Student nurses were part of the hospital workforce and were required to deliver a service while they were learning. Project 2000 changed the role of student nurses. They became 'supernumerary', in that students still spent half of their education learning in the clinical situation but received a bursary and were not required to deliver service. Nurse training had been at the academic level of certificate. Project 2000 proposed that nurse education should be raised to the academic level of diploma and in some cases degree. Consequently, nurse teachers also had to have their academic level of qualifications raised. These proposals were generally accepted by the government and the profession, and the new style courses were introduced from 1989. Project 2000 has now become the norm for nurse education in Great Britain.

PREPP

In 1990, the UKCC also made proposals for change to the continuing education of qualified practitioners. These were contained in the *Report of the Post-registration*

Education and Practice Project (PREPP) and were again designed to develop practitioners who could meet the future health needs of the population. This report recommended that all newly registered practitioners should engage in a period of preceptorship for the first 6 months after registration. The preceptor would provide support and mentorship to the new practitioner. PREPP also made it a statutory requirement for practitioners to demonstrate that they have maintained and developed their professional knowledge; this is recorded in a personal professional profile or portfolio. There are also recommendations about retraining for nurses who return to practice after a career break. Practitioners must also re-register every 3 years.

These recommendations have now been instated. There has been a significant growth in postregistration education for nurses and a cultural shift to a commitment to lifelong learning and updating as a means of delivering safe and effective care throughout the nurse's career.

Midwifery services

The practice of midwifery has always been considered to be distinct from that of nursing, and it has developed its own set of policy provision over the twentieth century. There were several attempts to introduce legislation to regulate the profession of midwifery during the nineteenth century. The main driver of this was the Matrons Aid Society, founded in 1881. This was a small group of educated midwives who wanted to improve standards of care and the professional status of midwives. In the late nineteenth century, eight Bills proposing a midwives register were introduced to parliament, but all failed. This was partly because the government did not give it priority, so the proposed legislation was consequently put forward by a Private Members Bill. The Bill was also opposed by the medical profession because it trespassed upon their professional territory. Equally, there was opposition from the developing nursing profession, led by Mrs Bedford Fenwick, who wished to see the professions united and regulated jointly.

A Midwives Act was eventually passed in 1902. Its main provision was to establish a Central Midwives Board (CMB), initially for England and Wales. Later, provision was made for Scotland and Ireland. The CMB was charged with maintaining a roll of certificated midwives. It also set up Local Supervising Authorities (LSAs) to supervise the practice of midwives. The CMB set out rules that governed midwifery practice. It also provided for the education of midwives and set up structures to maintain professional discipline.

In the first half of the twentieth century, the practice of midwifery took place largely in the client's home. Women had to pay a fee to the midwife and to the GP if he was required. Often, as the client could not afford a doctor, the midwife would pay the fee. The Midwives Act 1918 provided for the LSA to pay the fees

preceptor

a teacher or advisor who guides the development of new entrants to a profession, paying attention to its codes, ethics and standards

profile/portfolio

interchangeable terms that refer to a systematic record of the professional development and achievement of the practitioner. Sections from this record may be requested by the UKCC to provide evidence of continuing development

Activity
5

Use this chapter to develop your professional profile or portfolio. Identify your knowledge of health-care policy. List ways in which this knowledge supports your effectiveness in clinical practice. For further reading, see Hull and Redfern, 1996 and RCN, 1995.

of doctors who were called to obstetric emergencies. The Midwives Act 1936 made it compulsory for the LSAs to provide a salaried domiciliary midwifery service. The fact that midwives could now receive a salary allowed them to provide a fuller service, which included antenatal care.

The Second World War had an effect upon the organisation of obstetric care. As a result of the war effort, there were fewer friends and family available to support a woman through a delivery. Women were consequently drawn to having their babies delivered in hospital.

The advent of the NHS in 1948 again changed the nature of obstetric care. As the service was free, women took up the service more readily and were more prepared to have their babies in hospital.

As previously described, the 1974 reorganisation of the NHS moved community health services from the local authority to the health authority. This included community midwives and had the effect of integrating midwifery services and improving communication.

The 1979 Nurses, Midwives and Health Visitors Act created a statutory committee for midwives, which is very important in the regulation of the practice of midwives. It is required to make Midwives' Rules, which relate to the LSAs and midwives' practice.

Activity 6

Based upon your reading of this section and your observations in obstetric practice areas, make a list of the ways in which midwives differ from nurses with regard to the regulation of their profession. For further reading, see Bennett and Brown, 1993, pp. 727–40, 741–54.

Mental health care

Care for people with mental health problems in the nineteenth and the first half of the twentieth century was based in large asylums, later to be termed psychiatric hospitals. More recently, there has been a movement to assist clients to live independently in the community, and policy and legislation have been developed to support this movement.

Caring for people who have mental health problems sometimes involves having to use powers that infringe civil liberties. This area of client care is consequently subject to significantly more legal involvement. In their daily practice, mental health nurses have to be knowledgeable about the law that regulates mental health practice.

Mental Health Act 1959

A significant change occurred in mental health care in the late 1950s. Before this time, the focus of care delivery was large psychiatric hospitals. These were built in the nineteenth century. Admission to hospital was by a system of certification. All clients who were admitted to hospital were legally committed into the care of the hospital and detained against their will.

During the 1950s, there was considerable social change, which created the climate for the development of legislation that was revolutionary in its approach.

The Mental Health Act of 1959 repealed all previous mental health legislation, introduced a single code for all types of mental disorder and set out new definitions of mental disorder. Clients were enabled to be admitted for treatment on a voluntary basis, as for any other hospital. Provision was made for compulsory admission to hospital only for those who were a danger to themselves or others because of mental illness. A new type of body was created to safeguard clients' civil rights. This was the Mental Health Review Tribunal, consisting of legal, medical and lay members. It allowed clients who were detained to have a right of appeal. The Tribunal also has the power to discharge clients from hospital following a sucessful appeal. The effect of the Act was to reduce the number of clients who were compulsorily detained as clients could be admitted to hospital before they became severely ill. The stigma associated with mental illness was significantly reduced. Discharging clients from hospital became much easier, and staff could contemplate the concept of the client living in the community.

Hospital closure

In 1961, Enoch Powell, the then Minister of Health, announced a new policy, a programme of closure of the mental hospitals. He recognised that a huge proportion of the NHS budget was spent on maintaining mental hospitals and saw that this programme would lead to a reduction in spending on the NHS. Powell wanted to see the development of mental illness units within general hospitals. Thus a trend was begun to decrease institutional care and increase community services, although this did not happen with anything like the speed that Powell had anticipated.

Better services for the mentally ill

In 1975, the Department of Health and Social Security (DHSS) published a report showing that although the client population of mental hospitals had been reduced, not one hospital had been closed and the volume of work was increasing. The report drew a picture of how future services would be. Services would be centred in general hospitals, and there would be provision for hostels for recovering clients, outclient clinics and day care.

Mental Health Act 1983

As services developed in the community and more effective drug therapies were discovered, the nature of mental health care changed. Once again, the legal framework required amendment, and a Mental Health Amendment Act was passed in 1983. The main tenets of the 1959 Act were upheld, but new provisions were added. Clients who are detained under treatment orders may be treated without their consent for the first 3 months after admission. After this, a 'second opinion' has to be sought to continue treatment. The second opinion is supplied by a qualified psychiatrist who is appointed by the Mental Health Act Commission (MHAC) (see below). Treatment in this case is most often ECT or drug therapy.

The Act created a new body, the Mental Health Act Commission. This is a special health authority whose role is to be an independent inspectorate; its powers are limited to detained clients. MHAC members are charged with the duty of visiting and interviewing detained clients and investigating complaints. The MHAC also makes an annual report to parliament.

The Act also makes provision for social care. Social services departments are required to appoint approved social workers (ASWs). These have to be competent in the care of mentally ill people. The ASW has the duty to apply to the hospital for a client to be detained. Before doing this, the ASW must interview the client and ensure that there is no means of providing care other than compulsory admission. Health and social services are charged with a duty to provide aftercare for clients who have been detained on a treatment order.

The Act made a new provision for nurses: they were given the power to prevent a voluntary client leaving hospital for up to 6 hours if they believed the client to be a danger to himself or others. Nurses and other practitioners are also to be consulted by the doctor, who gives a second opinion for compulsory treatment.

Care programme approach

care programme approach

a systematic framework for mental health practice which ensures that the service user has an assessment, a care plan, a key worker and ensures she is fully involved

In 1991, the government responded to several incidents that caused public concern by developing a system of organising mental health care for people with severe mental illness living in the community. This approach is to be followed by all health practitioners who deliver care to people with mental health problems. The first essential element of the care programme approach (CPA) is a systematic assessment of health and social care needs. Based on this assessment, the client has an agreed care plan. A key worker is appointed to co-ordinate the care plan and liaise with all the agencies that contribute to the package of care. The client's progress is subject to regular review, and he is involved in decisions about his care at every stage.

It is recommended that a distinction is made between varying levels of severity and complexity. Three levels are advised. First is a minimal level in which the client requires a low level of intervention, usually from only one member of the multiprofessional team. There is an intermediate level, where the client is likely to need more than one type of service. Third, clients who have a severe mental illness are likely to have complex needs and require a full multi-disciplinary CPA. This categorisation helps service providers to distinguish between levels of need and to prioritise service delivery.

Supervision register

Another measure was introduced in 1994, which was designed to address the problem of responding to and monitoring the care of people with complex needs who might be at risk to themselves or to others. The supervision register is a list kept by each mental health care provider unit for three types of client: those at risk of suicide, of serious violence to others and of severe self-neglect. The decision to include someone on the register is made in consultation with all members of the mental health team. The client must have an opportunity to state her views. The final responsibility to include someone on the register lies with the consultant psychiatrist. The client must be informed of this decision both orally and in writing. The register constitutes a confidential health record, and computerised registers are subject to the provisions of the Data Protection Act.

Supervised discharge

A further measure, the supervised discharge order, came into effect in 1996. It is an arrangement by which a client who has been treated in hospital under the provisions of the Mental Health Act is subject to formal supervision when discharged. The aim of the order is to ensure that the client receives aftercare services.

Clients who are placed on this order will have been assessed to be at substantial risk to themselves and others. They would normally also be included on the supervision register. Arrangements for aftercare under supervision are drawn up as part of a normal discharge planning process, following the principles of the CPA. The supervision order has the power to require the client to live in a particular place and attend a particular place at set times for medical treatment, occupation, education and training. The client may also be required to allow access to his place of residence to the supervisor or anyone else authorised by the supervisor. Despite having the power to require the client to attend for treatment, the order does not give the power to impose medication or any other treatment against the client's wishes.

The Act specifies that a range of people must be consulted before the order is applied. These are the client, members of the team caring for him in hospital, the community team and informal carers and relatives.

The client has a supervisor, a member of the community mental health team who is suitably experienced and qualified. This can be any professional but is often a community mental health nurse. The supervisor is responsible for monitoring the implementation of the care plan and liaising with other members of the community team. The supervisor is also responsible for ensuring that the order and care plan are reviewed. Most importantly, the supervisor is responsible for ensuring that the client complies with the requirements of the order. The supervisor has the power to require entry to the client's place of residence and to

Activity 7

Some countries do not have a law to regulate mental health care. Make notes on what mental health law provides for citizens of the UK. For a detailed explanation of mental health legislation, read Dimond and Barker, 1997.

convey the client to a place where he is required to live or attend. The order is applied for a period of 6 months, and the client has the right to appeal against it to a Mental Health Review Tribunal.

All these legal measures have been devised in order to meet the demands of caring for people who have severe mental illness but can live in the community with support rather than staying in a large institution.

Working with children and young people

Children and young people are a group who are vulnerable, especially when in need of health and social care. Similarly to mental health care, there is a legal framework that supports and guides practitioners in their work with children.

The Children Act

The legal framework that currently supports practice is the Children Act 1989, which took effect from 1991. It is addressed mainly to the court and to local authority social services; there are parts, however, that are important for nurses to understand.

The main principles of the Act are all child and family focused. The welfare of the child is paramount, and the overall aim is that children should be brought up and cared for within their own family. If children are in danger, they should be protected by effective intervention. An important principle is that children should be kept informed about what happens to them and be involved in the decision-making process. Care should also be designed to support parents, ensuring that parental responsibility is maintained and that effective support is provided.

The Act requires that health practitioners should work with parents to enable them to care for their children to the best of their ability by enhancing their knowledge and understanding of child care and development. Working in the spirit of the Act means listening to the child, providing appropriate information and taking account of his feelings and wishes. Health-care professionals are also required to co-operate with the social service and education departments to meet the health needs of the child. Most important is the identification of children in need and referral to social services if that is appropriate.

The Act specifically defines a 'child in need' as one who:

> is unlikely to achieve or maintain, or to have the opportunity of achieving or maintaining, a reasonable standard of health or development without the provision for him of services by a local authority: his health or development is likely to be significantly impaired, or further impaired without the provision for him of such services, he is disabled... (Section 17(10))

The Act recognises the role of midwives, health visitors and school nurses as having contact with the child from birth. They are likely to be the first to recognise a child in need. They are expected to refer the child to social services using agreed health authority protocols. They are also expected to co-operate with social workers to provide the health care needed to promote the child's welfare.

The Act outlines a new concept of 'parental responsibility', which has replaced the phrase 'parental rights'. The emphasis is placed upon the ongoing obligations of the parents' role. It includes the duties, rights, powers, responsibilities and authority that a parent has in respect of a child and his property. Parental responsibility is not affected by parental separation or divorce.

The nurse may be involved in a case where a court order may be applied. It is important to be aware of of the different types of order that might be granted. A *care order* is made if a court decides that a child is suffering or likely to suffer significant harm through a lack of adequate parental care or control. The child is placed in the care of the local authority, which then has parental responsibility for the child, shared with the parents. It does not take parental responsibility from the parents, but the local authority may decide how the parents exercise it.

The *supervision order* is made if the court decides that the local authority should observe a child closely and give guidance. The child is then under the supervision of a local authority or probation officer. The local authority or the supervisor has parental responsibility under this order.

The *child assessment order* is for use in situations where there are reasonable grounds to suspect that the child is suffering significant harm but is not at immediate risk. The applicant may form the opinion that an assessment is needed but the parents are unwilling to co-operate. Either the local authority or the National Society for the Prevention of Cruelty to Children (NSPCC) may apply for this order. It has a maximum duration of 7 days, and the court decides about the nature of the assessment.

The *emergency protection order* is reserved for extremely urgent cases, where the child's safety is immediately threatened. This order can be applied for 8 days, with a additional 7 if needed. The order may be challenged by the parents after the first 72 hours of the order. Parental responsibility is given to the applicant but only insofar as it is necessary to safeguard the child and promote his welfare. All these orders can be made by the court under public law.

In addition, there are a number of orders that are at the disposal of the courts but which are under private law proceedings relating to cases of divorce, domestic violence or adoption.

The *residence order* states with whom the child will live. This order may be made while the child is in the care of the local authority. It can thus end any care order and give parental responsibility to the person with the benefit of the order.

A *contact order* requires the person with whom the child lives to permit the child to have contact with the persons named in the order.

Activity
8

Make notes on the ways you think the Children Act protects and supports the rights of children. A more complete outline of the provisions of The Children Act can be found in DoH, 1992.

A *prohibited steps order* prevents the child's parents or any other person taking steps as outlined in the order without first obtaining the permission of the court.

Nurses may be required to attend a child protection conference before an application is made for a court order. The conference has to be clear and certain about the evidence before applying for an order. Nurses must also be prepared to write reports for court proceedings. In a child protection case, the nurse is required to provide a report that describes the nature of the significant harm that has already happened to the child. In addition, a statement is required of future risk for the child.

Almost any nurse, midwife or health visitor may, at some time in their practice, encounter a child who is at risk, so having a working knowledge of the principles and powers of the Children Act is important for all practitioners.

Chapter Summary

This chapter has described the main institutions of government and the processes that are undertaken in order to enact social policy. It has outlined how the NHS came into being and its subsequent development, and discussed the statutory regulation of the profession and the development of education. In addition, social policy relating specifically to midwifery, children's nursing and mental health practice has been described in some detail. Finally, it is emphasised that nurses can sometimes be a support and help to service users because of their knowledge of the wider social context of care as much as because of their clinical skill.

Test Yourself!

1. How many stages must a Bill pass through in the House of Commons?

2. In which year did the National Health Service begin?

3. What are the three kinds of contract that a fundholding GP can have?

4. In which year did midwives have the power to establish a Central Midwives Board?

5. What is the name of the inspectorate created by the Mental Health Act 1983?

6. What is the name of the order of the Children Act in which the court decides that the local authority should observe a child closely and give guidance?

References

Allsop, J. (1995) *Health Policy and the NHS: Towards 2000*, 2nd edn. Longman, London.

Bennett, V.R. and Brown, L.K. (1993) *Myles' Textbook for Midwives*, 12th edn. Churchill Livingstone, Edinburgh.

DHSS (Department of Health and Social Security) (1975) *Better Services for the Mentally Ill*. HMSO, London.

DHSS (Department of Health and Social Security) (1980) *Inequalities in Health* (Black Report). HMSO, London.

DHSS (Department of Health and Social Security) (1983) *NHS Management Inquiry* (Griffiths Report). HMSO, London.

Dimond, B.C. and Barker, F.H. (1997) *Mental Health Law for Nurses*. Blackwell, Oxford.

DoH (Department of Health) (1989) *Working for Patients.* White Paper on the NHS. HMSO, London.

DoH (Department of Health) (1992) *The Health of the Nation*. HMSO, London.

DoH (Department of Health) (1992) *The Children Act 1989: An Introductory Guide for the NHS*. HMSO, London.

DoH (Department of Health) (1995) *Building Bridges: A Guide to Arrangements for Interagency Working for the Care and Protection of Severely Mentally Ill People*. HMSO, London.

DoH (Department of Health) (1997) *The New NHS; Modern. Dependable.* White Paper. HMSO, London.

Gough, P., Maslin-Prothero, S. and Masterson, A. (1994) *Nursing and Social Policy: Care in Context*. Butterworth Heinemann, Oxford.

Hanson, A.H. and Walles, M. (1990) *Governing Britain*, 5th edn. Fontana, London.

Hill, M. (1993) *Understanding Social Policy*, 4th edn. Blackwell, Oxford.

Holliday, I. (1995) *The NHS Transformed*, 2nd edn. Baseline Books, Manchester.

Hull, C. and Redfern, L. (1996) *Profiles and Portfolios*. Macmillan, Basingstoke.

Illich, I. (1976) *Limits to Medicine: Medical Nemesis*, 2nd edn. Marion Boyars, London.

McKeown, T. (1976) *The Modern Rise of Population and the Role of Medicine: Dream, Mirage or Nemesis?* Rock Carling Monograph. Nuffield Provincial Hospitals Trust, London.

Ministry of Health (1942) *Report of Committee on Social Insurance and Allied Services* (Beveridge Report), HMSO, London.

Ministry of Health (1946) *NHS Bill. Summary of the Proposed New Service*. HMSO, London.

Ranade, W. (1994) *A Future for the NHS?: Health Care in the 1990s*. Longman, London.

RCN (Royal College of Nursing) (1995) The really useful guide to portfolios and profiles. *Nursing Standard* 9(32): 3–12.

UKCC (United Kingdom Central Council for Nursing, Midwifery and Health Visiting) (1986) *Project 2000: A New Preparation for Practice*. UKCC, London.

UKCC (United Kingdom Central Council for Nursing, Midwifery and Health Visiting) (1990) *The Report on the Post-registration Education and Practice Project (PREPP)*. UKCC, London.

Nursing Practice in an Interprofessional Context

JANET McCRAY

Introduction

At the end of this chapter, the reader will be able to:

- Define the term 'interprofessional practice'

- Identify elements of good and bad practice in teamwork settings

- Highlight different professionals' contributions to teamwork

- Describe the role of the primary health-care team

- Discuss the challenges that the primary health-care team presents to different professionals

- Plan methods of working in practice that will support effective interprofessional teamwork.

What is Interprofessionalism?

interprofessional

teamwork that involves a group of different professionals working to achieve mutually agreed goals

multidisciplinary

often used to describe interprofessional teamwork in an academic context

'Interprofessional' is the most recent term used to describe professionals from different disciplines working together. The definition suggests that these professionals are working in collaboration to achieve the same goals for the client, patient or service user. Interprofessional practice can occur in a range of settings, from that of the acute medical ward to community support for elderly people.

Other terms are used in place of and in preference to 'interprofessional', most commonly 'multidisciplinary' and 'interdisciplinary'. Marshall *et al.* (1979, p. 12) define multidisciplinary practice as a group of individuals with different training backgrounds, for example nursing, medicine, occupational therapy, health visiting and social work, who share common objectives but who make a different but complementary contribution. Within the White Paper *Primary Care: Delivering the Future* (DoH, 1996), the term 'multidisciplinary' has been chosen to describe both professional practice and the activity of professionals learning together, for example on study days or workshops. The term 'multi-agency' is also used to describe the involvement of a range of services and professionals in the delivery of health and social care to an individual. To help the reader, the term 'interprofessional' will be used when describing teamwork that involves working towards the same goal for patients or clients.

'Interprofessional' may be a more radical or progressive description of practice. Some advocates of interprofessional work might include working across ordinary professional boundaries to meet the needs of the client or service user. For example, a nurse in the field of learning disability may give advice on housing or welfare benefits to a young man. In day-to-day practice, this would ordinarily be the role of the social worker.

Two key features of interprofessional practice are teamwork and collaboration. Thus the concept of interprofessional practice may be interpreted in a range of ways, which will be explored in this chapter.

Moves Towards Interprofessional Practice

In the past 30 years, changes in the delivery of health and social care have placed a different emphasis on the role and work of professionals. These changes have been created by government policy and concerns about the cost and focus of health and welfare provision. In addition, the developing role of some professional groups and the need to respond in order not to undermine the provision of service has required a new look at practice. Advances in technology that have reduced the time spent in hospital, and the deinstitutionalisation movement, have placed emphasis on care in the community. This has had an impact on a more vocal and questioning consumer or service user group seeking an understanding of, or participation in, decisions about treatment and services offered, together with welfare rights. These changes have not occurred in isolation, and all can be attributed to one or more of the factors identified. Because this chapter explores interprofessional work, it may be worth reviewing each of these elements separately.

Government Policy and the Focus of Health and Welfare Provision

Moves to introduce general management structures created by the Griffiths Report (DoH, 1983) refocused the activity and roles of professionals within the National Health Service (NHS). This is explored in greater detail in Chapter 12. One of the greatest changes was the movement of nurses and clinicians into general management. A second change was the split of the functions of delivery and purchasing of care. Owens and Petch (1995, p. 44) explain this move as an attempt by the government to control budgets and resources. These changes also occurred in social care and formed part of the NHS and Community Care Act of 1990. This separation of the functions of purchasing and providing health and social care was also to influence general practice and the role of the GP.

One development has been the creation of fundholding GPs – GPs holding budgets and determining priorities for the purchasing of services. This role is currently under review after the May 1997 change in government. The current implementation of the White Paper *The New NHS – Modern Dependable* (DoH, 1997) confirms the emphasis on primary health care, with the creation of primary care groups. These groups will be responsible for consulting with local communities on health-care needs as well as commissioning the health care needed from a range of services, for example acute health care. Such changes will continue to affect the way in which professionals work together and will create different partnerships and relationships for practice. For example, in primary care groups, practice nurses may take on responsibility for managing specific elements. Equally, some of the roles traditionally undertaken by the GP, for example caring for people who have a terminal illness in their own homes, may now be undertaken by community or practice nurses.

While GPs are funding posts within their own practices, they may question the cost-effectiveness of some professionals and choose to employ others. Therefore, while the NHS and Community Care Act has created a greater need for collaboration and interprofessional work, it has also created uncertainty for some individual professional groups.

primary care groups

groups of GP practices set within a specific locality

Role Expansion of Some Professional Groups

The Greenhalgh Report (Greenhalgh and Company, 1994) reviewed the role of junior doctors and recommended the reduction of their weekly working hours. One response to these changes has been that of a broader role for nurses. The document *The Scope of Professional Practice* (UKCC, 1992) identifies several areas in which nurses could take on broader and more autonomous roles, for example in nurse prescribing and nurse practitioner roles within community hospitals and in nurse-led clinics.

Finally, there has been a blurring of the boundaries between health visitors, district nurses and community nurses. All of this means a greater emphasis on teamwork and multiprofessional co-operation, as clinical work that was in the domain of the GP or hospital-based doctor is transferred to other professionals.

Changes in the Provision of Service

As technology and approaches to treatment have changed, for some patients or clients less time is spent in acute hospital settings. Many people are discharged and supported by community or district nurses in their own homes, the majority of care being provided by family members. Running parallel to these developments has been the deinstitutionalisation movement for people who are elderly or have a learning disability or a mental health need. The transition from institution to community care has seen a change in role for the professional groups of nurses, occupational therapists, psychologists and speech therapists. This has been compounded by the increasing emphasis on voluntary and independent sector provision in the community. Roles that might once have been undertaken by qualified professionals may now be carried out by support workers or vocationally trained employees. Professional roles have become more specific because of the different types of support required in community settings.

At the same time, the cost of some roles has been questioned and the need for a professionally qualified individual challenged. Interwoven throughout these changes has been an increased demand for interprofessional collaboration in order to co-ordinate service delivery in the community.

The Rights of Service Users, Clients and Patients

A recognition of the changing position of service users with regard to the services offered has gained momentum. An acknowledgement of fragmented services and a need to create a seamless service has built the foundation for change. Responses from service user groups have ranged from the formal voice of the Community Health Council and other representative bodies, to the radical position of others, notably those involved in the Council for Disabled People. Such activity has challenged the power of the professional and sets the scene for a partnership between the service user and professional, and a greater input into the making of decisions about the use of resources. This change in position for the service user or client has meant that the involvement of large numbers of professionals in their specific care group is no longer accepted – and greater collaboration within and across professional teams will be needed in order to minimise this and to ensure access to the appropriate services.

Activity
1

From your recent practice experience, identify all the different professionals you have come into contact with. What is their role and how does it link with yours?

Why is Interprofessionalism Important to the Nurse?

As a nurse practising in a range of health- and social care settings, the need for collaboration to meet service user needs will be a priority. Working together with other professionals will be part of everyday practice. In order to make sense of interprofessional working, and to enhance its success, it is necessary to have a clear picture of how nursing practice in the interprofessional team has evolved over time and what factors have impinged upon its success. In thinking about interprofessional practice, a greater understanding of the role of other professional groups may be gained. This may lead to greater confidence in collaboration for the nurse.

Teamwork

teamwork

involves a group of
identified professionals
working together to
achieve a specific
outcome or set of
outcomes

When interprofessional or multidisciplinary work is described, it is usually placed within a teamwork setting. For example, effective multidisciplinary teamwork is a target within the White Paper *Primary Care: Delivering the Future* (DoH, 1996). The World Health Organisation (WHO, 1984) describes teamwork as follows: 'A group who share a common health goal and common objectives determined by community needs, to the achievement of which each member of the team contributes, in accordance with his or her competence and skill and in coordination with the function of others.' Similarly, Rubin and Beckhard (1972) and Gilmore *et al.* (1974, pp. 5–6) describe it as follows: 'a team is a group of people who make different contributions towards the achievement of a common goal.'

Collaboration

Collaboration can be defined as 'work across boundaries, work with difference' (Loxley, 1997, p. 50). Successful collaboration is dependent on team members having clear ideas about what they hope to achieve. These ideas should be clear not just to the individual team members, but also to all those contributing to the team activity. Equally, team members should be working to meet the same goals or objectives for service users, patients or clients.

Effective collaboration requires mutual support and space for disagreement or the exploration of different views to take place. Part of the process of collaboration is deciding when it is needed and when individual team members can make autonomous decisions. For example, in emergency situations, there may be limited time for collaboration. This does not stop collaboration occurring in emergency or crisis intervention work. Instead, protocols or guidelines may need to be developed by team members that take into account the decision-making process so that they can be followed in difficult situations or circumstances.

Factors affecting teamwork

While in the definition, the route to teamwork may seem straightforward, it might in reality be a more complicated process. Many factors can influence the ability of a team to practise effective co-operation, all of which are occurring in the changing context of health and social care practice.

Financial

When budgets and resources are constrained, costs and who will pick up the bill for intervention can create tension in teams. Often, practitioners at ground level may wish to work collaboratively to solve problems with service users. However, managers who hold budgets may be constrained and less able to be facilitative, perhaps placing restrictions on the amount of collaboration that takes place.

Team support

A key factor in team development is that of co-ordination. Once again, resources may influence the level of support. Teams need accountable individuals to help the problem-solving process and take forward practice-focused solutions. These individuals may be identified as leaders or co-ordinators. Those teams which have an absence of leadership or co-ordination are not as likely to achieve effective outcomes for clients. As a result, the cost in terms of an individual leader's time has to be found. Equally, teams require a physical environment in which to meet, as well as diaried time to get together to discuss problems, evaluate progress and plan future developments. All of these have both obvious as well as hidden cost implications.

Endorsing teamwork

Activity

2

Once again, think about your recent practice experience. What sort of formal and informal methods of evaluation have you seen? How effective have they been? Consider, for example, reading case notes or care plans, or review meetings within social care agencies.

Team members need to be able to see benefits from a team-based model of care. When professionals are under pressure to maintain their current workload, finding time for additional means of collaboration and reviewing their current practice may seem a further and somewhat onerous task.

The lynchpin of good practice may be evaluation. Evaluation enables team members to consider the effectiveness of their intervention and whether it has achieved the outcome that was anticipated. Balancing the results of intervention with the time and cost involved may help team members to decide on the relevance of the team activity that they have undertaken. Team members may need to consider the best use of their time together and set priorities, all of which may change following review. As teams work together over a longer period of time, they may be able to make decisions more swiftly. However, ongoing evaluation may help the team to decide whether such teamwork processes ensure the best outcomes for service users or patients.

Professional Boundaries

For teamwork to be centred on clear outcomes for service users, clients or patients, team members need to be clear about what their role is within the team and what the boundaries of that role are. In other words, what is my professional role, and where does it end and become the responsibility of a different professional? Brown (1991) notes the significance of professional boundaries and the need for clarity with regard to professional roles. For example, what practice activity is defined as core and to be taken on by all members, and what is seen as specific and thus the role of one discipline? Without a clear specification, team members may drift towards a common ground, which means that some areas of practice might be neglected. This is illustrated in McGrath's (1993) study of community teams in the field of learning difficulties in the late 1980s. Her research reviews the practice of 27 teams in Wales. Within the teams, members were either nurses, social workers, psychologists, physiotherapists or speech therapists. One of the main team aims was to establish individual care plans for each person with a learning difficulty requiring a service intervention. Her research indicates that during the period of the study, a number of benefits were perceived by individual team members. However, these did not result in a higher level of individual programme or care plans being established. In contrast, collective responses to such developments as advocacy schemes increased, and individual team members felt that their knowledge of learning difficulty was heightened. However, the key aim of creating formal care plans made little progress.

All of the above are significant barriers to good practice that need to be overcome or acknowledged by both those working in teams and those co-ordinating them. Other elements can also inhibit or sustain good working practices.

Professional Socialisation

An individual's socialisation and integration within a specific professional group may impact upon their ability to work within an interprofessional team. For example, when a person enters a career pathway with the intention of registering as a professional nurse, a key element of the process is that of professional socialisation into the role. This may include, for example, guidelines about clothing to wear in practice, particular skills and competencies learnt in the common foundation programme and the way in which the client or patient is described, all manifesting themselves in how the role or identity of the nurse is developed by the learner. Similar processes will occur in all professional groups, a consequence being that when teamwork is practised, such factors may impinge on team integration. Some specific elements of professional socialisation are language, values and professional status.

professional socialisation

process of taking on a set of values and identity that are associated with and underpin a particular profession

Activity
3

Think about your first weeks of nurse education. What activities formed part of the socialisation process? Were you aware of this process at the time?

Language

Within each professional group, a vocabulary of terminology and abbreviations is used continuously to communicate information. The language may be unique to that profession. When teamwork is undertaken, the meaning of particular words and expressions will need clarification. If clarity is not sought, assumptions could be made about the meaning of specific language and actions, one result being conflict or conflicting views when language is interpreted in different ways by those who do not belong to that particular professional group.

Personal values

A value is something that an individual holds at the centre of their being. Values are developed over time and from experience. Personal values may reflect an individual's culture, moral stance or lifestyle. Values may be a product of age or historical tradition. Such values may be translated into action through the development of specific views or attitudes, either positive or negative. Values held may suggest that all individuals have the right to the same opportunities. For example, a person may believe that all people with learning disability should be part of ordinary community life. In this case, attitudes in terms of behaviour might involve becoming an independent advocate for an individual when the person needs help with communicating his wishes. In contrast, attitudes may remain observable only in terms of how positively or negatively an individual views a person or situation.

Professional values

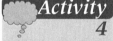

Activity
4

What do you think the values of the nurse are? What are these values based on? Do these values differ from your own?

In addition to personal values, individuals who participate in professional education may also develop a further set of values. Within teams, there may be assumptions made about the values of professional groups. All are working towards similar goals for the client or service user, ideally in partnership with that person. However, in reality, values may be different. For example, social work may be concerned with interprofessional practice and achieving outcomes for service users based on a recognition of oppression and inequality in society. The care plan or care management assessment set in place might reflect this. Equally, physiotherapists may be focused on physiological factors that inhibit good health for service users. In working towards collaborative practice, discussion based on values and what they mean to individual professions may work towards an understanding of professional action. If values are ignored, this may lead to greater tension in teams (Braye and Preston Shoot, 1994).

Interprofessional values

Loxley (1997, p. 92) describes the core values of interprofessional work as trust and sharing. She uses the word 'utilitarian', that is, being or having practical worth, to endorse their validity in teamwork. Essential components of trust and sharing are that they must remain two way. This means not just relying on people's commitment to the team's purpose or task, but also taking on the team members' belief in oneself as being able to deliver the goods or take on the role, and meeting these expectations. Achieving the ability to trust others and to share practice with them will require confidence and a clear understanding of one's own professional role. This may become more complex when individuals are of a different status.

Status

For teams to work effectively, mutual trust and respect for all members' contributions to the team is required. Part of the means of achieving this trust is to hold a greater understanding of the key role of other professional groups and to acknowledge the differences and similarities in language, values and models of practice used by other professions. The team co-ordinator or leader should be facilitating this process as a model for teamwork is developed. Nurses have traditionally been seen as semi-autonomous practitioners working to guidelines drawn up by medical staff. Doctors themselves have been seen as making autonomous clinical decisions and advising other members of the health and social care teams on practice. Speech therapists and physiotherapists, although autonomous practitioners, work largely on an individual basis with clients, advising on very specific areas of intervention. Because of these differences, power and status may become an issue when teamwork is undertaken. For example, doctors may have difficulty taking advice from other health-care professionals, whereas nurses may lack the confidence to advise or provide information related to a specific area of practice. Social workers' views of good practice in mental health services may clash with a more medically orientated response from a consultant psychiatrist. All of these factors can influence the way in which teams function and create future stress for team members.

Good Practice in Teamwork

At this point, nursing practice in an interprofessional context may seem fraught with complex and insoluble problems and to be avoided at all costs! Nevertheless, having realistic expectations of teamwork may help the nurse to prepare for practice with greater confidence and maintain a focus on what is significant to the outcomes for the client or service user. Some reasons for this follow.

Knowledge

Having knowledge that identifies some probable causes of friction within the teamwork setting can help to make sense of difficulties and begin to shape the problem-solving process: in other words, to help the practitioner to find a workable solution to the situation. Because of the knowledge held, an acceptance of team members' differences and different contributions to teamwork can lead to a gradual mutual trust. This will contribute towards a working environment in which it is safe to air conflict or state different opinions. A further spin-off will be the prevention of isolation and an increased willingness to share information.

Methods of practice intervention

Within a range of different professionals, the responses to client's or service user's needs may differ. A medical model approach may favour giving information and a course of treatment to individuals. This model may be used by doctors. Some nurses may also adopt an information-giving role. In contrast, some professionals may seek a more partnership-based model of practice, for example, as Oliver (1996) suggests, where the professional is seen as a resource to be used by the particular service user. In other words, the client or individual service user will direct the professional's approach, personally requesting specific information, action and responses from her. This approach is developing within social work and care management-type roles. The different models of practice among professional groups can lead to inconsistency of information for the client or service user and can cause greater confusion. The teamwork process should provide a framework in which issues such as what information to give and the level of commitment required by each professional are clearly stated and agreed upon. Pritchard (1995, p. 208) adopts Bruce's (1980) 'teamwork for presentation' matrix to identify stages of team co-operation (Table 13.1).

Table 13.1 ● Stages of team co-operation

Co-operation in:	'Nominal'	'Convenient'	'Committed'
Team goal-setting	No explicit goals	Follow doctors' goals	Shared explicit goals
Role perceptions	Stereotypes common	Some understanding	Roles clearly understood
Professional status	Wide differences	Differences inhibit co-operation	Differences ignored
Referral of patients	To agency rather than individual professional	Referral by delegation	Easy two-way referral and open access
Interaction within team	Very little and irregular	Some interaction	Close regular interaction, formal and informal
Mutual trust	Lacking	Guarded	Strong and developing
Communication failure	Often	Sometimes	Exceptional
Confidentiality	A problem	Problems partly solved	Not a problem
Advice to patients	Inconsistent	Poor co-ordination	Consistent
Preventative care	Not possible	Possible	Optimum conditions

Source: Modified from Bruce, (1980).

Pritchard's matrix illustrates the steps toward the committed team by describing co-operation in a range of teamwork activities. The main use of this tool has been in the assessment or diagnosis of a team's current position. Here it is used to give an example of what could be achieved within the teamwork setting. Moreover, as Pritchard (1995) notes, there is a need to link teamwork performance to outcomes for service users, and as such to begin to meet need.

Meeting need

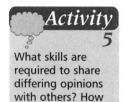

Activity 5

What skills are required to share differing opinions with others? How can these be used?

In a team where conflict is aired and individual members feel safe to share differing views, steps toward clear mutual goals can be made. These can help the teamwork forward, preventing obstruction or avoiding difficult issues. Rubin and Beckhard (1979) suggest that, in order to meet need, the team must be able to identify agreed objectives and be able to articulate and resolve differences. Finally, the team must be able to manage interpersonal issues – how the team feel about each other – and make a commitment to teamwork. In learning to manage all of these factors, the needs of service users or clients can remain central to the team's purpose.

Working in Teams

The first section of this chapter has reviewed some of the factors that can affect teamwork. These have been generic in setting and content. In the next section, the role of the primary health care team will be explored to give a specific example of teamwork and multiprofessional practice.

What is the primary health-care team?

primary health care

the continuing health and social welfare care offered appropriately to needful individuals living in private households

In the foreword to the summary of the White Paper *Primary Care: Delivering the Future* (DoH, 1996), primary health care is described as 'the NHS most people see – the NHS of the family doctor and their team, community nurses, therapists as well as pharmacists, dentists and optometrists'. It will also include midwives, district nurses and health visitors. With the implementation of the White Paper *The New NHS – Modern Dependable* (DoH, 1997), the role of the primary care team is currently developing and growing. Traditional teams based on health centres may now include counsellors and mental health nurses. Social workers will also be involved in areas such as child protection and the provision for elderly people. Plans set in place by the 1996 White Paper will review and expand the role of the nurse in learning further skills, such as prescribing medication. Equally, the role of the practice nurse may also expand to take on referrals from people who would ordinarily have seen their GP.

How has it evolved?

Jeffereys (1995, p. 193) writes that, as a result of the Family Doctor's Charter in 1966, arrangements were set in place for positive community-based practice. This charter established a positive role for non-hospital-based medicine, and a structure for interprofessional work was established. Jeffereys identifies the elements of this structure as allowances for GPs who worked together on one site and promotion of the employment of receptionists and practice nurses, by providing reimbursement of their services, and offering interest-free loans for more modern premises. The Health Services and Public Health Act 1968 endorsed a health-promotion role for general practice that involved the prevention of ill-health and support for families, and thus the role of the primary health-care team gradually emerged.

Further changes were to occur in the 1980s as the Conservative government responded in order to cut increasing public expenditure. Pietroni (1994, p. 81) writes that the White Paper *Priorities for Health and Social Services in England* (DHSS, 1976) and the NHS management enquiry (DoH, 1983) were to culminate in the NHS and Community Care Act 1990 (DoH, 1990). These placed further responsibilities for care within the primary care team, making it the first point of call for all referrals. Alongside this has been the devolvement of budgets to GPs, with practices taking on GP fundholding responsibilities. These moves enable GPs to decide on purchasing priorities for primary and secondary care across the spectrum of demographic needs. These developments have placed the GP at the centre of decision-making within the primary health-care team, despite suggestions that other professionals such as nurses might take on the initial assessment role. Chart 13.1 highlights the key developments within primary health-care nursing practice.

Quality services in the community

Towards the millennium, the primary health-care team faces the challenge of better teamwork and the need to develop further professional roles. The government's aim to achieve a seamless service remains, in order that clients or patients are not seen by vast numbers of different professionals and to prevent their continual assessment and attendance at different clinics. An emphasis on developing primary health care remains a top priority, and the principles of good primary care, shown in Figure 13.1, are highlighted with regard to quality. In addition, one of the key functions of primary care groups will be that of clinical governance, ensuring that effective, high-quality care is offered to a specific population.

Chart 13.1 ● Key development in primary health-care nursing

District nursing

1970s	Introduction of attachment schemes
	District nurses based at GP practices. Established primary health-care teams
1972	Report of the Committee on Nursing made recommendations for formal post-basic education, which became law in 1979
1974	Royal College of General Practitioners published *Nursing in General Practice in the Reorganised NHS*
1990s	Extended role of the district nurse may include the prescribing of medication, which has been the task of the GP
	Review of educational requirements of the role as part of the English National Board specialist pathway curricula

Practice nursing

1970s	Nurses attached to GP practice
1986	Cumberlege Report, *Neighbourhood Nursing, A Focus for Care*
	Recommended development of the nurse practitioner role – taking on direct referrals to take the pressure off GPs
1987	Government rejected these plans
1990s	Role of practice nurses under review
1996	White Paper *Primary Care: Delivering the Future* (DoH, 1996) advocates major change to practice nurse education and role within the primary health-care team
1998	Configuration of primary care groups may mean changes in practice nurse role

Health visiting

1976	Court Report identified the health visitor as a major agent of prevention in family work (Orr, 1975)
1970s and 80s	Central Council for Education Training of Health Visitors continued to assess the role of the health visitor, especially when the focus on child protection and children at risk increased
1980	Standing conference on health visitor education, *A Time to Learn,* looked at the changing role of health visiting
1990s	Role still unclear. Purchaser concern with cost of health visitor intervention
1998	Configuration of primary care groups may mean changes in the role of the health visitor

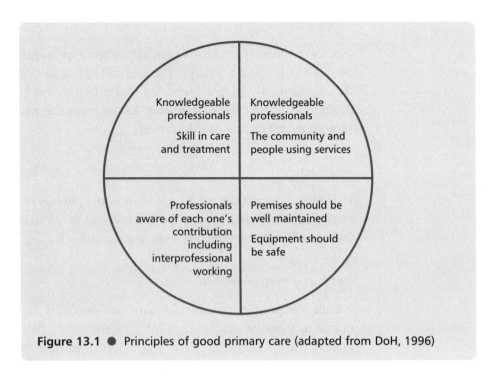

Figure 13.1 ● Principles of good primary care (adapted from DoH, 1996)

Role of the professional within the primary health-care team

There are still decisions to be made about the extended roles of nurses and how these will contribute to the primary health-care team. Equally, the need to use resources effectively remains an issue. What also remains unanswered is why there is still an ongoing need to re-emphasise interprofessional teamwork when primary health-care teams have been in existence for more than 25 years. Teamwork should be seen as an essential part of working together – yet some gaps still exist. Earlier in the chapter, some broad reasons for the difficulties in teamwork were raised. If we look specifically at primary health-care teams, all the factors identified may inhibit good practice. It is worth at this point looking at some further constraints on teamwork within primary care teams.

Location

It is likely that the core members of the primary health-care team are situated on one site within a local health centre. However, other professionals, such as social workers, who provide an input to the team may be based in different locations. As a consequence, they may miss out on informal contact and lines of communication.

Team size

Within the primary health-care team, a range of individual professionals may be involved in providing services. The size and extent of this may impact on team development. Too large a team may prevent clear and focused discussion and inhibit the decision-making process. Examples of this may be seen in the child protection and mental health services.

Payment

Individual professionals working as part of the primary health-care team will be employed on different rates of pay and conditions of service. This could lead to feelings of resentment among some team members.

Resource management

Within the primary health-care team, responsibility for practice and performance may not be clearly identified. In some teams, GPs may be the decision-makers when funding for services is allocated. In contrast, practice nurses and other nurse practitioners may have limited financial or budgetary control. While each practitioner may see himself as autonomous, issues such as payment and access to resources can lead to inequality of status, and individual contributors to teamwork may, as a consequence, be seen as being of more or less value.

In the changing climate of primary care, where GPs may have greater financial autonomy, the position of other professionals may be under greater scrutiny, for example in making decisions about the effectiveness of input of various professionals and, in doing so, questioning roles and performance. Part of this process may lead to a narrowing down of certain roles and limited input to primary health-care teams for some professionals. These activities may restrict good teamwork.

Activity 6

From your reading so far, highlight the key challenges to interprofessional teamwork in primary health care.

Moving Towards Co-operation

The place of interprofessional work at this point in time remains uncertain. Pockets of good practice are observable. Mutual co-operation and the desires of service users can be in conflict with government policy, how funding mechanisms operate and the struggle for power of some professional groups (Figure 13.2).

Responses So Far

Research and reports

A considerable amount of research and evaluation has been undertaken in the area of teamwork in primary and community care. Many of the findings of

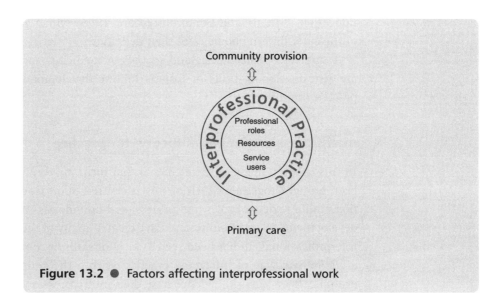

Figure 13.2 ● Factors affecting interprofessional work

earlier studies in the 1980s focusing on primary health-care settings were negative. The reluctance to collaborate of some specific professional groups, such as doctors, is well documented. More recently, however, the value of interprofessional work has become the focus of research and evaluation. Most of the work published emphasises the positive responses to collaboration across different professional groups. It is too early to review the impact of this research on practice development. However, as the body of research grows along with an increasing amount of research funding for such projects, it is likely that effective mechanisms for change will be identified and implemented. At the time of writing, several key reports have been published that focus on the value of collaboration, including the:

● Sainsbury Foundation for Mental Health report (1997)
● Medical and Nursing and Midwifery Advisory Committee report (1997)
● SCOPME Working Paper (1997).

Educational developments

Education has been one response to the interprofessional agenda. Providers of educational programmes have seen educational activity as a route to a greater understanding of the professional roles of others. Most of the activity that has occurred has been at postregistration or post-qualifying level. Individual professionals have come together to share units of study, an emphasis on problem-solving having been developed during the 1990s. Loxley (1997) reproduces a table from CAIPE 1996 (The Centre for the Advancement of Interprofessional

Education, Primary and Community Care, 1996) which gives a detailed review of the co-ordinating bodies and their activities.

A number of universities and schools of medicine, social work and nursing are also developing units or forums for the development of interprofessional practice initiatives.

Interprofessionalism as a 'theory' for practice

In this chapter, many of the elements that form interprofessional practice have been brought together. Much of this is centred upon teamwork and collaboration, and a review of roles and professional boundaries. We have seen how the developments in community care have created many of these changes. In reality, interprofessionalism has been seen as a set of skills or competencies rather than a whole new way of informing practice, with a theoretical underpinning. For example, from what knowledge base does interprofessional work come? Loxley (1997) suggests that assumptions are made about what knowledge from a certain discipline might be helpful but that this has not been investigated or studied in a coherent way. It is largely driven from what services need. Because of this, a sound theoretical framework has not yet developed.

A number of academics and practitioners are beginning to study and build a theory for interprofessional practice. As this develops, it is possible that those professionals who have been reluctant to make interprofessional practice a priority may begin to participate.

Personal responses

The moves forward outlined above take on complex issues at a societal service and organisational level. However, an individual in practice can still begin to create change. For a nurse practising in a multiprofessional setting, thinking about individual responses to teamwork and reflecting on their cause or foundation may be helpful. Observing professionals who hold effective team member skills may also provide ideas for personal knowledge and skill development.

From this perspective, individual methods of working that can help effective teamwork can be shaped. Part of this exercise should include active consideration of the role of service users in the process.

Chapter Summary

The route to interprofessional practice is a complex one. At times, the agendas of government, service managers, professionals and service users seem to be in conflict. Nevertheless, positive examples are occurring in practice. As practitioners, educationalists and service managers design the organisational structures needed to develop further multiprofessional work, professionals can build on their skills in collaboration. The interface of health and social care delivery can then become a positive one.

Test Yourself!

1. What does the term 'interprofessional practice' mean?

2. Provide examples from your own experience of good and bad teamwork.

3. How do different professionals contribute to teamworking?

4. What challenges does working in a primary health-care team create for the nurse?

References

Braye, S. and Preston Shoot, M. (1995) *Empowering Practice in Social Care*. Open University Press, Buckingham.

Brown, S. (1991) Professions in teams. In Thompson, T. and Mathias, P. (eds) *Standards and Mental Handicap*. Baillière Tindall, London.

Bruce, N. (1980) *Teamwork for Preventative Care*. Research Studies Press, John Wiley & Sons, Chichester.

CAIPE (Centre for the Advancement of Interprofessional Education, Primary and Community Care) (1996) *National Coordinating Bodies and Their Interests*. CAIPE, London.

DHSS (Department of Health and Social Security) (1976) *Priorities for Health and Personal Social Services in England*. HMSO, London.

DoH (Department of Health) (1983) *NHS Management Inquiry* (Griffiths Report). HMSO, London.

DoH (Department of Health) (1990) *Caring for People. Community Care in the Next Decade and Beyond*. HMSO, London.

DoH (Department of Health) (1996) *Primary Care: Delivering the Future*. HMSO, London.

DoH (Department of Health) (1997) *The New NHS – Modern Dependable*. Stationery Office, Norwich.

Gilmour, M., Bruce, N. and Hunt, M. (1974) *The Work of the Nursing Team in General Practice*. Council for the Education and Training of Health Visitors, London.

Greenhalgh and Company (1994) *The Interface Between Junior Doctors and Nurses: A Research Study for the Department of Health*. Cm/EL 94/75. HMSO, London.

Jeffereys, M. (1995) Primary health care. In Owens, P., Carrier, C. and Horder, J. (eds) *Interprofessional Issues in Community and Primary Health Care*. Macmillan, Basingstoke.

Loxley, A. (1997) *Collaboration in Health and Welfare*. Jessica Kingsley, London.

McGrath, M. (1993) *Multidisciplinary Teamwork*. Avebury, Aldershot.

Marshall, M., Preston, M., Scott, E. and Wincott, P. (eds) (1979) *Teamwork For and Against: An Appraisal of Multidisciplinary Practice*. British Association of Social Workers, London.

Oliver, M. (1996) *Social Work. Disabled People and Disabling Environments*. Jessica Kingsley, London.

Orr, J. (1975) Health visiting in the UK. In Hockey, L. (ed.) *Primary Care Nursing*. Churchill Livingstone, London.

Owens, P. and Petch, H. (1995) Professionals and management. In Owens, P., Carrier, J. and Horder, J. (eds) *Interprofessional Issues in Community and Primary Health Care*. Macmillan, Basingstoke.

Pietroni, P. (1994) Interprofessional teamwork. In Leatherhead, A. (ed.) *Going Interprofessional*. London, Routledge.

Pritchard, P. (1995) Learning to work effectively in teams. In Owens, P., Carrier, J. and Horder, J. (eds) *Interprofessional Issues in Community and Primary Health Care*. Macmillan, Basingstoke.

Rubin, I.R. and Beckhard, R. (1972) Factors influencing the effectiveness of health teams. *Millbank Memorial Fund Quarterly* **50**(3): 317–37.

Sainsbury Foundation (1997) *Pulling Together*. Sainsbury Centre for Mental Health, London.

SCOPME (1997) *Multiprofessional Working and Learning. Sharing the Educational Challenge*. SCOPME Working Paper. SCOPME, London.

Standing Medical, Nursing and Midwifery Advisory Committee (1996) *In the Patient's Interest: Multiprofessional Working across Organisational Boundaries*.

UKCC (United Kingdom Central Council for Nursing, Midwifery and Health Visiting) (1992) *The Scope of Professional Practice*. UKCC, London.

Vanclay, L. (1996) *Sustaining Collaboration Between General Practitioners and Social Workers*. CAIPE, London.

World Health Organisation (1984) *Health for All by the Year 2000*. WHO Regional Office, Copenhagen.

World Health Organisation (1984) *Glossary of Terms Used in the 'Health for All' Series*. WHO, Geneva.

14 Challenges to Professional Practice

MELANIE JASPER

● Introduction

The aim of this chapter is to start you thinking about some of the issues that influence the ways in which nurses operate as registered practitioners to manage and deliver nursing care. At the end of the chapter, you should be able to:

- Define professional practice and discuss the responsibilities involved

- Understand the *Code of Professional Conduct* in relation to your own roles and responsibilities as a student, with particular relationship to accountability

- Describe the role that personal, organisational and professional beliefs and values play in underpinning practice

- Identify the influence of models and frameworks of care in nursing practice

- Discuss the significance of quality assessment and standards in evaluating nursing care

- Identify your own responsibilities for evidence-based practice and lifelong learning.

By the time you reach the end of the common foundation programme, you will have gained some confidence in clinical skills, experienced a range of placements aimed at broadening your perceptions of nursing and your clients, and developed a foundational theoretical basis on which to build the more specialised theory of your chosen branch of nursing. The issues raised in this chapter can be seen as challenges that nurses have addressed in an effort to move from an occupation dominated and directed by medical practitioners, to one with a developing knowledge and skill base of its own, which has a direct influence on client care. All of these subjects will be addressed in more detail in your branch studies and are merely touched upon here in terms of raising your awareness of what the responsibilities of being a registered practitioner are.

registered practitioners

nurses, midwives or health visitors who are registered on the professional register with the UKCC

The issues to be considered are:

- Defining professional practice
- The responsibilities of professional practice
    - The United Kingdom Central Council for Nursing, Midwifery and Health Visiting (UKCC) *Code of Professional Conduct*
    - accountability
    - credibility
    - lifelong learning
- Evidence-based practice
- Philosophies and ideologies (beliefs and values)
- A knowledge base for nursing – frameworks of care, models and the nursing process
- Quality and standards.

However, before addressing the theoretical issues, it is worth taking time to consider just what we mean by 'professional practice'.

Defining Professional Practice

Activity
1

Take a few minutes to think back over your experience to date and note down the expectations you would have from any person that you consulted as a professional, for example, a lawyer, a doctor or an architect.

The debate about whether or not nursing is a profession has been raging for over a decade, and each of us has our own views on it (for an overview of this, see Rafferty, 1996). The whole issue is largely a sterile one that has little impact on the way in which nurses practise nursing. What is far more important for nursing students is how we choose for ourselves what constitutes 'professional' behaviour and how we enact that in our practice. So perhaps the best place to start this chapter is by identifying what we mean by professional practice. Try Activity 1.

Some of the issues that you identified probably relate to such things as:

- The knowledge that people have
- Their professional qualifications, or evidence of belonging to a professional body or organisation that licenses or registers them to practise
- The skill that they exhibit in their practice
- Their conduct – for example, the way in which they dress, their manner, the way they treat you, the respect they show you and the confidence they have in their ability to help you
- A recommendation from other people, or the fact that they are recognised for their particular expertise.

Hence we all carry with us a personal view of what professional practice is. Superimposed on that will be external definitions that arise from the professional bodies governing the people whom they license to practise, for example codes of practice, and criteria established by government policies. Similarly, there may be expectations of professional practice that come from your employer and a contract of employment. Moloney (1992) suggests that the set of attributes displayed by people in professional practice can be seen as 'professionalism' and that they relate essentially to the attitudes and attributes that they display. The first of these is that a profession is indeed 'practised' or engaged in rather than being a theoretical activity. Other attitudes may be a commitment to work and an orientation towards service rather than personal profit. Similarly, there may be a requirement for accountable practice that is based on evidence and an inherent motivation for learning and the development of a knowledge base. These arise, as we have seen, from a multitude of sources.

The responsibilities of professional practice

The UKCC and four National Boards were established in the 1979 Nurses, Midwives and Health Visitors Act as the regulatory bodies for the professions. Although the UKCC was intended to be an elected body, it functioned in its first years, from 1980 to 1983, as an appointed body as responsibilities were transferred from the previous authorities such as the General Nursing Council, the Central Midwives Council and the Council for the Education and Training of Health Visitors. One of the main functions of the UKCC is the maintenance of a 'live' register of qualified nurses, midwives and health visitors. However, according to the 1979 Act:

> The principal function of the Central Council shall be to establish and improve standards of training and professional conduct for nurses, midwives and health visitors. (Section 2(1))

In order to carry this out, four key objectives and priorities have been identified (UKCC, 1988).

Objective one

> To determine an education and training policy and programme to ensure that nurses, midwives and health visitors who are trained and registered meet the needs of society in the 1990s and beyond.

In order to achieve this objective, the UKCC established a set of training rules and for the first time included a statement of the outcomes of training. While clarifying and developing initial training for registration, the Council also developed a policy for the standards of post-qualifying education under the heading 'Post-registration Education Policy' (PREP). In 1995, the UKCC published the finalised standards to ensure a competent professional workforce.

In order to maintain registration on the professional register, each practitioner must:

Notification of Practice

the form completed every 3 years by practitioners wishing to maintain current registration on the 'live' professional register

personal professional profile

a collection of evidence that provides an up-to-date record of the practitioner's career and development, and how they meet the UKCC's requirements for registration

- Complete a Notification of Practice form every 3 years and if the area of practice changes
- Undertake a minimum of 5 study days or equivalent every 3 years
- Maintain a personal professional profile with details of professional development
- Undertake a return-to-practice programme if there has been a break in practice for 5 years or more.

Objective two

To promote a heightened awareness among nurses, midwives and health visitors of:

- professional standards and responsibilities
- the opportunities of being members of a profession.

These two issues have resulted in several publications that provide professional advice and guidelines for nurses, midwives and health visitors. The most significant of these for student nurses would probably be those relating to the *Code of Professional Conduct* (UKCC, 1992), *Exercising Accountability* (UKCC, 1989), *Confidentiality* (UKCC, 1987) and *Guidelines for Professional Practice* (UKCC, 1996).

The UKCC *Code of Professional Conduct* (1992) states that:

Each registered nurse, midwife and health visitor shall act, at all times, in such a manner as to:

- safeguard and promote the interests of individual clients
- serve the interests of society
- justify public trust and confidence
- uphold and enhance the good standing and reputation of the professions.

As a registered nurse, midwife or health visitor, you are personally accountable for your practice.

Chart 14.1 shows the responsibilities placed on practitioners by the Code of Conduct.

Chart 14.1 ● Responsibilities of registered practitioners

The code of conduct states that you are personally accountable for your practice and, in the exercise of your professional accountability, must:

1. act always in such a manner as to promote and safeguard the interests and well-being of patients and clients;

2. ensure that no action or omission on your part, or within your sphere of responsibility, is detrimental to the interests, condition or safety of patients and clients;

3. maintain and improve your professional knowledge and competence;

4. acknowledge any limitations in your knowledge and competence and decline any duties or responsibilities unless able to perform them in a safe and skilled manner;

5. work in an open and co-operative manner with patients, clients and their families, foster their independence and recognise and respect their involvement in the planning and delivery of care;

6. work in a collaborative and co-operative manner with health care professionals and others in providing care, and recognise and respect their particular contributions within the care team;

7. recognise and respect the uniqueness and dignity of each patient and client, and respond to their need for care, irrespective of their ethnic origin, religious beliefs, personal attributes, the nature of their health problems or any other factor;

8. report to an appropriate person or authority, at the earliest possible time, any conscientious objection which may be relevant to your professional practice;

9. avoid any abuse of your privileged relationship with patients and clients and of the privileged access allowed to their person, property, residence or workplace;

10. protect all confidential information concerning patients and clients obtained in the course of professional practice and make disclosures only with consent, where required by the order of a court or where you can justify disclosure in the wider public interest;

11. report to an appropriate person or authority, having regard to the physical, psychological and social effects on patients and clients, any circumstances in the environment of care which could jeopardise standards of practice;

12. report to an appropriate person or authority any circumstances in which safe and appropriate care for patients and clients cannot be provided;

13. report to an appropriate person or authority where it appears that the health or safety of colleagues is at risk, as such circumstances may compromise standards of practice and care;

14. assist professional colleagues, in the context of your own knowledge, experience and sphere of responsibility, to develop their professional competence, and assist others in the care team, including informal carers, to contribute safely and to a degree appropriate to their roles;

15. refuse any gift, favour or hospitality from patients or clients currently in your care which might be interpreted as seeking to exert influence to obtain preferential consideration;

16. ensure that your registration status is not used in the promotion of commercial products or services, declare any financial or other interests in the relevant organisations providing such goods or services and ensure that your professional judgement is not influenced by any commercial considerations.

Source: UKCC (1992).

Objective three

To develop professional conduct work positively and in dealing with matters of professional misconduct to ensure a consistency of approach throughout the UK.

Professional Conduct Committees

committees of the UKCC whose purpose is to hear cases of alleged professional misconduct

The UKCC offers professional advice about standards of conduct and ensures that practitioners have access to current information available. Professional Conduct Committees hear cases of alleged misconduct against any registered practitioner. They sit in different regional venues and are open to members of the profession. Additionally, there are two panels – the Panel of Professional Screeners and the Health Committee – that meet to consider other issues relating to practitioners' fitness to practise, such as alcohol or drug abuse.

Objective four

To make the Central Council financially viable and a cost-effective and efficient organisation.

One of the most significant issues to have been highlighted by the UKCC in terms of standards of professional practice is that of accountability.

What is accountability?

accountability

being answerable for one's actions

While we tend to talk in terms of *professional* responsibility, there are in fact four different types of accountability that can be identified for registered nurses:

1. Accountability to society under criminal and civil law
2. Accountability to the employer under a contract of employment
3. Accountability to the patient under existing law provision
4. Accountability to the profession under the Nurses, Midwives and Health Visitors Act 1979.

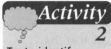

Activity 2

Try to identify examples from your own life that would fit under each type of accountability listed in the text.

Thus, although we usually focus on the latter in terms of professional issues, it is important to remember that nurses as individual members of society need to be accountable in terms of the expectations of any other member of society; that is, they cannot commit a criminal act and expect to be defended by a professional code.

professional accountability

being answerable to the UKCC for decisions made and actions taken in the course of practice

Features of professional accountability

Professional accountability means using your professional judgement and being answerable for it. We can, therefore, identify two features of it – decision-making, and an obligation to explain and justify actions taken. Hence, as a nurse, you are privileged to be allowed to make decisions about areas of care based on your knowledge, skills and experience. These will quite often be life-saving decisions or decisions that have a huge potential impact on your clients. Think, for example, about the responsibility behind a health visitor's decision to refer a suspected case of child abuse to the social services department. Practitioners are imbued with the power to make decisions because they are recognised to be competent in their area of practice, and their clients trust them to act in their best interests.

On the other side of this, however, is the expectation that all practitioners will be able to justify the basis on which their decisions were made if asked to do so. This implies that there is both a right and a duty attached to professional accountability. In recognition of the autonomy of the nurse, there is a concomitant responsibility to act in the best interests of the client.

The *Code of Professional Conduct* clearly states that 'each registered nurse, midwife and health visitor is accountable for his or her practice', and accountability is thus clearly a duty of all nurses. Accountability cannot be delegated to others; therefore, although the accountable nurse may delegate *responsibilities* to others, the accountability remains with her.

Clauses 10 and 11 of the Code refer specifically to accountability. Clause 10 identifies the environment of care, the adequacy of resources and a duty to inform others of any inadequacy of provision or threat to standards of practice. This suggests not only that the nurse is responsible for his or her own actions or omissions, but also that accountability relates to the whole environment within which care is provided. Hence, if an environment is not safe, or resources are inadequate, it is the nurse's responsibility to take action in order to remedy the situation.

Clause 11 deals with accountability with regard to workload pressures on colleagues and subordinates, and the action to be taken if circumstances jeopardise safe standards of practice. It is crucial that nurses realise the implications of this clause, in terms of working with inadequate staffing – either in number or in skill mix – and their own responsibility. It is often the case that nurses in charge of a shift report inadequate staffing numbers to a manager but agree to do the best they can. This is clearly bad practice, and, should an accident occur or clients suffer negligence or acts of omission, it is the nurse present at the time who is accountable.

Student nurses and accountability

Students clearly cannot be professionally accountable because they are not entered on the professional register, but they are accountable in the other three ways. For example, a registered nurse may delegate the task of giving an intramuscular injection to a student. The student is accountable for not causing harm to the patient and, therefore, should not give the injection if he or she does not feel competent to do so. The registered nurse, however, retains the professional accountability in terms of ensuring that the correct drug and dosage are administered, and for ensuring that the student is, in the registered nurse's opinion, competent to administer the drug. Thus students may be given responsibility by qualified nurses who themselves retain accountability.

The UKCC

The registered nurse is accountable for his or her actions as a professional at all times, whether or not engaged in current practice, and whether on or off duty. Ultimately, the nurse is accountable to the UKCC for any failure to satisfy the requirements of the introductory paragraph of the *Code of Professional Conduct*. The interests of the public and client must predominate over those of the practitioner and profession. As such, practitioners are accountable for both actions and omissions.

An essential part of accountability is the making of contemporaneous and accurate records of nursing care, and the consequences for clients if they have not been given the care they require. Increasingly in health care, records are being written and stored on computers so it is worth spending some time considering the implications of computer-held records for nurses.

The use of computers

The use of computer facilities in record maintenance and care-planning could provide definite advantages to the profession, providing that clear guidelines for practice are established. Issues that need to be considered before the implementation of any system on a large scale are:

- The acquisition and storage of client-related data
- The compilation of a database of nursing care practices, including the generation of alternatives
- Accountability for individualised care plans
- The maintenance of records
- Confidentiality, security and access.

The Data Protection Act 1984

This Act was designed to offer citizens of the UK protection in terms of information held about them on computer.

All users of computerised records need to be registered under this Act; employers have block registration that covers all employees using their facilities. Chart 14.2 shows the eight principles to be observed with reference to storing information about people.

Chart 14.2 ● The principles of the Data Protection Act 1984

1. The information to be contained in personal data shall be obtained, and personal data shall be processed, fairly and lawfully.
2. Personal data shall be held only for one or more specified and lawful purposes.
3. Personal data held for any purpose or purposes shall not be used or disclosed in any manner incompatible with that purpose or those purposes.
4. Personal data held for any purpose or purposes shall be adequate, relevant and not excessive in relation to that purpose or those purposes.
5. Personal data shall be accurate and, where necessary, kept up to date.
6. Personal data held for any purpose or purposes shall not be kept for longer than is necessary for that purpose or purposes.
7. An individual shall be entitled:
   a) at reasonable intervals and without undue delay or expense:
      i) to be informed by any data user whether he holds personal data of which that individual is the subject
      ii) to access any such data held by a data user
   b) where appropriate, to have such data corrected or erased.
8. Appropriate security measures shall be taken against unauthorised access to, or alteration, disclosure or destruction of, personal data and against accidental loss or destruction of personal data.

The Act also specifies four categories of sensitive data:

1. Racial origin
2. Political opinions and religious or other beliefs
3. Physical or mental health or sexual life
4. Criminal convictions.

These need to be dealt with carefully in record-keeping. They are all of relevance to health-care professionals as it is extremely likely that information that falls into these categories will be obtained. It is important to consider these principles when using computerised records in terms of data collection, resource management and research purposes.

These principles derive from society's beliefs about people's rights and responsibilities when living within it. They arise from a concern to promote fairness and equality. Each profession in society is, similarly, founded on a set of beliefs and principles that underpin the way in which it relates to society and the ways in which its members practise. These principles can be seen as philosophies and ideologies

philosophies

sets of beliefs and values that guide the way in which we operate in the world

ideologies

sets of ideas, assumptions and images that help people to make sense of society and provide individuals with distinctive social identities

Philosophies and Ideologies

Personal beliefs and values

Activity

3

Take a few minutes to list the beliefs and values that you hold that made you want to become a nurse. Can you attribute these to Jasper's sources listed in the text?

We all practise from a belief and value system that has arisen from our own personal experiences of life and what we have encountered. Jasper (1996) suggests that personal beliefs and values arise from the following six sources:

- Our religious beliefs and moral upbringing
- Our ethnic origins
- Our educational opportunities
- Our social class
- The environment in which we grew up
- Our life experiences.

In addition to these personal life experiences, we accumulate various other beliefs and values, which are accommodated into the way we practise as nurses.

You will already have encountered different ways of looking at the world from your nursing education, from the practitioners and educationalists you work with, and from your reading. You will have developed particular ways of looking at things that direct the way in which you give care. Think, for example, about concepts that you have met, such as 'holistic care', 'individualised care' or 'reflective practice'. Or even about the difference between your ideas of what nursing is now compared with what you thought it would be when you started your nursing education.

In addition to these beliefs and values, you will also have been exposed to professional ones as defined by the UKCC in the *Code of Professional Conduct* (1992) and illustrated in Chart 14.1. These professional codes of conduct clearly identify the standards of practice that are expected from any practitioner and provide them with a baseline of values and beliefs deemed appropriate at that particular time. Indeed, the UKCC possesses power to sanction any practitioners who contravene the code, even in their personal lives. The beliefs and values from the professional codes are absorbed into the individual belief and value system of the practitioner. Thus anyone calling themselves a nurse, midwife or health visitor is assumed to behave in the way expected of a registered practitioner, as set out in the *Code of Professional Conduct*.

The final sources of influence upon your personal beliefs and values are those arising from your employing organisation, and wider societal issues such as government policy relating to health and social care. These sources of beliefs are likely to change, or be modified, at an even more rapid rate than those arising from education or professional philosophies because they will be subject to political influences and trends, for example the impact that the introduction of the internal market has had on the provision of infertility treatment available from the NHS, or the decisions taken in some health authorities to restrict access to health care depending on the age of the client.

Wright (1986) suggests that the combination of all these sources of values and beliefs can be regarded as a personal philosophy that is used to shape our practice and education, provide motivation, prompt research and set our management style.

Nursing philosophies

As nurses, we tend to work in teams to provide nursing care. In the same way that our own style of nursing is directed by our beliefs and values, so will be the care delivered by a team of nurses working together. The use of the word 'philosophy' in nursing tends to refer to a way of doing things that is underpinned by a written statement of beliefs and values. Mawdsley (1991, p. 78) sees a nursing philosophy as:

> an invaluable tool which directs and influences patient care. It is a series of beliefs, values and outlooks that can be developed in any area concerned with patient care, with the purpose of demonstrating what nurses feel their particular specialty should be achieving both for patients and nursing staff.

For a philosophy to be a true representation of the care delivered by a team, there are two key elements that must be contained in it. First, it must be an agreed statement that reflects the shared perceptions, beliefs and values of all the people concerned. Second, it must be related to their own practice and have practical applications. Johns (1989, cited by Johns 1991, p. 1090) identifies the value of a philosophy when he says:

> Staff who share a common positive belief about nursing, within the context of their workplace, are more likely to give consistent and congruent care for the benefit of their patients.

Therefore a nursing philosophy is:

- A statement of intent and belief
- An explanation of how and why things are done
- A statement of the purpose of the organisation and individuals
- A statement of the ideas behind our behaviour and actions
- A reflection of members' ideals and ideas for nursing, which should be endorsed by peers
- An outlook that should include the future, expectations and reflection
- A consideration of the role of nursing.

All clinical areas providing place-ments are required to have a nursing philosophy. Think back to your last placement. Were you introduced to the philosophy? How was its relationship to care explained? Look again at the six components of a written philosophy. How successful is your example in covering these? To what extent are the characteristics of a philosophy present? Does your example really reflect the nursing care given in that clinical area?

A written philosophy includes:

- What you do
- Why you do it
- What you value and why
- What is important and why
- The uniqueness of your practice/ward and so on
- The qualities offered.

The success of a philosophy as a working document for a clinical area will often depend upon the way in which it was devised in the first place. If it is meant to reflect the combined values of the team or area to which it relates, it is essential that those people were involved in developing it. Described below are two approaches to philosophy development.

The top-down approach

In this case, the philosophy tends to be imposed by the managerial system and is a reflection of organisational beliefs, which are not necessarily applicable to the nursing care. As a result, a philosophy may become a paper exercise, the components not being shared by the nurses, who lack any ownership or motiva-tion to use it within their practice. This, however, may not necessarily be so, as organisations adopt change, and responsibility and accountability are delegated downwards. Many nurses are using broad policy statements created within an organisation and developing their own philosophies from them, incorporating the beliefs and values of their own nursing environment. These are fine as broad statements, but they do not necessarily relate to the specific environment of nursing in which teams of nurses are working and, although helpful as value statements, are not necessarily useful as operational policies.

The bottom-up approach

Try to find out the origins of the phil-osophy you used in Activity 4. Ask your supervisor how it was developed, for example who wrote it, where the underpinning beliefs and values came from, and how these were identified. What part did the members of the ward team play in its development?

In this case, it is the people who will have to use the philosophy who are involved in writing it. Philosophies developed in this way tend to include the 'how, what, when, why, who and where' of practice, which can then be used as a way of directing and delivering care within a specific environment. An excel-lent example of the creation of a philosophy in which all members of a team were part of the process is described by Johns (1991) in relation to the Burford Nursing Development Unit.

Purposes of a philosophy

Practical application

It can now be seen that a nursing philosophy, if it is to be effective, must have practical application to the area for which it has been written and must reflect the current practices that occur. It will, therefore, serve the purpose of stimulating nurses to reflect on their practice in terms of being able to justify the nursing care delivered and learning from their experiences. The philosophy can also be used to teach nursing care to students or other types of worker, and form the basis for the development of nursing care in that area.

Facilitating teamwork

Similarly, a philosophy as a working document will facilitate teamwork, as all members of the team will share common values and beliefs that have been made explicit and open. A published philosophy may even be used to recruit new members of the clinical team, as it could be used to advertise the beliefs and values underpinning care to potential applicants and form the basis for exploring whether a person will fit into the ward team. A philosophy will also encourage continuity of care while the client is being looked after in that clinical area, and enable a smooth transfer to other areas or upon discharge.

Setting a baseline for the development of quality and standards in practice

standards of care

these usually identify the minimum standard to which an aspect of care is expected to conform and provide the criteria against which the quality of care can be measured

quality of care

the measure of the standard of care that is used as a judgement to evaluate the services being delivered. The term 'quality' needs to be accompanied by an adjective describing the standard to be achieved, for example 'high'-quality care

It seems logical to assume that if a philosophy for a clinical area has been agreed by the team working in it, it will serve as a starting point for setting the standards of care and assessing the quality of care delivered. If the philosophy identifies your beliefs and values, and these are translated into the way in which you work and what you intend to provide, you have already set some *standards* to be achieved. The *quality* of your care can be measured by finding ways of evaluating the outcome of care against what your intentions were.

Quality

On the surface this seems very simple, but let us take some time to think about what we mean by quality.

Quality is a nebulous term that means different things to different people. One problem lies in the necessity to qualify the term with a value word such as 'high' or 'low' in order to give it some meaning. For example, it is clearly meaningless to talk about 'quality' care without defining the standard of quality that you are aiming for – 'quality' could refer to anything!

Another problem is that of who defines the quality. Think, for example, of the values that you might attribute to quality care in giving a blanket bath. You might identify privacy, time, skilled staff and other issues relating to assessing the condition of your client and completing the task in a certain amount of time. Your client, however, may well look for different measures of quality – what might these be? Your ward manager, on the other hand, may well think of good-quality procedures as relating to completing the work schedule, meeting the client's needs identified in the care plan and complying with treatment schedules.

Hence it is important, where any measurement or assessment of quality is attempted, to ask several overarching questions about what it is that is being attempted.

What is being assessed?

This evolves from the definition of quality that is in operation, from organisational needs, from externally imposed criteria such as government targets, and from the beliefs and values that underpin the model of quality that is used. Koch (1994) suggests that, in the past, there have been three generations of quality evaluation: measurement orientated, objective orientated and judgement orientated.

First, in a measurement-orientated approach, boundaries or quality criteria are selected by the health-care professionals, and data are collected in statistical terms. Examples of this might be the waiting times of clients attending a particular outpatient department, or the wound infection rates following specific surgical procedures.

Second, objective-orientated approaches use observational techniques to assess the strengths and weaknesses of care against stated objectives. Many of the well-known quality audit tools, such as Phaneuf's audit of documentary records (Phaneuf, 1976), use this approach.

Third, judgement-orientated techniques involve the evaluation of care against standards set by 'experts', usually in the form of quality assurance committees. Approaches within this category often have a dual purpose in terms of quantifiable standards of practice and the marketing of services, as labels such as 'excellent' or 'poor' are awarded. QUALPACs (Wandelt and Ager, 1974) can be seen as falling into this category of approaches as value assessments are made of the care given. Another recent initiative of this type is the assessment of nursing outcomes (Higgins et al., 1992, Griffiths, 1995), which relates the outcome achieved to the process used to achieve it.

These three categories of approach share the characteristics of the standards being set by health-care experts, thus ignoring client-generated concerns, and of being of a quantifiable nature, data being collected by a disinterested observer (Koch, 1994).

These might, however, not suit the purposes of nurses wanting to evaluate the quality of their own work, especially as few of these approaches involve client-generated issues relating to the everyday care received. Koch (1994) suggests that this can be achieved by using a fourth-generation approach to the evaluation of quality that is negotiation orientated, involving a skilled negotiator who acts as facilitator in setting the agenda for quality among all the stakeholders. Another approach to involving clients in assessing the quality of care has been the development of client satisfaction schedules (Bond and Thomas, 1992; Avis *et al.*, 1995; Simpson *et al.*, 1995). These have the advantage of enabling the clients' perspectives to be drawn into the quality debate and often use qualitative approaches to data-gathering, which generate material relating to clients' experiences, rather than quantitative approaches, which rely on objective statistics yet do not describe subjective experiences.

Thus, in exploring quality assessment in your own area of practice, it is important to be able to identify exactly what you are assessing; this leads to the next question of *what purpose you are assessing it for*.

Although at present you have probably not had to think very much about the quality of care that you deliver because you have been closely supervised in clinical practice, you will, as you move into your branch studies, need to make these decisions and clarify the purpose of evaluating that quality for your own personal and professional development. This is where the skills of reflective practice that you met in Chapter 11 will be useful to you. Now refer to Activity 6.

This activity highlights one purpose of quality assessment – individual practitioners' needs to ensure their own high-quality care. However, many other purposes can be identified if you refer back to the beginning of this section. These are listed briefly below and can be a stimulus to further reading as you go through your branch studies.

Quality may be assessed in order to:

- Ensure value for money
- Attract funding for a service
- Demonstrate target achievements
- Audit a service
- Award training status to a clinical area
- Verify that standards of practice are being achieved
- Publicise a service
- Provide new business or services.

The next question that needs to be addressed is *what structure will the approach take?* This is not the place to outline the strategies available for assessing quality; suffice it to say that there is a whole range of approaches depending on what it is you want to assess and the purpose of your assessment. Examples of nursing assessment tools are the Phaneuf audit (Phaneuf, 1976), QUALPACs (Wandelt and Ager, 1974) and DYSSSY (RCN, 1990).

---

qualitative reseach approaches

research approaches that use in-depth and holistic methods through the collection of narrative data and a flexible design

quantitative research approaches

the investigation of phenomena that lend themselves to precise measurement and quantification, often involving a rigorous and controlled design

Activity

6

Think of a recent encounter with a client where you worked independently in directly delivering care. Describe the scene in as much detail as possible. What was the main purpose of this interaction? What other purposes might there have been? Describe your part in the interaction. Did your actions/ interventions achieve the original purposes? How do you know this? Can you think of any other ways to evaluate the effectiveness of your interaction? What have you learnt as a result of this interaction about the quality of care that you gave?

Activity 7

Gather together from your clinical area as many examples as possible to attempt to assess the quality of care being provided. Consider such aspects as a tracking form for client care, the presence of written standards for procedures, the evaluation of care against the written philosophy and the collection of statistics relating to bed occupancy.

All of these issues have a direct link back to the philosophy of care that has been created for the clinical area. The philosophy sets the baseline for determining the focus that quality assessment will take and relates directly to the standards of care to be achieved.

The development of nursing

Although written philosophies tend to be the end result of values clarification and teamwork, they mark just one stage in the overall process of developing nursing knowledge. This is a process that starts when nurses start to think about what they are doing and why. Creating a philosophy of care for a clinical area, or being able to articulate your own philosophy, sets the baseline for thinking about and making connections between our knowledge base, our skills and our experience, and for considering how these can be taken forward.

Models and Frameworks of Care

Another purpose of a nursing philosophy is that it underpins the model of nursing that is used to direct care in the clinical area.

One of the major challenges that nurses have faced in the quest for professional practice is the development of a knowledge base that can be seen as specifically relating to nursing. Prior to the 1950s, there was very little theory that could be seen to be exclusively about the ways in which nurses practise in a specific capacity. Since that time, and related in particular to the move of nursing education into American universities, nurse theorists have attempted to identify a nursing knowledge base that is separate or is built eclectically from other foundational theory bases. Some authors, usually from outside nursing, argue that there is no specific knowledge that can be seen to belong to nursing, and they therefore justify the designation of nursing as a semiprofession. Others suggest that there is no such thing as a knowledge base belonging to *any* particular profession; instead, it is the special combination of the way in which knowledge from different sources is collected together and used to underpin clinical practice that provides the focus for a profession. Also, although nursing is still in the infant stages of creating nursing knowledge, this has developed effectively in the past 40 years. The creation of models of nursing was one of the first attempts at creating a knowledge base specific to nursing in this way.

What is a model?

Wright (1990) defines a nursing model as:

> a collection of ideas, knowledge and values about nursing which determines the way nurses as individuals and groups, work with their patients or clients

and therefore models:

> help nurses to organise their thinking about nursing and then set about their practice in an orderly and logical way.

Hence the primary purpose of a model is to help nurses to understand nursing from a particular viewpoint and use that to direct their care. But what do we mean by a model? In everyday life, a model is often seen in a physical way, as with a model house, boat or aeroplane. Although it does not contain all the elements or components of the real thing, it acts as a representation of that thing. So how does that help us with models of nursing? Models of nursing also act as a representation of reality but from a particular viewpoint: nursing models describe, or represent, nursing from the viewpoint of the writer and present different ways of looking at or understanding nursing. Hence nursing models are abstract models that help us to make sense of the way in which nursing happens.

These models do not have to be published, formal models written by theorists. Each one of us has our own informal model that we carry around in our head. These comprise individual collections of ideas about nursing, socialised behaviour and experience from both nursing and life, and determine a great deal of nursing care as they form the basis of the way in which each nurse practises. While these informal models are obviously important to the individual, there are certain problems associated with individuals practising their own model rather than one that is shared by others in the team. Informal models are usually value laden and are not necessarily based on commonly held values. In a way, they are 'secret' models, but at the same time we seem to make the assumption that everyone else shares our values!

Formal models occur, however, when the values, beliefs and ways of working are made explicit and shared by the team of nurses in the clinical area. They enable groups of nurses to think about, and carry out, nursing in a fairly similar way, with clear objectives for the delivery of care because the model purports to represent the nursing care to be achieved by that team.

In the past 60 years many models have been created that claim to represent the reality of nursing. While most of these originate in the USA, the most commonly used model in practice in the UK, the activities of daily living (ADL) model, was devised by Roper *et al.* in Edinburgh in the 1980s; it will be used as an illustration for the rest of this section. The ADL model developed out of Virginia Henderson's description of what nursing does in helping clients with 14 activities of living (Henderson, 1966). These were refined by Roper *et al.* (1980) as an educational model to help students learn about nursing.

Components of models

Philosophies and beliefs

The basic starting point for a model is a statement of the beliefs and values that underpin it; this is usually referred to as the philosophy of the model. Roper *et al.* (1980) use Henderson's (1966) definition of nursing as a starting point. This suggests that:

> The unique function of the nurse is to assist the individual, sick or well, in the performance of those activities contributing to health or its recovery (or to a peaceful death) that he (sic) would perform unaided if he had the necessary strength, will or knowledge, and to do this in such a way as to help him to gain independence as rapidly as possible.

Hence, the underpinning beliefs here relate to nursing as a 'helping' activity, by which, using the framework of the ADLs (Chart 14.3), the nurse aids a client to gain independence or die peacefully. There is a focus here on the individual as an active part of the nursing process because it identifies the notion of partnership in which the nurse will only do things for clients that they are unable to do themselves. There is also a notion of holism running through this definition, in that although the activities are identified as separate elements, there is no attempt to address each one without the presence of the individual client. The definition implies that all individuals can grow in some way, whether this is by direct nursing interaction, by the provision of information or by the support necessary to gain independence. There is also the underpinning assumption that the ADLs *are* indeed the activities that enable people to live and grow.

holism

a philosophy addressing the person as an irreducible whole

Chart 14.3 ● Roper *et al.*'s activities of daily living (1980)

1. Maintaining a safe environment
2. Communicating
3. Breathing
4. Eating and drinking
5. Eliminating
6. Personal cleansing and dressing
7. Controlling body temperature
8. Working and playing
9. Mobilising
10. Sleeping
11. Expressing sexuality
12. Dying

From this brief discussion, it can be seen that a philosophy is composed of many different ideas that together set the scene for each particular model. Every model has a different set, or combination, of these ideas that underpin it and will, therefore, see nursing, and the delivery of nursing care, in a different way. The ideas within the philosophy and which make up the model are usually referred to as 'concepts'.

Concepts

Activity 8

To illustrate what is meant by the fluid nature of concepts, write down the images, ideas or words that come into your head when you hear or read the word 'marriage'.

Concepts can be viewed not only as ideas, but also as a mental picture of the idea, which is made up of a collection of ideas and constructed within the mind (Walker and Avant, 1996). Immediately, we can see that concepts are thus open to individual interpretation depending upon experience.

Try Activity 8. The words you have written are likely to have arisen from your own experiences of marriage. For example, single readers may rely on memories from childhood, whether or not their parents were married, the socio-economic stability of marriage, religious beliefs and any experiences of a 'married' partnership. Other students may well have experienced happy or traumatic marriages personally and may indeed be divorced or separated, with experience of abuse or economic problems. So although we all have an understanding of the concept of 'marriage', the word and its meaning are likely to hold different components for each individual.

This immediately poses a problem for nurse theorists in constructing the philosophy of a model and its component parts. Hence it is extremely important for concepts to be defined within each model so that the reader can understand what the basis of the model is.

The metaparadigm of nursing

metaparadigm of nursing

the defining combination of concepts that are seen to make up nursing: man, the environment, health and nursing

There are four major concepts that are found in nursing models or frameworks, which are collectively known as the metaparadigm or grand framework of nursing. These concepts (constructs) are: man or the person; the environment; health; and nursing.

All nursing models describe and define these concepts, and it is the way in which these are combined that determines how the client will be approached and how the nurse will serve the client. Chart 14.4 summarises the metaparadigm concepts as defined by Roper *et al.* (1980).

Other concepts may be included in the model and give it the specific focus of that particular model. For example, in Peplau's (1952) model, the concept of 'interpersonal relations' is central; in Orem's (1980) model, we find the concept of 'self-care'; and in Roy's (1984) model, there is 'adaptation'. The concepts central to Roper *et al.*'s model are summarised in Chart 14.5.

Chart 14.4 ● Roper *et al.*'s metaparadigm concepts

The person – the model focuses on the client as an individual engaged in living throughout his or her life span, and moving from dependence to independence, according to age, circumstances and environment. The important ideas relating to the person are:

- the progression of a person along a life span
- a dependence/independence continuum
- the activities of daily living and influencing factors
- individuality.

Health – Roper *et al.* develop this concept in the third edition of the model (1990) and draw attention to the notion that the concept of health changes, as does society and current thought. They see health as a dynamic process with many facets.

Environment – this is defined as anything external to the person and is deemed to be an essential component of 'living activities' as it is one of the influencing factors that impinge upon all ADLs.

Nursing – is involved when an individual is unable to be independent in any of the ADLs and cannot draw on the support of family or social grouping to meet them. Nursing aims at:

1. The individual acquiring, maintaining or restoring maximum independence in the activities of living, or enabling him or her to cope with dependence on others if circumstances make this necessary
2. Enabling the individual to carry out preventing activities independently to avoid ill-health
3. Providing comforting strategies to promote recovery and eventual independence
4. Providing medically prescribed treatments to overcome illness or its symptoms, leading to recovery and eventual independence.

Source: Adapted from Pearson *et al.* (1996).

Chart 14.5 ● Other concepts in Roper *et al.*'s model

Life span – an individual begins living at conception and ends at death. As people engage in the process of living, their position on the life span influences their capacity for independence. Progress on the life span is, of course, unidirectional.

Dependence/independence continuum –this continuum is moved along dynamically and is affected by a whole range of factors.

Activities of daily living – 12 of these are defined in the model; the individual is seen as engaging in these in different capacities as he or she moves through the life span. The activities of daily living are listed in Chart 14.3. Each activity has five components:

● Physical
● Psychological
● Sociocultural
● Environmental
● Politico-economic.

Preventing activities – these are engaged in to prevent those things that will impair living, such as accidents and illness, for example by eating a balanced diet to maximise health or restricting alcohol intake to prevent car accidents.

Comforting activities – these are performed to give physical, psychological and social comfort; an example is doing stretching exercises to relieve muscle tension.

Seeking activities – these are activities carried out in the pursuit of knowledge, new experiences and answers to new problems.

The latter three activities tend to be interrelated and overlapping, and may occur simultaneously in actions taken by the individual.

Individuality in living – each person will be affected by a unique range of influencing factors, the result being that they will manifest differences in the way in which they live.

Source: Adapted from Pearson *et al.* (1996).

Hence we can see that each model of nursing will define and develop concepts in a way that 'fits' the overall nature of the model. Although it is important for understanding a model for concepts to be clearly defined and unambiguous, the concepts do not exist in isolation – the model itself needs in some way to explain the *relationship* between the concepts.

Statements

Statements are used to link two or more concepts together, and, according to Walker and Avant (1996), must be present before explanations or predictions can be made. Statements may occur in two forms:

1. *Relational statements* declare a relationship of some kind between two or more concepts, for example 'Water temperature above $X°C$ will cause skin damage'. Thus relational statements assert either association between concepts or causality – the effect of one concept on the other.
2. *Non-relational statements* either exert the existence of a concept or define a concept, and act as adjuncts to relational statements. They give meaning to concepts in a theory. An example is Roper *et al.*'s statement that:

> Basically, people are envisaged as carrying out various activities during a lifespan, from conception to death.

Once statements have linked concepts together, they can be built into theories.

Theories

Theories 'represent a scientist's best effort to describe and explain phenomena' (Polit and Hungler, 1997). They help us to make sense of what we observe and perceive by suggesting relationships between concepts and propositions. Walker and Avant (1996, p. 22) suggest that a theory is:

> an internally consistent group of relational statements (concepts, definitions and propositions) that presents a systematic view about a phenomenon and that is useful for description, explanation, prediction and control. A theory, by virtue of its predictive potential, is the primary means of meeting the goals of the nursing profession concerned with a clearly defined body of knowledge.

The key words in this definition are the ones that identify the dynamic qualities of theories in terms of description, explanation, prediction and control. These move us from the notion that knowledge is fixed and given, to the idea that knowledge is always in the process of being created or discovered. Dickoff *et al.* (1968) suggest that there are four levels of theory development to be seen through nursing history, shown in Chart 14.6, and that these can be linked to Walker and Avant's key words.

Chart 14.6 ● Levels of theory development in nursing

1st level – factor isolating – identification of factors and their variables, and their subsequent definition. Walker and Avant's 'description'

2nd level – factor relating – explains by identifying possible relationships between factors. Walker and Avant's 'explanation'

3rd level – situation relating – predicts what may occur if factors are varied and manipulated. Walker and Avant's 'prediction'

4th level – situation producing – control of the situation can be achieved where the nursing intervention is highly likely to accomplish the desired goals. Walker and Avant's 'control'

These clearly show how theory is inextricably linked to clinical practice; that is, theories have to have practical application or they are merely rhetoric or someone's ideas. However, you are likely to have experienced the frustration of learning theory relating to a particular aspect of practice (for example, the ideas behind the nursing process and nursing assessment) and then finding that this is not how it operates in practice at all. This is often referred to as the theory–practice gap and has perplexed many nurses over the past 20 years. Rolfe (1996) identifies this problem as originating with the notion of the separation between theory and practice in the first place. He suggests that 'nursing praxis' is a more realistic way of looking at the way in which nurses develop theories that originate and work in practice. He suggests that:

nursing praxis

a model that integrates reflection-on-action, reflection-in-action and formal and informal theory

paradigm

in this context, a 'prime example' or model case

nursing praxis begins with reflection-on-action, which except with very experienced practitioners, involves thinking about and analysing practice situations after the event and away from the clinical area. The outcome of reflection-on-action is personal knowledge about specific situations, which can be stored away for later use as paradigm cases, or which can be employed immediately in the construction of informal theory. (Rolfe, 1996, p. 36)

Rolfe goes on to describe a reflective, theory-proposing and testing model of the way in which nurses operate in everyday practice. While this model incorporates many of the previous ideas about the relationship between theory and practice, Rolfe provides a way of looking at the creation of nursing knowledge that acknowledges their interdependency, with the nurse as the catalyst for creating reality. There is a logical corollary to this approach – theory without practice is of little use to the practitioner; practice without theory is dangerous.

Activity 9

What knowledge base does nursing share with other disciplines? Think here about both the practice and theoretical components of your course and try to identify the disciplinary base that informs each one. What makes nursing different from other disciplines; that is, what is special about nursing? Where does the knowledge come from that informs the 'special' nursing components? Where does nursing theory come from? What is the purpose of nursing theory?

Thus we must explore the uses of theory and how the individual nurse can practice from an evidence basis that incorporates personal knowledge.

But why does nursing need to have theory at all? If nursing is just a conglomeration of facts and ideas generated within other disciplines, there does not appear to be a need for *nursing* theory. If, however, nursing has something special that delineates it from other disciplines, we need to develop a nursing knowledge base.

Now that you are probably at the end of your common foundation programme, it is important to identify just what nursing is to you as, from now on, you will increasingly be called on to defend your own practice as a nurse. Work your way down the questions in Activity 9 in an attempt to clarify your views at this time.

Having studied through these questions, you are likely to have made the links between nursing being a special discipline in its own right, having a specific knowledge base, and the role that theory generation will play in that. We need to have evidence on which to base our practice, and there is little purpose for theory if it does not relate in some way to practice. We need to know what to do and why we do it, and one of the purposes of theory is to enable us to practise from an informed basis. After all, that is why you are undertaking an educational programme in preparation for registered practice rather than working as an unqualified member of staff. But what are the other purposes of theory?

Purposes of theories

There are multiple purposes to which theories are put, one overall purpose being to make scientific findings meaningful and generalisable. In nursing, the main purpose must be to enhance nursing practice. Subpurposes include:

- The provision of knowledge
- Enhancing nursing's power by developing the knowledge base
- Explaining and predicting previously unexplained events
- The stimulation of new discoveries
- Aiding decision-making
- The support of professional autonomy in practice, education and research.

Finally, it is worth thinking about your own personal development in relation to being able to select appropriate nursing action. While much of the theoretical work that you have done so far is based on learning facts and skills, you must remember that your critical powers are also being developed. It is very important to see theory in a developmental light, in terms of how being able to discuss and differentiate, evaluate and justify, helps your critical thinking.

Chart 14.7 ● Levels of theory development

....

Meta-theories – these comprise the philosophical and methodological aspects of theory building, for example philosophical issues about relationships between nursing theory, the philosophy of science, and nursing knowledge or methodology (for example Dickoff *et al.*, 1968).

Grand theories – these define nursing broadly and abstractly from a global perspective, describing the 'whole of nursing's concern' (Chinn and Kramer, 1991). Theories at this level include nursing models that tend to provide a conceptual framework or overview of nursing. Because of the scope of nursing models, they tend not to provide testable theories but offer a direction for practice.

Middle-range theories – although these are still abstract, they contain elements of grand theories but have less scope and fewer variables, therefore making them more appropriate for testing. These include, for example, Watson's (1979) theory of caring and Peplau's (1952) theory of interpersonal relations.

Practice theory – this is the situation-relating theory of Dickoff *et al.* (1968) that relates to the way in which nurses practise. Examples are techniques such as the Waterlow scale to assess the degree of risk for pressure sores (see Chapter 8) and the management of incontinence.

....

Source: Adapted from Walker and Avant (1996) and Manley (1991).

Classification of nursing theories

Nursing's knowledge base has now developed to such an extent that, instead of nurses being able to say with certainty, 'This is how you do it', there are a multitude of alternatives to consider. While you may still find this confusing (especially when what you meet in practice bears little relationship to what you have learnt academically), you will, as you progress in your career, come to see that this points to the move by nursing from an occupation dependent on others, to a fledgling discipline in its own right. Chart 14.7 considers the types or levels of theory development that you may come across.

As you can see, nursing models fit into the category of *grand theory*. It is worth taking some time to consider this as it helps to explain the problems that nurses have with trying to enact a model in a clinical area.

Grand theory is abstract – it is made up of concepts related to each other in some sort of framework that enables us to gain an overview of what is happening. Thus nursing models are created by their author as a personal perspective on nursing. There is nothing fixed or 'true' about any one nursing model. If you take time to consider the plethora of models that we have (see, for

Activity **10**

Work your way through Chart 14.7 and try to identify examples from your own experience to illustrate each level.

example, Fawcett, 1984; Meleis, 1996), it becomes obvious that a model is an exposition of ideas that will help us to guide our practice. These ideas need to be operationalised and tested through middle-range and practice theory in order for them to be of practical use. Thus models are there to *guide* practice rather than to tell nurses *how* to practise.

Many clinical areas have attempted to import models written by theorists in order to give a more theoretical foundation to their practice. The problem with this approach is that models of nursing are rarely founded on evidence. For example, if we go back to Roper *et al.*'s model, the central concepts (apart from the life span continuum) are based on assumptions. Can we 'prove' that the 12 ADLs are in fact inclusive of all activities of daily living? Many nurses would argue that the concept of nursing within the model is too limited and does not cover many aspects of work carried out by community-based nurses. However, what the model does give us is a way of looking at and directing our nursing practice.

The most common example of the use of the ADL model is the way in which the assessment and planning of nursing care are enacted. The concept of the ADL has been used to develop comprehensive assessment strategies that enable nurses to gather data relating to the health status of the client. In turn, this informs nursing diagnosis, care-planning and much of the documentation that we see in nursing practice today. To what extent, however, does this interpretation of the ADL model represent the original model itself?

There have been numerous criticisms of the ADL model since its publication. These include the problem of mismatch between the concept of holism and the reductionist approach taken in the ADLs, and the largely physical focus of the model. However, as with any theory, it is up to readers to evaluate its usefulness for their own area of practice. It is extremely easy to engage in academic debate about the consistency between the concepts and the lack of proven theory within the model. Yet, Roper *et al.* achieved a great deal in creating a model that appeared to reflect nursing in Britain when previous models had originated in America, with the associated problems of a culturally different conceptual understanding and a totally different health-care system. At the time of writing, nursing care delivered using the ADL model is alive and well in Britain, despite attempts by other practitioners to create models in their own place of work.

There is, of course, a fundamental danger to the notion of being able to adopt a model wholesale for a clinical area. Consider the fundamental principles behind models, and nursing; by importing a ready-made model to guide practice there is little likelihood that the nursing team will share the underpinning philosophy. Look back at the section concerning philosophies and the importance of joint ownership, and the two models of change. Imposed models are likely to be poorly received by staff who have no part in their creation. If the staff do not give their commitment to the model as the way in which they practise, it is unlikely that the model itself will be implemented in its entirety. As a test, when you next visit your clinical area, ask the trained staff whether they have actually read the ADL model or whether they merely put into practice what they were told to do.

Finally, there is a fundamental problem with the idea of using a published model to guide all practice in one clinical area. Nursing today claims to provide holistic care and recognise clients as individuals with differing needs. How then can we assume that the same model can be applied to all the clients in one clinical area? The type of care that a client receives should be devised on an individual basis but it may vary depending on the model used in that particular area. If we can say that clients should receive care appropriate to their needs no matter which model is used, there is maybe no need for different models. Yet there are many models used to drive practice, all with differing starting points and complicated conceptual development – despite the fact that there is little contemporary evidence published to show that the use of a model in practice affects client outcomes.

What then is the purpose of using models in practice?

Effects on practice of using a model

While there is scant evidence to support the direct effect of a model on client outcomes, there are documented benefits to using a model.

Teamwork

Many nurses draw attention to the benefits of choosing or creating a formal model of care that the whole team can share. By identifying, or even merely talking about, beliefs and values, and identifying what is important to them in their practice, teams of nurses have found that their commitment to work and motivation have risen and that they feel valued as part of a team. In addition, the overt use of a model leads to a reduction in conflict between team members and is more likely to facilitate both continuity and consistency of care for clients.

Directing nursing care

Using a model can direct nursing care by providing a consistent focus for the way in which care is assessed, planned, implemented and evaluated. For example, the use of Roper *et al.*'s model provides a comprehensive way of determining needs by using the idea of activities of daily living. Whether a nurse personally believes in such an approach is irrelevant if it is the model used in that area; it will lead the way in which care is given.

Similarly, new ways of working or new policies for nursing care may arise from implementing a model as deficiencies can easily be identified through the application of the concepts.

Facilitating communication

The use of a model of care is usually accompanied by specific documentation or nursing records that comprehensively trace the client's progress through the system. These provide important data for charting progress and for enabling nurses to continue the chosen treatment regimen. They also force nurses to be accountable for their practice in a way unknown prior to the 1970s as detailed records have to be made, and signed by the supervising nurse. This has led to a vast improvement in the quality of nursing documentation as nurses learn to record their decision-making regarding client care as provision of the evidence on which their practice is based.

Selection of team members

There can be a more effective and appropriate selection of new team members if there is an active selection of people who share the same beliefs and values as the team. Active acknowledgement of the model to attract staff, and deliberate selection policies, will make it more probable that the right sort of people are selected.

Publicity of good work

Models may also be used as the vehicle for demonstrating good practice. Some quality audit systems, such as that of Phaneuf, make the assumption that good documentation is a valid measure of the standard or quality of nursing care delivered. (Space precludes a debate on this here, but you might like to consider whether you believe that this is necessarily so.) The overt use of models, with public displays of the team philosophy, client and relative information booklets, and active partnership in care, is likely to be seen by others as good practice. Similarly, other health professionals are likely to develop a greater understanding of the focus and direction of nursing care, and may well share it on a multidisciplinary basis, if a model is made public.

Aggleton and Chalmers (1990) suggest that models enable us to value what is effective in current practice, and encourage the search for new ways of improving care. There is thus an acknowledgement of the importance of nursing in health-care systems in its own right and not just as the enactor of others' directions. In addition, models and theories may indicate the area of practice that distinguishes nursing from other health professions by defining a specific body of knowledge and describing nursing practice. This is particularly so when nurses have the courage to reject the use of published models and take the long, difficult road of creating one that suits their own nursing team.

Finally, this section ends with an analogy coined by Visintainer (1986), who likens the idea of models to different kinds of map. Maps are chosen for a specific purpose. If you wanted to drive from Portsmouth to Edinburgh, you would probably use a road map that showed motorways and main roads. However, that would not be much use if you wanted to go rambling on the Isle of Wight. For that, you would need a large-scale ordnance survey map. The same principle applies to models: they will only work if they are selected for a specific purpose. They are clearly a positive tool for nursing but must be appropriate to the use to which it is intended to put them. Visintainer wisely says:

> The goodness of fit becomes the responsibility of the map-user not the map-maker, and the task can be a difficult one.

Nursing models and nursing process – the relationship

The nursing process has been fully covered in Chapter 1, and this ground will not be revisited here. However, it is important to explore briefly the relationship between models and the nursing process.

Models tend to provide us with a representation of what nursing is and how it can be approached. They define the type of care and the concepts behind it. To use another analogy, models delineate the parcels and packages of care that can be expected. The nursing process, however, is a system of delivery – the vehicle for delivering the 'parcels'. In no way can the process be seen as a nursing model. The process says nothing about the content of care, and is not specific to nursing; it is a sequence of steps passed through in order to achieve an end. Therefore, the process can only operate effectively within the beliefs and philosophies established by the model of care being used. Without the framework of the model, the process becomes just another form of work allocation.

Where to Next?

Congratulations – if you have read this chapter, you are probably about to embark on your chosen branch studies. This chapter has introduced many of the issues that you will meet in greater depth in the final 18 months of your course. What ties all of these issues together is the need for you to adopt the mantle of being a professional, registered nurse, with the accompanying privileges and responsibilities that this entails. On emerging from the branch programme, fully qualified, you will be expected to have adopted a professional ethos, to be competent and accountable for your practice, and to have acquired the necessary knowledge, skills and experience to give you professional authority.

However, learning does not, and cannot, stop on qualification. Quite apart from the UKCC's requirements for triennial registration, you will, as a qualified practitioner, need to be able to provide evidence-based practice (UKCC, 1995). In order to do this, you will continue to practise academic skills and will direct your own learning so that you can deliver care of the quality that you want to achieve. Courses for registration are only the beginning of a long and exciting journey – you will have acquired the skills needed for lifelong learning throughout the course. The next 18 months will consolidate those skills and enable you to take more responsibility for your own personal and professional development.

Test Yourself!

1. (a) What is meant by professional practice?
   (b) What are the responsibilities associated with professional practice?

2. (a) What is meant by the *Code of Professional Conduct*?
   (b) What are your roles and responsibility, as a student, under the *Code of Professional Conduct*?
   (c) What is your accountability as a student nurse?
   (d) How does this differ from the accountability of a registered practitioner?

3. How do beliefs and values influence nursing care?

4. How do models of care influence the care that a client receives?

5. Why is quality assessment important in profesional care?

6. Why is it necessary for registered practitioners to practise from a contemporaneous knowledge base?

References

Aggleton, P. and Chalmers, H. (1990) *Nursing Models and the Nursing Process*, 2nd edn. Macmillan, London.

Avis, M., Bond, M. and Arthur, A. (1995) Satisfying solutions? A review of some unresolved issues in the measurement of patient satisfaction. *Journal of Advanced Nursing* **22**(2): 316–22.

Bond, S. and Thomas, L.H. (1992) Measuring patients' satisfaction with nursing care. *Journal of Advanced Nursing* **17**(1): 52–63.

Chinn, P.L. and Kramer, M. (1991) *Theory and Nursing: A Systematic Approach*, 3rd edn. C.V. Mosby, St Louis.

Dickoff, J., Weidenbach, E. and James, P. (1968) Theory in practice discipline. *Nursing Research* **17**(5): 415–35.

Fawcett, J. (1984) *Analysis and Evaluation of Conceptual Models of Nursing*. F.A. Davis, Philadelphia.

Griffiths, P. (1995) Progress in measuring nursing outcomes. *Journal of Advanced Nursing* **21**(6): 1092–100.

Henderson, V. (1996) *The Nature of Nursing*. Collier Macmillan, London.

Higgins, M., McCaughan, D., Griffiths, M. and Carr-Hill, R. (1992) Assessing the outcomes of nursing care. *Journal of Advanced Nursing* **17**(5): 561–8.

Jasper, M. (1996) *Evaluating Care and Effecting Change*. Unit Study Guide. Distance Learning Centre, South Bank University, London.

Johns, C. (1991) The Burford Nursing Development Unit holistic model of nursing practice. *Journal of Advanced Nursing* **16**: 1090–8.

Jolley, M. and Brykcznska, G. (1995) *Nursing Beyond Tradition and Conflict*. C.V. Mosby, London.

Koch, T. (1994) Beyond measurement: fourth-generation evaluation in nursing. *Journal of Advanced Nursing* **20**(6): 1148–55.

Manley, K. (1991) Knowledge for nursing practice. In Perry, A. and Jolley, M. (eds) *Nursing: a Knowledge Base for Practice*, pp. 1–27. Edward Arnold, London.

Mawdsley, D. (1991) Who needs nursing philosophies? *Professional Nurse* **7**(2): 78–82.

Meleis, A. (1996) *Theoretical Nursing: Development and Progress*, 3rd edn. J.B. Lippincott, Philadelphia.

Moloney, M.M. (1992) *Professionalization of Nursing – Current Issues and Trends*. J.B. Lippincott, Philadelphia.

Orem, D.E. (1980) *Concepts of Practice*, 2nd edn. McGraw-Hill, New York.

Pearson, A., Vaughan, B. and Fitzgerald, M. (1996) *Nursing Models for Practice*, 2nd edn. Heinnemann, Oxford.

Peplau, H. (1952) *Interpersonal Relations in Nursing*. G.P. Putnam, New York.

Phaneuf, M.C. (1976) *The Nursing Audit: Self-regulation in Nursing Practice*. Appleton-Century-Crofts, New York.

Polit, D.F. and Hungler, B.P. (1997) *Nursing Research – Principles and Methods*, 5th edn. J.B. Lippincott, Philadelphia.

Rafferty, A.M. (1996) *The Politics of Nursing Knowledge*. Routledge, London.

RCN (Royal College of Nursing) (1990) *Quality Patient Care: The Dynamic Standard Setting System*. RCN, London.

Rolfe, G. (1996) *Closing the Theory–Practice Gap – a New Paradigm for Nursing*. Butter-worth Heinemann, Oxford.

Roper, N., Logan, W. and Tierney, A. (1980) *The Elements of Nursing*. Churchill Livingstone, Edinburgh.

Roper, N., Logan, W. and Tierney, A. (1990) *The Elements of Nursing*, 3rd edn. Churchill Livingstone, Edinburgh.

Roy, C. (1984) *Introduction to Nursing: an Adaptation Model*, 2nd edn. Prentice-Hall, Englewood Cliffs, NJ.

Simpson, R.G., Scothern, G. and Vincent, M. (1995) Survey of carer satisfaction with the quality of care delivered to in-patients suffering from dementia. *Journal of Advanced Nursing* **22**(3): 517-27.

UKCC (United Kingdom Central Council for Nursing, Midwifery and Health Visiting) (1987) *Confidentiality*. UKCC, London.

UKCC (United Kingdom Central Council for Nursing, Midwifery and Health Visiting) (1988) *UKCC – The First Five Years 1983–1988*. UKCC, London.

UKCC (United Kingdom Central Council for Nursing, Midwifery and Health Visiting) (1989) *Exercising Accountability*. UKCC, London.

UKCC (United Kingdom Central Council for Nursing, Midwifery and Health Visiting) (1992) *Code of Professional Conduct*. UKCC, London.

UKCC (United Kingdom Central Council for Nursing, Midwifery and Health Visiting) (1995) *PREP and You*. UKCC, London.

UKCC (United Kingdom Central Council for Nursing, Midwifery and Health Visiting) (1996) *Guidelines for Professional Practice*. UKCC, London.

Visintainer, M. (1986) The nature of knowledge and theory in nursing. *Image* **18**(2): 32–8.

Walker, L.O. and Avant, K.C. (1996) *Strategies for Theory Construction in Nursing*, 3rd edn. Appleton & Lange, Norwalk, CT.

Wandelt, M. and Ager, J. (1974) *Quality Patient Care Scale*. Appleton-Century-Crofts, New York.

Watson, J. (1979) *Nursing: the Philosophy and Science of Caring*. Little, Brown, Boston.

Wright, S. (1986) *Building and Using a Model of Nursing*. Edward Arnold, London.

Wright, S. (1990) *My Patient – My Nurse*. Scutari Press, London.

15 Answers to Test Yourself! Questions and Activities

● **Test Yourself!**

Chapter 1

1. ● Assessment
   ● Diagnosis
   ● Planning
   ● Implementation
   ● Evaluation

2. It enables the nurse to plan care for a client on an individual basis and to solve problems.

3. ● Physical health information
   ● Psychological information
   ● Social health information
   ● The activities of living.

4. Two: actual and potential.

5. ● Setting goals
   ● Identifying actions.

6. The MACROS criteria:
   ● Measurable and observable
   ● Achievable and time limited
   ● Client centred
   ● Realistic
   ● Outcome written
   ● Short

7. ● Nursing handover
   ● Reflection
   ● Patient satisfaction or complaint
   ● Reviewing the nursing care plan.

Chapter 3

1. These data are available from the infection control department of your hospital Trust. The national average for HAI in the UK is about 9 per cent.

The number of patients affected will vary depending on the number of beds in the hospital.

2. The infection control department usually produces guidelines for infection control as well as the names of the infection control team. You are advised to consult the infection control manager/sister.

3. The following criteria should be used to evaluate the quality of hand-washing:
   - The use of soap/detergent
   - The use of continuously running water
   - Positioning of the hands to avoid the contamination of surface areas
   - Rubbing the hands together vigorously
   - Rinsing and drying the hands thoroughly.

4. Refer to the 10-point code outlined in Chapter 3.

5. Diarrhoea, vomiting, abdominal pain, pyrexia.

6. The source should be isolated. Spread must be prevented by following the infection control guidelines, for example employing a good handwashing technique and protective clothing. Any further spread to staff/patients must be reported. Visitors should be restricted.

7. A general guide to ensure the patient's safety in the administration of medications is to check yourself against the five 'R's:
   - The right medication
   - The right amount
   - The right time
   - The right patient
   - The right route.

8. The ventrogluteal muscle, the deltoid muscle and the dorsogluteal muscle.

9. Special precautions when giving injections to children:
   - Take into account whether the infant has been walking for a year.
   - Sites for intramuscular injection in infants who have not been walking for a year are:
     - the vastus lateralis muscle
     - the ventrogluteal muscle
     - the mid-anterior thigh muscle.
   - Sites for intramusclar injections in older children who have been walking for more than a year are:
     - the vastus lateralis muscle
     - the dorsogluteal muscle
     - the deltoid muscle.

Chapter 4

1.
   - Fat: 37 kJ/g (9 kcal/g)
   - Alcohol: 29 kJ/g (7 kcal/g)
   - Carbohydrate: 17 kJ/g (3.75 kcal/g).
   - Protein: 16 kJ/g (4 kcal/g)

2. Fibre slows the release of glucose into the bloodstream (soluble fibre), and forms bulk to aid the passage of faeces (insoluble fibre).

3. Fruit, vegetables, whole grains, wholemeal bread, cereals, beans and pulses.

4. Fluid requirement is 30–35 ml/kg per day for adults with normal renal and cardiac function.

5. An antioxidant neutralises free radicals, the potentially damaging molecules within the body produced by normal processes such as digestion.

6. Vitamin A and beta carotene, vitamin C, vitamin E and selenium.

7. Take your weight in kilograms divided by the square of your height in metres to estimate your body mass index.

Chapter 5

1. ● The client's normal bowel habit
   ● The frequency/time of faecal/urinary elimination
   ● The presence of pain/discomfort when eliminating
   ● The amount eliminated
   ● Odour
   ● Diet/fluid intake
   ● Disease
   ● Mobility.

2. ● Drugs, resulting in reduced motility of the intestine
   ● Laxative abuse, resulting in a diminished normal reflex
   ● Pregnancy, due to reduced abdominal space and progesterone slowing peristalsis
   ● Disease processes, altering the time passage of the faeces
   ● Pain, causing the client to be reluctant to defaecate
   ● Psychiatric problems, causing a lack of interest in the surroundings and diet, or an altered dietary intake
   ● A diet low in fibre, or an inadequate intake
   ● Fluids not sufficient for the patient's needs
   ● Immobility, reducing intestinal motility
   ● Ignoring the call to defaecate, allowing more fluid to be absorbed from faeces, which, therefore, become harder and more difficult to eliminate
   ● Psychological factors, caused by unfavourable conditions so that the client delays defaecation process until more favourable conditions exist.

3. ● Stress incontinence
   ● Urge incontinence
   ● Reflex incontinence
   ● Overflow incontinence.

4. ● Ileostomy: an opening from the ileum; faecal material liquid
   ● Colostomy: an opening from the colon; faecal material ranges from semi-solid to more formed stools
   ● Urostomy: the bladder is removed and urinary excretion is diverted via a stoma formed on the abdominal wall.

5. ● Embarrassment (the most common factor)
   ● Depression
   ● Anorexia nervosa
   ● Chronic psychoses.

6. Calculated on a 30–35 ml/kg body weight, this equals 1950–2275 ml per 24 hours.

Chapter 6

1. 25 per minute.

2. Respiratory cycles of gradually decreasing rate and depth, followed by cycles of increasing rate and depth. Cheyne–Stokes respiration frequently indicates impending death.

3. ● Mucoid: raw egg appearance, due to chronic bronchitis
   ● Purulent: slimy and green, due to bronchopneumonial infection
   ● Haemoptysis: red and frothy, due to bleeding in the lungs
   ● Frothy: pink and bubbly, due to pulmonary oedema.

4. Jaw thrust is a method of opening the airway that maintains in-line stabilisation of the neck and is used if cervical injury is suspected.

5. ● Decreased urine output
   ● Muscle weakness
   ● Peripheral cyanosis
   ● Cool extremities
   ● Grey, mottled skin in infants
   ● Tachycardia.

6. Using the brachial pulse in the infant, and the carotid pulse for all other age groups.

7. 1. Sharp and clear
   2. Blowing and swishing
   3. Sharp but softer than 1
   4. Muffled but fading
   5. No sound.

8. By pressing one's thumb on a client's skin, causing it to blanch, and timing the return of the blood flow.

9. ● Verbal descriptor
   ● Visual analogue
   ● Pain behaviour
   ● Combined tool.

10. ● Circulatory overload
    ● Allergic reaction
    ● Disease transmission
    ● Pyrogenic reaction
    ● Haemolytic mismatch.

Chapter 7

1. See below.

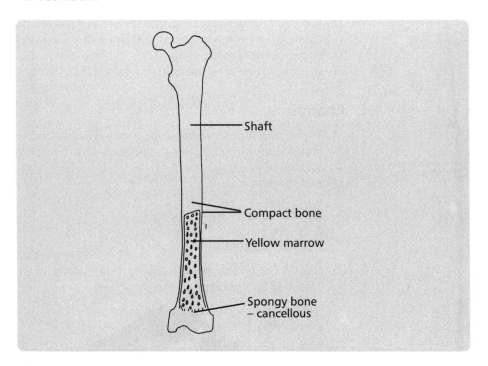

2. Collagen, calcium and phosphate, and bone cells.

3. The outer area of all bones, in the shafts of the long bones, and in the outer and inner parts of the flat bones.

4. Haversian systems.

5. To allow movement and aid the production of body heat.

6. The resistance offered to a passive stretch of the muscle. This is determined by the nerve supply to the muscle and its control, and also by the contractile and elastic properties of the muscle.

7. Twenty per cent.

8. To facilitate movement, to ensure that movements are stable and to help to maintain the posture.

9. The elbow joint.

10. The shoulder girdle, hand, foot and vertebral column.

11. Flexion, extension, abduction, adduction, external and internal rotation, and circumduction.

12. Exercise slows osteoporosis, interrupts bone loss and encourages new bone mass. It may lessen dependency in individuals.

13. The development of deep vein thrombosis and pulmonary embolism, chest infections, constipation, urinary tract infections and renal calculi, muscle weakness and atrophy pressure sores and the demineralisation of bones.

14. A skin ulceration occurring as a result of unrelieved pressure and a combination of other variables. Nursing care involves the relief of pressure, encouraging mobility, a nutritious diet and adequate fluid intake. If the client is incontinent, incontinence aids should be used.

Chapter 8

1. The accountability relationships within which professional practitioners are required to discharge their duty of care to the client include:
   - Legal
   - Managerial
   - Organisational
   - Professional
   - Governmental
   - Moral and ethical.

2. Any kind of breach in the integrity of the skin or underlying tissues can be described as a 'wound'.

3. Wounds can be classified as follows:
   - According to causal factor(s)
   - According to depth
   - As 'open' or 'closed'
   - By the anticipated method of healing.

4. The different types of risk assessment include:
   - Pressure area damage
   - Diabetic foot ulcer risk
   - Nutritional compromise
   - Manual handling.

5. The components of the skin are:
   - Epidermis
   - Dermis
   - Subcutaneous tissue
   - Hair and hair follicles
   - Nails
   - Sweat glands
   - Sebaceous glands
   - Sensory nerve receptors
   - Capillary network
   - Specialist cells, for example melanocytes.

6. The four main phases of wound healing are: haemostasis, inflammation, proliferation and maturation.

7. The factors affecting wound healing from the personal aspect include:
   - Age
   - Mental state

- Ability to communicate
- Nutritional status
- Cardiovascular status
- Respiratory status
- Mobility
- Continence
- Underlying pathophysiology
- Pain
- Type of wound
- Location of wound
- Condition of skin.

Those from the contextual aspect include:
- Socio-economic status
- Housing
- Access to the multidisciplinary team
- Access to voluntary organisations
- Method of care delivery
- Social network
- Exposure to environmental contaminants
- Ambient temperature
- Education
- Medication.

8. The optimum environment for wound healing includes the following elements:
   - Moisture
   - Protection from bacterial contamination
   - Protection from particulate and toxic contamination
   - Thermal insulation
   - Removal of excess exudate
   - Good blood supply
   - Protection from mechanical damage
   - Minimal disturbance.

9. The assessment criteria for wound management include:
   - General physical condition
   - Mental state
   - Mobility
   - Nutritional status
   - Continence
   - Concurrent disease
   - Cardiovascular status
   - Pain
   - Skin
   - Risk assessment.

10. The purpose of a nursing care plan in wound management is to provide a systematic, rational documentary review, using a problem-solving approach, of the prescribed care required to meet nursing care needs and achieve

specified nursing care objectives. The nursing care plan also provides documentary evidence of evaluations of nursing care, providing a 'decision trail' for the rationale underpinning any modifications to prescribed nursing care.

11. The term 'aseptic technique' refers to the method of carrying out procedures in an environment that is rendered as free from micro-organisms and contaminants as possible.

12. The evaluation of nursing care in wound management is concerned with the effectiveness of nursing interventions. The key considerations should be:
    - Current versus previous wound status
    - To what extent specified objectives have been achieved
    - What factors have facilitated or impaired the achievement of these objectives
    - Further assessment
    - Revisions to planned care.

Chapter 9

1.
   - Empathic understanding
   - Genuineness
   - Unconditional acceptance.

2. The six categories are:
   - Prescriptive
   - Informative
   - Confronting
   - Catalytic
   - Supportive
   - Cathartic.

3. Any of the interventions listed below could be used:
   - Open questions
   - Closed questions
   - Checking for understanding
   - Simple reflection
   - Paraphrasing
   - Logical building
   - Empathic building.

4. A primary group is a close intimate group that usually has face-to-face contact. A secondary group is usually a large group in which members have less direct contact.

5.
   - Task needs
   - Team maintenance needs
   - Individual needs.

6.
   - Forming
   - Storming
   - Norming
   - Performing.

7. ● Assertive
    ● Aggressive
    ● Submissive/passive.

8. ● Listening carefully
    ● Saying what you think and feel
    ● Saying what you want to happen
    ● Being persistent
    ● Being prepared to compromise.

9. For valid criticism, accept the criticism. If the criticism is invalid, reject it. If it is partially valid, accept the valid aspects and reject the invalid aspects of the criticism.

Chapter 10

1. The self-concept is the knowledge a person has about themselves. It is an organised set of beliefs and feelings that are self-referent.

2. Self-awareness is a constructive appreciation of the self. Self-consciousness is a concern for others' perception of self.

3. Stress occurs when the demands of the situation exceed the personal resources of the individual.

4. ● Personality
    ● Social support
    ● Emotion.

5. Attitudes are the sum of one's beliefs and opinions. They have three components: behavioural, cognitive and affective.

6. It is a person's attitude to health behaviours that influences whether people will modify risky health behaviours such as smoking, diet and so on.

7. ● Trust
    ● Like/dislike
    ● Credibility
    ● Perceived attractiveness
    ● Individual beliefs
    ● Self-esteem.

Chapter 12

1. Four.

2. 1948.

3. ● Block contracts
    ● Cost and volume
    ● Cost per case.

4. 1902.

5. Mental Health Act Commission.

6. A supervision order.

Chapter 13

1. Interprofessional practice is one of the terms used to describe a group of professionals working together to achieve mutually agreed goals. These goals should involve the service user and the carer. Other terms are often used in place of interprofessional, for example interdisciplinary, multi-professional and multidisciplinary. Interprofessional practice has been most common in primary care and community care settings. More recently, it has become an element of acute care practice.

3. With the establishment of primary care groups, the role of many professionals may change. For example, practice nurses, district nurses and health visitors may be involved in the management of primary care groups, bringing together the work of GPs and other professions. Social workers may also be represented, especially in child protection and mental health issues. In the hospital setting, nurses will be involved in the care-planning process for discharge in elderly care, and also in working alongside physiotherapists and occupational therapists in the field of stroke rehabilitation. Ensuring that the client's or patient's needs are met by the person with the appropriate skill and knowledge is the most significant role that all professionals bring to teamwork. Equally, the ongoing evaluation and review of practice intervention will mean that the most effective use of resources is being made.

4. Ensuring that the specific skills and knowledge held by the nurse are recognised by others in the team. If the nurse is employed by the GP, he or she may have limited involvement in the allocation of resources for the particular area of practice. Equally, a difference in payment can lead to differing levels of status within a team. Status may play a major part in the decision-making process, and nurses may have to work proactively to ensure that their views on good practice are heard and evaluated.

Chapter 14

1a. Professional practice can be viewed from many different starting points depending on who it is that is defining it. However, the common elements arise from expectations about a practitioner's behaviour as a professional that arise from the profession's code of conduct and from legal responsibilities.

1b. The responsibilities for professional practice are defined in the UKCC *Code of Professional Conduct* (1992) and encapsulated by the following statement:

> Each registered nurse, midwife and health visitor shall act, at all times, in such a manner as to:

- safeguard and promote the interests of individual clients;
- serve the interests of society;
- justify public trust and confidence and

- uphold and enhance the good standing and reputation of the professions.

As a registered nurse, midwife or health visitor, you are personally accountable for your practice.

Individual responsibilities are listed in Chart 14.1.

2a. The *Code of Professional Conduct* is the document produced by the UKCC that outlines the roles and responsibilities of a registered practitioner. It acts as a standard for professional practice, enabling the profession to judge practitioners in terms of misconduct.

2b. Students are given their own, amended, version of the *Code of Professional Conduct*. If you are not familiar with this, it is important that you read it before proceeding with your studies.

2c. You are accountable for your own actions as a citizen of this country and must therefore not undertake criminal activities. You are also accountable to your employer for your actions while working, and you are accountable under civil law for all of your actions, whether these occur at work or elsewhere.

2d. Students clearly cannot be professionally accountable because they are not entered on the professional register, but they are accountable in the other three ways listed in Answer 1b. This does *not*, however, mean that students are not responsible for their actions.

3. We all practise from a belief and value system that has arisen from our own personal experiences of life and what we have encountered in the way of experience, education and professional socialisation. In the same way that our own style of nursing is directed by our beliefs and values, so also will be the care delivered by a team of nurses working together.

4. The primary purpose of a model of care is to help nurses to understand nursing from a particular viewpoint and use that to direct their care. Formal models occur when the values, beliefs and ways of working are made explicit and shared by the team of nurses in the clinical area. They enable groups of nurses to think about, and carry out, nursing in a fairly similar way, with clear objectives for the delivery of care because the model aims to represent the nursing care to be achieved by that team.

5. Quality assessment measures the standard of care that is used as a judgement evaluating the services being delivered. It is used to evaluate services against the promises made to clients in the *Patient's Charter* and against targets set by purchasing agencies, and to provide information for improving nursing care.

6. The basic answer here is that this is required by the UKCC and written into Clause 3 of the *Professional Code of Conduct*. However, apart from that, you would consider it ethically wrong, wouldn't you, if you consulted a lawyer and she was not up to date with the pertinent laws relating to your case? Similarly, as professional nurses we must ensure that we provide the best possible care to our clients, and as professionals, it is incumbent upon us continually to keep abreast of developments in our speciality and practise appropriately.

Activity Answers

Chapter 4
Activity 6

The nurse needs to understand that, as the body is about 60 per cent water, it affects many physiological processes, including the circulation of the blood (Chapter 6) and elimination (Chapter 5). Fluid and electrolytes are gained in eating and drinking, and lost in urine and sweat. Intravenous therapy (Chapter 6) makes no sense without an understanding of fluid compartments.

Activity 7

The client's urine will be pale and plentiful, defaecation easy, the skin well hydrated and the eyes not sunken.

Activity 8

Look around the supermarket to identify wholegrain cereals, for example:

- wholemeal bread, flour, pasta and brown rice
- Weetabix, Shredded Wheat, muesli and porridge
- bran-enriched cereals such as All Bran and Bran Flakes.

A trip to the supermarket will also identify loaves fortified with folic acid, for example *Mighty White*.

Folic acid is needed in very early pregnancy, often before the woman realises that she is pregnant.

Activity 9

Lack of sunlight on the skin can deprive the person of this source of vitamin D. Vitamin B deficiency will lead to osteomalacia with muscle weakness and bone pain and tenderness.

Activity 10

Channel Islands' breakfast milk has 134 mg calcium per 100 ml, skimmed cows' milk has 124 mg/100 ml, semi-skimmed milk has 122 mg/100 ml, and whole cows' milk has 119 mg/100 ml.

Activity 12

Non-starch polysaccharides (NSP/fibre) are digested by colonic bacteria, with methane as a byproduct. Intestinal flora synthesise vitamin B6.

The products of bacterial metabolism vary according to the types of bacterium present, which are different in different people, and their numbers, which are also subject to wide variations. If the volume of food residue from the small intestine increases, their numbers go up. Thus, if the amount of NSP/fibre in the diet is increased, or the digestion of carbohydrate and protein in the small intestine is incomplete (for example because of enzyme deficiency), the bacterial population in the large intestine increases (Rutishauser, 1994, pp. 123–4).

The metabolic activities of colonic bacteria result in the protein products of ammonia, urea and nitrogen; NSP products – short-chain fatty acids, carbon dioxide, methane and hydrogen; primary bile salts producing secondary bile salts, stercobilin from bilirubin (Rutishauser, 1994, pp. 123–4).

Activity 13

Eggs are classified in the meat and alternatives section, and potatoes in the starchy foods section.

Activity 14

Anabolism is the building up of body substance, such as occurs during convalescence of body-building. There will be increased nutritional demands compared with the normal steady state.

Catabolism is the breakdown of body substance, the destructive phase of the acute stress response, as occurs, for example, after trauma or surgery. Muscle may be very much depleted, and nutritional support is directed to minimise the impact of this process.

Activity 23

The pH of gastric juice ranges from 1.0 to 7.0, depending on the stomach contents.

Activity 24

The eustachian (auditory) tube runs between the pharynx and the middle ear and can transmit infection introduced by nasogastric tube placement.

Chapter 13

Activity 3

You may have observed the following as part of your 'socialisation':

- The fitting of uniforms
- The language used
- Examples of practice from a nursing perspective
- The way in which people were described as patients.

Activity 4

The values of nursing include:

- All individuals should be seen holistically
- All individuals have a right to intervention and care
- A person's rights and wishes are to be respected
- Values may be based upon the concept of caring
- Care should be planned individually.

The values of nursing are not static and may or may not reflect your own personal values: it is worth considering the similarities and differences.

Activity 5

The skills involved in sharing opinions are:

- Listening
- Assertiveness
- Planning
- Offering valid evidence
- Timing
- Building positive professional relationships
- Acknowledging difference.

Activity 6

The main challenges to interprofessional teamwork are:

- The status of individual team members
- Differing professional values
- Location
- Team size
- Professional roles and boundaries.

Index

....

Page numbers printed in **bold** type refer to figures; those in *italic* to tables or charts. Asterisks (*) against page numbers indicate the presence of glossary points in the left-hand margin in addition to material in the main text.

A

abdominal thrusts 176–7
abduction 220
abrasions *243*
abscesses, as complication of
  intramuscular injection 78
acceptance 301
  see also unconditional acceptance
accessory muscles of respiration 170*
accidents, *Health of the Nation*
  targets 40
accountability 394*
  frameworks for *242*
  relationships *242*
  v. responsibility 241, 395, 395–6
  types of 394
  UKCC *Code of Professional
    Conduct* on 2, 16, 17, 18, 42,
    395, 396
  in wound management 241–2
  see also professional
    accountability
acidosis 172*
action planning 13–14
actions, *see* human actions
active reflection 328
activities of daily living (ADL) 7, 405,
  406 409
adduction 220
adenosine triphosphate (ATP) 185
adrenaline 195, 211
advice-giving 269
advocacy, and assertiveness 286
aetiology 39*
Agenda 21 (environmental action
  plan) 33–4

agglutination 211*
AIDS, *Health of the Nation* targets
  39–40
air, atmospheric 184
airway
  causes of obstruction *175*
  foreign bodies 176–7
  Guedel's (oropharyngeal) 175–6
  Heimlich manoeuvre 176–7
  maintenance 175–7
  suctioning 189–90
  see also respiration
albumin levels 124
alcohol 111–12
alkalosis 171*
alpha-linolenic acid 97
alpha-tocopherols 107
American Nurses Association 11
American Scenic Report 57
amino acids 96*, 246
anabolism 113*
anaemia 171*
  iron deficiency anaemia 109*
  nutritional 121*
anaphylaxis *175*, 211
anastomosis 144*
anger 307
angiogenesis 245*, 246
anomie 281
anorexia 109*
anorexia nervosa 103*
anosmia 118*
anticipatory reflection 328–9
active reflection 328
anti-embolic precautions 209–10
  exercise 210
  intermittent pneumatic
    compression 210
  stockings 210
antimuscarinic 156*
antioxidants 104, 106, 107, 109
apnoea 171*
appetite 119–20
approved social workers (ASWs) 364
aprons 57
arm, injection site 75

arrhythmia 208*
arteries
  injections into 79
  intra-arterial medication
    administration 71
artificial respiration, *see* resuscitation
ascites 127*
ascorbic acid (vitamin C) 104, 106,
  109, 246
aseptic technique *263*
assertiveness 284*, 284–90
  and advocacy 286
  broken record technique 288–9
  fielding the response 289
  fogging 290
  functions of 286
  gender 285
  managing criticism 289–90
  non-verbal communication 287*
  overview 290
  principles of 287
  reasons for 286
  saying no 288–9
  techniques 288–90
  see also leadership
assessment 3–10
  of breathing 7–8
  data collection 6–7
  data sources 3–4
  framework for 7–8
  information-gathering skills 4–6,
    251–2
  listening 5
  measurements 6
  observation 5
  of pain 8–10, *11*
  physical examination 5
  questioning 5
  in wound management 251–9
assessment of nursing outcomes 402
asthmatic breathing 172
asymptomatic 25*
atherosclerosis 243*
atrial fibrillation 194*, 196
atropine 195

attitude 309*, 309–13
    change of 311–12
    expectancy value model 311
    prejudice 312
    stereotype 312*
    three-component model 310–11
    see also behaviour; personality
auscultation 227*
authenticity, see genuineness
autolysis 260*
autonomy
    and health status 27
    v. shame and doubt 297
awareness, zones of 274

B

back pain, costs of 49
bad news, breaking of 278
basal metabolic rate (BMR) 112*
bed sores, see pressure sores
behaviour
    behaviour messages 284–6
    inconsistent with beliefs 312
    see also attitude; personality
beliefs, behaviour inconsistent with
    312
beta-blockers 195*
beta-carotene 104
beta-tocopherols 107
Beveridge Report 352, 353
Bianca hoists 54, 55
Bills (Parliamentary) 349*
biofeedback 157*
Biot's respiration 172
Black Report 32, 347
blood pressure 197–200
    arterial 197
    average values 200
    diastolic 197*
    factors determining 197
    hypertension 199*
    hypotension 200*
    Korotkoff sounds 198, 199
    measuring 198–9
    peripheral resistance 197*
    postural recordings 200
    systolic 197*
blood transfusion 210–12
    allergic reactions 211
    circulatory overload 211
    cold blood 212
    complications 211–12
    disease transmission 212
    and glucose solutions 211
    haemolytic mismatch 211
    observations during 211

pyrogenic reactions 212*
safety precautions 210–11
storage 210
types of blood/blood product
    210
body fat percentage 114
body language 274, 287
body mass index (BMI) 113*,
    113–14
bone marrow 219
bone matrix 219
bone resorption 224*
bones 218–19
    compact 218, 219
    composition 219
    demineralisation 225*
    functions 218–19
    Haversian systems 219
    trabecular (cancellous/spongy)
        218, 219
    types 218
    see also lever systems
boundaries, professional 372, 375–6
bovine spongiform encephalitis (BSE)
    28–9, 29
bradycardia 194*, 194–5, 195
bradypnoea 170*
bran 101
breastfeeding 94, 100
breathing, see respiration
British National Formulary 64, 66
British Pharmaceutical Codex 63
British Pharmacopoeia 63
BSE (bovine spongiform encephalitis)
    28–9, 29
Burford nursing development unit
    400
burns 243
buttocks, injection site 75–6

C

Cabinet (government) 348*
calciferol (vitamin D) 97, 106, 108
calcification 225*
calcium 97, 106, 107–8
calculi, see gallstones; kidney stones;
    urinary stones
calorie requirements 100, 124
Campylobacter infection, food
    poisoning 60
cancer, Health of the Nation targets
    39
capillary refill time 201
carbamino compound 185
carbohydrate(s) 95*, 95–6, 246
carbon dioxide 167*, 169, 185

carcinoma, colonic and rectal 136
cardiac arrest 177–8
    see also resuscitation
cardiac compression 180–2
    children 180
    infants 181–2
cardiac failure 171*
    congestive 201–2
    see also heart disease
cardiac monitoring 205–9
    see also electrocardiographs
cardiac muscle 217
cardiac output 197
care
    duty of 241
    imposing conformity 320–1
    thinking or unthinking? 317–19
    unnecessary 317
    see also nursing care
care models, see nursing models
care orders 367
care planning 12–14
    action planning 13–14
    goals, MACROS criteria 13
    information technology and 20–1
    REEPIG criteria 14
    stages 12
care plans
    example 21
    review of 20
care programme approach (CPA), in
    mental health care 364*
carotene 104
ß-carotene 104
cartilage 218*
caseload management 17–18
catabolism 113*
catalytic interventions 273*, 273–6
cathartic interventions 277*, 276–7
catheters
    nasal, for oxygen 188
    see also urinary catheters
Central Midwives Board (CMB) 361
challenge 307
chemoreceptors 169*
chemotaxis 245*
chest, shape 174
chest thrusts 176–7
Cheyne–Stokes respiration 172*
child assessment orders 367
children
    administration of medication 68,
        88–9
    bones 218, 219
    carbohydrates 96
    'child in need' 366–7
    development of self-concept
        296–7

ear treatment 84, **85**
energy requirements 96
enuresis 154*
eye treatment 84
faecal elimination development 135–6
fat requirements 97, 100
fluid requirements 102–3
heart rate 194, 196
injections 89
intramuscular injections 75, 76, 77, 78
oral stimulation 129
oxygen therapy 186–8, 189
parental responsibility 366, 367
rectal medications 86, 87
respiratory rates *171*
resuscitation 179, 180–2
urinary elimination development 149–50
Children Act 1989 366–8
court orders 367–8
chin lift 175, **176**, 178
chloride 108
chlorpheniramine 211
chlorpromazine 72
cholesterol 98, 99, 99–100, 111
sources 99
chronic obstructive airway disease 190*
circulation 191–212
anti-embolic precautions 209–10
assessment 192–205
blood pressure 197–200
blood transfusion 210–12
cardiac monitoring 205–9
fluid balance 201–2
heart rate 192–7
intravenous fluid therapy 212, *213*
nursing interventions 205–12
pain 202–5
peripheral perfusion 200–1
physical examination 192
pulmonary 191, 197
systemic 191, 197
see also pulse
circulatory system, mobility and 226–7
civil servants 350
CJD, *see* Creutzfeldt–Jakob disease
claudication 204*
client allocation 16*
clients, rights of 373
client satisfaction schedules 403
clinical waste 59
closed questions 5*
Clothier Report 2

Code of Professional Conduct (UKCC) 42, 392, *393*, 398
on accountability 2, 16, 17, 18, 42, 395, 396
on medicine administration 63, 66
cognitive post mortem 329
collaboration 374
research and reports on 384–5
see also teamwork
collagen 231, 247, 249
collagenases 246
collagen synthesis 245*, 246
colostomy 144*, 144–5, *145*, 147
colour, and respiration 173
comforting activities *409*
commitment 307
Committee on Medical Aspects of Food Policy (COMA) reports 95, 96, 101, 112
communication
benefits of nursing models 416
non-verbal 287*
see also therapeutic communication; therapeutic interventions
Community Health Councils 354
Community Psychiatric Nurses Association 346
competitiveness 307
compliance 88
computer records 20, 396–7
care planning 20–1
Data Protection Act 1984 396–7
conflict resolution
negative 299
positive 297
conformity 320–1
confronting interventions 277*, 277–8
congruence 270*
conjunctivae, infection precautions 57
constipation 138*, 138–42
causes 138–39
client care 140–2
and impaired mobility 227
manual evacuation 142
with overflow 138
signs and symptoms 140
contact orders 367
contracting 358
contraction, in wound healing 245, 246–7
contractures 228*, 249
control 284, 307
controlled drugs 65*

co-operation
moving towards 384
stages of 379–80
see also collaboration; teamwork
co-ordination, *see* leadership
coronary heart disease, *Health of the Nation* targets 37–9
Corrigan's pulse 195
cough 173–4
Council for Disabled People 373
counselling 269
see also therapeutic communication
counselling skills, *v.* counselling 269
Court Report *382*
CPA (care programme approach), in mental health care 364*
creatinine clearance test 151
Credé manoeuvre 156, *157*
crepitations 173
Creutzfeldt–Jakob disease (CJD) 28–9
new variant (nvCJD) 29
critical incident analysis 19, 329–34
criticism, handling 289–90
Crohn's disease 136*
cultural differences, in communication 277, 287
Cumberlege Report *382*
cuts, *see* lacerations
cyanocobalamin 105
cyanosis 173, 200, 256*
with dyspnoea 173
cystitis 157–8*
cytotoxic drugs, precautions 72
cytotoxic 158*

D

Data Protection Act 1984 396–7
decubitus ulcers, *see* pressure sores
deep vein thrombosis (DVT) 209, 210, 227
defaecation, *see* faecal elimination
defence cells 231
defence mechanism 301*
dehiscence, as complication of wound healing 249*
dehydration 103, 111
deinstitutionalisation 373
demineralisation 225*
Department of Health 350, 351
dependence
dependence/independence continuum *409*
v. independence 310
depolarisation 206*

Derbyshire chair 187
dermatitis 109*
    from drug contact 72
dermis 231
despair, v. integrity 298
detrusor muscle 156*
diabetes 129*
diagnosis, see nursing diagnosis
diarrhoea 142*, 142–3
    causes 142–3
    steatorrhoea 143*
diathermy 243*
dichotomous 275*
diet
    balanced 94–5, 110–11
    carbohydrates 95–6
    cultural issues 122–3
    economic influences 121
    ethnic practices 122–3
    healthy 94–5
    macronutrients 95–103
    micronutrients 104–11
    monitoring 123–4
    political influences 121
    proteins 96*, 96–7, 124, 246
    relative food group needs
        110–11, **111**
    religious practices 122–3
    social influences 121
    vegan 97, 105, 122
    vegetarian 97, 105, 122–3, **123**
    'yo-yo' dieting 130
    see also calorie requirements;
        fats/fatty acids; food;
        nutrients; nutrition; 'tilted
        plate'
dietary reference values (DRVs) 112
    Committee on Medical Aspects of
    Food Policy report 95, 96, 101,
    112
digoxin 195*
disability
    and adaptation 234–6
    social security benefits 234,
        236–7
    stereotyping 236
    see also mobility impairment
Disabled Living Centres 236
disaccharides 95
district nursing, key developments
    382
diuretics 201, 202
diurnal 150*
diverticular disease 138*
domestic waste 59
Do not resuscitate (DNR) orders 177
Doppler testing 201
doubt, v. autonomy 297

dressings, for wounds 250–1
drugs
    controlled 65*
    cytotoxic, precautions 72
    inhaled 190–1
    nebulisation 191
    see also medications
duty of care 241
Dynamic Standard Setting System
    (DYSSSY) 403
dyspareunia 147
dyspnoea 172*, 209
    with cyanosis 173

E

ears, medications 85
eating, see diet; food
ECGs, see electrocardiographs
echoing 274–5
economic efficiency v. caring society
    32–3
education and training
    handling operations and
        equipment 50
    interprofessional developments
        385–6
    lifelong learning 418
    National Boards 359, 360, 391
    Post-registration Education and
        Practice Project (PREPP) 334,
        360–1, 392
    Project 2000 360
    UKCC objective 391–2
    see also experiential learning;
        patient education
elastin 231
elbows **222**
    exercise 229
electrocardiographs (ECGs) 205
    arrhythmia 208*
    baseline 206
    chest lead placements **207**
    heart rate 208
    isoelectric line 206
    P wave 206, 208
    P–R interval **207**, 208–9
    Q wave 206, **207**
    QRS complex 206, **207**, 209
    regularity 208
    rhythm analysis and
        interpretation 208–9
    R wave 206, **207**
    sinus rhythm **207**
    S wave 206, **207**
    S–T segment **207**
    T wave 208

    waveforms 206–8
electromechanical dissociation 206*
elimination, see faecal elimination;
    urinary elimination
embolism, see anti-embolic
    precautions; pulmonary embolism
Emergency Medical Service 352
emergency protection orders 367
emotion, as source of stress 308–9
emotions, expression of 276–7
empathic building 276
empathic understanding 270*,
    270–1
empathy 270
employers, influence on personal
    beliefs and values 398–9
ENB, see English National Board
enemas 141
energy 100–2, 112
English National Board (ENB), health
    promotion as key characteristic
    44
enteral feeding 124–9
    contraindications 126
enuresis 154*
environment, concept *408*
environmental health 33–4
environmental health officers (EHOs)
    60
epidermis 231
    superficial break 242*
epithelialisation, in wound healing
    246–7
ergocalciferol 106
ergonomics 52*
    and nutrition 115–16
Erikson's psychosocial theory of
    personality development 297–8
eschar 258*
Escherichia coli 28, 29–30, 59
essential fatty acids 97
estimated average requirements
    (EAR) (of nutrients) 112
European Tissue Repair Society 241,
    265
European Wound Management
    Association 241, 264
evaluation, of nursing care 18–20
excision, surgical *243*
excoriation 145*
Executive Councils 353
exercise 221–3
    anti-embolic precautions 210
    effect of, on respiration 170
    isometric 227*, 228, 233
    joints 228–9
    passive 227*, 228, 229
experience, see knowledge; learning

experiential learning 334–9
  maximising learning opportunities 322–3
  reflection as learning tool 320, 325
experiential learning cycle 335, 338–9
expiratory reserve volume (ERV) 182, **183***
extension movement of joints 220
extravasation 245*
exudate 250*
eye contact 277, 287
eyes
  medications 83–4
  protection 57

F

face masks 187–8
faecal elimination 133, 134–47
  adolescents 136
  adults 136
  ageing adults 136
  altered 138–44
  constipation 138*, 138–42
  defaecation reflex 135
  development of 135–6
  diarrhoea 143*, 142–3
  incontinence 143–4
  in infants 135
  school-aged children 136
  specimen collection 136–7
  toddlers to preschool age 135
falls 225–6
Family Doctor's Charter 381
fasting 123
fats/fatty acids 97*, 97–100
  food energy from 97–8
  mono-unsaturated 97, 98, 99, 99
  omega-3 97, 98
  omega-6 97, 98
  polyunsaturated 97, 98, 98–9, 99
  saturated 97, 98, 98, 99
  sources 98, 99
  trans-fats/fatty acids 95, 97, 98, 99
  triglycerides 97
  types and sources 98, 99
  unsaturated 98
  in wound healing 246
  see also body fat percentage
feeding, see diet; food
fibre, see non-starch polysaccharide
fibroblasts 245–6, 247
flatus 147*
flavour, of food 119

flexion 220
fluid 102–3
fluid balance 201–2
fluid charts 124
fluid intake 102–3, 140
fogging 290
folate 105
folic acid 105
food
  choices in 119
  flavour 119
  gravity feeding 115
  habits 122
  hygiene, see food hygiene
  nurse's responsibility 62, 94
  preparing and cooking 42
  provision and serving, overview 118
  psychology of eating 119
  rejection or acceptance, factors in 119
  smell 119
  social factors 120
  taste 118, 119
  transporting 34
  see also diet; nutrition
food charts/diaries 113, 118, 124, **125**
food hygiene 59–63
  contamination sources 60
  food service on the wards 62–3
  nurses' code 62
food pathogen growth curve **61**
food poisoning 59–61, 60*
food safety legislation 60
foreign bodies, in airway 176–7
foundations theory of health promotion 27–8
Frank–Starling Law 197–8
free radicals 246*
fruit 101, **102**
fruitarians 122
fulcrum 221*
functional nursing (task allocation) 15–16
functional residual capacity (FRC) 182, **183***
fungating wounds 243

G

gallstones 129*
gastrocolic reflex 117, 135*
gastrointestinal system, mobility and 227
gastrointestinal tract, lower **134**

general adaptation syndrome (GAS) 304–5
General Nursing Council (GNC) 359
general practitioners, see GP fundholders
generativity 298*
  v. self-absorption 298
genuineness 270, 271*, 272
gloves 57, 72
glyceryl trinitrate (GTN) 205
goals 13*
goldfish bowl society 29, **30**
Gordon's phenomenological approach 296
government
  Bills 349*
  British 348
  Cabinet 348*
  civil servants 350
  Department of Health 350, 351
  finance 350–1, 351–2
  government ministers 348*, 348–9
  House of Commons 349
  House of Lords 349
  ministries 349–50
  policy implementation 351–2
  Treasury 348*, 350–1
  see also politics; and specific Acts of Parliament
GP fundholders 357, 372, 381
  contract types 358
graded compression stockings 210
Gram-negative bacilli 58
grand theory 413, 413–14
granulation tissue 246*
grazes, see abrasions
Greenhalgh Report 372
Griffiths Report 355, 371
groups 280–4
  description 280–1
  development stages 283
  group processes **283**
  leadership 281–4
  norms 281
  primary 281
  secondary 281
  self-help 302
grunting 173
Guedel's (oropharyngeal) airway 175–6
guilt, v. initiative 298

H

haematoma, as complication of wound healing 249*

haemolysis 211*
haemoptysis 174*, 209
haemorrhage, as complication of
    wound healing 249
haemoserous fluid 147*
haemostasis 245
HAI (hospital-acquired infection) 56,
    57
half-life 124*
handling, see manual handling
handwashing 57, 58, 58, 62
head tilt 175, **176**
healing, see wound healing
health
    challenges to 28–9
    concept of 408
    concepts of 26–8
    defining 25–6
    definition 27
    inequalities 32
    see also health promotion
Health and Safety at Work Act 1974
    49–50
    employees' duties 50
    employers' general duties 49, 50
health authorities 354–5, 356*, 358
health care teams
    members of 15
    see also primary health care
        teams
Health Committee, UKCC 394
Health for All by the Year 2000
    (WHO) 36–7
health gain 36–7
Health of the Nation (White Paper)
    36–40, 95
    accidents 40
    AIDS 39–40
    cancer 39
    coronary heart disease 37–9
    HIV infection 39–40
    initial key areas 37–40
    mental illness 39
    Portsmouth local authority
        response to **38**
    sexual health 39–40
    stroke 39
health policy 346*
health promotion 29–42
    aspects of 30–1, **45**
    collaboration in 24
    English National Board key
        characteristic 44
    environmental health 33–4
    foundations theory 27–8
    individual health 41–2
    organisational health 34–6
    political health 30–1, 36–40

resource strategy 32
role of nurse 42–4, **45**
social health 32–3
spiritual health 30–1, 40–1
Health Services and Public Health Act
    1968 381
Health Services Supervisory Board
    355
health visiting, key developments 382
health visitors, see registered
    practitioners
heart
    heart rate, from ECG 208
    see also pulse; and cardiac entries
heart disease, and diet 98, 99, 111
Heimlich manoeuvre 176–7
hemianopia 118*
heparin 67, 80, 210
hierarchy of needs 294–5, 303
hip(s)
    exercise 229
    injection site **76**, 77
HIV infection, Health of the Nation
    targets 39–40
hoists, for patient handling 54, **55**
holism 406*
Homan's sign 209
hospital-acquired infection (HAI) 56,
    57
Hospital Management Committees
    353
hospitals
    mental health 362, 363
    in NHS structure 353–4
    teaching hospitals 353, 354
hostility 307
House of Commons 349
House of Lords 349
human actions 320
    routine v. reflective 319
human tissue, disposal of 59
hydration 114*
    assisting with 114–18
    checking 124
    dehydration 103, 111
    rehydration techniques 124
hydrocephalus 26*
hydrocortisone 211
hydroxylation 246*
hyperaemia, reactive 232
hypercalcaemia 108*
hypercoagulability 209*
hyperpnoea 172*
hypertension 199*
hypertrophic scarring 249*
hypodermoclysis 124*
hypotension 200*
hypovolaemia 206*

hypoxia 175*, 184, 185–6, 195
hypoxic drive 189

I

iatrogenic 29*
ice-making machines 63
ICN (International Council of Nurses)
    12
identity 298*
    v. role confusion 298
ideologies 397*, 398–404
idiopathic 151*
ileal conduit 163
ileostomy 145*, 145, 147
immobility, see mobility impairment
'I'm OK, you're OK' quadrangle
    285–6
implementation, of nursing care
    14–18
impotence 147
incision, surgical 243
incontinence 153*
    faecal 143–4
    urinary 153–7
independence, v. dependence 310
individual health 41–2
individuality in living 409
industry, v. inferiority 298
infarction 195*
infection
    as complication of intramuscular
        injection 78
    as complication of wound healing
        249
    costs to NHS of 56
    hospital-acquired (HAI) 56, 57
    nosocomial 56*, 57
    see also aseptic technique
infection control 56–9
    handwashing 57, 58, 58, 62
    laundry 58
    patient protection 57
    universal precautions 57
    waste disposal 57, 58–9
inferiority, v. industry 298
inflammatory response 98*
information gathering skills 4–6,
    251–2
information technology, see
    computer records
informative interventions 278*,
    278–9
inhalation therapy 191
inhalers 191
initiative, v. guilt 298

injections
    administration 67
    to children 89
    equipment 71–2
    intradermal *72*, 81–2
    intramuscular, *see* intramuscular
        injections
    subcutaneous *72*, 79–81
    see also medication
        administration
inspiratory capacity (IC) 182*
inspiratory reserve volume (IRV) **183**
insulin, injection method **80**, 80
integrity, *v.* despair 298
interdisciplinary practice, *see also*
    interprofessional practice
intermittent positive-pressure
    ventilation 191
International Council of Nurses (ICN)
    12
interpersonal skills, *see* therapeutic
    communication
'interprofessional' 370*, 371
interprofessionalism 370–1
    importance to nurses 373
    as a theory 386
    see also teamwork
interprofessional practice 370–86
    collaboration, research and
        reports on 384–5
    educational developments
        385–6
    factors affecting **385**
    intervention models 379
    key features 371
    moves towards 371, 384
    personal responses 386
    role changes 372
    theory for 386
    see also interprofessionalism;
        primary health care teams;
        teamwork
interstitial fluid 231*
intervention analysis, *see* therapeutic
    interventions
interventions, *see* therapeutic
    interventions
intestines 134
intimacy, *v.* isolation 298
intra-arterial medication
    administration 71
intra-articular medication
    administration 71
intracardiac medication
    administration 71
intradermal injections *72*, 81–2
intradermal route 81*
intramuscular injections 72–9

    in children 75, 76, 77, 78
    complications 78–9
    deltoid muscle in upper arm 75
    dorsogluteal site in buttocks
        75–6
    drawing medication from
        ampoules and vials 73
    guidelines 74
    procedure 72
    reconstituting powdered
        medication 73
    sites 74–8
    syringe and needle sizes *72*
    vastus lateralis in thigh 77–8
    ventrogluteal site in hip area **76**,
        77
    Z-track 78
intramuscular route **72***
intrathecal medication
    administration 71
intravenous fluid therapy 212, 213
    complications 212
    drip rate calculation formula **213**
intravenous medication
    administration 71
inunction 82*
iodine 81, 108
iron 109, 246
iron deficiency anaemia 109*
irritable bowel syndrome 136*
ischaemia 201*
ischial tuberosities 252*
isolation, *v.* intimacy 298

J

jaw thrust 178, **178**
job insecurity 32
Johari window 299–302
Joint Consultative Committees 354
joints 218, 219–20
    exercising 228–9
    as fulcrum in lever systems 221,
        221–2
    movement types 220
    synovial 219–20
juvenile chronic arthritis 235, 237

K

keloid scarring 249*
keratin 231
key workers 17
kidney stones 97, 106, 108
kinins 245*
knees, exercise 229
knowledge
    experiential 334–5

    practice 334
    propositional 334
    quality and depth of 327
    tacit knowing 326
Korotkoff sounds *198*, *199*
Kussmaul's respiration 172

L

lacerations *243*
lacto-ovovegetarians 122
lactovegetarians 122
language, within teams 376–7
laryngospasm 175*
laundry 58
laxatives 138, 141
leaders, classification 282
leadership 281–4, 375
    maintaining the individual 284
    maintaining the task 284
    maintaining the team 282–3
    styles 281–2
    three circles model **282**, 282
    see also assertiveness
learning
    experiential, *see* experiential
        learning
    lifelong 418
learning disabilities, medication
    administration to clients with
    89–90
left lateral position **142**
legislation
    food safety *60*
    substances for medicinal use *64*
    *see also specific Acts of
        Parliament*
lever systems 221, **221–2**
life line **272**
lifelong learning 418
life span *409*
lifting, *see* manual handling
linoleic acid 97
α-linolenic acid 97
lipoproteins 99
listening 5, 274
Listeria infection, food poisoning 60
Local Supervisory Authorities (LSAs),
    for midwives 361, 362
logical building 276
lowering, *see* manual handling
lower reference nutrient intake (LRNI)
    112
lung volumes and capacities 172,
    182–3
lysyl oxidase 246

M

maceration 258*
macronutrients 95–103
MACROS criteria for writing goals 13
manual handling 48–56
   assisting with patient's
      movement 52–4
   definition 49
   equipment 54–6
   ergonomics 52
   guidelines **53**
   individual capability for 52
   injuries from 49
   instruction in 50
   legislation 49–50
   load 51
   patient handling principles 54
   risk assessment 50–2, 53
   task assessment 51
   and work environment 51–2
Manual Handling Operations
   Regulations 1992 49, 52
MAOIs, *see* monoamine oxidase
   inhibitors
Maslow's hierarchy of needs 294–5,
   303
Matrons Aid Society 361
mattresses, for pressure sores 233
Maximove hoists 54, **55**
measurements, in assessment 6
meatus 151*
meconium 135*
medication administration 63–90
   to children, *see* children
   to clients with learning difficulties
      89–90
   compliance 88
   errors in 90
   intra-arterial 71
   intra-articular 71
   intracardiac 71
   intrathecal 71
   intravenous 71
   nurses' responsibilities 63
   oral 69–71
   parenteral 71–2
   patient assessment before 64
   patient education 88
   right amount 66–7
   right medication 65–6
   right patient 68
   right route 68–9
   right time 67
   routes of *68*
   safety guidelines 65
   subcutaneous 79–81

see also injections; nasogastric
   tubes; prescriptions; topical
   medications
medications
   administration, *see* medication
      administration
   controlled drugs 65
   legislation *64*
Mental Health Act Commission
   (MHAC) 364
Mental Health Acts 1959 and 1983
   362–3, 363–4
mental health care 362–6
   care programme approach (CPA)
      364*
   hospital closure 363
   supervised discharge 365–6
   supervision register 365
Mental Health Review Tribunals 363,
   366
mental illness, *Health of the Nation*
   targets 39
metabolic acidosis 172
metaparadigm of nursing 407*,
   408–9
metered-dose inhalers (MDIs) 191
methicillin-resistant *Staphylococcus
   aureus* (MRSA) 28
micronutrients 104–11
microwave ovens 62, 63
micturition 141*
   see also urinary elimination
midwifery 361–2
midwives
   Local Supervisory Authorities
      (LSAs) 361, 362
   see also registered practitioners
Midwives Acts 1902, 1918 and 1936
   361–2
Midwives' Rules 362
minerals 107*, 107–11
Mini-Wright's meter 182, **183**
misconduct, and the UKCC 394
mistrust, *v.* trust 297
mobility
   definition 217
   impaired 223–6
   importance of 217
   see also pressure sores
mobility impairment
   aids (equipment) 236
   disorders resulting in 223–6
   elderly people 223, 226, 235
   family involvement 234
   negative self-image 235
   nurse's responsibilities 234
   physical health problems 226–9
   psychosocial health 233–4
   see also disability

monoamine oxidase inhibitors
   (MAOIs), food types and side-
   effects 64
monosaccharides 95
monosodium glutamate 119
morbidity 114*
movement, *see* mobility
MRSA (methicillin-resistant
   Staphylococcus aureus) 28
mucous membranes, infection
   precautions 57
multi-agency practice 371
'multidisciplinary' 370*
multidisciplinary practice 370–1
   see also interprofessional practice
muscle myopathy, as complication of
   intramuscular injection 79
muscles 217–18
   age changes 225
   cardiac 217
   as effort in lever systems 221,
      221–2
   smooth 217
   skeletal 218
muscle spasms 108
muscular dystrophy 223*, 223–4
musculoskeletal system 217–21
   bones 218–19
   joints 218, 219–21
   lever systems 221, **221–2**
   mobility and 228–9
   muscles 217–18
myocardium 191*
myofibroblasts 247

N

named nurse 15
NANDA (North American Nursing
   Diagnosis Association) 11
nasal cannulae/catheters/prongs 188
nasogastric tubes
   administering medication via
      70–1
   complications 126, 126–7
   feeding via 125–6
National Boards 359, 360, 391
National Health Service (NHS)
   beginnings of 352–4
   contracting 358
   development, continuing 358
   finance 350–1, 352
   general management 355–6, 371
   GP fundholders 357, 358, 372,
      381
   health authorities 354–5, 356*,
      358
   internal market 356

Management Board 355
Management Executive (NHSME) 350
'new managerialism' 356
NHS Trusts 357*
Policy Board 350
primary care groups 358, 372
purchaser–provider split 356, 371
reforms (1990s) 356–8
reorganisation (1974) 354–5, 362
structure (1948) **353**
National Health Service and Community Care Act 1990 356, 372, 381
National Society for the Prevention of Cruelty to Children (NSPCC) 367
neck **221**
exercise 229
necrotic 258*
needles, for injections *72*
needlestick injuries 57
needs, hierarchy of 294–5, 303
nerve damage, as complication of intramuscular injection **76**, 79
The New NHS – Modern Dependable (White Paper) 372, 380
New Right philosophies 347
NHS, *see* National Health Service
niacin 105
nicotinamide 105
nicotinic acid 105
nocturia 150
non-starch polysaccharide (NSP) 101*, 101–2
insoluble 101
soluble 101
non-verbal communication 287*
normative-re-educative approach 321
North American Nursing Diagnosis Association (NANDA) 11
nose, medications 86
nosocomial infection 56*, 57
Not for resuscitation (NFR) orders 177
Notification of Practice 392*
NSPCC (National Society for the Prevention of Cruelty to Children) 367
nurse–patient relationship
and attitude change 311–12
knowing the patient 43
partnership and respect in 42
nurses
back injuries 49
emotional support for 41
expertise 326

as health promoters 42–4, **45**
media image *v.* reality 316
personal professional profile/portfolio 361*, 392*
role expansion 372
skills conditional to registration 2
student nurses 49, 360, 395–6
see also registered practitioners
Nurses, Midwives and Health Visitors Acts 1979 and 1992 359, 362, 391
Nurses Registration Act 1919 359
nursing
aims *408*
definition 11, 406
development of 404
intuitive nature of 326, 328
regulation 359–60
nursing care
benefits of nursing models 415–16
management 15–18
see also care planning; care plans
nursing diagnosis 10–12
actual *v.* potential 12
definitions 11*, 11–12
key components *12*
nursing handover 19
nursing models
activities of daily living (ADL) 7, 405, *406*, *409*
components of 406–15
concepts 407–10
definition 404–5
effects on practice 415–17
formal and informal 405
as maps 417
metaparadigm of nursing 407*, *408*–9
and the nursing process 417
philosophy of 406–7
purpose 405
statements 410
see also theories
nursing praxis 411*
see also praxis
nursing problem 11*
nursing process 1–23
definition 1*
and nursing models 417
stages in 2–3
see also assessment; care planning; evaluation; implementation; nursing diagnosis
nutrients 112–14
changing requirements 112–13

dietary reference values (DRVs) 112
estimated average requirements (EAR) 112
lower reference nutrient intake (LRNI) 112
macronutrients 95–103
micronutrients 104–11
recommended daily allowances (RDAs) 95, 112
reference nutrient intake (RNI) 112
see also Committee on Medical Aspects of Food Policy (COMA) reports
nutrition 95*
assessment 113, 121, 123–4
function 117–18
see also diet; food
nutrition, assisting with 114–18
economic aspects 116–17
educational aspects 116–17
ergonomic aspects 115–16
nutrition function 117–18
physiological aspects 115–16
SEEN areas 114
social aspects 114–15
nutritional anaemia 121*
nutritional support 124–9
nasogastric tube feeding 125–7
percutaneous endoscopic gastrotomy (PEG) 127–9

O

obesity 129–30
objectives, *see* goals
observation, in assessment 5
obstetric care 361–2
oedema, peripheral 201
open questions 5*
oral medications 69–71
oral route 69*
oral stimulation 129
organisational health 34–6
oropharyngeal airway 175–6
oropharynx 175*
orthopnoea 172*
osteoarthritis 224*, 226
osteomalacia 106
osteoporosis 97, 107–8, 224*, 225, 226, 228
and exercise 223
outcomes, evaluation of 18
overflow incontinence 157
oxalates 110

oxygen 167*, 169
  consumption 185
  humidification 187, 188, 189
  in wound healing 246
oxygen delivery 184–9
  administration methods 186–7
  face masks 187–8
  nasal cannulae/catheters/prongs
    188
  oxygen concentration 188
  precautions 188–9
  system components 186
oxygen therapy 186
  complications 189
  prescription for 186
  see also oxygen delivery
oxyhaemoglobin 185

P

pain
  assessment 8–10, 11, 206
  circulatory problems, see pain,
    from circulatory problems
  definition 8
  duration 10
  intensity 9–10
  location 10
  nursing action planning 14
  nursing care goals 13
  onset 10
  responses to 11
  signs and associated responses
    10, 10
  site of 10
  type 9
pain, from circulatory problems
  202–5
  alleviating factors 205
  assessment 202–5
  effects of 205
  precipitating factors 204–5
  severity 202–3
pain assessment tools/scales 202–4
pain behaviour tools 203–4
Panel of Professional Screeners, UKCC
  394
panproctolectomy 145
pantothenic acid 105
paradigms 411*
paralytic ileus 126*
paraphrasing 275
paraplegia 138*
parental responsibility 366, 367
parenteral medications 71–2
parenteral route 71*
Parkinson's disease 309*

partial pressure 169*, 184
patient education 318
  medication 88
patient handling 52–4
  equipment 54–6
  hoists 54, 55
  policy 56
  principles of 54
  see also manual handling
patients, rights of 373
patient satisfaction 19–20
Patient's Charter 15
peak expiratory flow rate (PEFR)
  182*, 182–3
pelvic floor exercises 157–8
penicillin 67, 72
percussion 174*
  percutaneous endoscopic
    gastrotomy (PEG) 127–9
  complications 129
  contraindications 127
  tube design 127, **127–8**
pericardium 205*
peripheral oedema 201
peripheral perfusion 200–1
peripheral resistance 197*
peristalsis 115, 134*
persistent patent ductus arteriosus
  185*
personality
  core qualities for personality
    change 270
  hardy personality 306–7
  psychodynamic theory of 302
  and stress 306–7
  theory of development 297–8
  type A (coronary-prone) 307
  type B 307
  see also attitude; behaviour
personal professional
  profile/portfolio 361, 392
personal space 287
pethidine 67
phagocytosis 245
Phaneuf Nursing Audit 402, 403,
  416
phenomenological approach (who
  am I?) 296
philosophies 397*, 398–404
  bottom-up approach 400
  developing quality and standards
    401
  facilitating teamwork 401
  of nursing models 406–7
  nursing philosophies 399
  personal beliefs and values 398–9
  practical application 401
  purposes of 401

  top-down approach 400
  written 400
phosphorus 108
physical activity level (PAL) 112, 113
physical examination 5
physical health information 6
phytate 106, 110
pica 109*
Piriton 211
planning care, see care planning
platelet-derived growth factor (PDGF)
  245
polarisation 206*
political health 30–1, 36–40
politics
  decision making 347–8
  nurses' need for knowledge of
    345–6
  political process 345–52
  values and beliefs 346–7
  see also government; social policy
polyphenols 110, 111
polysaccharides, see non-starch
  polysaccharide
portfolio 361*
Portsmouth
  Fast Food Fit campaign 42
  local authority response to Health
    of the Nation 38
  University of, health promotion
    35–6
Post-registration Education and
  Practice Project (PREPP) 334,
  360–1, 392
postural drainage 174*
postural hypotension 200
posture, see manual handling
potassium 108
poverty 29
power-coercive approach 321
practice nursing, key developments
  382
praxis 43–4, 411*
preceptors 361*
prejudice 312
PREPP (Post-registration Education
  and Practice Project) 334, 360–1,
  392
prescriptions 64–5
  abbreviations used in 66
  for oxygen therapy 186
prescriptive interventions 279*
pressure sores 229*, 229–33, 243
  and age 232
  assessment 232
  causes 232
  cone of pressure 232, **233**
  costs 229

development 232–3
nursing interventions 232–3
nutrition 233
prevention 232–3
risk assessment tools 243
ulcers *243*
see also skin
preventing activities *409*
Primary Care: Delivering the Future
(White Paper) 370–1, 374, 380,
382
primary care groups 358, 372*
primary health care 380*
principles of **383**
primary health care teams
clinical governance 381
evolution 381
key developments in nursing
382
location 383
payment of members 384
professionals' role 383
quality services in the community
381
resource management 384
role of 380
size 384
see also teamwork
primary nursing 16, 17*
problem-solving approaches 3
professional accountability 394*
features of 394–5
registered nurses 16, 396
v. responsibility 395, 395–6
student nurses 395–6
see also accountability
professional boundaries 372, 375–6
Professional Conduct Committees,
UKCC 394*
professional practice
challenges to 389–420
defining 390–1
responsibilities of 391–4
see also accountability; registered
practitioners
professional socialisation 376*,
376–8
profile 361*
prohibited steps order 368
Project 2000 360
prophylactic 107*
prostaglandins 245*
prostate gland 149, **155**
proteins 96*, 96–7, 124, 246
protocols 284*
Pseudomonas 187
psychodynamic theory of personality
302

psychological information 6
psychosocial health, in impaired
mobility 233–4
psychosocial theory of personality
development 297–9
Public Expenditure Survey Committee
Report 351
publicity, benefits of nursing models
416–17
pulmonary embolism 174*, 209, 227
pulmonary oedema 172*, 201
pulse 192*, 192–7
apical 196–7
bounding 195
Corrigan's 195
measuring *193*
palpation sites **194**
radial **193**
rates 192–5
rhythm 196
strength 195
and systolic blood pressure **195**
thready 195
volume 195
waterhammer 195
pulse deficit 197*
pulse oximetry 184
puncture wounds *243*
purchaser–provider split 356, 371
pus 248*
in urine (pyuria) 150*
pyridoxine 105
pyrogenic reaction 212
pyuria 150*

Q

qualitative research approaches 403*
quality of care 401*, 401–2
assessment of 402–4
and care evaluation 18
nursing assessment tools 402,
403
statistics on 19–20
quality time, for clients 274
QUALPACs 402, 403
quantitative research approaches
403*
questioning
in assessment 5
open and closed questions 5*,
275–6

R

râles 173
rattle 173

RCN, *see* Royal College of Nursing
reactive hyperaemia 232
recommended daily allowances
(RDAs) (of nutrients) 95, 112
records
care planning 20–1
computerised 20–1, 396–7
Data Protection Act 1984 396–7
failure to keep 2
as legal documents 18
and models of care 416
prescribed medicines 65
sensitive data 397
as sources of assessment data 4
recovery position 178, **179**
rectal infusion 124
rectal medications 86–7
rectal route 86*
rectoplexy 144*
REEPIG criteria for care planning 14
reference nutrient intake (RNI) 112
reflection
active 328
anticipatory 328–9
as care evaluation method 19
definition 319–20
as learning tool 320, 325
on nursing procedures 317–19
in the practice setting 339–41
selective 275
simple 274–5
on stereotype of nurse 315–16
taking control 325–8
types of 328–9
reflection-in-action 328–9
reflection-on-action 329, 411
reflective action, definition 319
reflective framework 321–5
action 324
analysis of feelings and
knowledge 323–4
awareness of uncomfortable
feelings 322–3
identification of new learning
324–5
knowledge evaluation 324
situation description 323
reflective practice 315–44
critical incident analysis 19,
329–34
see also reflection; reflective
framework
reflex incontinence 156–7
reflux 115*
refrigerators 62–3
for blood storage 210
Regional Hospital Boards 353, 354

registered practitioners 390*
  maintaining registration 392
  responsibilities of *393*
  see also accountability
rehydration techniques 124
requests, refusal of 288–9
research, qualitative v. quantitative
  approaches 403*
residence orders 367
residual volume 182, **183***
resolution of conflict
  negative 299
  positive 297
resource management, in primary
  health care teams 384
respiration 167–91
  abnormal patterns of 172
  accessory muscles 170*
  apnoea 171*
  assessment 7–8, 168–74
  asthmatic breathing 172
  Biot's 172
  bradypnoea 170*
  chest shape 174
  Cheyne–Stokes 172*
  and colour 173
  cough 173–4
  depth 172
  dyspnoea 172*, 173
  effects of exercise on *170*
  hyperpnoea 172*
  involuntary 168–9
  Kussmaul's 172
  lung volumes and capacities 172,
    182–3
  orthopnoea 172*
  oxygen delivery 184–9
  physical assessment 170
  pulse oximetry 184
  purpose of 167
  rates 170–1
  rhythm 171–2
  sounds 172–3
  spontaneous 168
  tachypnoea 171*
  tidal volume 172*
  volume measurements 172,
    182–3
  see also airway
respiratory arrest 177–8
  see also resuscitation
respiratory centre 168–9
respiratory system 167–8
  mobility and 227
responses, behavioural 285–6
responsibility, v. accountability 241,
  395, 395–6

resuscitation
  aim 177
  cardiac arrest 177–8
  cardiac compression 180–2
  Do not resuscitate (DNR) orders
    177
  mouth-to-mouth 178–9
  Not for resuscitation (NFR) orders
    177
  see also cardiac arrest
retinol 104
retrolental fibroplasia 189
rheumatoid arthritis 224*, 224–5,
  226
riboflavin 104
rickets 106*, 107
rights, of service users, clients and
  patients 373
risk assessment, wounds 242–3
risk assessment tools 243
ritual 316–17, 318, 320–1
road transport, increase in 34
Rogers' model of self 303
role confusion, v. identity 298
rotation 220
roughage, see non-starch
  polysaccharide
routine 316–17, 317, 319
Royal College of Midwives (RCM)
  346
Royal College of Nursing (RCN) 346
  on hand hygiene 58
  on manual handling 52, 56

S

safety, see food hygiene; infection
  control; manual handling;
  medication administration
salbutamol 211
Salmonella typhimurium 59
salmonellosis 59–60, 61
  contributory factors 61
salt 108
Sara 2000 hoists 54, **55**
sciatic nerve, damage as
  complication of intramuscular
  injection **76**, 79
sclerosis 149*
Scope of Professional Practice (UKCC)
  326, 372
scurvy 106
sebaceous glands 230, 231
seeking activities *409*
selenium 109
self
  blind self 300–1
  categories of 296

hidden self 301–2
  ideal self 303
  Johari window 299–302
  public self 300
  Rogers' model of 303
  and sources of stress 303–4
  unconscious self 302
  understanding of 294–314
self-absorption, v. generativity 298
self-awareness 299*, 299–302
  v. self-consciousness 299
self-concept 295*, 295–6
  changes in 296
  development of 296–7
self-consciousness, v. self-awareness
  299
self-esteem 303
self-help groups 302
self-interrogation 324
self-monitoring 340
sensory receptors **230**, 231
septicaemia, as complication of
  intramuscular injection 78
septicaemic shock 212*
service provision, changes in 372–3
service users, rights of 373
sexual health, *Health of the Nation*
  targets 39–40
shame, v. autonomy 297
sharing 377–8
sharps 57, 59
shock 171*
  septicaemic 212*
shoulders, exercise 229
sickness, costs to employers 34
sinus arrhythmia 196*, 208
skeletal (striated) muscle 218
skin
  colour 173, 200
  cyanosis 173, 200
  dermis 231
  epidermis 231
  functions 230
  hairy and non-hairy 231
  infection precautions 57
  stratum corneum 231
  structure 230–1, 244
  temperature 201
  texture 201
  turgor 124*
  see also pressure sores
sleep apnoea 172
slough 258*
'slow virus' 28
smell, sense of 119
smoking 37, 40
  attitude to 311
snoring 172

social class, mortality and morbidity 32
social health 32–3
social health information 6
socialisation, professional 376*, 376–8
socialism 346*
social loafing 284
social policy 352–68
social readjustment rating scale 306
social security benefits for the disabled 234, 236–7
social support 307*
    buffering hypothesis 308
    direct effect hypothesis 308
    and stress 307–8
    types 308
social workers, see approved social workers (ASWs)
societal issues, influence on personal beliefs and values 398–9
sodium 108
sodium chloride 108
specimens 136*
specimen collection 136–7
    faeces 137
    sputum 174
    urine 150–3
spillages 57
spiritual health 30–1, 40–1
sputum
    specimen collection 174
    types 173–4
stab wounds 243
standards of care 401*
    see also quality of care
Staphylococcal infection 56
Staphylococcus aureus, methicillin-resistant (MRSA) 28
starches 95, 96
stasis 226*
    haemostasis 245
    urinary 149, 228
    venous 226
status epilepticus 26*
statutes, see legislation
steatorrhoea 143
stereotype 312*
    and the disabled 236
stockings, anti-embolic (graded compression) 210
stoma 144
    colostomy 144*, 144–5, 146, 147
    ileostomy 145*, 146, 147
    normal appearance 147
    postoperative care 147
    preoperative care 145–6
    sites to be avoided 146

stoma bags 146
stoma care 147
stones, see gallstones; kidney stones; urinary stones
stratum corneum 231
streptomycin 72
stress
    factors affecting 306–9
    general adaptation syndrome (GAS) 304–5
    information-processing model 305–6
    interactional model 305
    models of 304–6
    response-based model 304–5
    sources of, and self 303–4
    stimulus-based model 304
    stressful life events model 306
stress incontinence 154–6
stridor 172
strokes, Health of the Nation targets 39
stroke volume 197*
student health 35–6
student nurses 49, 360, 395–6
subcutaneous injections 72, 79–81
subcutaneous route 79*
sugars 95–6
superficial break 242*
supervised discharge orders 365–6
supervision orders 367
supervision register 365
support, emotional, for nurses 41
supportive interventions 279*, 279–80
suppositories 86–7, 141
surgical excision/incision 243
swallowing 116, 117
sweat glands 230, 231
sympathetic nervous system 115*
synovial fluid 219*, 220
syringes 72

T

tachycardia 193*, 193–4, 195
tachypnoea 171*
tacit knowing 326
tannins 110
task allocation 15*, 15–16
taste sensations 118, 119
TB (tuberculosis) 29
team nursing 16*, 16–17
teams, see groups
teamwork 374*
    benefits of nursing models 415, 416

collaboration 374
co-operation 379–80
endorsing 375
evaluation 375
factors affecting 374–5
financial aspects 374–5
good practice in 378–80
interprofessional values 377–8
knowledge 378–9
language 376–7
leadership and co-ordination 375
meeting need 380
personal values 377
philosophies facilitating 401
practice intervention methods 379–80
professional boundaries 372, 375–6
professional socialisation 376*, 376–8
professional values 377
research and reports on 384–5
roles of members 378
status 378
team support 375
see also primary health care teams
tetany 108
theories 410–15
    classification 413–15
    definition 410
    grand theory 413, 413–14
    levels of development 411, 413
    need for 412
    purposes of 412
    theory-proposing and testing model 411
theory–practice gap 411
therapeutic 268*
therapeutic communication 268*, 268–9
    congruence 270*
    core qualities 270–2
    counselling and 269
    empathic understanding 270*, 270–1
    genuineness 270, 271*, 272
    unconditional acceptance 270, 271*, 271–2
    see also therapeutic interventions
therapeutic interventions
    catalytic category 273*, 273–6
    cathartic category 276*, 276–7
    confronting category 277*, 277–8
    informative category 278*, 278–9
    prescriptive category 279*

six-category intervention analysis
272–3
styles of 279
supportive category 279*,
279–80
therapeutic skills, see therapeutic
interventions
therapeutic use of self, see
therapeutic communication
thiamin 104
thigh, injection site 77
three circles model, of leadership
282, 282
thrombophlebitis 212*
thrombosis 209*, 226–7
deep vein thrombosis (DVT) 209,
210, 227
precautionary measures 209–10
venous 209
thyroxine 195
tidal volume (TV) 172*, **183**
'tilted plate' 111, **111**, 113, 118
vegetarian *123*, **123**
time, for clients 274
time urgency 307
tissue viability 241*
Tissue Viability Society 241, 264
α-tocopherols 107
β-tocopherols 107
toes **222**
topical 82*
topical medications 82–7
administration guidelines 82
ears 85
eyes 83–4
nasal 86
rectal 86–7
transdermal application 82–3
vaginal 87
total lung capacity (TLC) 182*, **183**
touch 277, 287
trace elements 107
transactional analysis 285*
transdermal medication application
82–3
transdermal route 82*
trans-fats/fatty acids 95, 97, *98*,
99
Treasury 348*, 350–1
triglycerides 97
Trixie Lift hoists 54, **55**
trust 377–8
v. mistrust 297
tuberculosis (TB) 29

U

UKCC, see United Kingdom Central
Council for Nursing, Midwifery
and Health Visiting
ulcerative colitis 143*
ulcers *243*
unconditional acceptance 270,
271*, 271–2
unconditional positive regard, see
unconditional acceptance
understanding
checking for 276
of self 294–314
United Kingdom Central Council for
Nursing, Midwifery and Health
Visiting (UKCC) 359–60, 391
on decision-making 326
function 391
Health Committee 394
objectives and priorities 391–4
Panel of Professional Screeners
394
on patient feeding 62, 94
power of sanction 398
Professional Conduct Committees
394*
publications 392
Scope of Professional Practice
326, 372
see also *Code of Professional
Conduct*
universal precautions 57
universities, and health promotion
34–6
urethra
female *154*, **155**
male **155**
urethritis 149*
urge incontinence 156
urinary catheters 158–63
balloon sizes 159
catheter size *159*, 159
catheter types 159
client care principles *161*
closed urinary drainage system
160
indications for catheterisation
158
indwelling 159–61
intermittent self-catheterisation
161, 162
suprapubic 162–3
urinary elimination 133, 148–64
adolescents and young adults
149
adults 149
ageing adults 149

altered 153–8
development of 148–9
incontinence 153–7
infants 148
micturition 140*
school-aged children 149
specimen collection 150–3
toddlers to preschool age 148–9
see also urine specimens
urinary stasis 149, 228
urinary stones 150, *151*, 228
urinary system **149**
mobility and 228
urinary tract infection (UTI) 149,
150, 156, 161, 162
urine
colour **153**
and fluid intake 103
odour 153
urine specimens 150–3
24-hour collection 150
catheter specimen of urine (CSU)
152
early morning urine (EMU) 150
midstream specimen of urine
(MSU) 150–1
routine screening 150, 152–3
urostomy 163–4
urticarial hives 211*
UTI (urinary tract infection) 149,
150, 156, 161, 162
'utilitarian' 377*

V

vaginal medications 87
vaginal repair 156*
vaginal route 87*
Valsalva manoeuvre *156*, 157
value(s) 377*
interprofessional 377–8
personal 377
professional 377
vasoconstriction 184*
vegan diet 105, 122
vegetables 101, **102**
vegetarian diet 97, 105, 122–3, **123**
veins
injections into 79
intravenous fluid therapy 212, 213
intravenous medication
administration 71
venous stasis 226
venous thrombosis 209
ventricular septal defect 185*
verocytotoxic *Escherichia coli* (VTEC)
59

Virchow's triad 209
virus, *see* 'slow virus'
vitamins 104*
    vitamin A 97, 104, 246
    vitamin B group 104–5, 246
    vitamin C 104, 106, 109, 246
    vitamin D 97, 106, 108
    vitamin E 97, 107, 109, 246
    vitamin K 97, 107
VTEC (verocytotoxic *Escherichia coli*)
    59

W

waste, classification 59
waste disposal 57, 58–9
water, for drinking 102–3
waterhammer pulse 195
weight loss 120
welfare state 347*
wheeze 173
WHO, *see* World Health Organisation
'who am I?' 295–6
wine, red 111
Working for Patients 356
World Health Organisation (WHO)
    33
    Health for All by the Year 2000
        36–7
Wound Care Society 241, 264

wound exudate 250*
wound healing
    abnormal 249
    complications 248–9
    contractures 249
    dehiscence 249*
    dressings 250–1
    exudate 250*
    factors affecting 248, **248**
    granulation tissue 246*
    haematoma 249*
    haemorrhage 249
    haemostasis 245
    hypertrophic scarring 249*
    infection 249
    inflammatory phase 245
    keloid scarring 249*
    malignant disease 249
    maturation phase 247
    modes of *243*, 247–8
    optimum environment for 250–1
    phases 245–7
    primary intention 247*
    the process 245–9
    proliferative phase 245–7
    secondary intention 247*
    temperature variations 250
    third intention 247–8
wound management 240–66
    accountability in 241–2
    aseptic technique *263*

    assessment 251–9
    assessment criteria 252
    assessment summary 259
    care planning 251
    case study 252–62
    nursing care evaluation 262–3
    nursing care implementation
        261–2
    nursing care planning 251,
        259–61
    nursing diagnosis 251–9
    professional associations 241,
        264–5
    professional perspective 241
    tissue viability 241*
wounds
    classification 242, *243*
    definition 242*
    risk assessment 242–3
    superficial break 242*
    see also wound healing; wound
        management
Wright's meter 182, **183**

Z

zinc 109, 246
Z-track intramuscular injections 78